By looking here for help:

W9-AAM-746

THE BRIEF McGraw-Hill GUIDE

WRITING for COLLEGE, WRITING for LIFE

DUANE ROEN

Arizona State University

GREGORY R. GLAU

Arizona State University

BARRY M. MAID

Arizona State University

McGraw-Hill Higher Education

Boston   Burr Ridge, IL   Dubuque, IA   New York   San Francisco   St. Louis
Bangkok   Bogotá   Caracas   Kuala Lumpur   Lisbon   London   Madrid   Mexico City
Milan   Montreal   New Delhi   Santiago   Seoul   Singapore   Sydney   Taipei   Toronto

The McGraw·Hill Companies

McGraw-Hill
Higher Education

Published by McGraw-Hill, an imprint of The McGraw-Hill Companies, Inc., 1221 Avenue of the Americas, New York, NY 10020. Copyright © 2009. All rights reserved. No part of this publication may be reproduced or distributed in any form or by any means, or stored in a database or retrieval system, without the prior written consent of The McGraw-Hill Companies, Inc., including, but not limited to, in any network or other electronic storage or transmission, or broadcast for distance learning.

This book is printed on acid-free paper.

2 3 4 5 6 7 8 9 0 DOC / DOC 0 9

ISBN: 978-0-07-721399-2
MHID: 0-07-721399-8

Editor in Chief: *Michael J. Ryan*
Senior Sponsoring Editor: *Christopher Bennem*
Senior Developmental Editor: *Carla Kay Samodulski*
Executive Marketing Manager: *Tamara Wederbrand*
Editorial Coordinator: *Molly Meneely*
Lead Media Project Manager: *Ron Nelms, Jr.*
Production Editor: *Brett Coker*
Manuscript Editor: *Jan Fehler*
Art Director: *Jeanne M. Schreiber*
Cover Designer: *Jeanne M. Schreiber*
Interior Designers: *Linda M. Robertson and Kim Menning*
Art Editor: *Ayelet Arbel*
Senior Photo Editor: *Natalia Peschiera*
Photo Researcher: *Jennifer Blankenship*
Lead Production Supervisor: *Randy Hurst*
Composition: *Electronic Publishing Services Inc., NYC*
Printing: *45# New Era Matte by R.R. Donnelley & Sons*

Library of Congress Cataloging-in-Publication Data
Roen, Duane H.
  The brief McGraw-Hill guide: writing for college, writing for life / Duane Roen, Gregory R. Glau, Barry M. Maid. – 1st ed.
    p. cm.
  Includes bibliographical references and index.
  ISBN-13: 978-0-07-721399-2 (acid-free paper)
  MHID: 0-07-721399-8 (acid-free paper) 1. English language—Rhetoric. I. Glau, Gregory R. II. Maid, Barry M. III. Title.
PE1408.R644 2008
808'.042071173—dc22

                                        2007016459

The Internet addresses listed in the text were accurate at the time of publication. The inclusion of a Web site does not indicate an endorsement by the authors or McGraw-Hill, and McGraw-Hill does not guarantee the accuracy of the information presented at these sites.

www.mhhe.com

Brief Contents

v

Contents

PART SIX   Using Research for Informed Communication   825

19   Finding and Evaluating Information from Sources and the Field   827

About the Authors

Duane Roen is Professor of English at Arizona State University and Head of Humanities and Arts in the School of Applied Arts and Sciences. At ASU he served as Director of Composition for four years before directing ASU's Center for Learning and Teaching Excellence. Prior to that, he directed the Writing Program at Syracuse University, as well as the graduate program in Rhetoric, Composition, and the Teaching of English at the University of Arizona. Early in his career, he taught high school English in New Richmond, Wisconsin, before deciding to complete a doctorate at the University of Minnesota. In addition to more than 160 articles, chapters, and conference papers, Duane has published numerous books including *Composing Our Lives in Rhetoric and Composition: Stories about the Growth of a Discipline* (with Theresa Enos and Stuart Brown); *The Writer's Toolbox* (with Stuart Brown and Bob Mittan); *A Sense of Audience in Written Discourse* (with Gesa Kirsch); and *Views from the Center: The CCCC Chairs' Addresses, 1977–2005,* among others. In 2007, Duane was elected Secretary of the CCCC. Duane's interest in family history has motivated him to construct a database that lists more than 32,000 of his ancestors and to collaborate with his wife, Maureen, to write more than 14,000 pages of journal entries about their two children, Nick and Hanna.

Gregory R. Glau is Director of Writing Programs at Arizona State University, where he has taught since 1994. Greg received his MA in Rhetoric and Composition from Northern Arizona University and his PhD in Rhetoric, Composition, and the Teaching of English from the University of Arizona. Before he was appointed director in 2000, Greg directed ASU's basic writing Stretch Program. Greg is past Co-Chair of the Conference on Basic Writing (CBW) with Linda Adler-Kassner of Eastern Michigan University, and he coedited (with Linda) *BWe: Basic Writing e-Journal.* Greg is coeditor of the *Bedford Bibliography of Basic Writing,* also with Linda Adler-Kassner. Greg is also coauthor (with Craig Jacobsen) of

Scenarios for Writing. Greg has published in *WPA: Writing Program Administration*, *Rhetoric Review*, *English Journal*, *The Writing Instructor*, *IDEAS Plus*, and the *Arizona English Bulletin*. He regularly presents papers at CCCC and has also presented papers at WPA, MLA, RMMLA, the Western States Composition Conference, NCTE, and other conferences. As a teenager, Greg was an amateur magician. He maintains that interest today, and with his oldest son, Robert, he attends a convention for mentalism entertainers every year.

Barry M. Maid is Professor and Head of Multimedia Writing and Technical Communication at Arizona State University, where he led the development of a new program in Multimedia Writing and Technical Communication. He has spent most of his career in some form of writing program administration. Before coming to ASU in January 2000, he spent nineteen years at the University of Arkansas at Little Rock where, among other duties, he directed the Writing Center and the First Year Composition Program, chaired the Department of English, and helped create the Department of Rhetoric and Writing. He has written or coauthored chapters for more than a dozen books. His work has also appeared in *Kairos*, *Computers and Composition*, and the *Writing Lab Newsletter*, among other technology-oriented publications. More recently, Barry has coauthored articles on information literacy for library journals. His professional interests remain primarily with computers and writing, writing program administration, and partnerships between academia and industry. Barry enjoys long road trips. Over the past several years, he has driven along the Pacific Coast Highway from Los Angeles to Oregon, through national parks in Utah and Arizona, and through much of the Carolinas and Tennessee.

Dear Colleagues,

As longtime writing program administrators and instructors, we know that students need textbooks that address both their current and future needs. They need to see how important and valuable writing will be for them in the many diverse situations they will encounter. *The Brief McGraw-Hill Guide* grew out of our desire to help students learn to write more effectively not only in their college courses but also in their professional, civic, and personal lives. To do this, we designed a text that will help students to set goals for their writing, to use effective composing strategies to reach those goals, and to assess their progress toward achieving them.

In establishing goals for students, we've drawn on the learning outcomes established by the National Council of Writing Program Administrators because we know how important they have been in shaping discussions about writing curricula in the United States and other countries. These learning outcomes demonstrate the value of the full range of skills and knowledge that writers need to develop: rhetorical knowledge; critical thinking, reading, and writing; composing processes; and knowledge of conventions. *The Brief McGraw-Hill Guide* is the first rhetoric of its kind to be developed specifically with these outcomes in mind, and the result is a text that will help students achieve these outcomes while also helping instructors teach them.

As for the future, in the twenty-first century, all writers can expect to confront increasingly varied digital contexts. Whether they need to use visual elements, implement specific design features, employ a variety of digital media, or choose an alternate genre to communicate with their readers, effective writers today have a wide range of choices to make to accomplish the goals of any particular writing task. *The Brief McGraw-Hill Guide* helps students not only to make thoughtful choices, but also to ask thoughtful questions. We also aspire to help them find answers.

Sincerely,

Duane Roen   Gregory R. Glau   Barry M. Maid

The features of *The Brief McGraw-Hill Guide* are designed to help students answer three questions they typically ask:

- **Why** am I writing?
- **How** do I write?
- **Did** I achieve my writing goals?

Why am I writing?

Effective writers understand the situation—the purpose, context, and audience—in which they are writing. The most effective writers are strong communicators in any situation. The chapters in Parts 2 and 3 (Chapters 4–12), which present writing assignments, each focus on the purpose for which students need to write—exploring, analyzing, convincing, and so on—and provide comprehensive instruction on writing for various contexts in college and beyond.

Writing for College

SCENARIO 1   Exploring a Major or Career

For this scenario, assume you are taking a "Career and Life Planning" class—a class devoted to helping college students decide what discipline they might like to major in. This class gives you the opportunity to explore different career paths, to learn what the educational requirements are for various majors, and to find out what job opportunities will be available in various careers and what salaries and other forms of compensation different jobs might offer.

Writing Assignment: Select one college major or career that you may be interested in pursuing and construct an exploratory paper in which you consider the various aspects of that major or career from many angles, including the preparation you would need for it and the rewards and pitfalls you might encounter if you decide to pursue it. Asking and answering questions about the major or career you are considering will form the heart of your exploratory paper.

In Chapters 4–12, assignment options in the form of brief *scenarios* give students a context for writing.

A scenario gives students an audience, a purpose for writing, and a context. Each chapter in Parts 2 and 3 provides a *range* of scenarios, so students and instructors can select from academic, professional, civic, or personal scenarios.

The text focuses throughout on writing in all four areas of a student's life (academic, professional, civic, and personal). Although most students have an immediate need to improve their academic writing, students will see the benefits of learning to write more clearly if they examine their current literacy practices in the other areas of their lives as well.

Writing for Life

SCENARIO 3   Professional Writing: A Formal Report
Evaluating Advertisements

Almost every enterprise advertises in one form or another: in newspapers, in the Yellow Pages, online, on radio, on television, in movie theaters, in magazines—the list is large and growing. Even the U.S. Post Office advertises; the U.S. military advertises; and many nonprofit organizations such as hospitals advertise. For this assignment, assume that you work for the type of company or organization you hope one day actually to work for. (If you already are employed, you can write this assignment as an employee of your current employer or another organization.) One of your duties is to evaluate possible advertisements that are appropriate for this organization.

Choosing a Medium, Genre, and Technology for Your Communication

Chapter **17**

The text emphasizes different media and genres for writing. Because many writing situations will require the use of various media and genres, in the chapters in Parts 2 and 3, many of the "Writing for Life" assignment options call for students to publish their work in a format other than a traditional, plain text, printed academic essay. In addition, Chapter 17, "Choosing a Medium, Genre, and Technology for Your Communication," gives students practical advice on using both basic and advanced computer tools to prepare documents for, and communicate with, different audiences in various media and genres.

Writing in Action boxes show students examples of different genres. Found in the "Knowledge of Conventions" sections of the chapters in Parts 2 and 3, these boxes offer students brief, high-interest examples of writing in different genres, as well as a sense of the way writers address their audiences within these genres. Questions prompt students to consider the issues involved in writing in different genres and how they might apply to students' own writing.

WRITING IN ACTION

Convention in Genre and Design

University of Georgia student Phillip Kisubika provides a somewhat humorous but still thoughtful persuasive essay in the following newspaper opinion piece. His thesis is that many college-age students are not ready for marriage. Do you find his argument convincing?

(cont'd)

(continued)

MUCH TO DO BEFORE TYING THE KNOT

by Phillip Kisubika

We're living in strange times.

No, I don't mean the random wars, the crazy technology or the neglected disease pandemics and natural disasters. I mean that in this time of individualism, free thought and experimentation, so many of us contemplate and go through with tying the knot at a young age.

According to a CNN poll in 2002, 63 percent of people between the

According to the U.S. Census Bureau, two out of three marriages taking place under 30 years of age end in divorce.

Surprised? Don't be.

The trends of today's relationships sometimes make me wonder how any couple stays together.

In the past, couples did marry young, but it was more an arrangement of convenience instead of passion. Men chose women who they cared for and who could run a household and raise children. Divorces happened, but they weren't as common, probably because

How do I write?

Each chapter in Parts 2 and 3 illustrates the steps of the writing process with clear examples of a student writer adapting to a specific writing situation. In this way, *The Brief McGraw-Hill Guide* helps students achieve their own writing goals by introducing them to the principles and guiding them through the processes of effective writing.

Santi DeRosa's First Draft

In this brief draft, note how Santi DeRosa incorporates information and examples from his own life as well as from outside sources. As he wrote, DeRosa did not worry about grammar, punctuation, and mechanics; instead, he concentrated on getting his main ideas on paper.

> The Objectification of Woman. Who's Fault Is it?
>
> Are women at ASU being objectified by the very university that has a responsibility to treat women with equality and not as second class citizens?
>
> I say yes. All you need to do is look at the athletics department to see the way women are treated. What I don't understand is that in the year 2003, women are still allowing themselves to be used in such a way
>
> In the past week I have read a couple of news articles from the State Press that got me a little perplexed. Maybe it's the fact that I have a son

---

Examples of student writing show the entire process of responding to an assignment. Because students respond best to examples of student work, the "Writing Processes" section of each chapter in Parts 2 and 3 follows a student writer as he or she goes through a composing process, from invention through drafting and revising. In this way, students have an example for every step and can see the entire process of constructing a successful piece of writing.

The chapters in Parts 2 and 3 include a wide variety of student and professional readings. Each chapter includes the final version of the student essay as well as three professional selections by a range of authors including Maureen Dowd, P. J. O'Rourke, Roger Ebert, Elvis Mitchell, Juan Williams, and Thomas Friedman. The apparatus that accompanies each reading selection encourages students to think about how the Learning Goals apply to that particular selection, as well as about ideas for their own writing.

MAUREEN DOWD

Our Own Warrior Princess

Maureen Dowd won the Pulitzer Prize for Commentary in 1999. In 1992, she received the Breakthrough Award from Women, Men and Media at Columbia University. She won the Matrix Award from New York Women in Communications in 1994. In 1996, she was named one of *Glamour's* Women of the Year. In 1992, she was also a Pulitzer Prize finalist for national reporting.

In the following column, which first appeared in the *New York Times* on June 1, 2003, Dowd writes in a personal way about organ donation—telling the story of what her niece, Jennifer, did to help her brother, Michael. Although persuasive writing most often uses facts, statistics, and hard evidence to make its case, as you read Dowd's column consider how effective she is in using emotional appeals to persuade you.

Jennifer showed me her scar Friday. It's the most beautiful scar I've ever seen. A huge stapled gash on her stomach, shaped like the Mercedes logo. A red badge of courage. Jennifer is my niece, a 33-year-old lawyer. On Wednesday, she had half her liver taken out at Georgetown University

Each chapter in Parts 2 and 3 emphasizes multiple forms of research. Although there are two separate chapters on research in Part 6 (Chapters 19 and 20), each chapter in Parts 2 and 3 also includes coverage of conducting research.

Each chapter in Parts 2 and 3 offers advice on using visuals. Because many writing situations today require visual as well as verbal texts, throughout the writing assignments in Parts 2 and 3, "Thinking about Visuals" sections and "Visualizing Variations" boxes encourage students to consider how they can use visuals in their writing when appropriate.

Exploring Your Ideas with Research

Although you may be able to use information from your own experience as evidence, you will usually need to offer verifiable information from sources, such as facts, statistics, expert testimony, and examples. If you are writing about a local issue, for instance, a local official such as a member of the town council or a state senator might be a useful person to interview. His or her views on your issue could add ethos to your paper—if your audience will consider the official to be fair, knowledgeable, and honest.

To find evidence outside of your experience that you need to support your claim, look for answers to the following questions:

- What facts or other verifiable information can I find that will provide solid ev...
- What c...
  authori...

VISUALIZING VARIATIONS

Using Charts and Other Visuals to Support Your Claim

If you were writing in response to Scenario 2, which asks you to focus on a controversial issue, you might choose to write about global warming. Here is a dramatic image that you could use at the beginning of your paper:

The text reminds students of their responsibilities as writers. Chapter 1 includes a section on writing responsibly, and the chapters in Parts 2 and 3 reinforce this important aspect of writing, with boxes that remind students that writing has consequences and that good writing is ethical writing.

A WRITER'S RESPONSIBILITY

Establishing and Maintaining Credibility

Dealing Fairly with Opposing Views

An ethical writer must deal with opposing views fairly and honestly. If you ignore or distort opposing views, readers will think you are either ignorant, unaware, or dishonest, which will quickly weaken or destroy your ethos—your credibility.

It is perhaps only natural to tend to ignore what those who disagree with you have to say about your topic—after all, if you just ignore their views, your view will be stronger, right? However, ignoring the other side of an issue, the objections that others might have to your point of view, actually weakens your position, as your readers will most likely know of the objections and wonder why you did not deal with t...

TechNote One way to see argumentation and persuasion in action is to look at the political discussion boards on various Web sites, blogs, and online bulletin boards. Choose a topic thread, and as you skim or read the posts, ask yourself three questions about each post you see: 1) How much credibility does the writer seem to have as a person (*ethos*)? 2) How does the writer use reason and logic to make his or her points (*logos*)? 3) What is your emotional reaction to the writer's remarks (*pathos*)? You can determine the weight a writer's comments probably carry with others by assessing your impressions of that writer's credibility, reasoning, and emotional integrity.

TechNotes in each chapter offer hints on using technology throughout the writing process. These useful notes will help students get more from the resources that are available to them in the computer lab, in the library, and on the Web.

Did I achieve my writing goals?

The Brief McGraw-Hill Guide is designed to help students understand how others will evaluate their work and provides criteria they can use to judge their own work. Taking as their basis the Council of Writing Program Administrators *Outcomes Statement*, Chapters 4–12 integrate coverage of the four categories of learning outcomes that form the foundation of assessment practices at writing programs throughout the country: *rhetorical knowledge, critical thinking, writing processes,* and *conventions.*

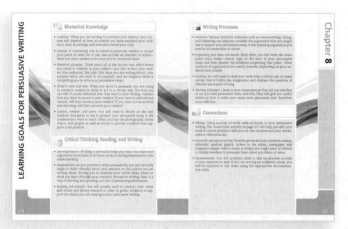

Each assignment chapter is structured around the Learning Goals, so students know what the book will *do* for their writing. The Learning Goals are introduced in Chapter 1. In addition, a chart at the beginning of each chapter in Parts 2 and 3 relates the Learning Goals to the type of writing covered in that chapter, and the organization of each chapter is based on the Learning Goals, to reinforce their importance.

Each assignment chapter ends with questions for self-assessment. In the self-assessment activity, students are prompted to consider how their progress on the chapter's assignment has helped them work toward attaining the goals for the chapter, thus helping them build their knowledge of themselves as writers and thinkers. A student sample of reflective writing is also included.

 ## Self-Assessment: Reflecting on Your Learning Goals

Now that you have constructed a piece of writing designed to convince your readers, go back and consider your learning goals, which you and your classmates may have considered at the beginning of this chapter (pp. 318–19). Then, reflect on all the thinking and writing that you have done in constructing your persuasive paper. To help reflect on the learning goals that you have achieved, respond in writing to the following questions:

Rhetorical Knowledge

- *Audience:* What have you learned about addressing an audience in persuasive writing?
- *Purpose:* What have you learned about the purposes for constructing an effective persuasive text?

Critical Thinking, Reading, and Writing

- *Learning/inquiry:* How did you decide what to focus on for your persuasive text? Describe the process you went through to focus on a main idea, or thesis. How did you judge what was most and least important in explaining your position to your readers?
- *Responsibility:* How did you fulfill your responsibilities to your readers?
- *Reading and research:* What did you learn about persuasive writing from the reading selections you read for this chapter? What research did you conduct? How sufficient was the research you did? Why? What additional research might you have done?

Chapter 2 on reading helps students hone their critical reading—and thinking—skills. To help students with the second category of the Learning Goals, Chapter 2 covers the skills students need for effective college-level reading. This chapter also provides ample opportunity for students to examine and reflect on their own reading practices and habits, suggests ways to improve their reading activities, and provides journaling ideas and activities. The chapter includes a strong focus on visual literacy.

Synthesizing Information in Readings

Synthesis is more than reassembling other people's ideas and information from different sources; it calls for the thoughtful combination or integration of ideas and information with your point of view.

Synthesis can take place in all four areas of your life. For example, suppose that you would like to see a particular movie this Saturday evening. You hope to convince a group of your friends to accompany you. Because you are a movie buff, you have read several reviews of the film, you know other work by the director, and you have even read the novel on which this movie is based. In other words, you have quite a bit of information to support your case that everyone should accompany you Saturday evening to see this film. At the same time, simply sending your friends all the information you have about the film might overwhelm them. Unless you effectively structure what you have to say, one piece of information may contradict some other point that you want to make. While you want to portray what you know about the film accurately, your primary purpose is to make the case to see the film.

So how would you go about organizing your information about the film in order to convince your friends? You could focus on what you see as the most compelling reasons your friends should see the film: the novel the film is based on, along with the director of the movie. You would then provide information on the following:

- How good the novel was, with specific examples to show what you mean
- How effectively the novel has been translated to film, again, with several examples—probably quotations from reviews or other information about the film—as evidence
- Other films by the same director that you know your friends like

---

"Round-Robin" activities help students learn writing conventions. The chapters in Parts 2 and 3 each include a collaborative "Round-Robin" activity in the "Knowledge of Conventions" section that asks students to focus on a particular writing convention. These activities help students learn sentence-level conventions in the context of their own writing. The text also includes a grammar handbook that students can use for easy reference. The handbook includes "Writer's Workshop" activities that can be done collaboratively.

WRITER'S WORKSHOP
Round-Robin Editing with a Focus on Fragments

Because exploratory writing often includes incomplete thoughts, writers sometimes inadvertently use sentence fragments to express their thinking. A sentence fragment is missing one or more of the following elements: a subject, a verb, or a complete thought. Some fragments lack a subject, a verb, or both:

FRAGMENT   College sports are popular. *Generating lots of money for schools with successful teams.*

Other fragments have subjects and verbs, but they begin with a subordinating word like *because* or *although* and so are not complete thoughts:

FRAGMENT   *Although I have played football in high school and college.* I'm not good enough to play on a professional team.

Some fragments are intentional, especially if they occur in dialogue. Unintentional fragments, however, need to be corrected. You can correct a sentence fragment by adding the element that is missing or connecting it to a sentence that precedes or follows it:

The Support Package for *The Brief McGraw-Hill Guide: Writing for College, Writing for Life*

The Brief McGraw-Hill Guide offers a rich support package for the composition classroom, with free and premium media options, a comprehensive Instructor's Resource Manual, and instructor access to *Partners in Teaching*—the McGraw-Hill faculty development Web site for Composition.

Online Learning Center powered by *Catalyst 2.0* Catalyst 2.0, McGraw-Hill's online resource for writing, research, and editing, is available with every student and instructor copy of *The Brief McGraw-Hill Guide.*

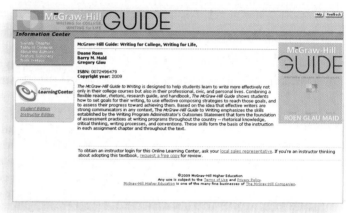

Features you'll find online include the following:

- Interactive tutorials for analyzing images and visual rhetoric
- Guides for avoiding plagiarism and evaluating sources
- Electronic writing tutors for composing informative, interpretive, and argumentative papers
- Bibliomaker software for MLA, APA, Chicago, and CSE styles of documentation
- Over 4,500 exercises with feedback in grammar, usage, and punctuation
- A state-of-the-art course management and peer review system

The McGraw-Hill Guide Online: This fully interactive version of the print text includes all the writing scenarios and readings from the text as well as the writing instruction and writing process coverage in a format optimized for online reading. Students can compose and submit papers in response to assigned writing scenarios, reading selections, or complete units online. In addition, they can take advantage of over two hundred "Ask the Author" video segments, all new interactive writing tutors, and a wide range of other activities and tools that facilitate writing and learning.

Partners in Teaching: **Faculty Development Web site for Composition (www.mhhe. com/englishcommunity)** McGraw-Hill is proud to partner with many of the top names in the field to build a community of teachers helping teachers. *Partners in Teaching* features up-to-date scholarly discourse, practical teaching advice, and community support for individual instructors, graduate student programs, and professional development seminars.

The site features two main parts:

The Teaching Comp Blog and Discussion Board

This online resource is the next stage of the successful *Partners in Teaching* listserv for composition. Join in the conversation about new topics each month to discuss the latest trends, strategies, and issues in composition in our new Teaching Comp blog, moderated by Chris Anson.

Teaching Topic Modules

Created by experts, the Teaching Topics modules explore key concerns in composition today. Each module contains a wealth of information on its topic: an introductory Background section, an extensive Bibliography, practical Teaching Strategies, and helpful Video Mentors. In addition, instructors can download resources for teaching, including Handouts, classroom PowerPoint Presentations, and Video Lecture Launchers. Combining the latest academic research with practical teaching tools, the modules provide incredible resources for new and experienced instructors.

Instructor's Resource Manual Written by the authors of *The Brief McGraw-Hill Guide,* this in-depth resource includes advice and chapter-by-chapter support by three of the discipline's preeminent rhetoricians. This valuable resource features suggested assignment sequences, sample syllabi, in-class activities, and discussion topics as well as classroom management techniques and advice for new instructors.

Acknowledgments

On a personal level, we'd like to thank our colleagues at Arizona State University, who've heard us talking about the project (probably more than they'd wished to!), offered constant support, and gave us good advice: Demetria Baker, O. M. "Skip" Brack, Barbara D'Angelo, Frank D'Angelo, Chitralekha Duttagupta, Ben Fasano, Janice Frangella, Maureen Goggin, Sonia Gracia-Grondin, Jeremy Helm, Glenn Irvin, Ruth Johnston, Keith Miller, Neal Lester, Silvia Llamas-Flores, Patricia Murphy, Camille Newton, Sherry Rankins Robertson, Dave Schwalm, and Linda Searcy. Duane would like especially to thank Hanna and Maureen Roen.

A number of people have made important contributions to this text and its media components. Cynthia Jeney of Missouri Western State University contributed most of the TechNotes, for which we thank her. Charlotte Smith of Adirondack Community College helped us locate reading selections, and Joanna Imm, Julie McBurney, and Judy Voss all provided editorial suggestions and guidance at various stages. Video producers Peter Berkow and Bruce Coykendahl have worked tirelessly on the videos that are part of *The Brief McGraw-Hill Guide Online* and the Faculty Development Web site. Debora Person of the University of Wyoming provided expert commentary on the sections on library and Internet research, for which we thank her.

At McGraw-Hill, we were fortunate to have some of the best in the business helping us with this project, including Steve Debow, president of the Humanities, Social Science, and Languages group; Mike Ryan, editor in chief; Sharon Loeb, director of marketing; Tami Wederbrand, our tireless and highly creative marketing manager; Ray Kelley, Paula Radosevich, Byron Hopkins, Audra Bussey, and Brian Gore, our terrific field publishers; and Jeff Brick, advertising design manager. Sherree D'Amico, our senior sales representative, and Mina Mathies, our regional manager, have both provided us with valuable advice. Betty Chen, Molly Meneely, and Mia Alvar have all made contributions both to the text and the supplements, and Paul Banks, media development editor, has worked tirelessly on the *The Brief McGraw-Hill Guide Online* and has provided us with useful comments on the text. Kim Menning and Jeanne Schreiber oversaw the beautiful design of the text, Janice Fehler copy edited the text, Jennifer Blankenship and Natalia Peschiera handled the photo research, and Brett Coker was responsible for seeing the text through production. We owe special thanks to Lisa Moore, now the publisher for history, arts, and the humanities, who originally helped us develop the concept and signed the project, and to Chris Bennem, senior sponsoring editor, who has guided us "editorially" in a thoughtful and kind manner. We also owe a special thanks to Carla Samodulski, senior development editor, who is quite simply the best developmental editor in the business. Thanks Lisa, Chris, and Carla.

The following instructors provided extremely useful advice about rhetorics at symposiums sponsored by McGraw-Hill, for which we thank them:

Edith Baker, Bradley University

Charles Boyd, Genesee Community College

Amy Braziller, Red Rocks Community College-Lakewood

Jo Ann Buck, Guilford Technical Community College

Susan Callender, Sinclair Community College

Sandra Clark, Anderson University

Mary Ann Crawford, Central Michigan University

Brock Dethier, Utah State University

Anthony Edgington, University of Toledo

Steve Fox, Indiana University-Purdue University Indianapolis

Elaine Fredericksen, University of Texas-El Paso

Carolyn Handa, University of Alabama-Tuscaloosa

Christa Higgins Raney, University of North Alabama

Kim Jameson, Oklahoma City Community College

Nanette Jaynes, Wesleyan College

Peggy Jolly, University of Alabama-Birmingham

Elizabeth Kessler, University of Houston-Houston

Sandra Lakey, Pennsylvania College of Technology

Barry Mauer, University of Central Florida

John Miles, University of New Mexico-Albuquerque

Dave Reinheimer, Southeast Missouri State University

Denise Rogers, University of Louisiana-Lafayette

Mary Sauer, Indiana University-Purdue University Indianapolis

> " I love the readings! They are one of the outstanding parts of the book. They are not simply didactic or chosen because they deal with politically correct topics, though they often do. They are just exceedingly well written and highly engaging pieces that both I and my students can enjoy. It's hard to choose a favorite, ... "
>
> —Geraldine Wagner, Johnson & Wales University

> " Students are critical consumers today, and they want to know what they're getting for their investment in time and money. Presenting the goals and objectives up front honors their intelligence. "
>
> —Christopher Twiggs, Florida Community College

Mark Saunders, Front Range Community College, Boulder City

Kip Strasma, Illinois Central College

Gordon Thomas, University of Idaho

Donna Thomsen, Johnson & Wales University, Providence

Jeffrey Weimelt, Southeastern Louisiana University

John M. Ziebell, College of Southern Nevada

As we developed this text, we needed to test each assignment chapter in actual classrooms. We are immensely grateful to the following instructors and their students for class-testing chapters from *The Brief McGraw-Hill Guide* and providing us with frank and valuable feedback:

Angela Adams, Loyola University-Chicago

Luisa Benton, El Centro College

Charley Boyd, Genesee Community College

Marybeth Bradley, Grand Rapids Community College

Robin Bryant, Phillips Community College of the University of Arkansas

Laura Butler, West Texas A&M University

Regina Clemens Fox, Arizona State University

Michelle Crummey, Southwest Missouri State University

Sarah Dean, Arizona State University

James Drake, Arizona State University

Darrel Elmore, Arizona State University

Malvina Engelberg, Nova Southeastern University

Katy Grant, Arizona State University

Gwen Gray Schwartz, University of Arizona

Nanette Jaynes, Wesleyan College

Ellen Johnson, Arizona State University

Sally Lahmon, Sinclair Community College

William Lamb, Johnson County Community College

Jeanne Levy, Arizona State University

Leanne Maunu, Palomar College

Examples are plentiful, directions are practical, and the readings are refreshingly current. Thank goodness there are many new topics and different authors!

—Cindy Catherwood, Metropolitan Community College

This book provides a sound, student-friendly approach to writing for many purposes and in many genres, with excellent professional readings. A highlight of the text is the integration of actual student work into the writing process section of each assignment chapter.

—Steve Fox, Indiana University-Purdue University Indianapolis

Mildred Melendez, Sinclair Community College

Susan Miller, Mesa Community College

Terry Moore, Arizona State University

Karyn Reidell, Arizona State University

Jill Richards-Young, Arizona State University

Jenny Rytting, Arizona State University

Sarah Schwab, St. Louis University

Tom Skeen, Arizona State University

Carol Smith, Coastal Georgia Community College

Dana Tait, Arizona State University

Laci Talley, Baton Rouge Community College

Jillian Toomey, University of Arizona

Julie Townsend, University of North Carolina

Anna Varley, University of Arizona

Keith Yokley, Greensboro College

Finally, we are extremely grateful to all of the instructors who have provided us with their insights and suggestions as we have developed this project:

Michelle Auerbach, Front Range Community College-Boulder

Adrian Ayres Fisher, Triton College

Edith Baker, Bradley University

Larry Beason, University of South Alabama-Mobile

Luisa Benton, El Centro College

Kyle Bishop, Southern Utah University

Vicki Bott, University of Wisconsin-Milwaukee

Charley Boyd, Genesee Community College

Barbara Brown, San Jacinto College-Pasadena

Robin Bryant, Phillips Community College of the University of Arkansas

Jo Ann Buck, Guilford Technical Community College

Polly Buckingham, Eastern Washington University

> *"This text comes more closely to fitting the way I teach my class in terms of building on assignments, the writing process, and the various components of the process and assignments than any other text I've used or surveyed. And as I mentioned at the beginning, I generally "force" a text to fit into my classroom; this textbook would not have to be forced to fit into my instructional goals and objectives as so many others are."*
>
> —Susie Kuilan, Northwestern State University, LA

Michael Burke, Southern Illinois University-Edwardsville

Laura Butler, West Texas A&M University

Sharon Buzzard, Quincy University

Susan Callender, Sinclair Community College

Vincent Casaregola, St. Louis University

Cindy Catherwood, Metropolitan Community College

Gary Christenson, Elgin Community College

Ann Christiansen, University of Houston-Houston

Ron Christiansen, Salt Lake Community College

Sandra Clark, Anderson University

Regina Clemens Fox, Arizona State University

Carol Conder, University of Nevada-Las Vegas

David Correll, Langston University

Mark Crane, Utah Valley State College

Mary Ann Crawford, Central Michigan University

Sarah Dean, Arizona State University

Debra Dew, University of Colorado

Anthony Edgington, University of Toledo

Jonell Farrar, San Jacinto College-Pasadena

Daniel Ferguson, Amarillo College

Steve Fox, Indiana University-Purdue University Indianapolis

Elaine Frederickson, University of Texas-El Paso

Lisa Gordon, Columbus State Community College

Jeanne Ann Graham, Ivy Tech Community College

Gordon Grant, Baylor University

Carolyn Handa, University of Alabama-Tuscaloosa

Anne Helms, Alamance Community College

Anneliese Homan, State Fair Community College

Phil Hutcheon, San Joaquin Delta Community College

Jon Inglett, Oklahoma City Community College

"The Brief McGraw-Hill Guide: Writing for College, Writing for Life is an exceptionally thorough approach to teaching composition skills. Its focus on rhetorical techniques and critical thinking, along with its attention to writing beyond the composition classroom, make it stand apart from other composition texts."

—Jessica Kidd, University of Alabama, Tuscaloosa

"This text approaches writing from an organic perspective—that is, the text demonstrates that good, effective writing does not come from strict adherence to genre formulas, but rather, good writing grows out of a writer's understanding of purpose, audience, and situation."

—James Krajewski, Kansas City Kansas Community College

Peggy Jolly, University of Alabama-Birmingham

Dennis Kasum, University of South Florida

Elizabeth Kessler, University of Houston

Jessica Kidd, University of Alabama- Tuscaloosa

James Krajewski, Kansas City Kansas Community College

Julie Kratt, Cowley County Community College

Susie Kuilan, Northwestern State University

Sally Lahmon, Sinclair Community College

Sandra Lakey, Pennsylvania College of Technology

William Lamb, Johnson County Community College

Marianne Liauba, South Suburban College

Lucinda Ligget, Ivy Tech Community College

Margaret Lindgren, University of Cincinnati

Michael Mackey, Community College of Denver

Martha Marinara, University of Central Florida

Kelly Martin, Collin County Community College- Plano

Barry Mauer, University of Central Florida

Leanne Maunu, Palomar College

Mary Pat McQueeney, Johnson County Community College

Elizabeth Metzger, University of South Florida

Philip Mitchell, Dallas Baptist University

Cindy Moore, Eastern Kentucky University

Lyle Morgan, Pittsburg State University

Robin Mosher, Kansas State University

Bonnie Noonan, Xavier University of Louisiana

Michelle Pichon, Northwestern State University

Shelby Pierce, Owens Community College

Erin Pushman, Limestone College

Christa Raney, University of North Alabama

David Reinheimer, Southeast Missouri State University

Lois Reynolds, Pellissippi State

> Overall, I think this book looks really good. I'm intrigued by how much this book will change how I teach this class while really supporting the goals I already incorporate into my classroom. Excellent work!
>
> —Sarah Dean,
> Arizona State University

> [The Brief McGraw-Hill Guide] ... teaches sound rhetorical theory in an accessible and engaging manner with effective support for both students and instructors ...this text would be a useful addition to the texts that our instructors choose among.
>
> —Martha Marinara,
> University of Central Florida

Paul Rodgers, Henry Ford Community College

Denise Rogers, University of Louisiana-Lafayette

Shirley Rose, Purdue University-West Lafayette

Mary Sauer, Indiana University-Purdue University Indianapolis

Mark Saunders, Front Range Community College-Boulder

Barbara Schneider, University of Toledo

William Schuh, Erie Community College

Nick Serra, Upper Iowa University

Michelle Sidler, Auburn University

Eric Stalions, Augusta State University

Ed Stieve, Nova Southeastern University

Denise Sutton, Grand Rapids Community College

David Tanner, Eastern Arizona College

Donna Thomsen, Johnson & Wales University

Christopher Twiggs, Florida Community College

Geraldine Wagner, Johnson & Wales University

Colin Wansor, Indiana University of Pennsylvania

William Waters, Northwest Missouri State University

Scott Weeden, Indiana University-Purdue University Indianapolis

Temple West, Old Dominion University

Rosemary Winslow, Catholic University of America

Lynn Woodbury, Oakton Community College

Keith Yokley, Greensboro College

Kathie Zemke, Western Illinois University

"*This is a text that addresses the many kinds of writing our students will be called upon to complete—not just in their academic lives, but in their personal and professional lives as well. This text will help faculty prepare students for the kinds of real world writing that will convince students that writing is integral to their success both in and beyond the college classroom.... We look forward to its publication.* "

—Donna Thomsen, Johnson & Wales University

Duane Roen
Gregory R. Glau
Barry M. Maid

WPA Outcomes Statement for First-Year Composition

Adopted by the Council of Writing Program Administrators (WPA), April 2000

For further information about the development of the Outcomes Statement, please see
> http://comppile.tamucc.edu/WPAoutcomes/continue.html

For further information about the Council of Writing Program Administrators, please see
> http://www.wpacouncil.org

A version of this statement was published in *WPA: Writing Program Administration* 23.1/2 (fall/winter 1999): 59-66

Introduction

This statement describes the common knowledge, skills, and attitudes sought by first-year composition programs in American postsecondary education. To some extent, we seek to regularize what can be expected to be taught in first-year composition; to this end the document is not merely a compilation or summary of what currently takes place. Rather, the following statement articulates what composition teachers nationwide have learned from practice, research, and theory. This document intentionally defines only "outcomes," or types of results, and not "standards," or precise levels of achievement. The setting of standards should be left to specific institutions or specific groups of institutions.

Learning to write is a complex process, both individual and social, that takes place over time with continued practice and informed guidance. Therefore, it is important that teachers, administrators, and a concerned public do not imagine that these outcomes can be taught in reduced or simple ways. Helping students demonstrate these outcomes requires expert understanding of how students actually learn to write. For this reason we expect the primary audience for this document to be well-prepared college writing teachers and college writing program administrators. In some places, we have chosen to write in their professional language. Among such readers, terms such as "rhetorical" and "genre" convey a rich meaning that is not easily simplified. While we have also aimed at writing a document that the general public can understand, in limited cases we have aimed first at communicating effectively with expert writing teachers and writing program administrators.

These statements describe only what we expect to find at the end of first-year composition, at most schools a required general education course or sequence of courses. As writers move beyond first-year composition, their writing abilities do not merely improve. Rather, students' abilities not only diversify along disciplinary and professional lines but also move into whole new levels where expected outcomes expand, multiply, and diverge. For this reason, each statement of outcomes for first-year composition is followed by suggestions for further work that builds on these outcomes.

RHETORICAL KNOWLEDGE

By the end of first year composition, students should

- Focus on a purpose
- Respond to the needs of different audiences
- Respond appropriately to different kinds of rhetorical situations
- Use conventions of format and structure appropriate to the rhetorical situation
- Adopt appropriate voice, tone, and level of formality
- Understand how genres shape reading and writing
- Write in several genres

Faculty in all programs and departments can build on this preparation by helping students learn

- The main features of writing in their fields
- The main uses of writing in their fields
- The expectations of readers in their fields

CRITICAL THINKING, READING, AND WRITING

By the end of first year composition, students should

- Use writing and reading for inquiry, learning, thinking, and communicating
- Understand a writing assignment as a series of tasks, including finding, evaluating, analyzing, and synthesizing appropriate primary and secondary sources
- Integrate their own ideas with those of others
- Understand the relationships among language, knowledge, and power

Faculty in all programs and departments can build on this preparation by helping students learn

- The uses of writing as a critical thinking method
- The interactions among critical thinking, critical reading, and writing
- The relationships among language, knowledge, and power in their fields

PROCESSES

By the end of first year composition, students should

- Be aware that it usually takes multiple drafts to create and complete a successful text
- Develop flexible strategies for generating, revising, editing, and proof-reading
- Understand writing as an open process that permits writers to use later invention and re-thinking to revise their work
- Understand the collaborative and social aspects of writing processes
- Learn to critique their own and others' works
- Learn to balance the advantages of relying on others with the responsibility of doing their part
- Use a variety of technologies to address a range of audiences

Faculty in all programs and departments can build on this preparation by helping students learn

- To build final results in stages
- To review work-in-progress in collaborative peer groups for purposes other than editing
- To save extensive editing for later parts of the writing process
- To apply the technologies commonly used to research and communicate within their fields

KNOWLEDGE OF CONVENTIONS

By the end of first year composition, students should

- Learn common formats for different kinds of texts
- Develop knowledge of genre conventions ranging from structure and paragraphing to tone and mechanics
- Practice appropriate means of documenting their work
- Control such surface features as syntax, grammar, punctuation, and spelling

Faculty in all programs and departments can build on this preparation by helping students learn

- The conventions of usage, specialized vocabulary, format, and documentation in their fields
- Strategies through which better control of conventions can be achieved

THE **BRIEF**
McGraw-Hill
GUIDE

WRITING for COLLEGE, WRITING for LIFE

1

Getting Started

Writing Goals and Objectives for College and for Life

Whenever you write in college, or for any other purpose in your life, you write to fulfill a goal. In school, you write papers and essay exam answers to demonstrate what you have learned and communicate your ideas to others. Writing is also a powerful tool for learning course material. You can use it every day to take notes during lectures and annotate assigned reading. Outside of school, you probably use—or will use—writing to perform your duties in the workplace and to make your voice heard in your community. You might also use writing to communicate with friends and family. Many of us keep in touch with our loved ones through daily e-mail exchanges or text messages.

Whether you are writing for a course or for a nonacademic reason, though, one of the most important principles of this book is that effective writers achieve their objectives with their writing. Throughout the ages, rhetoricians, scholars who study the subject of written and oral communication, have understood the importance of using language to get things done. Consider the following definitions of **rhetoric** by some well-known rhetoricians:

> Rhetoric is "the means whereby language, spoken or written, may be rendered effective."
>
> —Alexander Bain, *English Composition and Rhetoric,* 1866*

> Rhetoric is "the faculty of observing in any given case the available means of persuasion."
>
> —Aristotle, *Rhetoric*

> Rhetoric is the "symbolic means of inducing cooperation in beings that by nature respond to symbols."
>
> —Kenneth Burke, *A Rhetoric of Motives,* 1950

> Rhetoric is "the art of Speaking in such a manner as to obtain the end for which we speak."
>
> —John Getty, *Elements of Rhetoric,* 1831

> "Rhetoric is the art, practice, and study of human communication."
>
> —Andrea Lunsford

---

*You can find citations for all quotations in this text in the Acknowledgments section at the end of the book. For an explanation of the MLA and APA style for citing sources, which are used in many academic disciplines, see Chapter 20.

Rhetoric is "a study of misunderstanding and its remedies."
—I. A. Richards, *The Philosophy of Rhetoric*, 1936

You have probably noticed that in each definition, the rhetorician focuses on using words—either spoken or written—to achieve some goal. Other than perhaps the yell you release when you stub your toe, most discourse, whether spoken or written, has some goal or **purpose:** to explain, to inform, to persuade, to indicate how to do something. In your college, civic, professional, and personal worlds, you use words to *do* things, to accomplish your objectives.

Taking our cue from the rhetoricians quoted above, we have endeavored to give each chapter in this book—especially the chapters in Parts 2 and 3, which provide writing assignments—a *rhetorical* focus. Each chapter focuses on what you as a writer want your writing to *accomplish*. (The writing you will do for the chapters in Part 2 will have an informative or explanatory purpose; the writing you will do for the chapters in Part 3 will have a persuasive or argumentative purpose.) The first decision any writer makes, then, is rhetorical: what would you like this writing to *do* for a particular group of readers—your **audience**—at a particular place and time? All of your subsequent writing decisions follow from your goals. Once you have determined your goals, you are prepared to decide how much and what kinds of information your audience needs to know, what kind of research you might need to conduct to collect this information, what kind of evidence will be convincing to your audience, and the best format in which to present your information.

This rhetorical approach may be different from the kind of writing you have done in the past, where you were perhaps assigned to write an essay or a research paper on a particular topic, with no notion of an audience or a purpose for that paper. But if you think about the writing that you do on your own, outside of class, you will see that you do not decide to write a letter or send an e-mail or construct a formal proposal until you figure out your purpose—what you want that letter or e-mail or proposal to do. As noted in the next section of this chapter, this rhetorical approach applies to writing that you do in various settings—not just in the classroom.

Rhetoric is "the art of [a good person] speaking well."
—Quintilian, *Institutes of Oratory*, 95 C.E.

Writing in the Four Areas of Your Life

You may think that the writing skills you will learn in this course are meant to help you write successfully in your other classes as well, and of course the ability to write effective college papers is an important goal of

Rhetoric: "the ways one person attempts to act on another, to make him laugh or think, squirm or thrill, hate or mate"

—James Moffett, *Teaching the Universe of Discourse*, 1968

this course and this text. Writing skills are vitally important not just in college, however, but also in the professional, civic, and personal parts of your life.

Consider how you plan to spend the twenty-four hours in each day for the next week, the next month, the next year, the next four years, the next decade, and the next six decades. If you are like most students, during the next few years you will devote most of your time to your academic studies. If your college or university is typical, though, you and some of your classmates—possibly a majority of them—may spend anywhere from ten to forty hours a week working at paying jobs while attending college. Everyone in your class will also devote some time to their family and friends. Some will even become involved in their communities by working in a political campaign, doing volunteer work for a charitable or community organization, coaching a youth sport, or participating in another type of civic-oriented activity.

When you finish your academic studies, however, your time commitments will probably change. Although it is possible that you may still be a full-time student half a decade from now, it is more likely that you will devote more time to the other three parts of your life—especially to your professional life. In today's rapidly changing work world, though, you will probably need to return to the academic world at some point to keep developing your professional skills by acquiring new information, learning new skills, or mastering new technology.

WRITING ACTIVITY

Balancing the Four Areas of Life

Working with two or three of your classmates, answer the following questions about the bar graph shown in Figure 1.1. Compare and discuss your responses. Your instructor may ask your small group to share its findings with the rest of the class.

- Which bar graph (1, 2, 3, or 4) comes closest to representing the current balance in your life?

- Which bar graph comes closest to representing what you consider the ideal balance for someone enrolled full-time in college? For someone enrolled part-time? For a student with family responsibilities and/or a part-time or full-time job?

- Which bar graph best represents the balance that you would like to achieve a decade from now? Two decades from now? Five decades from now?

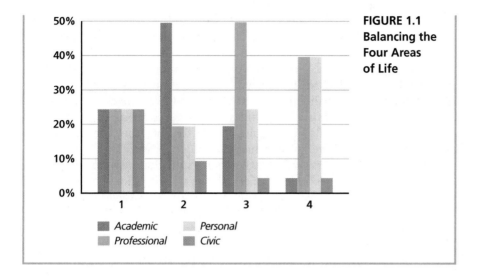

FIGURE 1.1 Balancing the Four Areas of Life

No matter how the four areas of your life are balanced, writing plays an important role in each of them.

Writing as a College Student

You will be expected to do a great deal of writing in college because writing is a powerful tool both for learning and for demonstrating that learning. Students who use writing to explore course material generally learn more—and get higher grades—than students who do not. The reason for this enhanced performance is fairly simple: Writing is an effective way to become more involved with your course material.

Many instructors will expect you to demonstrate what you have learned by writing. Your composition course will provide you with skills you will need to compose essays, lab reports, case studies, and other forms of writing you will be expected to do in the disciplines. The in-class writing, journal entries, and papers you write in this course will help you develop the skills and knowledge you will need to write throughout the rest of your college career.

See Chapter 3 for writing-to-learn strategies.

Writing as a Professional

Almost all jobs require some writing; some require a great deal of it. Furthermore, there is a general correlation between the prestige of a job—and the level of income it generates—and the amount of writing required for that job. That is, people in important jobs that pay higher salaries tend to write more than people in lower-level jobs. The time to build essential writing skills is now while you are an undergraduate student.

At the beginning of each semester, David Sudol, a professor at Arizona State University, asks students in his business and professional writing classes to interview a professional person in a position like the one they hope to have one day. Students ask about the types and amount of writing their subject handles every day. No matter what the position, Professor Sudol's students are always astonished at how much writing is involved. Whether the students aspire to be nurses, attorneys, teachers, accountants, or business owners, the professionals holding and doing the jobs they are training for *always* routinely do more writing than the students expect.

Surveys of employers consistently yield results that bear out the importance of writing in the work world: employers want to hire people who can write and speak clearly and effectively, think critically, solve problems efficiently, work well in teams, and use technology thoughtfully. In other words, they prefer employees who have already developed these soft skills in college. Of course, developing these skills takes many years, so the most competitive job seekers are those who begin honing these skills as early as possible.

Writing as a Citizen

As Thomas Jefferson frequently noted, democracies—and societies in general—work best when citizens are well-educated and get involved. If you have strong feelings about certain issues and want to have a voice in how your society functions, you need to participate in your community. Of course, you can get involved by volunteering your time: for example, by building homes with Habitat for Humanity or serving as a Big Sister or Big Brother. You can also get involved by studying candidates' positions and ballot initiatives before voting on them. But an important way to make your voice heard in a representative democracy is to write. You can write to elected officials at the local, state, and federal levels to let them know what you think about an issue and why you think the way that you do: "I'm in favor of this pending legislation because . . .". You can write letters to your local newspaper. You can also write brochures, newsletters, or other documents to further the work of your volunteer organization or to advance a cause you care about. In the civic part of your life you most often will work with others—neighbors or other citizens who are involved and interested in solving problems that affect them, their neighborhood, and their community.

Writing as a Family Member or Friend

Even though writing in the academic, professional, and civic areas of life is important, the writing that you do in your personal life is probably the most important of all. We write to the people who are important to us—whether on paper or in cyberspace—to accomplish life's daily tasks and to fulfill our needs. For instance, we write letters or e-mail messages to family and friends to sustain our relationships with them. We maintain Web sites with information about our personal interests. We write letters to a child's teacher or a parent's doctor. We participate in Web logs (blogs) about topics that matter to us—a favorite sports team, a hobby, a travel destination. We write daily journals to record and reflect on our experiences.

WRITING ACTIVITY

Your Writing in the Four Areas of Life

Think of all the writing that you have done in the past week in each of the four areas of your life. Using the chart below, make a list of that writing. We have provided an example to get you started. When you have finished, compare notes with two or three classmates. What are the major similarities and differences in the lists that the group members constructed? How can you explain the differences?

Writing in the Four Areas of My Life

Area of Life	Topic	Audience	Purpose
ACADEMIC	Summary of chapter in biology textbook	myself	To spend time thinking about biology concepts so that I understand them better
PROFESSIONAL			
CIVIC			
PERSONAL			

 ## Writing in the Four Areas in This Course

Because the academic, professional, civic, and personal parts of our lives are all important, this book offers numerous opportunities to write in all four areas. In each chapter in Part 2, you have the option of writing in response to an academic, professional, civic, or personal situation. You and your instructor may decide that you want to focus on one area or more than one, and this book gives you that choice.

Because any writing you do will have various rhetorical goals and purposes, what you will learn in this book will help you make the right kinds of writing choices whether you are writing an academic essay, working with others to construct a business proposal, writing a letter to the editor about a community problem, or writing to console an unhappy friend. In addition, the writing assignments in Parts 2 and 3 are built around **scenarios**—simulated but realistic writing situations. For each assignment, you will have a specific purpose for constructing your writing and a specific audience you are writing to. In each chapter, we have provided two scenarios focused on academic writing and three scenarios that you might encounter outside of college.

 ## Learning Goals in This Course

Whether you are writing for an academic, a professional, a civic, or a personal audience and purpose, you will need to draw on the same set of writing skills. Your work in this course will help you both to learn and to apply these skills to specific writing situations. To this end, throughout the text we have taken care to incorporate the learning goals developed by the Council of Writing Program Administrators (WPA), a national organization of instructors who direct composition courses. WPA has worked for years to develop this set of learning goals, which its members consider crucial for students in first-year writing courses to master. The goals are organized into four broad areas: **rhetorical knowledge; critical thinking, reading, and writing; writing processes;** and **knowledge of conventions.** (If you want to read more about these learning goals, visit the WPA's Web site at http://www.wpacouncil.org/positions/outcomes.html.) At the beginning of each chapter in Parts 2 and 3, a chart relates these four areas to the type of writing covered in the chapter, and each chapter is then organized into sections based on these four broad areas.

Rhetorical Knowledge

As we have noted, all writing is done for a particular purpose, in response to the needs of a specific audience. In other words, writers write in response to a **rhetorical situation.** Although each rhetorical situation is unique, there are general types of situations that require writers to use the appropriate conventions of format and structure in their writing. For example, if you are writing a lab report for a biology course, your instructor will expect you to structure your report in a certain way and use a neutral, informative tone. If you are proposing a solution to a problem in your community, your readers will expect you to describe the problem first and explain how your solution can be implemented, using a reasonable, even-handed tone and giving some attention to those who might raise objections to your proposal. The established forms of writing that are used to respond to each of these situations are known as **genres.** In your writing for the courses in your field, as well as in the writing you do for the other three areas of your life, you will be expected both to understand how genres work and to use them appropriately. Genre in writing means that you follow the conventions of a kind of writing and provide, generally, what readers expect from that genre. In a formal report, for example, readers expect information and analyses, as well as data that supports any conclusions in the report. Likewise, a business letter will be more formal than, say, a memo, which will usually be somewhat informal. A paper for one of your college classes will generally be more formal and detailed than an e-mail you might write to your classmates, asking them to vote in an upcoming election.

From a rhetorical standpoint, you select the format to use (a letter, an e-mail, a memo, a formal report) based on what you want to accomplish. Think of format as the overall structure of the piece of writing you are constructing. For example, a letter will have a salutation, a body, and a signature. The format of that letter could vary widely. For instance, in the body of the letter, you will usually have sentences organized in paragraphs. However, you could just as easily have a bulleted or numbered list in a paragraph.

To write for others successfully, then, you need to determine how to adapt your writing to meet their expectations and needs. In other words, you need to focus on where there is a meeting of minds—yours and theirs—and where there is not. For example, if you were to write the following grocery list and take it to the store, you would probably know precisely what you had in mind. Take a moment to think about what you would bring home.

Grocery List
cereal
milk
coffee
bread
paper

If you were sick, however, and had to rely on a close family member to do your grocery shopping for you, you might have to revise the list by adding a few more details:

A Version of the Grocery List for a Family Member
Cereal
1% milk
Coffee beans
White bread
Sunday paper

If you handed the list to a neighbor, though, you would probably have to add much more specific information:

A Version of the Grocery List for a Neighbor
Grape Nuts Flakes
1% milk (half gallon)
whole bean Starbuck's Columbian coffee
Grandma Sycamore's white bread
The New York Times

In each case, you need to adjust your list depending on the person who will be acting on the information. When you share a great deal of lived experience with your reader, you can leave gaps in information without causing serious problems. The fewer experiences you have in common with your audience, however, the more you need to fill in those gaps while you write and revise, rather than after you have finished writing. The best way to identify those gaps is to share your writing with as many people as possible so that they can point them out.

> "Rhetoric is a form of reasoning about probabilities, based on assumptions people share as members of a community."
> —Erika Lindemann

The Rhetorical Knowledge section in each chapter in Parts 2 and 3 includes a discussion of academic as well as professional, civic, and personal writing situations that call for the type of writing covered in the chapter. The section also includes two academic writing scenarios and a professional, civic, and personal writing scenario. The academic scenarios call for academic essays; the professional, civic, and personal scenarios call for a variety of genres including reports, letters to the editor, Web sites, and e-mails.

Critical Thinking, Reading, and Writing

To get the most out of your reading, and to accomplish your goals as a writer, you need to develop and use critical thinking skills. In Chapter 2 we offer some informal reading and writing activities that promote critical thinking. While these activities will help you read more thoughtfully, many of them are also tools for generating ideas and material for the more formal writing tasks you will do in all four parts of your life—especially in college, where critical thinking is one of the most universally valued skills.

In general, you use **critical thinking** when you examine an idea from many perspectives—seeing it in new ways. For example, when you write a formal argument, you will need to address others' objections to your ideas if you hope to persuade your audience to accept your point. You can also apply critical thinking to understand the relationships among language, knowledge, and power. That is, language often has a greater effect when it is used by people in positions of social, political, or economic power. For instance, if you were to utter the words, "I declare that our army will invade Country A," your sentence would *not* result in any military action. It might result in a psychological examination, though. If, on the other hand, the President of the United States utters those same words, military action is likely to follow. This is not to say, though, that powerful people are the only ones who can use language powerfully. When a news anchor reads a letter from a soldier in a war zone, that letter has the power to move listeners.

Recognizing the power of language, Victorian novelist Edward Bulwer-Lytton asserted that "beneath the rule of men entirely great, the pen is mightier than the sword" (*Richelieu*, act 2, scene 2). What that means for us in the twenty-first century is that language, when used effectively, is often far more powerful than physical weapons. Modern civilizations have written constitutions and written laws derived from those constitutions. The most politically and economically powerful people in societies tend to be those who use language most effectively to present their ideas.

To foster your critical reading skills, we start the section on Critical Thinking, Reading, and Writing in the chapters in Parts 2 and 3 with a discussion of the qualities of the type of writing covered in that chapter. Three professional reading selections follow, giving you a chance to practice critical reading skills and learn strategies that you can apply to your writing. The section ends with a consideration of visual texts that exemplify the kind of writing covered in the chapter and a brief section on an important kind of critical reading: conducting research.

Writing Processes

Almost anyone can become an effective writer. As with any skill, however, it takes work and helpful coaching to develop into such a writer. The good news is that this book, your teacher, and your classmates are available to coach; you simply need provide the work. A major focus of that work will be the processes of composing.

Although writing processes vary from writer to writer and from situation to situation, effective writers generally need to go through the following processes:

- Generating initial ideas
- Relating those ideas to the writing situation or assignment
- Conducting research to find support for their ideas
- Organizing ideas and support and writing an initial draft
- Revising and shaping the paper, frequently with the advice of other readers
- Editing and polishing the paper

The order of these processes can vary, and often you will need to return to a previous step. For example, while drafting you may discover that you need to find more support for one of your ideas; while revising you may find a better way to organize your ideas. In addition, effective writers develop many strategies for generating ideas, for drafting, for revising, and for editing.

One common strategy effective writers use is to revise, revise, revise, and revise even more. When writers revise, they add or delete words, phrases, sentences, or even whole paragraphs, and they often modify their ideas. After they have revised multiple times, they then edit, attending to word choice, punctuation, grammar, usage, and spelling—the "surface features" of written texts. To have time for multiple rounds of revising and editing, of course, a writer needs to begin a writing task early. Beginning a formal paper the day before it is due rarely results in satisfactory work.

Efficient writers do not concern themselves with the surface features of their writing—spelling, usage, grammar, punctuation, word choice—until after they have finished revising their paper. As Ann Duin, a writing professor at the University of Minnesota, puts it, editing before revising is analogous to painting a room before remodeling it. You *could* paint the walls early in the process, but you would run the risk of painting a wall that may get ripped out later during remodeling. Another problem with obsessing about surface features early in the process is that while you are paying attention to punctuation or grammar it can be difficult to attend to other tasks—such as generating, developing, supporting, and organizing ideas.

Effective writers also understand the principle that two heads are better than one. Therefore, they ask others to help them generate and refine their ideas and polish their prose. Published writers in academic, civic, and professional fields rely heavily on others as they work, often showing one another drafts of their writing before submitting a manuscript to publishers. Once submitted, the manuscript is then reviewed by several experts in the field before it is printed as an article or book. Further, every reputable journal or publishing house relies on copy editors who improve the quality of the prose and proofreaders who catch mistakes in grammar, usage, punctuation, mechanics, and spelling. For this book project, a number of professors and others read and made suggestions—you can get a sense of how many of them helped us on page xxxix.

Because effective writers get help from others, this book provides many opportunities for your classmates—your **peers**—to help you. As you work through the writing assignments in Parts 2 and 3, you will find Writer's Workshop activities and other suggestions for working with peers. One key to working productively with others is to understand that they bring differing backgrounds, experiences, knowledge, and perspectives to the writing task, so it is critical to treat what others think and have to say with respect, no matter how much you agree or disagree with them.

You should also remember when working with others that the suggestions and comments they make are about your *text*, not about you. If someone says she likes the introduction to your text, that does not necessarily mean she likes you—or, conversely, if she says that part of your writing is confusing, that does *not* mean that she thinks you are confused! Too often writers tend to take comments and suggestions personally, as if those comments were directed at them, rather than at their text.

In the chapters in Parts 2 and 3, the section on Writing Processes gives you guidelines, writing activities, and models for generating ideas through revising your assignment. (Editing and polishing are covered in the next section, Knowledge of Conventions.) The models show a student developing his or her essay in response to an assignment; the final version of the student's essay appears at the end of the chapter. Each Writing Processes section includes a Visualizing Variations box that gives you ideas and guidelines for using visuals in your essay or choosing a more visual genre for your assignment.

Knowledge of Conventions

Conventions are the table manners of writing. At times, they matter; at other times, they do not. Writing for yourself to learn course material is like eating breakfast alone at home. Just as nobody will care—or even notice—if you eat your cereal with your fingers while wearing your pajamas, nobody will notice if you misspell words or make sentence-level errors in notes you make for yourself. When you are having dinner with your employer or the president of your college, though, table manners do matter. The same principle applies when you write for readers. Effective writers know which writing conventions they should use in particular settings.

Rhetoric: "the art of using language effectively"

—Cleanth Brooks and Robert Penn Warren, *Modern Rhetoric*, 3rd ed. 1970

Of course, writers who are striving to make their writing more appealing to readers need to master many kinds of conventions: spelling, punctuation, sentence structure, word choice. While some conventions are considered signs of the writer's respect for readers (correctly spelling someone's name, for instance), other conventions make it easier for readers to understand what you are saying. Consider the following string of words:

- "that that is is that that is not is not is it not it is"

Even if we give you the hint that this string is a philosophical observation, you still probably cannot make sense of it.

Now consider the same string of words with some punctuation:

- "That that is, is. That that is not, is not. Is it not? It is."

Just as the punctuation helps to guide the reader, other conventions—such as the organization of an essay, the paragraph breaks, the use of headings and white space, tone, and documentation style—can be equally helpful to readers.

A round-robin activity in the Knowledge of Conventions section of each chapter in Parts 2 and 3 helps you work with peers to edit your paper by looking for sentence-level problems and problems with other conventions such as proper documentation. The section also covers genres, documentation, and format.

Assessing Your Strengths and Weaknesses

Assess your strengths and weaknesses in each of the four goal areas: rhetorical knowledge; critical thinking, reading, and writing; writing processes; and knowledge of conventions. Once you have completed your assessment, share your list with two or three classmates.

 ## Becoming a Self-Reflective Writer

By evaluating your strengths and weaknesses in each of the four learning outcomes, you have taken a step toward becoming a more reflective—and therefore a more successful—writer. Throughout this course, you will continue to build on this foundation. The chapters in Parts 2 and 3 also give you an opportunity to reflect on your work following each writing assignment. Toward the end of each chapter, you will be asked to reflect on the work you did for that chapter, so that similar writing tasks will be easier for you to complete, and so that your results will be even better in the future. When you reflect—in writing—on your own writing activities, such thinking helps you learn what worked for you (and perhaps what did not work). That kind of activity helps you the next time you face a similar writing task because the reflective activity will help you remember the best aspects of your process. Reflection, too, is a major component of the WPA's and our goals and objectives: what we hope you will learn as you work with this text.

 ## Writing in Today's World

Regardless of whether they are writing for an academic, a professional, a civic, or a personal purpose, writers today have more responsibilities than ever before because with online technology it is easy to make writing available to a wide spectrum of readers. Writers who are careless in representing themselves or who use technology negligently can live to regret their lack of caution. Wise writers ask themselves the following question before publishing any of their writing electronically: what would the consequences be if this piece of writing were to appear on the front page of a local or national newspaper, a radio show, a television news program, the home page of a Web site, or a blog?

Writing Responsibly

When you write responsibly, you establish your character for your reader. The Greek philosopher and rhetorician Aristotle suggested that a writer's or speaker's *ethos*, his or her character, is one of the ways people are persuaded: readers believe you because of who you are, how you portray yourself, how you present your information, the logic you use, and the language you employ. How a writer presents himself or herself establishes that *ethos*.

Not only do writers need to present their arguments accurately and fairly, they also need to be aware of how they "sound" to their readers. You present a positive image of yourself to readers through the persona you create by the words you use. If you call opponents names and use incendiary language to describe or explain the issue you are writing about, you will come across in one way to your readers. If you are logical and well-prepared and provide solid evidence to support your case, with citations for all of your sources, you will come across in another way. Which way, do you suppose, is the most convincing to readers?

Because fulfilling your responsibilities and establishing your ethos as a writer are so important to the writing you do in any area of your life, we pay special attention to these issues in this text. Throughout the chapters in Parts 2 and 3, in the sections on Critical Thinking, Reading, and Writing, we include boxes that discuss the responsibilities that writers have for each type of writing.

Writing Technologies

As you make decisions about writing for various audiences and purposes in the four areas of your life, you will also need to make decisions about how and when to use various kinds of technology. Recently, researchers, educators, and others have been focusing on the ways in which digital technologies are affecting—positively or negatively—how people write. Such discussions are not really that new, though. For at least several thousand years humans have understood that writing is inseparable from the technologies that make it possible. For our purposes here, **technology** is a system or practice that extends human capabilities. The system of writing that we use is actually a technology for extending human thought across time and space. You can read the thoughts of the Greek philosopher Plato even though he has been dead for over two thousand years—searchable versions of Plato's writings are now available on the World Wide Web.

Other technologies facilitate the act of writing. For example, a person can write by using an index finger to inscribe letters on sand or even soft clay tablets. With your fingernails, you can inscribe less pliable surfaces such as soft wood or a wax tablet. However, the limitations of an index finger or a fingernail are obvious. To write more efficiently in sand, you could use a stick; to write more clearly on soft clay tablets, ancient people used a stylus (a sharp stick); to write on wood, charcoal is superior to a fingernail; to write on paper, a ballpoint pen is easier to use than the quill pens wielded by the signers of the Declaration of Independence. The point, of course, is that throughout history writers have always used the best technologies available to work more effectively and efficiently.

TechNote You and your friends and classmates can help each other get more out of the writing technologies that are available now or will soon become available. Let some of your friends or the members of your study group know that you would be willing to exchange knowledge by showing them shortcuts and tools in programs you are familiar with. Don't be shy about asking friends and classmates for tips and tricks they've picked up while writing their papers with computer software. You can use your own computing knowledge as social collateral in classes where students use computers to complete assignments because some students will be more comfortable than others with the available software.

For an interesting history of writing instruments, visit the About.Com Web site at http://inventors.about .com/library/weekly/ aa100197.htm.

A generation ago it was relatively difficult to integrate words and pictures because the technology for doing so was expensive and time-consuming. With the advent of the personal computer and the software that is available in this first decade of the third millennium, however, it is now relatively easy to mix words, still pictures, video segments, audio segments, and Web links in a single digital text. These capabilities have enabled writers to become more imaginative as they compose, but these capabilities have also given writers many more choices to make as they construct texts.

This book recognizes the way writing technologies affect the writing you will do in college, on the job, in your community, and in your home. Tech-Notes in each chapter offer advice on using computer technology to your best advantage. Throughout this text, you will be encouraged to make informed choices about the most appropriate technology to use for your audience and purpose. Chapter 17 offers additional advice on choosing a medium, genre, and technology for your written communication.

WRITING ACTIVITY

Assessing Your Uses of Technology

Think about the ways that you have used digital technologies in the past year. List a few tasks that you have done with technology in the grid below. When you have finished listing tasks, compare your list with those of several classmates.

Technological Tool	Academic Situation	Professional, Civic, or Personal Situation
E-mail		
Word-processing software		
Web browser (e.g., Internet Explorer, Mozilla FireFox)		
Web site composing tools (e.g., *Dreamweaver, Frontpage, Netscape Composer*)		
Web logs (blogs)		
Other		

Reading Critically for College and for Life

In Chapter 1, we considered how writing skills will serve you in the academic, professional, civic, and personal parts of your life—especially in your academic life. This chapter focuses on an activity that reinforces and helps you improve your writing skills: **reading.**

In your college classes, you will be asked to read (and write about) all kinds of print and digital texts—books, articles, Web sites, reports, newspaper stories, listservs, and others—for all kinds of purposes. More often than not, you will use some of what you read in the papers that you write for your college classes. The connection between what you read and how you use that material in your writing is stressed throughout this book. That connection requires you to read not just casually, but *critically*. If an instructor assigned you to "read this essay critically," what would you expect to do? How would you know if you had done the assignment correctly?

To define the term *reading critically*, we might begin with the first word: *reading*. When we read, of course, we make meaning out of words on a page or computer screen and try to understand what the writer meant when he or she composed the selection. We can even extend our definition to include "reading" photographs, charts and graphs, Web pages, and other visual images. Actually, reading is not simply a process of figuring out, or decoding, what words mean, but rather it is the active process of constructing meaning. In this way, reading parallels what writers do. Just as a writer works to say something through the words and sentences of a piece of writing—to provide information, perhaps, or to make a point—a reader likewise has to work to construct the meaning of that same piece of writing.

If reading is constructing meaning, what about the second word: *critically*? When you read a text critically, you are not reading to *criticize* that text, to comment on how effective or ineffective it is, but rather to question what you read, to make connections to other articles, books, and Web pages that you have read as well as to your own experiences, and to think about how the information in the text you are reading might help you as you develop your own writing. To read critically means to read *thoughtfully*, keeping in mind what you already know. To read critically also means to read *actively*, interacting with the text as you bring your prior knowledge into play. Critical readers underline, make notes, and ask questions as they read. This chapter will give you some strategies and methods for reading actively and critically.

As you think and write about what you read in college, as well as what you read in your personal, civic, or professional life, this process of reading actively and critically will enable you to do the following:

- **Consider an issue, a problem, or a topic in its full complexity:** Reading and thinking critically about a subject means that you examine it from many points of view. You consider its relevant history and background, what perspectives people have on it, and what is really important about it—what is at stake. You do not have to accept every viewpoint as valid, but you do need to recognize that other viewpoints have validity and try to understand them.

- **Pose substantial questions that probe and test the information you are reading:** When you read actively, the questions you raise about the text will require careful analysis before you can answer them.

- **Synthesize or put together all of the information:** Once you have read a text actively and critically, you should then be able to gather the relevant information, data, and ideas that you have gleaned from the reading and construct a **synthesis,** a clear, accurate outline or summary of your perspective on the issue, problem, or topic, based on your knowledge and your reading. Your synthesis should combine the new information you have just read with what you already know and should make sense out of that combination.

WRITING ACTIVITY

How Do You Read?

Take a few minutes to write your answers to these questions:

- What kinds of books do you like to read? What kinds of magazines do you like to read? Newspapers? Web sites? Blogs?
- How does the way you read a text from the World Wide Web differ from the way you read an article from a magazine or a newspaper?
- How do you read your college textbooks? How do the strategies you use to read a text for one course differ from those you use to read texts for another course?
- What strategies do you use to read long, complex nonfiction texts?
- What strategies do you use to help you understand and remember what you have read?

After you have answered the questions, share your comments with several classmates. How do your responses compare with theirs? What strategies do they use that might be helpful to you?

Using Prereading Strategies

When you write something, you usually have a purpose in mind: To borrow some money from Aunt Christina, say, or to jot down what you need to remember for a test. As we noted in Chapter 1, that reason for writing is called your **rhetorical purpose**—what you are hoping to accomplish. Likewise, before you read an article, a textbook chapter, a letter from a friend, or another piece of writing, think about your rhetorical purpose: what are you trying to accomplish by reading this text? Are you reading to be entertained, to learn new information, to understand a complex subject in more detail, or for some other reason? If you consciously think about *why* you are reading, as well as *how* you plan to read a particular text, you will have a strategy you can follow as you begin reading.

In your college classes, of course, you will probably read mostly to learn information about the subject of the course, whether it is literature, math, biology, or art history. You will learn new definitions and concepts, and you will be asked to apply those definitions and concepts to various writing tasks. In your personal life, you will read for pleasure or to learn about subjects that interest you, such as sports, film, or music. In your professional and civic worlds, you will read to learn how to perform different tasks, how to work more effectively with others, how to solve problems, or how new laws or rules might affect you and your family.

Whatever your purpose for reading, before you start to read any text, take a few minutes to preview its content and design. As you preview the text, look for the following elements:

- The title of the work, or of the particular section you are about to read
- Headings that serve as an outline of the text
- Boxes that highlight certain kinds of information
- Charts, maps, photographs, or drawings that are meant to help readers understand the information the author is providing
- Numbered or bulleted lists (such as this one) that set off certain information

Scanning these textual elements can help you get a quick sense of what you are about to read.

Think about what you bring to your reading task: In what ways does the text seem similar to or different from others of this type or on this topic that you have already read? What can you bring to the new reading that you have learned from your past experiences? Readers always bring a map to whatever they read, some notion of what they can expect from the text. For example, when you sit down with a magazine such as *Time* or *Sports Illustrated*, you probably expect to read in-depth reports about news or sporting events, letters to the editor of the magazine, profiles of famous (and infamous) news or sports personalities, and so on. If you sit down to read poetry, you expect each poem to form mind images and to involve you emotionally as well as intellectually. If you sit down with a novel, you know the story is fictional and will not assume it is truthful in the full sense of that word. If you are actively involved in the reading process and if you think of reading rhetorically—that is, if you think about what you want to get from the reading (for example, information, an explanation, directions)—then you will start with a useful map for any text you read.

After your preview, **skim** the text by reading the first and last sections or paragraphs as well as any elements that are highlighted in some way, such as boxes, section titles, headings, or terms or phrases in bold or italic type. Sometimes a box or highlighted section at the beginning of an article—often called an **abstract**—will give you a quick summary of what is ahead. Skimming the text will help you gain a broad perspective on the article, chapter, or section. If you are reading a textbook, read the preface, which usually offers a broad overview of the text, and the introduction, which is often written to help students understand and use the textbook.

As a final step before you start to read, consider again what you are hoping to accomplish by reading this particular text. Ask yourself the following questions:

- What information—facts, statistics, graphs, data—have I noticed as I previewed the text that might help me with my writing task?
- How have I reacted so far to what I have seen in the text? Has anything startled me? Pleased me? Made me curious? Made me angry?
- What questions do I have?
- What in this text seems to relate to other texts that I have read?

 ## Reading Actively

Now that previewing has given you a sense of what the text is about, you are ready to read actively. Here are some questions to ask yourself as you read your college texts or any other type of material:

- What is the writer's thesis or main point? What evidence does the writer provide to support that point? Does the writer offer statistics, facts, and expert opinion, or anecdotes (stories)? Which kind of evidence has the most validity, in your mind? Why?
- How reliable is the information in this text? How conscientiously does the writer indicate the sources of his or her data, facts, or examples? How reliable do these sources seem? Information from a reputable newspaper such as the *New York Times* or the *Washington Post* is probably more dependable than a story from a tabloid newspaper such as the *National Enquirer*. Statistics from an article in an academic

journal by a recognized authority on a given subject are more reliable than statistics quoted by an industry spokesperson and appearing on a company's Web site.

- What else do you know about this topic? How can you relate your previous knowledge to what this writer is saying? How consistent is your knowledge with what you are reading? In what ways do you agree or disagree with the point the writer is making?

- Has the writer included examples that clarify the text? Are there photographs, drawings, or diagrams that help you understand the writer's main points? Graphs or charts that illustrate data or other statistical information? Maps are a perfect example of visuals that can make information easier to understand. Consider how you are reading the visual information in the text: why might the writer have chosen the particular perspective that an illustration provides? In what way(s) do the examples and visuals help you better understand the text? What information do they give you that the written text does not provide?

FIGURE 2.1   Fans at an Eastern Kentucky University Homecoming Game

- What kinds of emotional impact do the photographs or other visual texts have? For example, a sociology textbook might include photographs of two kinds of group activities—a community-building activity, such as fans cheering at a sporting event (Figure 2.1), and a confrontational activity, such as a group of protestors in a face-off with police (Figure 2.2). How does such a pair of photographs affect you as a reader?

FIGURE 2.2 An Anti-War Protest in Oregon in March 2003

- What information or evidence is not in this text? (Your past experience and reading will help you here.) Why do you think that the author might have left it out?
- If what you are reading is an argument, how effectively does the writer acknowledge or outline other points of view on the issue at hand? How does the way the writer handles opposing views make his or her position more, or less, credible?

For more on counterargument, see Chapter 14.

Annotating Effectively

When you **annotate,** you interact actively with the text as you read. Of course, you should only mark texts that you own—if you want to annotate a text you have borrowed, consider annotating a photocopy or making notes on a separate sheet of paper or in your journal. To annotate a reading, make the following kinds of notes:

- Underline the main point or thesis of the reading or otherwise mark it as the key point.
- Underline key supporting points and indicate in the margins next to the corresponding paragraphs why you think each point is important.

Look for a photo of loon.

find website with loon call

16.5
x 6
‾‾‾‾
99 feet

As I was paddling along the north shore one very calm October afternoon, for such days especially they settle on to the lakes, like the milkweed down, having looked in vain over the pond for a loon, suddenly one, sailing out from the shore toward the middle a few rods in front of me, set up his mild laugh and betrayed himself. I pursued with a paddle and he dived, but when he came up I was nearer than before. He dived again, but I miscalculated the direction he would take, and we were fifty rods apart when he came to the surface this time, for I had helped to widen the interval; and again he laughed long and loud, and with more reason than before. He manoeuvred so cunningly that I could not get within half a dozen rods of him. Each time, when he came to the surface, turning his head this way and that, he cooly surveyed the water and the land, and apparently chose his course so that he might come up where there was the widest expanse of water and at the greatest distance from the boat. It was surprising how quickly he made up his mind and put his resolve into execution.

What is milk weed?

rod = 16.5 feet

16.5
x50
‾‾‾‾
725 feet

This reminds me of the gopher in our yard.

He attributes human qualities to the loon = anthropomorphism

FIGURE 2.3   Example of Annotations on a Page   Excerpt from the chapter "Brute Neighbors" in *Walden* by Henry David Thoreau

TechNote Are you faced with one of those jargon-filled college reading assignments? When the glossary at the back of the book just isn't enough, try searching the World Wide Web for a definition. A number of good dictionaries and glossaries are available online. One trick is to use a Web search engine to find substantial definitions of complex terms. For example, if you're looking for a working definition of *existentialism,* type "define: existential" into a search engine's search screen. Often your top results will include dictionary sites, academic Web sites, and technical sites that have developed working glossaries for students, experts, and professionals.

- List any questions you have (you may find the answers as you read further).

- Respond to the text with your own remarks—especially ideas you can relate to other ideas you are familiar with.

- Jot down key terms—and their definitions—in the margins.

- Mark sections that summarize material as summary, so you will be able to spot them more easily when you return to the text.

In the example shown in Figure 2.3, a student has annotated several paragraphs of an excerpt from the chapter "Brute Neighbors" in Henry David Thoreau's classic *Walden*. Notice how the different kinds of annotations, including definitions, comments, and even mathematical calculations, enrich the student's understanding of the passage.

WRITING ACTIVITY

Annotating "A Purpose Greater Than Oneself"

"A Purpose Greater than Oneself" is an advertisement that appeared in the *New York Times* on September 23, 2001, shortly after the terrorist attack on the World Trade Center. This advertisement does not dwell on that event, however, but rather offers a statement about how the school that placed the advertisement feels and thinks about the concept of "community" and its students.

Annotate this advertisement by underlining, adding questions in the margins, and so on. As you work, keep in mind that this *is* an advertisement—yet it really does not seem to be trying to sell a product or service. To what extent do you agree? What do you think it is advertising? Why?

Share your annotations with several of your classmates, noting places where your annotations are similar as well as places where they differ.

A PURPOSE GREATER THAN ONESELF

MISS HALL'S SCHOOL

"It is in the shelter of each other that the people live." The Irish Proverb came to mind as girls and adults gathered in the school living room to hear about the wrenching terrorist attacks on this country a week and a half ago. Together, as we articulated our shock and our anger, we confirmed the power of collective spirit, determination, and resilience. Confronted with unfathomable loss, we knew that our country would prevail. In community, we performed the ancient task of teaching the next generation that hope and trust are stronger than hate.

Perhaps it took the image of America uniting after tragedy for us to understand how important it is to resist the loss of community in contemporary culture. Recent studies argue that Western societies have experienced a noticeable decrease in social capital or social connectedness over the past few decades. Suburban sprawl, busy parents, and the scatter of extended families have reduced the time we spend together and imperiled our collective strength.

And now researchers tell us that the rise in social disconnectedness parallels the rise in children's anxiety. How could it be otherwise? When our communities weaken, the individuals in them first become distrustful, then anxious. Young people need sustained, healthy interactions in order to learn how to trust themselves and others.

Adding to the rise in anxiety is girls' awareness that we expect more of them than ever before. In *The Hurried Child*, David Elkind says that today's youngsters are the "unwilling, unintended victims [of] constantly rising expectations." As a result-oriented society, we are fixated on high growth rate and strong performance as we try to compensate for the fractures in our collective life. These goals may be perfect for the GNP, but they are not sufficient for adolescents trying to become effective and balanced adults.

We are all familiar with the demands placed on young people. We expect high achievement, high test scores, admission to elite colleges, and early steps toward a brilliant career. At one time, the important challenges of school were tempered by the warmth of family and the relaxation of unscheduled time with friends. Now, every minute not in school is scheduled. The bewildering changes in our society leave us with kids who sometimes seem to be drowning in a sea of adult requirements.

Even without the added pressure from this culture, adolescence is an uneasy time. Think of what a girl will accomplish between the ages of fourteen and eighteen. She must establish an identity, become independent from parents, learn about relationships, clarify ethical positions, grow physically, overcome awkwardness, deal with peer pressure, and maneuver through the social land mines, confronting sex, drugs, and our media-fired culture. Then, of course, she's expected to excel in Biology, Calculus, and U.S. Government and compete in team sports. Add onto that list getting into her first-choice college and keeping her room clean, and we will acknowledge that there is a lot to be uneasy about.

But a girl should not have to absorb all of the worries of the adult world just to grow up. She should not have to experience life as an unrelenting test in order to achieve. A strong community guided by wise and caring adults will empower her genius. It will let her know that she is not the only person who has ever encountered difficulty and frustration. It will connect her to others who have met serious challenges and accomplished great works. She will learn to trust the sufficiency of her person, and she will develop a purpose that is greater than herself. Instead of feeling small and anxious, she will be expansive and confident. She will relax and work from inside herself. She will do everything she needs to do and more.

Reading Visuals

While college students are most often asked to read words on paper—such as the ones you are reading now—other types of texts can be read, usually by using the same strategies you use to read sentences and paragraphs critically. However, because you see so many visual images in a typical day—on television, on billboards, in newspapers, and on the Internet—you might think that they are easy to read and to understand. You might even think that visuals are easier to read than plain old written text, but this assumption is not accurate. In fact, you often have to pay more attention to visual images, not only because they are sometimes subtler than written text, but because you are not accustomed to reading them critically.

While the process of understanding photographs, bar and line graphs, diagrams, and other visuals may seem different from that of reading and understanding textual information, you are essentially doing the same kind of work. When you read a text, you translate letters, words, and sentences into concepts and ideas; when you read a photograph or a chart (or another kind of visual image), you do the same kind of translation. And your purpose is usually the same. Just as you read a printed text such as an article in your local newspaper for information, you also read the photographs in the newspaper or the images on your television screen to be informed. In the past, instructions on how to put together a bicycle were provided as a print document. These days, they are just as likely to come on a videotape or DVD—or you can read the product's documentation on your computer. However they are presented, you read the instructions with the same purpose in mind: you want to put together your bicycle.

As you read visuals, here are some questions to consider:

- What words can I use to describe the visual? That is, how can I use words to tell what the visual shows?

- If the visual is combined with written text, what does the visual add to the verbal text? What would be lost if the visual were not there? How necessary is the visual?
- Why has the writer included the visual?
- Why do you think that the writer chose this particular format—photo, line drawing, chart, graph—for the visual?
- If you were choosing or designing a visual to illustrate this point, what would it look like?
- How accurately does the visual illustrate the point?
- What emotions does the visual evoke?

WRITING ACTIVITY

Reading Text and Visuals in an Advertisement

Select a full-page advertisement from a newspaper or magazine and read both the written text and the visual elements carefully, keeping in mind that nothing in an advertisement is left to chance. Each element, from the kind and size of the typeface to the colors to the illustrations or photographs, has been discussed and modified many times as the advertisement was developed and tested. On a separate piece of paper, jot down answers to the following questions:

- What is this advertiser trying to sell?
- What kinds of evidence does the advertisement use to convince you to buy the product or service?
- In what ways does the advertisement appeal to your emotions?
- What strategies does the advertiser employ to convince you of the credibility of the ad's message?
- How effective is this advertisement? Why?
- How might the various elements of the advertisement—colors, photos or other visuals, background, text—be changed to make the ad more, or less, effective?
- How much does the advertisement help potential buyers make informed decisions about this product?

   If your instructor asks you to do so, share your advertisements and notes with several of your classmates. What similarities did you find in the advertisements that you selected? In what ways did the advertisements make use of visuals? What were the most effective elements of the advertisements?

Reading Web Sites

Today many of us read Web sites, which can include not only text, with type in different colors and various sizes, but also photographs or other visual elements, videos that readers can click on to view, and music. To read Web sites actively and critically, you need to examine the information on your screen just as carefully as you would a page of printed text or a visual in a magazine or newspaper, asking the questions you would ask when reading a print or visual text critically (see pp. 23–25 and 28–29). Because there are more aspects of the text to examine and consider, however, and also because it is often harder to establish where a text on the Web comes from, active reading becomes even more important. Consider the following additional questions when you are reading a Web page:

- The uniform resource locator (URL) of a site, its address, can give you clues about its origin and purpose. The URL for the Library of Congress, for example, is www.loc.gov. The final three letters, (*gov*), indicate that the site is maintained by a government agency. For any page you visit, consider what the URL tells you about the page, especially the last three letters—*edu* (educational), *gov* (U.S. government), *org* (nonprofit organization), or *com* (commercial). Is the page you are visiting located on a personal site—often indicated by a name preceded by a tilde (~) in the URL—or on a site that is hosted or sanctioned by an educational, an organizational, a governmental, or a commercial agency? What difference does it make who sponsors the site?

- How reputable is the person or agency that is providing the information on this page? You can check the person's or agency's reputation by doing a Web search (in Google or Yahoo, for instance), using the name of the person or the agency as your keyword.

- What clues do you see to the motive of the person or agency that is providing this information? Is there a link to an explanation of the purpose of the site? Usually such explanations are labeled something like "About [name of organization or person]."

For further details about evaluating information on the Web, see Chapter 19, Finding and Evaluating Sources.

- How current is the information on this page? Can you find a date that indicates when the page was last updated?

- If there are links on the page, how helpful is the description of each link? Are the links working, or do they lead to dead ends?

WRITING ACTIVITY

Reading Web Pages: What You Can Really See

Using the questions above, read the following Web page. Respond in writing to as many of the questions as you can. Compare your responses with those of your classmates.

Image above: High-resolution, digital scan of a full frame from the original Apollo 16 film showing the object in question (top center) and its position relative to the moon. Reflections in the window are also visible (left and right). Credit: NASA

Beginning their return from the moon to an April 27, 1972, splashdown, Astronauts John Young, Thomas Mattingly and Charles Duke captured about four seconds of video footage of an object that seemed to look a lot like Hollywood's version of a spacecraft from another world.

Image on right: Image enhancement of the object and linear feature. Credit: NASA

The thing was described as "a saucer-shaped object with a dome on top." The images were captured with a 16mm motion picture camera shooting at 12 frames per second from a command/service module window. The object appears momentarily near the moon. As the camera pans, it moves out of the field of view. It reappears as the camera pans back. It appeared in about 50 frames.

Using Postreading Strategies

After you have read an essay or other text actively and annotated it, your final step is to spend a bit of time thinking about what you have learned from it and even writing in response to it. Review your annotations and answer the following questions.

- What is the main point or idea you learned from working through this text?

- What new ideas did you glean from this reading?

- What did you learn that surprises or interests you?

- How does the information in this text agree with or contradict information on this topic you have already read or learned from your own experience?
- What questions do you still have about this text?
- Where can you find answers to those questions?
- What in this reading might be useful in your own writing?

One useful method for storing and keeping track of what you have learned from your reading is to keep a writer's journal. A journal is a handy and accessible place to write down the information and ideas you gather, as well as your reactions to and insights about the texts you read. You can use the information in your journal as a source of ideas and research for your own writing.

Starting Your Writer's/Research Journal

A writer's journal is a place where you keep track of the notes, annotations, and summaries that you make from your reading. When you keep a record of your ideas, comments, and questions in your journal, whether on paper or in a computer file, it is easy to refer to and continue to expand on what you have learned. Because any writing project longer than a page or two demands more information than you can usually store in your memory, it is vital to keep a written record of information that you discover. You can use the entries in your journal as the basis for group discussions as well as for writing tasks.

Putting what you have learned on paper also helps you to discover what you really think. As we noted in Chapter 1, we all learn as we write. Writing theorist Peter Elbow suggests that "meaning is not what you start with but what you end up with . . . [so view] writing not as a way to transmit a message but as a way to grow and cook a message." Your ideas will expand and become more complex as you write about them in your journal.

The information that you include in your journal can vary, based on the needs of the project you are working on, and the format and design will also vary to suit your purpose. In other words, your rhetorical situation will have an impact not only on the material you collect, the notes that you take, and the summaries and syntheses that you write (see pp. 35–38), but also on the physical makeup of your journal. If you are working on a project that requires a large number of illustrations, for example, you will need to include space in your journal to store them.

Whatever format you decide to keep it in, you can use your journal in a number of ways:

- To jot down notes and ideas about the issues that you see as critical to your writing project; using it as your "research log."
- To record questions as they come up (and the answers you discover).

- To keep summaries that capture the essence of what you have read (for help with writing summaries, see p. 35).

- To list questions for further research, as well as ideas suggested by your instructor and classmates as they read what you have written.

- To reflect on your writing progress and process, as you write your way through a project.

It is usually a good idea to keep a journal of some sort for *each* writing project you are working on, as different kinds of projects lend themselves to different kinds of journals. Consider the following questions for each journal:

- What kinds of information (data, charts, anecdotes, photos, illustrations, and so on) should you collect for this project?

- What information will help you get your message across to your intended audience?

- What information might you jot down that may lead to more complex ideas? Why would more complexity be desirable?

- What questions do you have and how might you go about finding answers to those questions?

- What kinds of illustrations might help you *show* what you mean? Or help you explain a concept or directions about how to do something? Or present statistical information to your readers more effectively?

As you write in your journal, you should note where ideas or quotations come from in the original texts, so that you will be able to properly cite them in your own writing. Get in the habit of noting the information you will need to cite your source, including the page number an idea or quotation comes from, and you will then have that information on hand when you write and document your papers.

For more on taking notes from and properly citing sources, see Chapter 20.

WRITING ACTIVITY

Reading a Text Critically

Assume that you have been asked to read "Choosing the Sex of Your Baby" for your Human Life Experiences class. Based on what you have learned in this chapter, put yourself in the role of student and consider how you should go about reading this text.

As you read the editorial, which appeared in the *New York Times* in September 2001, use the critical reading skills you have learned to do the following:

- Explain what you already knew about this topic, just from the title.

- In a brief paragraph, explain what you did before you read this text. Did you read the main headings? Did you skim it?

- Annotate the first paragraph.
- Finally, jot down your answers to the following postreading questions, providing no more than two sentences for each response.
  - What was your initial reaction and response to this text?
  - What is the main idea you learned from working through this text?
  - What new ideas did you glean from this reading?
  - Did you learn anything that surprises or interests you?
  - In what ways does the information in this text reinforce or contradict other texts you have read or what you know from your own experience?
  - What questions do you still have about this text?

CHOOSING THE SEX OF YOUR BABY

THE *NEW YORK TIMES*

The public is already deeply concerned about whether the onrush of biomedical science is pushing our society into ethically troublesome areas. So it can hardly be reassured by the cavalier way in which the American Society for Reproductive Medicine has just endorsed the use of in vitro fertilization techniques to help parents determine the sex of their next child.

When last heard from on this issue, in a detailed ethics report in 1999, the society said that selecting and implanting embryos of a particular sex solely for the purpose of guaranteeing parents that their child would be a boy or a girl "should be discouraged" because of serious ethical concerns. But now, as reported by Gina Kolata in Friday's *Times*, the acting head of the society's ethics committee has ruled in a brief letter that such sex selection is permissible if parents who already have a child of one sex want to ensure that the next child is of the opposite sex.

However modest that suggestion may seem to some, it raises enormously complicated ethical issues for individuals and for the larger society. Many fertility specialists were appalled when they learned that the society had modified its position. Some cited a "slippery slope" argument, worrying that allowing parents to determine the sex of their children will inevitably lead, as science learns more and more about genetics, to designing the eye color or intelligence or other characteristics that are currently left to chance. Others worried that allowing parents to choose the sex of their children could reinforce gender discrimination in society and, if practiced widely, upset the natural balance between men and women in the population.

Such arguments must be weighed against the strong desire of some parents to have a child of a particular sex, or a mix of boys and girls, or a preferred gender order among their children. They plead that they should have maximum freedom to choose in reproductive matters that, by their lights, harm no one. The in vitro fertilization process that would be used is expensive and would thus limit the number of people who could take advantage of sex selection. The stipulation that sex selection should apply only to a second child, not to the first, eases fears of gender discrimination and the balance between men and women in the population.

Given these difficult issues, the society's latest position seems a hasty response driven by competitive pressures in the fertility industry, where some clinics see a potentially big demand for sex selection. The society, in a detailed report in May, concluded that it would be permissible to use a different method—sorting sperm to greatly increase the odds of having a child of a particular sex—for the limited purpose of achieving gender variety in a family. But extending that approach to the selection and discarding of embryos based on their sex surely deserves more consideration than a brief letter from an ethics committee chairman to the head of a fertility organization that immediately announced it would offer sex selection at its clinics in New York and Chicago. The American Society for Reproductive Medicine owes its members, and the public, a fuller examination of this issue.

Writing Effective Summaries

After they have read and annotated a text, many readers find that summarizing it also helps them to understand it better. A **summary** is a concise restatement of the information that a text contains. It includes only the most important information in the text—its main point and major supporting points.

Writing a Summary: To write an effective summary, start by listing the main points of the text, in effect outlining what you are reading. This outline forms the basis of your summary. Remember, however, that a summary is more than just a listing of the main points in an essay, book chapter, or other kind of text (the outline does that); rather, a summary provides a brief narrative structure that connects these main ideas.

STEPS FOR WRITING A SUMMARY

1. Read the text relatively quickly to get a general sense of what it is saying.

2. Read the text again, this time noting the main point of each paragraph. Mark or highlight a sentence that expresses the main point of each paragraph, and paraphrase that point—put it entirely into your own words—in the margin.

3. For a longer text, label the major sections. If the writer has provided subheadings, use them as they are or paraphrase them. If not, write subheadings.

4. After considering what you have done in the first three steps, write a statement that captures the writer's main point or thesis.

5. Working backward from Step 4, craft a paragraph—in your own words—that captures the gist of what the writer is saying.

SUMMARY OF "CHOOSING THE SEX OF YOUR BABY"

1. Read the text relatively quickly to get a general sense of what it is saying.

   This seems to be an issue with several perspectives.

2. Read the text again, this time noting the main point of each paragraph. Mark or highlight a sentence that expresses the main point of each paragraph, and paraphrase that point—put it entirely into your own words—in the margin.

   Paragraph 1: People are concerned that ASPM is moving too quickly.
   Paragraph 2: The ASPM has altered its position on choosing the sex of a child—if parents already have one child.
   Paragraph 3: The new ASPM suggestion has raised concerns among fertility specialists who worry about the "slippery slope" of this—that parents might be allowed to choose other features in the future.
   Paragraph 4: Some parents want the freedom to choose the sex of their children.
   Paragraph 5: The ASPM seems to have moved too quickly, and it should examine the issue more fully.

3. For a longer text, label the major sections. If the writer has provided subheadings, use them as they are or paraphrase them. If not, write subheadings.

   This reading is too short to have major sections.

4. After considering what you have done in the first three steps, write a statement that captures the writer's main point or thesis.

   Some people want the American Society for Reproductive Medicine to reconsider its recent endorsement of allowing parents to choose the sex of their children.

5. Working backward from Step 4, craft a paragraph that captures the gist of what the writer is saying.

   Some people think that the American Society for Reproductive Medicine (ASPM) moved too quickly when it endorsed the use of in vitro fertilization methods to allow parents to choose the sex of their children. When the ASPM altered its position on choosing the sex of a child (if parents already have one child), the move raised concerns among fertility specialists and the general public who worry about the "slippery slope" of this—that parents might be allowed to choose other features in the future. Even though some parents want the freedom to choose the sex of their children, some people think that the ASPM needs to review the ethical issues of this new science.

WRITING ACTIVITY

Summarizing "A Purpose Greater Than Oneself"

In no more than one page, summarize "A Purpose Greater Than Oneself" (pp. 27–28). If your instructor asks you to, share your summary with several of your classmates.

Synthesizing Information in Readings

Synthesis is more than reassembling other people's ideas and information from different sources; it calls for the thoughtful combination or integration of ideas and information with your point of view.

Synthesis can take place in all four areas of your life. For example, suppose that you would like to see a particular movie this Saturday evening. You hope to convince a group of your friends to accompany you. Because you are a movie buff, you have read several reviews of the film, you know other work by the director, and you have even read the novel on which this movie is based. In other words, you have quite a bit of information to support your case that everyone should accompany you Saturday evening to see this film. At the same time, simply sending your friends all the information you have about the film might overwhelm them. Unless you effectively structure what you have to say, one piece of information may contradict some other point that you want to make. While you want to portray what you know about the film accurately, your primary purpose is to make the case to see the film.

So how would you go about organizing your information about the film in order to convince your friends? You could focus on what you see as the most compelling reasons your friends should see the film: the novel the film is based on, along with the director of the movie. You would then provide information on the following:

- How good the novel was, with specific examples to show what you mean
- How effectively the novel has been translated to film, again, with several examples—probably quotations from reviews or other information about the film—as evidence
- Other films by the same director that you know your friends like

When you synthesize information, then, you organize the information that you have gathered to support the point that *you* want to make. When you synthesize effectively, you take the jumble of facts, data, information, and other knowledge you have on hand and put it into an understandable format that fulfills the purpose you want to accomplish. And, of course, when you cite reviewers' opinions (in the hope of convincing your friends which movie to see), you will need to indicate where the comments came from—to properly attribute what the reviewers had to say and to lend their authority to your argument. Failure to properly attribute ideas to original sources constitutes plagiarism, so you always want to indicate where your ideas and information come from.

For more on avoiding plagiarism, see Chapter 20.

As we have noted, to fully understand information and then be able to synthesize it effectively, to integrate what you read with what you already know, you must read critically, questioning, challenging, and engaging the text as you work through it. One strategy that will help you improve your critical thinking and reading is to work with others. For this reason, many of the exercises and activities in this book can be done collaboratively. When you work with your classmates, you learn how they read and understood a given selection. You hear their perspectives and ideas and have the opportunity to consider various points of view. Working with others encourages you to abandon any simplistic notions that you might have, and it will also help you learn to construct the most effective questions to ask, to help you become an active reader.

WRITING ACTIVITY

Synthesizing Information

Begin by making a list of the five features of your college or university that you like best. (If you have just begun taking classes at your school, list five features that caused you to choose this particular college or university.) After you have constructed your list, exchange it with two classmates. After the three of you have read and discussed each other's lists, combine the three lists into a single list of what the three of you agree are the top ten features of your school. List the ten items in rank order with number one as the best liked item. Your instructor may ask you to share the group's list with the whole class.

Using Your Reading in Your Writing

Information that you find in your reading, can be used in many ways in your writing. If you have annotated the texts that your instructor asked you to read for a writing project in this course or another course, or the sources that you drew on for another project, you can often use those annotations in your own writing. Likewise, if you have summarized sources for a research project, you can refer to and use those summaries to spot the important points of each text you have read, and then use relevant information as evidence to support your main idea when you start composing your text. If you have found statistical information that can be better understood in graphical form, or photographs, drawings, maps, or other illustrations, these too can become part of your text. Of course, it is always important to indicate where you found information, whose ideas you use in your text, and where statistical information came from in order to establish your credibility and avoid *plagiarizing*—representing the words or ideas of others as your own ideas or words.

In the chapters in Parts 2 and 3 of this book, you will read various kinds of selections. Most of these texts will model the kinds of essays that you will be writing. Also, for many of the writing assignments in Parts 2 and 3, you will need to conduct library and/or Web research to find support for your writing. As you read both kinds of texts, you will find it helpful to use the reading strategies we have described in this chapter.

Writing to Discover and to Learn

Most of the chapters in this book focus on learning to write for an audience—to accomplish a purpose involving other people. This chapter, though, provides some tried-and-true strategies for using writing to discover ideas and to learn—to accomplish a purpose for yourself. As you probably are finding out as you do more of it, writing is a way of learning, of figuring out what you know and understand about a subject and, in the process, of coming to know and understand it better. Many famous writers have commented that they cannot really know what they think about something *until* they write about it. They learn as they compose. We learn in this way, too, and we think that if you explore and experiment with some of the strategies in this chapter, writing to discover and to learn will become one of your most effective educational tools.

In addition to using strategies such as the muddiest point and invented interview to learn material from lectures, discussions, and readings in your courses, you can use some as invention strategies for formal writing assignments. Furthermore, although people typically use these tools in academic settings, they can be equally effective in professional, civic, and personal settings. For example, when creating a plan for a yard, a landscape contractor might write down everything he or she knows about a prospective customer along with ideas for plants, trees, and other features, just to learn what possible suggestions to make—a process that might help win the job. As we introduce some of the more common writing-to-discover and writing-to-learn strategies in this chapter, we offer examples from a range of academic fields as well as a few from the professional, civic, and personal areas of life.

The strategy of rewriting your in-class notes to help you learn the material might seem obvious, but you can use writing to learn in many other ways. As we discussed in Chapter 2, writing about what you read for your classes can help you learn that information better, not just by rewriting to summarize your notes, but by jotting down your questions and comments, reflecting on what you have read, and noting how any new ideas and information relate to other ideas and information. In your professional life, consider how writing about what was useful in a recent business meeting, what problems came up, and what issues did not get solved might help you conduct more effective and efficient meetings in the future.

For more on critical reading strategies, see Chapter 2, pp. 23–32.

If you are asked to construct a text that explores an idea, an issue, or a concept, writing about what you already know and about what questions you still have will help you compose a more effective paper. If you are asked to write an informative text—a newsletter, for example, or a set of instructions on how to do something—writing about what you already know and what questions you still have will help you construct a more relevant newsletter or a more useful set of instructions.

For more on writing to explore, see Chapter 5. For more on writing to inform, see Chapter 6.

In almost any situation, writing (immediately afterward) about what you *learned* from an experience will give you useful information for any similar situations you might face in the future. If you get into the habit of writing about the events, situations, and issues in your life, more often than not you will come to a more thoughtful and thorough understanding of those events and issues—so that you will be able to deal with them more effectively.

The strategies that follow are all ways that writers have used to figure out what they have learned and what they still need to know. Try a variety of strategies. Some may work better for you than others.

Using Invention Strategies to Discover Ideas

As you begin to explore your subject, it is a good idea to use more than one invention activity to help you generate ideas. No matter what your purpose is for writing—to share an experience, to argue a position, to propose a solution to a problem—you will need to generate information and knowledge about your topic through invention activities. (Doing your invention work in electronic form, rather than on paper, makes it easier to use the writing you generate in your paper at the drafting stage.)

Listing

For an example of a writer using listing to explore a personal experience, see Jessica Hemauer's list on pages 99–100.

When you use listing, you jot down keywords that will remind you of ideas as you write more later. You might find it effective to establish categories within your lists to help jog your memory. If you are exploring an experience, for instance, you might organize keywords under the following categories: "Participants," "Location," "Visual Images," "Sounds," "Activities," "Smells." If you wanted to propose a solution to a problem, you might organize keywords under "history of the problem," "how the problem affects my readers," "possible solutions," "failed solutions," and "objections to a solution."

Freewriting

When you freewrite, you simply write for a set period of time—perhaps five or ten minutes. You jot down, or type, everything that comes to mind, even if you cannot think of anything (in that case, you might write, "I can't think of anything to write," until your ideas start to flow).

An early proponent of freewriting is writing teacher and theorist Peter Elbow, who suggests (and we agree) that an effective way to get started writing about any subject is to find out what you already know and think about that subject—and the best way to do that is to get what you know down onto paper. Freewriting allows you to do so.

Questioning

One useful way to generate information and ideas is to ask questions about your topic, audience, and purpose:

- What am I trying to accomplish in this paper?
- What do I already know about my topic?
- What might my readers already know?
- What would readers need to know to understand my point?
- What kind(s) of information (for example, graphs, tables, lists) might be useful to *show* my readers (rather than just to tell them)?
- What kinds of details and explanation can I provide?
- Where might I learn more about this subject (in the library, on the Internet, by interviewing people)?
- What verifiable information about my subject is available, and where can I find it?
- What do I know about my audience? What don't I know that I should know?

Answering the Questions *Who? What? Where? When? Why? How?*

You can expand the questioning approach (above) by spending a few minutes jotting down answers to the reporter's questions: *who, what, where, when, why,* and *how*. You may find that your answers lead to still more questions.

- Whom does this subject affect? In what ways?
- Who is involved in making a decision about this subject?
- Who is my audience?
- What am I trying to get my audience to do?
- What can't I ask my readers to do?
- What is important here?
- What are the historical aspects of this topic?
- When might something happen to affect this situation?
- When would I like something to happen?
- Where does all of this take place?
- Why should my readers care about my paper?

For an example of a writer using freewriting to explore his ideas about a topic, see Rick Mohler's freewriting on the subject of finding a career on page 161.

- Why is this topic important?
- Why will _____ happen?
- Why would someone want _____ to happen?
- How does the context—the "where"—affect the situation?
- How might _____ happen?
- How might _____ react to the topic I am writing about?

For an example of how a writer might use the reporter's questions to explore an issue, see page 359 in Chapter 8.

Brainstorming

For an example of a writer using brainstorming to help focus her ideas, see Deborah Schlegel's brainstorming on the topic of global warming on page 493.

When you brainstorm, you record on paper or on-screen the information you already know about the topic you are exploring. Once you have written down several possible topics or ideas or possible ways to focus your paper, you may have an easier time finding the one that seems most promising.

Clustering

Clustering is especially useful for figuring out possible cause-and-effect relationships. For more on clustering and an example, see page 58.

Keeping Notebooks and Journals

Writers and learners frequently maintain notebooks and journals because these forms of informal writing are useful places for recording and/or exploring ideas. Leonardo da Vinci, for example, kept notebooks for years, compiling 1,566 pages of ideas in words and images.

Double-Entry Notebook

One useful type of notebook is what composition scholar Anne Berthoff calls a **dialectical notebook** or **journal.** In a dialectical notebook, you write notes and observations on one page and then write your questions and comments about those notes on the facing page. (Some people prefer to draw a line down the center of a page.) In effect, the two pages "speak" to each other. The **double-entry notebook,** which is a type of dialectical notebook, is one of the most commonly used writing-to-learn strategies because it can be easily adapted to so many contexts. As the name suggests, the double-entry notebook has two columns. The left column is used to present whatever kind of information is appropriate to the context. Thus, in this column, you might record lecture, lab, field, or reading notes; list the steps in a math problem; construct a timeline, or list events in chronological order. The right column is used to respond to, comment on, question, and apply the information in the left column.

For instance, Judy Bowden is enrolled in an art history course to fulfill one of the general studies requirements at her school. To understand some of the artworks that she is studying in the course, Bowden uses a variety of writing-to-learn strategies, but she frequently uses the double-entry notebook. Because her journal is electronic, she downloads public-domain artwork from the Web and pastes it into the left column of her notebook. In the right column, she writes about the work. Here is an example from Bowden's double-entry notebook.

Artwork	My Thoughts
	This is the *Black Bull* cave painting from Lascaux, France. It's amazing that this and other paintings in the cave are 10,000 to 30,000 years old. It's also amazing that 2,000 paintings and drawings in the cave have survived for so long. The details seem very sophisticated for such an old piece of art. I wonder what the four teenagers thought when they discovered the cave on September 12, 1940. If I were in an anthropology course instead of an art history course, I wonder what other things we'd learn about this painting and the others.

These comments and questions help Judy to think about and appreciate, and then to remember, the artwork and relevant details about it.

WRITING ACTIVITY

Your Dialectical Notebook

Select one of your college classes and go over your notes for the most recent week of classes. Construct a dialectical notebook that outlines your notes and also your reactions to, comments on, and questions about those notes.

Your instructor may want you to share your notebooks with your classmates.

Field Notebook

For more on field research, see Chapter 19, pages 861–69.

Fairly common in the sciences and social sciences, **field notebooks** are useful for students who are doing field research. A field notebook can take many forms, depending on the observations that you are making. Usually, though, it is a good idea to set up the notebook ahead of time so that you can quickly take your notes in an organized way.

For instance, Lindsay Hanson is enrolled in a summer session biology course for nonmajors. One of the requirements of the course is to pick a natural habitat and observe some life-forms in that habitat. Lindsay chooses to do some bird-watching in a marsh near her campus. She decides to set up her field notebook in columns with headings, an organization that makes it easy for her to record her observations.

Date and Time	Location	Common Name	Scientific Name	Sex	Comments
6/6/06 6:20 p.m.	west shore of Widespread	red-winged blackbird	Agelaius phoeniceus	♂	The bird was sitting on the top of a weed, which was swaying in the breeze. Partly cloudy, 61°, windy
6/6/06 6:35 p.m.	south shore of Widespread	yellow-shafted flicker	Colaptes auratus	♀	The bird took off from some 8"–10" grass. Partly cloudy, 61°

WRITING ACTIVITY

Writing Your Own Field Notebook

If you have a class that requires you to do some fieldwork, construct a field notebook, including drawings or other images and your notes on your field research. If you do not have a class that requires field research, spend an hour at some place on your campus, observing and making notes on what you see in a field notebook. Use these reporter's questions to guide you:

• Who is there? What are they doing? How are they dressed? What are they carrying or working with?

- What does the Place look like? Can you take photos or make drawings? What kinds of activities are going on? What sounds and smells are in this place? What is the weather like?
- Where is this place? How does it connect or relate to other places on campus?
- When did you visit? Why? What makes that time different from another time you might observe this place?
- Why did you select this particular spot? What other places did you consider? Why?

Vocabulary Journal

One of the most challenging aspects of any course in a field that is new to you is learning the vocabulary of that field. One way to address that challenge is to keep a list in your journal of new terms that you encounter in your reading and in class lectures and discussions. These lists should include definitions and examples to help you better understand the terms. One way to construct such lists is to make them immediately following the class in which you encountered the vocabulary. If you run across new words as you read, get out a dictionary and jot down their meaning immediately.

For example, in her Introduction to Philosophy course, Meghan Wilson kept a list of terms that were new to her. For each term she recorded, Meghan not only wrote a definition but also added something else in order to better understand and remember the term; she might comment on the term, use it in a sentence, or list a synonym, a near-synonym, or an antonym. Here are two examples from Wilson's vocabulary journal.

Term	Definition	My Comment
epistemology	the branch of philosophy that focuses on theories of knowledge	"Episteme" is related to "epistemology." I recall that we discussed this in my philosophy course earlier this semester.
dialectic	a conversational method of argument that relies on question and answer	"Dialectic" comes from the Greek word meaning "to converse." This is sort of like dialogue.

Expanding the Journal Concept

Learning in academic settings is most effective when students can connect what they learn to the other three areas of life—the professional, the civic, the personal. Often, though, students are so focused on the academic task at hand that they do not take the time to make these important connections. By making a conscious effort to contemplate the ways that you can use course knowledge and skills in the rest of your life, you increase the possibility that you will have that knowledge and those skills at your disposal when you need them. Consider keeping a journal in which you jot down any connections you see, any ideas you learn in your classes that might be useful in the other areas of your life.

Here are possible entries from various courses.

Course	Knowledge/Skills	Application to Another Arena of Life
Geology	Weathering from the elements, especially wind and rain	How long-lasting will the material be for the new roof we're considering? What's its wind-speed rating? Would the more expensive brand be a safer choice?
Writing	*Ethos:* The character of the speaker or writer	Aristotle says someone's *ethos* is often the best way to persuade someone—how can I, in any speaking or writing job, create *ethos*?
Communications	How to get an audience's attention	For that speech I have to give next month, what's the best way to start—a joke? A question? A provocative statement?

Rewriting Your Class Notes

Whether you use a double-entry notebook or some other method, make rewriting your class notes part of your own "homework" assignment each day. Many students who use this strategy find it helpful because, when they rewrite their class notes, they do the following:

- Put them into a more readable form than the jottings they made during class.
- Organize them so they are more understandable.
- Think of questions about the information that had not occurred to them when they were taking the notes during class.
- Discover areas of interest that they want to find out more about.

Think of the "re" in the word *rewriting* and what it means: to resee, to reenvision, to reconsider, perhaps even to reorganize. Put another way, when you rewrite your in-class notes, use the writing as a way to help you learn, not just by transcribing your notes, but by reconsidering them and asking questions, by reseeing what you wrote (and jotting down connections you make with other ideas and texts), and by reorganizing them so they make more sense than they might have made in class. The strategies that follow can help you not just to rewrite your class notes but to comprehend and, perhaps, go beyond them.

After each of your college classes, convert your in-class notes to e-notes in a computer document. Doing so encourages you to reread your notes and put them into a more readable form. Just reading them over again helps cement the ideas into your memory—and writing them down again helps you remember them, too. Also, your notes will be easier to read when exam time comes around. Finally, your notes will be searchable, and you can copy and paste them, as needed, into your college papers.

Minute Paper

A minute paper is a quick, useful way to reflect on a class lecture or discussion, but first we need to make a confession: this really is not a paper, but a chance just to jot down—in a minute or two—your answers to two questions:

1. What is the most important thing that I learned in class today?
2. What is the most important question that I have about today's class lecture/discussion?

For example, Conner Ames, who was enrolled in a general studies course in sociology, responded at the end of a particular class as follows:

1. Today we learned that group behavior often is different from individual behavior: people will act differently in groups than they might act alone. This is especially true for male adolescents when a group interacts with other male adolescent groups.
2. What are more of the real-life implications of group behavior (and I also want to know more about *why* young males like me act as they do when they're in a group).

Ames could use his question to guide further reading about group behavior. Or he could raise his question in class or on the course Web site or listserv.

Muddiest Point

As its name suggests, this strategy involves jotting down some concept or idea that is unclear or confusing and, if possible, exploring it through writing. This does not mean looking up the definition of a concept you might find confusing, but instead writing about it to clarify your thinking.

TechNote When you take a college class, remember that your classmates can be a valuable resource. Create communication spaces on the Internet for study groups or for just yourself and one study-partner. Exchange contact information with classmates, and use it. You can exchange notes using personal blogs, e-mail, chat, instant-messaging, and other social networking/messaging sites.

Remember, though, that if you post text or images straight from sources (such as textbooks or reference works), you must cite them properly. If you want to share copyrighted work online, you must obtain permission from the source before posting someone else's intellectual property on a public site.

For more on e-mail, instant messaging, and blogs, see Chapter 17.

Your muddiest point may come from a paragraph in a chapter that you are reading for a course, or it may come from a class lecture or discussion. In many instances, you may be able to work through your confusion by writing. At the very least, you will crystallize the issue and provide yourself with a reminder to raise a question during the next class meeting, in an office-hour visit, in an e-mail to the professor, or on the online discussion board for the course. Alternatively, while writing about the problem you may generate a keyword that can help you search for a clear explanation in a book or on a Web site.

As an example, in Gabe Johnson's chemistry course, the professor briefly mentioned the distinction between beneficial and harmful ozone. After class Johnson realized that he wasn't clear about what the distinction is; he also was not certain that he knew what ozone is. He jotted down the following note:

> Professor Barkuloo mentioned that some ozone is beneficial to us and that some is harmful. What is the difference? Also, I heard Professor Barkuloo indicate that ozone is represented as O_3. So that tells me that ozone molecules have three atoms of oxygen, but I'm still a little unclear. I know that oxygen is part of what we breathe every day, so that can't be harmful, so why is ozone a problem? And isn't that something I read about the other day—a hole in the ozone? Now I remember: the hole in the ozone shrinks and grows at different times of the year, and the ozone keeps us safe from some ultraviolet rays or something—again, why is that harmful sometimes?

Johnson decided not to wait for the next class meeting to raise his questions. Instead, he used a search engine to do an advanced search on "ozone." Although the search yielded scores of hits, one of the first sites was that of the Environmental Protection Agency (http://www.epa.gov/oar/oaqps/gooduphigh/#what), where he found answers to his questions (Figure 3.1).

After reading this information, Johnson might have added the following note:

> Okay, now I understand better, and the title of this article really says it all: we need ozone, but we don't want to be very close to it!

After writing a muddiest-point entry, use any key terms in the entry to do an online search. You will find definitions and detailed explanations of the terms.

Preconception Check

A *preconception* is something you think you know about a subject, before you learn more about it in class, through your reading, and from other sources of information. For example, what do you think of when you hear the words "Grand Canyon"? Even if you have never seen Arizona's Grand Canyon, you

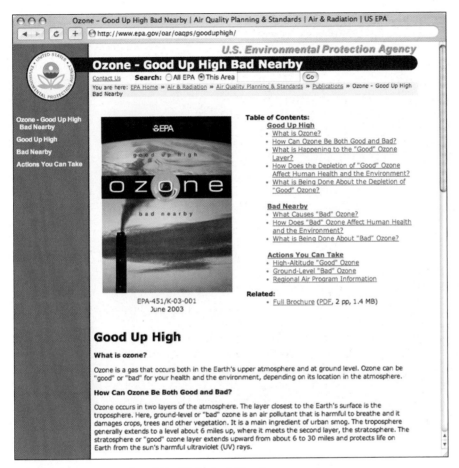

FIGURE 3.1 Ozone: Good Up High, Bad Nearby

may have seen photographs of it, such as the one shown in Figure 3.2 on page 52; you may think that it is located in the hot desert. However, if you have visited the Grand Canyon, you know that it is located in northern Arizona. The elevation is high there, so the site is much cooler than the desert of southern Arizona.

One strategy for overcoming preconceptions is to become aware of them, which is not always easy to do. In some of your courses, professors may ask you about your preconceptions so that they can confront them head on. If they do not, you can confront them yourself by writing about your preconceptions to see if they are actually misconceptions.

For instance, Tom Ambrose was enrolled in an astronomy course that fulfilled the science portion of his general studies requirements. As he read a chapter about the solar system, he encountered a subsection entitled "Why Are There Seasons on Earth?" Before he read the subsection, he realized that

FIGURE 3.2   Arizona's Grand Canyon

he had some preconceptions about why the seasons occur. He wrote the following in his learning journal for that course:

> I think that Earth has the four seasons because of the elliptical path of the planet as it orbits the Sun. When that path takes us farthest from the Sun (December–March), we have winter. When the path takes us closest to the Sun (June–August), we have summer.

This short explanation may seem trivial, but it served to make Ambrose more attuned to the explanation in his astronomy textbook. When he read that the seasons are caused by Earth's tilt on its axis, he was better prepared to process that information. He noted,

> Yes, of course. When I read the textbook's explanation, I realized the problem with my preconception—my misconception. If the elliptical path of Earth's orbit were the cause of the seasons, then the whole planet would have summer in June–August. I forgot that when it's summer in the northern hemisphere it's winter in the southern hemisphere.

Incidentally, his misconception about what causes the seasons is a fairly common one—even among college graduates.

Paraphrasing

When you are having difficulty understanding material in a reading assignment, lecture, or class discussion, one strategy you can use to make the material more understandable is to paraphrase it—to restate it in your own words. If you have ever tried to teach something to someone, you know that the act of teaching—explaining, demonstrating, answering questions— often aids your understanding of the subject or concept. This is the rationale behind paraphrasing—by explaining something in your own words, you come to understand it better.

Jack Johnson was taking an introductory physics course for nonmajors. Early in the course, during a lecture on choosing between theories, the instructor mentioned "Ockham's razor" but did not define it. Using a popular search engine to find some definitions of the term, Johnson found that it is defined as the principle of economy, or of parsimony, stated, for example, as "entities should not be multiplied unneccessarily." After reading several Web sites, Johnson felt he understood the term and wrote the following in his course journal:

> In a nutshell, Ockham's razor means this: if two theories have equal explanatory power, choose the simpler one. That is, keep it simple, Stupid—K.I.S.S. But how might I apply that to my other coursework? Well, in my geology class we did discuss the Grand Canyon and I kind of now see how the simplest answer to its formation—a river and other natural weather conditions, acting over a long period of time, actually makes the most sense. If I try to get too complicated about something, I need to remember the Ockham razor notion that if two or more ideas seem to explain something, the simpler is probably the better answer.

For more on paraphrasing, see Chapter 20.

 ## Organizing and Synthesizing Information

Finding and collecting information is part of learning, but effective learners need to organize and synthesize information to make it usable. Clearly, you do not want to write down everything you find . . . or highlight every word of every page of information you locate! As you conduct research and locate information that might be useful for your writing, do the following:

- Organize what you learn in a logical, useful manner. Often an effective way to organize your notes is to put them into a computer document; you can then use its search function to locate particular words or phrases.

- Organize your notes by putting them into a spreadsheet like Excel. If you format the spreadsheet cells to "wrap text," you create a database or what appears to be a card file:

  INTERVIEW with Jordon Hockings re: recycling project on campus, 2/22/07. Hocking said that our recycling program will double in capacity over the next two years (he is the President of CRC: Campus Recycling Club)

  NOTES from campus newspaper, 2/23/07: letter to the editor from student Matt Wilson, noting how "messy the south side of campus has become." (page 5)

  BOOK on recycling that looks useful: here's the info from the library: **Make a difference in your school [electronic resource]: a how-to guide for engaging students in resource conservation and waste reduction.** Gov doc # EP 10.2:SCH 6

For more on summary and synthesis, see pages 35–38.

- As you take notes, synthesize the information: condense it into a brief form, where the important aspects are listed, along with the reference, so you can easily locate the complete information.

Invented Dialogue

An invented dialogue is a useful tool for bringing divergent views together. When you read what might seem like contradictory information in your college assignments, or present views on a subject that seem diametrically opposed to one another, you can use the invented dialogue technique to recast the information in a way that (perhaps) will clarify the similarities and differences for you.

- In a psychology course, you could have Sigmund Freud and Carl Jung discuss how they would treat a specific case. Or you could have B. F. Skinner and Jean Piaget discuss the views of behaviorists and cognitivists.
- In a political science course, George III and Thomas Jefferson could discuss the relative merits of absolute monarchy and democracy.
- In an economics course, Adam Smith, a classical economist, and Milton Friedman, a monetary economist, could discuss the relative merits of the importance of a free market economy, especially in light of their respective historical periods.
- In a physics course, Newton and Einstein could discuss time and space.
- In an astronomy course, Ptolemy and Copernicus could discuss Ptolemy's reasons for thinking that Earth is at the center of solar system.

Invented Interview/Unsent Letter

In an invented interview, you are the interviewer. The interviewee could be a person or a character whom you are studying or a person associated with a concept that you are studying. If you *really* could interview someone for a college class, what would you ask that person? What questions can you generate? What issues or concepts would you focus on? How would you phrase your questions? It is often useful to put your questions into an unsent letter format so that you have a specific audience you are writing to as you generate interview questions. Often such an audience is just what a writer needs to clarify what he or she is trying to say.

Here are some sample questions:

- In a geometry course, you might interview Pythagoras to ask him about the process that led to his development of the Pythagorean Theorem.

- In a music history course, you might interview Tchaikovsky to ask him what was the inspiration for his "1812 Overture" and what he hoped to accomplish by composing it.

- In a botany course, you might interview George Washington Carver to ask about the significance of the epitaph on his grave marker: "He could have added fortune to fame, but caring for neither, he found happiness and honor in being helpful to the world."

- In an entrepreneurship course, you might interview Bill Gates to ask him what drove him to found Microsoft.

- In an anthropology course you might interview a group of Cro-Magnons to ask about their interactions with Neanderthals.

- In a United States history course, you might ask President Harry Truman why he decided to drop atomic bombs on two Japanese cities in 1945.

Taking this concept of an invented interview further, you can conduct research to determine how your questions might have been answered if you were able to conduct such an interview.

The key to writing such interviews—and this is the case for any of the writing-to-learn strategies in this chapter—is that you need to move beyond the limits of your initial response to an event or a person, especially if your response is emotional. Use the interview as an opportunity to explore a topic from an intellectual perspective as well as an emotional perspective. For example, to conduct the interview with President Truman on his decision to use the atom bomb on Japan, you would need to do some basic research to find out about the context of Truman's decision to drop the bombs on Hiroshima and Nagasaki and about his deliberations leading up to the decision. Then, of course, to *answer* your questions, you would conduct even more research (what interviewers really did ask Truman about his decision; what his answers and his diaries and notes reveal).

Résumé/Vita

In some courses you will read paragraphs, chapters, or even whole books about people who are influential in their field. When such biographical information appears in prose form over many pages, it can be a challenge to keep the most important facts and events in mind. One strategy for doing so is to write a résumé or a vita for the influential person. The principal differences between the two are that résumés tend to be used outside academia, and vitae to be used within, and that résumés tend to be short (generally no more than a page or two), and vitae tend to be long, mainly because they include lists of publications and presentations.

For the purposes of learning course material, it is not crucial that you carefully follow the formatting conventions of résumés or vitae, and your document can be whatever length is appropriate to the material.

In a course on the history of architecture, Maureen Goggin read a biography of architect Frank Lloyd Wright. Here is part of the résumé/vita that she developed on Wright. Notice that Goggin includes some information that would not be included in a real résumé or vita (for example, a section with personal information; a note that he was fired in 1893).

```
                    Frank Lloyd Wright
Personal Information
   Born: June 8, 1867; Richland Center, Wisconsin
   Died: April 9, 1959; Taliesin West, Arizona
   Married: Catherine Tobin; 1889

Education
   Second Ward School, 1879-1883
   University of Wisconsin-Madison (a few engineering
   courses), 1884-1887

Employment History
   Firm of J. L. Silsbee
   Drafting Position, Firm of Adler and Sullivan
   Louis Sullivan), 1887-1893 (fired)
   Established Own Architectural Firm, 1893
   Designed 41 buildings between 1893 and 1901.
   . . .
   Founded Taliesin West Fellowship, October 1932
   . . .

Selected Architectural Projects
   Unity Temple, 1906
   Frederick C. Robie House, 1909
   Fallingwater, 1936
```

```
Johnson Wax Administration Building, 1936
    . . .
Guggenheim Museum, New York, 1959
```

Selected Publications

An Autobiography, 1932

Frank Lloyd Wright Collected Writings: 1949–1959

    . . .

Bio-Poem

The bio-poem is another useful tool for organizing information about a person or character whom you are studying. Here is one possible format, but feel free to deviate from it as you construct your own poem. The idea here is to get basic, essential information down, and while this is called a "poem," remember that poems do not always need to rhyme!

Line 1: First name

Line 2: Three or four traits that describe the person

Line 3: Relationship to someone else

Line 4: Lover of _____ (three items or people)

Line 5: Three feelings

Line 6: Three needs

Line 7: Three fears

Line 8: Who gives _____ (three items)

Line 9: Three things liked

Line 10: Residence

Line 11: Last name

Here is an example that Mary Lee Carlson wrote for her film studies course:

Steven
dedicated, talented, innovative, visionary, prolific
favorite son of Cincinnati, Ohio
Lover of films with adventure, drama, and comedy
Who feels sadness for victims of the Holocaust, wonder at the thought of
    extra-terrestrials, and a drive to keep working on the next great film
Who needs to direct films that engage viewers, that provoke thinking, and
    that evoke a range of emotions
Who fears that he might make a mediocre film, that he might lose his
    creativity, and that his career will eventually end
Who has given millions of viewers many opportunities to cry, to laugh, and
    to experience worlds that would be otherwise unavailable

Who would like to make more great films
Resident of Los Angeles, California
Spielberg

Using Charts and Visuals to Discover and to Learn

If you are like many people, you may be a visual learner: seeing something often really helps you understand it. Just as charts, graphs, tables, photographs, and other visuals help readers understand what you write about, using visuals is often a way for writers to explore ideas and really see and understand what they are writing about.

Clustering and Concept Mapping

Concept maps help us to visualize ideas that may otherwise seem abstract and also to understand relationships among ideas. A concept map is the same as the invention strategy known as clustering: in a cluster or concept map, you construct a visual representation of your ideas—how they might connect to each other. For example, Figure 3.3 shows how student writer Santi DeRosa might have developed a cluster map to help him get started with his paper about how female students help recruit male athletes for his school. According to an article in the campus newspaper, women serve as campus guides when potential athletes visit the school. When he read the article, DeRosa had

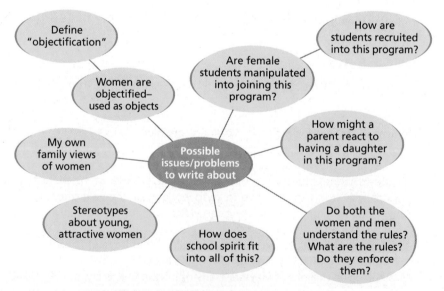

FIGURE 3.3   A Possible Cluster Map on the Topic of Recruiting Practices

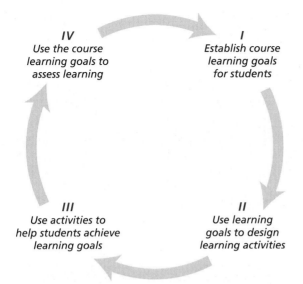

FIGURE 3.4   A Concept Map for an Education Course

concerns about the ethics of this practice, so he decided to respond by writing an essay on the issue (you can read his complete essay in Chapter 8).

Sometimes this kind of visual helps us better understand how a cause might lead to an effect, how events are related to one another, and other logical relationships.

WRITING EXAMPLE: CONCEPT MAPPING

Mary Beth Peterson was enrolled in an introductory course in education because she hoped to teach high school biology. In the course she read about the ways in which reflective teachers begin with course learning goals and then use those goals as the foundation for their courses. She used PowerPoint software to construct the concept map shown in Figure 3.4.

Process Flowchart

A process flowchart is another visually useful tool for converting information from verbal to visual form. A flowchart allows you to translate several paragraphs of information into a clear, succinct visual that can make difficult concepts easier to understand. While concept mapping focuses on relationships in a system (how ideas or concepts might connect to one another), a flowchart indicates how things *move* through a system. Think of your progress as a student:

No credit hours → 30 credit hours → 60 hours → 90 hours → 120 hours

Freshman class → Sophomore → Junior → Senior → graduate

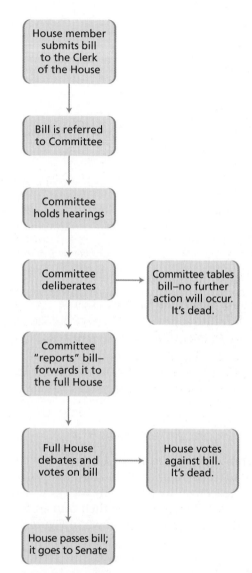

FIGURE 3.5   Following a Bill through the U.S. House of Representatives

In his political science course, Brian Flores studied the process by which a bill moves through the U.S. House of Representatives. After reading a few pages on the process, Brian converted the material into the flowchart shown in Figure 3.5. Note that a flowchart was the best choice here instead of, say, a concept map, because a bill follows clear and specific steps as it works its way through the legislative process.

You will also find flowcharts useful for many situations you will deal with in your professional life. While flowcharts for explaining computer systems are typical, organizational charts are also common.

Timeline/Chronology

In some courses, you will study information that you cannot fully understand unless you have a clear sense of the chronology involved. In textbook and classroom discussions, however, this information may not be presented chronologically. You can help yourself by constructing a timeline. In a geology course, for example, your timeline might delineate the geological eras and periods in the history of the Grand Canyon. In a literature course, you might construct a timeline for the events in a novel. In a philosophy course, you might construct a timeline listing famous philosophers and their main ideas—a timeline that will help you understand how concepts and ideas developed over time.

Timelines or chronologies can be set up horizontally or vertically, of course. Here is an example: Krista Williams was enrolled in a United States history course. One unit focused on the Civil War. Using the information from her textbook's chapter on the Civil War, Williams constructed the following chronology of events:

November 6, 1860: Lincoln elected President
December 20, 1860: South Carolina secedes from the Union
February 9, 1861: Jefferson Davis is selected as President of Confederacy
April 12, 1861: Confederate soldiers attack Fort Sumter in Charleston, S.C.
July 21, 1861: Confederates win Battle of Bull Run—just southwest
of Washington, D.C.
March 8–9, 1862: The Confederate Merrimac and the Union Monitor,
both ironclads, battle to a draw
September 17, 1862: 26,000 soldiers are wounded or killed at Antietam
January 1, 1863: Lincoln issues Emancipation Proclamation
July 1–3, 1863: Battle of Gettysburg
September 19–20, 1863: Battle of Chickamauga
November 19, 1863: Lincoln delivers Gettysburg Address
November 8, 1864: Lincoln reelected
January 31, 1865: Congress approves Thirteenth Amendment
to the Constitution, which the states eventually ratify; it abolishes slavery.
April 9, 1865: Lee surrenders to Grant at Appomattox Court House
in Virginia
April 14, 1865: John Wilkes Booth shoots Lincoln at 10:13 p.m.
at Ford's Theater in Washington
April 15, 1865: Lincoln dies at 7:22 in the morning
December 6, 1865: The states ratify the Thirteenth Amendment

Pedigree Chart

With some material, it can be a challenge to understand the pedigree—the ancestral lines or, more generally, the origin—of a person, a character, or even an idea. Creating a chart that traces that pedigree can help.

Brian Thomas read the plays *Oedipus Rex* and *Antigone* in a humanities course. To understand and keep in mind the relationships among some of the major characters in the plays, Brian constructed the pedigree chart shown in Figure 3.6.

Studying for Exams

Course grades are often based largely on tests. If you study for tests strategically, you can usually anticipate the questions that will be asked and review the course material more efficiently.

Test Questions

TechNote One way to learn material more thoroughly is to help someone else learn about it, too. Offer to help one of your former teachers from middle school or high school create a Web site about a topic you are learning more about in college. Or if you have a younger brother or sister or a child in school, offer to help his or her teacher. Use your new knowledge to create links and study notes that will help younger learners.

For advice on creating an effective Web site, see Appendix C.

One way to prepare for tests is to write questions that you think your instructor may pose on them. Anticipating test questions also gives you the opportunity to anticipate your answers, thus simulating the test itself.

When one of the authors of this text was in graduate school, one of his professors told the class, "You can Figure out what questions we're going to ask you, pretty easily." The author tried it, and he was right—it required some thought as well as taking a different perspective than he was used to (thinking as a teacher rather than as a student), but he soon found writing his own questions to be an effective way of preparing for tests and learning about a subject.

If you are using questions to prepare for a test, the first step is to ask the instructor about the kinds of questions that you should anticipate. Your instructor will probably indicate the formats that the questions will be in—for example, whether they will be multiple-choice, true/false, matching, short answer, and/or essay questions—and might also indicate the levels of thinking they will require: comprehension, application, analysis, synthesis, and/or evaluation.

Once you understand the kinds of questions you will be expected to answer, the next step is to pay close attention in class to what the instructor emphasizes because that content is important to understanding the subject and may very well appear on tests.

One of the most effective strategies for writing test questions is to go through your class notes and reading notes marking sections that you think are likely to be covered on the test. Then, as soon as possible after class or after reading the textbook, write a few questions and think about the

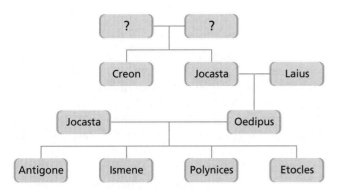

FIGURE 3.6 A Pedigree Chart

answers. If you write some questions each week, you will learn much more than if you wait until just before the test, and you will be more thorough in your coverage of the material you have studied.

Maggie Simpson is enrolled in a music appreciation course. On the first day, her instructor mentioned that the tests and exams would include a mixture of question types—multiple-choice, matching, and short answer. Her instructor also mentioned that the questions would require a range of thinking levels—comprehension, analysis, synthesis, and evaluation. With this in mind, Maggie constructed, for a test that she knew would cover the Romantic period, questions that included the following:

1. What are the major features that distinguish music of the Romantic period from music of the Classical period? [This question asks for analysis of the material covered in the class.]
2. What are the most identifiable characteristics of Chopin's concertos? [This question asks for analysis of material covered in the class.]
3. What are the similarities between music and literature of the Romantic period? [This question asks for synthesis of material.]
4. How effectively did German literature inform the music in the Romantic period? [This question asks for evaluation of material.]
5. Why has music of the Romantic period remained popular into the twenty-first century? [This question asks for analysis and evaluation.]
6. Who composed *Ring of the Nibelung*?
   a. Wagner
   b. Liszt
   c. Schumann
   d. Offenbach [This question asks for comprehension.]

Of course, Maggie also wrote responses to each of her questions—to make certain that she knew how to answer them and to practice for the real thing.

For advice on taking essay examinations, see Appendix B.

Mnemonic Play

Although in many courses you will need to learn course material without having to memorize facts, there may be times when you will need to develop memory aids for some material. Here is an example that may already be familiar to you:

Erin Wilson was enrolled in a general science course for nonmajors. To help her remember the order of the planets in the solar system (before Pluto's status as a planet was changed), she used the sentence: "<u>M</u>y <u>v</u>ery <u>e</u>ducated <u>m</u>other just <u>s</u>erved <u>u</u>s <u>n</u>ine <u>p</u>izzas." That is, the order, beginning with the planet closest to the sun, is Mercury, Venus, Earth, Mars, Jupiter, Saturn, Uranus, Neptune, Pluto.

PART TWO

Using What You Have Learned to Share Information

Rhetorical Knowledge

- *Audience:* Readers may or may not know you or the people you are writing about personally, but you will want to make your experience relevant to them regardless.

- *Purposes:* You may want to entertain readers and possibly to inform and/or persuade them.

- *Rhetorical situation:* Consider the constellation of factors affecting what you write—you (the writer), your readers (the audience), the topic (the experience that you're writing about), your purpose (what you wish to accomplish), and the exigency (what is compelling you to write).

- *Writer's voice and tone:* You have a *stance*—or attitude—toward the experience you are sharing and the people you are writing about. You may be amused, sarcastic, neutral, or regretful, among many possibilities.

- *Context, medium, and genre:* Your writing context, the medium you are writing in (whether print or electronic), and the genre you have chosen all affect your writing decisions.

 ## Critical Thinking, Reading, and Writing

- *Learning/inquiry:* You need to learn the features of writing to share experiences so that you can do so effectively in any writing situation.

- *Responsibility:* You have a responsibility to represent your experiences accurately, with sensitivity to the needs of others.

- *Reading and research:* You will need to draw on your own memories, memories of relatives and friends, photographs and documents, and ideas you develop from your reading.

Chapter 4

Writing Processes

- *Invention:* You will need to choose invention strategies that will help you recall details about your experience or experiences.

- *Organizing your ideas and details:* You will usually be organizing a series of events.

- *Revising:* You will need to read your work with a critical eye, to make certain that it fulfills the assignment and displays the qualities of this kind of writing.

- *Working with peers:* Classmates and others will offer you comments on and questions about your work.

Conventions

- *Editing:* When writers share experiences, they tend to use dialogue to report what they have said and what others have said to them. The round-robin activity in this chapter (on p. 115) addresses the conventions for punctuating dialogue.

- *Genres for sharing experiences:* Genres include personal essay, memoir, autobiography, magazine or newspaper essay, blog, letter, and accident report, as well as other possibilities.

- *Documentation:* If you have relied on sources outside of your experience, you will need to cite them using the appropriate documentation style.

Writing to Share Experiences

This brief section of an article about the aftermath of Hurricane Katrina in September 2005, written by three reporters from the *Houston Press*, is a news item—but at the same time the writers are focusing on *stories* about real people at the Houston Astrodome, and each person, such as Nikki Ramey (shown in the smaller photograph), has an important tale to tell:

> Nikki Ramey, a 24-year-old mother, heard the media reports about refugees and volunteers who were turned away at the gate. Still, she was determined to get inside the Dome and invite a family back to her home in north Houston. So she and her friend lied to [security guard Nathan] Njakoy. They told him they were hurricane victims who had ridden one of the buses from New Orleans.
>
> "Do I look like a hurricane victim?" Ramey later asks a *Houston Press* reporter. "I'm wearing a full face of makeup and my hair is freshly straightened. Duh."
>
> The hoax worked—maybe the fresh hair and makeup helped—and Ramey could see what journalists from across the nation still could not: the Dome's ground floor, which was lined with rows of narrow cots set inches apart.
>
> Once inside, Ramey says, she approached seven families and offered to house them for free. Each family declined. Many said they wanted to stay in hopes that their own family members would eventually come to find them.

Ramey's was just one story from this monumental event. Many stories were told visually. The other photograph on the facing page tells a compelling part of the story of Hurricane Katrina strictly through the image it presents.

In sharing her experience with the reporters from the *Houston Press*, Nikki Ramey was engaging in a common activity. On any given day, you share your experiences in a variety of ways. At breakfast, you might tell your roommate about the nightmare that awakened you at 3:00 in the morning, or at dinner you might tell your family about the argument that you had with your supervisor at work. In a courtroom, you might narrate the experience you had when an intoxicated driver lost control of his vehicle and hit your car. In a recommendation written on behalf of a friend, you might illustrate her character by telling a story about how she helped you achieve an important goal. At work, you might share your experiences in using a particular piece of software because you think that your co-workers should use the same software. Or you might brag to officemates about how you negotiated a contract with a persnickety client.

Although you may think that you share your experiences most frequently in your personal life, you have also shared your experiences in your academic life if you wrote an autobiography for your college application packet. You may need to do the same again if you apply for admittance to graduate or professional school. In your professional life, you will need to narrate your experiences in résumés and letters of application, and you also will tell about your experiences in order to teach others how to do their work. In your civic life, you may decide to appear before the city council to describe how the lack of a streetlight at a busy intersection led to an automobile accident. Or you may need to tell voters how your experiences make you well qualified for political office—whether as a member of a local school board or neighborhood association, the city council, the state legislature, or—someday, perhaps—the United States Congress.

There are many reasons to share your experiences with other people. Writing about your experiences helps you as a writer because the act of writing requires reflection, which is a powerful tool for gaining insight into and understanding about life. Also, when you share your experiences with others, you are also offering others insight into what has worked well—and not so well—in your life. After all, for thousands of years humans have shared stories about experiences to establish and nurture social connections with one another.

Rhetorical Knowledge

When you write about your experiences in a private journal, you can write whatever and however you wish. When you write for other people, though, you need to make conscious choices about your audience; purpose; voice and tone and context, medium, and genre. You need to consider what your audience may already know about the experience that you are sharing and what your purpose is in sharing this experience with this particular audience. You also need to think about how much of your attitude toward this topic and your audience you want to reveal. Further, the effectiveness of your narrative will also be influenced by the medium and genre you choose.

Writing to Share Experiences in Your College Classes

Throughout your college career, you will often be called on to share your experiences in writing. Such writing can help you learn more effectively because it encourages you to reflect on your academic experiences. Furthermore, much academic writing takes the form of **narrative**—stories about the physical or human world. In the book *The Man Who Mistook His Wife for a Hat*, for example, neurologist Oliver Sacks shares stories about patients suffering from neurological and psychological disorders. Author Sandra Cisneros draws on her rich heritage as she crafts work of fiction such as *The House on Mango Street*. One of the best-known philosophers in history, Plato, used stories as powerful teaching tools. In the *Republic*, Plato tells "The Allegory of the Cave" to illustrate what it's like to think like a philosopher.

Likewise, in your own academic life—your life in college—you may be asked to share experiences in the following ways:

- A math instructor may ask you to write about some experience in which you used a math principle or procedure to solve a problem in your everyday life.

- A chemistry teacher may ask you to write about an accident or near-accident in a chemistry lab.

- A music instructor may ask you to attend a concert and then write about the experience.

- A history instructor may ask you to write about a personal experience as if you were a historian, placing the experience in a broader context.

- A psychology instructor might ask you to write about a personal experience and its psychological significance.

- An education instructor might assign you to observe a classroom and write about your observations.

- Your college or university may ask you to write about your experiences at the institution so that the administrators can assess the quality of the educational programs they offer.

Writing to Share Experiences for Life

As humans we tend to organize our lives as ongoing narratives. While your life is one long narrative, within it are thousands of shorter narratives. Those are the kinds of events you will most likely focus on when you write to record and share experiences in the professional, civic, and personal parts of your life.

Curt Schilling, one of the most successful major league baseball pitchers in recent years, partially attributes that success to his ritual of recording his experience with every batter that he faces. Although you may never have a multi-million dollar contract as a major league pitcher, you can still follow Curt Schilling's example by using writing to record and analyze your **professional** experiences so that you can learn from them.

To participate effectively in **civic** life, writers also frequently need to share their experiences. For democratic institutions to function effectively, citizens need to be involved with their government, especially at the local level. Suppose people are dumping trash in a vacant lot near where you live and where young children play. To draw attention to this problem, you may need to write to your city council, narrating a recent incident during which a child was injured while playing in the trash to emphasize the potential danger.

In **personal** settings, you have many opportunities to record and share experiences every day. At dinner, you may entertain your friends or family by recounting a humorous incident that occurred at work that day. At the wedding of two friends, you may be asked to tell the story of how you introduced them in high school. Or, at your grandfather's funeral, you may be asked to tell about the time your grandfather taught you how to play chess or showed you how to build a birdhouse.

WRITER'S WORKSHOP

Applying Learning Goals to Writing That Shares Experiences

Writing to share your experiences with others may seem personal and intimate, but as with any piece of discourse, when you write about your life for others, you should consider what you are trying to accomplish, who your audience consists of, and the context that surrounds the writing. As a group, think of a writing situation in which you would need or want to share your experiences with your audience. Perhaps the situation is a college assignment, a piece of workplace writing, a piece of writing for a civic group or organization, or a personal circumstance. With the other members of your group, discuss your writing situation in terms of the learning goals listed on pages 66–67. Consider how you would address each of these goals in the situation you have chosen. For example, what would your purpose be? Who would your reader be, and what would your stance, or attitude, be toward your subject?

 ## Scenarios for Writing: Assignment Options

Your instructor may ask you to complete one or more of the following assignments that call for you to write about your experiences. Each assignment is in the form of a *scenario*, a brief story that provides some context for your writing. The scenario gives you a sense of who your audience is and what you need to accomplish with your writing. The list of rhetorical considerations on pages 76–77 encourages you to think about your audience; purpose; voice, tone, and point of view; and context, medium, and genre for the scenario you have chosen.

As in the other chapters in this text, we have provided two scenarios focused on academic writing and three scenarios that you might encounter outside of college. Starting on page 97, you will find guidelines for completing the assignment option that you choose or that is assigned to you.

Writing for College

SCENARIO 1   Fostering Learning

This is at least your thirteenth year of formal education. Throughout your formal education, you have worked with dozens of teachers. Some of them have been especially influential in helping you learn to succeed in academic settings—and, of course, their influence may have spilled over into the other three parts of your life. You may have chosen your future profession because of a specific teacher's influence. In "On Becoming a Writer" (p. 81), Russell Baker describes one teacher's influence on his development as a writer. One of the authors of this textbook decided in junior high school to become an English teacher because he admired his eighth-grade English teacher, much as the student in Figure 4.1 admires her professor.

Writing Assignment: Write a narrative about your work with a teacher who has been especially influential in your academic life. Your narrative can be for a general academic audience, or it can be for a specific course in a specific discipline such as education or your academic major.

**FIGURE 4.1
A Graduating
Student with a
Favorite Professor**

SCENARIO 2   Examining and Writing about a Significant and Positive Experience

This scenario asks you to examine and write about an experience in your life that you are interested in and would like to know more about—something that affected you in a positive or useful way. Such events do not always seem to be life-changing when they occur, but when we reflect back, we find that they affected us in a significant way.

For example, at a sophomore-senior picnic in high school, several male seniors, including one of the authors of this text, threw one of the female seniors into a river. When she walked out, she asked the author, "Why don't you like me?" He responded, "But I do like you." Several years later they were married. As of this writing, they have been married for 41 years. Would you agree that this was a fairly significant event?

Writing Assignment: Write a narrative in which you tell about an experience that affected you or someone you know in a positive way. Sometimes experiences like this are major occurrences. You might remember when a relative went off to war and how your correspondence with him or her helped you mature and grow. As an alternative, you might use a version of a tactic that disk jockeys call "brushes with greatness" or "encounters with celebrity": they ask listeners to call in and relate encounters with someone who is famous. Your narrative can be for a general academic audience, or it can be for a specific course in a discipline such as psychology or marriage and family.

Writing for Life

SCENARIO 3   Personal Writing: A Memoir or Biographical Sketch

Much of the writing that you will do to record and share your experiences will be personal writing—entries in journals or diaries, blogs, letters, e-mails to friends. Because many of us have easy access to computers and the Internet, a popular topic for writers who want to record and share experiences is family history. In a narrative about a family's history, the writer tries to look back in time at his or her relatives, both current and distant, and to paint a picture of who they were—which may provide some insight into who the writer is.

Writing Assignment: Write a narrative for a family reunion, such as the one shown in Figure 4.2, in which you tell of a recent event in your life, or of an incident in a family member's life that you have researched, that will be of interest to members of your family.

FIGURE 4.2
A Family Reunion

SCENARIO 4   Civic Writing: A Letter to the President of your College

Think about some problem on campus that has directly affected you. The problem could be inadequate street lighting, a lack of bicycle racks, long lines at the bookstore, litter on the sidewalks (Figure 4.3), missing periodicals in the library, insufficient Internet access in the residence hall, stray cats starving on campus, the need for more evening or online classes, the lack of daycare for children of students, the lack of access for students with disabilities, or any other problem that needs attention.

FIGURE 4.3
Litter on a Sidewalk

Writing Assignment: Write a letter to the president of your college in which you narrate your first-hand experience with the problem that you have identified. At first glance writing to the president of your school might seem presumptuous, but most (if not all) college presidents want to hear from students and are willing to act on student concerns. The president of the school where we teach, Arizona State University, even maintains a blog so that students can interact with him in writing.

SCENARIO 5   Professional Writing: A Letter to a Prospective Employer

In the other scenarios, we have asked you to write about personal experiences from the recent or distant past. In this scenario, we ask you to focus on a recent experience that you have had as an employee or a volunteer. Consider how that experience has made you think about your future. For example, when one of the authors of this book was in college, he worked the graveyard shift (11:00 p.m. to 7:00 a.m.) in a plastics factory. As he operated the machines each night, he was reminded that he wanted a job—a career—that would allow him to work directly with people, a job that would allow him to feel the satisfaction derived from helping people achieve their goals.

Writing Assignment: Write a letter to a prospective employer narrating some experience that you have had as an employee, volunteer, or student. Indicate how that experience has prepared or inspired you for future work.

Rhetorical Considerations in Sharing Your Experiences

Especially because you are constructing a paper for your college class, it is vital to consider the rhetorical aspects of your text—what you are trying to accomplish, who you see as the audience for your work, and how you will establish your credibility with your readers. Before you begin the process of writing in response to one of the scenarios presented above, take a few minutes to consider the following aspects of your writing situation.

Audience: Who is your primary audience? Who else might be interested in this subject? Why? In one paragraph, outline the readers you see as your audience for this assignment.

Purpose: Your narrative could have several interrelated purposes. For example, if you are writing in response to Scenario 1, your narrative can serve both to thank the teacher who has been most influential in your academic life and to honor that teacher. If you choose to address your narrative to other students considering teaching careers, your purpose might also be to remind them of what constitutes effective teaching. If you write about your family's history, your purpose will probably be mostly informative, whereas a narrative about a campus problem could be both informative and persuasive.

Voice, Tone, and Point of View: Depending on the assignment, you may or may not be a major character in your narrative. If you are relating a story in which you are a participant, you have two roles: you are its writer, and you are also a major character in it. If you are not a participant, you will need to use the third-person point of view. Your attitude toward your characters will help determine the tone of your narrative, which could be humorous, such as in "On Becoming a Writer" by Russell Baker (pp. 81–83), or more straightforward and serious, such as in the excerpt from *All Deliberate Speed* by Charles Ogletree (pp. 91–94).

Context, Medium, and Genre: You will always need to understand the situation that creates the occasion to write. Although you are writing this narrative to fulfill an assignment for a college course, you may choose an audience and purpose that go beyond the course. Keeping the context of the assignment in mind, decide on a medium and a genre for your writing. How will your writing be used? Obviously, your instructor will use your writing to help determine your grade for the course, so you should follow his or her instructions carefully. If you are writing for an audience beyond the classroom, consider what will be the most effective way to present your information to this audience. For example, if you are writing a letter to the president of your college in response to Scenario 4, you will need to learn, and follow, the conventions of a business letter.

For more on point of view, see page 79. For more on choosing a medium and genre, see Chapter 15 and Appendix C.

Critical Thinking, Reading, and Writing

Before you begin writing to share your own experiences, you need to consider the qualities of this kind of writing. It also helps to read one or more examples to get a feel for writing about experiences. Finally, you might consider how visuals could enhance your writing, as well as the kinds of sources you might consult.

Writing about experiences has several qualities—a clear sense of purpose, a significant point, a lively narrative, and an honest representation. The writer also has a responsibility to respect the privacy of anyone who appears in a narrative because there are some parts of our lives that should remain private. In the pages that follow, you will learn more about these qualities and responsibilities. The reading selections and the visual text that appear in this section exemplify these qualities. Further, they may serve to stimulate your own inquiry and writing.

Learning the Qualities of Effective Writing about Experiences

Successful writing about experiences—often called *narrative writing*—engages your readers and keeps them interested. One of the best ways to engage readers when narrating your experiences is to incorporate real dialogue. Other strategies include providing telling details and description. The old advice to "show, don't tell" is especially important when writing about experiences.

Even when you are sharing experiences that seem self-evidently fascinating, you need to have a reason for writing about those experiences. In other words, you need to make a point.

Most readers expect the following qualities in writing that shares experience:

- A clear sense of purpose. When you write about your experiences, you need to provide your readers with clues that will help them understand why you are sharing this narrative. Your tone is one important clue. If you are sharing the experience to amuse your readers, for example, you might use obvious exaggerations or add self-deprecating remarks. The amount of explanation and reflection that you include is another clue. If you are simply recording the event so that others can experience it vicariously, for example, you might include very little explanation or reflection. If, however, you want readers to learn something from your experience, or you are trying to convince them of something, you will probably use part of your paper to reflect on the significance of your experience.

- A significant point. Just as you need to have a clear purpose for what you are writing, you also need to use the experience you are relating to say something significant and not just ramble on aimlessly. Writers sometimes use their experiences to make a sweeping, clichéd point such as "if I knew then what I know now," which usually leads to boring, obvious writing. Points have significance for readers when they are fresh and—often—unexpected. In her struggles to learn Spanish, for example, Tanya Barrientos is confounding preconceived ideas her readers may have of her as a Latina (pp. 85–89).

  One way to show significance is to explain—with examples—how the event you are telling about affected you, changed you, or improved your life. You may or may not express your point in a thesis statement, however. Many writers who share their experiences use their language, tone, and the details they choose to make their points implicitly.

- A lively narrative. Although your writing may include other elements, such as reflection, the foundation for writing about experience is a lively narrative. A narrative needs to answer the following questions: Who? What? Where? When? Why? and How? To answer these questions, most narratives include elements that you know well from reading, hearing, and seeing stories—characters, setting, vivid details, and actions. To make these elements come alive for readers, you can use the following conventions of narrative writing:

  - *Dialogue:* Natural-sounding dialogue helps make a piece of writing immediate and lively. Dialogue—what people have to say—brings a narrative to life. Dialogue also can reveal something about the character of the people in your narrative.

- *Vivid description:* Detailed descriptions of the people, or *characters,* mentioned in the narrative, the place where it occurs, and the actions that take place all help involve the reader in your story. Describing people, places, actions, and objects so that your readers will recognize them and relate to them will help make your narrative memorable.

- *Point of view:* While you will most often relate personal stories from your own point of view (first-person perspective, usually told using the pronouns *I* and *me*), it may be more interesting or effective to tell the story from a third-person perspective—perhaps from the point of view of another participant in the event (called the "third-person limited perspective") or from the point of view of an observer who knows what each participant is doing and thinking (called the "third-person omniscient perspective"). All three of the reading selections in this chapter (pp. 81–93) are told from a first-person perspective. The brief account of Nikki Ramey's experience in the Astrodome at the beginning of the chapter is told from the third-person limited perspective.

- *A climax or crisis:* Effective narrative *leads* to something: a point the writer wants to make, an idea the writer wants to explain, a concept the writer wants the reader to understand. By constructing your narrative to lead readers to your main idea or point, you keep them interested, all through your narrative. Sometimes, to build suspense, your narrative can lead up to a crisis, which may or may not have already been resolved.

For more on narration and description, see Chapter 13, pages 687–702.

- **An honest representation.** As you relate, discuss, and examine your experiences—as you share them, in other words—it's important to represent them to readers as accurately as possible. Although you can present your own perspective on any situation, it is usually important to present events without unnecessary embellishments, unless you are exaggerating for an obviously humorous purpose. When writing about your experiences, you may be tempted to make them more interesting than they actually were. When you are striving for accuracy, however, you need to resist that temptation. Usually you are not trying to convince readers to change their ways with this kind of writing, but to honestly relate your experiences so readers can understand their significance. Often you'll be recording family information, which future generations may rely on.

If you keep the qualities of effective writing about experiences in a computer document, you can refer to them as you work. Rewriting the qualities in your own words will help you keep them in mind as you write your own paper.

A WRITER'S RESPONSIBILITIES

Sharing Experiences Responsibly

When you share your experiences with other people, you need to make careful decisions about what to reveal about yourself. As you write, you will need to decide how to fulfill your responsibilities not only to your readers but also to those people who are characters in your narratives.

If you are recording an experience for your eyes only (for example, in a journal or private diary), you may be tempted to think that you have relatively little responsibility to be accurate. After all, you are probably the only person who will ever read the account. But even if the record is for your own purposes, others may be affected by it. On page 72, for example, we mention major league pitcher Curt Schilling who shared the title of Most Valuable Player of the 2001 World Series, won by the Arizona Diamondbacks, and who then helped another team, the Boston Red Sox, win the 2004 World Series. Schilling owes at least part of his phenomenal success to his routine of recording his experiences with every hitter he faces. Even though he keeps those records for the purpose of improving his performance, all of his teammates, as well as thousands of ticket-buying fans, are counting on him to do well—and those records are part of the reason he has been successful.

In other cases, your responsibility to recount your experiences accurately is even greater. For instance, if you are recording the procedures you followed during an experiment in a lab, other scientists are depending on you to be accurate. If you are testifying in a criminal or civil trial, you have not only an ethical but also a legal responsibility to narrate your experience as truthfully as possible. If you agree to serve as a reference for a colleague who is searching for a job, you have a responsibility to portray your experiences with that person accurately because the potential employer, as well as the employer's clients or customers, will rely on that person to perform the job well. Also, if the person for whom you are serving as a reference does excellent work and has good character, you have a responsibility to describe your experiences with your colleague in such a way that you help him or her obtain the desired job.

You also have another responsibility: if you write about criminal activity, your teacher or your classmates may feel compelled to report that activity to the proper authorities. For certain kinds of criminal behavior—domestic violence or sexual abuse, for instance—state law may require your teacher to report the activity to the police. Only you can decide whether you want to write about such experiences, but you need to consider the consequences of doing so.

Reading, Inquiry, and Research: Learning from Narratives That Share Experiences

The selections that follow are examples of writing that share experiences. We think you will both enjoy and learn from them. As you go through each of the selections your instructor asks you to read, consider the following questions:

- How does the author make his or her experiences understandable and indicate their significance?
- What parts of the reading selection could be improved? How?
- What qualities of writing that share experiences does each selection exemplify?
- How can you use the techniques of sharing experiences exemplified in the selection in your own writing?

As you read an essay, take notes, jot down questions, and make observations about the essay in a computer file. Then, if you want to use the information in your own writing, you will already have the main points in a digital format.

RUSSELL BAKER
On Becoming a Writer

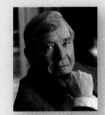

Born in Virginia in 1925, Russell Baker began his professional writing career with the *Baltimore Sun* in 1947, after attending Johns Hopkins University. In 1973 he won a Pulitzer for commentary for his nationally syndicated column, "Observer," which he wrote for the *New York Times* from 1962 to 1998. Baker is the author of a Pulitzer-winning memoir *Growing Up* (1982) and *Looking Back: Heroes, Rascals, and Other Icons of the American Imagination* (2002) and has edited numerous books. Baker's writing regularly appears in the *New York Times Magazine, Sports Illustrated,* and *McCalls*. The following selection is excerpted from *Growing Up*.

The only thing that truly interested me was writing, and I knew that 1 sixteen-year-olds did not come out of high school and become writers. I thought of writing as something to be done only by the rich. It was so obviously not real work, not a job at which you could earn a living. Still, I had begun to think of myself as a writer. It was the only thing for which I seemed to have the smallest talent, and, silly though it sounded when I told people I'd like to be a writer, it gave me a way of thinking about myself which satisfied my need to have an identity.

The notion of becoming a writer had flickered off and on in my head 2 since the Belleville days, but it wasn't until my third year in high school that the possibility took hold. Until then I'd been bored by everything associated with English courses. I found English grammar dull and baffling. I hated the assignments to turn out "compositions," and went at them like heavy labor, turning out leaden, lackluster paragraphs that were agonies for teachers to read and for me to write. The classics thrust on me to read seemed as deadening as chloroform.

When our class was assigned to Mr. Fleagle for third-year English I 3
anticipated another grim year in that dreariest of subjects. Mr. Fleagle
was notorious among City students for dullness and inability to inspire.
He was said to be stuffy, dull, and hopelessly out of date. To me he looked
to be sixty or seventy and prim to a fault. He wore primly severe eye-
glasses, his wavy hair was primly cut and primly combed. He wore prim
vested suits with neckties blocked primly against the collar buttons of
his primly starched white shirts. He had a primly pointed jaw, a primly
straight nose, and a prim manner of speaking that was so correct, so
gentlemanly, that he seemed a comic antique.

I anticipated a listless, unfruitful year with Mr. Fleagle and for a long 4
time was not disappointed. We read *Macbeth*. Mr. Fleagle loved *Macbeth*
and wanted us to love it too, but he lacked the gift of infecting others
with his own passion. He tried to convey the murderous ferocity of Lady
Macbeth one day by reading aloud the passage that concludes.

> . . . I have given suck, and know
> How tender 'tis to love the babe that milks me.
> I would, while it was smiling in my face,
> Have plucked my nipple from his boneless gums. . . .

The idea of prim Mr. Fleagle plucking his nipple from boneless gums was
too much for the class. We burst into gasps of irrepressible snickering.
Mr. Fleagle stopped.

"There is nothing funny, boys, about giving suck to a babe. It is the— 5
the very essence of motherhood, don't you see."

He constantly sprinkled his sentences with "don't you see." It wasn't 6
a question but an exclamation of mild surprise at our ignorance. "Your
pronoun needs an antecedent, don't you see," he would say, very primly.
"The purpose of the Porter's scene, boys, is to provide comic relief from
the horror, don't you see."

Late in the year we tackled the informal essay. "The essay, don't you 7
see, is the . . ." My mind went numb. Of all forms of writing, none seemed
so boring as the essay. Naturally we would have to write informal
essays. Mr. Fleagle distributed a homework sheet offering us a choice of
topics. None was quite so simple-minded as "What I Did on My Summer
Vacation," but most seemed to be almost as dull. I took the list home
and dawdled until the night before the essay was due. Sprawled on the
sofa, I finally faced up to the grim task, took the list out of my notebook,
and scanned it. The topic on which my eye stopped was "The Art of
Eating Spaghetti."

This title produced an extraordinary sequence of mental images. 8
Surging up out of the depths of memory came a vivid recollection of
a night in Belleville when all of us were seated around the supper

table—Uncle Allen, my mother, Uncle Charlie, Doris, Uncle Hal—and Aunt Pat served spaghetti for supper. Spaghetti was an exotic treat in those days. Neither Doris nor I had ever eaten spaghetti, and none of the adults had enough experience to be good at it. All the good humor of Uncle Allen's house reawoke in my mind as I recalled the laughing arguments we had that night about the socially respectable method for moving spaghetti from plate to mouth.

9   Suddenly I wanted to write about that, about the warmth and good feeling of it, but I wanted to put it down simply for my own joy, not for Mr. Fleagle. It was a moment I wanted to recapture and hold for myself. I wanted to relive the pleasure of an evening at New Street. To write it as I wanted, however, would violate all the rules of formal composition I'd learned in school, and Mr. Fleagle would surely give it a failing grade. Never mind. I would write something else for Mr. Fleagle after I had written this thing for myself.

10   When I finished it the night was half gone and there was no time left to compose a proper, respectable essay for Mr. Fleagle. There was no choice next morning but to turn in my private reminiscence of Belleville. Two days passed before Mr. Fleagle returned the graded papers, and he returned everyone's but mine. I was bracing myself for a command to report to Mr. Fleagle immediately after school for discipline when I saw him lift my paper from his desk and rap for the class's attention.

11   "Now, boys," he said, "I want to read you an essay. This is titled 'The Art of Eating Spaghetti.'"

12   And he started to read. My words! He was reading *my words* out loud to the entire class. What's more, the entire class was listening. Listening attentively. Then somebody laughed, then the entire class was laughing, and not in contempt and ridicule, but with openhearted enjoyment. Even Mr. Fleagle stopped two or three times to repress a small prim smile.

13   I did my best to avoid showing pleasure, but what I was feeling was pure ecstasy at this startling demonstration that my words had the power to make people laugh. In the eleventh grade, at the eleventh hour as it were, I had discovered a calling. It was the happiest moment of my entire school career. When Mr. Fleagle finished he put the final seal on my happiness by saying, "Now that, boys, is an essay, don't you see. It's—don't you see—it's of the very essence of the essay, don't you see. Congratulations, Mr. Baker."

14   For the first time, light shone on a possibility. It wasn't a very heartening possibility, to be sure. Writing couldn't lead to a job after high school, and it was hardly honest work, but Mr. Fleagle had opened a door for me. After that I ranked Mr. Fleagle among the finest teachers in the school.

QUESTIONS FOR WRITING AND DISCUSSION: LEARNING OUTCOMES

Rhetorical Knowledge: The Writer's Situation and Rhetoric

1. **Audience:** Who is Baker's primary audience for this piece of writing? What makes you think that?

2. **Purpose:** What is Baker's purpose in telling this story about becoming a writer?

3. **Voice and Tone:** What is Baker's attitude toward his topic and his audience? How do you know that?

4. **Responsibility:** What has Baker done in this essay to be a responsible writer?

5. **Context and Format:** Even though this piece is excerpted from Baker's book-length memoir, *Growing Up*, what makes it work as a stand-alone essay?

Critical Thinking: Your Personal Response

1. What were some of your most memorable experiences with writing in high school?

2. Which of your writing experiences in high school were most pleasant? Why? Which of your writing experiences in high school were most unpleasant? Why?

3. How do Baker's experiences in high school English compare with your experiences?

Critical Thinking: The Writer's Ideas

1. What caused Baker to dislike writing so much in school?

2. What caused Baker to change his mind about writing?

3. How does Baker help readers understand what it means to become a writer?

Composing Processes and Knowledge of Conventions: The Writer's Strategies

1. Why do you think Baker uses dialogue in describing Mr. Fleagle's class rather than simply summarizing or paraphrasing what Fleagle said?

2. How does Baker establish his *ethos* (credibility) in this essay?

3. Baker is well known for his use of precise language, carefully selecting just the right word to express what he means. Where is that care most evident in this essay?

4. Baker is also known for his carefully crafted sentences—not one more word than is necessary. Where is that quality most evident in this essay?

Inquiry and Research: Ideas for Further Exploration

1. In *Growing Up*, Baker narrates many other stories from his life. In your school library, or online, read more stories about Baker's life. Find one that you consider to be especially compelling. What are the qualities or features of that story that you can use in your writing?

2. What else would you like to know about Baker's development as a writer? Why?

TANYA BARRIENTOS

Se Habla Español

Tanya Maria Barrientos has written for the *Philadelphia Inquirer* for more than twenty years. Barrientos was born in Guatemala and raised in El Paso, Texas. Her first novel, *Frontera Street*, was published in 2002, and her second, *Family Resemblance*, was published in 2003. Her column "Unconventional Wisdom" runs every week in the *Inquirer*. This essay originally appeared in the collection *Border-Line Personalities: A New Generation of Latinas Dish on Sex, Sass & Cultural Shifting*.

The man on the other end of the phone line is telling me the classes   1
I've called about are first-rate: native speakers in charge, no more than six students per group.

"Conbersaychunal," he says, allowing the fat vowels of his accented   2
English to collide with the sawed-off consonants.

I tell him that will be fine, that I'm familiar with the conversational   3
setup, and yes, I've studied a bit of Spanish in the past. He asks for my name and I supply it, rolling the double *r* in Barrientos like a pro. That's when I hear the silent snag, the momentary hesitation I've come to expect at this part of the exchange. Should I go into it again? Should I explain, the way I have to half a dozen others, that I am Guatemalan by

birth but pura gringa by circumstance? Do I add the humble little laugh I usually attach to the end of my sentence to let him know that of course I see the irony in the situation?

This will be the sixth time I've signed up to learn the language my parents speak to each other. It will be the sixth time I've bought workbooks and notebooks and textbooks listing 501 conjugated verbs in alphabetical order, with the hope that the subjunctive tense will finally take root in my mind.   4

In class, I will sit across a table from the "native speaker," who won't question why the Irish-American lawyer, or the ad executive of Polish descent, has enrolled but, with a telling glance, will wonder what to make of me.   5

Look, I'll want to say (but never do). Forget the dark skin. Ignore the obsidian eyes. Pretend I'm a pink-cheeked, blue-eyed blonde whose name tag says Shannon. Because that is what a person who doesn't innately know the difference between corre, corra, and corrí is supposed to look like, isn't it? She certainly isn't supposed to be earth-toned or be from my kind of background. If she happens to be named García or López, it's probably through marriage, or because an ancestor at the very root of her family trekked across the American line three or four generations ago.   6

I, on the other hand, came to the United States at age three, in 1963, with my family and stopped speaking Spanish immediately.   7

College-educated and seamlessly bilingual when they settled in West Texas, my parents (a psychology professor and an artist) embraced the notion of the American melting pot wholeheartedly. They declared that their two children would speak nothing but inglés. They'd read in English, write in English, and fit into Anglo society beautifully. If they could speak the red, white, and blue without a hint of an accent, my mother and father believed, people would be forced to look beyond the obvious and see the all-American kids hidden inside the ethnic wrapping.   8

It sounds politically incorrect now. But America was not a hyphenated nation back then. People who called themselves Mexican-Americans or Afro-Americans were considered dangerous radicals, while law-abiding citizens were expected to drop their cultural baggage at the border and erase any lingering ethnic traits. Role models like Vikki Carr, Linda Ronstadt, and Raquel Welch[1] had done it and become stars. So why shouldn't we?   9

To be honest, for most of my childhood I liked being the brown girl who defied expectations. When I was seven, my mother returned my older brother and me to elementary school one week after the school year had already begun. We'd been on vacation in Washington, D.C., visiting the   10

---

[1] Three popular entertainers of Hispanic orgin.

Smithsonian, the Capitol, and the home of Edgar Allan Poe. In the Volkswagen, on the way home, I'd memorized "The Raven," and I'd recite it with melodramatic flair to any poor soul duped into sitting through my performance. At the school's office, the registrar frowned when we arrived.

"You people. Your children are always behind, and you have the nerve to bring them in late?"   11

"My children," my mother answered in a clear, curt tone, "will be at the top of their classes in two weeks."   12

The registrar filed our cards, shaking her head.   13

I did not live in a neighborhood with other Latinos, and the public school I attended attracted very few. I saw the world through the clear, cruel vision of a child. To me, speaking Spanish translated into being poor. It meant waiting tables and cleaning hotel rooms. It meant being left off the cheerleading squad and receiving a condescending smile from the guidance counselor when you said you planned on becoming a lawyer or a doctor. My best friends' names were Heidi and Leslie and Kim. They told me I didn't seem "Mexican" to them, and I took it as a compliment. I enjoyed looking into the faces of Latino store clerks and waitresses and, yes, even our maid, and saying "yo no hablo español." It made me feel superior. It made me feel American. It made me feel white.   14

It didn't matter that my parents spoke Spanish and were successful. They came from a different country, where everyone looked alike. In America, fitting in with the gringos was key. I didn't want to be a Latina anything. I thought that if I stayed away from Spanish, the label would stay away from me.   15

When I was sixteen, I told my father how much I hated being called Mexican—not only because I wasn't, but also because the word was hurled as an insult. He cringed and then he made a radical plan. That summer, instead of sending me to the dance camp in Aspen that I wanted to attend, he pointed me toward Mexico City and the Ballet Nacional.   16

"I want you to see how beautiful Mexico is," he said. "That way when anybody calls you Mexican, you will hold your head up."   17

I went, reluctantly, and found out he was right. I loved the music, the art, the architecture. He'd planted the seed of pride, but it would take years for me to figure out how to nurture it.   18

Back at home, my parents continued to speak only English to their kids while speaking Spanish to each other.   19

My father enjoyed listening to the nightly Mexican newscast on television, so I came to understand lots of the Spanish I heard. Not by design, but by osmosis. So, by the time I graduated from college, I'd become an odd Hispanic hybrid—an English-only Latina who could comprehend Spanish spoken at any speed but was reluctant to utter a word of it. Then came the backlash. In the two decades I'd worked hard to   20 isolate myself from the stereotype I'd constructed in my own head, society shifted. The nation had changed its views on ethnic identity.

College professors had started teaching history through African-American and Native American eyes. Children were being told to forget about the melting pot and picture America as a multicolored quilt instead.

21

Hyphens suddenly had muscle, and I was left wondering where I fit in. The Spanish language was supposedly the glue that held the new Latino-American community together. But in my case it was what kept me apart. I felt awkward among groups whose conversations flowed in and out of Spanish. I'd be asked a question in Spanish and I'd have to answer in English, knowing that raised a mountain of questions. I wanted to call myself Latina, to finally take pride, but it felt like a lie. So I set out to learn the language that people assumed I already knew.

22

After my first set of lessons, which I took in a class provided by the newspaper where I worked in Dallas, I could function in the present tense. "Hola Paco, ¿qué tal? ¿Qué color es tu cuaderno? El mío es azul."[2] My vocabulary built quickly, but when I spoke my tongue felt thick inside my mouth, and if I needed to deal with anything in the future or the past I was sunk. I suggested to my parents that when I telephoned we should converse only in Spanish, so I could practice. But that only lasted a few short weeks. Our relationship was built in English and the essence of it got lost in the translation.

23

By my mid-twenties I had finally come around to understanding that being a proud Latina meant showing the world how diverse the culture can be. As a newspaper reporter, I met Cubans and Puerto Ricans and brown-skinned New Mexicans who could trace their families all the way back to the conquistadores. I interviewed writers and teachers and migrant workers, and I convinced editors to put their stories into print. Not just for the readers' sake, but for my own. I wanted to know what other Latinos had to say about their assimilation into American culture, and whether speaking Spanish somehow defined them. What I learned was that they considered Spanish their common denominator, linking them to one another as well as to their pasts. With that in mind, I traveled to Guatemala to see the place where I was born, and basked in the comfort of recognizing my own features in the faces of strangers. I felt connected, but I still wondered if without flawless Spanish I could ever fill the Latino bill.

24

I enrolled in a three-month submersion program in Mexico and emerged able to speak like a sixth-grader with a solid C average. I could read

25

---

[2] Hello Paco. What's happening? What color is your notebook? Mine is blue.

Gabriel García Márquez with a Spanish-English dictionary at my elbow, and I could follow ninety percent of the melodrama on any given telenovela.

But I still didn't feel genuine. My childhood experiences were different from most of the Latinos I met. I had no quinceañera, no abuelita teaching me to cook tamales, no radio in the house playing rancheras. I had ballet lessons, a high school trip to Europe, and a tight circle of Jewish friends. I'd never met another Latina like me, and I began to doubt that they existed. 26

Since then, I've hired tutors and bought tapes to improve my Spanish. Now I can recite Lorca. I can handle the past as well as the future tenses. But the irregular verbs and the subjunctive tense continue to elude me. 27

My Anglo friends call me bilingual because I can help them make hotel reservations over the telephone or pose a simple question to the women taking care of their children. But true speakers discover my limitations the moment I stumble over a difficult construction, and that is when I get the look. The one that raises the wall between us. The one that makes me think I'll never really belong. Spanish has become a pedigree, a litmus test showing how far from your roots you've strayed. Of course, the same people who would hold my bad Spanish grammar against me wouldn't blink at an Anglo tripping over a Spanish phrase. In fact, they'd probably be flattered that the white man or woman was giving their language a shot. They'd embrace the effort. But when I fumble, I immediately lose the privilege of calling myself a full-fledged Latina. Broken Spanish doesn't count, except to set me apart from "authentic" Latinas forever. 28

My bilingual friends say I make too much of it. They tell me that my Guatemalan heritage and unmistakable Mayan features are enough to legitimize my membership in the Latino-American club. After all, not all Poles speak Polish. Not all Italians speak Italian. And as this nation grows more and more Hispanic, not all Latinos will share one language. But I don't believe them. I think they say those things to spare my feelings. 29

There must be other Latinas like me. But I haven't met any. Or, I should say, I haven't met any who have fessed up. Maybe they are secretly struggling to fit in, the same way I am. Maybe they are hiring tutors and listening to tapes behind the locked doors of their living rooms, just like me. I wish we all had the courage to come out of our hiding places and claim our rightful spot in the broad Latino spectrum. Without being called hopeless gringas. Without having to offer apologies or show remorse. 30

If it will help, I will go first. 31

Aquí estoy.[3] 32

Spanish-challenged and pura Latina. 33

---
[3] I am here.

QUESTIONS FOR WRITING AND DISCUSSION: LEARNING OUTCOMES

Rhetorical Knowledge: The Writer's Situation and Rhetoric

1. **Audience:** For whom do you suppose Barrientos is writing about these experiences?
2. **Purpose:** What do you see as Barrientos's purpose in writing this essay?
3. **Voice and Tone:** Barrientos has specific attitudes toward her subject matter. What parts of her essay can you cite to show what her attitudes are?
4. **Responsibility:** How reliable does Barrientos seem in the way that she presents factual information? What specific details in her essay seem most credible? Why?
5. **Context and Format:** While Barrientos presents her experiences as true, she still relates them almost in the form of a story. How effective is this strategy for writing about such experiences?

Critical Thinking: Your Personal Response

1. What is your response to "Se Habla Español"?
2. Barrientos writes that "this will be the sixth time I've signed up to learn the language my parents speak to each other." What subject area are you still trying to learn?
3. Have you ever tried learning a language your family spoke at home but you did not know? If so, how successful were you? Why?
4. In many ways, this essay is about how Barrientos is trying to fit in to American culture and society. Where have you tried to fit in, and what have your struggles been?

Critical Thinking: The Writer's Ideas

1. Barrientos says that her parents "declared that their two children will speak nothing but inglés." What were their motives for saying that? What do you think about that declaration?
2. What are the potential advantages of being multilingual?
3. Is it, as Barrientos suggests, "politically correct" for someone to give up their home language to learn English? Why?

Composing Processes and Knowledge of Conventions: The Writer's Strategies

1. While she is telling her readers of her personal experiences, Barrientos includes quotations from real people (for example, the school registrar

in paragraph 11 who says, "You people. Your children are always behind, and you have the nerve to bring them in late?"). How effective is this writing strategy? Why?

2. Barrientos tells of her experiences in the first person. How would it alter the effectiveness and interest of this essay if it had been written in the third person? Why?

3. Barrientos now and then writes in Spanish. How do the Spanish sentences affect her essay?

Inquiry and Research: Ideas for Further Exploration

1. Interview several family members about their language background and experiences. In a brief paper, explain how their experiences compare to those related by Barrientos.

2. Barrientos notes that through her newspaper experience, she met people "who could trace their families all the way back to the conquistadores." How far back can you trace your family? Spend some time researching your family history and how your ancestors fared when they first arrived in a new community or country or situation. In a brief paper, describe their positive and negative experiences.

CHARLES OGLETREE

From *All Deliberate Speed: Reflections on the First Half-Century of Brown v. Board of Education*

Charles J. Ogletree, a professor of law at Harvard University, began his career as an attorney in the Washington, D.C., Public Defender's Office. He is now the executive director of the Charles Hamilton Houston Institute for Race and Justice, named for the African American lawyer credited with the legal strategy that overturned racial segregation in Brown v. Board of Education. Ogletree has published two books on the subject of integration: *Brown at 50: The Unfinished Legacy*, which he co-authored with Stanford University professor Deborah Rhode, and *All Deliberate Speed: Reflections on the First Half-Century of Brown v. Board of Education,* a historical memoir. He has contributed to dozens of books about race and justice, and his editorials regularly appear in the *New York Times, Boston Globe,* and other national newspapers.

The following is an excerpt from the second chapter of *All Deliberate Speed*.

I recall that my first experiences in elementary school were fond ones. My classmates, all poor and working class, were predominantly black and brown, with a few whites. The topic of race never came up in those   1 early days, and we all felt we were equal. However, when we left public school and returned to our respective homes, race mattered very much. The black, brown, and white families all lived in largely segregated communities. There was no interaction between our families. We did not play together outside of school. We did not dine or socialize in the same areas. There seemed to be an unspoken agreement that people would be cordial to one another, interact when necessary, but never raise the uncomfortable issue of race voluntarily.

The significance of race was evident in the economic disparities between the two sides of town, but I was too young even to know that we were economically inferior to our white counterparts. It was not the economic disparities that brought race to the forefront. No, it was the interaction with white students that made me realize that being black meant being different and that, in the minds of some of my white peers, it meant being inferior.   2

One of the numerous moves my family made landed us for a short time in a rural section of Merced, where schools were almost exclusively white and the families were generally poor. My mother had gained the support, or possibly sympathy, of a public assistance employee who placed us in a crowded home. My siblings and I were enrolled in the Franklin Elementary School, a school with few black or brown students. I embraced the label "good student" and earned recognition for being so, even in my all-white sixth-grade class. There were occasions, however, when on reflection I might have misinterpreted a special honor as a reflection of my academic achievements rather than of my racial identification. Although *Brown* was by 1964 settled law in the United States, there was little evidence that it had changed the hearts or minds of those to whom it was addressed.   3

There was no more enjoyable period of the school day than morning and afternoon recess. In California, the sun would shine generously and the clouds strike dramatic poses in the skies, making the weather conditions perfect. We could not wait to get outside and run around. Although new to the school, I was fortunate to make friends easily. I recall that the guys stuck together, throwing rocks on the pond, shooting marbles, or playing a little touch football. The girls played jump rope, hopscotch, or on the playground swings. At that age, our recess activities usually divided along gender lines or, as we preferred to call it in those days, boy-girl.   4

One nice day, the boys decided to play a game of touch football. Since I had some speed and decent moves, I was pleased that one of the teams quickly chose me to be on their side. Since recesses lasted only twenty to thirty minutes, these games had to be quick. We were   5 doing well in the game and scored first. We then kicked off to our opponents, one of whom made a pretty good runback, but did not score. On an ensuing play, one of our opponents caught a pass, but I tagged him before he could score. Although it was unintentional, our bodies collided, and he fell down. He seemed more embarrassed than hurt. But it was his spontaneous response that changed everything that day. "You nigger!" he shouted and stormed off the field, startling me and everyone else who heard it. I was only eleven years old and had never been called a "nigger" before. I was shocked and deeply hurt by the experience and to this day cannot understand why I responded the way I did. I laughed and pretended that maybe I hadn't heard it, or that he hadn't really said it, or maybe that it didn't matter. My teammates wanted to follow my lead, before responding. No one said a word. Although I'm sure it was only a matter of minutes, it felt like an eternity before the recess ended. I was no longer reading a story, trying to anticipate what was next. I was living a very uncomfortable moment and had no clue how to proceed. We were spared further awkwardness when the bell rang.

I wanted to put the incident out of my mind and to forget that it had ever happened. Unfortunately, I did not have that luxury. For some reason that I cannot recall, I was the last student to return to the classroom after our recess. The class was unusually quiet after a recess, with the students in their seats, and all eyes on me when I walked in. Our teacher appeared particularly somber, for someone had obviously shared the recess incident with him. He began a discussion about the need for us to respect each other. He, too, was struggling with how to talk about race, without obviously talking about race. As he rambled on, it was clear that he had to confront the issue: a white student had called me, the only black in the class, a "nigger," intending to hurt me. He expressed how upset he was with all that had happened. He then went on personally to apologize to me on behalf of the class and asked whether I wanted to talk about it further. Being the only black student in the class, I could not imagine any benefit from discussing the incident any more, so I declined his invitation. I wanted to ignore the incident, and he wanted to hold a class discussion on the use of the "N" word. Although very well intentioned, my teacher's effort to discuss race did not make me feel any better. It was at that moment when I sat in that classroom as the only black student that I grasped the significance of my blackness and concluded that being black was not a good thing. What did the boy mean when he called me a "nigger"? I know, at a minimum, the word was intended to hurt me, and it did. I also know that it changed the way I saw myself going forward.

Later that year, one of my teachers organized a play depicting   7
California's early history. Our teacher announced the different roles
that each student would portray in the school play, and let me know
that I was selected for a special role, that of master of ceremonies for
the event. It was my job to introduce my fellow fifth-graders, describe
the characters they were playing, and offer a narrative describing the
California gold rush of the 1840s. My classmates were playing the roles
of proud American pioneers who battled the terrain, disease, weather
conditions, and other barriers as they sought to make California the
state where their dreams would come true. As I watched the play
unfold, I realized that there was no role or character for me in this
story. Those in the gold rush were white women and men. If there was
to be a mention of African-Americans, it would require the discussion
of the difficult topic of slavery. Race was not mentioned at all that day.
While I was told that my selection as master of ceremonies was a
reward for being a good student, a subtle, more disturbing factor also
was evident. The teacher created a role for me to play that I, as a black
student, could play credibly in the discussion of this topic. It is true that
I was a good student, but apparently not good enough to have a character role in a play about the gold rush.

QUESTIONS FOR WRITING AND DISCUSSION: LEARNING OUTCOMES

Rhetorical Knowledge: The Writer's Situation and Rhetoric

1. **Audience:** For whom do you suppose Ogletree is writing about these experiences?

2. **Purpose:** What is Ogletree's purpose in writing this section in his book?

3. **Voice and Tone:** Based on this excerpt from Ogletree's book, what do you know about his personality? What are his attitudes toward the topic and toward readers?

4. **Responsibility:** How responsibly does Ogletree deal with the other characters in his narrative such as the teacher? What can you point to in the text to support your claim?

5. **Context and Format:** While Ogletree's experiences are presented as true, he still relates them almost in the form of a *story*. How effective is story writing in relating someone's personal experiences? Why?

Critical Thinking: Your Personal Response

1. What is your response to this passage from Ogletree's book, *All Deliberate Speed*?

2. This passage of Ogletree's text opens with the comment that in elementary school, "the topic of race never came up," but when Ogletree and his classmates "returned to our respective homes, race mattered very much" because their "families all lived in largely segregated communities" (paragraph 1). Why do you suppose people were reluctant to discuss this topic?

3. Have you ever experienced a situation that you wanted to ignore but others insisted on talking about (as Ogletree's elementary school teacher did)? Describe the experience.

Critical Thinking: The Writer's Ideas

1. Using a personal story from his childhood, Ogletree offers evidence that he was changed by an incident on a school playground. How effective is Ogletree's use of this personal story as evidence?

2. At the end of this excerpt, Ogletree tells of the experience of participating in his school play—and how it made him feel. What point is Ogletree making in telling this story?

Composing Processes and Knowledge of Conventions: The Writer's Strategies

1. Ogletree tells of his school experiences in the first person. How effective and interesting would this section of *All Deliberate Speed* have been if he had written it in the third person? Why?

2. Ogletree explains that his elementary school teacher wanted "to talk about race, without obviously talking about race" (paragraph 6). How well do the details about what that teacher says and how the teacher acts support Ogletree's contention? Why?

Inquiry and Research: Ideas for Further Exploration

1. Ogletree's book, *All Deliberate Speed*, is not just about Ogletree's personal experiences with race and education. In your school library or online, read more of what Ogletree has to say. In a few pages, detail how Ogletree's career was shaped by his experiences.

2. In your college library, find several other books that deal with a writer's school experiences. Judging from the chapter titles, what might be the similarities with Ogletree's story?

**FIGURE 4.4
A Grandmother
and Her Grandson**

Thinking about Visuals That Share Experiences

As numerous advertisements have claimed, photographs can also serve to share experiences, sometimes more effectively than written text. On any given day, we are surrounded by images that tell stories—some mundane, some tragic, some comic, and so on.

The photograph in Figure 4.4 shares an experience with which most people are familiar. As you look at this photograph, consider these questions about the effective use of photographs to share experiences:

- What kind of story does this photograph tell?
- What details in the picture speak to you?
- What might this grandmother have to say if she were to write about this experience?
- What can you tell infer about this experience from the photograph? Is this the first time this grandmother has fed her new grandson? Is she singing or talking to him? How is he responding?
- Does this photograph speak to a larger theme about how fragile people are when they are young? About the relationship between young and old? Is a photograph more, or less, effective at making a point or expressing a theme than a written narrative about this relationship would be?

Drawing on Research about Experiences

While a paper in which you share experiences may not seem to require research, even mining your memory—and looking through childhood memorabilia—is a form of research. One of the authors of this text once found some of his own childhood writing on a yellowed sheet of paper with lines drawn to help young students form their letters:

```
_____
-------------------------------------------------
_____
```

On the page, the sentence, "There is no such word as 'can't'," was written over and over. He must have said something in class like "I can't do my homework." Perhaps he even had what seemed, to him, a good reason for saying "can't". . . so the teacher suggested this writing assignment. A find such as this one can help you recall long-buried events and feelings and add compelling details to your writing.

For more on using research to discover your experiences, see pages 100–1.

 # Writing Processes

As you work on the assignment scenario that you have chosen, keep in mind the qualities of effective writing about experiences (see pp. 77–79).

Technote

Are your files stored in folders (directories) on your computer? If so, have you established a system of organization for them? Have you ever lost track of where you've stored a song, video, project, or paper on your computer? Before it happens again, take some time to organize your folders and files.

- Start by looking at the names of all of the folders you've already created. Did you use some principle for naming and organizing them? That is, are they alphabetized? Named according to project or media type (such as music, video, and so on)?

Or are the names more or less random?

- See if you can find relationships among the names of your folders, and look for ways to group folders and files and store them together in one folder.

- Establish a separate folder for each course you are taking.

Taking a little time to organize your files and folders today can save you time and prevent confusion when you need to retrieve files you are working on and quickly locate documents you must print and hand in.

In the pages that follow, you will engage in various writing processes to help you generate ideas and draft, revise, and edit your writing. These processes are *recursive*, which means that you will probably revisit each stage numerous times as you work.

If you are considering several possible topics, put your notes into a separate computer document for each one. Once you determine which topic you will write about, it will be easy to access and use those notes. As you work on your project, make certain that you save your computer files frequently because any work that you don't save could be lost. Many experienced writers save their files every fifteen minutes or so. Also, savvy writers back up their computer files in two or more places—on an internal or external hard drive of the computer, on a USB flash drive, and/or on a rewritable CD or DVD.

Invention: Getting Started

As you begin to explore your subject, it is a good idea to use more than one invention activity to help you come up with ideas. Especially when you are writing to share experiences, the more detail that you generate about the experience through invention, the better you will be able to convey the experience and its meaning to your readers. As you begin the process, consider the following questions:

- What do I already know about the experience that I am writing about?
- What feelings, attitudes, or notions do I already have about this experience?
- What questions can I ask about the experience? That is, what gaps do I have in my memory of it or knowledge about it that might help me understand what information a reader might need?
- Who would know about my experience (a relative or friend)? What questions might I ask that person in an interview?
- What do I know about my audience? What don't I know that I should know? Why might they be interested in reading my text?
- What might my audience already know about my subject? Why might they care about it?
- To what extent will sensory details—color, shape, smell, taste—help my reader understand my topic? Why?

For more on descriptive writing, see Chapter 13.

- What visuals might I use to help my readers understand my experience?

Completing invention activities such as the ones suggested in the first writing activity should yield a wealth of information that you can draw on for your first draft. (Doing your invention work in electronic form, rather than on paper, lets you easily use the writing you generate in your paper at the drafting stage.)

If you already keep a journal, you might skim through it to find ideas for your writing. If you don't already keep a journal, you might do so while you are getting started on this writing project. Who knows—you might even start a lifelong habit of writing in a daily journal.

WRITING ACTIVITY

Listing, Questioning, and Freewriting

When you use listing, you jot down keywords that will remind you of ideas as you write more later. You might find it effective to establish categories for your lists to help jog your memory. If you are exploring an experience, for instance, you might organize your keywords under the following categories: "Participants," "Location," "Visual Images," "Sounds," "Activities," "Smells."

Especially if your experience consists of a single event, you can generate some of the basic details about that event by simply responding to the five questions that are commonly asked by reporters:

- *Who* are the participants in this event and what useful information about those participants will help me tell my story?
- *What* are the participants doing? *What* are they saying?
- *Where* did the event occur?
- *When* did the event occur, and what is the significance of when it happened?
- *Why* did the participants do what they did? That is, what motivated their actions?

Finally, a good way to get your ideas about an experience down on paper or into a computer file is to use freewriting.

TechNote Use technology to help you "unjam" that writer's block! Some writers find it hard to get started when they are asked to share personal experiences in class, either because they are overcome by shyness or overwhelmed by the number and variety of experiences and interests they are excited to write about. If writer's block sets in, one way to get your ideas and memories flowing is to use your personal network and communication skills to tap a vital resource: the people who know you well. Send a couple of e-mails, a text message, an instant message, or even an I-Voice message to family members or close friends. Ask them to reminisce briefly about events, occurrences, or activities you've shared. You might be pleasantly surprised at the memories and ideas they share that will inspire you.

Jessica Hemauer's Listing and Freewriting

Jessica Hemauer, a student in a first-year composition course, generated the following list about her experience of growing up on a farm.

For help with listing, questioning, and freewriting, as well as other strategies for discovery and learning, see Chapter 3.

small town
farm chores—endless
Dad worked hard; we did too
coffee
siblings
Orange, multi-stained Carpet
Oversized, cluttered Table
Stuffed, pine Shelves
Steep, creaky Stairs
Bathroom
Basement
Loud, Plastic runners covering the multi-stained orange carpet
Warm, rustic steel Woodstove

Blinds
Navy blue, understuffed, corduroy Sofa that has one cushion
    burnt b/c it was too close to the woodstove
White, clean carpet
Clean table set for 2
Neatly lined bookshelves
Round staircase with a wood banister

Jessica Hemauer also used freewriting to explore her ideas about growing up on a farm.

An Excerpt from Jessica Hemauer's Freewriting

Small town girl. What's special about that some might ask. Well, I actually have a lot to share. My background makes me who I am. It shapes your personality, values, and morals. I am who I am because of where I grew up. For me, the place I will forever call home, even after moving half way across the country to go to college. The place that I never thought I would want to return to, I long for in my dreams. I think of waking up to the smell of my mom's hot coco and my dad's coffee brewing. Sometimes it's burnt coffee, depending if the cows need to be fed before he feeds himself. That's another part of me. I grew up on a dairy farm. When the wind blew from the west, you didn't want to go outside; it was the worst smell you could imagine. I remember having pool parties outside in our yard with my friends from school and once the wind was blowing from the wrong way and everyone was complaining about the smell. I tried not to notice, but even I was getting nauseous from the putrid smell . . .

 ## Exploring Your Ideas with Research

Depending on the scenario you are responding to, you may need to interview family members or friends about the experiences you are exploring. Be sure to record their stories carefully; their recollections will enliven your text. Always try to ask them for remembered dialogue—what people said—as those remembered sentences will help you show (rather than just tell) the experience you are writing about.

Especially if you are responding to Scenario 3, you may find it useful to go back through old family files, letters, documents, and photo albums—all wonderful sources of information. See the box on pages 101–2 for more on generating ideas from photographs and documents.

Many families have one or two members who, over time, become the family historians, the ones who collect letters and photographs and use computer programs (like Family Tree Maker) to record a history of the family.

What members of your family might have such records that you could look at?

Use an electronic journal to record images, URLs, and other electronic pieces of information that you find as you are conducting your research. Such an e-journal makes it easy for you to add those e-documents once you start drafting your paper.

For more on conducting interviews, see Chapter 19, pages 863–65

VISUALIZING VARIATIONS

Using Photos and Documents as Sources

If you are writing in response to Scenarios 1, 2, or 3 (pp. 73–74), you may be able to use photographs and documents to help you generate ideas and recall or reconstruct events. The photograph above is of the great-great-grandparents of the wife of one of the authors of this book. Look at a photograph or photographs of your teacher (Scenario 1), of the experience you are writing about in your past (Scenario 2), or of one or more of your relatives or ancestors (Scenario 3), and speculate about the person or people, using the following questions:

1. What do the clothes the people in the photograph are wearing tell you about them?
2. What do their expressions reveal—or fail to reveal—about them?
3. Are you looking at old photographs similar to this one? If so, compare the facial expressions in your photos to the one above. Does everyone in your old photographs always look glum (ours do!)?

The photograph on the following page, taken in Wisconsin circa 1955, includes one of the authors of this book and his siblings. Use the following questions to speculate about this photograph or a similar one from your past.

1. On what day of the week do you think the photograph was taken? What evidence supports that assumption?
2. During what time of year was the photograph taken? Why do you think that?
3. What do the expressions on the people's faces tell you about the situation?

(cont'd)

(continued)

In addition to photographs, you might have a letter, diary, or other document that you, your teacher, or your relatives or ancestors wrote that can give you insight into your experience or their experiences. Use the following questions to generate more ideas about this assignment:

1. When and where was the document written? What was the writer's purpose in writing it? How can you tell?
2. What does the document reveal about the writer's experiences or about your experiences at the time? If the document was written by someone else, in what ways, if any, can you relate the experiences that writer describes to your own?
3. How significant does the experience seem? In what ways did the experience in the document change the writer's, or your, life?
4. What insight, if any, does the photograph or photographs you have looked at give you into the document? What insight, if any, does the document give you into the photograph(s)? What do both the photograph(s) and the document, taken together, tell you about yourself, this person, or these people?

If you participated in the experience shown in the photograph or described in the document, use the following questions to generate ideas about it:

1. How is your memory of the experience the same as, or different from, the experience as it is depicted in the photograph(s) or document?
2. If you wanted to write a brief story about the people in one of the photographs above, or in one of your photographs, what would you say?
3. What experiences have you had in taking photographs? What stories do you try to tell when taking photographs or videos? How do you try to do so?

Consider including a copy of the photograph or a selection of photographs and quoting from the document in your final paper.

WRITER'S WORKSHOP

Reacting to Your Classmates' Invention Work and Research

As with any kind of writing, invention activities improve with peer feedback and suggestions. Working with several classmates, share the invention work that you have done so far. Tell the members of your group the scenario you are responding to and the experience you are writing about. Offer one another the following kinds of comments and ask one another the following kinds of questions:

Comments

- The part about _____ is not clear to me—can you clarify?

- I like _____ in what you've generated so far.

- I can see that _____ is important to you—can you tell me more?

Questions

- What is a _____?

- How would you describe the purpose of the _____ that you mention?

- What did you do/think/feel when _____ did _____ or when _____ happened?

- What do you think is the significance of the experience?

- What makes the experience memorable or important for you?

Make sure you address all the questions your classmates ask. You do not necessarily need to change what you have written just because someone has asked a question. However, you do need to understand the concern and make changes where they are appropriate. You should also pay close attention to your classmates' comments. If someone makes a positive statement about what you have written, make sure you understand why that reader felt that way. Knowing the reason for a positive comment may help you generate more information that will evoke the same feelings in your readers.

Organizing Your Ideas and Details

Once you have generated ideas and details about your subject using invention activities and, if necessary, research, consider how you might organize this material. The questions that you need to ask yourself when deciding on your organization are all rhetorical:

- Who is your audience?
- Why might they be interested in your narrative—and how can you make them interested?
- What is your purpose for writing—that is, what do you want your readers to understand about you or the event you are narrating?

The answers to these questions can help you decide what you need to emphasize, which in turn will help you choose an organization.

It is usually helpful to try *several* organizational strategies in early drafts because seeing your words on paper—in various ways—will help you decide what strategy will work best for you. Most often, writing about experiences is linear or sequential: the writer starts at some specific point in the past and then moves to a later time or to the present. This kind of writing can also lend itself to less linear approaches. For example, you might start in the present, then look back at the experiences and events you are writing about, and then reflect on the significance of your subject.

Another alternative would be to use the narrative technique known as **flashback.** In a flashback, commonly used in film, something that happened in the past is shown "just the way it happened" and then the narrator returns to the present to reflect on the event's significance.

For example, suppose when you were younger you had a memorable experience at either a soccer match or a concert. You might have been a player or a member of the audience. To write about this experience, you could do the following:

- Start by describing the experience in detail and explaining how it sparked your interest in athletics or music, and then move to the present and talk about your involvement with music or athletics (perhaps you have a continuing interest in participating in and listening to music, or in watching a particular kind of athletic event, or perhaps you encourage your children to take part).
- Start by discussing your current interest in and involvement with the type of music or game, and then narrate the past experience and reflect on its significance.

Here are three possible organizational structures that you might use for a piece of writing that shares experiences:

Options for Organization

First Approach	Second Approach	Third Approach
• Straightforward chronology—narrate the experience from beginning to end. • Relate key details surrounding the event or experience. • Note the impact of the experience on your life or the lives of others who were part of the experience. • Reflect on the significance of the experience. (optional)	• Begin in the present. • Flash back to the events and experiences you want to share and relate them in sequence. • Relate key details surrounding the events or experiences. • Look back on those events and experiences in terms of the impact they had on you and your life, or the lives of other family members. • Reflect on the significance of the experiences. (optional)	• Begin with the crisis point in the event or experience. • Go back to the beginning and tell the story to the end. • Relate key details surrounding the event or experience. • Reflect on the significance of the event and experience. (optional)

WRITING ACTIVITY

Deciding on an Organizational Approach

Before you construct a full draft about your experiences, consider the organizational approaches that are available to you and decide which one will best serve your writing purpose and help your audience see and understand your meaning. Try writing a page or two using at least two organizational approaches before you settle on one. Trying out different approaches will give you a sense of which one might be the most effective for this particular writing task. For example, it may be easiest to use the first approach— narrating the event using a straightforward chronology that moves from beginning to end. However, using the second, flashback approach might offer your readers some hindsight that will help them interpret your narrative. Alternatively, using the third approach can help your readers feel more urgency in the narrative. You might try out several organizational approaches on the computer before deciding on one. Be sure to save each attempt with a different file name. That makes it easy to recall the one that seems best and start to develop your draft using that organization.

Jessica Hemauer's Organization

Jessica Hemauer looked over her invention material and then put together a rough outline for her draft. She decided to use the third approach, beginning at the crisis point.

Begin as a 10-year-old girl—waking up to feed calves
Describe daily family routine
Good feelings about being in charge when feeding calves
Describe parents
    Impact of their relationship on me
School WAS social life
    Being a farm girl made me different
    How I didn't fit in
Playing Basketball in 8th grade
    Started to feel included—but worked harder than others
    Falling asleep in class
THE FAMILY MEETING
Freed from farmwork and being involved
Why I'm still different and that's ok.

Constructing a Complete Draft

Once you have chosen the organizational approach that works best for your audience and purpose, you are ready to construct the rest of your draft. Before you begin your draft, review all your invention material to see what needs to be included and what might be left out. To make these decisions, consider your purpose for sharing this experience with others. The overriding questions are these: What is the significance of the experience? How can I help readers see the significance?

If you have received comments from classmates, you will want to take their views into consideration. However, remember that you must make the final decisions about what to include and what to leave out.

You will also want to discover the method of writing a first draft that works best for you. Some writers prefer drafting large chunks at once. Others prefer drafting small pieces over time. Remember that you do not have to compose your essay in a linear way—from beginning to end. You might find it easiest to jump in somewhere in the middle. You might also find that it is much easier to write the introduction last.

Introduction: One of the qualities of a successful narrative is that it grabs and holds readers' attention—from the beginning, the narrative interests them in the story and in its characters. A number of strategies for beginning your narrative can help get your readers interested, including the following:

- *Start your narrative with a surprising event or piece of dialogue.* Tanya Barrientos (her essay appears on p. 85) starts her essay by telling of a phone conversation and then adds a word readers may not know or expect: "*Conbersaychunal.*"

- *Start with interesting details*, to draw the reader in through sensual, descriptive words and phrases. George Orwell begins his essay "A Hanging" in this way: "It was in Burma, a sodden morning of the rains. A sickly light, like yellow tinfoil, was slanting over the high walls into the jail yard. We were waiting outside the condemned cages, a row of sheds fronted with double bars, like small animal cages."

- *Start with a comment that might startle your readers.* John McPhee, in writing about the formation of continents in *Basin and Range*, starts this way: "The poles of the earth have wandered. The equator has apparently moved."

For more on introductions, see Chapter 13.

Body: The main part, or body, of your narrative is the place to tell your story. Use dialogue and telling details to develop the story and reveal the character of the people in your narrative. To hold your readers' interest, you should usually build your narrative to a crisis or climax, unless you are writing for an informative purpose and are required to maintain a neutral tone (or unless you are beginning with the crisis point of the narative—see p. 105). Choose the verb tense that will best serve the purpose of your narrative. If you use past-tense verbs to narrate the experience, you remind readers that it happened in the past and that you've had time to reflect on it. If you use present-tense verbs, you make the event seem as if it is happening now, and you will seem to reveal its significance to yourself and to your readers at the same time. Also, you might consider using photographs to complement the words you're using to tell the story. If the event you are relating occurred when you were nine years old, for example, you might show readers what you looked like then.

Conclusion: Your conclusion should tie things together for your readers by explaining or suggesting the significance of the experience or experiences you have shared: why your story is important and why it has made a difference in some way. Here are some strategies for concluding a paper in which you have shared experiences:

- Review the subject's most important aspects. For example, if you chose Scenario 1, you might summarize the ways in which the teacher you are writing about has influenced you.

- Explain the subject's significance. At the end of the excerpt from *All Deliberate Speed*, Charles Ogletree notes the significance of his experiences in Franklin Elementary School.

- Suggest avenues for a reader's further inquiry. If you chose Scenario 4, you might recommend that readers do some research into the community problem themselves.

For more on conclusions,
see Chapter 13.

- Refer back to the introduction of your narrative. At the end of Jessica Hemauer's essay, she thinks back to her childhood on the farm.

Title: You might think that you need to come up with a title before you start writing, but often it is more useful to get a first draft down on paper or into a computer file and then consider possible titles. As with the introduction, an effective title for a narrative intrigues readers and makes them want to read the text. Jessica Hemauer, for instance, uses the word *girl* in her title since "Life on the Farm" or "My Early Years" did not seem as interesting to her as the title "Farm Girl."

WRITING ACTIVITY

Constructing a Full Draft

Starting with the writing that you did in order to choose an organizational approach, write a complete draft of your paper that shares an experience.

A Portion of Jessica Hemauer's First Draft

After deciding on her organizational approach, Jessica Hemauer wrote the first draft of her essay on growing up on a farm. The following is a portion of her first draft. Like all first drafts, it includes problems with grammar, spelling, and punctuation. (The numbers in circles refer to peer comments—see p. 113.)

Farm Girl

Jessica Hemauer

BEEP! BEEP! BEEP! It's 5:00 a.m. My eyes are heavy with sleep and struggle to open. I think to myself, "A typical ten-year-old child does not have to wake up at five in the morning to do chores!" I hit the snooze button with disappointment, hoping desperately that the cows would for once, feed and milk themselves. Seconds away from falling back into a deep sleep, I hear the heavy footsteps of what could only be my father coming near my bedroom door. They stop and my door opens with a creak. "Jessica, are you awake yet?" my father asks. Without a word, knowing from the past that an argument doesn't get me anywhere, I stagger out of my warm twin bed, trudging dejectedly past the figure at the narrow doorway. I continue down the hall toward the small bathroom to find my sisters, Angie and Melissa, and my brother Nick already awake. ❶

We all proceed with our usual morning routine, which consists of washing our faces, brushing our teeth and taking turns on the white porcelain throne. In the lower level of the old farmhouse our outside clothes await. My mother made it a rule to keep them there so that they wouldn't stink up the rest of the house. As soon as you opened the door to the basement, you can smell the putrid aroma of cows that has seeped from our clothing into the damp cool air.❷ We took our turns going down the steep, narrow steps, using the walls on either side for extra guidance. As we dressed not a single word was spoken because we all felt the same way, "I hate this!" Although most of the time our choice of vocabulary was much more creative.

Nick opened the basement door leading outside to the barn. There was a brisk and bitter wind accompanied by snowflakes that came down fast and hit us, making it feel like needles digging into our faces. We didn't turn back. We desperately wanted to, but we knew my father was patiently waiting for us to help him milk and feed the cows before school started at 8:30 a.m. We lifted our scarves and pulled down our hats so only our squinted eyes showed. We lowered our bodies to dodge the fierce winds and trudged a half mile to the red barn, which was somehow standing sturdy in the dreadful blizzard.

When we finally reached the barn, Nick, leading the pack, grabbed the handle of the heavy wood door and propped it open for my sisters and I to pass through. Nick went immediately to help my father heard the cows and get them into their proper stalls to be milked. Meanwhile, my sisters and I went to the milk house to sanitize the milk machines, prepare all the milking equipment and set up a station with towels and charts of the cows that are being medicated.

While Melissa and my father milked the 100 cows, Nick and Angie fed the cows, and I went to feed the newborn calves.❸ Being the youngest in the family, this was my favorite chore because I rarely had the chance to look after someone or feel like I was taking care of them. I have always had older siblings who looked after me, watching every step I took, being sure that I didn't get into trouble. When feeding the calves, I was finally the one in charge. It was a nice feeling, being on the opposite end of the spectrum. They were my responsibility. I was in charge of them and caring for them during feeding time every morning and evening. Little did I know at that time, this was the beginning of a lifetime of responsibilities.

When the calves were fed, other chores had to be done. Cleaning out various huts and pens and laying down fresh straw were apart of our daily duties. This was the worst of the jobs I had to do. It was so dusty that I could hardly breathe at times, but we all knew it had to be done so there was no sense in complaining. My family and I worked together to get the work done as quickly as possible. The more we worked together, the faster we were able to get out of the bitter cold and into the warmth of the farm house. Typically, we would finish with the chores and return to the house around 7:30 in the morning.

When we made our way back to the farmhouse, we draped our clothes on a folding chair next to the washing machine in the basement and crawled up the stairs. The delicious smell of smoked bacon and cheese omelets grew more intense with each step. As our stomachs ached with hunger, we took turns in the shower, cleaning ourselves as fast as possible in order to get to the breakfast table. My brother would be the first to the table because as we all know, girls take longer to get ready than boys. My father would eat and be back outside on the farm by the time my sisters or I would run by the kitchen grabbing a glass of fresh squeezed orange juice and a piece of toast as we yelled frantically at the bus, "Wait!" It seemed our daily lives operated in shifts, not like a real family. ❹

When we left for school, my mother would clean up the half eaten breakfast and finish getting ready for work at the office. She worked from nine to five wearing business suits and a mink coat. The relationship between my mother and father seemed strange. They were completely opposite of each other. My mother loved diamonds and pearls. My father didn't seem to care much for material things. I guess their many differences made their relationship an exciting roller coaster. ❺

Watching my parents as I grow up, I notice how their relationship has made a strong impact on me. I have a hard time focusing on relationships. I seem to get extremely involved in my job and school that I don't make time for the other person. I learned this behavior from my parents. My father was always very consumed with the farm and my mother had her own interests. They rarely made time for each other and neither of them seemed to care. They never went out on dates or went out with friends. Everything revolved around the farm. Therefore, I tend to focus on one or two things and don't make time for someone special.

When I finally arrived at school I had already been up for four hours doing chores on the farm in the bitter cold. The other kids in my private grade school just rolled out of their beds inside their subdivision homes an hour before the bell rang. The school day always went by fast. While my other classmates were thinking about what television show they were going to watch after school, I was thinking about the chores that await me once I get off the yellow school bus. . . .

Revising

Just finishing a complete draft may give you a justified sense of accomplishment. However, you are only part of the way to a successful piece of writing; you still need to revise and then edit the draft. It is a good idea to let your draft sit for a while after you have finished it. When you return to it, you are much more likely to find sections that need to be revised, places where details need to be added, other places where details may need to be removed, still others where some of your words or sentences need to be shifted from one place to another.

Technology can help you revise and edit your writing more easily. Use your word processor's track-changes tool to try out revisions and editing changes. After you've had time to think about the possible changes, you can "accept" or "reject" them. Also, you can use your word processor's comment tool to write reminders to yourself when you get stuck with a revision or some editing task. If your classmates are offering feedback on your draft, they can also use track changes, the comment tool, or the peer-commenting feature of the software.

At this point in the process, feedback from others can prove especially valuable. Your instructor may ask you to share your work with classmates and request suggestions and ideas. Friends or family members may also be willing to read your draft and offer useful suggestions.

WRITER'S WORKSHOP

Responding to Full Drafts

Working with one or two classmates, read each paper and offer comments and questions that will help each of you see your papers' strengths and weaknesses. You might share your comments and questions in a conversation, or you may have each reader write comments and questions (either with pen or pencil or electronically) on the writer's draft. Consider the following guidelines and questions as you do:

(cont'd)

(continued)

- Write a brief narrative comment that outlines your first impression of this draft. How effectively does the title draw you into the narrative? Why? Do you have any suggestions for improving the title?

- In a paragraph, indicate what you like about the draft—that is, provide positive and encouraging feedback to the writer.

- Comment specifically on the introduction: What is effective about it? What suggestions can you make on how to improve the introduction?

- What significant point is the writer making about the experience or experiences he or she is relating? How easily can you articulate the writer's point? How might the writer be able to make that point more clearly?

- Why is the writer relating this experience or these experiences? How successful has the writer been in fulfilling his or her purpose? What in this piece of writing helps you see why the experience or experiences were important to the writer?

- How lively is the narrative? Where has the writer gone beyond simply telling readers about the experience or experiences to showing it or them? For example, one way of showing is to use dialogue. How might the writer use more dialogue?

- How has the writer used description to make people, places, and scenes vivid for readers? Where is more description needed?

- How effectively does the story build in terms of reaching a climax, holding the readers' attention throughout, and making logical sense in how one action follows another?

- How honestly has the writer explained the experience? What specific details in the narrative lead you to believe that it is honest? If not, why do you question it?

- Reread the conclusion. What could be added or changed to make it more effective? How well does it bring the narrative to a satisfying conclusion?

- In another paragraph, outline what you see as the main weaknesses of this piece of writing—and suggest how the writer might improve the text.

Student Comments on Jessica Hemauer's Draft

Here are some comments that student reviewers made about Jessica Hemauer's draft keyed to the first draft on pages 108–11.

① "I really liked the description of you getting up early and getting ready. I could almost feel the cold and smell the farm smells."

② "I like how the real details (like all of the smells) help me 'be there' with you."

③ "I think you're writing this because you want to tell people that all those awful farm chores really helped you."

④ "I think your point was that all the time you wanted to fit in, and then when you could do things normal kids do, you found out you were different anyway."

⑤ "I don't see why the information about your parents is important— can you clarify or explain?"

⑥ "I'd like to hear more about school and the people there."

As with the comments you will receive from your teacher and classmates, Jessica had to determine which comments and suggestions made sense—and then to revise her paper accordingly.

Responding to Readers' Comments

Once they have received feedback from peers, teachers, writing tutors, and others, all writers have to determine what to do with that feedback. Since the draft is *your* paper, you as the writer are responsible for dealing with reader responses to your work.

The first thing to do with any reader feedback is to consider carefully what the reader has to say. For example, Jessica Hemauer's readers indicate the following reactions:

- Two readers really like some of the descriptive passages in the paper. Hemauer needs to consider whether more description could be added since this strategy has been effective.

- Another reader was confused about the parts of the paper where Hemauer gives details about her parents. She needs to look for ways to clarify those sections or, perhaps, to delete them altogether.

- A reader has outlined what seemed to him to be the point, or thesis, of Hemauer's paper. When you get such feedback on your papers, make sure that the reader does in fact understand and reiterate your point. If the reader does not get your point, then perhaps you are not being clear and explicit enough.

Pay close attention to what your readers tell you. You may decide to reject some comments, of course, and that decision is yours. As with any group of readers, some of your peer reviewers might not understand your point, or they may misunderstand something you wrote. It is up to you either to accept or to ignore their comments and suggestions. Other comments, though, deserve your attention because they are the words of interested, caring readers speaking to you about how to improve your text. They offer perspectives that you may not have. You may find that comments from more than one reader contradict each other. In that case, use your own judgment to decide which reader's comments are on the right track.

In the final version of her paper on pages 117–21, you can see how Jessica Hemauer responded to these comments as well as to her own review of her first draft.

Knowledge of Conventions

When effective writers edit their work, they attend to the conventions that will help readers understand their ideas. These include genre conventions, documentation, format, usage, grammar, punctuation, and mechanics. By attending to these conventions in your writing, you make reading a more pleasant experience for readers.

Editing

After you revise, you need to go through one more important step: editing and polishing. When you edit and polish your writing, you make changes to your sentence structure and word choice to improve your style and to make your writing clearer and more concise. You also check your work to make sure it adheres to conventions of grammar, usage, punctuation, mechanics, and spelling.

Because it is sometimes difficult to identify small problems in a piece of writing you have been mulling over for some time, it often helps to distance yourself from the text before your last read so you can approach the draft with fresh eyes. Some people like to put the text aside for a day or so; others try reading aloud; and some even read from the last sentence to the first so that the content, and their familiarity with it, doesn't cause them to overlook an error. Because checking conventions is easier said than done, though, we strongly recommend that you ask classmates, friends, and tutors to read your work to find sentence problems that you do not see. Another option is to post your paper on a course Web site and invite everyone in class to read your paper. You may get only one or two takers, but one or two is better than none.

To assist you with editing, we offer here a round-robin editing activity focused on punctuating dialogue, which is a common concern in writing to share experiences.

WRITER'S WORKSHOP

Round-Robin Editing with a Focus on Punctuating Dialogue

When writers share their experiences, they often use dialogue to make the scenes and events vivid for readers. Writers who use dialogue need to be aware of the conventions for punctuating it, in particular the use of quotation marks, as well as commas, periods, and question marks.

All dialogue needs to be enclosed in quotation marks to set it off from the rest of the text. The conventions for punctuating dialogue are straightforward. If the dialogue is presented within the context of a sentence, the phrase that introduces the dialogue ends with a comma and then the dialogue begins with a quotation mark:

> Raising my head, feeling embarrassed that she caught me sleeping, I said quickly, "No, Ms. Cain, I'm fine. I'm sorry for being rude and causing a disruption. I promise to be more attentive."

If the dialogue is not introduced within a sentence, it usually starts a new paragraph that begins with a quotation mark.

> "Hey Carrie, how was basketball practice last night?" Susan asked as she pulled out a chair from the lunch table and set her plastic tray down next to the tall, broad, blond-haired girl.

If the dialogue goes on for more than a paragraph, an opening quotation mark begins each new paragraph, but a closing quotation mark appears only at the end of the speaker's words. Periods and commas go inside the quotation marks:

> "He made us run sprints for every shot we missed. And Kelly was missing all her shots last night. I'm so sore today."

Question marks and exclamation points go either inside or outside of the quotation marks, depending on whether they are part of the quotation itself.

> "Jessica, are you awake yet?" my father asks.

> "It was terrible! Coach was in such a bad mood!"

Work with two peers to edit one another's papers for problems in punctuating dialogue. Each student should hand his or her paper to the classmate on the left. Read your classmate's paper, focusing on whether the dialogue has been punctuated correctly. After no more than ten minutes, pass the papers to the left again, and focus on the punctuation of dialogue in the second paper. After two peers have read each paper, compare notes to see if you have any questions about the conventions for punctuating dialogue. If you are uncertain about a rule, consult the examples above, check the rules in a grammar handbook, or ask your instructor for assistance.

 ## Genres, Documentation, and Format

If you are writing an academic paper, follow the conventions for the discipline in which you are writing and the requirements of your instructor. If you have written a letter to the president of your college (in response to Scenario 4), you should check Appendix C to see what the requirements are for length and format and what information you need to include when you send a business letter. If you have chosen to write a letter to a prospective employer, you should also follow the conventions of a business letter.

WRITING IN ACTION

Convention in Genre and Design

An experience almost everyone shares at one time or another is trying to find a job. In "Ed's Girl on the Hunt," the writer has shared her experience of searching for, and finding, a job in a Web log, or *blog*, a Web site that is a kind of online journal to which anyone can post their comments. In the blog entry below, the writer tells of finally finding an internship at a magazine. Do these comments seem true to your experiences? How effectively does this writer relate her joy at landing a summer job? Why do you suppose she chose to share her experiences in a series of blog entries?

ED'S GIRL ON THE HUNT
What Does It Take To Get A Job in This Town? One Woman's Hunt for That Elusive First EA Job in the World of New York City's Magazine Industry

Friday, March 31, 2006
26 Days and I'm Out!

At 10:34 am on Wednesday, the day after my interview, I got a call. I didn't mean to pick up. I was on my way to lunch with a friend and had just sent out an email to someone who could advise me on good/bad career moves.

The voice on the other end said they liked me and wanted to offer me the internship, did I want it?

Yes. Of course.

What followed next were a few phone calls to my family and friends filled with nervous laughter. Did I really just accept? I meant to think about it more. But with all of the congratulations rolling in from the other line, my smile grew. And with each hour that passed thereafter I couldn't stop thinking about it or calling people to talk about it. I came home that night after a few beers with friends and kept singing the name of the magazine to my roommates—they thought I'd had too many, but I was euphoric.

I can't think of another magazine I'd take an internship for. I was prepared to settle for anything—*Cats Weekly, Knowing Knitting, Dissecting Diesel Engines*. Or even a stand-up magazine that I really had no interest in besides the salary they were offering. Even that would be a struggle—I have a hard time working towards something I don't believe in.

But this magazine, THIS magazine is the one I eventually want to write for and I emulate the people who do. This month one of their articles blew me away—and I'm a tough critic. I can't wait to check out all of the back issues from the library and learn every article and nuance from the past few years. I'm an excited nerd.

And it all started with a cold email to the assistant editor. I didn't know him, I didn't know anybody that knew him. I thought I barely left an impression during the informational interview. But one person backed out of the internship and four days later, I'm a summer intern for my dream magazine.

Now to figure out what to do with the next two months.

Thanks for reading, thanks for listening, and thanks for responding everyone. Thank YOU Ed. And with a little luck, I'll have an exciting update like Ed's first girl around August.

Take care.

Love, love, love,

Ed's Girl The Second

Considering Genre and Design

1. Sometimes bloggers make sensational statements to gain attention. Often these statements are unsupported or too revealing. How would you define the tone of this blogger? Compare her tone with that of others, at other blogs.
2. Bloggers frequently include lists, *blogrolls,* of other Web logs that they like to read. Why do you think that this practice has become so common?
3. What can you point to in this blog entry that shows how the writer makes her experiences interesting to the readers of the blog?
4. Would you like to read more from this blogger? Why? What about her blog entry makes you feel this way?
5. Given that family members and potential employers may read blog entries, what kinds of material would you not include in your blog?

A Writer Shares Her Experiences: Jessica Hemauer's Final Draft

The final draft of Jessica Hemauer's essay "Farm Girl" follows. As you read Hemauer's essay, think about what makes it an effective example of writing about experiences. Following the essay, you'll find some specific questions to consider.

JESSICA HEMAUER

Farm Girl

BEEP! BEEP! BEEP! It's 5:00 a.m. My eyes are heavy with sleep and struggle to open. I think to myself, "A typical ten-year-old child does not have to wake up at five in the morning to do chores!"   1

I hit the snooze button, hoping desperately that the cows will, for once, feed and milk themselves. Seconds away from falling back into a deep sleep, I hear my father's heavy footsteps outside my bedroom door. They stop and my door opens with a creak. "Jessica, are you awake yet?" my father asks. Without a word, knowing from past experience that an argument won't get me anywhere, I stagger out of my warm twin bed, trudging dejectedly past the figure at the narrow doorway. I continue down the hall toward the small bathroom to find my sisters, Angie and Melissa, and my brother, Nick, already awake.

We all proceed with our usual morning routine, which consists of washing our faces, brushing our teeth, and taking turns on the white porcelain throne. In the lower level of the old farmhouse, our outside clothes await. My mother makes it a rule to keep them there so that they won't stink up the rest of the house. As soon as we open the door to the basement, we can smell the putrid aroma of cows that has seeped from our clothing into the damp cool air. We take our turns going down the steep, narrow steps, using the walls on either side for extra guidance. As we dress, not a single word is spoken because we all feel the same way, "I hate this!" However, most of the time our choice of vocabulary is much more creative.

Nick opens the basement door leading outside to the barn. There is a brisk and bitter wind accompanied by icy snowflakes that feel like needles digging into our faces. We don't turn back. We desperately want to, but we know my father is patiently waiting for us to help him milk and feed the cows before school starts at 8:30 a.m. We lift our scarves and pull down our hats so only our squinted eyes show. We lower our bodies to dodge the fierce winds and trudge a half mile to the red barn, which is somehow standing sturdily in the dreadful blizzard.

When we finally reach the barn, Nick, leading the pack, grabs the handle of the heavy wood door and props it open for my sisters and me to pass through. Nick goes immediately to help my father herd the cows and get them into their proper stalls to be milked. Meanwhile, my sisters and I go to the milk house to sanitize the milking machines, prepare all the milking equipment, and set up a station with towels and charts of the cows that are being medicated.

While Melissa and my father milk the one hundred cows, Nick and Angie feed them, and I feed the newborn calves. Because I am the youngest in the family, this is my favorite chore because I rarely have the chance to look after someone or feel like I am taking care of him or her. I have always had older siblings who look after me, watching every step I take, making sure that I don't get into trouble. We all work together — that's critical. When I feed the calves, I am finally the one in charge. It is a nice feeling,

2

3

4

5

6

One of Hemauer's peer readers wrote the following comment:

I like how the real details (like all of the smells) help me "be there" with you.

Notice the sensory details in this paragraph.

being on the opposite end of the spectrum. They are my responsibility. Little do I realize it, but this is the beginning of a lifetime of responsibilities.

After the calves are fed, other chores have to be done. Cleaning out various huts and pens and laying down fresh straw are a part of our daily duties. This is the worst of the jobs I have to do. It is so dusty that I can hardly breathe at times, but we all know it has to be done so there is no sense complaining. My brother, sisters, and I work together to get the chores done as quickly as possible. Typically, we finish with the chores and return to the house around 7:30 in the morning.

We make our way back to the farmhouse, drape our clothes on a folding chair next to the washing machine in the basement, and crawl up the stairs. The delicious smell of smoked bacon and cheese omelets grows more intense with each step. Our stomachs aching with hunger, we take turns in the shower, cleaning ourselves as fast as possible in order to get to the breakfast table. My father eats quickly and is back outside on the farm by the time my sisters or I run by the kitchen, grabbing a glass of fresh squeezed orange juice and a piece of toast as we yell frantically at the bus, "Wait!" It seems our daily lives operate in shifts, not like a real family.

When I finally arrive at school, I have already been up for four hours doing chores on the farm in the bitter cold. The other kids in my private grade school have just rolled out of their beds inside their subdivision homes an hour before the bell rang. The school day always goes by fast. While my other classmates are thinking about what television show they are going to watch after school, I am thinking about the chores that await me once I get off the yellow school bus.

School has always been my social life. I want to join teams or different clubs, but I always have to consider how my chores on the farm will get done, which makes it difficult for me to get involved. If I join a team that practices after school, I can't participate. If I join a club that meets before school, I can't attend the meetings. Being a farm girl means that I can't be like the other kids in my class. Not being able to participate in school activities like my friends makes me feel left out and depressed. The topic of conversation at the lunch table never involves me.

"Hey, Carrie, how was basketball practice last night?" Susan asks as she pulls out a chair from the lunch table and sets her plastic tray down next to the tall, broad, blond-haired girl.

"It was terrible! Coach was in such a bad mood!" Carrie shoves a handful of French fries into her mouth, spilling catsup down the front of her white tee shirt without noticing. "He made us run sprints for every shot we missed. And Kelly was missing all her shots last night. I'm so sore today."

7

8

Again, note the sensory details in Hemauer's paper: the smells, being hungry, fresh OJ, etc.

9

One peer reader had the following comment:

I don't see why the information about your parents is important—can you clarify or explain?

Hemauer has deleted two paragraphs about her parents that took the essay off track.

One peer reviewer made this suggestion:

I'd like to hear more about school and the people there.

Note the details and specific examples that Hemauer provides to really show what she means (rather than just telling).

10

11

Carrie starts rubbing her legs when she notices the streak of catsup   12
on her shirt. She begins to wipe it off with one of her napkins, with little
success.

"Hey, Carrie, how was the student council meeting this morning? Did   13
you decide if we're going to have a formal dance this winter?"

"Yeah, we're having it on the Saturday before Christmas. Are you   14
going to come?"

I sit listening in silence. The twenty-minute lunch period always   15
feels like eternity. While everyone around me continues talking and
laughing, I sit there next to them silently eating my French fries, listening carefully, trying to laugh at the right times.

In eighth grade I really want to play basketball, and after begging and   16
pleading with my parents, they finally say I can join the team as long as I
continue to help with chores in the morning before school and after practice. I quickly agree. I become the basketball team's starting point guard. I
am thrilled to be on a team, and I finally feel like I am starting to have a life
like the other kids. Now I am included in the conversations at lunch, and I
feel like a part of the group. I never tell anyone that I have to go home after
practice and work on the farm, or that I wake up every morning at five to
help with chores. None of my friends, teachers, or coaches know. I don't
think they would care and I don't want them to know that I am different.

In high school I become more involved with the school. Coincidently,   17
my father's farm continues to grow. We are now up to two hundred cows,
and my dad still wants to expand the farm. During my freshman year I
continue to work on the farm before and after school, making sure that I
can still play on the basketball team. A few times a teacher catches me
with my eyes closed during class. One time my teacher, Ms. Cain, comes
over to my wooden desk, where my head is resting on top of a math textbook. She taps her knuckles on the hollow wood and says, "Jessica, are you
okay? Do you need to go to the health room?" Raising my head, embarrassed
that she caught me sleeping, I say quickly, "No, Ms. Cain, I'm fine. I'm sorry
for being rude and causing a disruption. I promise to be more attentive."

Shortly after freshman year, my father arranges a meeting with my   18
entire family. He explains that he wants our farm to continue to grow, and
this means that he needs more help on the farm than his children can
provide. In fact, he says that he would rather not have us work on the farm
anymore, unless we want to. He would rather have us be more involved in
school and go on to college. After this meeting, I feel happy and relieved,
and I can tell my father is relieved too. He knows that my siblings and I
have sacrificed our school activities and social lives to help with the family business, and I know that this is his way of saying thank you.

From this moment on, I become more involved with my school. I join   19
the homecoming club, audition for musicals and plays, serve as the

president of the student council as well as president of my class. I also became more social with my friends. I even take on a waitressing job at a resort in a neighboring town. During all these activities, I always notice that I stick out from the group. In school people come up to me and ask how I manage my time so well, without getting stressed out. When I'm with a group of my friends, I always seem to be more mature than they are, leading the group while others try to follow in my footsteps. When it comes to my job, I am always on time, never calling in sick and never complaining about a task I have been asked to do.

One night after work, I sit down in front of the full-length mirror in my bedroom and start thinking about the past years. I had believed that joining various clubs and social activities would make me fit in with my peers. But in fact, it has not. I still stick out. And the more I think about it, the more I realize why. My life growing up has been much different from the lives of my peers. From an early age, I had to learn how to manage my time so that I could do my chores and attend school. When I started to play basketball, I had to manage my time even more carefully. I have always had a challenging amount of responsibility, and I have learned to complete tasks in a timely fashion. The work that I had to do on the farm was far from glamorous. I have done some of the worst jobs conceivable, so I have a higher tolerance for work than most people. Though I hated it growing up, working on the farm has taught me many lessons about life, and it has shaped me into the individual I am today.   20

Each day of my life there are times when I reflect back to working on the farm. And every day people notice that I am different from the rest of my peers. At school, teachers and organization leaders are impressed by my time management skills and the amount of responsibility I take on. At work, my boss continues to ask me where he can find some more hard working people. I simply tell him, "Try hiring some farm girls. I hear they turn out pretty good."   21

QUESTIONS FOR WRITING AND DISCUSSION: LEARNING OUTCOMES

Rhetorical Knowledge: The Writer's Situation and Rhetoric

1. **Purpose:** Why did Hemauer write this essay? How might different audiences see different purposes?

2. **Audience:** Who do you see as Hemauer's audience? What can you point to in the text that supports your claim?

3. **Voice and Tone:** How does Hemauer establish her *ethos*—her credibility—in this essay?

4. **Responsibility:** What is Hemauer's responsibility to her readers? To the members of her family? How does she fulfill those responsibilities?

5. **Context and Format:** Hemauer is writing an essay for readers who are probably not familiar with life on a farm. How does this context affect her essay?

Critical Thinking: Your Personal Response

1. What is your first impression of Jessica Hemauer's essay? What does the essay say about Hemauer?

2. Even though you may have had a much different childhood from Hemauer's, can you relate to some of her experiences? What does she do to develop interest in the subject of her essay?

3. Which of Hemauer's experiences would you most like to experience? Why? Which of Hemauer's experiences would you least like to experience? Why?

Critical Thinking: The Writer's Ideas

1. What insights do you now have about Hemauer?

2. What insights do you now have about Hemauer's family?

3. What do you see as the significance of Hemauer's story?

4. Why does Hemauer mention the mirror toward the end of the essay?

Composing Processes and Knowledge of Conventions: The Writer's Strategies

1. How do descriptive and narrative details function in the essay? Point to several places where Hemauer "shows" instead of "tells."

2. What is the main point of Hemauer's essay? How do the details in the essay support that point?

3. How does Hemauer use dialogue in the essay? What other methods does she use to show readers what her life as a farm girl was like?

Inquiry and Research: Ideas for Further Exploration

1. Search the Web to find other narratives—especially blog entries—in which college students' reflect on their life and work experiences. How do they compare to Hemauer's narrative about her farm-life experience?

2. If you were considering hiring Jessica Hemauer for a job, which of her qualities would make her an effective employee? Based on the information in this essay, are there any qualities that might make you hesitate to hire her?

3. What other childhood experiences might give a person the qualities that Hemauer claims growing up as a farm girl taught her?

Self-Assessment: Reflecting on Your Learning Goals

Now that you have constructed a piece of writing to share experiences, revisit your learning goals, which you and your classmates may have considered at the beginning of this chapter (see pp. 66–67). Here are some questions to help you focus on what you have learned from this assignment. Respond to the questions in writing and discuss your responses with classmates. If you are constructing a course portfolio, your responses to these questions can also serve as invention work for the portfolio.

Rhetorical Knowledge

- *Audience:* What did you learn about your audience as you wrote about your experience or experiences?
- *Purpose:* How successfully do you feel you fulfilled your purpose? What makes you think that?
- *Rhetorical Situation:* What was your rhetorical situation? How have you responded to the rhetorical situation?
- *Voice and Tone:* How did you reveal your personality? What tone did you use?
- *Context, Medium, and Genre:* What context were you writing in? What medium and genre did you choose, and how did those decisions affect your writing?

Critical Thinking, Reading, and Writing

- *Learning/Inquiry:* What did you discover about writing about experiences while you were working on this assignment? What did you discover about yourself? About your experiences?
- *Responsibility:* How did you fulfill your responsibility to your readers? To the people you wrote about?
- *Reading and Research:* Did you rely on your memories, or did you conduct additional research for this assignment? If so, what sources did you consult? How did you use them? Did you use photographs and/or documents?

Writing Processes for Sharing Experiences

- *Invention:* What invention strategies were most useful to you?
- *Organizing Your Ideas and Details:* What organization did you use? How successful was it?
- *Revising:* What one revision did you make that you are most satisfied with? What are the strongest and the weakest parts of the paper you

wrote for this chapter? Why? If you could go back and make an additional revision, what would it be?

- *Working with Peers:* How did your instructor or peer readers help you by making comments and suggestions about your writing? List some examples of useful comments that you received. List some examples of how you revised your essay based on those comments and suggestions. How could you have made better use of the comments and suggestions you received? How could your peer readers help you more, on your next assignment? How might you help them more, in the future, with the comments and suggestions you make on their work?

- Did you use photographs or other visuals to help you describe your experience or experiences? If so, what did you learn about incorporating these elements?

- What "writerly habits" have you developed, modified, or improved on as you constructed the writing assignment for this chapter? How will you change your future writing activities, based on what you have learned about yourself?

Knowledge of Conventions

- *Editing:* What sentence problem did you find most frequently in your writing? How will you avoid that problem in future assignments?

- *Genre:* What conventions of the genre you were using, if any, gave you problems?

- *Documentation:* Did you use sources for your paper? If so, what documentation style did you use? What problems, if any, did you have with it?

 ## Jessica Hemauer Reflects on Her Writing

Once she completed the polished version of her essay, student writer Jessica Hemauer reflected on the process. Here is an excerpt from her reflection:

> I learned a lot about audience while working on this project. Because most of my classmates had not grown up on farms, I had to work hard to describe farm activities so that city residents would understand them. That's often not easy to do, so I always was thinking, what might my readers know about farm life? What wouldn't they know? What kinds of details and examples would show them, like they were actually there on the farm with me?
>
> I knew I had to have a thesis or point to make. At first, I thought that I'd just like to tell a story about growing up on a farm in Wisconsin, but

then I realized that my story had a lesson for me and for others. Once I understood that my story had a bigger purpose, I had to keep that purpose in mind. It helped me make decisions about what to include in my story.

I also wanted my personality to come through in my essay, which meant that I had to use expressions that say who I am. I have some good examples of that in the story, I think.

I loved writing about some of my early experiences—both good and bad—and telling what life was like for me, a "farm girl." I learned a lot about myself but also about the relationships with my parents and especially about my relationships with the other students I went to school with. I was surprised that much of my writing was a reflection — I wrote, "Each day of my life there are times when I reflect back to working on the farm," and I guess that's true. I like to reflect back . . .

I think writers are supposed to be responsible and accurate in what they say—and sometimes that's hard when you're going from memory. I think that I was responsible in how I represented my family to readers. I told my story as accurately as I could, but I left out some details that readers don't need to know or shouldn't know.

In a lot of college papers, students have to conduct research. My "research" for this paper consisted of drawing on memories of my experience. I learned that I have a pretty good memory—I was able to remember a lot from when I was younger and growing up, lots of good details about the farm and farm life and the smells and all.

I did a lot of different "invention" work for this paper. It was helpful to do invention activities because I needed to have rough lists of ideas before I began constructing a draft. Even after I began drafting, though, I still had to do some brainstorming to generate more ideas to flesh out the draft. Once I had generated ideas for the essay, it was pretty easy to organize the narrative in chronological order. It was a little more of challenge to weave reflection into the paper. Although I was able to do some revisions on my own, my peers asked questions and offered suggestions that helped me revise. They especially asked for more examples and details, which I tried to add, about smells and sounds and things that would help make my paper come alive.

My peers were great. They told me what they did and did not understand in my earlier drafts. Once I knew what they didn't understand, I was able to add needed details.

I learned that I'm a decent writer of description but not so good at dialogue, writing what people said, or what I remember they said. Sometimes I couldn't remember their exact words, but our teacher told us that it was okay to vary from the exact words as long as I was true to the spirit of what they said. I also had to work at fixing my verb tenses, as they didn't always match the rest of the sentence.

Rhetorical Knowledge

- *Audience:* Because you are learning as you write, you will often be the main audience. Who else can you visualize reading your work? What will that person or those people expect to find in it? How can you appeal to those readers as well?

- *Purposes:* Your purpose might be simply to learn more about the topic, but often exploratory writing leads to the unexpected and unfamiliar, so you need to be prepared to be surprised.

- *Rhetorical situation:* Consider the myriad of factors that affect what you write—you (the writer), your readers (the audience), the topic (the subject you are exploring), your purpose (what you wish to accomplish), and the exigency (what is compelling you to write). In an exploratory essay, you are writing to raise questions and to let them guide your inquiry; your readers are reading your text so that they can grapple with those same questions.

- *Writer's voice and tone:* Generally, exploratory writing has an inquisitive tone. Of course, sometimes an exploratory essay can have a humorous tone—see, for example, P. J. O'Rourke's "Memoir Essay" (p. 151).

- *Context, medium, and genre:* The genre you use to present your thinking is determined by your purpose: to explore. You will need to decide on the best medium and genre to use to present your exploration to the audience you want to reach.

Critical Thinking, Reading, and Writing

- *Learning/inquiry:* By reading and writing as an explorer, you gain a deeper understanding of diverse and complex perspectives.

- *Responsibility:* You have a responsibility to represent diverse perspectives honestly and accurately.

- *Reading and research:* Your research must be accurate and as complete as possible, to allow you to consider the widest possible array of perspectives.

Writing Processes

- *Invention:* You will need to choose invention strategies that will help you thoughtfully contemplate diverse perspectives.

- *Organizing your ideas and details:* You will need to find the most effective way to present perspectives to your readers, so they can easily understand them.

- *Revising:* You will need to read your work with a critical eye, to make certain that it fulfills the assignment and displays the qualities of effective exploratory writing.

- *Working with peers:* Your classmates will make suggestions that indicate parts of your text they find difficult to understand so you can work to clarify.

 Conventions

- *Editing:* When you explore, you might tend to leave your thoughts—and sentences—incomplete. To help you avoid this pitfall, the round-robin activity for this chapter (on pp. 176–77) deals with sentence fragments.

- *Genres for exploratory writing:* Possible genres include exploratory essays, profiles, and more informal types of exploratory writing such as blogs, journals, and diaries.

- *Documentation:* If you have relied on sources outside of your own experience, you will need to cite them using the appropriate documentation style.

A. Photo taken on July 20, 1969, by Neil A. Armstrong of Edwin E. "Buzz" Aldrin during the Apollo 11 mission to the moon.

B. The Mars Rover, one of two "robot geologists" that landed on the surface of Mars in January 2004.

C. A view of the star cluster NGC 346 in the Small Magellanic Cloud, a satellite galaxy of the Milky Way, taken by the Hubble Space Telescope.

Writing to Explore

When you hear the word *exploration*, you may envision astronauts or explorers of earlier centuries, people who physically ventured to previously uncharted territory. When astronauts Neil Armstrong and Edwin E. "Buzz" Aldrin went to the moon in 1969, they were looking for answers to questions that humans have asked for thousands of years: What is the moon like? What is it composed of? What is its surface like? Has there ever been water there? What does Earth look like from the moon? More recently, the Hubble Space Telescope has enabled explorers to view remote parts of the universe such as the brilliant star cluster NGC 346. And today's space explorers are often not astronauts but robots—like the Mars Rover, also shown here.

Although we commonly associate exploration with physical travel, there are many other kinds of explorations. Indeed, some of the most valuable explorations are those that take place in your own mind. Often, through the act of writing, you can discover new ideas or new perspectives. Exploratory writing can take you places you do not expect to go. It is not unlike the experience of following links on the Internet. Starting at one site, you follow one link, then another, then another. Before you know it, you find yourself in a totally unexpected—but extremely interesting—place.

Playwright Edward Albee once noted, "I write to find out what I'm talking about." Albee's insight offers a way of thinking about exploratory writing as writing that allows you to understand both what you know about a subject and what you do not know. In addition to exploring what you already know, exploratory writing gives you the chance to ask questions and to consider what else you would like to find out. These questions often lead to research that can give you the answers you need.

Exploring various perspectives on issues, concepts, places, or people will help you to work your way through ideas and problems in college and in the professional, civic, and personal areas of your life. You may already have used exploratory thinking and writing in deciding where to go to college. If you were choosing between a local community college and a state university some distance away from your hometown, for example, you probably noted that the community college had the advantages of being close to home and less expensive, while the university offered more extracurricular activities and a wider range of majors, along with the experience of living in a different place—but at a higher cost. In your professional life, you might be asked to research possible locations for a new branch office of your company, exploring the advantages and disadvantages of each. Or, at some point in your personal life, you may need to decide whether to stay home with a young child or find an appropriate daycare facility so that you can work outside the home or attend school. In your civic life, you may research a charity to which you are thinking of donating to make sure it is what it claims to be.

In each of these explorations, you investigate a particular subject closely. You will often need to explore an idea or a concept—or a decision you need to make—in detail, from various perspectives, before you can really see and understand the overall situation, gain some insight, or make a difficult decision.

 ## Rhetorical Knowledge

When you write to explore, consider how your exploration will help you gain some greater understanding and how you can help your readers understand your topic in a new way and why you want them to gain this understanding. You will also need to decide what medium and genre will help you communicate your exploration most effectively to your audience.

 ## Writing to Explore in Your College Classes

Your college classes, which are generally designed to fulfill requirements for a specific major and college degree, give you wonderful opportunities to explore your current interests and discover new ones. Taking a college class in almost any field allows you to begin exploring that field, reading its literature, and listening to and interacting with people who are experts in the field. Each class you take also gives you the chance to explore the subject area in writing. During your college career, you may write the following kinds of papers:

- In a history class, your instructor may encourage you to explore several perspectives on the Cuban Missile Crisis in 1962. Such an exploration might then lead to a writing project in which you argue that certain events and factors were the actual causes of this crisis.

- In a nutrition class, your instructor asks you to explore several perspectives on vegetarian diets. Here, too, your exploration could lead to a paper in which you demonstrate specific effects of vegetarianism or in which you argue for or against such a diet.

- For a communication course, your instructor may ask you to explore whether there is evidence that men and women have different communication styles.

- In a philosophy course, you might be asked to write a dialogue in which two characters discuss a complicated ethical issue—such as what to do if bird flu becomes a human pandemic and there is not enough vaccine available to protect all people in the United States.

- In a chemistry course, your instructor may ask you to combine several chemicals, observe the reactions, and then record them in a lab report.

For all of these writing situations, think about what you might need to do to communicate your ideas effectively: what information you might need to include, how you would describe your exploration, what visuals or examples you might use, and so on.

For information on writing a cause-and-effect analysis, see Chapter 10. For information on writing to convince, see Chapter 8.

 ## Writing to Explore for Life

Just as you will undoubtedly write to explore in your academic life, you are likely to use different kinds of exploratory writing in other areas of your life. You may enjoy keeping a journal of your personal life. In your professional life, creating scenarios may help you explore options and make difficult decisions. In your civic life, you may also have opportunities to use exploratory writing.

In much of the exploratory writing you will do in your **professional** life, you will find yourself exploring various options. To what extent will hiring Ms. X instead of Mr. Y make a difference to the business or institution? A teacher might ask what effect one lesson plan would have on a group of students compared to a different lesson plan? Parents might explore the possibilities of different places for a vacation, or different schools for their

TechNote The ultimate form of writing to explore might be a personal or professional online journal, or *blog*. A blog can be a fun place to explore issues and events of the day while developing your voice, style, and expressive self. If your teacher recommends blogging, a good place to get started with ideas for a blog might be Maggie Mason's book *No One Cares What You Had for Lunch: 100 Ideas for Your Blog* (Peachpit Press; August 11, 2006).

For more on blogs, see Chapter 17.

children, or different neighborhoods to live in. While it is impossible to predict the future, by engaging in exploratory writing we can often better understand the consequences of taking a particular action. Putting alternatives in writing makes them clearer and helps us understand cause-and-effect relationships.

People working for the good of a community often deal with *best options*—solutions to problems for which there may not be a single perfect result but rather many possible outcomes. Therefore, those involved in **civic** life can find exploratory writing especially useful. For example, if a community is threatened with a mosquito-spread disease such as West Nile virus, community leaders can use writing to explore the advantages and disadvantages of alternatives for dealing with the threat.

Your **personal** life offers many opportunities for exploratory writing. You may respond regularly to e-mails or notes from friends, family members, and classmates in which you explore the possibilities for a group gift for someone important to all of you, propose convenient times for getting together to study, or consider a new wireless phone carrier. You may keep a journal or diary, where you can explore your thoughts, ideas, responses, and feelings in a private conversation with yourself.

WRITER'S WORKSHOP

Applying Learning Goals for Exploratory Writing

One of the most powerful ways to use writing is as a tool to "write to learn" or "write to discover." The act of writing can produce results writers are not able to anticipate until they begin putting words on paper or on the computer screen. Often your first response to or thoughts about a particular situation are not the best ones. By engaging in exploratory writing, you can discover new and sometimes better options. As a group, think of a writing situation in which you need or want to explore a topic. Perhaps the situation is a college assignment, a piece of workplace writing, a piece of writing for a civic group or organization, or a personal circumstance. Exploratory writing allows you to learn as you write, to delve into a subject and discover through the act of writing. With the other members of your group, discuss your writing situation in terms of the learning goals listed on pages 126–27. Consider how you would address each of these goals in the situation you have chosen. For example, what would your purpose be? Who would your reader be, and what would your stance, or attitude, be toward your subject?

Scenarios for Writing: Assignment Options

Your instructor may ask you to complete one or more of the following assignments that call for exploratory writing. Each assignment is in the form of a *scenario*, a brief story that provides some context for writing. The scenario gives you a sense of who your audience is and what you need to accomplish with your writing. The list of rhetorical considerations on page 136 encourages you to think about your audience; purpose; voice, tone, and point of view; and context, medium, and genre for the scenario you have chosen.

As in the other chapters in this text, we have provided two scenarios focused on academic writing and three scenarios that you might encounter outside of college. Starting on page 159, you will find guidelines for completing whatever assignment option you choose.

Writing for College

SCENARIO 1 Exploring a Major or Career

For this scenario, assume you are taking a "Career and Life Planning" class—a class devoted to helping college students decide what discipline they might like to major in. This class gives you the opportunity to explore different career paths, to learn what the educational requirements are for various majors, and to find out what job opportunities will be available in various careers and what salaries and other forms of compensation different jobs might offer.

Writing Assignment: Select one college major or career that you may be interested in pursuing and construct an exploratory paper in which you consider the various aspects of that major or career from many angles, including the preparation you would need for it and the rewards and pitfalls you might encounter if you decide to pursue it. Asking and answering questions about the major or career you are considering will form the heart of your exploratory paper.

SCENARIO 2 Writing a Profile to Explore a Personal Interest

In this writing option, you will explore a subject that interests you personally and write a profile of it. Instructors sometimes allow students to focus on an issue or area of interest; this assignment gives you the chance to do just that: to explore something or someone you are interested in and would like to know more about.

Writing Assignment: Think of a subject that fascinates you and that you would like to know more about—your subject might be a type of music or musician, a sport, a popular singer or actor, a local hangout, a community center, or something completely different. This assignment offers you the opportunity to research and write about a topic you are interested and/or involved in. Use this opportunity not only to learn about the subject but also to examine your perceptions of and reactions to it.

FIGURE 5.1   A Conference in a Professional Setting

Writing for Life

SCENARIO 3   Professional Writing: A Report on Planning a Meeting

You are working for a large organization with offices all over the country. Your supervisor informs you that she would like you to organize a planning meeting for several high-level managers of your company (Figure 5.1). Because the meeting will be held in January and most of the participants live in cold-weather climates, she would like you to look for a warm-weather site for the meeting. She suggests that Orlando, Florida; Palm Springs, California; or Bermuda might be nice locations and asks you to explore the pros and cons of each site. She also tells you that the meeting should run from Monday morning through Thursday afternoon. Three people will be attending from the Buffalo, New York, office; two from the Cincinnati, Ohio, office; two from the Denver, Colorado, office; two from the Philadelphia, Pennsylvania, office; and one from the Los Angeles, California, office.

Writing Assignment: Write a report that explores the different options for a meeting location. You will need to explore the cost and convenience of the three possible sites for this meeting. It should be relatively easy to determine how much it would cost to fly the people to each location and house them for several days. Keep in mind that although one location might be less expensive than the others, it might not be the most convenient. For example, if the meeting were held in Bermuda, all the participants would need passports.

FIGURE 5.2   A Poster for the United Way, a Nonprofit Agency

SCENARIO 4   Civic Writing: A Profile of a Local Agency

What local nonprofit agencies exist in your area? What do you know about how they function? What do you know about the work that they do in your community? Do you interact with any local, county, state, or federal agencies or departments? What experiences (good or bad) have you had with such entities?

Select one local nonprofit *or* government agency or organization in which you are interested and about which you would like to learn more. The agency or organization may be your city or county government, your local school system, or a nonprofit organization such as United Way (Figure 5.2).

Writing Assignment: Investigate the nonprofit or government agency or organization you have chosen. Explore what it does, where and how it functions, where its funding comes from, who works for it, and how its functions relate to other aspects of your community. Then construct a paper in which you explain your exploration of the agency or organization. Since this is not an informative paper, your focus should be on the exploratory process you used to learn about your subject.

SCENARIO 5   Constructing a Personal Exploration in a Letter to a Friend

For this exploratory writing assignment, think of something you really believe in. You might want to discuss your views on raising children, supporting aging parents, choosing a simpler lifestyle, discovering some important truth about yourself, or some other quality or belief that makes you who you are. (Because religious beliefs are so personal, you may want to select a strongly held opinion that does not involve your religion.)

Writing Assignment: Write down in a sentence or two something you believe in strongly. Now explore the basis for your belief. Consider what in your background, education, history, family, friendships, upbringing, and work experiences has helped you come to the conclusions you have reached about the topic. Why do you believe what you do? Put your text into the form of a letter to a good friend.

Rhetorical Considerations for Exploratory Writing

Audience: Although your instructor in your college class is your main audience for this paper, you are also part of your audience—this assignment is designed to help you think through some possible educational and career choices, to explore an interest, to practice planning a business meeting, or to explore some of your personal beliefs. Your classmates are also your audience, as some of them may also be considering these issues and ideas, and they will learn from your research and perhaps ask questions and think of ideas they had not yet considered.

Purpose: Your purpose is to explore the various aspects of your topic in enough detail and depth to lead you to a greater understanding of it and what you believe about it.

Voice, Tone, and Point of View: As a student, you already have your own ideas, knowledge, background, and experiences. As you explore your topic, you will step back to consider whether your preconceptions about it are accurate. Your stance should be objective, and you should be open to the different possibilities you will discover. The point of view you take should be one of *questioning:* what can you learn by exploring your topic? The tone you use can range from humorous to serious, just as the essays in this chapter run from funny (O'Rourke) to serious (Wolff).

For more on choosing a medium and genre, see Chapter 15 and Appendix C. For more on writing a causal analysis, see Chapter 10. For more on writing a proposal paper, see Chapter 11.

Context, Medium, and Genre: Since you will be exploring an area you are already interested in, you will have the incentive to learn more as you research and write. The knowledge you gain may benefit you later. For example, you may be able to use the information you have acquired from this assignment to write a causal analysis or a proposal paper. Obviously, your instructor will use your writing to help determine your grade for the course, so follow his or her instructions carefully. If you are writing for an audience beyond the classroom, consider what will be the most effective way to present your information to this audience. You might write an e-mail message to a friend, prepare a formal report for colleagues at work, or construct a Web site for members of your community.

◼ Critical Thinking, Reading, and Writing

Before you begin to write your exploratory paper, consider the qualities of successful exploratory writing. It also helps to read one or more examples of this type of writing. Finally, you might consider how visuals could enhance your exploratory writing, as well as the kinds of sources you will need to consult.

As with any other kind of writing, certain qualities make an exploratory text effective and useful. Unlike many other kinds of writing, where writers have a good idea of their intent, exploratory writing frees writers to take intellectual chances and to see where different, and sometimes unusual, possibilities may lead.

There are, of course, certain cautions that you need to be aware of. Although effective exploratory writing involves taking intellectual chances and finding alternatives that you may not have thought of before, your writing will not be successful if you simply write anything you please. Effective exploratory writing is based on reasonable options and uses information culled from solid research.

Learning the Qualities of Effective Exploratory Writing

As you think about how you might construct an exploratory paper, consider that readers probably expect the unexpected from this kind of text. Effective exploratory writing will include the following qualities:

- **A focus on a concept or question.** Rather than focusing on a specific, narrowly provable thesis, exploratory writing is more open-ended. Writers are more than likely trying to answer a question, to lay the groundwork for a solution to a problem, or to redefine a concept. For instance, a writer might pose a question such as this one: "We had a large number of traffic fatalities in my city last year. What possible solutions might I explore?"

- **An inquisitive spirit.** Any explorer begins with an interest in finding out more about the subject. Ask questions that you really want to answer, and let the answers lead you to further questions. While you want to make sure your queries are grounded in reality, you should not feel constrained by conventional thinking. For instance, Albert Einstein used "thought experiments" to explore time and space in ways conventional experiments could not. As a result, he developed his revolutionary theory of relativity.

- **A consideration of the range of perspectives in a subject.** As you explore your subject, you need to be willing to see it from different vantage points and to consider its positive and negative aspects. Effective exploratory writing looks at a topic from as many angles as possible. This can be difficult to do sometimes, as we often get locked in to our own way of thinking. In exploratory writing, however, it is vital to look at alternative views and to understand that others may have a different perspective than yours. For example, in the essay "Bipolar

Iraq" (p. 145), Michael Wolff explores two different perspectives on the United States's efforts in Iraq. Once you have identified alternative views, look at the arguments and evidence supporting those views as well as the arguments and evidence that support your initial point of view.

- **Expansive coverage of a subject.** Effective exploratory writing does not try to make a case or attempt to persuade you as writer or your reader of something, but rather examines all aspects of the topic, often developing a **profile** of its subject. You need to look at as much information about your subject as possible, while realizing that not all information is good or relevant. You will use your critical reading and thinking skills to help determine the reliability and relevance of the information you have gathered. Just as respected newspapers such as the *New York Times* and the *Washington Post* are more reliable than supermarket tabloids, some Web sites are more reliable than others. Because exploratory writing is often inductive in nature, you might find it useful to organize your details in categories, using a cluster chart or listing.

For more on inductive thinking, see Chapter 14. For more on cluster charts and listing as strategies, see Chapter 3.

In a computer document, you might find it helpful to put the above qualities of effective exploratory writing into your own words, and then refer to those notes as you conduct research and write your paper.

A WRITER'S RESPONSIBILITIES
Exploring Ideas

Writers who are considering and examining multiple viewpoints have a responsibility to their readers to present those viewpoints as accurately as possible. In exploratory writing, you can express your opinions, responses, and reflections, but you must be careful not to misrepresent the viewpoints of others.

When writing about alternative perspectives, it is especially important to be honest with both yourself and your readers. Because you may not feel comfortable, at least initially, with all the points of view you will be exploring, you need to make sure you are using reliable information that readers can verify themselves. You do not have to accept all of the perspectives you examine, but you do have an ethical responsibility to treat them all honestly and with respect.

Your purpose is to open yourself and your readers to different possibilities. If you find yourself limiting the perspectives you explore because you feel uncomfortable with some of them, you are limiting your and your readers' options.

Reading, Inquiry, and Research:
Learning from Texts That Explore

The readings that follow are examples of exploratory writing. Each offers perspectives on a subject. As you read each one, consider the following questions:

- What makes this reading an interesting and useful exploration?
- After reading the selection what else do you want to learn about the subject? Why?
- In what ways can you use the techniques of exploratory writing as demonstrated in the selection in your writing?

As you read an essay and respond to the questions that follow it, take notes, jot down questions, and make observations about the essay in a journal, preferably in a computer file. Then, if you want to use any ideas in your own writing, you will already have the main points in a digital format.

KENNETH CHANG

Scientist at Work: Terence Tao; Journeys to the Distant Fields of Prime

After working on his Ph.D. in physics at the University of Illinois for seven years, Kenneth Chang transferred to the University of California, Santa Cruz to study science writing. He has written for numerous outlets, including the *Los Angeles Times*, the *Greenwich Times*, the *Newark Star-Ledger*, and ABCNews.com. Since 2000, Kenneth Chang has regularly written science articles for the *New York Times*. A good example of a profile exploring the world of a mathematician, the following article was first published in the *New York Times* in March 2007.

Four hundred people packed into an auditorium at U.C.L.A. in January to listen to a public lecture on prime numbers, one of the rare occasions that the topic has drawn a standing-room-only audience. 1

Another 35 people watched on a video screen in a classroom next door. Eighty people were turned away. 2

The speaker, Terence Tao, a professor of mathematics at the university, promised "a whirlwind tour, the equivalent to going through Paris and just seeing the Eiffel Tower and the Arc de Triomphe." 3

His words were polite, unassuming and tinged with the accent of Australia, his homeland. Even though prime numbers have been studied for 2,000 years, "There's still a lot that needs to be done," Dr. Tao said. "And it's still a very exciting field." 4

After Dr. Tao finished his one-hour talk, which was broadcast live on the Internet, several students came down to the front and asked for autographs. 5

Dr. Tao has drawn attention and curiosity throughout his life for his prodigious abilities. By age 2, he had learned to read. At 9, he attended college math classes. At 20, he finished his Ph.D.   6

Now 31, he has grown from prodigy to one of the world's top mathematicians, tackling an unusually broad range of problems, including ones involving prime numbers and the compression of images. Last summer, he won a Fields Medal, often considered the Nobel Prize of mathematics, and a MacArthur Fellowship, the "genius" award that comes with a half-million dollars and no strings.   7

"He's wonderful," said Charles Fefferman of Princeton University, himself a former child prodigy and a Fields Medalist. "He's as good as they come. There are a few in a generation, and he's one of the few."   8

Colleagues have teasingly called Dr. Tao a rock star and the Mozart of Math. Two museums in Australia have requested his photograph for their permanent exhibits. And he was a finalist for the 2007 Australian of the Year award.   9

"You start getting famous for being famous." Dr. Tao said. "The Paris Hilton effect."   10

Not that any of that has noticeably affected him. His campus office is adorned with a poster of "Ranma 1/2," a Japanese comic book. As he walks the halls of the math building, he might be wearing an Adidas sweatshirt, blue jeans and scruffy sneakers, looking much like one of his graduate students. He said he did not know how he would spend the MacArthur money, though he mentioned the mortgage on the house that he and his wife, Laura, an engineer at the NASA Jet Propulsion Laboratory, bought last year.   11

After a childhood in Adelaide, Australia, and graduate school at Princeton, Dr. Tao has settled into sunny Southern California.   12

"I love it a lot," he said. But not necessarily for what the area offers.   13

"It's sort of the absence of things I like," he said. No snow to shovel, for instance.   14

A deluge of media attention following his Fields Medal last summer has slowed to a trickle, and Dr. Tao said he was happy that his fame might be fleeting so that he could again concentrate on math.   15

One area of his research—compressed sensing—could have real-world use. Digital cameras use millions of sensors to record an image, and then a computer chip in the camera compresses the data.   16

"Compressed sensing is a different strategy," Dr. Tao said. "You also compress the data, but you try to do it in a very dumb way, one that doesn't require much computer power at the sensor end."   17

With Emmanuel Candès, a professor of applied and computational mathematics at the California Institute of Technology, Dr. Tao showed   18 that even if most of the information were immediately discarded, the use of powerful algorithms could still reconstruct the original image.

By useful coincidence, Dr. Tao's son, William, and Dr. Candès's son attended the same preschool, so dropping off their children turned into useful work time. 19

"We'd meet each other every morning at preschool," Dr. Tao said, "and we'd catch up on what we had done." 20

The military is interested in using the work for reconnaissance: blanket a battlefield with simple, cheap cameras that might each record a single pixel of data. Each camera would transmit the data to a central computer that, using the mathematical technique developed by Dr. Tao and Dr. Candès, would construct a comprehensive view. Engineers at Rice University have made a prototype of just such a camera. 21

Dr. Tao's best-known mathematical work involves prime numbers— positive whole numbers that can be divided evenly only by themselves and 1. The first few prime numbers are 2, 3, 5, 7, 11 and 13 (1 is excluded). 22

As numbers get larger, prime numbers become sparser, but the Greek mathematician Euclid proved sometime around 300 B.C. that there is nonetheless an infinite number of primes. 23

Many questions about prime numbers continue to elude answers. Euclid also believed that there was an infinite number of "twin primes"— pairs of prime numbers separated by 2, like 3 and 5 or 11 and 13—but he was unable to prove his conjecture. Nor has anyone else in the succeeding 2,300 years. 24

A larger unknown question is whether hidden patterns exist in the sequence of prime numbers or whether they appear randomly. 25

In 2004, Dr. Tao, along with Ben Green, a mathematician now at the University of Cambridge in England, solved a problem related to the Twin Prime Conjecture by looking at prime number progressions—series of numbers equally spaced. (For example, 3, 7 and 11 constitute a progression of prime numbers with a spacing of 4; the next number in the sequence, 15, is not prime.) Dr. Tao and Dr. Green proved that it is always possible to find, somewhere in the infinity of integers, a progression of any length of equally spaced prime numbers. 26

"Terry has a style that very few have," Dr. Fefferman said. "When he solves the problem, you think to yourself, 'This is so obvious and why didn't I see it? Why didn't the 100 distinguished people who thought about this before not think of it?'" 27

Dr. Tao's proficiency with numbers appeared at a very young age. "I always liked numbers," he said. 28

A 2-year-old Terry Tao used toy blocks to show older children how to count. He was quick with language and used the blocks to spell words like "dog" and "cat." 29

"He probably was quietly learning these things from watching 'Sesame Street,'" said his father, Dr. Billy Tao, a pediatrician who immigrated to Australia from Hong Kong in 1972. "We basically used 'Sesame Street' as a babysitter."   30

The blocks had been bought as toys, not learning tools. "You expect them to throw them around," said the elder Dr. Tao, whose accent swings between Australian and Chinese.   31

Terry's parents placed him in a private school when he was 3½. They pulled him out six weeks later because he was not ready to spend that much time in a classroom, and the teacher was not ready to teach someone like him.   32

At age 5, he was enrolled in a public school, and his parents, administrators and teachers set up an individualized program for him. He proceeded through each subject at his own pace, quickly accelerating through several grades in math and science while remaining closer to his age group in other subjects. In English classes, for instance, he became flustered when he had to write essays.   33

"I never really got the hang of that," he said. "These very vague, undefined questions. I always liked situations where there were very clear rules of what to do."   34

Assigned to write a story about what was going on at home, Terry went from room to room and made detailed lists of the contents.   35

When he was 7½, he began attending math classes at the local high school.   36

Billy Tao knew the trajectories of child prodigies like Jay Luo, who graduated with a mathematics degree from Boise State University in 1982 at the age of 12, but who has since vanished from the world of mathematics.   37

"I initially thought Terry would be just like one of them, to graduate as early as possible," he said. But after talking to experts on education for gifted children, he changed his mind.   38

"To get a degree at a young age, to be a record-breaker, means nothing," he said. "I had a pyramid model of knowledge, that is, a very broad base and then the pyramid can go higher. If you just very quickly move up like a column, then you're more likely to wobble at the top and then collapse."   39

Billy Tao also arranged for math professors to mentor Terry.   40

A couple of years later, Terry was taking university-level math and physics classes. He excelled in international math competitions. His parents decided not to push him into college full-time, so he split his time between high school and Flinders University, the local university in Adelaide. He finally enrolled as a full-time college student at Flinders when he was 14, two years after he would have graduated had his parents pushed him only according to his academic abilities.   41

The Taos had different challenges in raising their other two sons, although all three excelled in math. Trevor, two years younger than Terry, is autistic with top-level chess skills and the musical savant gift to play back on the piano a musical piece—even one played by an entire orchestra— after hearing it just once. He completed a Ph.D. in mathematics and now works for the Defense Science and Technology Organization in Australia. 42

The youngest, Nigel, told his father that he was "not another Terry," and his parents let him learn at a less accelerated pace. Nigel, with degrees in economics, math and computer science, now works as a computer engineer for Google Australia. 43

"All along, we tend to emphasize the joy of learning," Billy Tao said. "The fun is doing something, not winning something." 44

Terry completed his undergraduate degree in two years, earned a master's degree a year after that, then moved to Princeton for his doctoral studies. While he said he never felt out of place in a class of much older students, Princeton was where he finally felt he fit among a group of peers. He was still younger, but was not necessarily the brightest student all the time. 45

His attitude toward math also matured. Until then, math had been competitions, problem sets, exams. "That's more like a sprint," he said. 46

Dr. Tao recalled that as a child, "I remember having this vague idea that what mathematicians did was that, some authority, someone gave them problems to solve and they just sort of solved them." 47

In the real academic world, "Math research is more like a marathon," he said. 48

As a parent and a professor, Dr. Tao now has to think about how to teach math in addition to learning it. 49

An evening snack provided him an opportunity to question his son, who is 4. If there are 10 cookies, how many does each of the five people in the living room get? 50

William asked his father to tell him. "I don't know how many," Dr. Tao replied. "You tell me." 51

With a little more prodding, William divided the cookies into five stacks of two each. 52

Dr. Tao said a future project would be to try to teach more nonmathematicians how to think mathematically—a skill that would be useful in everyday tasks like comparing mortgages. 53

"I believe you can teach this to almost anybody," he said. 54

But for now, his research is where his focus is. 55

"In many ways, my work is my hobby," he said. "I always wanted to learn another language, but that's not going to happen for a while. Those things can wait." 56

QUESTIONS FOR WRITING AND DISCUSSION

Rhetorical Knowledge: The Writer's Situation and Rhetoric

1. **Audience:** Who is the audience for Chang's essay? What makes you think that?

2. **Purpose:** What is Chang's primary purpose for writing this profile of Terence Tao? How effectively does he fulfill that purpose? Why do you think that?

3. **Voice and Tone:** What is Chang's tone in this profile?

4. **Responsibility:** How has Chang acted responsibly in writing this essay?

5. **Context and Format:** Chang wrote this profile for the *New York Times*, a major daily newspaper. If he had written it for an academic journal, what might he have done differently?

Critical Thinking: Your Personal Response

1. What do you find most interesting in Chang's essay about Terence Tao? Why do you find this aspect of the essay interesting?

2. What is the most surprising information about Terence Tao in Chang's profile?

3. How much would you like to have a life like Terence Tao's? Why?

4. What would it be like to have a gifted child like the young Terence Tao?

5. What would it be like to have a sibling like Terence Tao?

Critical Thinking: The Writer's Ideas

1. Why do you think Chang includes information about three areas of Tao's life—the academic, the personal, and the professional?

2. Why do you think Chang focuses so much attention on Tao's childhood?

3. Why does Chang write about Tao's family in the profile?

Composing Processes and Knowledge of Conventions: The Writer's Strategies

1. Why does Chang use so many quotations in the profile? Why do you think he uses quotations instead of paraphrases in particular places? Which of the quotations could easily be changed to paraphrases?

2. Because he writing for a newspaper, Chang cites his sources within the body of his article rather than using a formal system of documentation. How do his sources lend credibility to his writing? What other sources of information might he have cited?

Inquiry and Research: Ideas for Further Exploration

1. Conduct a Web search to find more information about Terence Tao. What are some interesting details that Chang does not include in his essay? How might those details be added to Chang's profile?

2. Conduct some research on Terence Tao. Once you have done this research, write your own profile of him.

3. Conduct research on some person whom you find interesting. Write a profile of that person.

MICHAEL WOLFF

Bipolar Iraq

Michael Wolff, who grew up in New Jersey, has written widely about the Internet since 1991. Among his most popular books are *Net Guide*, a manual for using the Internet, and *Burn Rate*, a exposé on the early days of the Internet business boom. A regular columnist for *Industry Standard* and for *New York Magazine*, Wolff frequently tackles controversial and complex topics. The essay the follows was first published in *New York Magazine* in November 2003.

Here are the two opposite story lines: 1

(1) It's working. 2

(2) It's a quagmire. 3

Let's fill them out a little more: 4

(1) Iraqis are back in the markets and on the street; schools are 5 opening, businesses getting going again, institutions returning to life. By virtually every happiness-quotient measure, the state of being among the vast majority of Iraqis is more positive now than it was during the reign of Saddam Hussein—and it will be even more positive in the near future. As social experiments go—revivifying a materially and psychologically broken nation—there is every reason to be optimistic (and even proud) about this one.

(2) We've gotten ourselves into an ever-expanding war with a fanati- 6 cal and well-armed resistance. What's more, growing numbers of ideological defenders are traveling to this battlefield, which threatens to turn Iraq, along with Israel and the Palestinian territories, into a permanent

Muslim versus non-Muslim front and international tripwire. We're stuck in a situation with consequences and financial burdens that we cannot estimate. This is the definition of quagmire. And by the logic of quagmire, the situation only ever becomes more intractable and the consequences more fearful and destabilizing.

As you read those quick précis, your inclination is, invariably, to pick one. They can't, after all, really exist together. Or, if perchance they do exist together now, one will inevitably come to overshadow the other. Obviously, if you're a Bush person, you choose the former, and if you're an anti-Bush person, you choose the latter. In some sense, in fact, these are not even alternative views of the reality in Iraq as much as opposite worldviews applicable to almost any situation.

(1) There is, quite simply, the patent superiority of the American way. When people are exposed to it, it spreads like a virus. We have not only righteousness on our side but modernity and economic reality. Eighty-seven billion dollars changes any equation. Everything seems messy, inchoate, ugly, fraught, without organization; but at some point in the organizational process, rationality and benefit will begin to become clear. Upside will outweigh downside. Ambivalence and self-doubt are the real killers here. Long-term investment and staying the course are the solutions and the way to get a big return.

(2) An incredible arrogance chronically pervades the American mind-set. Our lack of self-doubt makes us stupid. We're blinded to the intractable problems set against us: not just to a deep cultural antipathy but to a million details on the ground that the guys at the Pentagon or at Centcom HQ in Florida don't have the patience or the language skills or the in-country intelligence to think through. What's more, because we pride ourselves on "can-do" and turn up our noses at intellectual and abstract analysis, we never really or accurately appreciate cause and effect. We're always the victims of the law of unintended consequences. Because we're too big and too quick, we necessarily upset the ecology in ways that will certainly come back to haunt and terrorize us.

(1) Essentially good news.

(2) Inevitably bad news.

Which brings us to the Chinook helicopter—and before that the attack on the Al Rashid Hotel, and before that the U.N. attack.

The fervent bad-news-ites seem to believe that the Bushies understand the kind of mess they're (we're) in and are doing everything they can to disguise (spin) it and to blame someone else for it. But the more interesting and complex and difficult possibility is that they don't see it as a mess at all.

For them, these bad-news incidents represent an illusion created by the small resistance, the leftover Baathists. These thugs and irregulars.

What we have here are isolated acts meant to sow widespread fear—it's just, well, terrorism. The odd thing, of course, is that such terrorism is exactly why we went to war—so it's rather disorienting to have it dismissed now as somehow inconsequential in relation to the bigger picture.

It's not bad news, the Bushies seem to be saying, as much as bad 15 PR—or the other side's good PR. The bad guys have effectively influenced the media coverage without, the Bushies seem genuinely convinced, affecting the reality. Life in Iraq gets better and better—except for the fact that these scumballs know how to generate bad press for the Americans who are making life in Iraq better and better.

Hence the Bushies have countered with a campaign to generate 16 good news. There is even the sense—again, a reality inversion—that the best way to deal with terrorism is in the court of public opinion rather than on the battlefield.

So the good-news offensive. The mainstream media—because it is 17 overly liberal and crassly superficial—is emphasizing the (minimal) bloodshed and ignoring the story of a liberated nation. And there has been the careful parsing of the story: carving the Sunni triangle from the rest of a (largely) pacified country; rushing in American pollsters (and then parsing those results); separating good imams from bad imams.

And, indeed, there has been a sudden rush of not unconvincing 18 good-news accounts. Life was terrible. Life is better. Nothing worked. Now many things are working. Average Iraqis may not be embracing the American occupation, but they are sure grateful not to have Saddam around (cue the torture tapes that the Pentagon released to Fox News). Life, as seen by in-country reporters, is returning to normal.

But there are the bodies. 19

The Bush people, as they argue their story line, have to distract peo- 20 ple's attention from the dead. The president doesn't mention the bodies; doesn't attend funerals. Body-bag shots are on the media proscribed list. You can sense their frustration in this regard—that the bodies are always, annoyingly, the story. This is partly a military-civilian disconnect. Our job, you can hear Rumsfeld saying, is to minimize casualties, not to eliminate them. In sheer military terms—troops deployed versus casualties sustained—it's not even that bad. Arguably (although it's an argument you lose by making it), the kill ratio indicates a big success. I mean, you can't really fight a war if everybody is precious—if nobody is expendable.

And yet, the great nonmilitary sensibility of the country, and of the 21 media, sees each body as a story, and multiple bodies as a bigger story, and the aggregate of bodies as a really damning piece of evidence.

There is a socio-military calculation on the part of reporters and 22 politicians (both Democrats and Republicans) and, one would assume, military people as well, as to how much is too much. What's sustainable and what's a big problem?

When the number of soldiers killed in the aftermath exceeded the number of people killed in the actual war, that was seen as a problematic milestone. 23

When the total number of people killed in Iraq II surpassed the total number killed in Iraq I, that got serious. 24

Oh yes, and significant multi-casualty incidents are major bad news. Mogadishu levels would be very dicey. Beirut levels in the Reagan era might well put the whole proposition over the top. 25

Now, what the Bush administration is arguing is, in effect, that our enemies know these numbers. That they cannot damage us enough to truly harm us or even to actually hamper our mission, but they can inflict enough damage to frighten us (or frighten you—or frighten the media)—precisely because our tolerance for damage has been set artificially low. 26

Not least of all by Democrats and by the biased media! 27

And so we move from a military war to a political one. 28

This is the exact opposite of the wars of the last generation—of the Clinton approach or even of the first Bush administration—that constant and obsessive cost-reward analysis. 29

Of not being caught out there without a way back. Retreating from Mogadishu. Not following Saddam into Baghdad. Of always making the calculation about when the consensus might divide. Of not making people choose sides. Of not letting there be two stories told at once. 30

The Bush people don't believe there are two sides. Not two right sides, anyway. This mission is sacrosanct. The WMD canard and the sexing of intelligence reports happened, not least of all, to protect the mission. Nobody is going to go for broke in an elective war—it had to be a necessary war. 31

There's no debate. There's polling (of course) but no interest in consensus. Stubbornness (Rumsfeldness) is both virtue and strategy. If you refuse to engage in any back-and-forth but just say what you believe relentlessly, repetition eventually changes perceptions. 32

Righteousness went out of favor in the post–Cold War world (incrementalism, globalism, complex systems analysis came in). But righteousness is surely back. The righteous don't compromise, don't negotiate, don't wimp out. The righteous (even if they had planned not to have to) take casualties (unlike that thoroughly nonrighteous Clinton, who hated to take casualties). 33

There's no longer even a pretense that this is about conventional success measures (indeed, failure suddenly seems part—even a necessary part—of the great ultimate success). The *we're-not-quitters* stance of 34 the Bushies (and that the Democrats are, ipso facto, quitters) is explicitly disconnected from any talk about how we're actually going to win.

The arguable merit of the Bush position—life is certainly better in Iraq—is subsumed by its larger, relentless, messianic, and fatalistic ambitions. 35

We're at the bear-any-burden stage. That is, in most political terms, a wildly unpopular place to be. We are, after all, selfish, self-obsessed Americans. 36

So the only way they're going to sell this is to turn it from a problem-solving issue into an ideological one. "We are fighting that enemy in Iraq, in Afghanistan today so that we do not meet him again on our own streets, in our own cities," said the president. 37

It's a setup. We're going to have to choose position (1) or position (2). 38

The Democrats and Howard Dean play into that hand (Bush-bashing is probably good for the Bushies). 39

It's them or us. 40

Winners or losers. 41

Lefties or real Americans. 42

We've been here before, and we know how badly it turns out. 43

QUESTIONS FOR WRITING AND DISCUSSION

Rhetorical Knowledge: The Writer's Situation and Rhetoric

1. **Audience:** On its Web site, *New York Magazine* indicates that 54% of its 2.2 million readers are between ages 18 and 34, and that 64% are "professional, managerial, or top management." Given those readership demographics, why would the magazine want to publish an essay like Wolff's?

2. **Purpose:** What purpose do you think Wolff had for writing this essay? How can you tell? Cite evidence from the essay for your answer.

3. **Voice and Tone:** What passages can you find in Wolff's essay that give him credibility? What do you find most and least convincing about his stance toward his topic?

4. **Responsibility:** What preconceptions about his topic does Wolff reveal in this exploration? How responsibly does he treat his own point of view and those of others?

5. **Context and Format:** This essay originally appeared in *New York Magazine*. Look at the magazine's Web site at http://www.newyorkmetro .com/. What can you say about the readers of this magazine, based on its Web site?

Critical Thinking: Your Personal Response

1. What is your immediate response to Wolff's exploration of the United States's activities in Iraq?

2. To what extent do your views of the United States's involvement in Iraq correspond to those offered by Wolf—that "it's working" or that "it's a quagmire"?

Critical Thinking: The Writer's Ideas

1. In the end, which of the two story lines does Wolff seem to embrace?

2. Why does Wolff offer so many dichotomies in his essay? How would Wolff's essay be different if he had used continua rather that dichotomies? That is, what if he had tried to figure out how the situation might lie somewhere on the following continuum:

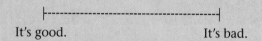

It's good.   It's bad.

Composing Processes and Knowledge of Conventions: The Writer's Strategies

1. How effectively does Wolff present the alternative perspectives in this piece? How might he improve his presentation?

2. What exactly is Wolff exploring?

3. What organizational strategy does Wolff use in this essay? How successful is it? Would another strategy have been more effective?

Inquiry and Research: Ideas for Further Exploration

1. With several of your classmates, discuss Wolff's essay and positions. Your teacher may ask each small group to report its collective thoughts to the rest of the class.

2. Given what has happened in Iraq since Wolff's essay was published on November 17, 2003, how might Wolff revise the essay to reflect the current situation in Iraq?

3. Given the current situation in Iraq, use Wolff's two story lines—"it's working" and "it's a quagmire"—to reflect on the United States's involvement in Iraq.

P. J. O'ROURKE

Memoir Essay

P. J. O'Rourke was born in Toledo, Ohio, in 1947. Although he was a political liberal in his college days at Miami University and Johns Hopkins University, he is now considered a libertarian or conservative. He has written columns for many magazines, with a stint as a staff writer for *Rolling Stone*. He has also served as a commentator for the television news show *60 Minutes*. He has published a dozen books, including *Peace Kills: America's Fun New Imperialism* (2004). "Memoir Essay" was first published in the *New York Times Book Review* in 1998 under the title, "Putting *Moi* Back in Memoir."

After years of effort in the author trade, I've discovered an ideal topic, an inexhaustible subject of discourse, a literary inspiration—me. I'm writing a memoir. I don't know why I didn't do this ages ago. It's so liberating to sit down at the keyboard and just be myself, as opposed to, say, being you, which I don't have the clothes for.

1

Actually, my memoir is still in the idea stage. But I'm full of enthusiasm. I'll give the secret of my success—the success I plan to have as a memoir writer. As far as I can tell, the secret is thinking about myself all the time. No doubt my memoir will be inspirational, inspiring others to think about themselves all the time. They'll see the meaning in their lives: They've been meaning to write a memoir, too.

2

So what if it's a crowded field? My memoir will stand out. It will show readers a side of life they little guessed at, the side with the writer sitting in his boxer shorts surrounded by six empty coffee cups and three full ashtrays playing Go Fish on his laptop.

3

Maybe they *had* guessed at that. But I'm going to recount my personal struggles, such as having to come up with things to write about all the time. I've spent decades looking for stories that would interest other people. I've surmounted enormous obstacles—thinking about other people, just for instance.

4

But enough about them. This isn't going to be a mere self-help book. This is the story of how one young man grew up to be . . . a lot older. That is probably the most serious issue I need to work through in my memoir. The issue being that I haven't really done much. But I don't feel this should stand in my way. O. J. Simpson wrote a memoir, and the jury said he didn't do anything at all.

5

There's also a lot of anger I need to deal with. I'm angry at my parents. For memoir purposes, they weren't nearly poor enough. They weren't rich either. And they failed miserably at leading colorful lives. My mother did belong to Kappa Kappa Gamma, which is a secret society, I believe. And my father was a veteran of the Pacific war, but the only casualty in his battalion was one fellow crushed by a palm tree. Furthermore, we lived in Toledo, Ohio. I suppose I could write a comic memoir. But, in today's society, there are some things you just don't make fun of and chief among these is yourself.   6

My parents also neglected to abuse me. They're gone now, alas. (Downside: no publicity-building estrangement when memoir is published, to be followed by tearful reconciliation on the *Oprah* show. Upside: I'm an Adult Child of the Deceased.) I've thought about asking my wife's parents to abuse me, but it seems too little, too late. I did have a step-father who bowled.   7

Perhaps I'll keep the section on my childhood brief, just emphasize that I'm a survivor. That's what's unique about me, and there are 5.7 billion people in the world who know how unique I feel. This should guarantee excellent sales. And—here comes that literary inspiration again—memoirs do sell. Readers want to know what real people really did and really felt. What a shame that the writing geniuses of the nineteenth century wasted their time making things up. We could have had Jane Austen Reality Prose: "Got up. Wrote. Went out. Came back. Wrote some more. Vicarage still drafty."   8

Modern book buyers have become too sophisticated for imaginary romance and drama. They want facts—Roswell, New Mexico;[1] the missile that shot down TWA flight 800;[2] the Congress/Clinton balanced budget deal. Unfortunately, I don't have many facts like that, but I do have some terrific celebrity gossip. I've read all their memoirs.   9

I also know about some awful things my friends have done. I've noticed, while memoir-reading, that one of the main points of the genre is ratting on your pals. So I was gathering that material together and was about to commit it to paper when I realized that other memoir writers, as a class, seem to have very few friends who weigh two hundred pounds and own shotguns.   10

Probably confession is a safer route. I've done all kinds of loathsome deeds myself and am perfectly willing to admit them, if it sells books. But, thumbing through my memoir collection, I noticed another thing. Good memoir writers only confess to certain of the more glamorous sins—   11

---

[1] The site of an alleged crash landing of a UFO in 1947.
[2] A disputed plane crash in 1996, ultimately blamed on a fuel tank explosion.

drastic sexual escapades, head-to-toe drug abuse, bold felonies after the statutes of limitation have run out. Nobody confesses to things that just make him look like a jerk-o. Nobody admits that he got up at four a.m. with a throbbing head after five hours of listening to the kid's pets squeaking in the exercise wheel and drowned the gerbils in the toilet. Most of my transgressions fall into this category and will need to be excised. I don't want to get caught writing one of those "unauthorized autobiographies."

This brings me to the other little problem I'm having with the story of my life, which is remembering it. There were the 1960s. I recall they started out well. Then there were the 1970s. I recall they ended badly. In between, frankly, I am missing a few candles on the cake. Also there were the 1950s, when nothing memorable happened, and the 1980s, when everything memorable was happening to somebody else. And the 1990s have gone by in a blur. But, no worries, I've been keeping a diary. "Got up. Wrote. Went out. Came back. Wrote some more. Drowned the gerbils." 12

Maybe I can make up for my lack of reminiscences by inserting various vivid fantasies I've had. But this is cheating on the memoir form since I'm admitting that those things—the *New York Review of Books*[3] swimsuit issue, for example—never happened. 13

Or, perhaps I should go back to all those challenges I've faced. I've had to endure enormous prejudice. True, since I'm a middle-aged white male Republican, the enormous prejudice came from me. But I still had to endure it. This is one reason that learning to love myself was another huge challenge. But I've overcome that, too. Although, now that I'm completely self-infatuated, I keep waiting for me to give myself a promotion. It's been a bitter disappointment. 14

Thank goodness. Bitter disappointments are crucial to memoirs. Thinking of something to write in this memoir has been a bitter disappointment so far. That means I can write about not being able to write. Should be good for a chapter, if I can make it sound bitter enough. 15

Wait. I'm forgetting spiritual transformation. I've been touched by an angel—and a big one, too, all covered in glitter. It got me right in the forehead last month when the dog knocked over the Christmas tree. 16

And I have a good title: "My Excuse for Living." That should count for something. 17

Anyway, I'm not daunted. The memoir is the great literature of the current era. All that we ask of art, the memoir provides. Beauty is truth, truth beauty, and if we can get a beauty to tell the truth then Kathryn Harrison's *The Kiss* is all ye need to know. Art justified God's ways to man 18

---

[3] An influential book review that has historically had a liberal point of view.

like *The Art of the Comeback* does. God is going to fry Donald Trump in hell, and He is perfectly justified. As with all art, the memoir holds a mirror up to life and if there are some lines of cocaine on that mirror, so much the better. Out of chaos the memoir brings order—a huge order from a major bookstore chain, it is to be hoped. The memoir is nature's handmaiden and also nature's butt boy, bagman, and patsy if *Behind the Oval Office* by Dick Morris[4] is anything to go by. The memoir exists on its own terms, art for art's sake, if you happen to be named Arthur—vide *Risk and Redemption: Surviving the Network News Wars* by Arthur Kent. The memoir speaks to us, indeed it won't shut up. *Vita brevis est, memoir longa.*[5]

And mine is going to be really long. I've got a major book happening   19
here. After a whole morning spent wrestling with my muse, I've made a vital creative breakthrough. I now know how to give my memoir the moral, intellectual and aesthetic impact that the works of Shakespeare, Goethe, Dostoyevsky had on previous generations. As with all insights of true originality, it's very simple. It's called lying.

---

[4] An advisor to President Bill Clinton who later became a political commentator.
[5] Life is short, memories are long.

QUESTIONS FOR WRITING AND DISCUSSION

Rhetorical Knowledge: The Writer's Situation and Rhetoric

1. **Audience:** Memoirs are very popular. How would a voracious memoir reader respond to O'Rourke's essay?

2. **Purpose:** What does the last sentence of the essay reveal about O'Rourke's purpose?

3. **Voice and Tone:** What is O'Rourke's attitude toward memoirs? Toward memoir writers? Toward readers of memoirs?

4. **Responsibility:** How does O'Rourke demonstrate that he feels responsible to his family?

5. **Context and Format:** What would O'Rourke need to do to revise his humorous satire into a serious editorial? What change in context would call for such a revision?

Critical Thinking: Your Personal Response

1. What is your general reaction to O'Rourke's exploration of writing a memoir?

2. What do you see as the strengths and weaknesses of O'Rourke's essay? Why?

3. To what extent do you share O'Rourke's views about the nature of memoirs? Why?

Critical Thinking: The Writer's Ideas

1. According to O'Rourke, what are the features of memoirs? Which of those features do you think is the most useful for a memoir to have? Why?

2. What is the point of O'Rourke's exploration of the nature of memoirs?

Composing Processes and Knowledge of Conventions: The Writer's Strategies

1. In satire, writers ridicule people or institutions or societies for their weaknesses or failures. They often do so by directly or indirectly showing that certain behaviors are not within the realm of what we consider "normal" behavior. How does O'Rourke appeal to readers' sense of what is normal behavior?

2. How effective are O'Rourke's examples? Why?

3. What strategies does O'Rourke use to make his essay humorous?

Inquiry and Research: Ideas for Further Exploration

1. In your school's library or on the Web, find a memoir. Read it to see how much it exhibits the qualities that O'Rourke satirizes.

2. If you were to write a memoir, how could you write it so that it didn't have the qualities that O'Rourke satirizes?

 ## Thinking about Visuals That Explore

Visuals are helpful tools for exploring because they often compress a great deal of verbal and numerical information into a single element. Here, for example, is a bar graph from the United States Bureau of Labor Statistics showing projected job growth in service-providing industries over a decade. In the box on pages 156–57, notice the relationship between the information presented in the bar graph and the verbal information that accompanies it.

Excerpted from "Tomorrow's Jobs"

U.S. Bureau of Labor Statistics
(http://www.bls.gov/oco/oco2003.htm)

Service-providing industries

The long-term shift from goods-producing to service-providing employment is expected to continue. Service-providing industries are expected to account for approximately 18.7 million of the 18.9 million new wage and salary jobs generated over the 2004–14 period (*Chart 4*).

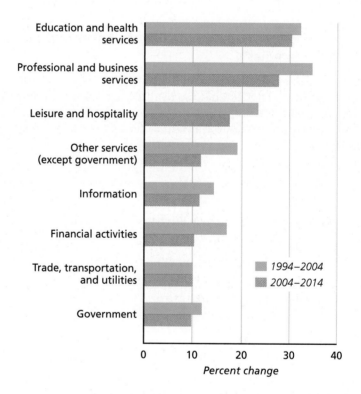

Education and health services

This industry supersector is projected to grow faster, 30.6 percent, and add more jobs than any other industry supersector. About 3 out of every 10 new jobs created in the U.S. economy will be in either the healthcare and social assistance or private educational services sectors.

. . .

Professional and business services

This industry supersector, which includes some of the fastest growing industries in the U.S. economy, will grow by 27.8 percent and add more than 4.5 million new jobs.

. . .

Information

Employment in the information supersector is expected to increase by 11.6 percent, adding 364,000 jobs by 2014. Information contains some of the fast-growing computer-related industries such as software publishers; Internet publishing and broadcasting; and Internet service providers, Web search portals, and data processing services.

Leisure and hospitality

Overall employment will grow by 17.7 percent. Arts, entertainment, and recreation will grow by 25 percent and add 460,000 new jobs by 2014. Most of these new job openings will come from the amusement, gambling, and recreation sector. Job growth will stem from public participation in arts, entertainment, and recreation activities—reflecting increasing incomes, leisure time, and awareness of the health benefits of physical fitness.

. . .

Government

Between 2004 and 2014, government employment, including that in public education and hospitals, is expected to increase by 10 percent, from 21.6 million to 23.8 million jobs. Growth in government employment will be fueled by growth in state and local educational services and the shift of responsibilities from the Federal Government to the state and local governments . . .

Other services (except government)

Employment will grow by 14 percent. More than 1 out of every 4 new jobs in this supersector will be in religious organizations, which is expected to grow by 11.9 percent. Other automotive repair and maintenance will be the fastest growing industry at 30.7 percent. Also included among other services is personal care services, which is expected to increase by 19.5 percent.

If you were using the graph on page 156 and the accompanying text to explore potential college majors (Scenario 1), you might consider the following kinds of questions:

1. How does the bar graph help you to see future trends in service-industry job categories?

2. How do these trends influence your thinking about potential careers?

3. How do the bar graph and the verbal text complement each other? For example, what do the bar graph and the text tell you about the prospects for employment in the teaching profession?

4. What does the bar graph show you that the text does not? What does the text explain that the bar graph does not?

Drawing on Research to Explore Your Subject

While your opinions and ideas—and especially your questions—are central to any exploratory writing that you do, as you explore your subject, you need to answer the questions you raise. Getting those answers usually requires research, which can include reading books and periodical articles at the library, reading articles in your local newspaper, interviewing people who know more than you do about your subject, conducting searches online, and using other means of gathering information. The information that you discover through your research, such as data, statistics, examples, descriptions, images, and expert testimony, can help you respond to the questions that prompted your exploration.

TechNote

Writing to explore is not about getting and giving information or simple answers. Exploration involves the hard work of experiencing and understanding *different perspectives*. A good way to learn about different or unusual perspectives is to read news reports from around the world—not just those published by American news services such as the Associated Press and Knight-Ridder, but news reports published in foreign newspapers and newsmagazines. Most of the major publications (and plenty of smaller ones) are now available in English translation. The following are some examples of Web sites maintained by foreign news organizations:

Pravda (Russian)
http://english.pravda.ru/

London Times
http://www.timesonline.co.uk/tol/global/

Japan Times
http://www.japantimes.co.jp

Agence France-Presse
http://www.afp.com/english/home/

You could conduct several kinds of research in response to the scenarios on pages 133–34:

- For Scenario 1, in which you explore potential majors, you might visit the Web sites of various departments to gather information about degree programs, courses offered, and careers of alumni. You might also visit the Web sites of companies that hire graduates in the fields that you are exploring. You could even search newspapers and the Internet to find job advertisements in those fields. You might interview graduating seniors to ask them about their experiences in the majors that you are exploring or people who hold the kinds of jobs that require those majors. Finally, you could search for and read blogs maintained by people who write about their professional fields and careers.

- For Scenario 3, in which you explore cities for an organization's meeting, you might visit Web sites put up by the visitors bureaus for those cities to find information. (Keep in mind, though, that any visitors bureau will focus on only positive information about that city because the job of the bureau is to attract visitors.) You might also use a Web site such as http://www.weather.com to find factual information about the weather in any city in the country.

For more on primary research, see the Writing in Action *about primary research on pages 307–8. For more on conducting research and citing your sources properly, see Chapters 19 and 20.*

Writing Processes

As you work on the assignment you have chosen, remember the qualities of an effective exploratory paper, which are listed on pages 137–38. Also remember that writing is recursive—you might start with an invention activity or two and then conduct some research, which leads to more invention work and then a first draft; but then you might need to do more invention work to help flesh out your draft and conduct more research to answer questions that come up as you explore your ideas further, and then you'll revise your draft and possibly find another gap or two. . . . Writing, in other words, is more a circular than a linear process. So while the activities listed below imply that writers proceed step-by-step, the actual process of writing is usually messier. You will keep coming back to your earlier work, adding to it and modifying it to be more accurate as you conduct further research and become more familiar with your topic.

For a tip on organizing your computer files, see page 97.

As you work on your project, make sure that you save your computer files frequently because any work that you don't save could be lost. Many experienced writers save their files every fifteen minutes or so. Also, savvy writers back up their computer files in two or more places—on an internal or external hard drive of the computer, on a USB flash drive, and on a rewritable CD or DVD, for example.

Invention: Getting Started

The invention activities below are strategies that you can use to help you get some sense of what you already know about a subject. These activities can lead to all sorts of questions that will help guide your research on your topic. You may find it effective to use one or more of these approaches to start exploring your subject. Whatever invention method(s) you use (or that your instructor asks you to employ), try to answer questions such as these:

- What do I already know about my subject?
- What preconceptions—positive, negative, neutral—do I have?
- Why am I interested in exploring this subject?
- What questions about the subject would I most like answers to? Where might I find those answers? Who might I be able to talk to about this subject?
- What do I know about my audience? What can I say to interest them in my subject?
- What might my audience already know about my subject? What questions might they have?
- What is my purpose in exploring this subject? What would I like the end result of my research and writing to be? More knowledge? Information that I might use to pursue some goal?

Doing your invention work in electronic form, rather than on paper, lets you easily use this early writing as you construct a draft.

WRITING ACTIVITY

Freewriting, Listing, and Clustering

Using the questions above, freewrite for ten minutes, writing everything you can think of about your subject. Remember, even if you cannot think of anything to say, you must keep writing. The idea is that if you keep writing words, your mind will keep generating ideas.

Or, answering the questions above, list your ideas about the subject you are focusing on. You might come up with categories for your list that will help jog your thinking; for example, you might list various perspectives or types of information you want to research for your exploratory writing.

Once you have generated ideas by freewriting or listing, use cluster-ing to determine how those ideas relate to one another. Write your subject in the center of the page and put your other ideas around it—drawing lines between the ideas that relate to one another. Often, one idea in your cluster will cause you to think of another idea. Clustering is a useful visual way to think on paper.

For help with freewriting, listing, and clustering, as well as other strategies for discovery and learning, see Chapter 3.

Rick Mohler's Freewriting, Listing, and Clustering

Rick Mohler was taking a "Career and Life Planning" class at his local com-munity college, so he decided to respond to Scenario 1 on page 133. Rick was interested in a lot of areas—especially sports—but he was not quite sure what he might want to pursue as a career. Here is a portion of his freewriting, which reflects his questions and concerns about finding a career that he will enjoy:

> I think what I like most is sports—playing them, thinking about them, learning new rules and games. Football is my game! But I know I probably won't have a professional career—not many people make it to the NFL. I'm not a very fast runner. I can work at it and try, but I need some fallback position, if I'm not good enough. I can't think of anything, maybe an analyst? Sportswriter? Coach? Sports medicine? Photographer? Trainer? Do something with the physical aspect of football?
>
> But if I can't be an NFL player, what can I do? Do I want to stay with sports? What other careers beside being an athlete goes with sports, especially football? Careers in sports, jobs in sports, jobs about sports. Are there college classes I can take to lead me there?

Rick Mohler also used listing to explore his ideas about a career.

Rick Mohler's Listing

- Sports
- Football
- High school success
- Jobs
- Player
- Coach
- Agent
- Trainer
- Scout

Finally, Mohler combined ideas from his freewriting and list into a cluster.

Rick Mohler's Clustering

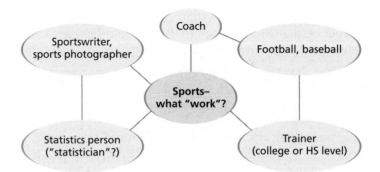

Exploring Your Ideas with Research

Before you begin your research, consider how you are focusing your exploration. For example, if you are writing in response to Scenario 4, you may want to focus your research on how an agency deals with a social problem that is important to you, such as teenage drinking or adult literacy. Notice how Rick Mohler focuses his research in the example that follows. Before you start your research, review your invention work to remind yourself of all that you know about your subject and the questions you have about it. Use the reporter's questions of *who, what, where, when, why*, and *how* to get started. After you have decided what information you need, determine what kind of research you need to conduct to gather that information, and conduct research in the library and on the Internet.

For help with locating sources of information, see Chapter 19; for help with taking notes and documenting your sources, see Chapter 20.

WRITING ACTIVITY

Conducting Research

In college writing assignments, your research will frequently begin in your college or university library. There you will find practically anything you need to learn about your subject: books, popular magazines, academic journals, and access to databases and the Internet. As you think about the subject that you are exploring, consider where you might look for answers to your questions. If you are exploring an issue in forest management, for example, a quick Web search will lead you to the United States Department of Agriculture's Forest Service Forest

Management Web site. To get a potentially different perspective, you might check out the Sierra Club's Web site.

Gather, read, and take notes on your topic from outside sources. You might use an electronic journal to record images, URLs, and other electronic pieces of information that you find as you are conducting your research. Keeping an e-journal makes it easy for you to add those e-documents once you start drafting your paper.

One of the challenges of exploratory writing is knowing when you are finished with your research. Sometimes writers discover that digging around and finding all kinds of information on their subject is so much fun that they want to continue indefinitely. However, because most writers have deadlines, they need to know when to stop. The easiest way to manage your research is to set certain parameters when you begin. Your parameters might be time-induced: "I only have two weeks to work on this." Or you might limit the number or type of sources you can survey: "I will not use Interlibrary Loan on this assignment." While you might decide to reconsider one of your initial limitations, it is usually best to save new issues that emerge as subjects for further inquiries.

For help with conducting research, see Chapter 19.

Rick Mohler's Research

Student writer Rick Mohler wanted to explore possible careers in the world of sports other than being an athlete. In addition to sitting at his computer and browsing the World Wide Web, he went to his college library and examined recent issues of his school newspaper, some magazines, and several books. To find helpful articles, he used the search term "sports—careers." He used the same search term to search his school's online library indexes. Based on what he read, he made some notes to himself in order to try to find some direction. Here are some of Mohler's notes:

1. Read through back issues of the campus newspaper—College Press— there were some interviews with several coaches, all from different sports. Interview them to find out more?
2. Also lots of photos of athletes. That might be an interesting career choice: sports photographer. Probably gets into the games free, too.
3. Checked out this old Vince Lombardi book—Run to Daylight—looks interesting. I think there was another Lombardi biography a few years ago, When Pride Still Mattered. He's been dead for years, and they're still writing about him.
4. Someone has to write all those articles in Sports Illustrated. I wonder: how do you become a big-time sportswriter?

5. Someone has to train athletes, too—to help them know what to eat and how to work out and weight training and how to effectively use all those machines and about conditioning . . .

6. I always read the columns on Page 2 at ESPN.com. I bet it would be fun to do that kind of writing.

 ## Reviewing Your Invention and Research

After you have conducted your research, you need to review your invention work and notes and think about the information you have collected from outside sources. You may be tempted to decide on a thesis statement—a statement that summarizes the main point of your exploration—at this point. Even though you might already have a general idea of the conclusion your research is leading you to, until you get some of your ideas and information down on paper or into a computer file, it is often hard to know for certain what your thesis will be. Your thesis should come *from* your exploration. It is best to decide on your thesis after you have done a lot of invention work (listing, brainstorming, clustering, and so on) and research, or even after you construct your first draft.

For more on developing a thesis, see Chapter 13.

WRITING ACTIVITY

Considering Research and Focusing Ideas

Even though you may not be ready to formulate a working thesis statement at this time, you should look closely at the information you have found and try to find patterns that you might use to organize your ideas.

- Ask yourself, "Are there any significant trends or patterns in what I've found?" For example, in looking at the preliminary work Rick Mohler has done, you may have noticed a trend emerging about how sports appear in the media. Some careers in sports journalism might be worth further exploration.

- Since exploratory writing can lead in many directions, make sure you stay focused on paths that have potential for you. Rick Mohler might be interested in a career in sports medicine or as an agent for professional athletes. However, both of those careers take extensive training that he may not have the time for or an interest in pursuing.

WRITER'S WORKSHOP

Reacting to Your Classmates' Invention Work and Research

With any writing assignment, your invention materials and research can improve with peer feedback and suggestions. Working with several of your classmates, provide comments and suggestions and ask one another questions, with the overall goal of helping one another to understand your rhetorical situations more clearly and to generate more useful information:

Comments

- _____ in what you have so far is familiar/unfamiliar to me, so you might _____.

- I like _____ in what you've generated so far.

- I don't see how _____ fits as part of your exploration.

- I'm confused when you write about _____.

- These aspects of your subject— _____ and _____—seem really interesting. Have you thought about exploring them further?

- The part about _____ seems promising, but the part about _____ seems underdeveloped.

- I'd suggest that you include these ideas or this information:

  _____   _____

  _____   _____

Questions

- What is a _____ ? (Ask this kind of question when something is unclear.)

- I still have questions about _____.

- How would you describe the purpose of the _____ that you mention?

- How do _____ and _____ work together?

The comments and questions that you receive are intended to guide you, to suggest areas where your readers might be intrigued or confused and where they need more information about the subject of your exploration and its various aspects.

Organizing Your Ideas and Details

Because the purpose of writing an exploratory text is to examine an idea or concept from various perspectives, you will need to organize your thoughts in a useful manner. The questions that you need to ask yourself when deciding on your organization are all rhetorical.

- Who is your audience?
- Why might they be interested in your exploratory writing, or how can you make them interested in it? One way to emphasize the importance of your exploration to your audience is to show them why your subject is interesting to you.
- What is your purpose for writing—that is, why do your readers need to explore this topic with you? What will your readers learn about your subject by reading your exploratory writing?

Here is a brief outline of three possible organizational approaches to writing an exploratory paper:

Options for Organization

Classifying Ideas	Comparing and Contrasting Idea	Relating Causes and Effects
• Begin with your questions, perhaps from the least to the most important. • Explain each question in detail—and then provide possible answers. By looking at each question in detail, you may find that classifying both questions and answers is a useful method of organization. • Offer follow-up questions that may lead to further exploration. • You may conclude by suggesting that your exploration does not answer all the	• Note how many possible perspectives there may be on your subject and how they relate and connect to one another. • Explore each perspective in detail, so your reader can really understand what you are writing about. Because you began by noting multiple perspectives, comparison and contrast might be a useful method of organization. • By exploring your topic through various lenses, you come to a better understanding of your	• Start from what happens first and move to later events. • Explore and explain the various possible causes or effects. • Use specific examples to show how one cause or effect logically leads to the next. This is a variation on a cause-and-effect paper. In an exploratory paper you consider possible causes and effects; in a cause-and-effect paper, you argue that specific phenomena are causes or effects. • You may choose to end your paper with what seems like the final effect—

Options for Organization (*continued*)

Classifying Ideas	Comparing and Contrasting Idea	Relating Causes and Effects
questions and that other, specified, questions now need to be asked.	subject and are able to explain it for your readers, especially in relation to the different points of view on it. • Having presented multiple perspectives on your topic, indicate which conclusion your exploration has led you to.	keeping the entire paper chronological.

For more on classifying and comparison and contrast as organizing strategies, see Chapter 13. For more on causal analysis, see Chapter 10.

WRITING ACTIVITY

Deciding on an Organizational Approach

As you begin to draft your exploratory paper, try to envision what approach might serve you best. For instance, you might ask a number of questions and then answer them in a logical order. You might present a situation and then follow it through in an understandable—perhaps a chronological—order. You might define multiple perspectives and then explore the possibilities of each one. Try out several organizational approaches on the computer before deciding on one—and be sure to save each first attempt with a different file name. That strategy makes it easy to recall the one that seems best. You can then start to develop your draft using that organization.

 ## Constructing a Complete Draft

Once you know your subject, have your ideas down on paper or stored in a computer file, and have conducted research, you are ready to construct your initial draft. It is possible that you will find a suitable organizational approach before you begin drafting, but you may also find it—or decide to change it—as you are drafting or even after you have constructed a draft.

As you write the first version of your exploratory paper, do not worry about editing your work. At this point, you are just organizing your thoughts and research into some coherent form.

Introduction: One of the qualities of a successful piece of exploratory writing is that it grabs and holds readers' attention. There are a number of strategies for beginning your paper that will help you hook your readers. Here are some possibilities:

- *Take your readers on the journey.* Let your readers know from the beginning that this is an exploration. Let them be your travel companions. In "Scientist at Work: Terence Tao; Journeys to the Distant Fields of Prime," Kenneth Chang (p. 139) indicates that his essay will be a journey through his title and his opening anecdote, in which Tao promises an audience at a lecture "a whirlwind tour."

- *Ask one or more questions.* By asking a question or questions, you present options and directions. Your exploratory writing will help you and your reader find solutions. Rick Mohler uses this strategy in his exploration of possible careers in sports: "If you ask most people about a career in sports, they'll usually say, 'professional athlete,' as that is the most visible (and well-paid) career option. But what about those of us who will never make a professional team?"

- *Establish multiple perspectives.* Let your readers know from the very beginning that they will look at an issue from different points of view. In the opening to "Bipolar Iraq," Michael Wolff offers two conflicting story lines for the U.S. military involvement in Iraq:

  "It's working."
  "It's a quagmire."

Body: The body of your paper will lead you and your readers through your exploration process. You may choose one or several different kinds of organization. You might try classification, for example, where by grouping ideas in like categories, you discover similarities. However, comparison and contrast, where you discover both similarities and differences, might be more helpful. Michael Wolff uses this approach as he considers two perspectives on his subject in "Bipolar Iraq." Or you might discover that cause and effect, where you consider whether one event or phenomenon has caused, or was caused by, one or more other events or phenomena, might be the most powerful kind of organization for your paper.

Conclusion: Following your exploration, your conclusion should leave your readers feeling satisfied. You have several options for concluding an exploratory paper.

- If in your exploration you discover that there will be consequences if certain events occur, you may choose to present these final consequences. After explaining how he will write his memoir in "Memoir Essay" (p. 151), P. J. O'Rourke announces his "vital creative breakthrough."

- If you discover that your exploration has only led to even more questions, you may simply state the new questions that need to be researched. If you have explored options for your company, for example, but all of them have proved unsatisfactory for one reason or another, you would end your report in this way.

- Finally, if your exploration does lead you to a reasonable conclusion, state that conclusion, explaining to readers how you reached it.

Title: You might think that you need to come up with a title before you start writing, but often it is more useful to get a first draft down on paper or into a computer file and then consider possible titles. For an exploratory paper, your title should indicate your subject and give your reader a reason to want to explore it with you. The titles "Bipolar Iraq" and "Memoir Essay," for example, indicate that their authors have a unique approach to their subjects.

VISUALIZING VARIATIONS

Using Visuals to Make Your Exploration Clear

An appropriate image can add visual appeal to any exploratory writing. If you have chosen Scenario 2 because you wish to explore some personal interest, consider using a visual or visuals to show why you find your topic appealing. Suppose you collect state quarters, which first appeared in 1999 when the Delaware quarter was issued. As your collection has grown, you've become more interested in the images on the backs of the quarters, the stories behind them, and the artists who designed them.

   As you think about presenting your profile of quarter collecting to your readers, you decide which of the quarters' images will be most intriguing to them and which will best demonstrate your exploration. You might choose the Nevada quarter, for instance, released in 2006.

(cont'd)

(continued)

The image on the Nevada quarter tells a story about the state, but you need to do some exploration to discover what that story is. Your exploration might lead you to the Web site for the United States Mint (http://www.usmint.gov), where you find the story behind the "design of three galloping wild horses, sagebrush, the sun rising behind snow-capped mountains and the State's nickname, 'The Silver State,' inside a banner" and how it was chosen from five candidates.

Although you could certainly use words, as the United State Mint has, to describe the image on the Nevada quarter, the photo of the image will help readers see it more clearly. Using this image as an example, consider the best way to use an image or images to enhance your exploratory writing for your readers. Use the following questions to guide you:

- What can an image or images add that the words alone cannot show?
- How can I use the image to surprise readers—to offer them something unexpected?
- Should the image(s) I use be in color or black-and-white? What would be most effective?
- What kinds of images would draw readers into my text, make them want to read and learn more?
- How can the image(s) I select help show my exploration?

WRITING ACTIVITY

Constructing a Complete Draft

To prepare to construct the first draft of your exploratory essay, review the information you have gathered from your invention activities and research. When you draft exploratory writing, you don't necessarily need to begin your first draft with a clear thesis statement. Your thesis will probably emerge from your exploration.

Write your draft, exploring your subject in as much depth as possible and using the organizational scheme you think will work best. Make it as detailed as possible: the more you get down on paper initially, the easier it will be for you to flesh out and revise your paper later. Remember that this draft of your exploration will probably lead to additional questions and answers that you will want to include in your revision(s).

Rick Mohler's First Draft: A Sporting Career?

After doing research and deciding on an organizational approach, Rick Mohler was ready to begin his first draft. As he wrote, he did not concern himself with grammar, punctuation, or mechanics, but instead tried to get his questions and answers and ideas on paper. Note that Mohler started his paper with a series of questions—one of the organizational methods described above. Note also that Mohler incorporated some of his research information into his paper. (The numbers in circles refer to peer comments—see pp. 174–75.)

A Sporting Career?

If you ask most people about a career in sports, they'll usually say, "professional athlete," as that is the most visible (and well-paid) career option. But what about those of us who will never make a professional team? We may have enough desire, but what if we're not big enough, or fast enough, or have enough talent to "make the pros"? Are there other career options available to us and if so, what are they? How can we learn about them? What are some of the good things about those careers, and what are some of the bad things?? What might their work entail? What are the opportunities for promotion?❶

Those are just a few of the questions that I will explore in this paper, as I'm one of the people described above—I'll never be big enough or fast enough to "make the pros," but I also want to pursue a career in sports.❷

My favorite sport is football—and it's also America's choice, especially NFL football. In addition to the players, what other careers might be associated with the NFL? A few come to mind, including coach, weight-trainer/conditioning coach, publicity folks, and others. I want to explore two that interest me:

- Sportswriter
- Sports photographer ❸

One important part of either of these careers is that they are everywhere. Local newspapers as well as national television companies need them, so there are plenty of employment opportunities.

Since I've always been a pretty good writer, the idea of becoming a sportswriter strikes me as an interesting career. Last week's College Press, for example, carried seven sports-related articles, all written by student writers. Two touched on football, and perhaps the most interesting article was about spring workouts for our football players.

John Wilson, the spring workouts College Press writer, was kind enough to give me an interview. I asked him what kind of background you needed. "It's not as easy as it sounds," Wilson told me. "I'm an English major, which really helps, and while that combined with my interest and knowledge of sports is good, what's hard for me is the process of writing."

I asked John what he meant, and he said "it's just a lot of work. You have to go to the game and take notes. Then you interview some of the people involved—the coaches, the players, etc. Then you figure out some angle or slant that you want to focus on—one big play, or how a coach made a great call, or whatever. Then, finally, you have to write it all into a coherent form." I told John that the process he described was just what I was learning in my college writing class. He also told me that much of the writing has hard deadlines. You have to write fast as well as accurately. John said that he likes the challenge. I can see that appealing to my competitive nature.

Since I wanted to find out what a professional sportswriter might do John also suggested I email Brad Taylor, the high school sports editor of a large local newspaper.

My email correspondence and subsequent phone conversation with Brad Taylor proved even more interesting. Taylor explained to me the path he took to become a sportswriter. Like me, he had played football in high school but wasn't big enough or good enough to play in college. He was a history major in college but also wrote for the College Press, being sports editor his senior year. As much as he enjoyed working on the newspaper, he didn't think it was a real career. He expected to either go to law school or graduate school in history and become a history professor.

I was amazed to hear that he had been accepted by some really good law schools and grad schools but chose to start work on a masters degree instead. For a number of reasons, school wasn't as exciting as he thought it would be. On a whim, he went to the sports department of the large local paper. They asked if he had clippings. He brought them some of his college articles. They offered him a job as a stringer covering high school football.

Taylor told me that something clicked when he started covering high schools. He got a real thrill talking to the coaches and the players. Eventually, he dropped out of grad school when offered a full-time reporting job. Over time he became editor for all of high school sports. I could hear the excitement in his voice. It reminded me of the times in my old high school locker room. ❹

Revising

Revising means reseeing and rethinking your exploratory text. The most effective way to revise your work is to read it as if you are reading it for the first time. Reading your work in this way is difficult to do, of course—which is why writers often put their work aside for a period of time so that when they reread it, the experience is something like seeing it as a new piece of writing. The more you can see your writing as if for the first time, the more you will respond to it as your real readers might, questioning and probing and exploring it. When you reread the first draft of your exploratory writing, be sure to begin at the beginning. Here are some questions to ask yourself:

- What are the most important questions, the ones I would really like to have answered? How well have I answered them?
- How well have I answered the questions that will help me understand every facet of my subject?
- How well do I understand the draft? What parts are confusing or need more information? What research might I need to conduct to further clarify my ideas?
- What information, if any, might I provide as a visual?

Technology can help you revise and, later, edit your writing more easily. Use your word processor's track-changes tool to try out revisions and editing changes. After you've had time to think about the possible changes, you can "accept" or "reject" them. Also, you can use your word processor's comment tool to write reminders to yourself when you get stuck with a revision or some editing task. If your classmates offer feedback on your draft, they can also use track changes, the comment tool, or the peer-commenting feature of the software.

Because it is so difficult even for experienced writers to see their emerging writing with a fresh eye, it is almost always useful to ask classmates, friends, or family members to read drafts.

WRITER'S WORKSHOP

Responding to Full Drafts

As you read and respond to your classmates' papers (and as they comment on yours), focus on the exploratory nature of this assignment, but from a reader's perspective. Be sure to ask questions of their writing and respond to their ideas by exploring your reactions and responses to their thoughts.

Working in pairs or groups of three, read each others' papers, and then offer your classmates comments that will help them see their papers' strengths as well as places where they need to develop their ideas further. Use the following questions to guide your responses to the writer's draft, whether you respond directly on your classmate's text, on a separate sheet of paper, or online:

(cont'd)

(continued)

- Write a brief comment that gives your first impression. How interested are you in reading beyond the first paragraph? Why? What might the writer add to the beginning? Do you have any suggestions for improving the title?
- In a paragraph, indicate what you like about the draft—that is, provide positive and encouraging feedback to the writer. How interesting, educational, or useful did you find this exploration? Why?
- How interesting is the introduction? How appropriate are any questions or statements that the writer offers in the introduction? What suggestions can you make to improve the introduction?
- What is the focus of the paper? How does the focus emerge as you read? How well do you understand how the writer comes to the conclusion?
- How easily can you follow the writer's thought process? What explorations might be better left out of the draft? Comment on how the writer's exploratory writing helps you better understand the questions or problems posed in the introduction.
- How thoroughly does the writer explore the subject? How might the writer explore it more fully? If there are places in which the writer is simply restating information that is already known and obvious, how might those parts be changed?
- How viable are the differing perspectives? When the writer presents information, what makes you think that it is the best possible information? How appropriate are the writer's sources?
- Reread the conclusion. How logically does it follow from the rest of the paper? Were you surprised by the conclusion? What are other possible conclusions based on the information the writer has presented?
- In another paragraph, outline what you see as the main weaknesses of this paper—and suggest how the writer might improve the text.

Student Comments on Rick Mohler's First Draft

Rick Mohler got comments on his first draft from several readers. Below are comments on his draft, keyed to the first draft on pages 171–72.

❶ The above are really useful questions, but maybe you should kind of build up to the most important ones and leave the rest for the body of the paper. Another question I thought of is about how many possible careers in sports are there?

❷ That's a really interesting point. Most sports fans think it's either the pros or nothing, so I like the way you're trying to be realistic and still come up with a career that lets you do what you like most.

❸ Why are you interested in these two careers? What about them attracts you? I really do not know what a person in either position does all day long. Maybe to focus the paper a little more, you ought to focus on just one career?

❹ This is a good story, but I'd like to see more in your conclusion. What's so good about your old locker room?

Responding to Readers' Comments

Once they have received feedback on their writing from peers, teachers, friends, and others, all writers have to figure out what to do with that feedback. Since your text is *your* responsibility, you must determine how to deal with reader responses to your work.

The first thing to do with any feedback is to consider carefully what your readers have to say about your text. Rick Mohler's readers indicate the following reactions:

- One reader likes the details that point to the fact that Mohler may not end up playing professional ball, which means he is considering other careers. How might he pursue that line of thinking?
- Another reader thought Mohler had a weak conclusion and requested more information. How might he respond to this suggestion?

It is important to consider seriously what your readers are saying to you. You may decide to reject some comments, of course; other comments, though, deserve your attention, as they are the words of real readers speaking to you about how to improve your text. You may find that comments from more than one reader contradict each other. In that case, you need to use your own judgment to decide which reader's comments are on the right track.

In the final version of his paper on pages 180–81, you can see how Rick Mohler responded to these comments as well as to his own review of his first draft.

 # Knowledge of Conventions

When effective writers edit their work, they attend to the conventions that will help readers move through their writing effortlessly. These include genre conventions, documentation, format, usage, grammar, and mechanics. By paying attention to these conventions in your writing, you make reading a more pleasant experience for readers.

Editing

The last task in any writing project is editing—the final polishing of your document. When you edit and polish your writing, you make changes to your sentence structure and word choice to improve your style and to make your writing clearer and more concise. You also check your work to make sure it adheres to conventions of grammar, usage, punctuation, mechanics, and spelling. Use the spell-check function of your word-processing program, but be sure to double-check your spelling personally. If you have used sources in your paper, make sure you are following the documentation style your instructor requires.

See Chapter 20 for more on documenting sources using MLA or APA style.

As with overall revision of your work, this final editing and polishing is most effective if you can put your text aside for a few days and come back to it with fresh eyes. Because checking conventions is easier said than done, though, we strongly recommend that you ask classmates, friends, and tutors to read your work to find sentence problems that you do not see. Another option is to post your paper on a course Web site and invite everyone in class to read it. You may get only one or two takers, but one or two is better than none.

To assist you with editing, we offer here a round-robin editing activity focused on sentence fragments, a common concern in all writing.

WRITER'S WORKSHOP

Round-Robin Editing with a Focus on Fragments

Because exploratory writing often includes incomplete thoughts, writers sometimes inadvertently use sentence fragments to express their thinking. A sentence fragment is missing one or more of the following elements: a subject, a verb, or a complete thought. Some fragments lack a subject, a verb, or both:

FRAGMENT   College sports are popular. *Generating lots of money for schools with successful teams.*

Other fragments have subjects and verbs, but they begin with a subordinating word like *because* or *although* and so are not complete thoughts:

FRAGMENT   *Although I have played football in high school and college.* I'm not good enough to play on a professional team.

Some fragments are intentional, especially if they occur in dialogue. Unintentional fragments, however, need to be corrected. You can correct a sentence fragment by adding the element that is missing or connecting it to a sentence that precedes or follows it:

> *They generate*
> ➤ College sports are popular. ₍Λ₎~~Generating~~ lots of money for schools with successful teams.

> ➤ Although I have played football in high school and college₍Λ₎, I'm not good enough to play on a professional team.

Work with two peers to look for sentence fragments in each other's papers. As you consider each fragment, determine whether it is intentional. If it is not, decide whether to connect it to a nearby sentence or to recast it into a complete sentence.

Genres, Documentation, and Format

If you are writing an academic paper, follow the conventions for the discipline in which you are writing and the requirements of your instructor. If you are exploring potential majors (Scenario 1), you might choose to write a letter or an e-mail message to family members, especially if any of them are providing financial support for your education. If you are planning a meeting for an organization (Scenario 3), you might write a memo, an e-mail message, a blog entry, or a report to the membership. If you are doing a personal exploration (Scenario 5), you might want to write a journal entry—one that does not have a wide public readership. If you have chosen to do a personal exploration, you might avoid writing a blog entry, because blogs can have thousands of readers—including potential employers.

For advice on writing in different genres, see Appendix C. For guidelines for formatting and documenting papers in MLA or APA style, see Chapter 20.

If you have used material from outside sources, including visuals, give credit to those sources, using the documentation style required by the discipline you are working in and by your instructor.

WRITING IN ACTION

Convention in Genre and Design

Here is a page from the Web site for Denver's Cow Parade. What could a "cow parade" possibly be? Does seeing the photos make you want to explore the subject in more detail? Are there other parades like this that other communities offer? Can you tell what this Web page is all about? (If you live in a city that the cow parade has visited, then you will already know something about the event.)

(cont'd)

(continued)

Considering Genre and Design

1. What does the Web page tell you about this organization? In what ways does the Web page let you explore the Cow Parade?
2. What relationships do you see between the photos of the cows and their names?
3. How do the photos function? What do they tell you about the organization?
4. How effectively is information provided? How does the presentation make you want to explore further?
5. What more would you like to know about a cow parade?

 # A Writer Shares His Exploration: Rick Mohler's Final Draft

As you read the final version of Rick Mohler's exploratory paper, consider what makes it effective. Following the reading you will find some questions to help you conduct your own exploration of this paper.

RICK MOHLER

A Sporting Career?

One of Mohler's classmates made this comment on his paper:

Another question I thought of is about how many possible careers in sports are there?

Notice how he provides information to answer this peer-review question.

One of Mohler's classmates wrote this comment on an early draft:

Why are you interested in these two careers? What about them attracts you? I really do not know what a person in either position does all day long. Maybe to focus the paper a little more, you ought to focus on just one career.

Notice how in his final version, Mohler does just what his classmate suggested, focusing on one specific career path.

If you ask most people to name a career in sports, they'll usually say, "professional athlete," because that is the most visible (and well-paid) career option. But what about those of us who have the desire, but not the size, speed, or talent? Are there other career options available to us, and if so, what are they?

I'm one of those people. I doubt that I have the size or speed to make the pros, but I want a career in sports, as do many others. Perhaps my "wonderings" here can help others as they try to decide what career path they may want to follow.

My favorite sport is football—and it's also America's choice. While the players have the faces and names that fans recognize, they are only one part of the big picture that is NFL football. Many other people make the games happen, keep the players in good condition, and tell the rest of America all about the sport. Coaches, weight trainers and conditioning coaches, publicists, writers, and photographers all have a part to play in the game of football.

The career path that excites me most is being a sportswriter. The job has an artistic element that appeals to me. As a sportswriter, I wouldn't just describe what took place at a game or event—I would really try to paint a picture. Maybe someday I'll even be able to write something as famous as Grantland Rice's description of the Notre Dame football team:

> Outlined against a blue-gray October sky, the Four Horsemen rode again. In dramatic lore they are known as Famine, Pestilence, Destruction and Death. These are only aliases. Their real names are Stuhldreher, Miller, Crowley and Layden. They formed the crest of the South Bend cyclone before which another fighting Army football team was swept over the precipice at the Polo Grounds yesterday afternoon as 55,000 spectators peered down on the bewildering panorama spread on the green plain below.

Though not all sportswriters become as famous as Rice, they are everywhere. Local newspapers as well as national television networks need them, so there are plenty of employment opportunities. Just as most sports have both amateur and professional athletes, a sportswriter can start as an amateur and advance to the pros. It seems to make sense to begin working for a student newspaper, especially since I've always been a fairly good writer.

Last week's College Press, for example, included seven sports-related articles, all written by student writers. Two touched on football, and perhaps the most interesting article was about spring workouts for our football players.

John Wilson, the spring workouts <u>College Press</u> writer, was kind enough to give me an interview. I asked him what kind of background an aspiring sports-writer needs. "It's not as easy as it sounds," Wilson told me. "I'm an English major, which really helps, and while that combined with my interest in and knowledge of sports is good, what's hard for me is the process of writing." 7

I asked Wilson what he meant about writing and effort, and he gave me a description of how he typically covers a game: 8

> It's just a lot of work. You have to go to the game and take notes. Then you interview some of the people involved—the coaches, the players, etc. Then you figure out some angle or slant that you want to focus on—one big play, or how a coach made a great call, or whatever. Then, finally, you have to write it all into a coherent form.

I told Wilson that the process he described was just what I was learning in my college writing class. "You have to write fast as well as accurately," Wilson said. He also told me that he likes the challenge. I can see that appealing to my competitive nature. 9

Because I wanted to find out what a professional sportswriter might do, Wilson also suggested I contact Brad Taylor, the high school sports editor of a large newspaper in my hometown. 10

My communications with Brad Taylor proved even more interesting. Taylor explained the path he took to become a sportswriter. Like me, he had played football in high school but wasn't good enough to play in college. He was a history major in college but also wrote for the <u>College Press</u>, becoming sports editor his senior year. As much as he enjoyed sportswriting, he didn't think it was a real career. He expected to go either to law school or graduate school in history and become a history professor. 11

Despite being accepted by some really good law schools and graduate schools, he chose to start work on a masters degree at a local college. For a number of reasons, school wasn't as exciting as he thought it would be. On a whim, he went to the sports department of the large local paper. They asked if he had clippings, and he brought some of his college articles. They offered him a job as a stringer covering high school football. 12

Taylor told me that something clicked when he started covering high schools. He got a real thrill talking to the coaches and the players. 13

Eventually, he dropped out of graduate school when offered a full-time reporting job. Over time he became editor for all of high school sports. I could hear the excitement in his voice. It reminded me of the times in my old high school locker room—the joy after winning and the disappointment after losing, the camaraderie among teammates, the team meetings to discuss strategy. I wouldn't mind reliving that again—even if it's a vicarious experience. 14

Mohler ended his first version with the words "locker room," and a peer reviewer asked,

This is a good story, but I'd like to see more in your conclusion. What's so good about your old locker room?

Notice how Mohler has now added some information to answer his classmate's question.

Works Cited

Rice, Grantland. "The Four Horsemen." University of Notre Dame Archives.
    5 May 2003. <http://lamb.archives.nd.edu/rockne/rice.html>.
Taylor, Brad. Personal E-mail. 7 May 2003.
--- Personal Interview. 9 May 2003.
Wilson, John. Personal Interview. 30 Apr. 2003.

QUESTIONS FOR WRITING AND DISCUSSION

Rhetorical Knowledge: The Writer's Situation and Rhetoric

1. **Audience:** Who is the intended audience for Mohler's essay? What in the essay makes you think so?

2. **Purpose:** What does Mohler hope will happen when people read his essay?

3. **Voice and Tone:** How would you describe Mohler's tone in his essay?

4. **Responsibility:** How responsibly has Mohler reported information about being a sportswriter to you? To himself? Why do you think so?

5. **Context and Format:** Mohler wrote this paper for a college course. If you were an editor for your local newspaper, would you consider hiring Mohler as a sportswriter? Why or why not? What qualities in his exploratory essay would help you make this decision?

Critical Thinking: Your Personal Response

1. What is your first reaction to Rick Mohler's exploratory paper?

2. How easily can you relate to what Mohler writes about? Why?

3. What career do you see yourself pursuing? What did you learn from Mohler's exploratory essay that might help you explore your career path?

Critical Thinking: The Writer's Ideas

1. What is the main point of Mohler's essay? How well does he focus the essay? How does he support his main idea? What questions do you still have about his subject?

2. How well has Mohler convinced himself that he should consider a career in sportswriting? Why do you think so? How well has he convinced you? Why?

Composing Processes and Knowledge of Conventions: The Writer's Strategies

1. In what ways does Mohler establish his *ethos*, or his credibility, in this exploratory essay?

2. How effective is Mohler's introduction? Why?

3. How effective is Mohler's conclusion? Why?

4. How effectively does Mohler make an argument that sportswriting is a good career choice for him?

Inquiry and Research: Ideas for Further Exploration

1. How might Mohler's exploration have led him in other directions? What other professions might he have investigated?

2. In what other ways might Mohler have researched his choice? What sources might he have investigated?

3. Spend some time in your college library exploring the career you see for yourself. In no more than two pages, outline your career ten years from today.

 # Self-Assessment: Reflecting on Your Learning Goals

Now that you have constructed a piece of exploratory writing, go back and consider your learning goals, which you and your classmates may have considered at the beginning of this chapter (see pp. 126–27). Reflecting on your writing process and the exploratory text you have constructed—and putting such reflections down *in writing*—is another kind of exploration: you are exploring, thinking about, and commenting on your own work as a writer. Here are some questions to answer that focus on what you have learned from this assignment:

Rhetorical Knowledge

- *Audience:* What have you learned about addressing an audience in exploratory writing?

- *Purpose:* What have you learned about the purposes of exploratory writing?

- *Rhetorical Situation:* How did the writing context affect your exploratory text? How did your choice of topic affect the research you conducted and how you presented your exploration to your readers?

- *Voice and Tone:* How would you describe your voice in this project? Your tone? How do they contribute to the effectiveness of your exploratory essay?
- *Context, Medium, and Genre:* How did your context determine the medium and genre you chose, and how did those decisions affect your writing?

Critical Thinking, Reading, and Writing

- *Learning/Inquiry:* How did you decide what to focus on in your exploratory writing? Describe the process you went through to focus on a main idea, or thesis. How did you judge what was most and least important in your exploratory writing?
- *Responsibility:* How did you fulfill your responsibility to your readers?
- *Reading and Research:* What did you learn about exploratory writing from the reading selections you read for this chapter? What research did you conduct? How sufficient was the research you did? Why? What additional research might you have done?
- As a result of writing this exploration, how have you become a more critical thinker, reader, and writer? What critical thinking, reading, and writing skills do you hope to develop further in your next writing project? How will you work on them?

Writing Processes for Exploration

- *Invention:* What invention strategies were most useful to you? Why?
- *Organizing Your Ideas and Details:* What organization did you use? How successful was it?
- *Revising:* What one revision did you make that you are most satisfied with? What are the strongest and the weakest parts of the paper or other piece of writing you wrote for this chapter? Why? If you could go back and make an additional revision, what would it be?
- *Working with Peers:* How did your instructor or peer readers help you by making comments and suggestions about your writing? List some examples of useful comments that you received. List some examples of how you revised your exploration based on those comments and suggestions. How could you have made better use of the comments and suggestions you received? How could your peer readers help you more on your next assignment? How might you help them more, in the future, with the comments and suggestions you make on their texts?
- If you used photographs or other visuals to help present your exploration to readers, what did you learn about incorporating these elements?
- What "writerly habits" have you developed, modified, or improved on as you constructed the writing assignment for this chapter? How will you change your future writing activities, based on what you have learned about yourself?

Conventions

- *Editing:* What sentence problem did you find most frequently in your writing? How will you avoid that problem in future assignments?
- *Genre:* What conventions of the genre, if any, gave you problems?
- *Documentation:* If you used sources for your paper, what documentation style did you use? What problems, if any, did you have with it?

Rick Mohler Reflects on His Writing

Once he completed the polished version of his exploratory writing, Rick Mohler wrote a reflection on his work. Here is a brief excerpt from his reflective comments:

> Although I initially resisted the thought of invention work (mostly because I had never done it before), I found it helpful for getting ideas on paper. I used three kinds of invention tools—listing, freewriting, and clustering. I came to understand that each tool has a slightly different purpose, so it was helpful to use all three of them. These different invention tools are sort of like the different activities that we used on the practice field when I was in high school; each one is useful, but collectively they result in even better performance.
>
> Doing the research for my paper was a challenge. However, after I got suggestions from my classmates, teacher, and several librarians, I was able to find the materials that I needed. Of course, then the big challenge was deciding when to stop researching. In doing my research, I found interesting magazine articles, Web sites, and people to interview. If there were more time, I could have done more research, but time is hard to find when you're taking five courses and working at a part-time job.
>
> Next time I want to start working at research much sooner than I did for this paper so that maybe I can interview more than two people. I think being able to quote real people in my paper made it more effective. I didn't even <u>think</u> of asking some people I know what they thought. The library research I did was fine and interesting and useful, but I sure would have liked to talk to some more people about this paper. I'll be sure to do that, next time.
>
> My peers were pretty helpful when they responded to my invention work and my drafts. I probably could have written an okay paper without them, but they helped me strengthen my paper by helping me see things that I didn't notice or hadn't thought about.
>
> As I worked on the project, I came to realize how much I love sports, especially football. Writing this paper has encouraged me to think further about a career as a sportswriter. I know that the field is a tough one to break into, but I think that I have the drive and determination to get there. Wish me luck.

Rhetorical Knowledge

- *Audience:* Consider what your readers need to know—and how you can interest them in that information. What about your subject might your audience be *most* interested in? What information might readers consider unusual?

- *Purposes:* You want readers to understand the information you are sharing, so your writing must be clear. Considering what your audience might *do* with the information you provide will help you decide how best to provide the information to your readers.

- *Rhetorical situation:* In an informational essay, you are writing to share information; your readers are reading your text to learn about (and—you hope—to understand) that information.

- *Writer's voice and tone:* Generally, informational writing has a neutral tone because you as the writer are trying, not to convince or explore, but rather to inform your readers. Of course, sometimes an informational essay can have a humorous tone—see Peterson's *The Man Who Invented Baseball* (p. 199).

- *Context, medium, and genre:* The genre you use to present your information is determined by your purpose: to inform. Decide on the best medium and genre to use to present your information to the audience you want to reach.

Critical Thinking, Reading, and Writing

- *Learning/inquiry:* Because you are helping your readers learn about the subject of your text, decide on the most important aspects of your topic and explain them in a clear, focused way.

- *Responsibility:* You have a responsibility to represent your information honestly and accurately.

- *Reading and research:* Your research must be accurate and as complete as possible, to allow you to present thoughtful, reliable information about your subject.

- *Invention:* You will need to choose invention strategies that will help you generate and locate information about your topic.

- *Organizing your ideas and details:* You will need to find the most effective way to present your information to your readers so they can easily understand it.

- *Revising:* You will need to read your work with a critical eye, to make certain that it fulfills the assignment and displays the qualities of good informative writing.

- *Working with peers:* Your classmates will make suggestions that indicate the parts of your text they found difficult to understand so you can work to clarify.

Conventions

- *Editing:* Informative writing benefits from the correct use of modifiers, so the round-robin activity on pages 239–40 focuses on avoiding misplaced or dangling modifiers.

- *Genres for informative writing:* Possible genres include newspaper or magazine articles, informative letters, informative essays, and Web documents.

- *Documentation:* If you have relied on sources outside of your experience, cite them using the appropriate documentation style.

Chapter

6

| HOME PAGE | MY TIMES | TODAY'S PAPER | VIDEO | MOST POPULAR | TIMES TOPICS | | TimesSelect ▼ | Welcome, samod1 | Member Center | Log Out |

The New York Times

Friday, February 23, 2007 Last Update: 10:12 AM ET

| | NYT Archive Since 1981 ▼ | Search |

 ▸ Get Home Delivery | New York Partly Sunny 30°F

JOB MARKET
REAL ESTATE
AUTOS
ALL CLASSIFIEDS

WORLD
U.S.
Politics
Washington
Education
N.Y./REGION
BUSINESS
TECHNOLOGY
SPORTS
SCIENCE
HEALTH
OPINION
ARTS
Books
Movies
Music
Television
Theater
STYLE
Dining & Wine
Fashion & Style
Home & Garden
Weddings &
Celebrations
TRAVEL NEW

Blogs
Cartoons
Classifieds
Corrections
Crossword/
Games
First Look
Learning
Network
Multimedia
NYC Guide

U.S. Used Base in Ethiopia to Hunt Al Qaeda in Africa

By MICHAEL R. GORDON and MARK MAZZETTI

The counterterrorism effort was described by U.S. officials as a qualified success that disrupted terrorist networks in Somalia.

Long Iraq Tours Can Make Home a Trying Front

By LIZETTE ALVAREZ

For many soldiers and their families, the repercussions of deployments are one of the toughest, least discussed byproducts of the conflicts in Iraq and Afghanistan.

· 📷 Photographs: Strain at Home
· Iraq Rebels Expected to Use More Chlorine Gas in Attacks
· Senate Democrats in Bid to Limit U.S. Role in Iraq

📊 GRAPHIC

The Presidential Candidates on Iraq

What the candidates have said about one of the threshold issues of the '08 presidential election.

· Go to Complete Coverage »

Anne MoQuary for The New York Times

Giuliani Is Seeing Only Softballs
By RICHARD PÉREZ-PEÑA

Rudolph W. Giuliani has limited himself to events with narrowly defined, friendly audiences.

PTAs Go Way Beyond Cookies
By WINNIE HU

As some PTAs have become more corporatized, they have clashed with other parents, teachers and principals.

Springtime for Hit's End: 'The Producers' to Close
By CAMPBELL ROBERTSON

The Broadway musical that broke a batch of records will play its final performance on April 22.

MORE NEWS

· Cheney Criticizes China's Arms Buildup 8:40 AM ET
· 46 Nations Call for Cluster Bomb Ban 51 minutes ago
· Detour From High Road in Clinton-Obama Clash

ON THE BLOGS

· The Lede: On Naming a National Fish
· DealBook: Mixed Reactions on Hedge Fund Report
· The Carpetbagger's Oscar Picks
· The Caucus Blog: Lieberman and the G.O.P.

ESCAPES »
Spending a Day at the Rockefellers'

In the tranquil hamlet of Pocantico Hills, N.Y., the imprint of the Rockefeller family is everywhere and visitors will delight in exploring its rich legacy.

Confessions of a Golf School Junkie

In a vicious circle, golf school brings confidence that the course promptly snatches away.

OPINION »
· 📷 Krugman: Green Ideas
· 📷 Friedman: Foreign Policy
· 📷 The Opinionator
· Editorial: On JetBlue

MARKETS 10:01AM ET BigCharts

DOW	12,639.47	-46.55	-0.37%
NAS	2,516.74	-8.20	-0.32%
S&P	1,452.58	-3.80	-0.26%

My
Portfolio »   Stock Quotes: [ ] Go

· Tools: Alerts | Stocks | Sectors

The *New York Times* Online (February 23, 2007)

Writing to Inform

We all deal with *information* every day of our lives. We learn about facts, ideas, and ways of doing things and then communicate such information to others through spoken or written words and, at times, graphic or other visual means. In other words, in some way we are all both learners and teachers, and consequently there is a strong teaching component to informative writing.

Many newspaper articles are examples of informative writing. The headlines from the *New York Times Online* do not seem to contain elements of persuasion, argumentation, or evaluation—the primary goal of headline writers is simply to provide information. We could argue, of course, that any type of writing has elements of persuasion, and by selecting certain words and emphasizing particular facts, a writer will influence a reader's response. No piece of writing is completely neutral. However, the goal of most informative writing, especially the informative writing you will do in college, *is* to be as neutral as possible, so it is the writer's responsibility to present information impartially.

Not all newspapers or magazines make a similar effort to present information in an unbiased way, of course. A tabloid like the *National Enquirer* does not even attempt to appear neutral. Readers can assume that most of the information the *National Enquirer* provides is sensationalized and meant to entertain them. Even in less flamboyant settings, however, informative writing does not need to be dull.

As a college student, you read informative writing in your textbooks and other assigned reading and are expected to write informative responses on tests and provide information in the papers your teachers assign. While you may think that you encounter informative writing only in your textbooks and in newspapers or magazines, you can easily find examples of such reading and writing in each area of your life. In your professional life, for example, you may need to read (or construct) a training manual, while in your civic life, you may be called on to write a voter guide about two candidates, presenting their positions without revealing your personal views.

 # Rhetorical Knowledge

When you provide information to readers, you need to consider what your readers might already know about your topic as well as what other information you have learned about through your research that would be useful to them. You will also need to decide what medium and genre will help you get that information across to your audience most effectively.

 ## Writing to Inform in Your College Classes

Much of the writing you will do for your college classes will be informative. The purpose of most of the reading you will do in college is to learn new information—and many writing assignments will require you to relate new facts and concepts to other facts and concepts you have already read and learned about, as in the following examples:

- Your psychology instructor may ask you to read several essays or books about recovered memory and to *synthesize* the information they contain—to explain to a reader the most important points made in each text and how the information in one text agrees or disagrees with the information in the others. While it is sometimes necessary to repeat memorized information, it is often more useful to synthesize—comparing and contrasting and relating various pieces of information to one another.

- Your biology instructor may ask you to compose a report on the growing danger of avian (bird) flu—what some are calling an upcoming *pandemic*. You may be asked not only to explain the details of this potential disaster but also how this strain of bird flu differs from other pandemics in the past, so you will have to present the data and synthesize what you have read and learned.

- Your art instructor may ask that you trace the development of a specific approach to art, providing examples and details that show its evolution over time.

- Your political science instructor may ask you to examine "presidential bloopers," where presidential candidates did or said something awkward—and explain in writing how those instances affected the next election.

Writing to Inform for Life

In addition to your academic work, you will also construct informative texts for the other areas of your life, including your professional career, your civic life, and your personal life.

Much of the writing done in **professional settings** is designed to inform and often to teach. If you have or have had a job, for example, consider what you know about this job, including everyday activities and interactions, the tools or equipment you use or used, and so on. Now consider how you would explain the details of your job to someone who is going to take it over: What information would that person need to know to do your job effectively? How can you best relay that information to your replacement?

What you have just considered are the details that make up a training manual, a type of informative writing that most businesses have in one form or another. As employees change positions, new employees need information on how to do an effective job. Being able to write effectively in professional settings will prove beneficial to you.

Likewise, much **civic writing** is designed to provide information to residents, voters, neighbors, and other citizens to help them decide issues or take advantage of community resources and programs. Perhaps citizens are being encouraged to participate in a community program such as a citizen's watch campaign, a civic event that would almost certainly require informative writing.

You will also do a great deal of informative writing in your **personal life,** ranging from notes to family members to e-mail conversations with relatives and friends. While you no doubt feel more comfortable jotting down information for your friends and family than you do for other audiences, you probably feel especially obligated to provide accurate and useful information because you care about your personal relationships. Notice how easily the writer of the following e-mail anticipates the questions her friend would probably have about the restaurant she is suggesting for lunch.

How about meeting at Julio's Restaurant for lunch at 1:00 tomorrow? It's only a few steps east of Mama's Pizza. I know that you like Mexican food, and I remember you mentioned one time that you really like the more traditional kind. That's what Julio's serves. The music is not too loud, so we can talk. Lunch specials are under $8.00, and come with a drink.

Scenarios for Writing: Assignment Options

The following writing assignments call for you to construct informative texts. Each is in the form of a *scenario*, a brief story that provides some context for your writing. The scenario gives you a sense of who your audience is and what you need to accomplish.

As in the other chapters in this text, we have provided two scenarios focused on academic writing and three scenarios that you might encounter outside of college. The list of rhetorical considerations on page 196 encourages you to keep in mind your audience; purpose; voice, tone, and point-of-view; and context, medium, and genre for the scenario you have chosen. Starting on page 219, you will find guidelines for completing whatever assignment option you choose or that is assigned to you.

Writing for College

SCENARIO 1   Are Students Really Slobs?

Does your room—whether on campus or in a private home—look like the student's dorm room shown in Figure 6.1?

Your sociology class has been focusing on student behavior. Just last week a classmate mentioned the problem of trash on campus: "Our campus is a big mess because students just don't care," she said. "They ignore the trash cans and recycling boxes and just toss their garbage everywhere!"

Although the following scenario focuses on littering, if you prefer you may write about some other issue on your campus. Your task is not to propose

**FIGURE 6.1
A Student's
Dormitory Room**

a solution for the issue; rather, your task is to inform other members of the campus community that a problem exists.

Writing Assignment: Construct an informative paper, based on two sets of information: (1) your observations of the problem on campus, and (2) interviews you conduct with at least two of your classmates, asking them what their thoughts are on why some students don't use trash cans as they should, or on the alternate problem you have chosen to write about.

SCENARIO 2 A Subject You Are Curious About

This scenario asks you to examine and write about a subject you would like to know more about for an academic audience that knows less about it than you do. What subjects are you interested in but have never had the time to read and learn more about? Your topic can be from a course you have taken or are currently taking, or a subject area that you have an interest in but have not—or not yet—studied formally.

Writing Assignment: Select a topic that you would like to gather more information on, and construct an informative text that outlines and explains the information you uncover in your research.

TechNote A digital camera is an ideal tool for any assignment that asks you to make observations. Once you have transferred the photographs of your subject to your computer, it is easy to add them to your text. Be sure, though, to get written permission from any people you photograph before using photographs of them in your work.

Writing for Life

SCENARIO 3   Professional Writing: Instructions for Doing Your Job

Consider what you do now in your job. (If you don't currently have an outside job, think of what you have done as a volunteer, in a past job, or in a routine task at home.) What are your daily tasks? Weekly or monthly tasks? How do you plan your time? What do you do during each hour of the day? (from 8:00–9:00 a.m.? from 9:00–10:00 a.m.?) If you were to leave your job for a period of time, what would your replacement need to know in order to perform your job successfully?

Writing Assignment: In no more than three pages, explain to someone who knows nothing about your work what you do every day on your job. Keep the text neutral in tone—do not include your opinion of your boss or co-workers or ideas on how to improve procedures. Instead, explain in a dispassionate, informative manner what you are expected to do and how someone new to the position can do it well.

SCENARIO 4   Civic Writing: An Article about a Community Problem

As a reporter, you have been assigned to write about a community problem for your local newspaper. Select an important problem that your community is concerned about. To find a problem, read recent issues of your local paper and also speak to some residents of your community. For example, if you live in Bend, Oregon, and happen to glance through the online version of *Central Oregon Online*, you might see a list of local stories about the need to fund bridge repairs, an attempt to save horses, or problems with the water supply. All are aspects of civic life that you could write about.

Here, for example, is a headline about a local problem from the *Seattle Times* that you might want to focus on if you were a college student in Seattle:

The state allows hundreds of doctors, counselors and others to keep practicing despite their sexual misconduct.

Writing Assignment: Write an article for your local newspaper in which you explain the local problem or issue that interests you in detail so your readers will understand all aspects of and perspectives on it. Keep in mind that your article will be published on the front page of the newspaper, not in the editorial section, so your text must be as neutral as possible. (As an alternative, you can create a Web site, poster, or brochure about the problem—see the Visualizing Variations box on pp. 232–33.)

FIGURE 6.2 Poster for a stage performance

SCENARIO 5 Personal Writing: An E-mail Message about a Performance, Exhibit, or Sporting Event

Your friends and family members may sometimes ask you to provide information about—but not evaluations of—movies, concerts, shows, museum exhibits, or sporting events to help them make decisions about whether to spend money to see them. For instance, if an art museum in your area were exhibiting works by Dutch painter Vincent Van Gogh, friends or family members who live some distance away might want to know which paintings were on display before deciding to spend their time and money to see the exhibit.

Writing Assignment: In an e-mail message to a friend or family member, describe a performance, exhibit, or sporting event that you recently saw or that is coming up. Try to avoid evaluating it. Instead, present what you know about the subject in a nonjudgmental, informative manner.

Rhetorical Considerations in Informative Writing

Regardless of the scenario you have chosen, you need to keep the following rhetorical considerations in mind as you construct your informative writing.

Audience: Who is your primary audience? Who else might be interested in your subject? Why?

Purpose: As noted in Chapter 3, writing can be a powerful tool for learning, so use the information you collect and write about as a way to increase your knowledge of your subject, as well as the knowledge of your readers. Bear in mind as you write that your purpose is not to convince readers to agree with an opinion you hold about your subject, but rather to inform them about it in neutral terms.

Voice, Tone, and Point of View: If you have a fairly limited knowledge of your topic, your stance, or attitude, will be that of an interested investigator and your tone will usually be neutral. If you are writing about a topic that you know well, you will need to take care to keep any biases out of your writing and present all aspects of your subject. If you are writing about a problem, you should present all opinions about the problem, including those you disagree with, fairly. Your point of view will usually be third person.

Context, Medium, and Genre: Keeping the context of the assignment in mind, decide on a medium and a genre for your writing. How will your writing be used? Obviously, your instructor will use your writing to help determine your grade for the course, so follow his or her instructions carefully. If you are writing for an audience beyond the classroom, consider what will be the most effective way to present your information to this audience. For example, if you are writing a newspaper article in response to Scenario 3, you will need to learn, and follow, the conventions of that genre.

For more on choosing a medium and genre, see Chapter 15 and Appendix C.

 # Critical Thinking, Reading, and Writing

Before you begin to write your informative paper, you need to consider the qualities of successful informative writing. It also helps to read one or more examples of informative writing. Finally, you might consider how visuals can also inform readers, as well as the kinds of sources you will need to consult.

Writing to provide information has several qualities—a strong focus, relevant, useful information that is provided in an efficient manner, and clear, accurate explanations that enable readers to understand the information easily. In the following pages, you will learn more about these qualities as well as your responsibilities as a writer. The reading selections and the visual text that appear in the next sections exemplify these qualities. Further, they can serve to stimulate your inquiry and writing. Finally, informative writing almost always requires that you go beyond your current knowledge of a topic and conduct careful research.

Learning the Qualities of Effective Informative Writing

As you think about how you might compose an informative paper, consider what readers expect and need from an informative text. As a reader, you probably look for the following qualities in informative writing:

- **A focused subject.** In *The Elements of Style*, his classic book of advice to writers, author and humorist E. B. White suggests, "When you say something, make sure you have said it. The chances of your having said it are only fair." White's comment is especially applicable to informative writing. The best way to "make sure you have said" what you want to say is to have a clear focus. What information about your subject is the most important? What is unusual? (Unusual details may make your readers even more interested in your subject.) If you could boil down your information into one sentence, what would it be? Condensing the important aspects of your information into a single sentence forces you to craft a thesis statement, which in turn helps you connect all your details and examples back to that main point.

  For more on thesis statements, see Chapter 13.

- **Useful and relevant information.** People often read to gain information: they want to learn how their favorite sports team is doing, to find the best way to travel from one place to another, to learn why high blood pressure is a health concern. In constructing an informative text, you should consider why your readers need the information and use that insight to make your subject interesting and relevant to them. How can you present your information so that readers understand how it relates to their lives and what they might do with it? Perhaps there is an unusual or a humorous angle on your subject that you can write about. And if you synthesize the information you have—explain the most important points made in each source you have consulted and how the information in one source agrees or disagrees with that in the other sources you have read—you will provide readers with a more thorough understanding of your subject.

- **Clear explanations and accurate information.** Information needs to be presented clearly and accurately so it is understandable to readers who do not have background knowledge about your subject. Consider

For more on using examples and comparison and contrast, see Chapter 13. For more on conducting research and taking notes, see Chapters 19 and 20.

your information as if you knew nothing about the subject. What terms or ideas might be confusing? How might you best explain them? Examples are almost always a useful way to help explain ideas and define terms. *Comparison and contrast* can be useful when you need to explain an unfamiliar subject—tell the reader what a subject is like and what it is not like. One strategy that will help you write clear, accurate papers is to take careful notes when you conduct research.

- **Efficiency.** Information should usually be presented concisely, with no more or no less detail than your readers need. To help them grasp the information, you might want to provide them with a road map, an outline of what you have in mind, at the beginning of the paper so they will know what to expect. Another way to present data efficiently is to "chunk" your writing—put it into sections, each dealing with a different aspect of the subject, making it easier for readers to understand. As you plan your paper, you should also consider whether it would be helpful to present your information in a table, graph, chart, or map. How might pictures or drawings make the information more understandable? Consider how the title of your informative text not only will help your reader understand your focus, but also will help to draw readers in, motivating them to read your paper.

For more on the use of visuals to enhance your explanations, see Chapter 17.

In an electronic form that you can copy and paste, you might jot down the main ideas from the qualities of effective informative writing above. Later, you can paste them into your working draft to remind you of the qualities that make an effective informative text.

A WRITER'S RESPONSIBILITIES

Presenting Informative Writing Conscientiously

People often use information from their reading to help them make a decision, to support an idea in their writing, or to teach someone else. It is important, therefore, that you present accurate information and that you are aware of any biases, or preconceived ideas, you may bring to your writing about a topic—biases that might cause you to present that information in a way that is other than neutral. Ethical writers also take care to present reliable data. For example, you cannot say, "the majority of students who attend this college think that the school does a good job of recycling on campus," unless you have asked a sufficiently large and representative group of your classmates and are reasonably certain that you are presenting a true majority opinion.

In addition, in informative writing situations you will often need to present information to audiences with varying levels of knowledge about your subject. Think, for example, of the safety information recited by flight attendants to airline passengers before a plane is allowed to take off. Even though many of the passengers have heard this presentation multiple times, some passengers may be hearing it for the first time. The airlines have a legal responsibility to give their passengers this information. They try to do so in a clear, concise, and helpful manner.

Reading, Inquiry, and Research:
Learning from Texts That Inform

The following reading selections are examples of informative writing. We think you will enjoy and learn from the selections that your instructor asks you to read.

As you read these informative selections, consider the following questions:

- What makes this reading selection useful and interesting? What strategies does its author use to make the information understandable for readers?

- What parts of the reading could be improved by the use of charts, photographs, or tables? Why? How?

- How can you use the techniques of informative writing exemplified here in your writing?

As you read an essay and respond to the questions that follow it, take notes, jot down questions, and make observations about the selection in a journal, preferably in a computer file. Then, if you want to use the information in your writing, you will already have the main points in a digital format.

HAROLD PETERSON

From *The Man Who Invented Baseball*

Born in Illinois, Harold Peterson graduated from Harvard College, was a reporter for *Sports Illustrated*, and is the author of *The Last of the Mountain Men* (1969). In *The Man Who Invented Baseball* (1973), Peterson tells the story of Alexander Joy Cartwright and his contributions to baseball. By describing how Cartwright invented the rules of baseball, Peterson's book dispels the widely accepted cultural myth that our national pastime was invented by one Abner Doubleday. This essay is excerpted from the book. As you read this selection, consider what you thought you knew about baseball . . . that you learn is not correct after all.

On a quiet, sunny morning in the spring of 1845, six years after   1
Abner Doubleday did not invent baseball in Elihu Phinney's Cooperstown cow pasture (or anywhere else), a black-whiskered twenty-five-year-old volunteer fireman named Alexander Joy Cartwright, Jr., walked off the pleasantly shaded Eastern Post Road, an old maple- and oak-lined New England-bound country lane on Manhattan Island, into a dewy meadow.

**Alexander Joy
Cartwright**

The meadow, which was situated under the rocky schisted promi- 2
nence of Murray Hill called the Inclenherg, lay next to a pastoral little
lake, Sunfish Pond. Stagecoaches had but recently stopped here to
water their horses on the way to the little villages of Yorkville and
Harlem and, eventually, to Bostontown. Through the meadow ran a
large, pretty brook, much inhabited by trout and fishermen. Named Old
Wreck Kill for a pioneer Dutch ship sunk off its mouth, the brook rose
in a large crystal spring among the crags and hills of the interior, rushed
in little waterfalls through the boulders and fields and vernal green of
mid-Manhattan, and tumbled into turbulent Kipps Bay on the glisten-
ing East River. . . .

This one cool, warming morning burly Alexander Cartwright joined 3
a group of young men at their usual play, a lighthearted game of ball
remembered from their childhood—a game, like most children's games,
whose antecedents were mysterious and whose rules were subject to
constant change and much laughing dispute. He had often done so
before. But this particular day he swung off the brightly lacquered, elab-
orately decorated omnibus coach which clopped up the Post Road with a
carefully drafted diagram in his hand. Stilling the friendly badinage that
greeted his arrival (for he was a favorite among his friends, the young
businessmen of the city), he beckoned his fellows to gather around.
Soberly, he announced that he had a Plan.

Good-natured hoots and cries of derision met this declaration. It 4
was amid considerable cheerful raillery that Cartwright stationed his
friends at positions around a perfect ninety-foot square and placed the
batter at the fourth "home" base instead of in a special batter's box several feet toward the first base. Even Cartwright smiled at the jibes as he
solemnly dictated that there be only three men in the outfield, removed
two roving short fielders, put one of them at an entirely new position he
called Short Stop, and abolished one of the two catchers behind the batter. But "Alick" was so popular and so persistent that they decided to
humor him.

Whoops of delight replaced teasing complaint after a few ground 5
balls had been hit to the basemen, so precisely located by Cartwright
that their positions have remained almost exactly the same ever since.
Throwing to bases to make outs—as he prescribed—instead of throwing wildly at dodging runners tightened and rationalized the game
remarkably; it immediately ceased to be a mere children's amusement.
Another sophistication was Alick's new rule of "three hands out, all
out." Now, when only three men (instead of the whole team) need be
retired to end an inning, scoring runs became difficult enough to require
some skill and care.

Moreover, the rapid succession of innings rescued Cartwright's game 6
of Base Ball from the dawdling pace of cricket. Unlike cricket, it encouraged and rewarded good fielding by offering an imminent prospect of getting in out of the sun and getting a chance to hit. Another revolutionary inspiration, the provision of foul lines, accomplished the same laudable purposes by concentrating most of the action within a ninety-degree quadrant of the field. . . .

Cartwright also prescribed flat bases instead of the casually arranged 7
posts or random rocks, found on the site of the game, which had served in the past. There should be only nine men on a side, instead of the irregular mob usually scattered about. They would bat in a regular order, prescribed before the game.

He thought of some very modern small refinements, too. A "balk" 8
by the pitcher allowed the runner to advance. A run scored before a third force-out did not count. Later he originated the idea of the nine-inning game. (Before that innovation, matches ended when one side had scored twenty-one runs or "aces.") But this notion was not immediately accepted.

The game that Cartwright and his friends tried out beneath Murray 9
Hill was phenomenally successful from the start. The standardized shape and dimensions of the playing field meant that teams could meet on equal terms whenever they played, as did the standardized rules. But the best evidence of Alexander's inventive intuition was his setting the distance between bases at ninety feet. He was exactly right, uncannily so. Five feet less would have given base runners an enormous advantage. Five feet more would have given infielders too much time to scoop up a ground ball and get it to the first baseman. But at ninety feet, plays at first base are decided by a step.

Cartwright's innovations meant the beginning of fast team play, the 10
development of the art of the shortstop (who was needed because most balls are hit between second and third bases) and the first baseman (who was the least important baseman in the old games). It necessitated the accurate umpiring of games, suddenly essential because of the closeness of plays. The effect of newly vital umpiring was to bring order to all aspects of the game. Relatively uncredited by the most diligent archivists of the world's most documented sport, almost unknown to fans who have computer memories for statistics, long vanished and forgotten, Alexander Cartwright is the father of modern baseball.

And baseball, what of that? Of what importance is that? 11

Baseball is a social phenomenon. It was a social phenomenon in the 12
nineteenth century, when it was the central fact of most American men's leisure, almost the only way they knew how to play. It was a social

phenomenon in the early twentieth century, when it became an obses-sion, the very originator and prototype of a radical change in attitudes: the sea change of Americans from vigorous, unself-conscious amateur jack-of-all-trades participants into the sedentary, self-conscious, critical spectators they are now. Exactly one full century after Cartwright "invented" it, it was certainly a social phenomenon when soldiers in the biggest and bloodiest war in history said in real, recorded words that they were fighting for Mom's apple pie and for—yes—baseball.

13 If you don't understand where baseball came from and why it captured Americans so completely, you don't quite understand the United States. (Since nobody but an American understands baseball, a corollary—one supposes—is that only Americans fully understand the United States. Which is correct.)

14 Not that baseball is like tobacco or the turkey, a native weed or fauna sprung direct from our peculiar soil. The myth that Abner Doubleday invented baseball is one of the most amusingly fraudulent pieces of manufactured history extant. Yet what it lacks in authenticity it amply makes up in obstinate durability, like many myths. Ask who invented baseball at any bar in Brooklyn, Hoboken, St. Louis, or Sacramento. Your average incipient inebriate, who may have trouble remembering the name of the second President, his Senator or his wife's sister, will instantly ejaculate, "Abner Doubleday." Ask any stan-dard, informed, educated quasi-intellectual. Whether he last suffered baseball to cross his mind sometime before the Braves left Boston or whether he just this morning unfavorably compared the style of the 1972 Mets with the 1962 Originals, chances are he will say, "Abner Doubleday, wasn't it?" Better yet, ask any average major leaguer. If he talks at all, he will probably mention Doubleday. Some women have even heard the name. Doubleday, that is.

15 Apart from the fact that he never had anything to do with baseball, General Doubleday did make a nice figurehead. Handsome, distinguished, he was the holder of a heroic Civil War record that dated from Fort Sumter, where he was credited with firing the first Union shot. At the close of the first day at Gettysburg, he commanded the entire Union Army. He was also an excellent writer and a commanding public speaker. Unfortunately, in all his extensive writings and speeches there is not a solitary reference to baseball. In fact, there is no evidence that he ever played or even saw the game.

16 Albert Goodwill Spalding, the superb pioneer professional player for the Chicago White Sox and the Rockford Forest Citys, founder of the sporting-good firm, deserves the blame for Doubleday's odd immortali-zation. Henry Chadwick, the first sportswriter to cover baseball (he saw

his first game in 1848), had written numerous, now forgotten, historical sketches, the last in 1903, in which he traced the game's origins to the old English game of rounders. Somewhat unfortunately, the periodical in which these sketches appeared was Spalding's *Baseball Guide.* Spalding so hated the idea that any part of the sport might have started outside the United States that he virtually drafted as inventor the poor general, who would have much preferred to be remembered for his military exploits but who, having died in 1893, was helpless to defend himself.

The bit of fiction that replaced Cartwright with Doubleday was a   17
report made by the Mills Commission, formed by Organized Baseball in 1904 "to determine the origins of the great American pastime." Its chairman was starchy, long-faced old Abraham G. Mills, who had been third president of the National League and was a close friend of Spalding. The mission of the Mills Commission was to purify baseball of any taint of British influence. It was made up of seven men. Among them were Mills himself and two old-time players who had also become involved with the manufacture of baseball equipment, Al Reach and George Wright. . . .

Whatever historical material the Mills Commission accumulated   18
was conveniently destroyed in a fire that burned the office of the American Sports Publicity Company. Mills issued the report alone in 1907. He was the only person to write it. The report, not surprisingly, concluded that baseball was a purely American sport, not derived from rounders. What was surprising—confabulating, in fact—was the astounding information that the method of playing baseball had been devised by Major General Doubleday at Cooperstown in upstate New York in 1839.

The entire document was a classic example, as it will soon become   19
abundantly clear, of instant improvised history. It depended almost entirely on the uncorroborated ramblings of octogenarian Abner Graves. The one, the only proof that assigned to Doubleday the mysterious paternity of baseball was Graves's vague remark that, sixty-eight years earlier, "Doubleday improved Town Ball to limit the number of players, as many were hurt in collisions" and that "Doubleday called the game 'Base Ball' for there were four bases to it."

Graves said that Doubleday had been a boy, a Green Select School   20
student, playing daily in Cooperstown fields, when he made his momentous limitation in the interest of public safety. In reality, in 1839 Doubleday was a second-year cadet at distant West Point. And he didn't even get a summer vacation.

That merely begins to summarize the cornucopia of reasons why   21
Doubleday couldn't have created baseball. But at the time, no one cared.

Although it already had James Fenimore Cooper, author of *Leather-stocking Tales, The Last of the Mohicans, The Deerslayer,* and *The Pathfinder* to vaunt as native son, the beautiful village of Cooperstown gladly suppressed its surprise and clutched another claim to greatness to its breast. Pretty soon its citizens were remembering that the young'uns had indeed customarily played in Mr. Phinney's pasture and deciding that it was there young Abner, bless his heart, had first felt solicitude for the victims of town-ball conditions.   22

Of course, when organized baseball again cranked up the publicity machines to celebrate the glorious centennial of this event in 1939 and decided that a regulation field should be constructed and a game played between major-league teams on the site, hoary tradition was not allowed to conflict unreasonably with practicality. A field a couple of miles removed from Phinney's farm but more convenient to the center of town and the business district was deemed more suitable a location for the stadium. Phinney's pasture, a pretty spot between Route 80 and Ostego Lake, remains an unglorified bean field.   23

That was one of the easier parts of the "centennial" observation. A little further digging in the dirt about the roots of the national institution very rapidly became acutely embarrassing to all concerned. Exactly how embarrassing will be made obvious. Suffice it to say for the moment that Cooperstown nearly lost not only its legend but also the game, the celebration, one of the world's more famous museums, and a steady flood of tourist business that continues to the present day. Cooperstown and baseball reinterred the skeleton almost as quickly as they exhumed it and smoothed over the ground remarkably effectively. But it took some time for the snickering to subside. For quite a while, the truth was out.   24

Abner Doubleday didn't invent baseball. Baseball invented Abner Doubleday.   25

QUESTIONS FOR WRITING AND DISCUSSION: LEARNING OUTCOMES

Rhetorical Knowledge: The Writer's Situation and Rhetoric

1. **Audience:** What audience is the information in this reading selection intended for? How effective is Peterson at addressing this audience? What can you point to in the article to support your position?

2. **Purpose:** What is Peterson's primary purpose in writing about this topic? What other purposes might he have?

3. **Voice and Tone:** What can you point to in this selection that gives Peterson his *ethos* in writing about this subject? How does his tone contribute to—or detract from—his credibility? Peterson often writes in a humorous manner—some might call his tone tongue-in-cheek. What can you cite from the essay to illustrate his tone?

4. **Responsibility:** In writing about this topic, Peterson is debunking a long-held myth of American social history. What is his responsibility to his readers in this situation? How well does he handle it?

5. **Context and Format:** This reading selection was excerpted from a book that was published in 1969, the year of the "Miracle Mets" and an era of widespread public affection for the game of baseball. How do you think Peterson's information was received at that time? How do you think today's sports fans would receive it?

Critical Thinking: Your Personal Response

1. What was your response when you read that Abner Doubleday did not invent baseball? Why? What are some other "truths" that you believed in at one time—only to learn that they really are not true?

2. What was the most interesting information in this selection? Why? The least interesting? Why?

3. Peterson writes that "Throwing to bases to make outs—as he prescribed—instead of throwing wildly at dodging runners tightened and rationalized the game remarkably; it immediately ceased to be a mere children's amusement" (paragraph 7). How did you respond to the information that when baseball was originally played, whoever caught the ball evidently threw it at the base runner?

4. What information in this selection surprised you? Why?

Critical Thinking: The Writer's Ideas

1. Despite the publication of Peterson's book in 1969, the idea that Abner Doubleday invented baseball still persists. Why do you think this is so?

2. Peterson notes that baseball fans in the mid-nineteenth century did not want to believe that the game had its origins in England. What might be a similar situation today, in sports or in another area of popular culture?

3. Peterson notes that much was gained when Cartwright regularized the rules of the game of baseball. Was anything lost? If so, what?

Composing Processes and Knowledge of Conventions: The Writer's Strategies

1. Peterson provides a lot of details and information in his text. How do those details add to the effectiveness of this selection?

2. How does Peterson organize his information? How effective is this method of organization? Why?

3. What is your opinion of the conclusion?

Inquiry and Research: Ideas for Further Exploration

1. Conduct some research in the library and on the Internet on the origin of your favorite sport. What myths about its origins, if any, did you find? In no more than two pages, report on what you learn.

2. Find out how cricket is played, and in no more than two pages, describe the similarities and differences between it and modern baseball.

3. Conduct further research on baseball, and write a brief paper explaining any changes that have been made to the game during the past twenty-five years.

4. Peterson writes that "Cartwright's innovations meant the beginning of fast team play, the development of the art of the shortstop (who was needed because most balls are hit between second and third bases) and the first baseman (who was the least important baseman in the old games)" (paragraph 10). In a brief paper, explain why "most balls are hit between second and third bases."

5. Using online information available at www.mlb.com, confirm or refute the assertion that most balls are hit between second and third bases. Hint: You could look at assists and put-outs.

CAROL EZZELL

Clocking Cultures

Carol Ezzell has been a science writer since the early 1990s and currently works as a writer and an editor at *Scientific American,* specializing in biology and biomedicine. She has also worked for *Nature, Science News, Bio/World* and the *Journal of NIH Research.* An award-winning writer, Ezzell has been recognized for her science journalism by the National Association of Science Writers and the Pan American Health Organization. In 2000, she won a Science in Society Journalism award for her article "Care for a Dying Continent," about how AIDS has affected women and girls in Zimbabwe. This article was originally published in the September 2002 issue of *Scientific American.*

Show up an hour late in Brazil, and no one bats an eyelash. But keep someone in New York City waiting for five or 10 minutes, and you have some explaining to do. Time is elastic in many cultures but snaps taut in others. Indeed, the way members of a culture perceive and use time reflects their society's priorities and even their own worldview.

Social scientists have recorded wide differences in the pace of life in various countries and in how societies view time—whether as an arrow piercing the future or as a revolving wheel in which past, present and future cycle endlessly. Some cultures conflate time and space: the Australian Aborigines' concept of the "Dreamtime" encompasses not only a creation myth but a method of finding their way around the countryside. Interestingly, however, some views of time—such as the idea that it is acceptable for a more powerful person to keep someone of lower status waiting—cut across cultural differences and seem to be found universally.

The study of time and society can be divided into the pragmatic and the cosmological. On the practical side, in the 1950s anthropologist Edward T. Hall, Jr., wrote that the rules of social time constitute a "silent language" for a given culture. The rules might not always be made explicit, he stated, but they "exist in the air. . . . They are either familiar and comfortable or unfamiliar and wrong."

In 1955 he described in *Scientific American* how differing perceptions of time can lead to misunderstandings between people from separate cultures. "An ambassador who has been kept waiting for more than half an hour by a foreign visitor needs to understand that if his visitor 'just mutters an apology' this is not necessarily an insult," Hall wrote. The time system in the foreign country may be composed of different basic units, so that the visitor is not as late as he may appear to us. You must know the time system of the country to know at what point apologies are really due. . . . Different cultures simply place different values on the time units.

Most cultures around the world now have watches and calendars, uniting the majority of the globe in the same general rhythm of time. But that doesn't mean we all march to the same beat. "One of the beauties of studying time is that it's a wonderful window on culture," says Robert V. Levine, a social psychologist at California State University at Fresno. "You get answers on what cultures value and believe in. You get a really good idea of what's important to people." Levine and his colleagues have conducted so-called pace-of-life studies in 31 countries. In *A Geography of Time*, published in 1997, Levine describes how he ranked the countries by using three measures: walking speed on urban sidewalks, how quickly postal clerks could fulfill a request for a common stamp, and the accuracy of public clocks. Based on these variables, he concluded that the five fastest-paced countries are Switzerland, Ireland, Germany, Japan and Italy; the five slowest are Syria, El Salvador, Brazil, Indonesia and Mexico. The U.S., at 16th, ranks near the middle. Kevin K. Birth, an anthropologist at Queens College, has examined time perceptions in Trinidad. Birth's 1999 book, *Any Time Is Trinidad Time: Social Meanings and Temporal Consciousness*, refers to a commonly used phrase to excuse lateness. In that country, Birth observes, "if you have a meeting at 6:00 at night, people show up at 6:45 or 7:00 and say, 'Any time is Trinidad time.'" When it comes to business, however, that loose approach to timeliness works only for the people with power. A boss can show up late and toss off "any time is Trinidad time," but underlings are expected to be more punctual. For them, the saying goes, "time is time." Birth adds that the tie between power and waiting time is true for many other cultures as well.

The nebulous nature of time makes it hard for anthropologists and 6 social psychologists to study. "You can't simply go into a society, walk up to some poor soul and say, 'Tell me about your notions of time,'" Birth says. "People don't really have an answer to that. You have to come up with other ways to find out."

Birth attempted to get at how Trinidadians value time by exploring 7 how closely their society links time and money. He surveyed rural residents and found that farmers—whose days are dictated by natural events, such as sunrise—did not recognize the phrases "time is money," "budget your time" or "time management," even though they had satellite TV and were familiar with Western popular culture. But tailors in the same areas were aware of such notions. Birth concluded that wage work altered the tailors' views of time. "The ideas of associating time with money are not found globally," he says, "but are attached to your job and the people you work with."

How people deal with time on a day-to-day basis often has nothing 8 to do with how they conceive of time as an abstract entity. "There's often a disjunction between how a culture views the mythology of time and how they think about time in their daily lives," Birth asserts. "We don't think of Stephen Hawking's theories as we go about our daily lives."

Some cultures do not draw neat distinctions between the past, pres- 9 ent and future. Australian Aborigines, for instance, believe that their ancestors crawled out of the earth during the Dreamtime. The ancestors "sang" the world into existence as they moved about naming each feature and living thing, which brought them into being. Even today, an entity does not exist unless an Aborigine "sings" it.

Ziauddin Sardar, a British Muslim author and critic, has written about   10
time and Islamic cultures, particularly the fundamentalist sect Wahhabism.
Muslims "always carry the past with them," claims Sardar, who is editor of
the journal *Futures* and visiting professor of postcolonial studies at City University, London. "In Islam, time is a tapestry incorporating the past, present
and future. The past is ever present." The followers of Wahhabism, which is
practiced in Saudi Arabia and by Osama bin Laden, seek to re-create the
idyllic days of the prophet Muhammad's life. "The worldly future dimension
has been suppressed" by them, Sardar says. "They have romanticized a particular vision of the past. All they are doing is trying to replicate that past."

Sardar asserts that the West has "colonized" time by spreading the   11
expectation that life should become better as time passes: "If you colonize time, you also colonize the future. If you think of time as an arrow,
of course you think of the future as progress, going in one direction. But
different people may desire different futures."

QUESTIONS FOR WRITING AND DISCUSSION: LEARNING OUTCOMES

Rhetorical Knowledge: The Writer's Situation and Rhetoric

1. **Audience:** Who is the audience for Ezzell's essay? How can you tell?

2. **Purpose:** What realm (academic, professional, civic, or personal) does Ezzell's essay best fit into? Why?

3. **Voice and Tone:** How would you describe Ezell's tone in this essay? How does her tone contribute to her believability?

4. **Responsibility:** Ezzell discusses the notions of time across different cultures in her essay. How respectful of those cultures is she? Why do you think that?

5. **Context and Format:** This essay was published during a time of worldwide fears of terrorism. How does that context affect your reading of this essay?

Critical Thinking: Your Personal Response

1. What is the most interesting piece of information in Ezzell's article? Why? The least interesting? Why?

2. What evidence supports the observation that Americans are living a fast-paced lifestyle? Reread paragraph 5, where Ezzell reports a study in which

the United States ranks "16th . . . near the middle" in pace-of-life. To what extent do you agree? Why?

3. Ezzell writes that "Interestingly, however, some views of time—such as the idea that it is acceptable for a more powerful person to keep someone of lower status waiting—cut across cultural differences and seem to be found universally" (Paragraph 2). To what extent do you agree? Why?

4. How does time operate in your life? When does it control what you do and when you are allowed to do it? When have you pushed back against time's constraints?

Critical Thinking: The Writer's Ideas

1. What is the main idea—or thesis—in Ezzell's essay? How well does Ezzell provide support for this idea? Why do you think that?

2. Ezzell writes that "Most cultures around the world now have watches and calendars, uniting the majority of the globe in the same general rhythm of time. But that doesn't mean we all march to the same beat" (Paragraph 5). Consider the people you know. Describe the "beat" they "march to."

3. Ezzell notes that some cultures perceive time as "a revolving wheel in which past, present and future cycle endlessly" (Paragraph 2). Using this metaphor, think of the passage of time in your life. What insights does this metaphor give you?

Composing Processes and Knowledge of Conventions: The Writer's Strategies

1. Ezzell uses information and quotations from experts throughout her essay. How does she present this information? What does the presence of these experts add to the essay?

2. Prepare a quick outline of this essay. What does this outline reveal about the way Ezzell has organized her information for readers?

3. Comment on the opening and concluding paragraphs of the essay. How effective are they? Why?

4. Ezzell uses examples from different cultures throughout her essay. Point out one example that you think is especially effective, and explain why it works as well as it does.

Inquiry and Research: Ideas for Further Exploration

1. Prepare a list of questions that you still have about time and cultures. Interview several of your friends, asking them the questions that you

have listed, and then explain, in no more than two pages, their answers to your questions.

2. Ezzell writes that "Sardar asserts that the West has 'colonized' time by spreading the expectation that life should become better as time passes: 'If you colonize time, you also colonize the future. If you think of time as an arrow, of course you think of the future as progress, going in one direction. But different people may desire different futures'" (paragraph 11). In a brief essay, explain whether or not you agree with Sardar's assertion—and why.

KATIE HAFNER

Growing *Wikipedia* Revises Its "Anyone Can Edit" Policy

Katie Hafner has written widely about technology. Her books include *Cyberpunk: Outlaws and Hackers on the Computer Frontier* (with John Markoff, 1991), *The House at the Bridge: A Story of Modern Germany* (1995), *Where Wizards Stay Up Late: The Origins of the Internet* (with Matthew Lyon, 1996), and *The Well: A Story of Love, Death and Real Life in the Seminal Online Community* (2001). She writes regularly for the *New York Times* and *Newsweek*. She also has written articles for *Wired,* the *New Republic,* and *Esquire*. As a student, she studied German literature and culture. This article, published in the *New York Times* in 2006, concerns *Wikipedia,* an online encyclopedia. As you read Hafner's article, think about your experience with conducting research—and how you decide what is correct and accurate information and what is not.

W ikipedia is the online encyclopedia that "anyone can edit." Unless you want to edit the entries on Albert Einstein, human rights in China or Christina Aguilera. 1

Wikipedia's come-one, come-all invitation to write and edit articles, and the surprisingly successful results, have captured the public imagination. But it is not the experiment in freewheeling collective creativity it might seem to be, because maintaining so much openness inevitably involves some tradeoffs. 2

At its core, *Wikipedia* is not just a reference work but also an online community that has built itself a bureaucracy of sorts—one that, in response to well-publicized problems with some entries, has recently grown more elaborate. It has a clear power structure that gives volunteer 3 administrators the authority to exercise editorial control, delete unsuitable articles and protect those that are vulnerable to vandalism.

Those measures can put some entries outside of the "anyone can edit" realm. The list changes rapidly, but as of yesterday, the entries for Einstein and Ms. Aguilera were among 82 that administrators had "protected" from all editing, mostly because of repeated vandalism or disputes over what should be said. Another 179 entries—including those for George W. Bush, Islam and Adolf Hitler—were "semi-protected," open to editing only by people who had been registered at the site for at least four days. . . .   4

While these measures may appear to undermine the site's democratic principles, Jimmy Wales, *Wikipedia*'s founder, notes that protection is usually temporary and affects a tiny fraction of the 1.2 million entries on the English-language site.   5

"Protection is a tool for quality control, but it hardly defines *Wikipedia*," Mr. Wales said. "What does define *Wikipedia* is the volunteer community and the open participation."   6

From the start, Mr. Wales gave the site a clear mission: to offer free knowledge to everybody on the planet. At the same time, he put in place a set of rules and policies that he continues to promote, like the need to present information with a neutral point of view.   7

The system seems to be working. *Wikipedia* is now the Web's third-most-popular news and information source, beating the sites of CNN and Yahoo News, according to Nielsen *NetRatings*.   8

The bulk of the writing and editing on *Wikipedia* is done by a geographically diffuse group of 1,000 or so regulars, many of whom are administrators on the site.   9

"A lot of people think of *Wikipedia* as being 10 million people, each adding one sentence," Mr. Wales said. "But really the vast majority of work is done by this small core community."   10

The administrators are all volunteers, most of them in their 20's. They are in constant communication—in real-time online chats, on "talk" pages connected to each entry and via Internet mailing lists. The volunteers share the job of watching for vandalism, or what Mr. Wales called "drive-by nonsense." Customized software—written by volunteers—also monitors changes to articles.   11

Mr. Wales calls vandalism to the encyclopedia "a minimal problem, a dull roar in the background." Yet early this year, amid heightened publicity about false information on the site, the community decided to introduce semi-protection of some articles. The four-day waiting period is meant to function something like the one imposed on gun buyers.   12

Once the assaults have died down, the semi-protected page is often reset to "anyone can edit" mode. An entry on Bill Gates was   13 semi-protected for just a few days in January, but some entries, like the article on President Bush, stay that way indefinitely. Other semi-protected subjects as of yesterday were Opus Dei, Tony Blair and sex.

To some critics, protection policies make a mockery of the "anyone can edit" notion. 14

"As *Wikipedia* has tried to improve its quality, it's beginning to look more and more like an editorial structure," said Nicholas Carr, a technology writer who recently criticized *Wikipedia* on his blog. "To say that great work can be created by an army of amateurs with very little control is a distortion of what *Wikipedia* really is." 15

But Mr. Wales dismissed such criticism, saying there had always been protections and filters on the site. 16

Wikipedia's defenders say it usually takes just a few days for all but the most determined vandals to retreat. 17

"A cooling-off period is a wonderful mediative technique," said Ross Mayfield, chief executive of a company called Socialtext that is based on the same editing technology that *Wikipedia* uses. 18

Full protection often results from a "revert war," in which users madly change the wording back and forth. In such cases, an administrator usually steps in and freezes the page until the warring parties can settle their differences in another venue, usually the talk page for the entry. The Christina Aguilera entry was frozen this week after fans of the singer fought back against one user's efforts to streamline it. 19

Much discussion of *Wikipedia* has focused on its accuracy. Last year, an article in the journal *Nature* concluded that the incidence of errors in *Wikipedia* was only slightly higher than in *Encyclopaedia Britannica*. Officials at *Britannica* angrily disputed the findings. 20

"To be able to do an encyclopedia without having the ability to differentiate between experts and the general public is very, very difficult," said Jorge Cauz, the president of *Britannica*, whose subscription-based online version receives a small fraction of the traffic that *Wikipedia* gets. 21

Intentional mischief can go undetected for long periods. In the article about John Seigenthaler Sr., who served in the Kennedy administration, a suggestion that he was involved in the assassinations of both John F. and Robert Kennedy was on the site for more than four months before Mr. Seigenthaler discovered it. He wrote an op-ed article in *USA Today* about the incident, calling *Wikipedia* "a flawed and irresponsible research tool." 22

Yet Wikipedians say that in general the accuracy of an article grows organically. At first, said Wayne Saewyc, a *Wikipedia* volunteer in Vancouver, British Columbia, "everything is edited mercilessly by idiots who do stupid and weird things to it." But as the article grows, and citations slowly accumulate, Mr. Saewyc said, the article becomes increasingly accurate. 23

Wikipedians often speak of how powerfully liberating their first contribution felt. Kathleen Walsh, 23, a recent college graduate who majored in music, recalled the first time she added to an article on the contrabassoon. 24

"I wrote a paragraph of text and there it was," recalled Ms. Walsh. "You write all these pages for college and no one ever sees it, and you write for *Wikipedia* and the whole world sees it, instantly." 25

Ms. Walsh is an administrator, a post that others nominated her for in recognition of her contributions to the site. She monitors a list of newly created pages, half of which, she said, end up being good candidates for deletion. Many are "nonsense pages created by kids, like 'Michael is a big dork,'" she said. 26

Ms. Walsh also serves on the 14-member arbitration committee, which she describes as "the last resort" for disputes on *Wikipedia*. 27

Like so many Web-based successes, *Wikipedia* started more or less by accident. 28

Six years ago, Mr. Wales, who built up a comfortable nest egg in a brief career as an options trader, started an online encyclopedia called Nupedia.com, with content to be written by experts. But after attracting only a few dozen articles, Mr. Wales started *Wikipedia* on the side. It grew exponentially. 29

For the first year or so, Mr. Wales paid the expenses out of his own pocket. Now the Wikimedia Foundation, the nonprofit organization that supports *Wikipedia*, is financed primarily through donations, most in the $50 to $100 range. 30

As the donations have risen, so have the costs. The foundation's annual budget doubled in the last year, to $1.5 million, and traffic has grown sharply. Search engines like Google, which often turn up *Wikipedia* entries at the top of their results, are a big contributor to the site's traffic, but it is increasingly a first stop for knowledge seekers. 31

Mr. Wales shares the work of running *Wikipedia* with the administrators and four paid employees of the foundation. Although many decisions are made by consensus within the community, Mr. Wales steps in when an issue is especially contentious. "It's not always obvious when something becomes policy," he said. "One way is when I say it is." 32

Mr. Wales is a true believer in the power of wiki page-editing technology, which predates *Wikipedia*. In late 2004, Mr. Wales started Wikia, a commercial start-up financed by venture capital that lets people build Web sites based around a community of interest. Wiki 24, for instance, is an unofficial encyclopedia for the television show "24." Unlike *Wikipedia*, the site carries advertising. 33

Mr. Wales, 39, lives with his wife and daughter in St. Petersburg, Fla., where the foundation is based. But Mr. Wales's main habitat these days, 34 he said, is the inside of airplanes. He travels constantly, giving speeches to reverential audiences and visiting Wikipedians around the world.

Wikipedia has inspired its share of imitators. A group of scientists has 35 started the peer-reviewed *Encyclopedia of Earth*, and *Congresspedia* is a new encyclopedia with an article about each member of Congress.

But beyond the world of reference works, *Wikipedia* has become a 36 symbol of the potential of the Web.

"It can tell us a lot about the future of knowledge creation, which 37 will depend much less on individual heroism and more on collaboration," said Mitchell Kapor, a computer industry pioneer who is president of the Open Source Applications Foundation.

Zephyr Teachout, a lawyer in Burlington, Vt., who is involved with 38 *Congresspedia*, said *Wikipedia* was reminiscent of old-fashioned civic groups like the Grange, whose members took individual responsibility for the organization's livelihood.

"It blows open what's possible," said Ms. Teachout. "What I hope is 39 that these kinds of things lead to thousands of other experiments like this encyclopedia, which we never imagined could be produced in this way."

QUESTIONS FOR WRITING AND DISCUSSION: LEARNING OUTCOMES

Rhetorical Knowledge: The Writer's Situation and Rhetoric

1. **Audience:** How would you describe the audience that Hafner had in mind when she wrote this article?

2. **Purpose:** What purpose(s) would someone have for reading Hafner's article? In addition to its informative purpose, how is Hafner's writing also persuasive? How might it alter readers' perceptions of *Wikipedia*?

3. **Voice and Tone:** How does Hafner establish her authority? To what extent do you believe what Hafner has to say? How does her tone contribute to her credibility? Why?

4. **Responsibility:** One important quality of any successful informative text is *clarity*, especially when the author is dealing with a complex subject. How does Hafner meet her obligation to her readers to be clear? Where might she have been clearer?

5. **Context and Format:** Given Hafner's topic, it seems natural that her piece appeared in an online format, with hyperlinks, but it also appeared in the print edition of the *New York Times*. How does appearing in both

print and online formats affect the credibility of Hafner's comments? Why?

Critical Thinking: Your Personal Response

1. How would you feel if you came across an online entry about you, one that was written without your knowledge or permission? How might you react if that entry included false information? What steps might you take to solve the problem? What if the information about you was on *Wikipedia* and no one would correct it?

2. Have you ever looked up a "fact" only to discover later that the information was incorrect?

3. For your college papers, will you use *Wikipedia* as a research source? How might you evaluate the information you find on it, now that you have read the information in Hafner's essay?

Critical Thinking: The Writer's Ideas

1. What are the three most interesting pieces of information you learned from Hafner's text? Why are they interesting?

2. What in Hafner's text do you want to learn more about? What questions do you still have?

3. What solutions might you propose to address the problem of inaccurate or malicious information on *Wikipedia*? Or should this problem be solved? How well or poorly does such an open informational system serve the public?

4. Hafner addresses the delicate balance between the importance of accuracy and the advantages of openness—that anyone can contribute to *Wikipedia*. If you were an editor of *Wikipedia*, how would you maintain that balance? How would you specifically handle the dispute about the entry for Christina Aguilera?

Composing Processes and Knowledge of Conventions: The Writer's Strategies

1. How effective is Hafner's use of the anecdote about John Seigenthaler Sr. to illustrate a larger problem with *Wikipedia*'s accuracy? What writing strategy, if any, might have been more effective here?

2. Hafner covers a good deal of ground in this reading selection, yet she has a central idea. What is her central idea, or focus? How does she maintain it?

3. Because she is a journalist writing for a newspaper, Hafner cites her sources within the body of her article rather than using a formal system of documentation. How do her sources lend credibility to her writing? What other sources of information might she have cited?

Inquiry and Research: Ideas for Further Exploration

1. What questions do you have after reading Hafner's essay? Spend a few minutes and jot down as many as you can.

2. Conduct a search (at your school library or on the Web), focusing on one of the questions you generated above. Try to find an answer to your question, and write a two-page paper explaining your answer.

3. Research a concept or issue on the Web. Make a list of the information you collect that seems contradictory. How might you reconcile those inconsistencies, to figure out what is accurate?

4. Peruse *Wikipedia* to see if any of your favorite celebrities, places, concepts, or events is missing. Either alone or with classmates, compose an entry and submit it to *Wikipedia*. If anyone revises your entry, ask, "Why would someone make this particular change?"

 ## Thinking about Visuals That Inform

Tables, graphs, and charts are all excellent ways to inform readers about statistical data. These visual tools appear frequently in various forms of informative writing and are used in a wide variety of ways.

For more on using visuals in your own writing, see Chapter 17.

Figure 6.3 on page 218 is a bar graph showing the national debt of the United States. As you look at this bar graph, consider these questions about the effective use of bar graphs and other visuals to inform readers:

- How do you react to this graph?

- How do you comprehend numbers that are so large? What does this information mean to you, personally? How might a table or another type of chart be used to convey this information?

- How do you think our (rapidly) growing national debt might affect you and your family in the future?

- Is this visual neutral, or does it have a point of view? Look for other visuals that describe the national debt, either in a print publication or on the Web. How are those visuals used?

FIGURE 6.3   National Debt from 1940 to Present

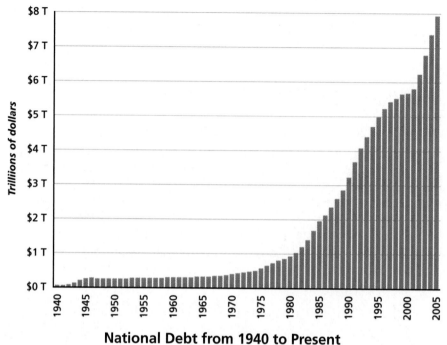

National Debt from 1940 to Present

Source: U.S. National Debt Clock
http://www.brillig.com/debt_clock/

 Drawing on Research to Inform Your Readers

While you can sometimes draw exclusively on your experience in a piece of informative writing, especially in personal writing contexts, in academic, professional, and civic writing situations you will usually need to include information gained from outside research.

Assume, for example, that you would like to inform a group of your friends about a local homeless shelter. You would probably want to list the services the shelter provides, indicate the various ways people can become involved with the shelter, and cite financial data on what percentage of each cash donation goes to support the shelter's clients. To provide this information to your readers, you would need to conduct some form of research.

Research provides you with the statistical data, examples, and expert testimony that will enable you to give your audience enough information, and the right kind of information, on your topic. As with any other aspect of your writing, the kind and amount of research you will need to do will depend on your rhetorical situation: who your audience is and what you are trying to accomplish. If you are writing a paper for a sociology course on aspects of male group behavior, you would need to locate articles in scholarly journals, as well as statistical data, which you could present in a chart. If you are writing about a problem in your community, you would need to read articles and government documents, and you might also interview government officials. As you work on the scenario you've chosen (see pp. 192–96), you could conduct several kinds of research:

- For Scenario 1 or 3, where you are researching a problem on campus or in your community, you will need to conduct interviews with students or with people affected by the problem. As an alternative, you might consider conducting a survey of a representative sample of students or people within the community. You will also need to observe the problem.

- For Scenario 2, where you are researching a topic that interests you, you will need to conduct preliminary research in the library and on the Web to get an overall sense of your topic. If you are researching a topic in one of your courses, reading about your topic in your course textbook, and looking for references in your text, is a good first step. Your course text also can provide you with keywords that you can use to search for further information in a library database or on a search engine.

For more on conducting research and citing your sources properly, see Chapters 19 and 20.

◢ Writing Processes

As you work on the assignment scenario you have chosen, keep in mind the qualities of an effective informative paper (see pp. 197–98). Also remember that writing is always recursive—you might start with an invention activity or two and then conduct some research, which leads to more invention work and then a first draft, but then you might need to do more invention work to help flesh out your draft and conduct more research to fill in the gaps in information you spot, and then you'll revise your draft and possibly find another gap or two. . . . Writing, in other words, is more a circular than a linear process. So while the activities listed below imply that writers go through them step-by-step, the actual process of writing is usually messier. You will keep coming back to your earlier work, adding to it and modifying the information to be more accurate as you conduct more research and become more familiar with your topic.

For a tip on organizing your computer files, see page 97.

As you work on your project, make certain that you save your computer files frequently because any work that you don't save could be lost. Many experienced writers save their files every fifteen minutes or so. Also, savvy writers back up their computer files in two or more places—on an internal or external hard drive of the computer, on a USB flash drive, and/or on a rewritable CD or DVD.

Invention: Getting Started

Use invention activities to explore, on paper or on your computer screen, the information that you want to include in your first draft. Completing one or more of the following invention activities should yield a wealth of information.

For more on using journals, see Chapters 2 and 3.

It is also useful to keep a journal as you work on any writing project, for your journal is a place where you can record not just what you learn but also the questions that arise during your writing and research activities.

Try to answer these questions while you do your invention work:

- What do I already know about the topic that I am writing about?

- What feelings, attitudes, or notions do I already have about this topic? How can I keep them out of my text so that my writing is as free of bias as possible?

- What questions can I ask about the topic? That is, what gaps do I have in my knowledge about it that might help me understand what information a reader might need?

- Where might I learn more about this subject (in the library, on the Web)? What verifiable information on my topic is available?

- Who would know about my topic? What questions might I ask that person in an interview?

- What do I know about my audience? What don't I know that I should know? Why might they be interested in reading my text?

- What might my audience already know about my subject? Why might they care about it?

For more on descriptive writing, see Chapter 13.

- To what extent will sensory details—color, shape, smell, taste, and so on—help my reader understand my topic? Why?

- What visual aids might I use to better inform my readers?

Doing your invention work in electronic form, rather than on paper, lets you easily use this early writing as you construct a draft.

WRITING ACTIVITY

Brainstorming, Freewriting, and Clustering

Working with the questions above, spend a few minutes brainstorming— jotting down everything you can think of about your topic. Also using the questions above, and perhaps using an idea from your brainstorming to get you started, jot down everything you can think of about your topic for a specific period of time. During that time frame, just keep writing (even if you have to write, "I can't think of anything to say"), because the very act of putting words on paper or keyboarding them on a computer will help you generate more ideas. Once you have generated a number of promising ideas and details, use clustering or another mapping strategy to indicate relationships between or among them.

For more on brainstorming, freewriting, and clustering, as well as other strategies for discovery and learning, see Chapter 3.

Craig Broadbent's Brainstorming

Craig Broadbent, a first-year student, chose to respond to Scenario 1 on page 192. Broadbent decided that he would brainstorm to get onto paper what he already knew about the litter issue on his campus before he interviewed his friends about it:

—I see stuff every day—newspapers, those extra advertising things they put into the paper, cups, plates, and—especially—cigarette butts.
—It's always worst around where ashtrays are—that's really weird.
—The paper stuff is always worst around where the newspapers are.
—Oh—they do put a box or some container next to the paper stands for students to toss those inserts, if they don't want to read them. Not sure why so many end up on the ground.
—Bad in the men's rooms, too, at times—towels on the floor almost always.
—Classrooms: stuff tacked or taped to the walls, old soda cups and crumpled-up hamburger wrappers and old napkins and candy wrappers . . .

Craig Broadbent's Freewriting

After interviewing two students, Broadbent did the following freewriting on the subject of littering on campus:

I've got a lot of information—so what to use? Joe Morris, a friend in my English class, had some really disgusting examples—stuff that had "been in the dorm hallway for years," he said—old cigarette butts (and a cigar butt!), papers, some old clothing, drinks that had obviously been spilled—he said that hallway was disgusting.

And Matt Elmore, who lives in the old dorm—says that the *elevators* are horrible. They never get cleaned and people just leave everything in them on their way in or out of their rooms.

The two interviews made me want to do another interview, this time with some of the people who pick up litter on campus. I can't think of what to write, I can't—oh, and maybe I can get some photos of the dorm at North Campus, where there's always a lot of litter, it's always horrible right by the front door. The wind seems to catch trash and papers and stuff and blow it right up to the big glass entry doors. . . .

Craig Broadbent's Clustering

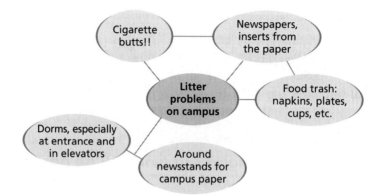

Exploring Your Ideas with Research

Most informative assignments require you to conduct research because your personal experiences usually will not provide enough information. Without research it is usually impossible to write an effective and useful informative

---

TechNote

The results of a search for sources on your topic can let you know if your informative topic is unwieldy. If a search brings up thousands of Web sites with information about your topic, it is probably too broad to be manageable. For example, when a search engine such as Google returns more than 1 million links for the topic "West Nile Virus," you'll need to use strategies that will narrow the topic so that your ideas and your research will be more focused. Adding search terms based on your specific interests and concerns can help.

Adding search terms narrows your exploratory Web search to an aspect of the West Nile Virus. (Tip: Separate your terms or phrases in the search window with quotation marks.) The terms "West Nile Virus" + "horse vaccine" narrows the results to 1,150 sites that are likely to give information about equine vaccination against West Nile virus—a more focused topic, but still fairly broad. Adding a third term—"Missouri"—narrows the topic further, resulting in 108 sites and getting you closer to a topic of immediate interest. Adding yet a fourth term—"Kansas City"—yields only 5 sites, possibly indicating a topic of interest to others, yet limited enough to provide the focus needed for an essay.

For an essay-length informative piece, then, think about focusing on a local—or even a personal—aspect of a larger issue. "West Nile Virus: Is Kansas City Doing Its Part?" is a working topic that may glean information that is fresh, new, and useful.

For more on using search engines, see Chapter 19.

paper. In a college setting, research sometimes begins and ends in the library, but you can also search the Web, conduct interviews or surveys, and make field observations.

Using the questions on page 220, decide what information you need from outside sources, determine what kind of research you need to conduct in order to gather that information, and conduct research in the library and on the Web. You may also find it necessary to do field research.

Gather, read, and take notes on your topic from outside sources. You might use an electronic journal to record images, URLs, and other electronic pieces of information that you find as you research. Such an e-journal makes it easy for you to add those e-documents once you start drafting your paper.

For help with locating sources of information, see Chapter 19; for help with documenting your sources, see Chapter 20.

Craig Broadbent's Research

For his informative paper on the litter problem on his campus, Craig Broadbent thought it would be useful to include data that show how long it takes certain waste products to decompose. By searching with the keywords "campus litter," using the search engine Dogpile, he found this table on a Web site maintained by the University of British Columbia.

Rate of Biodegradability

Product	Time It Takes
Cotton Rags	1–5 months
Paper	2–5 months
Rope	3–14 months
Orange Peels	6 months
Wool Socks	1–5 years
Cigarette butts	1–12 years
Plastic coated paper cartons	5 years
Plastic bags	10–20 years
Leather shoes	25–40 years
Nylon fabric	30–40 years
Tin cans	50–100 years
Aluminum cans	80–100 years
Plastic 6-pack holder rings	450 years
Glass bottles	1 million years
Plastic bottles	Never

Using the same search terms on Google, Broadbent found this photograph:

He also found information he might be able to use, which he copied into his research journal, carefully noting its source:

> **Hidden Litter Is a Problem**
> On Thursday, 06 February 2003, the Litter Patrol picked-up a small area near the Computer Technology and Mathematics building on the beautiful SCC campus. I had noticed that this area contained hidden litter. The pick-up (which lasted almost an hour) yielded 423 cigarette butts and one wasted glove. [This area could not be cleaned using a litter picker-upper.]
>
> **Author:** G. D.Thurman [gdt@deru.com]
> **Created:** 07 Feb 2003
> **URL:** http://azlitter.org/adopt-a-campus/hiddenlitter.html
> **Last Modified:** 02/11/2003 08:04:34
>
> from <http://azlitter.org/adopt-a-campus/hiddenlitter.html>. downloaded 11/11/03.
> (You have to wonder who counted those cigarette butts . . .)

Reviewing Your Invention and Research

After you have conducted your research, review your invention work and notes and think about the information you have collected from outside sources. You may be tempted to decide on a thesis statement—a statement that summarizes your main point—at this time. Even though you might already have a general idea of what you want your informative paper to focus on, until you get some of your ideas and research on paper, it is often hard to know what your thesis will be. Your thesis should come *from* the writing you do about your topic. Once you have done a lot of invention work (listing, brainstorming, clustering, and so on) and research, you may be ready to decide on your working thesis. Or you can wait until after you construct your first draft.

For more on deciding on a thesis, see Chapter 13.

WRITING ACTIVITY

Considering Your Invention and Research to Help Focus Your Ideas

To get some idea of what your main point (or thesis) might be, as well as how you might start your informative text, review the notes you have taken from your invention and research, thinking about what you now know about your subject:

- Start by trying to find connections between the pieces of information you have collected. By looking for connections, you are synthesizing the information from your sources. As you will see, Craig Broadbent noticed several instances where the recycling program on his campus seemed to be "invisible"—no one knew much about it. This discovery became the main idea of his informative paper.

- Decide on the most important piece of information that you collected. One writing strategy is to put this information right at the start of your paper, not only to get your reader involved, but also to indicate its importance. Craig Broadbent learned from his interviews that his friends did not know about the campus recycling program. To emphasize this significant fact, he decided to begin his paper with it: "We seem to have a case of invisible blue barrels on campus—when was the last time you saw one and what is unusual or unique about it?"

- Decide on the most unusual or surprising piece of information you collected. As with the most important information, you can put the most unusual or surprising information at the beginning of your paper. Craig Broadbent might have started his paper by noting that "If you don't recycle a glass bottle, the glass from that bottle will last a million years," using information from the table he found from the University of British Columbia.

Craig Broadbent's Review of His Research

Craig Broadbent wanted his paper to include some of the information about recycling that he learned from his research. He investigated the issue on his campus, he interviewed two of his classmates about it, and he did a brief search of back issues of the campus's newspaper, the *Campus Reporter*, for information about campus recycling. His review of his research helped him decide on an effective way to start his paper. Here are some of his notes:

1. Jim Roberts (roommate) told me that no one had mentioned the school's recycling program to him, at orientation or anywhere else.
2. Tracy Worsam (friend and classmate) told me that she'd even asked about the program at her orientation, and no one there seemed to know much about it, other than "we have some blue barrels around campus."
3. The last ten or twelve issues of the <u>Campus Reporter</u> had only one small advertisement and no articles about the program. Why so little?
   All of those things make me wonder if I should start with a question, perhaps like, "Why doesn't anyone on campus know about our recycling program?" And, maybe a title something like, "A big campus secret: Our blue barrels."
4. I also looked on the Web and found this, from the University of Nebraska at Lincoln. It's cute and might help make my point with a neat visual:

Did you know...

✓	UNL spends in excess of $180,000 per year just "picking-up" litter?
✓	An average of 10,700 labor hours were spent last year to pick-up campus litter?
✓	Cigarette butts are the #1 litter problem

Help us keep Campus clean.
Don't Litter.

from <<u>http://busfin.unl.edu/LS/litter/litter.html</u>>. Downloaded 6/27/03. University of Nebraska-Lincoln.

That would also be an interesting way to start my paper—with that little table and the "did you know?" drawing.

WRITER'S WORKSHOP

Reacting to Your Classmates' Invention Work and Research

As with any kind of writing, invention activities and research improve with peer feedback and suggestions. Working with several of your classmates, ask one another the following questions, and provide comments and suggestions, with the overall goal of helping one another to understand your rhetorical situation more clearly and to generate more useful information.

Comments

- I think you're trying to explain _____ to me, but it's not clear to me. Can you provide more information?

- I like how you've explained _____.

- I'm not sure how _____ relates to what you're trying to tell me.

- The part where you explain _____ seems promising, but the part where you talk about _____ seems underdeveloped.

- I'd suggest that you include these ideas or this information:

  _____   _____

  _____   _____

Questions

- What do you mean when you say, _____? (Ask this kind of question when something is unclear.)

- What additional information can you give me about _____?

- How would you describe the purpose of _____ that you mention?

Use the suggestions and comments that you receive on your invention work and the results of your research to guide you as you continue to gather information. The comments and suggestions indicate areas where your readers may not understand what you are trying to get across, as well as show you places where they need more information about your subject.

> **TechNote**
>
> Here are some tips for e-mailing professors and classmates with ideas about your informative paper or a draft of your paper:
>
> - Avoid sending attachments (unless they are requested). Sometimes other people's computers cannot open and display attached documents properly.
>
> - If you do send attached files, include information about the download in the subject line of your message:
>
> "paper draft attached." This subject line lets the recipient know that you haven't accidentally sent a hitchhiker virus or spyware.
>
> - Write in whole words, not instant-message abbreviations—you'll make a better impression!
>
> - In your message, state who you are, or end with a signature file so that busy classmates and teachers will know immediately whom the message is from.

Organizing Your Information and Research

Once you have some sense of what you would like your informative paper to include—information generated by completing various invention activities and through research—you need to consider how you might organize this material. The questions you need to ask yourself when deciding on your organization are all rhetorical:

- Who is your audience?
- Why might they be interested in your subject, or how can you make them interested in it? (One way to indicate why your subject is important to your audience is to explain how your audience will be affected by it.)
- What is your purpose for writing—that is, what do you want to *inform* your readers about?
- What are the most important ideas, concepts, or statistics that you want your readers to learn about from your text?

The answers to these questions can help you decide what you need to emphasize, which in turn will help you choose an organization.

Here is a brief outline of three possible organizational approaches for writing an informative paper:

Options for Organization

Option 1	Option 2	Option 3
• Start with an unusual or surprising piece of information about your subject.	• Begin with a question to help readers see why they might want to read about your topic.	• Set the stage—what is the situation that your readers may be interested in?

Options for Organization (*continued*)

Option 1	Option 2	Option 3
• Present the information, starting from the least unusual or surprising idea and moving to the most. • Use specific examples, quotations, statistics, and so on to illustrate your topic. • End your paper by restating a unique or surprising aspect of your topic.	• Outline the information, starting with the smallest, narrowest, or least significant piece of information and working toward the largest, the broadest, or the most important. • Use specific examples, quotations, statistics, and so on to illustrate your topic. • Your conclusion might answer the question that you started with.	• Broaden your initial explanation with specific details, quotations, and examples so your reader can "see" what you are writing about. • Compare and contrast your subject with another one, to help readers understand the information. • Conclude your paper by again relating the information to your reader, reinforcing his or her connection to your topic.

WRITING ACTIVITY

Deciding on an Organizational Approach

Before you construct a full draft, consider the organizational approaches that are available to you and decide which one will best serve your writing purpose and help your audience to understand the information you are presenting. Try writing a page or two using at least two organizational approaches before you settle on one. Trying out different approaches will give you a sense of which one might be the most effective for this particular writing task. Try out the approaches on the computer—and be sure to save each first attempt with a different file name. That makes it easy to recall the one that seems best and start to develop your draft using that organization. You might try to compare and contrast your subject with another subject readers are more familiar with. You can use vivid and clear description to help your reader see your subject, or you might want to explain how one thing leads to or causes another to happen.

For more on these strategies, see Chapter 13.

Craig Broadbent's Organization

Craig Broadbent looked over his invention material and then put together a rough outline for his first draft. He decided to start with a question and to use the second approach described above.

> Set the stage, so to speak, by asking if readers know what the blue barrels are and how they work.
> State my purpose: informational.
> Explain recycling and how it works.
> Include tables, photos, charts to show my ideas.
> Explain the cost aspects of recycling.
> Let people know how to find out more information.

Constructing a Complete Draft

Once you have chosen the organizational approach that works best given your audience and purpose, you are ready to finish constructing your draft. Look back over the information you have generated through your invention activities and collected through your research, as well as any comments made by your classmates.

You should also re-examine your focus or your thesis (if you have one) and decide if you need to modify it. If you do not have one yet, consider whether you are ready to develop a working thesis. Determine the most important points you will present, and choose the strategies you will use to explain this information.

As you write your first draft, draw on what you have learned and use the organizational approach you want to try. Remember that you will learn more about your subject as you write, and your ideas will probably change as you compose the first draft of your informative essay. Consider, too, what visual aids your readers might find useful—just as Craig Broadbent did when he constructed his initial draft.

Introduction: A successful piece of informative writing grabs and holds readers' attention. The following strategies can help you hook your readers:

- *Define any important terms that the reader might not know.* Defining terms does not mean listing their dictionary definitions, but rather explaining those terms in the context of your explanation of your subject. For an especially effective opening, you might get readers' attention by defining a familiar term in an unexpected way. For example, you could say that "Recycling really is *not* recycling when you put the wrong items into a blue barrel. Here is a list of 'no-nos' for the campus recycling barrels:" followed by a list of things students might think are acceptable for recycling, but which really are not.

- *Start your text with unusual or surprising information.* Harold Peterson starts (p. 200) with a statement sure to catch a reader's attention:

On a quiet, sunny morning in the spring of 1845, six years after Abner Doubleday did not invent baseball in Elihu Phinney's Cooperstown cow pasture (or anywhere else), . . .

- *Start with a provocative example or two:* For example, in "Clocking Cultures" (p. 206), Carol Ezzell involves her readers with two compelling examples, given in the second person:

Show up an hour late in Brazil, and no one bats an eyelash. But keep someone in New York City waiting for five or 10 minutes, and you have some explaining to do.

- *Get down to business by bluntly stating your thesis.* A straightforward statement like "Denver's new sign code is causing businesses to lose money" often gets readers' attention. Journalists, who are trained to put the most important information up front, often use this approach.

Body: Think of the body of your informative text as the place to provide all of the information that you want your readers to know and to understand. This is the section where you will present your data: quotations, graphs, tables, charts. The body of your paper is always the longest part, and, while you are not trying to prove anything in an informative essay, you are providing information to your readers, and most of it will appear in the body.

Conclusion: Your conclusion should tie your paper together for your readers by explaining or suggesting the significance of the information you have given them: why it is useful or interesting to them. Here are some strategies for concluding an informative paper:

- *Summarize your main points.* In a brief paragraph, Harold Peterson summarizes his main points at the end of the selection from *The Man Who Invented Baseball*: "Abner Doubleday didn't invent baseball. Baseball invented Abner Doubleday" (p. 204).
- *Outline again the subject's most important aspects.* Craig Broadbent does this at the end of his essay on campus recycling programs (p. 245).
- *Explain the subject's most critical part.* Carol Ezzell uses a quotation from an expert to indicate what is most significant about her topic: "If you colonize time, you also colonize the future" (p. 209).

Title: You might think that you need to come up with a title before you start writing, but often it is more useful to get a first draft on paper or into a computer file and then consider possible titles. Your paper's title should indicate what your paper is about, but it should also capture your readers' interest and invite them to read your paper.

- *Use a title that readers will wonder about.* For example, "Clocking Cultures" makes readers wonder what this essay could be about.
- *Start with something current.* Katie Hafner titles her article, "Growing *Wikipedia* Revises Its 'Anyone Can Edit' Policy." Anyone familiar with *Wikipedia* will want to read more.

Which of the following possible titles for Craig Broadbent's essay do you think is the most effective? Why?

The Million-Year-Old Glass Bottle?
You Students Are a Bunch of Slobs
Watch for the Blue Barrels

VISUALIZING VARIATIONS

Using a Web Site, Poster, or Brochure to Inform Your Readers

If you are working with Scenario 3 (p. 194), which calls for civic writing, one way to present your information to your readers would be to construct a Web site, poster, or brochure instead of a newspaper article.

The following Web site from EasyVoter.org is designed to provide information on issues that are important to California voters, as well as information on how to vote.

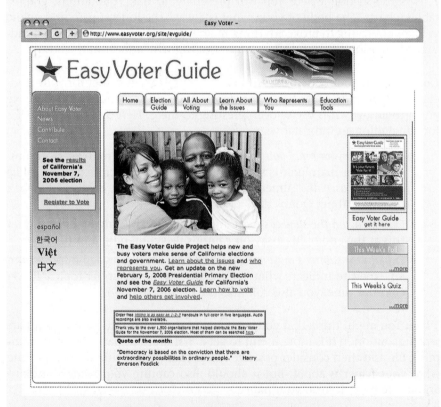

Using this Web site as an example, consider the best way to present the information you have researched to the voters in your area. Use the following questions to guide you:

1. Who do you see as your audience for your document? What information do you already know about them? What questions do you have about your audience?
2. What is the best format in which to put your information? Which format—a Web site, poster, or brochure—would be easiest for your audience to gain access to? In other words, what is the best way for you to reach these readers?
3. Should you illustrate your Web site, poster, or brochure with tables of data or photos of some kind? Why?
4. If you use photographs, what should they include? Not include?
5. What kind(s) of charts would be effective? Ineffective? How might you test a chart to see if it would be useful to include in your document?
6. If you create a Web document, what hyperlinks would you want to include? How much explanation would you need to include so readers would understand where each link might lead them? How effective are the hyperlinks in the document on page 232, and what makes them that way?

Writing Assignment: Using the information you have gathered through invention and research, construct a voter's guide about the problem you are focusing on for this assignment. Your voter's guide could be either a Web site such as the one on page 232 or a poster or brochure. (For advice on constructing a Web site or a brochure, see Appendix C.)

Craig Broadbent's First Draft

After deciding on an organizational approach, Craig Broadbent was ready to begin his first, or working, draft. As he wrote, he did not worry about grammar, punctuation, mechanics, or proper documentation style; instead, he concentrated on getting his main ideas on paper. Here is the first draft of his recycling paper.

Watch for the Blue Barrels

Have you ever wondered what all of those blue barrels are, around campus . . . and if you know what they're for, do you wonder why students don't seem to use them?

Joan Meyers, who coordinates our campus recycling program, says that it has been around for more than ten years now, but receives little publicity (Meyers). My purpose here is to outline what we're doing here on campus, what the costs and income are from the program, and finally, based on several interviews, to suggest reasons why students don't use the blue barrels.

What is recycling and why should we care about it? Recycling is the re-use of some product. We all know that reusing plastic, aluminum cans, newspaper, glass, and other items through a recycling program saves energy (and thus helps our air pollution problem) and also can save money. Recycling is environmentally sound—the more paper, plastic, etc. that we can reuse, the less we have to make. That saves trees and other resources.

Our campus program not only keeps the campus cleaner, since items are collected in the blue barrels instead of perhaps being thrown on the ground, but also makes some $5,000 a year for the school (Meyers). Ms. Meyers also told me that our college could make as much as $30,000 a year from recycling, if we all recycled all the newspapers, cans, etc., that we now throw away. Here is some cost information from another college:

Did you know...

✔	UNL spends in excess of $180,000 per year just "picking-up" litter?
✔	An average of 10,700 labor hours were spent last year to pick-up campus litter?
✔	Cigarette butts are the #1 litter problem

Help us keep Campus clean.
Don't Litter.

from <http://busfin.unl.edu/LS/litter/litter.html>.
Downloaded 6/27/03.
From the University of Nebraska-Lincoln.

Students, though, don't use the program, sometimes because they're not aware of it. Student Jim Roberts told me that at orientation or anywhere else no one had mentioned the school's recycling program to him (Roberts). And Tracy Worsam even asked about the program at her orientation, and no one there seemed to know much about it, other than "we have some blue barrels around campus" (Worsam).

A search of several issues of the <u>Campus Reporter</u> perhaps explains why not many students are really aware of the blue barrel program. During the last few months, there has been only one small advertisement about the campus recycling program, and no articles about the program were published.

In order to know about and understand the recycling program, Meyers suggests that information be provided at all orientation meetings, and that weekly advertisements are run in the <u>Campus Reporter</u> (Meyers).

 ## Revising

Revising means reseeing and rethinking your informative text. The most effective way to revise your work is to read it as if you are reading it for the first time. Reading your own work in this way is difficult to do, of course—which is why writers often put their work aside for a period of time so that when they reread it, the experience is something like seeing it as a new piece of writing. The more you can see your writing as if for the first time, the more you will respond to it as your real readers might, questioning and probing and exploring it. When you reread the first draft of your informative writing, be sure to begin at the beginning. Here are some questions to ask yourself:

1. What else might my audience want or need to know about my subject?
2. How else might I encourage my audience to learn more about my subject?
3. What information did I find that I did not include in my paper? (Effective research always results in more information than you can include, so consider what you left out that you might include in your next draft.)
4. Have I clearly explained and defined any terms my readers might not know?
5. Could some of my information be better presented as a graph or chart or in a photograph?

Technology can help you revise and edit your writing more easily. Use your word processor's track-changes tool to try out revisions and editing changes. After you've had time to think about the possible changes, you can "accept" or "reject" them. Also, you can use your word processor's comment tool to write reminders to yourself when you get stuck with a revision or some editing task. If your classmates are offering feedback on your draft, they can also use track changes, the comment tool, or the peer-commenting feature of the software.

Because it is so difficult to see our emerging writing with a fresh eye (even for experienced writers), it is almost always useful to ask classmates, friends, or family members to read and comment on drafts of your papers.

WRITER'S WORKSHOP

Responding to Full Drafts

As you read and respond to your classmates' papers (and as they comment on yours), focus on the informative nature of this assignment, but from a reader's perspective. Be sure to ask questions of their writing and respond to their ideas by exploring your reactions and responses to their thoughts.

Working in pairs or groups of three, read each others' drafts, and then offer your classmates comments that will help them see their papers' strengths as well as places where they need to develop their ideas further. Use the following questions to guide your responses to the writer's draft, whether you respond directly on your classmate's text, on a separate sheet of paper, or online.

- Write a brief narrative comment that outlines your first impression of this draft. How effectively does the title draw you into the paper? Why? How might the title be improved?

- Indicate what you like about the draft—that is, provide positive and encouraging feedback to the writer.

- Comment on the writer's focus: that is, how well does the writer stay on track or how much does the paper wander off course? If the paper loses focus, indicate where.

- Comment on how informative you found this paper to be. Explain, in a brief paragraph, whether you learned anything from reading this paper. What part(s) of the text are especially informative? What information was interesting and/or new to you?

- Comment specifically on the introduction: What is effective about it? What suggestions can you make on how to improve the introduction?

- What do you think is the author's thesis or main point? How could it be expressed or supported more effectively?

- In the main part of the paper, are there parts that are confusing? Where would you like more details or examples to help you see what the author means? What parts could use more explanation or definitions?

- How clear is the author's informative writing? If there are places that seem wordy or unclear, how might the author revise to address those problems?

- How accurate does the information seem? Are there statistics or concepts that seem questionable? How carefully does the author indicate the sources of statistics and other information that are not common knowledge?

- Reread the conclusion. What could be added or changed to make it more effective? How well does it tie everything together? To what extent does it make you want to learn more about this topic?

- In another paragraph, outline what you see as the main weaknesses of this paper—and suggest how the writer might improve the text.

- If you are working with what might be called a non-traditional text (a Web page, for example, or a brochure), comment on the special attributes of that kind of text and how effectively the piece functions *as* a brochure, Web page, or other example of an informative genre.

- If there are visual aspects of the document, comment on how effectively they illustrate the point being made. How much do the visuals add to a reader's overall understanding of the information? What other types of visuals might be even more useful?

Student Comment on Craig Broadbent's Draft

Here is a comment that a student reviewer made about Craig Broadbent's draft:

> It seems to me that the strongest part of your paper are the examples, especially the little drawings and all the statistics. The weakest part is the interview information, which made me want to read more of what other people had to say. I thought your introduction "worked" and made me want to read more. I'd like more tables and charts, if you have them—they help me see what you mean. Your conclusion was weak—maybe you could add what students ought to be doing now? Put another way, what do you want your readers to do with this (interesting) information?

As with the comments you will receive from your teacher and classmates, Broadbent had to determine which comments and suggestions made sense—and then to revise his paper accordingly.

Responding to Readers' Comments

Once they have received feedback from peers, teachers, and others, all writers have to decide what to do with that feedback. Because the text is *your* paper, you as the writer are responsible for dealing with reader responses to your work.

The first thing to do with any feedback is to consider carefully what your reader has to say. Craig Broadbent's reader has told him the following:

- The examples are good, as well as the visual aids. It might make sense, then, for Broadbent to consider adding more examples and visuals to his paper.

- The reader needed more from the interview information. Broadbent might consider how he can add more information from interviews to his paper.

- The reader thought Broadbent's conclusion was weak because he did not ask his reader to do anything. When you write an informative paper, you might think about what you would like your readers to do after they finish reading it. For a piece of civic writing, you might want the reader to vote or to write a letter to the editor of your local paper. For a paper written in a professional situation, you might want the reader to request more information or to sign a contract. Consider adding a call to action to your conclusion.

Pay close attention to what your readers tell you. You may decide to reject some comments, of course, and that decision is yours. As with any reader, some of your peer reviewers might not understand your main point, or they may misunderstand something you wrote—so it is up to you either to accept or to ignore their comments and suggestions. Other comments, though, deserve your attention, as they are the words of real readers speaking to you about how to improve your text. You may find that comments from more than one reader contradict each other. In that case, you need to use your own judgment to decide which reader's comments are on the right track.

In the final version of his paper on pages 242–45, you can see how Craig Broadbent responded to these comments, as well as to his own review of his first draft.

 # Knowledge of Conventions

When effective writers edit their work, they attend to the conventions that will help readers—the table manners of writing. These include genre conventions, documentation, format, usage, grammar, punctuation, and mechanics. By attending to these conventions in your writing, you make reading a more pleasant experience for readers.

Editing

The last task in any writing project is editing. When you edit and polish your writing, you make changes to your sentence structure and word choice to improve your style and to make your writing clearer and more concise. You also check your work to make sure it adheres to conventions of grammar, usage, punctuation, mechanics, and spelling. Use the spell-check function of your word-processing program, but be sure to double-check your spelling personally. If you have used sources in your paper, make sure you are following the documentation style your instructor requires.

See Chapter 20 for more on documenting sources.

As with overall revision of your work, this final editing and polishing is most effective if you can put your text aside for a few days and come back to it with fresh eyes. We strongly recommend that you ask classmates, friends, and tutors to read your work as well. Another option is to post your paper on a course Web site and invite everyone in class to read your paper. You may get only one or two takers, but one or two is better than none.

To assist you with editing, we offer here a round-robin editing activity focused on finding and correcting problems with modifiers.

WRITER'S WORKSHOP

Round-Robin Editing with a Focus on Modifiers

Because informative writing benefits from the careful use of **modifiers,** words or groups of words that describe or limit other words, focus in this workshop on the conventions for using modifiers in sentences—adjectives, adverbs, infinitives, participles, prepositional phrases, relative clauses. Consult the section of a grammar handbook that covers modifiers, then read one another's papers, looking for problems with modifiers. Two problems to watch for are misplaced or dangling modifiers. When a modifier is misplaced, it is too far away from the word or phrase it is modifying so that it appears to be modifying something else. To correct the problem, the modifier needs to be moved.

MISPLACED   Student Jim Roberts told me ~~at orientation or anywhere else~~ no one
                                        at orientation or anywhere else.
            had mentioned the school's recycling program to him, ∧

A modifier is dangling when the word or phrase it modifies does not appear in the sentence at all. You can correct the problem by adding the word or phrase.

DANGLING   In order to know about and understand the recycling
                    students need to be provided with
            program, ∧ ~~Meyers suggests that~~ information ~~be provided~~ at all
                                                            need to be
            orientation meetings, and ~~that~~ weekly advertisements ∧ are run in
                ,according to Meyers.
            the <u>Campus Reporter</u>, ∧

(cont'd)

(continued)

If you are uncertain about a specific convention for using modifiers, underline the problem sentence and put a question mark in the margin. To resolve such questions, consult the handbook or ask your instructor.

Genres, Documentation, and Format

For advice on writing in different genres, see Appendix C. For guidelines for formatting and documenting papers in MLA or APA style, see Chapter 20.

If you are writing an academic paper (which you will be if you work with Scenarios 1 or 2), follow the conventions for the discipline in which you are writing and the requirements of your instructor. If you are constructing an article for your local newspaper (Scenario 3), check the newspaper's editorial page or its Web site to see what the requirements are for length and format and what information you need to include when you submit your manuscript. If you have used material from outside sources, including visuals, give credit to those sources, using the documentation style required by the discipline you are working in and by your instructor.

WRITING IN ACTION

Convention in Genre and Design

While you might think that informative writing is usually dull, it certainly does not have to be. Newspaper reporters, who most often construct informative writing, are experts at capturing their readers' attention. The headline of reporter Scott Seckel's article undoubtedly catches your eye. Note also how Seckel sets the stage in the first paragraph, provides a quotation from a local resident, supplies some historical background by noting the "state laws dating back to the Old West," and then, having captured his readers' interest, goes into the main body of his story.

Considering Genre and Design

1. How effective is the headline of this newspaper article at getting a reader's attention? Why?
2. While only a portion of the article is reprinted here, how accurately does the headline represent the content of the article?
3. How effective is the first part of the article in making you want to read more? Why?
4. In what ways is the small map useful?
5. With one or two classmates, brainstorm about the requirements of a newspaper article. In what ways does this article fulfill the requirements of this genre? (You might compare this article to one or two other articles in your local newspaper.)

Rotting cows rile nearby residents

Law lets livestock owner leave carcass where it dropped

BY SCOTT C. SECKEL
TRIBUNE

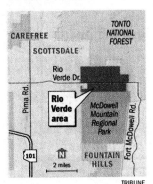

TRIBUNE

Coyotes and vultures found the reeking dead cow 20 feet from Julie White's property line the same way she did.

"We could smell it," the Rio Verde woman said.

Folks in the rural area north of Scottsdale are raising a stink about bloated bovines, but state laws dating back to the Old West allow owners to leave them where they fell.

The 18-square-mile county pocket has boomed over the past eight years as an increasing number of urbanites seek desert living and horse properties within commuting distance of city lights.

White called the sheriff's office when she and her boyfriend found the cow, which died as it was giving birth.

She said the deputy who answered said there was nothing he could do about the carcasses of free-range animals. "I was thinking, 'Shouldn't he still have to pick it up because it's so close to somebody's house?' I think the laws are a little outdated."

The state livestock inspec-

Please see **COWS**, Page **A9**

 ## A Writer Informs His Readers: Craig Broadbent's Final Draft

The final draft of Craig Broadbent's essay "Watch for the Blue Barrels" follows. As you read Broadbent's essay, think about what makes it effective. Note, too, how he used the suggestions his classmates offered during peer review to make his informative paper more effective. Following the essay, you'll find some specific questions to consider.

CRAIG BROADBENT

Watch for the Blue Barrels

Have you ever wondered what all of those blue barrels that are scattered around campus are for . . . and if you know what they're for, do you wonder why students don't seem to use them? Those blue barrels are the heart of our campus-wide recycling program, and it is critical not only that students know what they are, but also that they *use* the barrels.   1

Joan Meyers, who coordinates our campus recycling program, says that it has been in place for more than ten years now, but receives little publicity. My purpose here is to outline what we're doing about recycling on campus, to show what the costs and income are from the program, and finally, based on several interviews, to suggest the reasons that students don't use the blue barrels.   2

What is recycling and why should we care about it? Recycling is the reuse of some product. We all know that reusing plastic, aluminum cans, newspaper, glass, and other items by recycling them saves energy (and thus helps our air pollution problem) and can also save money. Recycling is environmentally sound—the more paper, plastic, and metal products that we can reuse, the less we have to make. That's the case even though things are usually not recycled into what they were to start with. That is, aluminum cans, Meyers told me, rarely are recycled to make more aluminum cans. But they *are* recycled and made into other products (frying pans, for instance). Therefore, recycling saves trees and other natural resources.   3

Not only that, but if certain items are *not* recycled, they can be around forever. That is, if we don't recycle some household items, they never seem to "waste away." For example, the University of British Columbia reports that some items can last huge amounts of time: glass bottles last a million years and plastic bottles *never* go away, as shown in Table 1.   4

One peer suggestion Broadbent received was the following:

I'd like more tables and charts, if you have them—they help me see what you mean.

To address this reader's concern, Broadbent added this paragraph and also Table 1.

Table 1
Rates of Disintegration of Common Waste Products

Product	Time it takes
Cotton Rags	1–5 months
Paper	2–5 months
Rope	3–14 months
Orange Peels	6 months
Wool Socks	1–5 years
Cigarette butts	1–12 years
Plastic coated paper cartons	5 years
Plastic bags	10–20 years
Leather shoes	25–40 years
Nylon fabric	30–40 years
Tin cans	50–100 years
Aluminum cans	80–100 years
Plastic 6-pack holder rings	450 years
Glass bottles	1 million years
Plastic bottles	Never

Source: "Facts about Litter." UBC Waste Management Litter Reduction Program. University of British Columbia. 23 June 2003 <http://www.recycle.ubc.ca/litter.html>.

Even seemingly minor items like cigarette butts can last as long as   5
twelve years, and empty soda cans—unless they are recycled—can last
for up to one hundred years. They can also cost the college a great deal
of money to clean up. Fig. 1 shows some cost information from the University of Nebraska at Lincoln, a school comparable to our own.

?

Did you know...

✓	UNL spends in excess of $180,000 per year just "picking-up" litter?
✓	An average of 10,700 labor hours were spent last year to pick-up campus litter?
✓	Cigarette butts are the #1 litter problem

Help us keep Campus clean.
Don't Litter.

FIG. 1   Costs of cleaning up litter at the University of Nebraska—Lincoln
Botanical Garden and Arboretum. "Did You Know?" <u>The Garden</u>. 6 Sept.
2002. University of Nebraska—Lincoln. 3 June 2003. <http://busfin.unl.edu/
LS/litter/litter.html>.

Joan Meyers notes that our recycling program not only keeps the   6
campus cleaner, since items are collected in the blue barrels instead of
perhaps being thrown on the ground, but it also generates some $5,000
a year in revenue for the school. Ms. Meyers also told me that our college could make as much as $30,000 a year from recycling if we all

recycled all the newspapers, cans, and other waste that we now throw away.

Students, though, don't use the program, sometimes because they're not aware of it. Student Jim Roberts told me that no one had mentioned the school's recycling program to him, at orientation or anywhere else. Another student, Tracy Worsam, even asked about the program at her orientation, but no one there seemed to know much about it, other than to say "we have some blue barrels around campus." Finally, I interviewed several students who live in that old house on the edge of campus. It's not really a fraternity but more of a boarding house. They all told me that *they* never littered, even though their yard was a mess (Wilson, Marble, and Addams). Maybe my interview with them—and the information I gave them about the blue barrel program—will help. Maybe if they understood recycling and had blue barrels in a convenient location, they would recycle their plastic, paper, and glass items.

A search through several back issues of the Campus Reporter may explain why not many students are really aware of the blue barrel program. During the last few months, only one small advertisement about the campus recycling program has appeared in the Reporter, and no articles about the program were published.

In order to know about and understand the recycling program, students need to be provided with information at all orientation meetings, and weekly advertisements need to be run in the Campus Reporter, according to Joan Meyers. In the meantime, students who would like to learn more about the recycling program on campus, and how they can help, can contact Meyers at JoanMeyers@Ourcollege.edu.

Works Cited

"Did You know?" The Garden. 6 Sept. 2002. University of Nebraska—Lincoln Botanical Garden and Arboretum. 27 June 2003 <http://busfin.unl.edu/LS/litter/litter.html>.

Meyers, Joan. Personal interview. 17 Mar. 2004.

"Facts about Litter." UBC Waste Management Litter Reduction Program. University of British Columbia. 23 June 2003 <http://www.recycle.ubc.ca/litter.html>.

Roberts, Jim. Personal interview. 15 Mar. 2004.

Wilson, James, Stacy Marble, and Sam Addams. Personal interview. 17 Mar. 2004.

Worsam, Tracy. Personal interview. 15 Mar. 2004.

7

8

9

Another comment Broadbent received from his peer review session pointed out a problem:

The weakest part is the interview information, which made me want to read more of what other people had to say.

Note how he has now included a good deal of information from the students he interviewed.

Broadbent's peer made this comment on his earlier draft:

Your conclusion was weak—maybe you could add what students ought to be doing now? Put another way, what do you want your readers to do with this (interesting) information?

Note how he now addresses what students can do to become more involved with their campus recycling program.

QUESTIONS FOR WRITING AND DISCUSSION: LEARNING OUTCOMES

Rhetorical Knowledge: The Writer's Situation and Rhetoric

1. **Audience:** How effective is Broadbent at appealing to the audience that this information is intended for—students at a college or university? What can you point to in the article to demonstrate what you mean?

2. **Purpose:** In addition to its informative purpose, what other purposes does this paper have?

3. **Voice and Tone:** What is Broadbent's attitude toward his subject? How does he indicate this attitude in his tone?

4. **Responsibility:** What can you point to in Broadbent's informational essay that gives the text its ethos? To what extent do you believe the information that Broadbent presents here? Why?

5. **Context and Format:** How has Broadbent's context—his college campus—affected his paper? How might he have written about the same subject differently in another context?

Critical Thinking: Your Personal Response

1. What was the most interesting piece of information in Craig Broadbent's essay? Why? The least interesting? Why?

2. To what extent does this information make you want to learn more about the recycling program on your campus? Why?

3. What was the most surprising piece of information in this essay? Why was it surprising?

Critical Thinking: The Writer's Ideas

1. What ideas in Broadbent's essay seem the most important to you? Why?

2. How effectively does Broadbent inform the reader? What examples can you point to in the text that provide useful information?

Composing Processes and Knowledge of Conventions: The Writer's Strategies

1. What internal strategies does Broadbent use to present his information? What other strategies might he have used?

2. How effective are the visuals that Broadbent includes? What is your opinion of the sources he uses? What other sources might he have consulted?

3. What is your opinion of Broadbent's conclusion?

Inquiry and Research: Ideas for Further Exploration

1. What questions do you still have about recycling? Where would you go to look for further information?

2. Go to your college's main Web page and search for "recycling." In no more than one page, outline what you learn.

 # Self-Assessment: Reflecting on Your Learning Goals

Now that you have constructed a piece of informative writing, go back and consider your learning goals, which you and your classmates may have considered at the beginning of this chapter (see pp. 186–87). Write notes on what you have learned from this assignment.

Rhetorical Knowledge

- *Audience:* What did you learn about your audience as you wrote your informative paper?

- *Purpose:* How successfully do you feel you fulfilled your informative purpose?

- *Rhetorical situation:* Consider some of the aspects that you have to think about, as a writer: How did the writing context affect your informational text? How did your choice of topic affect the research you conducted and how you presented your information to your readers? What do you see as the strongest part of your paper? Why? The weakest? Why?

- *Voice and tone:* How would you describe your voice in this essay? Your tone? How do they contribute to the effectiveness of your informational essay?

Critical Thinking, Reading, and Writing

- *Learning/inquiry:* How did you decide what to focus on in your informative paper? Describe the process you went through to focus on a main idea, or thesis. How did you judge what was most and least important in your information?

- *Responsibility:* How did you fulfill your responsibility to your readers?
- *Reading and research:* What did you learn about informative writing from the reading selections you read for this chapter? What research did you conduct? How sufficient was the research you did? Why? What additional research might you have done?

Writing Processes for an Informative Paper

- *Invention:* What invention strategies were most useful to you?
- *Organizing your ideas and details:* What organization did you use? How successful was it? Why?
- *Revising:* What one revision did you make that you are most satisfied with? What are the strongest and the weakest parts of the paper or other piece of writing you wrote for this chapter? Why? If you could go back and make an additional revision, what would it be?
- *Working with peers:* How did your instructor or peer readers help you by making comments and suggestions about your writing? List some examples of useful comments that you received. List some examples of how you revised your essay based on those comments and suggestions. How could you have made better use of the comments and suggestions you received? How could your peer readers help you more on your next assignment? How might you help them more, in the future, with the comments and suggestions you make on their texts?
- Did you use photographs or other visuals to help you inform your readers? If so, what did you learn about incorporating these elements?
- What "writerly habits" have you developed, modified, or improved on as you constructed the writing assignment for this chapter? How will you change your future writing activities, based on what you have learned about yourself?

Knowledge of Conventions

- *Editing:* What sentence problem did you find most frequently in your writing? How will you avoid that problem in future assignments?
- *Genre:* What conventions of the genre you were using, if any, gave you problems?
- *Documentation:* Did you use sources for your paper? If so, what documentation style did you use? What problems, if any, did you have with it?

 ## Craig Broadbent Reflects on His Writing

Once he completed the final draft of his essay, Craig Broadbent reflected on his writing process. Here is an excerpt from his reflection:

I saw this paper as an informative essay where I wanted others on campus to learn about our campus problems and how they might help, through the recycling program that already exists on campus. I didn't want to ask people to go out and pick up litter (I don't think they'd do that), but rather to see and understand that there was a problem and that our recycling program was a way to help solve that problem.

I know students—I am one and live in the dorm—so I know they might be semi-aware that we have a recycling program, that they probably have seen the blue barrels around campus, but that they're going to be way more interested in the football game this Saturday, or the dance on Friday, or the new scary movie that just came out, than they would even notice the barrels. So, I thought I'd better work hard to get their attention, with some facts and maybe photos, to show the problem.

I know informative writing is supposed to be pretty neutral, but I guess I'm not completely so, as I wanted to show we had a problem and tell about the recycling program. That was the purpose of my paper. But I guess my purpose, or the thesis of my paper, would be more that here is the problem and here is how you can help, without trying to really persuade people to get involved (that'd be a different kind of paper). Here, I knew there was a problem and just started looking around me and taking some digital photos (which I probably should have inserted into my paper, but didn't think of it at the time) and wondering who I might talk to to find out about what's happening on campus, to get rid of the stuff that everyone just walks by and sort of ignores.

I got the campus directory and found out the people to go talk to. They were very open and helpful and wanted to do the same thing I wanted to do: to let students know we had a problem and what we might do about it.

I especially enjoyed the research part of writing this paper, and the interviews were a lot of fun—even if they were a lot of work to do. I also found it useful to find tables and charts with information—the one I liked best was the little chart from the University of Nebraska because it provides a lot of important and useful information, information that my classmates ought to be able to relate to. So this chart combines good information with a good visual aid plus useful research and is in a form (and color) people will read and respond to—they'll pay attention to it, which is the whole idea here. . . .

Rhetorical Knowledge

- *Audience:* You should determine who will benefit from your analysis. Who needs the clarification? What do the audience members probably already know? What will you need to tell them?

- *Purpose:* When you analyze a complex situation, process, or relationship, you can help others understand the subject more thoroughly. Your purpose is usually informative, although you also in a sense intend to persuade the reader that your analysis is insightful.

- *Rhetorical situation:* In an analysis, you break down your subject into parts or categories to help your reader understand it more clearly. If you are a teacher or parent analyzing a school bond proposal, however, you may have a different stance toward your subject than a member of the town council or a senior citizen on a fixed income.

- *Writer's voice and tone:* When you write an analysis, you are trying to give readers a better understanding of something. You need to be detailed and thorough, but you should avoid an all-knowing attitude that might be interpreted as arrogant.

- *Context, medium, and genre:* You will need to decide on the best medium and genre to use to present your analysis to the audience you want to reach. Often, you can use tables, charts, and graphs as well as words to depict an analysis.

Critical Thinking, Reading, and Writing

- *Learning/inquiry:* By reading and writing analytically, you gain a deeper understanding of issues and the ability to make more informed decisions. This kind of thinking will help you avoid easy answers to complex issues.

- *Responsibility:* Effective analysis leads naturally to critical thinking. When you engage in analysis, you see the nuances of all the potential relationships involved in your subject.

- *Reading and research:* Analysis can involve close observation as well as interviews and online and library research.

Chapter 7

Writing Processes

- *Invention:* Various invention activities—brainstorming, listing, clustering—can help you consider the parts of your subject and how they relate to one another. The writing-to-learn strategies from Chapter 3 can also help you explore your subject.

- *Organizing your ideas and details:* If your subject is large, you might break it down into more understandable parts, or you might begin with individual parts and examine each one in detail. You will need to make sure that the individual pieces of information you are analyzing are presented clearly and logically.

- *Revising:* You will need to read your work with a critical eye, to make certain that it fulfills the assignment and displays the qualities of good analytical writing.

- *Working with peers:* Listen to your classmates to make sure that they understand your analysis. What do they say about how well your details justify your conclusion?

 ## Conventions

- *Editing:* Wordiness can be a problem in any kind of writing. The round-robin activity on pages 305–06 will help you check your analysis for wordy sentences.

- *Genres for analytical writing:* Usually analyses are written as formal documents (as opposed to, say, a letter that might be intended to inform a reader), so most times your analysis will be a formal report or an academic essay.

- *Documentation:* If you have relied on sources outside of your own experience, you will need to cite them using the appropriate documentation style.

What are you afraid of?

Writing to Analyze

To get a clearer understanding of a subject such as the irrational fear of spiders or snakes that many people suffer from, scientists need to analyze it, to break it down. An **analysis** examines an issue or topic by identifying the parts that make up the whole. You can gain a much clearer understanding of your subject when you look closely at the individual pieces that constitute the whole. Perhaps you have read an analysis of a current news story in a magazine such as *Time* or *US News and World Report.* Maybe you've heard a film critic analyzing the trends in summer movies, or read an analysis of a provocative new advertising campaign that started with a controversial ad first run during the Super Bowl. An analysis of a *phobia,* defined as an uncontrollable (and sometimes irrational) fear of some situation, object, or activity, would require you to examine the various aspects of that phobia. Think about what makes you or someone you know afraid of one or more of the following:

- Heights
- Insects
- Flying
- Water
- Caves
- Snakes
- Dogs, bats, or other mammals

Analyzing phobias is an area of study in colleges and universities, including the University of Texas at Austin. Following is an excerpt from an essay about the fear of snakes.

Fear can be a good thing.

Being afraid makes us heed severe weather warnings and keeps us from running across busy freeways. It is a survival mechanism for most, but for some people their fear has become consuming and out of control.

Since 1988 Dr. Michael Telch and the Laboratory for the Study of Anxiety Disorders (LSAD) in the Department of Psychology at The University of Texas at Austin have been researching treatments for anxiety-related disorders such as panic disorder, obsessive-compulsive disorder, social anxiety disorder, and specific phobias, including claustrophobia, arachnophobia and cynophobia (dog phobia).

"Anxiety is part of being a human being," Telch said. "The question is when does it become a disorder? Mother Nature gave us an alarm system of anxiety and panic to cope with threats. This signal system is critical to our survival. The bad news is that this mechanism is capable of sending a false alarm.

"It can become a disorder when the alarm is out of proportion to the threat," he added. "The hallmark is that the brain is receiving danger messages when the danger isn't there. While many people have these false alarms, it becomes a disorder when it interferes with daily functioning or when the response is above and beyond what is called for. Anxiety disorders are the largest—and one of the most treatable—classes of psychiatric disorders."

Rapid breathing, pounding heart and a desire to flee are typical—and reasonable—reactions to perceived danger, but for someone experiencing an anxiety disorder, these feelings become overwhelming. The fight or flight response kicks into overdrive when a person is experiencing the symptoms of an anxiety disorder. Research has shown that anxiety disorders in the U.S. cost more than $42 billion each year, about one third of the amount spent on mental health care in this country.

> . . .

While psychologists analyze subjects such as phobias to understand mental processes better and, perhaps, bring unwanted anxieties under control, analysis can also be a helpful tool in your everyday life. You have probably analyzed the college you are currently attending: examining its catalog to consider the variety of courses offered, perhaps reading through faculty lists to consider who you might be able to study with, and considering other

Some people do not have a fear of snakes.

factors. Many businesses ask employees to analyze their time by keeping a daily record of what they do and how long each task takes. Such an analysis may help businesses become more efficient. Likewise, as a college student, if you keep a log of how and when you study, you may be able to see emerging patterns that will enable you to study more efficiently. Using analysis in your writing can help you come to a deeper understanding of your subjects and share that understanding with your readers.

Rhetorical Knowledge

When you write an analysis, you need to consider how it will help your readers understand your topic in a new way and why you want them to gain this understanding. You will also need to decide what medium and genre will help you get your analysis across to your audience most effectively.

Writing to Analyze in Your College Classes

Much of the writing and thinking you will be asked to do in college will be analytical. You will encounter assignments that call for analysis in the humanities, the natural sciences, and the social sciences. Although academic disciplines vary widely, all of them use the process of analysis because when you analyze something, you almost always come to a more complete understanding of that idea or item. The thinking you do while working through your analysis—through reading and talking with others—necessarily causes you to learn more about the subject of your analysis.

In your college career, you may be asked to construct written analyses in many of your classes:

- In a chemistry class, you might be asked to break down an unknown compound to find what elements are present and write a lab report on your findings.

- In a social-psychology class, you might do a statistical analysis of the behavior of male college students in groups compared to their behavior as individuals.

- In a business class, you might analyze whether a certain corporation's stock is a safe investment by investigating such factors as its market share, earnings statements, track record in the field, and potential for growth.

- In a literature class, you might be asked to analyze how an author develops the hero of a novel to be a sympathetic character.

- In a nutrition class, you may have to analyze potential diets to see whether they meet particular nutritional needs.

- In an American history class, you may analyze what political circumstances led to the ratification of an amendment to the U.S. Constitution.

The work needed to perform an analysis usually requires you to make close observations or conduct research so you will have a command of your subject. Writing an analysis also forces you to put your understanding of that subject into your own words. Whenever you express something in your own way, you automatically learn more effectively.

Writing to Analyze for Life

In the professional, civic, and personal areas of your life, you also will construct analyses of various ideas, products, and situations.

The kind of analytical writing you do in your **professional life** will depend on your career, yet the odds are that at some point you will be asked to do an analysis and write a report on your findings. For example, teachers analyze textbooks to determine which one will best suit the goals of their course. An attorney analyzes legal rulings, the strengths and weaknesses of a client's case, and the arguments presented in court. A physician analyzes her patient's symptoms as she attempts to diagnose the illness and prescribe a cure. The list of possibilities is endless, but it's clear the quality of your analytical thinking and writing will influence your ultimate success.

All too often our first impulse in our **civic life** is emotional. You may get angry when the city council decides to demolish an old building, or you might enthusiastically support a local developer's plan to buy unused farmland to build a twenty-four-screen movie theater. Despite your personal feelings on the issues, your voice will be taken much more seriously if you engage in a balanced, in-depth analysis.

Interestingly, in our **personal lives,** we often tend to analyze events or conversations after they have happened, determining what was useful, what was a problem, and what we might do the next time. You may have had a conversation with a close friend that left both of you feeling unhappy, angry, or resentful. After the frustrating encounter, you replay the conversation in your mind, trying to take apart what was said by whom and figure out what went wrong. You may then write a note to the other person, explaining your analysis of the situation and what you propose to do to make amends.

WRITER'S WORKSHOP

Applying Learning Goals to Analytical Writing

As we have seen, analysis is the act of breaking something down into its component parts and working to understand the relationships among those parts. What is most crucial in any analysis is identifying the parts and understanding how they fit together to form the whole. In all areas of life, you are likely to face complex situations, and often your initial impulse may be to respond with a simple reaction or solution. Unfortunately, this may not be the best response. Analyzing a situation carefully helps you understand its complexity and respond in the most appropriate and effective fashion. As a group, think of a writing situation where a detailed analysis might provide a much more reasoned response than an instant, knee-jerk reaction. Perhaps the situation is an increase in fees at your university, or perhaps the requirement that you pay sales tax on a car you purchased in another state. With the other members of your group, discuss your writing situation in terms of the learning goals listed on pages 250–51. How would you address these goals? Does it matter who your reader might be?

Scenarios for Writing: Assignment Options

Your instructor may ask you to complete one or more of the following analytical writing assignments. Each assignment is in the form of a *scenario*, a situation that provides some context for the analysis you will construct. The scenarios are designed to provide a sense of who your audience is and what you want to accomplish with your analytical writing. The list of rhetorical considerations on page 262 encourages you to consider your audience; purpose; voice, tone, and point of view; and context, medium, and genre.

As in the other chapters in this text, we have provided two scenarios focused on academic writing and three scenarios that you might encounter outside of college. Starting on page 285, you will find guidelines for completing the assignment option that you choose or that is assigned to you.

Writing for College

SCENARIO 1   An Analysis of a Campus Issue

As we have seen, in your college classes you will often be asked to analyze—to help your readers understand why something happens as it does. Analysis helps people understand whether an idea is a good one or not, or whether a policy should be followed or not.

For example, as we were writing this chapter, there was a discussion on our campus about giving the student government the responsibility to operate the student union. The university would allow the students to decide what restaurants and stores would operate in the building, how meeting rooms would be used, and other matters. Interested parties were considering whether this change would be a good idea. An analysis of the issues involved in a decision such as this one could help the decision makers understand what would be at stake, and they could then make an informed choice when they voted on the issue.

On your campus there are many issues that you might analyze:

- Tuition increases: Where does the money go? How does the tuition compare to that of other schools? As the graph shown in Figure 7.1 indicates, tuition increases at one school declined over a period of five

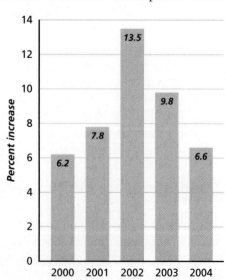

FIGURE 7.1   Tuition Increases at Penn State

years—on a percentage basis. But when you add up the cumulative total for the five years shown, the total increase comes to about 44 percent.

- Extra fees: Why are they necessary? Where does that money go?
- Availability of professors during their office hours (and at other times)

Writing Assignment: Think about what is happening on your campus. Select a complex problem that affects you or others, whether the issue is specific to a course, to students on your campus, or to students nationwide. Construct a report that analyzes the problem and offers insights about it. An analysis will help you as a writer and your readers understand the issue so an informed decision can be made.

SCENARIO 2   Analyzing a Subject That Matters to You

This scenario asks you to construct an analysis of a subject from any area of your academic life. Choose a complex subject that you would like to look at in depth and about which you think you have insights to offer.

Writing Assignment: Think of something that functions effectively. Possibilities include a championship sports team, a successful business, an effective charitable organization, or a popular TV show. Analyze the topic you selected by breaking down its components, describing and explaining what they are and how they function, outlining how each piece works in conjunction with the others, and offering insights into the subject. Your analysis

FIGURE 7.2   A College Student Analyzes His Data

should be for a course in the subject area to which the topic belongs; for example, you would analyze a championship sports team for a physical education course or a successful business for a business administration course.

Writing for Life

SCENARIO 3   Civic Writing: A Letter to the Editor
Analyzing Leadership Styles

One of the most important ways in which you can participate in your civic life is to vote, and most often you will vote for a person: a school board member, a state senator or governor, the President of the United States. Almost anyone in public life seeks to serve as a leader, to help advance ideas that he or she believes in.

This is an opportunity to analyze leadership style. As part of the project, you will need to define the term *leadership* and to conduct research and find examples of various people whom you consider to be effective leaders.

You will want to look for examples in the public sector, considering leaders who are known nationally or even globally as well as those who are serving in your community. Some local examples might include the following:

- A public figure who campaigns to improve literacy
- A professor who has fought for fair treatment for campus support personnel
- A local mayor or council member who has improved life in your community

Writing Assignment: Write a paper, as a letter to the editor, that analyzes the leadership style of someone you view as a successful leader. You will need to define *leadership* and then analyze what you see as that person's leadership style. There are many qualities of strong leadership, so you will need to describe and define those you deem important, and then analyze the person you focus on in terms of those leadership qualities.

SCENARIO 4   Personal Writing: Report on Options for a Trip

Think about several options for a trip that you would like to take with family or friends. Look over the following list of considerations that might be part of your planning for the trip:

- Possible destinations
- Time frame
- Cost
- Transportation
- Room and board

FIGURE 7.3   A Possible Vacation Option

Writing Assignment: Research the top three options for a trip you would like to take (Figure 7.3), and then write a report analyzing your findings for your traveling companions. You will need to cover all of the details of the trip—the parts—well enough to allow everyone to make informed choices about the whole plan. Since this assignment is an analysis and not just an informative paper, your paper should explain how the various aspects of the trip will work together to make a whole experience.

**SCENARIO 5   Professional Writing: A Business Report
Analyzing Part of Your Future Career**

Think forward to the day when you are ready to apply for jobs in your chosen field. Select an image or advertisement related to your future career—the position you plan to seek after you graduate from college. You might select the following, for example:

- A movie advertisement, if you are planning to work as an actor, director, screenwriter, or in another field in the film industry

- An advertisement for a product produced by or a service provided by the company you hope to work for
- An image from a company's annual report
- A company's logo
- An advertisement or a photograph of a product you hope to manufacture or sell
- A Web page from a nonprofit or government agency for which you hope to work

Writing Assignment: For this writing project, analyze the image or advertisement that you selected. Your task is not to evaluate the image or advertisement, but rather to analyze its various aspects (color, point of view, text, size, shading) to understand how the image or advertisement works.

Rhetorical Considerations in Analytical Writing

Audience: Although your teacher and classmates are your initial audience for your analysis, also consider a wider audience. Assume that your audience already knows something about the focus of your text, but they have probably not tried to analyze it. What kinds of analysis will be most interesting to this group of readers?

Purpose: By researching and analyzing the problem, issue, concept, options, or object, you will be providing your readers with an analysis that will allow them to make more informed decisions.

Voice, Tone, and Point of View: You have probably chosen your topic because you have a personal interest in the subject. What preconceptions do you have? How can you avoid letting them oversimplify your analysis? How can you use voice and tone to establish credibility, so your readers believe your analysis? Put another way, how will your analysis be most effective: if you write in a shrill or sarcastic tone, or a more professional, even-tempered tone?

Context, Medium, and Genre: Keeping the context of the assignment in mind, decide on a medium and a genre for your writing. How will your analysis be used? Who might be interested in reading your analysis? Obviously, your instructor will use your analytical writing to help determine your grade for the course, so you should follow his or her instructions carefully. If you are writing for an audience beyond the classroom, consider what will be the most effective way to present your analysis to this audience.

For more on choosing a medium and genre, see Chapter 15 and Appendix C.

Critical Thinking, Reading, and Writing

Before you begin to write your analysis, consider the qualities of successful analytic writing. It also helps to read one or more examples of analysis to see these qualities in action. Finally, you might consider how visuals can add to an analysis, as well as the kinds of sources you will need to consult.

As we have seen, effective analytical writing focuses on a complex subject, thoroughly explains the parts of that subject and their relationship to one another, and is almost always based on research rather than on personal experience. An analysis is usually presented in a focused, straightforward way, with insights and a conclusion that ties the aspects of your subject together for readers. The guidelines and reading selections that follow will help you learn more about the qualities of successful analytical writing.

 ## Learning the Qualities of Effective Analytical Writing

An effective analysis will help you and your readers better understand your subject. To accomplish this, you need to make sure your analysis includes the following qualities:

- **A focus on a complex subject.** Any subject worth analyzing—a political position, a book, a war strategy—will be complex (if it were not complex, you would not need to analyze it). It will consist of many parts or features, and these parts will interact with one another in complicated ways.

- **A thorough explanation of the parts and how they relate to one another.** An effective analysis identifies and explains the parts of a subject in sufficient detail and builds the foundation for your analysis. Your first step will be to identify the component parts or aspects of your subject and then consider how those component parts function separately and together. For a subject such as a new school tax bond, you might consider aspects like the following:

- Benefits
  - to the students
  - to the local tax base
  - to the teachers, administration, and support staff
- Problems and costs
  - costs in the form of debt that will need to be paid off
  - interest charges

- What happens if the community does not fund the schools in this way?
  - Will school taxes need to be raised?
  - Will the quality of the school suffer?

After you have identified the parts or aspects of your subject, you need to gain a thorough understanding of each one so that you can explain it to your readers.

- **Research-based rather than personal-based writing.** With the exception of an informal analysis of a subject you know well, such as an analysis of a film or restaurant for a friend or family member, a formal analysis usually requires research. Your understanding of the subject is seldom enough to inform a thorough analysis. If you were analyzing the bond proposal, for example, you would need to read the entire proposal, interview the officials or citizen groups behind it, and examine recent school budgets.

For more on conducting research, see Chapters 19 and 20.

- **A focused, straightforward presentation.** An effective analysis focuses on the subject's component parts, always working to show how they combine to make up the whole subject. All aspects of your text must focus on some central theme or idea that connects all parts or aspects of the analysis together.

  Suppose in a Western civilization class you have been asked to analyze the construction of some of the great medieval cathedrals. You might want to examine the traditional layout of medieval churches first and then look at the architectural innovations such as flying buttresses that medieval architects incorporated into the construction of the cathedrals. While some of your analysis may deal with structural elements and innovations, you may also want to look at the aesthetic features of these giant structures. Incorporating aesthetic elements into your analysis, you would probably look at the use of stained glass and decorative work such as gargoyles to get a sense of the effect the entire structure has on those who experience it.

  Like an informative text, an analysis is usually neutral in tone—the writer's primary purpose is not to persuade, but rather to explain how the writer's subject functions.

- **Insights.** The purpose of analysis is to provide more meaningful insights into a topic or an issue. Taking something apart (even metaphorically) to analyze it provides insights into how each part functions, how each aspect relates to every other aspect and to the whole. Consider your family relationships: you know who gets along well and who might have issues with other members of your family. But to understand those relationships more fully, you need to analyze them in detail, to learn about the background and history of how various members of your family have interacted and how they have solved (or not solved) problems.

- **A conclusion that ties parts together.** Any writing project needs to reach a conclusion, but for an analysis a thoughtful conclusion is critical, because this is where the writer sums up the analysis. In other kinds of writing, this part of your paper could be called the *thesis statement*, but in an analysis your conclusion does much more than just state your major claim (as a thesis statement usually does). While your paper serves to outline and explain each aspect of the subject you are analyzing, in your conclusion you have the opportunity to outline how those parts function together and also to explain whether you believe (based on your analysis) that those parts function—or have functioned—together effectively or not.

For more on thesis statements, see Chapter 13.

In a computer file, you might summarize each quality of an effective analysis in your own words, and then refer to that summary as you conduct research and write your paper. Later, you can paste this list of qualities into your working draft to remind yourself of them.

A WRITER'S RESPONSIBILITIES

Constructing Analytical Writing in the Sciences

Effective analytical writing is thorough, examining and explaining as many details as possible. If you are working in a field that has particular procedures in place, you have an obligation to follow the accepted procedures faithfully. Scientists must follow specific procedures and policies in order for their experiments to be considered valid, for example. If you are working in a scientific field, you will need to document everything you do—from taking notes on your process, to constructing drawings that illustrate the process, to verifying measurements with specific instruments. You also must clearly and accurately present any statistical data, with all supporting evidence and detail; you must explain in detail any relationships between variables in your experiment; and you must carefully follow other requirements for reporting your results.

To construct an effective scientific analysis, rely on and follow the four-step *scientific method* because your readers will understand and know the method and will expect you to use it:

1. You observe and describe a phenomenon or group of phenomena.
2. You formulate a hypothesis to explain the phenomena. In physics, for example, the hypothesis often proposes a cause for the phenomenon.
3. You then use your hypothesis to predict the existence of other phenomena or to predict quantitatively the results of new observations.
4. You and other independent researchers test your predictions by conducting experiments.

Source: The four steps are adapted from Frank Wolfs. "Appendix E: Introduction to the Scientific Method." http://teacher.nsrl.rochester.edu/phy_labs/AppendixE/AppendixE.html. Downloaded 12/13/03.

> ## Reading, Inquiry, and Research: Learning from Texts That Analyze

The reading selections that follow are examples of analytical writing. We think you will both enjoy and learn from them. As you read the texts, ask yourself the following questions:

- What makes this analysis effective? What might you point to in the reading selection that helps you understand the analysis?
- What qualities of an effective analysis (see pp. 263–65) does the reading selection exhibit?
- What parts of the analysis still leave you with questions?
- How can you use these analytical techniques to construct an analysis in your writing?

As you read a selection and respond to questions that follow it, take notes, jot down questions, and make observations about the essay in a journal, preferably in a computer file. Then, if you want to use the information in your writing, you will already have the main points in a digital format.

JAMES M. LANG

Putting In the Hours

James M. Lang is a public speaker, workshop leader, and assistant professor of English at Assumption College. Essays from his regular column for the *Chronicle of Higher Education* about life on the tenure track were compiled into the book *Life on the Tenure Track: Lessons from the First Year* (2005). Lang is also the author of *Learning Sickness: A Year with Crohn's Disease* (2004). This essay was originally published on May 16, 2003, as part of Lang's column in the *Chronicle*.

Most casual observers of the North American professor assume his   1
natural habitat to be the classroom, where he engages in those behaviors commonly associated with his species: speaking to audiences of young people in a loud voice, marking with writing utensils on green or white boards, receiving and distributing pieces of paper.

But the casual observer may overlook that this species usually   2
spends an equal, if not greater, part of his week in his den, holding what his institution terms "office hours." At small, liberal-arts colleges in New

England, like the one where our observations have been centered, he and his colleagues are, in fact, required to hold 10 office hours each week—time set aside for advisees and students who want to consult with the professor outside of the normal classroom hours.

Working our way up and down the halls of one faculty office building, checking out the office-hour schedules posted below the nameplates, and observing the work and leisure habits of these specimens through their half-opened doors, we have been able to classify, according to their office-hour behavior, some subspecies of the North American professor.

The Early Bird: Whether he actually likes mornings or not, the Early Bird schedules all of his office hours before 10 a.m.—in other words, before most of his students have rolled out of bed. The Early Bird can be assured that he will have fewer office visits than his next-door neighbor, who has scheduled all of her hours after noon.

The Early Bird has done nothing technically wrong, of course; he probably keeps his office hours more regularly than most faculty members. But the Early Bird also knows exactly what he is doing. He doesn't particularly want students visiting during office hours, and he has found the best legal means of ensuring that they don't.

The Door Closer: The Door Closer knows that students are far more likely to knock on an open door than a closed one, so he wards off all but the most desperate and devoted of his students by keeping his door completely shut during office hours. For extra effect, he will lock it, forcing students to realize that they are interrupting him by compelling him to walk to the door and open it.

We have actually observed students walk up to a professor's office, see the door closed, and walk away dispirited—only to watch the office's occupant emerge moments later, heading to the departmental office for a coffee refill. Like the Early Bird, the Door Closer has not violated the letter of his contract; he relies instead upon simple and subtle discouragement.

The Counselor: The Door Closer's antithesis, the Counselor props his door open as wide as it will allow, faces his desk towards the doorway, and peeks out expectantly at every passing footfall. The Counselor wants students to visit him in his office. The Counselor wants to know how they're doing. The students actually divulge this information to the Counselor: They tell him about their roommates, and their relationships, and their home lives. The Counselor loves it.

Other faculty members are baffled by the Counselor, and slightly suspicious of him. They suspect—and they are probably right—that their own names come up occasionally in the Counselor's office, and that the Counselor listens to student complaints about them with a sympathetic ear.

The Chatterer: Chatterers, whether they want students in their office or not, like to spend their office hours socializing. They stop in to visit other colleagues who are having office hours, they linger in the departmental office to check their mail or fill their coffee mug, and they welcome long lines at the copy machine. As a rule, nonchattering faculty members tend to appreciate Chatterers most at paper-grading time, when frequent interruptions to their work are happily tolerated. When they are trying to prepare for a class they have to teach in 30 minutes, the average faculty member sees his Chattering neighbor as a nuisance. 10

Most Chatterers are people who simply like to talk, and practice their chatting habits in other realms of their lives as incessantly as they do at the office. 11

We have noticed a subspecies of Chatterers, though: people who live by themselves, especially those newly arrived at the college, without much of a social network outside the campus. For this species, the time they spend in the office provides them with their primary socializing opportunity. Back in their apartments, it's a book or the television. During office hours they get to communicate with other members of their species. 12

The Fugitive: The counterpart to the lonely Chatterer, the Fugitive has a houseful of living creatures—spouses, children, dogs, cats, hermit crabs—and sees the office as his refuge from the chaos that constantly threatens to overwhelm his home life. Fugitives can best be recognized by their relaxed attitude during office hours. However much work they have to do at the office, it can't be any more stressful than what they have to deal with at home. Fugitives usually have at least one extremely comfortable chair in their office, and can occasionally be spotted sitting in that chair and staring off into space, just enjoying the peace and quiet. 13

In the interests of scientific objectivity, we should disclose that the author of this paper is a Fugitive. 14

He has a recliner purchased from the Salvation Army, and the most relaxing part of his day are those moments when he can balance a cup of tea on the armrest, kick off his shoes, and read the material he has assigned for class. He has a little refrigerator in his office, and he has expressed his desire to install a television/VCR as well. 15

"If you ever kick me out," he has been known to remark to his wife, with just a hint of hopefulness, when he has all three kids in the tub and the phone and the doorbell are ringing and the cats are scratching at the door, "I'll be able to move right into my office." 16

"Don't get your hopes up," she has been known to respond. 17

But the truth of the matter is, he is not always or exclusively a Fugitive. Sometimes he engages in behaviors associated with the Chatterer, and the Door Closer, and sometimes the Early Bird too (he draws the line at the Counselor—much as he loves his students, he does not want to hear about their latest relationship problems).   18

He holds one office hour on Friday morning from 8:30 to 9:30 a.m., before his first class. In an entire semester, he has had one visitor during that office hour, and she came under extreme duress, when all other options were exhausted. He counts three Chatterers in his department among his closest friends, so he often welcomes the opportunity to talk with them, even occasionally instigating such conversations. And he will close his door when he is having one of those weeks when the paper stack never seems to diminish, no matter how many he grades. So we have begun to suspect that these observations are perhaps more appropriately classified as behaviors rather than subspecies types.   19

Most North American professors do have a dominant behavior that characterizes their office-hour activity, but most also engage in multiple behaviors in the course of a single week.   20

Given the early and exploratory nature of these observations, we would welcome notes from fellow field researchers who have studied the office-hour habits of the North American professor, and have observed other forms of both common and unusual behaviors.   21

QUESTIONS FOR WRITING AND DISCUSSION: LEARNING OUTCOMES

Rhetorical Knowledge: The Writer's Situation and Rhetoric

1. **Audience:** The *Chronicle of Higher Education* is a weekly newspaper for college professors. How effectively does Lang understand and reach his audience? What can you point to in Lang's essay that supports your claim? Who else—besides college teachers and students—might be interested in reading Lang's analysis?

2. **Purpose:** Why, do you suppose, did Lang write this essay? What was he trying to accomplish?

3. **Voice and tone:** What can you point to in Lang's use of tone that helps to establish his ethos?

4. **Responsibility:** What can you cite from the essay that shows how Lang was fulfilling his responsibilities as a writer when he wrote "Putting In the Hours"?

5. **Context and format**: Lang's essay appeared in a respected academic periodical, the *Chronicle of Higher Education*. Is Lang's essay typical of the kind of writing you would expect in such a journal? Why?

Critical Thinking: Your Personal Response

1. What is your initial reaction to Lang's analysis? Do you find it humorous? Why?

2. Without naming names, think of your professors and how they fit into any of Lang's categories. Using Lang's categories, how would you describe their behavior?

3. How do you react to Lang's "confession" of his office-hour habits, labeling himself a "Fugitive"?

Critical Thinking: The Writer's Ideas

1. How accurate are Lang's categories and sub-categories? Why? How much do you agree with his analysis? Why?

2. What new ideas about college professors did you learn from Lang's analysis?

3. How well do Lang's comments let you know what his real attitude is toward professors' office hours? How does he reveal his attitude?

Composing Processes and Knowledge of Conventions: The Writer's Strategies

1. Consider Lang's overall organization by making a sentence or scratch outline of it (outline the text by writing, in one sentence, what each paragraph has to say). How effective is his organization? Why? In what other way(s) might this essay be organized?

2. Lang starts his essay with this line: "Most casual observers of the North American professor assume his natural habitat to be the classroom, where he engages in those behaviors commonly associated with his species . . ." (paragraph 1). What effect does Lang have by making his essay sound like an animal observation?

3. What label or classification do you find the most interesting or humorous? Why?

4. Lang organizes his essay by classifying various types of professors. How effective is it to label his comments about each "type" of professor in this manner? Why?

Inquiry and Research: Ideas for Further Exploration

1. Visit two of your professors in their offices. How do they compare to Lang's professors? Be specific in your description.

2. Give a copy of Lang's analysis to your favorite teacher and then, after he or she has read Lang's essay, interview that teacher. In no more than two pages, explain the teacher's reaction to Lang's comments.

JOHN ROCKHOLD

Pay Less at the Pump: The Hybrid Revolution

John Rockhold is the managing editor of *Mother Earth News*, a bi-monthly magazine that aims to help readers become more "self-sufficient, financially independent and environmentally aware." He has written numerous articles on environmental issues. This article was first published in *Mother Earth News* in 2005.

Six years after the release of the Honda Insight—the bulletlike two-seater that was the first gasoline/electric hybrid vehicle available in the United States—high fuel economy without compromise is here to stay. Praised by motorheads and environmentalists alike, hybrids represent the most exciting advancement in personal transportation since, well, the internal-combustion engine. Spearheaded by the Toyota Prius, hybrids' popularity surge shows that a rapidly growing number of people want to be on the cusp of the hybrid revolution. Furthermore, with skyrocketing gas prices and dwindling global oil supplies, hybrids are becoming an increasingly wise investment.

In 2004, more than 83,000 hybrids were sold. In just the first half of this year, more than 90,000 were sold; final 2005 sales may eclipse 200,000. Right now, hybrids account for less than 1 percent of the automobiles sold in the United States. But given their growth rate and the dozens of new models that will be available in the next several years—Toyota alone plans to introduce 10 more hybrid models within the next seven years—hybrids will soon have a significant share of the auto market. Already there are more hybrids in more size categories than most thought possible when the Insight arrived. Meanwhile, sales of large sport utility vehicles and trucks are dwindling.

Car-buyers also are willing to pay extra for hybrids—anywhere from $1,000 to $10,000 more than conventional vehicles. . . . But with tax incentives for hybrids and the rising cost of gas, it's possible to make up the low end of that hybrid premium in about five years. For example, compare a conventional vehicle with the average U.S. fuel economy of 21 miles per gallon to a 46-mpg hybrid (the average of the Accord, Civic, Escape, Insight and Prius hybrids). Assume you pay $2.20 a gallon for gasoline, with that price rising 10 cents annually (a modest estimate; inflation alone will increase prices by at least 5 cents a year). After five years, you'll save $4,658 with a hybrid; after 10 years, $10,287. (See the chart below for more examples.)

Still, the hybrid premium can be intimidating at first glance. In   4
a survey conducted by the Polk Center for Automotive Studies, 61

Hybrid Payback

To calculate when you'll see payback from a hybrid's gas savings, compare savings at the pump versus the premium for a hybrid. Also consider tax incentives: hybrid-buyers are eligible for a $2,000 tax deduction through 2005 or tax credits between $250 and $3,400 for 2006 through 2009.

FUEL COSTS*

Vehicle mpg	21 mpg	46 mpg	55 mpg
Years 1–5	$8,577	$3,913	$3,273
Savings vs. 21 mpg	—	$4,658	$5,298
Years 6–10	$10,357	$4,728	$3,954
Savings vs. 21 mpg	—	$5,629	$6,403
Total savings	—	$10,287	$11,701

APPROXIMATE COST DIFFERENCES

Toyota Prius vs. Toyota Camry = $1,000

Honda Civic Hybrid vs. Honda Civic = $4,500

Ford Escape Hybrid vs. Ford Escape = $7,000

Honda Accord Hybrid vs. Honda Accord = $10,000

21 mpg = Average fuel economy of U.S. passenger vehicles.
46 mpg = Average fuel economy of the Accord, Civic, Escape, Insight, and Prius hybrids. **55 mpg** = Average fuel economy of Toyota Prius and Honda Insight.
*Assumes gas price per gallon of $2.20 in year one, rising 10 cents annually. Assumes 15,000 miles driven annually, at a ratio of 45-percent highway, 55-percent city driving.

percent of those polled said the extra cost would be a deterrent to buying a hybrid. But if we're willing to pay hundreds or thousands extra for options such as larger engines, four-wheel drive or leather seats, why not invest in a technology that will actually pay dividends for years to come?

"There are a lot of features that aren't worth the extra cost, but people pay for them because they want those features," says Terry Penney, technology manager for advanced vehicle technologies at the National Renewable Energy Laboratory (NREL). Penney and his team have worked to develop and improve hybrid systems since the early 1990s. "You have to take the longer view, the real cost of gas and the environmental consequences of pollution. People have recently seen how gas prices can be volatile. Oil is now about $60 a barrel—where's it going to stop?"

How Hybrids Work

At the heart of every hybrid is the tandem of an internal-combustion engine (powered by gasoline) and an electric motor (powered by batteries). In conventional vehicles, automakers size gas engines to provide enough power for peak acceleration, but that level of power isn't needed most of the time. The addition of an electric motor allows for a smaller gas engine that uses less fuel and can run more often at its peak efficiency.

In most hybrids, when the vehicle idles, the gas engine shuts off and the electric motor is the sole source of power. The electric motor also powers the hybrid at low speeds and supplements the gas engine with extra *oomph* when the driver accelerates quickly.

To recharge their batteries, hybrids capture kinetic energy as the vehicle slows down, a process called regenerative braking. In conventional vehicles, this energy is lost as heat when brakes apply friction. But in hybrids, the electric motor helps slow the car and transfers some of the kinetic energy to the batteries, which store the power for future use. Hybrids' conventional brakes kick in when needed, such as with sudden stops. Because hybrids recharge themselves, there's no need to plug them into an electrical outlet overnight...

Types of Hybrids

The 10 hybrid models available today utilize these characteristics in different ways and to varying degrees. There are gray areas among the different types, but the foremost distinction is whether or not the electric motor can operate independently from the gasoline engine. In **full hybrids,** the gasoline engine remains off for short periods at low speeds and the electric motor alone powers the vehicle. The net effect significantly boosts city fuel economy, and while moving in electric-only mode, these hybrids release almost zero tailpipe emissions. Full hybrids available today are those from Ford—the Escape Hybrid and the Mercury Mariner Hybrid—and those from Toyota—the Prius, Highlander Hybrid and Lexus RX 400h.

Mild hybrids have all the hybrid features except electric-only drive. The gasoline engine kicks on once the vehicle begins to move and continues running until the driver turns off the ignition. The electric motor lightens the gas engine's load and boosts power when needed. Two of Honda's hybrids—the Insight and Civic Hybrid—are in this category. The 2006 Civic Hybrid, though, will be a full hybrid—it will include electric-only drive at low speeds. 10

Some hybrids do not have smaller gasoline engines in conjunction with their electric motors. These **muscle hybrids** deliver improved horsepower and acceleration, with slightly improved fuel economy. They also have idle-off and regenerative braking. The main example is the Honda Accord Hybrid, which has a six-cylinder engine and delivers up to 255 horsepower with fuel economy estimates of 29 mpg in city driving and 37 mpg in highway driving. The nonhybrid Accord with a six-cylinder engine has 15 less horsepower and achieves about 21/30 mpg. Some consider the Highlander Hybrid and RX 400h muscle hybrids because of their six-cylinder engines. 11

Described by some as **hollow hybrids**, the Chevrolet Silverado Hybrid and GMC Sierra Hybrid have the most limited hybrid characteristics. These trucks do not have electric-only drive, but they do have idle-off and regenerative braking. However, their regenerative braking only recharges the batteries—the batteries do not store extra kinetic energy for use with hard acceleration. The batteries do help power on-board accessories, such as air conditioning, and plug-in devices, such as electric tools. These trucks have a net fuel economy increase of about 10 percent over their conventional counterparts. . . . 12

Buying and Owning a Hybrid

A year ago, long waiting lists greeted those who wanted to buy just about any hybrid model. Some shoppers remained in limbo for six months or more. Demand was intense and supply was limited—looking for a hybrid became a year-round version of shopping for the hottest, hard-to-find toy of the Christmas season. Production of hybrids, though, is constantly increasing in an effort to keep up with demand. Although unsold hybrids are rare on dealers' lots—most are spoken for before they arrive—wait time is usually just a few weeks. 13

High demand also has driven up the price of hybrids. Odds are you 14 won't successfully haggle dealers for a bargain—in high-demand areas, hybrids frequently sell for several thousand dollars more than their retail prices. Some used hybrids, especially recent years of the Prius, sell for as much or more as they cost when brand-new. That's at least a good sign for resale value—most new cars sharply decline in value as soon as they leave dealers' lots. To get the best deal on a hybrid, be patient and search high and low. Arm yourself with knowledge so you don't get gouged; several Web sites list prices recently paid for automobiles. Two examples are *www.hybridcars.com* and *www.kbb.com*, the online version of the Kelley Blue Book. Also read about others' hybrid-buying experiences in the numerous Internet blogs and forums devoted to hybrids. . . .

If you buy a hybrid before 2006, you can take a $2,000 deduction on 15 your federal income taxes. Basically, this deduction will reduce your federal taxable income by $2,000. For hybrids bought after Jan. 1, 2006, the recently enacted energy bill set up tax credits—ranging from $250 to $3,400, depending on the vehicle's fuel economy. The credit would go toward your tax liability, the amount you owe before any withholdings.

Over the long term, the credit will be more advantageous to those 16 who buy newer hybrid models and less helpful to those who buy better-selling hybrids such as the Prius. The energy bill established a complex formula to reduce the credits once an automaker sells more than 60,000 hybrids after Jan. 1. Hybrid buyers in 14 states also can take advantage of state-level incentives, including tax credits and exemptions from sales tax. Hybrid buyers in Colorado, for example, are eligible for tax credits of more than $4,500. There also are nonfinancial incentives—such as being allowed to drive in lanes for high-occupancy vehicles and park without paying meter fees. Visit *www.hybridcars.com* to see if there are programs where you live.

Owning a hybrid should be a worry-free experience—don't believe 17 naysayers who claim they come loaded with extra maintenance costs. Their regular maintenance needs are no different than gasoline-only vehicles, and the Honda Civic Hybrid and Toyota Prius have earned the highest ratings for reliability and owner satisfaction from *Consumer Reports*. In a now-famous quote within the hybrid community, Toyota mechanic Gus Heredia told the *Los Angeles Times*, "I'd go broke if the Prius was all I worked on."

Hybrids also are backed by the same warranties you'd expect with 18 any new automobile. Additional warranties cover the hybrid systems and typically last for eight years or 100,000 miles. The hybrid components do not require any routine maintenance, and the batteries will work for about 200,000 miles or more. When they do expire, they can be recycled.

Tune-ups and routine service for hybrids probably should be handled   19
by a dealer-based mechanic—unless you know and trust an independent
mechanic with hybrid experience. Dealers' higher rates probably are
worth paying to keep your hybrid in knowledgeable hands. Expect,
though, to save some money on brake maintenance—regenerative braking reduces the use of mechanical brakes, extending their life.

In terms of safety, hybrids pose no more danger in a collision than   20
any conventional vehicle. In fact, many hybrids offer the best in newer
safety technologies, such as stability control, anti-lock brakes and side
air bags. Here's more good news: given those safety features, you may
even save money on insurance for a hybrid, especially if you're upgrad-
ing from an older vehicle and have a good driving record.

Driving a Hybrid

Initially, some hybrid owners find that their actual gas mileage doesn't live   21
up to what's advertised. For many, the effort to improve their fuel economy
becomes a diligent pursuit. Once drivers understand how hybrids work,
they can adjust their driving habits to improve their mileage—for example, learning just when to press and release the accelerator to maximize
coasting on the electric motor helps improve miles per gallon.

Consider, though, that the advertised fuel economy numbers may be   22
slightly exaggerated. The Environmental Protection Agency (EPA) uses a
30-year-old methodology for calculating fuel economy. The tests do not
account for modern influences on gas mileage such as air conditioning and
speeds greater than 60 mpg. The final numbers can be inflated by as much
as 10 percent. . . .

Properly driven hybrids, though, will match their EPA-rated fuel   23
economy more closely than nonhybrids, according to Amory Lovins,
senior author of *Winning the Oil Endgame* and chief executive officer of
Rocky Mountain Institute, an independent, nonprofit think tank devoted
to energy and resource efficiency.

Lovins recommends "pulse" driving: "When you see that you'll need   24
to slow or stop, start braking gently and as early as possible so you can
recover the most braking energy for later use. If you brake too late—
hence too hard—the mechanical brakes will override, and they simply
turn motion into useless heat."

Hybrids also are a justified excuse to accelerate with vigor. "Contrary   25
to what we were taught in high-school driver's education, when you're
accelerating up to cruising speed, do so briskly," says Lovins, who owns a
Honda Insight that gets 63 mpg. "The engine is most efficient at high

speed and torque, so you'll use less fuel accelerating aggressively for a short time than accelerating slowly for a long time."

Also, take advantage of hybrids' computerized monitors that show 26 which components are delivering power and report your fuel economy. "Consistent with attentive driving, keep an eye on the real-time mpg display and use the feedback to improve your driving habits," Lovins says.

Exactly how much your fuel economy will improve by driving a 27 hybrid depends on numerous personal factors, but compared to gasoline vehicles, today's hybrids generally get 20 percent to 25 percent better fuel economy in highway driving, and 40 percent to 100 percent better mileage in city driving. Gas mileage in high-speed driving can improve if you avoid short trips and take a road with at least some hilly sections— the electric motor will kick in with steep inclines, aiding the gas engine's efficiency. For example, Penney—who drives a Prius—gets better results when he's on highways in Colorado's mountains than when driving through the city of Golden to reach the NREL office.

But stop-and-go driving does have the statistical edge. "It's generally 28 true that stop-and-go driving is better [for hybrids' fuel economy] because you get regenerative braking, and that's always better than no regenerative braking," Penney says. "So if a hybrid is better for someone, it's for someone who does a lot of starting and stopping."

Translation: *everyone.* The bottom line is that driving a hybrid can be 29 empowering—a personal, patriotic and environmental rush. The next time you spend $20 to $30 at the gas station, imagine not returning for another 500 miles.

QUESTIONS FOR WRITING AND DISCUSSION: LEARNING OUTCOMES

Rhetorical Knowledge: The Writer's Situation and Rhetoric

1. **Audience:** *Mother Earth News* is a magazine intended for people who are concerned about the environment. How does Rockhold's article target this particular audience? How well does he also address a larger audience?

2. **Purpose:** What information do you think Rockhold is trying to convey in this article?

3. **Voice and tone:** To what extent does Rockhold reveal his opinion about hybrid cars? Where do you think he does so? How would you describe his tone, and what does it contribute to his analysis?

4. **Responsibility:** How well does Rockhold fulfill his responsibility to accurately represent hybrids?

5. **Context and format:** Rockhold uses a table in the essay. How effective is this visual element? What other kinds of visual elements would be useful here?

Critical Thinking: Your Personal Response

1. How do you respond to Rockhold's analysis? Would you be interested in looking into buying a hybrid vehicle as a result of what you've read? Why or why not?

2. Which argument might you find more persuasive when it comes to thinking about buying a hybrid—that it is environmentally friendly or that it will save you money on gas? Why?

3. How necessary is it for a reader to understand the technical aspects of Rockhold's article?

Critical Thinking: The Writer's Ideas

1. Rockhold implies that at the gas prices that were prevalent when he wrote the article (Fall 2005), it would take approximately five years for a buyer to recoup the extra cost of a hybrid. How reasonable is that time span for most consumers?

2. What did you learn about hybrid vehicles from Rockhold's article?

3. If all things were equal with regard to cost (even if costs evened out over time), is there a reason why you wouldn't buy a hybrid over a conventional automobile?

Composing Processes and Knowledge of Conventions: The Writer's Strategies

1. Rockhold's first paragraph consciously attempts to appeal to diverse, and sometimes opposing, groups of readers. How successful is he? What other groups might he have included?

2. Rockhold provides a great deal of technical information in his analysis, including many numbers. How helpful is this information? How could Rockhold have used visual elements to present this information?

3. How well does Rockhold's final paragraph represent his analysis? How effective is the drama of this paragraph?

Inquiry and Research: Ideas for Further Exploration

1. The situation regarding hybrid vehicles has changed from what it was when Rockhold wrote this article. Do some research to discover the

current state of hybrids. By today's standards, how cutting edge is Rockhold's analysis?

2. Based on current technologies and the current prices and availability of gasoline, what kinds of vehicles make the most sense for today's car buyer?

TAMARA DRAUT

All Work and No Play

Tamara Draut is the director of the Economic Opportunity Program at Demos, a public policy center. She has written widely on economic security, and her op-ed pieces frequently appear in major newspapers. She is also a frequent guest commentator on television and radio talk shows. The following selection is an excerpt from her book *Strapped: Why America's 20- and 30-Somethings Can't Get Ahead* (2006).

In the fall of 1997, Shaney, who is now 27, enrolled in the University of Arkansas. She chose the state college because it was close to home and the nearby private colleges were financially out of the question. Shaney's excellent grades in school scored her a $10,000 scholarship to help cover the cost of tuition for four years. The scholarship was an enormous relief for Shaney and her family. Neither of her parents had gone to college and they couldn't offer any financial support for her studies. With tuition covered by the scholarship, Shaney was confident she could earn enough for room and board through part-time jobs. She opted out of living in the dorms, choosing instead to get an apartment with a friend from high school.

Shaney worked a lot of hours during school, holding down two or three jobs at all times. During summers, Shaney was unable to capitalize on internship opportunities that would have helped her gain better work experience because the pay was too low and she had to continue to earn. She waited tables instead, trying to save as much money as she could before school started again in the fall. She regrets not being able to accept an internship that would have helped her build more impressive and relevant experience for her résumé.

Shaney's college days were a far cry from the keg parties and dorm room shenanigans that dominate our popular conception of college.

Tuition increases made her scholarship money run out sooner than expected. Because Shaney was a French major, she opted to study abroad in France for a year, which she paid for with student loans. She also took out loans to deal with tuition increases. All told, Shaney left school with $25,000 in student loans. After working two or three jobs for the last four years, Shaney was looking forward to being done with school and having a regular nine-to-five job and her nights once again free.

For all of Shaney's hard work, she graduated into one of the worst job markets in recent history and has yet to find a job. Staring down the barrel of $25,000 in loans, Shaney is understandably worried about her financial future. She's begun to question the value of going to college and finds herself wondering whether it wasn't all a waste of time. 4

Stress-filled college days like Shaney's are much more common than they were twenty or thirty years ago. Full-time on-campus students work more hours at paying jobs while in college than did students in the 1970s or 1980s. According to an analysis of U.S. Department of Education survey data, today three quarters of full-time college students are holding down jobs. Like Shaney, nearly half of them work twenty-five hours or more a week. Working while going to school isn't inherently a bad thing—in fact, some studies show that working on-campus for fifteen hours or less per week can help foster better academic performance. On-campus jobs, which are often work-study slots, provide a chance for students to deepen their connections to the campus through contact with other students, faculty, and staff. The problem is that more and more students are working off-campus at multiple jobs and for longer hours. Students who work twenty-five hours or more a week are much more likely to report that work affected their grades and interfered with their class schedule. Grades suffer as studying time declines and so does the free time to participate in academic clubs and social activities. 5

Not everyone can handle the added stress of long work hours on top of college. Too often students give up under the pressure. As anyone who has made it past their first two years of college can attest, the second half is when college becomes really interesting; it's the whole four-year package that provides the analytical, problem-solving, and writing skills that distinguish a bachelor's degree from an associate's degree. But when an 18-year-old is borrowing $8,000 or more a year and working twenty-five hours a week to pay for college, it changes the equation. Under these conditions, a boring class is no longer just a snooze fest—it's an extremely *expensive* snooze fest. It's not surprising that under a debt-for-diploma and work till you drop environment, one third of students drop out after their first year of college. And first-generation college students are almost 6 twice as likely as students with college-educated parents to drop out before their second year.

This is why the percentage of students who actually earn their bach- 7 elor's degree hasn't risen nearly as fast as enrollments would suggest. Just over half (53 percent) of all students who enroll in four-year colleges end up getting their bachelor's degrees within five years. Not surprisingly, there are wide disparities by class and race in who completes college. Within five years of entering college, 40 percent of students from the top socioeconomic quartile (25 percent) will earn a four-year degree as compared to only 6 percent of students in the lowest quartile. Over a quarter of white students who enter college will earn a bachelor's degree, whereas only about 15 percent of black and Hispanic college students will complete their degrees.

QUESTIONS FOR WRITING AND DISCUSSION: LEARNING OUTCOMES

Rhetorical Knowledge: The Writer's Situation and Rhetoric

1. **Audience:** From reading this short excerpt from *Strapped*, what inferences can you make about the intended audience for the book?

2. **Purpose:** What is Draut's purpose for analyzing the experiences of college students such as Shaney?

3. **Voice and tone:** How would you characterize Draut's tone in this piece? What does it contribute to her credibility?

4. **Responsibility:** Draut makes attending college appear to be fraught with financial worries. Is she merely being honest, or is she over-sensationalizing the situation? What makes you think so?

5. **Context and format:** This piece is an excerpt from a book. What clues from the piece, if any, indicate that this is an excerpt from a book, rather than a self-contained essay?

Critical Thinking: Your Personal Response

1. As a college student, what is your initial reaction to Draut's analysis?

2. To what extent is your life as a college student similar to or different from what Draut presents? To what extent is your college career clouded by the need to make ends meet?

3. How does it make you feel to know that a large number of college students may never graduate as a result of financial problems?

Critical Thinking: The Writer's Ideas

1. We have many cultural myths about what the "college experience" should be like. Draut's essay seems to explode some of these myths. How accurate and fair is she?

2. Draut mentions that Shaney is a French major. Why does she include that information? What does Shaney's major tell you about her?

3. What point do you think Draut is trying to make here? What conclusions is Draut drawing from her analysis of the information she is presenting here?

4. After reading Draut's piece, what are your thoughts about the worth of a college education?

Composing Processes and Knowledge of Conventions: The Writer's Strategies

1. Draut begins this piece with an example of one particular student who found herself in financial straits because of student loans. She then generalizes to other groups and shows how financial problems can lead to dropping out. How effective do you find this organizational method—starting with an example of a real person?

2. Draut uses many statistics, which she works into her text. How effective is this strategy?

3. Draut contrasts Shaney's stressful, work-filled life with the supposedly carefree life of the party-going college student. How fair is this contrast? How effective is it?

Inquiry and Research: Ideas for Further Exploration

1. Find out the graduation rate for your college or university. Is your school doing anything to improve it? If so, what? If the problem is primarily financial, what, if anything, can an institution of higher education do to address it?

2. How many hours a week do you and your best friends work while going to school? How does working at a job affect your educational experience?

Thinking about Visuals That Analyze

Often businesses use flowcharts to visually describe how something happens within their company. Such a visual aid not only provides a description of how items, products, ideas, or people move through their business, but also serves as a visual analysis of how things work.

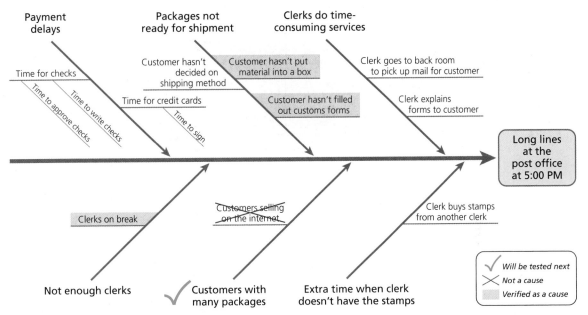

FIGURE 7.4   A Flowchart Illustrating a Problem at a Post Office

Figure 7.4 is an example that illustrates a post office problem. Figure 7.5 on page 284 is an example of a flowchart showing which aspects of a transaction are "costs" to the business and which aspects are "value added." As you look at both of these flowcharts, consider these questions about the effective use of flowcharts in analyses:

- How does each flowchart provide information on how things fit together?
- How does each flowchart show how the parts of the whole work in an ideal setting?
- How does each flowchart show how the parts work in real settings?
- What does the chart show that would be hard to show with text alone?

 ## Drawing On Research to Analyze Your Subject

Research is critical to any analysis. If you do not examine and consider each aspect of your subject in depth, how can you analyze it? Researching a subject for analysis can include reading books and articles, interviewing those who may know more about your subject than you do, conducting searches

**FIGURE 7.5
A Flowchart
Illustrating
Aspects of a
Transaction**

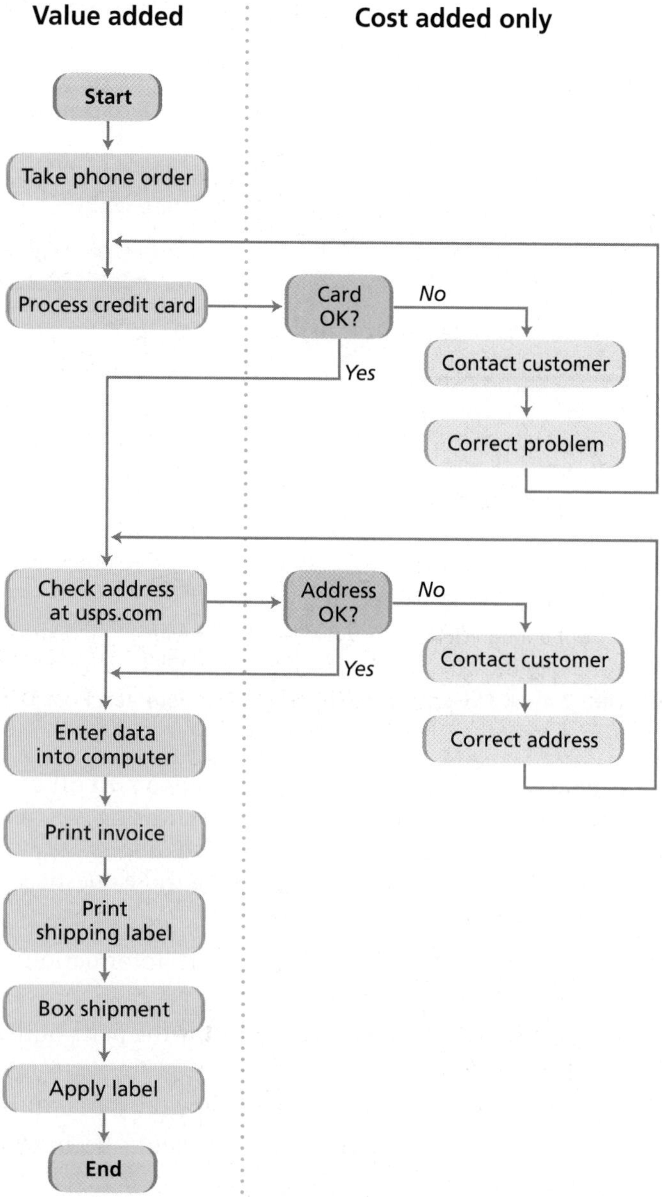

online, and other means of gathering information. Research materials such as data, figures, statistics, examples, descriptions, images, and testimony can help you explain the different parts or aspects of your subject.

You almost always will get the most useful information for an analysis if you conduct what is called *primary research:* you examine the subject and collect the data yourself. Primary research can include interviewing, field research where you take notes or measurements, making your own direct observations, and surveys.

For example, if you were working with Scenario 1 (p. 258) on a campus issue and your focus was on increasing tuition costs, you would conduct primary research by interviewing students and administrators on recent tuition increases. You might also visit the college library, where you could read through archived newspapers to learn about the long-term history of tuition changes at your college.

For more on primary research, see the Writing in Action *about primary research on pages 307–8. For more on conducting research and citing your sources properly, see Chapters 19 and 20.*

Writing Processes

As you work on the assignment you have chosen, remember the qualities of an effective analytical paper, which are listed on pages 263–65. Also remember that writing is recursive—you might start with an invention activity or two and then conduct some research, which leads to more invention work and then a first draft; but then you might need to do more invention work to help flesh out your draft and conduct more research to fill in any gaps in information you spot; and then you'll revise your draft and possibly find another gap or two. . . . Writing, in other words, is more a circular than a linear process. So while the activities listed below imply that writers go through them step-by-step, the actual process of writing is usually messier. You will keep coming back to your earlier work, adding to it, modifying your analysis as you conduct more research and become more familiar with your topic.

For a tip on organizing your computer files, see page 97.

As you work on your project, make certain that you save your computer files frequently because any work that you don't save could be lost. Many experienced writers save their files every fifteen minutes or so. Also, savvy writers back up their computer files in two or more places—on an internal or external hard drive of the computer, on a USB flash drive, and/or on a rewritable CD or DVD, for example.

Invention: Getting Started

As with your other writing assignments, the more invention activities you can draw on, the more information you will have available. Try to answer these questions while you do your invention work:

- What do I already know about the subject that I am considering for my analysis?
- What insights do I already have to offer?
- Where might I learn more about the topic I am considering? Should I go to the library, use the Web, interview people, and/or make observations? What verifiable information am I likely to find?

- What do I know about my audience? What don't I know that I should?

- What might my audience already know about my possible topic? How can I make my insights convincing for them?

- What questions do I need to answer before I can begin (and complete) my analysis?

Doing your invention work in electronic form rather than on paper lets you easily use your invention work as you construct a draft.

WRITING ACTIVITY

Freewriting, Listing, and Interviewing

Using the questions above, jot down everything you can think of about your subject. During that time, just keep writing (even if you have to write, "I can't think of anything to say") because the very act of writing will help you generate more ideas.

Another invention tool you can use is a list, which forces you to put your ideas into a sequence—perhaps from smallest to largest or least to most important. In constructing an analysis, a list is often especially useful as it helps you categorize each aspect of your subject. Once you have put your information in a list, you can move each item around as you see fit.

Once you have some ideas down, a helpful way to learn more is to ask others what they know about your subject—what they see as its component parts, what they think are its important aspects, and how they think those parts or aspects work together. A useful way to conduct such interviews is to center on the *who, what, where, when, why,* and *how* interview questions that a newspaper reporter generally tries to ask.

While we present various invention strategies in a particular order here, remember that every writing project is different, and you may find yourself using invention techniques in a different order, depending on the requirements of your project.

For more on freewriting, listing, and other strategies for discovery and learning, see Chapter 3. For more on interviewing, see Chapter 19.

Sarah Washington's Freewriting

Student writer Sarah Washington decided to respond to the scenario about a campus issue. When her instructor mentioned the issue of campus parking, Sarah knew she had found her subject. In class, Sarah used freewriting to get her initial ideas on paper. A portion of her freewriting follows:

Yes, I've been frustrated by the parking situation since I first started school here. While talking to other students, I've discovered that we're all not very happy about it. It's too expensive, and there are never enough spots. I've talked to other students who are juniors and seniors, and they say it's been like this since they started. Every year it seems as though the parking fees go up, and every year it seems as though it's harder to find a good parking spot. Then again, that's a typical reaction, I guess, to parking here—saying "it's a problem" without really understanding why. Maybe this analysis will help me understand all the ins-and-outs of the situation. . . .

Sarah Washington's Interviewing

Sarah Washington decided to interview Michael Nguyen, who heads her college's Parking & Transit office, and to focus on the reporter's questions. Here is a portion of that interview:

Question: Can you tell me a little about who you are and what your background is?

Answer: I have a degree—believe it or not—in Public Parking, and I'd worked with two businesses before I came here. When I started here, I had to start at the bottom and slowly worked my way up and I've had this position for nearly five years.

Q: What exactly does Parking & Transit do? What does it cost to park on campus?

A: P&T has 4,500 parking spaces available—most are in paved lots, but we also handle the Elm Street garage, which has six levels of covered parking, and the garage on Maple with five levels. We handle the cleaning, the paving and repair work, selling parking permits to students and faculty, and so on. We also patrol the campus, giving parking tickets to anyone illegally parked.

Lately, we've spent a lot of time talking to dorm residents, to see how we might provide better and more parking for their use. But it's a battle—we only have so much space on campus, and we're growing every semester in terms of students. That's a good problem to have.

Parking costs for the covered garage are $250 a semester; for the surface lots it's $200 a semester. However, it costs us about $150 a semester to maintain a surface parking space, and about $200 a semester to maintain a garage space in the garage—so we really lose money.

Q: When does most of your work take place?

A: Well, we're really busy right before classes start, selling permits. But we also get busy at mid-term as the lots and garages are pretty dirty by then—lots of litter—so there's an ongoing cleaning program. And we're busy all the time patrolling—we give out a lot of parking tickets.

Sarah Washington's Listing

Sarah Washington decided to use a list to organize the information she obtained from her interview with Michael Nguyen, to give her some sense of what the most important facts were. She found that listing prompted her to ask more questions—thus continuing the research process. Here is a portion of Sarah's list:

> Parking loses money for our college. Why? Do parking tickets subsidize parking costs?
> 4,500 parking spaces for how many students? I wonder how they decide how many students (or faculty) are on campus at any given time and day?
> Do the lots fill up?
> Interesting info on when P&T is busy, but does it fit into my analysis paper?

 ## Exploring Your Ideas with Research

Before you begin your research, consider what your focal point should be. For example, you may want to research how electronic telecommunications such as cell phones and the Internet are helping families to keep in touch more often and to share more information. You may choose to focus on how college students who live away from home are keeping in touch with their parents. You can see this kind of focusing activity at work in Sarah Washington's work below. Look over your invention work to remind yourself of all that you know about your subject, and the questions you came up with about it. Use the reporter's questions of *who, what, where, when, why,* and *how* to get started on your research. After you have decided what information you need, determine what kind of research you need to conduct in order to gather that information, and conduct research in the library and on the Internet. You may also find it necessary to do field research.

For help with locating sources of information, see Chapter 19; for help with taking notes and documenting your sources, see Chapter 20.

Use an electronic journal to record images, URLs, interview notes, and other electronic pieces of information that you find as you are conducting your research. Such an e-journal makes it easy for you to add those e-documents once you start drafting your paper.

WRITING ACTIVITY

Conducting Research

Consider your subject for analysis and, in no more than two pages, outline a research plan. In your plan, indicate the following:

What you already know about your subject
What questions you still have

Who or what sources might be able to answer your questions

Who (roommates, college staff, professors) might be able to provide other perspectives on your subject

Where you might look for further information (library, Web, primary documents, other sources)

When you plan to conduct your research

Sarah Washington's Research

As we have seen, Sarah Washington began her invention and research on college parking by writing what she already knew and the questions she still had. During the early stages of her invention work, she realized that she was having an emotional response to parking and really did not have good information about the reasons for the situation. She then set out to get that information. She started her formal research by interviewing Michael Nguyen. She then interviewed others affected by college parking to find out what they thought about their situation, focusing on the reporter's *who, what, where, when, why*, and *how* questions; she also learned what other colleges do in terms of parking; examined how parking permits are issued; and determined whether the parking costs at her college are in line with what other similar colleges charge for parking. All of this research helped her analyze and therefore understand the parking situation at her school.

After interviewing several people on campus, she made the following notes in her research journal.

> There needs to be sufficient parking for all the students who live in campus housing who have or are allowed to have cars. Of course, this number could vary from semester to semester.
> We have 4,500 parking places, in the garages and in surface lots (Nguyen interview).
> There also needs to be sufficient parking for the staff who drive to work during regular business hours. Faculty needs are more difficult to determine. Their time on campus is inconsistent. While it is easy to know when they teach and hold office hours, other times (class preparation, grading, writing, researching in labs or the library, attending meetings, etc.) all vary from week to week. They need a parking spot, but they might not all be on campus at the same time. The trick is to figure out what pecentage is likely to be on campus.
> Mr. Nguyen told me that there were 13,845 total students enrolled this semester. Of that total, 6,735 live on campus. 2700 of the resident students have cars. There are 512 full time faculty and 193 part-time faculty. In addition, there are 398 staff people who work at the university.
> Commuter students—there are about 6,500 of them, according to Mr. Nguyen—may be the group whose parking needs are most difficult to

determine. They often lead complicated lives balancing school, work, and family obligations. They come to campus for class, but also likely come to campus at other times to use the library, other campus facilities, or to take part in other activities. It's difficult to determine when they will be on campus. I should ask some commuter students in my English class when they actually *are* at school—in class or at the library or whatever—to get some sense of how much that group of students is on campus.

Finally, all campuses need to provide parking spaces for visitors. Again, the needs of visitors vary. They can be prospective students, business people, government employees, or industry leaders who need to meet with the faculty or administration. Sometimes they are members of the general public who want or need to use university facilities that may be open. Who can I talk to about how many visitors we have, on average?

I also did a bit of research on the Web and learned that there's a wide variation in what places charge for parking. For example, at

the University of Georgia, "prime parking" is up to $336 a year
the University of Texas at Austin, students can park in surface lots
    for $89 a year, but if they live off-campus and want garage parking,
    it runs $510 per year
Iowa State University, students park for only $45 per year

Reviewing Your Invention and Research

For more on developing a thesis, see Chapter 13.

After you have conducted your research, you need to review your invention work and notes and think about the information you have collected from outside sources. You may be ready to decide on a thesis statement—a statement that summarizes the main point of your analysis—at this point. Even though you might already have a general idea of the conclusion your analysis is leading you to, until you get some of your ideas and research on paper, it is often hard to know for certain what your thesis will be. Your thesis should come *from* your analysis. It is helpful to decide on your thesis when you have done a lot of invention work (listing, brainstorming, clustering, for example) and research. You might even wait until after you construct your first draft.

WRITING ACTIVITY

Considering Your Research and Focusing Your Ideas

Examine the notes you have taken from your research. Then, using the *who, what, where, when, why,* and *how* questions as a starting point, see what information you have. For example, if you were analyzing a potential tuition increase at your college (see Scenario 1), your research notes might look like this:

who: students and faculty are the ones affected. Jerome Armor (librarian) told me a tuition increase will allow the library to be open longer, helping students, but estimates show that two percent of students will have difficulty staying in school if tuition goes up, and many (check statistics from President's office) will need a part-time job . . .

what: the President proposed a 6 percent tuition increase for next fall. She also wants an additional $40 per semester for a health-services fee, to support the Health Center. I interviewed Helen Symbol, who directs the Health Center, and she told me . . .

WRITER'S WORKSHOP

Reacting to Your Classmates' Invention Work and Research

With any writing assignment, your invention materials and research can improve with peer feedback and suggestions. Working with several of your classmates, provide comments and suggestions and ask one another questions, with the overall goal of helping one another to understand your rhetorical situation more clearly and to generate more useful information:

Comments

- _____ in what you have so far is familiar/unfamiliar to me, so you might _____.

- I like the way you explain the relationships _____ in what you've generated so far.

- I don't see how _____ fits as part of your analysis.

- These aspects of your subject—_____ and _____— don't seem related, so I'm not sure why you're thinking of including them.

- The part about _____ makes sense, but I don't see how the part about _____ fits in.

- I'd suggest that you include these ideas or this information:

  _____   _____

  _____   _____

Questions

- What is a _____ ? (Ask this kind of question when something is unclear.)

(cont'd)

(continued)

- I'm confused when you write about _____. Can you break it down a bit more?
- I still have questions understanding _____.
- How can you describe the relationship of _____ to _____ better?
- How do _____ and _____ work together?

The suggestions and comments that you receive are intended to guide you, to suggest areas where your readers might become confused and where they need more information about the subject of your analysis and its various aspects.

Organizing Your Information

Once you have some sense of what your analysis will include, you need to consider how you might organize this material. The questions that you need to ask yourself when deciding on your organization are all rhetorical:

- Who is your audience?
- Why might they be interested in your analysis, or how you can make them interested in it? (One way to emphasize the importance of your analysis to your audience is to show them why they need to understand your subject.)
- What is your purpose for writing—that is, why do your readers need this analysis? What will your readers learn about your subject by reading your analysis?
- What is the most important part or aspect of the subject you are analyzing?

For more on classification and cause-and-effect, see Chapter 13.

The answers to these questions can help you decide on what you need to emphasize, which in turn will help you choose an organization.

Here are three organizational structures that you might consider for your analytical paper.

Options for Organization

Defining Parts	Classification	Relating Causes and Effects
• Explain why the subject you are analyzing is important to your readers. • Provide examples of how readers might be affected by the subject. • Provide background information, so readers can see the whole subject of your analysis. • Use a strategy of description to explain each aspect or part of your subject. • Provide examples to show what you mean. • Conclude by showing how each aspect or part works together.	• Start with a question about your subject that readers probably do not know the answer to. • Explain why knowing the answer to this question will benefit your readers. • Using the writing strategy of *classification* to explain your subject, label and explain each aspect or part. • Provide specific examples to illustrate each category. • Conclude by showing how the aspects or parts function together to make up the whole of your subject.	• Begin with information about your subject that may surprise your readers. • Explain how an analysis of your subject will lead to more surprises and better understanding. • Use the writing strategy of *cause-and-effect* to show how each aspect or part of your subject causes or is affected by the other aspects or parts. • Provide specific examples to show what you mean. • Conclude by outlining how all parts of your subject function together.

WRITING ACTIVITY

Deciding on an Organizational Approach

Before you construct a full draft of your analysis, consider which organizational approach will serve you best. As with any kind of writing, it is always useful to try several organizational approaches to see which one is most effective for your specific purpose, audience, and rhetorical situation. Try writing a page or two using at least two organizational approaches before you decide on the one you will use. You can try out several organizational approaches on the computer before deciding on one. Be sure to save each first attempt with a different file name. That makes it easy to recall the one that seems best and start to develop your draft using that organization.

Sarah Washington decided to use the first organizational approach—defining parts—so she wanted to explain, right at the start of her paper, why her readers should care about her subject. Note how Washington's first paragraph tells of her frustrations and then draws her readers into the text because they probably share those frustrations:

> Like many others, I've been frustrated by the parking situation since I first started school here. While talking to other students, I've discovered that we're all not very happy about the parking. It's too expensive, and there are never enough spots. I've talked to other students who are juniors and seniors, and they say it's been like this since they started. Every year it seems as though the parking fees go up, and every year it seems as though it's harder to find a good parking spot . . .

Constructing a Complete Draft

Once you have chosen the most effective organizational approach, you are ready to construct the rest of your draft. Consider how you might use the invention materials you have generated, how you might integrate the research information you have gathered, and how you should respond to the comments on your invention work that you have received from your classmates. While you already have an organizational approach in mind for your draft, this is a good time to reconsider your organization: What are the most and least important aspects of your subject? What terms do you need to define? How might you use classification to explain your subject by breaking it down into categories? How do the parts relate to each other and to the whole of your subject?

As you write your first draft, remember the main point that you are trying to make (if you have decided on one). In an analysis, you will want to make sure that your discussion of the parts or aspects of your subject helps to support what it is that you are trying to say about the whole.

There are many ways to write a first draft. It may seem to make the most sense to you to start at the first sentence and then move to the end; however, sometimes that straightforward approach is not the most effective way to draft. Many writers, once they are comfortable with their organization, write individual pieces of their draft and then put them all together.

Introduction: Regardless of the organizational approach that you have chosen, you need to begin with a strong introduction that captures your readers' attention and introduces the subject you are analyzing. To accomplish these two goals in an introduction, you might use one of the following strategies:

- *Provide a brief outline of what most people know about your subject.* Sarah Washington begins her analysis of the parking situation on her campus with a brief overview of what most students think they know about the problem (see p. 309).

- *Explain (briefly) why an analysis of your subject might be of interest.* In "Putting In the Hours" (p. 266), James Lang suggests that it might be interesting to consider a little-known aspect of the behavior of his subject, the North American college professor: "But the casual observer may overlook that this species usually spends an equal, if not greater, part of his week in his den, holding what his institution terms 'office hours.'"

- *Explain (briefly) why your analysis is important.* Just as Tamara Draut does in "All Work and No Play" (p. 279), you may want to look at how the problem affects one person and then generalize to show that your analysis affects many people.

- *Provide a fact about the subject you are analyzing that will surprise or concern your readers.* Consider how John Rockhold, in "The Hybrid Revolution" (p. 271), shows how hybrid vehicles are becoming more and more popular.

Body: You can use various writing strategies to effectively analyze your subject:

- *Classify and label each aspect of your subject.* In "Putting In the Hours" (p. 266), James Lang organizes his descriptions of professors and their offices by labeling them: the "Early Bird," the "Door Closer," the "Chatterer," and so on. He then describes each type.

- *Define the various parts of your subject—explaining what each is and how it relates to the other parts.* If you were to analyze a PDA (personal digital assistant, sometimes called a "Smartphone"), for example, you would probably focus on its features: operating system, software, phone, memory, processor speed.

- *Compare and contrast each aspect of your subject, so readers can see the differences and similarities.* For instance, you might compare the functional features of two PDAs.

- *Focus on the cause-and-effect relationship of each aspect of your subject*, to show how one aspect causes, or is caused by, one or more other aspects. This approach would work well if you were analyzing a complex machine such as a car or an airplane.

For more on classification, definition, comparison and contrast, and causal analysis, see Chapter 13.

Conclusion: In your conclusion, review the major parts or aspects of your subject, explaining the following:

- How they relate to one another

- How they function together
- How they affect one another
- How all of the aspects of your subject lead to the conclusion you have reached

James Lang accomplishes this in "Putting In the Hours" by noting at the end of his essay that he—like most professors—fits into each category at one time or another, which becomes his conclusion:

> Most North American professors do have a dominant behavior that characterizes their office-hour activity, but most also engage in multiple behaviors in the course of a single week.

Title: As you compose your analysis, a title may emerge, but often it won't occur to you until late in the process. The title should reflect the topic that you are analyzing. Because an analysis is by definition complex, you are probably not going to be able to summarize your main ideas in your title, but it should be something that catches your readers' attention and makes them want to read your essay. "Putting In the Hours" suggests the topic of James Lang's essay without stating it in an obvious way. "The Hybrid Revolution" (p. 271) lets readers who are curious about hybrid cars know what John Rockhold's article will be about.

VISUALIZING VARIATIONS

Using Charts and Graphs to Make Your Analysis Clear

If you decided to respond to Scenarios 1 or 2 (pp. 258–60) for one of your classes, you might discover that an effective way to show your analysis is by means of a chart or graph such as a flowchart (see pp. 282–83), a pie chart, a bar graph, or a line graph.

For example, the data below focus on the changes in tuition costs at a fictional college, in percentages, between 2004 and 2008:

Changes in Tuition, 2004–2008

	Our College	Other Colleges
2004	4.00%	5.60%
2005	6.50%	7.70%
2006	4.70%	5.00%
2007	3.70%	6.10%
2008	5.20%	7.10%

If you wanted to show these data in a graph, you could present it in several ways. A line graph would look like this:

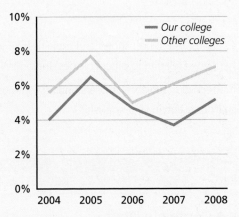

If you displayed the same data in a column graph, it would look like this:

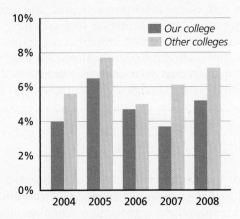

If you displayed the data as a bar graph, it would look like this:

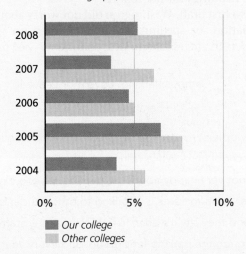

(cont'd)

TechNote If you are working with numbers and statistical information for your analysis, consider putting them into an Excel document. The Excel program can automatically convert your data into a table or graph.

(continued)

- What type of chart or graph best shows and explains how your college's tuition has changed in relation to other colleges' tuition? Why?

- How would it affect your audience's understanding if you used more than one kind of chart or graph in your analysis?

WRITING ACTIVITY

Constructing a Complete Draft

After reviewing your notes, invention activities, and research and carefully considering all of the information that you have generated and the comments you have received, construct a complete first draft of your analytical paper, using the organizational approach that you have decided on. Remember that your analysis will evolve as you write, so your ideas will most likely change as you compose this first draft.

Sarah Washington's First Draft

After reviewing all her work, Sarah Washington decided to write her first draft. She started with a portion of her original freewriting as an opening paragraph and one of the three organization schemes outlined above. Note also that she uses headings for her report

Because this is a first draft, Washington did not worry about errors in usage, grammar, punctuation, or spelling. She concentrated on getting her ideas down. (The numbers in circles refer to peer comments—see page 304.)

(The numbers in circles refer to peer comments—see page 304.)

Campus Parking: Love it or Leave It

Sarah Washington

Like many others, I've been frustrated by the parking situation since I first started school here. While talking to other students, I've discovered that we're all not very happy about the parking. It's too expensive, and there are never enough spots. I've talked to other students who are juniors and seniors, and they say it's been like this since they started. Every year it seems as though the parking fees go up, and every year it seems as though it's harder to find a good parking spot. ❶

I finally decided to do something about it. I started by going to the Student Government Office to see if they had information on why the parking was so bad on this campus and what they were planning to do about it. I was told the best person to talk with was Michael Nguyen, the head of our parking department.

Campus Data

I interviewed Mr. Nguyen and received the following background information:

There were 13,845 total students enrolled this semester. Of that total, 4,735 live on campus. 2,700 of the resident students have cars. There are 512 full-time faculty and 193 part-time faculty. In addition, there are 398 staff people who work at the university.❷

Analysis

Looking at those numbers, I was able to make the following quick determinations. If everyone drove themselves to campus and needed to be there at the same time, the campus would need 12,913 parking spots (the total of all the faculty and staff and students who are either non-residential or have cars). That means the university would have to be looking at close to 13,000 parking spots, which is especially important because Nguyen told me that the campus presently has 4,500 parking spots.

My initial response was no wonder I always felt I could never find a parking spot.❸ However, I soon realized that even at 9:00 am on Monday not every one of those 13,000 people will be on campus and not everyone drives. I knew I had friends who lived in apartments close enough to campus that they walked to class. And, after talking to Nguyen, I realized that not only are all students not on campus at the same time, but all faculty aren't necessarily on campus at the same time either. In addition, some students, and to a lesser degree, faculty and staff, carpool. All of these variables act to reduce the number of parking spaces that is really needed.

We can get a better idea of how great the need really is by looking❹ at the following scenario. By looking at staff surveys done by the Parking Office, we learn that 15% of the staff either carpool or use some other means of transportation. That gives us around 340 spots that are necessary to support employees not counting the faculty.

If we then assume, at the busiest time of day, 60% of the full time faculty and 50% of the part time faculty need to be on campus, and they all drive their own vehicles and don't carpool, that will cause us to have an additional need of around 410 spots.

It may be more difficult to determine the real number of spots that students need. However, if we assume that at the time of highest traffic, 70% of students are there, we can see there will then be a need for approximately 4,500 student spaces—not counting the necessary 2,700 spaces by the resident halls.

Adding all of these numbers, we discover that the campus may need around 7950 parking spots or a little more than 61% of the initial estimate of more 13,000 spots. It also becomes evident that the campus really can use a lot more parking at peak periods—not my initial thought of 5,500 spots.

Parking Costs

Parking on our campus—which for students runs $200 per semester—does not seem out of line with what other universities cost, except for Iowa State University, which charges students only $45 per year to park ("ISU Proposes Parking Enhancement, Fee Increase").

Here are some other examples:

the University of Georgia, "prime parking" is $336 a year (Stroer)

the University of Texas at Austin, students can park in surface
    lots for $89 a year, but if they live off-campus and want garage parking, it runs $510 per year ("Spring 2004 Garage Student Permit Availability")

Conclusion

I also became acutely aware that determining how many parking spots needed is not an exact science. There are many variables and they may change from semester to semester. In addition to the raw numbers, I discovered that part of the problem exists as a result of the desirability of the lots. Everyone wants to be close to where they're going, but that "where" keeps changing. During the morning, students all want to park in the lots closer to the academic buildings where their classes were being held. Later in the day, more vehicles could be found in the lot that serves the student union and the library. One thing that might help is simply having students plan their days on campus a little better. For example, if they have classes in the morning and plan on staying on campus for most of the day, they might have a much easier time looking for a parking spot over by the library rather than the classroom buildings. ⑤

Revising

Many writers find that it is useful to let their work sit for a period of time—to put it aside for a day or two and then revise it. Taking a break lets them come back to their paper as if they are seeing it for the first time. When you approach your work this way, you will find it easier to notice parts that are not explained in enough detail, or examples that are confusing, or places where an illustration or graph might show what you mean more clearly than the text does.

As you revise your early drafts, hold off on doing a lot of heavy editing. When you revise you will probably change the content and structure of your paper, so time spent working to fix problems with sentence style or grammar, punctuation, or mechanics at this stage is often wasted.

Think of revision as re-envisioning your work, reconsidering what you mean to say, not just editing for surface features. When you reread the first draft of your analysis, be sure to begin at the beginning. Here are some questions to ask yourself:

- What else might my audience want or need to know about my subject?
- How else might I interest my audience in my analysis of this subject?
- What did I find out about my subject that I did not include in my paper? (Effective research always results in more information than you can include, so consider what you left out that you might include in your next draft.)
- Have I clearly explained and defined any terms my readers might not know?
- Could some aspects of my analysis be better presented as a graph or chart?

Technology can help you revise and edit your writing more easily. Use your word processor's track-changes tool to try out revisions and editing changes. After you've had time to think about the possible changes, you can "accept" or "reject" them. Also, you can use your word processor's comment tool to write reminders to yourself when you get stuck with a revision or some editing task. If your classmates are offering feedback on your draft, they also can use track changes, the comment tool, or the peer-commenting feature of the software.

Because it is so difficult to see emerging writing with a fresh eye (even for experienced writers), it is almost always useful to ask classmates, friends, or family members to read drafts of your papers and comment on them.

WRITER'S WORKSHOP

Responding to Full Drafts

As you read and respond to your classmates' papers (and as they comment on yours), focus on the analytical nature of this assignment, but from a reader's perspective. Be sure to ask questions of their writing and respond to their ideas by exploring your reactions and responses to their thoughts.

Working in pairs or groups of three, read one another's papers, and then offer your classmates comments that will help them see their papers' strengths as well as places where they need to develop their ideas further. Use the following guidelines and questions to guide your responses to the writer's draft, whether you respond directly on your classmate's text, on a separate sheet of paper, or online:

- In a paragraph, comment on your first impression of this draft. How effectively does the title draw you into the paper and make you want to read it? Why? How might the writer improve the title?

- Indicate what you like about the draft—that is, provide positive and encouraging feedback to the writer.

- Comment specifically on the introduction: What is effective about it? What suggestions can you make on how to improve the introduction?

- Comment on the writer's focus. How well do you understand what the author is trying to do in this paper? How well does the writer stay on track? Does the paper wander a bit? If so, point out where. What questions are left unanswered?

- How has the writer demonstrated an awareness of readers' knowledge, needs, and/or expectations for the analysis? How might the writer demonstrate greater awareness?

- Comment on how effective you found this paper to be as an analysis. Explain how well the paper did what it was supposed to do. How has the writer covered—or failed to cover—all of the parts or aspects of the subject adequately? What other aspects of the subject should be included? That is, what did the author miss in this analysis that would help you better understand the subject?

- What is your opinion of the author's insight into the subject? How meaningful is it? Does it pass the "so what?" test?

- What do you think is the author's thesis or main claim for the analysis? How could it be expressed or supported more effectively?

- In the main part of the paper, are there parts that are confusing or concepts that are unclear? Where would you like more details or examples to help you see what the author means? What kind(s) of information would be useful?

- Comment on the writer's tone. Is it straightforward and neutral? Point out places where the tone needs work.

- How accurate and appropriate is the supporting evidence? Point out any questionable statistics, inaccurate facts, or questionable authorities. How clearly does the author indicate the sources for statistics and other supporting information?

- Reread the conclusion. What could be added or changed to make it more effective? How well does it tie everything together?

- How might visuals such as charts, tables, or photos strengthen the writer's case?

- If you are working with what might be called a nontraditional text (a Web page, for example, or a brochure), comment on the special attributes of that kind of text and how effectively the piece functions *as* a brochure, Web page, or other example of an analytical genre.

- If there are visual aspects of the document, comment on how effectively they illustrate the point being made. How much do the visuals add to a reader's overall understanding of the information?

- In another paragraph, outline what you see as the main weaknesses of this paper—and suggest how the writer might improve the text.

Student Comments on Sarah Washington's First Draft

Sarah Washington got comments on her first draft from several readers. Below are comments on her draft, keyed to the first draft on pages 298–301.

❶ Interesting introduction, but I'm not sure what the purpose of your paper is. Are you going to try to inform readers of parking problems or persuade us to do something?

❷ These numbers are confusing like this—maybe put them into a list?

❸ Also interesting, but you have a lot of your personal feelings in your paper. If I understood your paper's purpose, I'd know better whether it's appropriate for them to be in it.

❹ Who is "we" here? I'm not sure why you're using "we"—sounds strange.

❺ Now you're ending, and you're back to the number of parking spaces, without ever explaining what all that information about parking has to do with anything.

Responding to Readers' Comments

Once they have gotten feedback from peers, teachers, and others, writers have to decide how to deal with those comments and suggestions. Since the text is your paper, you as the writer are responsible for dealing with reader responses to your work.

The first thing to do with any feedback is to consider carefully what your readers have to say. Sarah Washington's readers indicate that they have the following reactions:

• One reader does not get the point of the paper, at least at the start, and expresses some confusion as to what Washington is trying to accomplish. How might she clarify her purpose and express her point?

• Another reader is confused by some of the data Washington presents. The reader makes a suggestion: "These numbers are confusing like this—maybe put them into a list?"

• Her first reader wonders about the personal feelings Washington is expressing in the text, noting again that if the reader clearly understood the purpose of the essay, he would better know if those personal feelings were appropriate.

It is important to consider carefully what your readers are saying to you. You may decide to reject some comments, of course, because they are not consistent with your goals for your paper. For example, some readers may disagree with your point of view or conclusion. Their perspective may have an impact on their comments. Other comments, though, deserve your attention, as they are the words of real readers speaking to you about how to improve your text. You may find that comments from more than one reader contradict each other. In that case, you need to use your own judgment to decide which reader's comments are on the right track.

In the final version of her paper on pages 309–11, you can see how Sarah Washington responded to these comments, as well as to her own review of her first draft.

Knowledge of Conventions

When effective writers edit their work, they attend to the conventions that will help readers—the table manners of writing. These include genre conventions, documentation, format, usage, grammar, punctuation, and mechanics. By attending to these conventions in your writing, you make reading a more pleasant experience for readers.

Editing

The last task in any writing project is editing—the final polishing of your document. When you edit and polish your writing, you make changes to your sentence structure and word choice to improve your style and to make your writing clearer and more concise. You also check your work to make sure it adheres to conventions of grammar, usage, punctuation, mechanics, and spelling. Use the spell-check function of your word-processing program, but be sure to double-check your spelling personally. If you have used sources in your paper, you should make sure you are following the documentation style your instructor requires.

See Chapter 20 for more on documenting sources.

As with overall revision of your work, this final editing and polishing is most effective if you can put your text aside for a period of time and come back to it with fresh eyes. Because checking conventions is easier said than done, though, we strongly recommend that you ask classmates, friends, and tutors to read your work to find editing problems that you may not see. Another option is to post your paper on a course Web site and invite everyone in class to read your paper. You may get only one or two takers, but one or two is better than none.

To assist you with editing, we offer here a round-robin editing activity focused on finding and correcting problems with wordy sentences, a constant challenge for many writers.

Round-Robin Editing with a Focus on Wordiness

Wordiness—using more words than necessary—is a common concern for writers and their readers. For instance, in the first draft of Sarah Washington's paper on pages 309–11, she wrote the following:

> I've talked to other students who are juniors and seniors, and they say it's been like this since they started. (20 words)

This sentence could easily be made more concise:

> Juniors and seniors say that it's been this way since they came here. (13 words)

As this example illustrates, wordy sentences take longer to read. Because they slow your readers down, they make your writing more difficult to read. An occasional wordy sentence will not matter that much, but a large number of them will increase your readers' workload and decrease your paper's effectiveness.

In this activity, work with two peers to edit one another's papers for wordiness. Each student should hand his or her paper to the classmate on the left. Read your classmate's paper, circling sentences that can be made more concise and making suggestions on how to tighten them. After no more than ten minutes, pass the papers to the left again, and repeat the process. After two peers have read each paper, compare notes to see if you have any questions about wordiness. If you are uncertain about a rule, consult a grammar handbook or ask your instructor for assistance. Also, think about ways to make sentences more concise. Ask yourself questions like, "Am I repeating myself?" "Have I included phrases that don't add meaning to the sentence?"

Genres, Documentation, and Format

For advice on writing in different genres, see Appendix C. For guidelines for formatting and documenting papers in MLA or APA style, see Chapter 20.

If you are writing an academic paper (which you will be if you work with Scenarios 1 or 2), you will need to follow the conventions for the discipline in which you are writing and the requirements of your instructor. If you are constructing a letter to the editor for Scenario 3, you will want to keep the letter brief and to the point. If you are working on Scenario 4, which asks for a report on travel options for friends or family, you can be fairly informal and may even want to provide your analysis as an e-mail. On the other hand, if you are constructing a formal business report for Scenario 5, you will need to follow the model for a business analysis report.

If you have used material from outside sources, including visuals, credit to those sources, using the documentation style required by the discipline you are working in and by your instructor.

WRITING IN ACTION

Convention in Genre and Design

The following pages from the Library of Congress's Web site offers a short analysis of a complex subject: primary source materials for research. *Primary sources* are original works of literature or art, documents, letters, and research; *secondary sources* comment on or interpret the primary source. For example, if you were writing a literary analysis of Joseph Conrad's *Heart of Darkness*, the novel is the primary source, while any critical commentary you read (what others have written about the book) would be a secondary source. Notice how the Web site presents different categories of primary source material—taking the large category and breaking it down into its constituent parts.

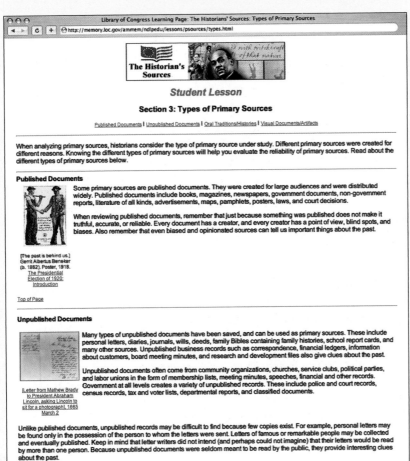

(cont'd)

(continued)

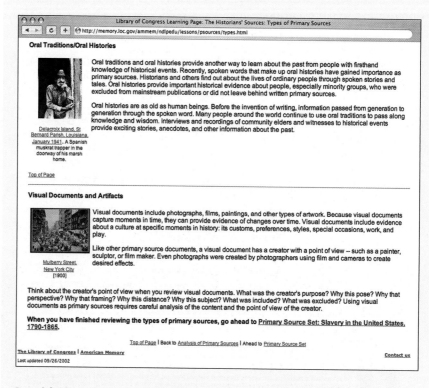

Library of Congress Learning Page: The Historians' Sources: Types of Primary Sources

http://memory.loc.gov/ammem/ndlpedu/lessons/psources/types.html

Oral Traditions/Oral Histories

Oral traditions and oral histories provide another way to learn about the past from people with firsthand knowledge of historical events. Recently, spoken words that make up oral histories have gained importance as primary sources. Historians and others find out about the lives of ordinary people through spoken stories and tales. Oral histories provide important historical evidence about people, especially minority groups, who were excluded from mainstream publications or did not leave behind written primary sources.

Oral histories are as old as human beings. Before the invention of writing, information passed from generation to generation through the spoken word. Many people around the world continue to use oral traditions to pass along knowledge and wisdom. Interviews and recordings of community elders and witnesses to historical events provide exciting stories, anecdotes, and other information about the past.

Delacroix Island, St Bernard Parish, Louisiana, January 1941. A Spanish muskrat trapper in the doorway of his marsh home.

Top of Page

Visual Documents and Artifacts

Visual documents include photographs, films, paintings, and other types of artwork. Because visual documents capture moments in time, they can provide evidence of changes over time. Visual documents include evidence about a culture at specific moments in history: its customs, preferences, styles, special occasions, work, and play.

Like other primary source documents, a visual document has a creator with a point of view -- such as a painter, sculptor, or film maker. Even photographs were created by photographers using film and cameras to create desired effects.

Mulberry Street, New York City [1900]

Think about the creator's point of view when you review visual documents. What was the creator's purpose? Why this pose? Why that perspective? Why that framing? Why this distance? Why this subject? What was included? What was excluded? Using visual documents as primary sources requires careful analysis of the content and the point of view of the creator.

When you have finished reviewing the types of primary sources, go ahead to Primary Source Set: Slavery in the United States, 1790-1865.

Top of Page | Back to Analysis of Primary Sources | Ahead to Primary Source Set

The Library of Congress | American Memory   Contact us

Last updated 09/26/2002

Considering Genre and Design

1. How effective are the headings on these Web pages in getting a reader's attention? Why?
2. How effective is the overall visual layout of this Web material? Does the layout make you want to read more? Why?
3. What functions do the photographs have?
4. With one or two classmates, brainstorm about the requirements of a Web page. In what ways does this one fulfill the requirements of this genre? (You might compare this Web page to several others.)

A Writer Shares Her Analysis: Sarah Washington's Final Draft

After meeting with peer reviewers, Sarah Washington continued to revise her paper and eventually constructed a finished draft. The final draft of "Campus Parking: Love It or Leave It" follows. As you read the essay, think about what makes it effective. Following the essay, you'll find some specific questions to consider.

SARAH WASHINGTON

Campus Parking: Love It or Leave It

Like many others, I've been frustrated by the parking situation since I first started school here. While talking to other students, I've discovered that we're all not very happy about the parking. It's too expensive, and there are never enough spots. I've talked to other students who are juniors and seniors, and they say it's been like this since they started. Every year it seems as though the parking fees go up, and every year it seems as though it's harder to find a good parking spot. An analysis of the parking situation on campus will help anyone concerned with parking (and that includes most students) understand how parking "works" at our college. I am focusing my analysis on two aspects of campus parking: the number of spaces, including how many spaces are actually needed, and also the costs for parking on campus, especially compared to what other colleges charge.

Campus Data

When I interviewed Mr. Michael Nguyen, head of Parking and Transit, he gave me the following background information:

A total of 13,485 students are registered this semester.
Of those, 4,735 live on campus.
A total of 2,700 resident students (that is, students who live on campus) have cars.
There are 512 full-time faculty members; 193 part-time faculty.
There are 398 staff employees.

Analysis

Looking at the numbers Mr. Nguyen provided, I was able to make the following quick determinations. If everyone drove to campus and needed to be there at the same time, the campus would need 12,913 parking spots (the total of all the faculty, staff, and students who are either non-residential or have cars). That means the university would have to provide close to 13,000 parking spots, or around 5,500 additional spots. This is especially important because, according to Nguyen, the campus presently has 4,500 parking spots.

However, even at 9:00 am on Monday not every one of those 13,000 people will be on campus, and not everyone who is on campus drives. I have friends who live in apartments close enough to campus to allow them to walk to class. And, after talking to Nguyen, I realized that not

1

2

3

4

One classmate wrote this comment on Washington's paper:

Interesting introduction, but I'm not sure what the purpose of your paper is. Are you going to try to inform readers of parking problems or persuade us to do something?

In her revision, Washington clearly indicates what she is trying to accomplish: to analyze the parking situation.

In her earlier draft, Washington got this comment from one of her peer reviewers to this sentence from her first draft: "My initial response was no wonder I always felt I could never find a parking spot."

Also interesting but you have a lot of your personal feelings in your paper. If I understood your paper's purpose I'd know better whether it's appropriate for them to be in it.

Note that in her final version she has removed her personal comment as she continues to outline the details of her analysis.

only are all students not on campus at the same time, but all faculty aren't necessarily on campus at the same time either. In addition, some students, and to a lesser degree, faculty and staff, carpool. All of these variables act to reduce the number of parking spaces really needed on campus. Clearly the severity of the parking problem requires further analysis.

Staff surveys done by the Parking Office indicate that 15% of the staff either carpool or use some other means of transportation. Therefore, around 340 spots are necessary to support employees, not counting the faculty. Assuming that, at the busiest time of day, 60% of the full-time faculty and 50% of the part-time faculty need to be on campus, and they all drive their own vehicles and don't carpool, then the campus will need around 410 additional spots.   5

It may be more difficult to determine the real number of spots that students need. However, assuming that at the busiest time of the day 70% of the nonresident students are present on campus, since many students live close enough to walk and are more likely to carpool, 70% of those students will probably need parking. At these times, then, the campus will need approximately 4,500 student spaces—not counting the necessary 2,700 spaces by the resident halls.   6

Therefore, when all of these numbers are added together, it seems that the campus may need in the neighborhood of 7,950 parking spots or a little more than 61% of the initial estimate of more 13,000 spots. The campus really can use some more parking at peak periods, but only around 500 spots—not my initial estimate of 5,500 spots.   7

Parking Costs

This analysis reveals that the college is close to the number of parking spots it needs, but cost is another part of the whole campus parking picture. The cost of parking on our campus—which for students is $200 per semester—does not seem out of line with what other universities cost, except for Iowa State University, which charges students only $45 per year to park ("ISU Proposes Parking Enhancement, Fee Increase").   8

Other schools charge varying amounts: 9

The University of Georgia: "prime parking" is $360 a year (Stroer).
The University of Texas at Austin: students can park in surface
    lots for $89 a year, but if they live off-campus and want garage

A classmate asked this question and made this comment on Washington's draft:

Who is "we" here? I'm not sure why you're using "we" so much—sounds strange.

She revised her draft to remove the word *we*, which also helped to make her sentences more concise.

parking, it runs from $240 to $336 per year ("Spring 2004 Garage Student Permit Availability").

Parking costs at our school, it appears, are not out of line with other colleges.

Determining how many parking spots are needed on a campus is not an exact science. There are many variables involved and those variables may change from semester to semester. In addition to the raw numbers, I discovered that part of the problem with parking is a result of the desirability of the lots. Everyone wants to be close to where they're going, but that "where" keeps changing. During the morning, students all seem to want to park in the lots closer to the academic buildings where their classes are being held. Later in the day, more vehicles can be found in the lot that serves the student union and the library. Students can help the situation by simply planning their days on campus a little better. For example, if they have classes in the morning and plan on staying on campus for most of the day, they might have a much easier time finding a parking spot over by the library rather than in crowded lots near the classroom buildings. Where parking is concerned, a little strategy can go a long way.

10

In her first draft, Washington received this comment from a classmate:

Now you're ending, and you're back to the number of parking spaces, without ever explaining what all that information about parking has to do with anything.

Note how she now offers a more effective conclusion to her text.

Works Cited

"ISU Proposes Parking Enhancement, Fee Increase." 3 Feb. 2004. <http://www.iastate.edu/~nscentral/releases/2002/jan/parking.shtml>.

Nguyen, Michael. Personal interview. 2 Feb. 2004.

"Spring 2004 Garage Student Permit Availability." 4 Feb. 2004. <http://www.utexas.edu/parking/parking/springStudentPermit.htm>.

Stroer, Joan. "Proposed parking plan drives costs up dramatically." 4 Feb. 2004. <http://www.onlineathens.com/stories/021902/uga_0219020032.shtml>.

QUESTIONS FOR WRITING AND DISCUSSION: LEARNING OUTCOMES

Rhetorical Knowledge: The Writer's Situation and Rhetoric

1. **Audience:** What audience does Washington have in mind for this essay? How can you tell?

2. **Purpose:** An analysis should help readers understand a subject. What can you point to in Washington's paper that indicates her purpose?

3. **Voice and tone:** How would you describe the tone Washington uses in her paper? Would a different tone (more strident, perhaps, or more subdued) have made her analysis more, or less, effective? Why?

4. **Responsibility:** How accurately does Washington represent statistical information? How can you tell? How credible is Washington's analysis? Why?

5. **Context and format:** Washington is writing as a college student concerned about parking on her campus. How does this context affect her use of language, appeals, and evidence in her analysis?

Critical Thinking: Your Personal Response

1. What is your initial response to Washington's analysis? What in her text causes your response?

2. To what extent does Washington's report give you insight into how parking might work at other public places serving large groups of drivers?

3. What new information did you learn that might help you understand the parking situation at your college?

Critical Thinking: The Writer's Ideas

1. In her conclusion, Washington talks about educating students on ways to alleviate the parking situation. How might her university accomplish this?

2. What is the most unusual idea in Washington's analysis? Why?

Composing Processes and Knowledge of Conventions: The Writer's Strategies

1. Construct a scratch or sentence outline of Washington's analysis (jot down, next to each paragraph, no more than a one-sentence description of what that paragraph contains. You will end up with a brief outline). How effective is her organization? Why?

2. How effectively does Washington use statistics or data to support her claims? What can you cite from her essay to demonstrate your conclusion?

Inquiry and Research: Ideas for Further Exploration

1. Consider an issue on your campus or in your neighborhood that you would like to understand more clearly. In no more than two pages, write down what you already know about this subject and what questions you would like answers to.

2. Focusing on the same subject, in no more than one page, outline a research plan—for example, whom you might interview and where you might search for more information.

3. At your library find a journal or magazine that covers the area you think you want to major in, and locate an example of an analysis. In no more than two pages, explain why that text is or is not an effective analysis.

 # Self-Assessment: Reflecting on Your Learning Goals

Now that you have constructed a piece of analytical writing, go back and consider your learning goals, which you and your classmates may have considered at the beginning of this chapter (see pp. 250–51). Write notes on what you have learned from this assignment.

Rhetorical Knowledge

- *Audience:* What have you learned about addressing an audience in analytical writing?

- *Purpose:* What have you learned about the purposes for constructing an analysis?

- *Rhetorical situation:* Consider some of the aspects that you have to think about, as a writer: How did the writing context affect your analytical text? How did your choice of topic affect the research you conducted and how you presented your analysis to your readers? What do you see as the strongest part of your analysis? Why? The weakest? Why?

- *Voice and tone:* How would you describe your voice in this essay? Your tone? How do they contribute to the effectiveness of your analytical essay?

Critical Thinking, Reading, and Writing

- *Learning/inquiry:* How did you decide what to focus on in your analysis? Describe the process you went through to focus on a main idea, or thesis. How did you judge what was most and least important in your analysis?

- *Responsibility:* How did you fulfill your responsibility to your readers?

- *Reading and research:* What did you learn about analytical writing from the reading selections you read for this chapter? What research did you conduct? How sufficient was the research you did? Why? What additional research might you have done?

- As a result of writing this analysis, how have you become a more critical thinker, reader, and writer? What critical thinking, reading, and writing skills do you hope to develop further in your next writing project? How will you work on them?

Composing Processes

- *Invention:* What invention strategies were most useful to you?

- *Organizing your ideas and details:* What organization did you use? How successful was it?

- *Revising:* What one revision did you make that you are most satisfied with? What are the strongest and the weakest parts of the paper or other piece of writing you wrote for this chapter? Why? If you could go back and make an additional revision, what would it be?

- *Working with peers:* How did your instructor or peer readers help you by making comments and suggestions about your writing? List some examples of useful comments that you received. List some examples of how you revised your analysis based on those comments and suggestions. How could you have made better use of the comments and suggestions you received? How could your peer readers help you more on your next assignment? How might you help them more, in the future, with the comments and suggestions you make on their texts?

- Did you use photographs or other visuals to help you explain your analysis to readers? If so, what did you learn about incorporating these elements?

- What "writerly habits" have you developed, modified, or improved on as you constructed the writing assignment for this chapter? How will you change your future writing activities, based on what you have learned about yourself?

Conventions

- *Editing:* What sentence problem did you find most frequently in your writing? How will you avoid that problem in future assignments?

- *Genre:* What conventions of the genre you were using, if any, gave you problems?

- *Documentation:* Did you use sources for your paper? If so, what documentation style did you use? What problems, if any, did you have with it?

If you are constructing a course portfolio, file your written reflections so that you can return to them when you next work on your portfolio.

Sarah Washington Reflects on Her Writing

In this brief excerpt from her reflective writing, notice how Sarah Washington addresses her knowledge and skills, as well as some connections between the academic and personal areas of her life:

> Writing this analysis of the parking situation on campus really helped me understand it. I thought parking was this huge major problem but now I see that we have <u>almost</u> enough parking, and also that the cost doesn't seem high, when compared to other colleges.
>
> The really interesting thing was that everyone seems to feel that <u>we</u> pay more for <u>less</u>, but when I looked at what some other colleges charge, we don't look so expensive here—and I wanted my analysis to show that, so anyone reading it could come to the same conclusion.
>
> I learned that it was pretty easy to find out all sorts of information and data about parking and costs and all, but it was more difficult to figure out how it was all related. Mr. Nguyen was very helpful and gave me a lot of good information, but I still had to analyze it. I wish I had interviewed more of the people (students!) directly affected by parking issues. I think more interviews of students would have added to my own perspective and given me even more useful information for an analysis. Maybe a survey would also be useful, as those students involved would also be my audience if I wanted to make my analysis into a report or letter for the campus newspaper. I can now see so many more ways in which I could do more research for this project, if I only had more time to do it.
>
> I also learned that my first draft had way too much of a personal stance—I kept writing "I feel this" and "I feel that," when what I should have been doing (as some of my classmates told me in peer review) was providing information that I could analyze and so better understand the

situation. So I took out my personal feelings, and I think that made for a stronger paper.

I also didn't have much of a conclusion in my early drafts—several of my classmates told me so—so I spent the time needed to really "pull things together" at the end of my paper. That (hopefully) will help readers come to the same conclusions that I have.

3
Using What You Have Learned to Write Arguments

Rhetorical Knowledge

- *Audience:* When you are writing to convince your readers, your success will depend on how accurately you have analyzed your audience: their knowledge and attitudes toward your topic.

- *Purpose:* A convincing text is meant to persuade readers to accept your point of view, but it can also include an element of action—what you want readers to do once you've convinced them.

- *Rhetorical situation:* Think about all of the factors that affect where you stand in relation to your subject—you (the writer), your readers (the audience), the topic (the issue you are writing about), your purpose (what you wish to accomplish), and the exigency (what is compelling you to write your persuasive essay).

- *Writer's voice and tone:* When you write to persuade, you are trying to convince readers to think or act in a certain way. The tone you use will of course influence how they react to your writing: consider how you want to sound to your readers. If your tone is subdued and natural, will that convince your readers? If you come across as shrill and shouting, will that convince your readers?

- *Context, medium, and genre:* You will need to decide on the best medium and genre to use to present your persuasive essay to the audience you want to reach. Often, you can use photographs, tables, charts, and graphs as well as words to provide evidence that supports your position.

Critical Thinking, Reading, and Writing

- *Learning/inquiry:* Writing to persuade helps you learn the important arguments on all sides of an issue, so such writing deepens your own understanding.

- *Responsibility:* As you prepare to write persuasively, you will naturally begin to think critically about your position on the subject you are writing about, forcing you to examine your initial ideas, based on what you learn through your research. Persuasive writing, then, is a way of learning and growing, not just of presenting information.

- *Reading and research:* You will usually need to conduct inter- views and online and library research in order to gather evidence to support the claims you are making in your persuasive writing.

Chapter 8

Writing Processes

- *Invention:* Various invention activities such as brainstorming, listing, and clustering can help you consider the arguments that you might use to support your persuasive essay, or the opposing arguments you need to accommodate or refute.

- *Organizing your ideas and details:* Most often, you will state the main point—your thesis—clearly right at the start of your persuasive essay and then present the evidence supporting that point. Other methods of organization are useful, however, depending on your audience and context.

- *Revising:* You will need to read your work with a critical eye, to make certain that it fulfills the assignment and displays the qualities of effective persuasive writing.

- *Working with peers:* Listen to your classmates as they tell you whether or not you have persuaded them, and why. They will give you useful advice on how to make your essay more persuasive and, therefore, more effective.

Conventions

- *Editing:* Citing sources correctly adds authority to your persuasive writing. The round-robin activity on page 377 will help you edit your work to correct problems with your in-text citations and your works-cited or references list.

- *Genres for persuasive writing:* Possible genres include academic essays, editorials, position papers, letters to the editor, newspaper and magazine essays—even e-mails or letters you might send to friends or family members to persuade them about a problem or issue.

- *Documentation:* You will probably need to rely on sources outside of your experience, and, if you are writing an academic essay, you will be required to cite them using the appropriate documentation style.

THE OLDEST CITY OF THE AMERICAS.
MYSTICAL MONTE ALBAN, OAXACA.
ONLY IN MÉXICO.

Founded more than 1,200 years ago, Monte Alban was a bustling urban center 600 years before Columbus was even born. Come discover the magic of a lost civilization. Live the mystery. Only in Mexico.

1 800 44 MEXICO   www.visitmexico.com

MÉXICO

BEYOND YOUR EXPECTATIONS

◆ Please remember that as early as January 23, 2007, passports will be required for US Citizens of all ages returning to the US.

Writing to Convince

Think of the last time you wrote something. Whether it was a formal academic paper, a letter, or an informal note such as a text message to a friend, your writing was most likely designed to convince someone about something—to persuade your reader that he or she should accept your particular point of view. Whether you write a letter to share your experiences, construct a report to provide information, or write an article to analyze or to evaluate a product, very often you will write to convince. Perhaps you will even try to move your reader to take action. And even the other purposes for writing just mentioned—to inform, to explain, to analyze—to some degree almost always involve persuasion.

You encounter **persuasive writing**—writing designed to convince readers to agree with the writer's position—many times a day. For instance, when you read a newspaper or magazine or visit a Web site, you will find scores of product advertisements such as the one that appears on the facing page. Notice the persuasive appeals in the advertisement. The top line noting that Monte Alban is "The oldest city of the Americas" is an ethical appeal because it shows that the ad writers are knowledgeable about the area's history. The same holds true for the details that appear below the photograph ("founded more than 1200 years ago"; "bustling urban center 600 years before Columbus was even born"). At the same time, these historical details can be considered logical appeals because they are fairly straightforward pieces of information. "Live the mystery" is, of course, an emotional appeal, as is the color photograph that showcases the breathtaking natural beauty of Monte Alban. How effectively does this advertisement convince you to visit this place?

Advertisements, of course, are clearly intended to convince the reader to buy something—a product or service or trip to Mexico. For most of the persuasive writing you will do, you will have a more limited audience than the audience for an advertisement or a newspaper editorial, but the strategies that you will use to assert your point of view and persuade readers are the same. Consider for a moment some of the writing you might do during any given day:

- You e-mail a friend about a music CD you just heard, recommending it to her.

- In your history class, you write about the main reasons behind a historical event (why your community voted to ban smoking in all public buildings, for example, or why your state decided to change emission rules for automobiles, or raise the minimum wage).

- You write a memo to your supervisor about a problem with office procedures.

When you compose your e-mail, you attempt to convince your friend that the CD is worth purchasing, and in your writing assignment for your history class, you try to persuade your teacher that you not only have read the material but can use what you learned to construct a convincing argument. Similarly, when you write your memo, you attempt to convince your supervisor that the problem exists.

 # Rhetorical Knowledge

When you write to persuade, you need to have a specific purpose in mind, a good sense of your audience, and an idea of what might be an effective way to persuade that audience. You need to make a point and provide evidence to support that point, with the goal of persuading your readers to agree with your position.

 ## Writing to Convince in Your College Classes

Many—if not most—of the papers you will be asked to write for your college classes will be persuasive. While your college assignments will often specifically require that you inform or analyze, they will frequently include an element of persuasion. Here are some examples:

- In a literature course, your instructor asks you to write a persuasive essay in which you argue that the concept of the Oedipal complex is appropriate for analyzing Hamlet's behavior.

- Your sociology professor asks you to develop and support a thesis about deviant behavior in prisons.

- In a physics course, your instructor asks you to argue for or against an explanation of a specific physical phenomenon.

- Your mechanical engineering professor asks you to argue for or against using a particular material in a specific situation.

- In a history course, your instructor asks you to argue for or against the decision to drop the atomic bomb on Hiroshima, Japan, in 1945.

Writing to Convince for Life

Although persuasive writing is common in college and university courses, it plays an even larger role in professional, civic, and personal settings. Many times a day you try to convince others to see your perspective. Consider these examples of **professional writing**:

- A product-development team writes a memo to company executives to convince them to manufacture a product it has designed and tested.

- An attorney writes a memo to fellow members of the local bar association, asking them to work *pro bono* (for free) for a specific group.

- An electronics retailer writes a letter to convince potential customers that its products are superior to those of its competitors.

- A high school teacher writes to other teachers in her district, encouraging them to volunteer their time at a local literacy center.

- A division manager writes an e-mail to convince the human resources manager to hire a particular applicant.

This list could go on and on. As you can see, persuasive writing is prevalent throughout the business and professional world.

Persuasive writing is also present in **civic settings**. Civic leaders and other participants in the political process—mayors, city council members, school board members, town supervisors, volunteers, and ordinary citizens— are all involved in persuasion. In fact, it is difficult to imagine a political process without persuasion as its major component. For instance, concerned citizens might write to their city council to argue that a streetlight needs to be installed at an intersection where many accidents have occurred.

In **personal settings**, you constantly negotiate with those around you as you make life decisions, often working to convince others that your views and ideas are best.

- You might write an e-mail to convince your long-distance boyfriend or girlfriend to visit you next month.

- You might write to persuade a family member to send you money for tuition.

- You might write to a friend or family member to encourage him or her to have a medical test if that person is having trouble making a decision.

Scenarios for Writing: Assignment Options

Your instructor may ask you to complete one or more of the following assignments that call for persuasive writing. Each of these assignments is in the form of a *scenario,* which gives you a sense of who your audience is and what you need to accomplish with your persuasive writing. The list of rhetorical considerations on pages 328–29 encourages you to think about your audience; purpose; voice, tone, and point of view; and context, medium, and genre for the scenario you have chosen.

   As in the other chapters in this text, we have provided two scenarios focused on academic writing and three scenarios that you might encounter outside of college. Starting on page 357, you will find guidelines for completing whatever scenario you decide—or are asked to—complete.

Writing for College

SCENARIO 1   An Academic Argument about a Controversial Issue

What controversial issues have you learned about in other college classes? Here are some possibilities:

- **Political science:** In what ways did the ethical issues some senators and members of the House of Representatives faced immediately before the 2006 election affect the results of that election?

- **Business ethics:** How effective is the threat of criminal punishment in preventing insider trading of stocks?
- **Psychology:** How should the courts use the concept of insanity to determine culpability in criminal cases?

Writing Assignment: Select a controversial issue or problem from one of your classes and compose a paper convincing readers in that class that your position on the issue is valid.

SCENARIO 2 An Argument on an Issue That Matters to You

This scenario asks you to select an issue that is important to you and construct a convincing essay about it for an audience of your classmates. Choose an issue you are interested in, feel strongly about, and would like to explore in more depth.

Writing Assignment: What interests you? What upsets you? What do you feel strongly about? Answering these questions may lead you to a topic and a thesis. Issues to consider might include the following:

- A local or national issue that you are interested in or involved with, such as traffic problems, environmental problems, immigration (Figure 8.1), work rules for welfare recipients, health care. For instance, you could

**FIGURE 8.1
Protesters Carrying
Flags, Banners, and
Picket Signs**

FIGURE 8.2
A Group of Anti-Fur
Protesters

write about the acceptability and need for animal testing—whether scientists use animals in appropriate or inappropriate ways as they try to find cures for various diseases. Other topics might include whether it is acceptable to raise animals for their fur (Figure 8.2) or whether calves raised for veal are treated humanely.

- A classroom issue, such as the condition of the building or the time classes are scheduled.

- A campus issue, such as campus safety, student fees, athletics. For example, you could argue that your campus needs more visitor parking or that the walkways are not safe at night and so need more lighting.

Writing for Life

SCENARIO 3   Civic Writing: An Editorial about a Campus–Community Problem

Every college campus has problems, ranging from scarce parking to overcrowded computer labs to too much vehicle traffic to too little community involvement. Many of these problems, such as too much traffic, extend into the neighborhoods near the campus.

Writing Assignment: Write an editorial for your campus newspaper in which you identify a campus problem that also affects the surrounding community and then persuade your readers that the problem exists and that it needs to be taken seriously. Although you need to do more than simply provide information about the problem (that is an informative paper, covered in Chapter 6), you do not need to suggest detailed solutions to the problem (that is a proposal, covered in Chapter 11). Your goal is to convince your readers that your campus has a serious problem and that this problem has a negative impact on the surrounding neighborhoods.

SCENARIO 4   Personal Writing: A Letter about an Issue That Affects Your Family

Think about an issue that is or should be important to your family. It may be an issue that concerns your family now or one that will be a concern in the future.

The following is a list of typical issues that can arise in families:

- Planning for college expenses
- Dealing with medical expenses
- Maintaining health (for example, eating properly, getting regular exercise)
- Arranging for child care
- Maintaining a budget
- Choosing a good school
- Sports programs for children and young adults
- After-school programs for children and young adults
- Leisure activities

Writing Assignment: Write a letter to the members of your immediate family in which you persuade them to take an issue seriously. It could be one of the issues listed above or another issue that is important to your family.

SCENARIO 5   Professional Writing: A Reference for a Job Application

Picture yourself in the job that you hope to have one day, and assume that you need to hire someone who will work under your supervision. The position for which you will be hiring calls for someone who has the following qualities:

- Is a leader
- Works well with people
- Is a hard worker
- Is trustworthy

Think of a friend or acquaintance of yours who might be the best person for the position that you have described.

**FIGURE 8.3
A Job Fair**

Writing Assignment: Write a persuasive letter to the hiring committee for your company, explaining exactly why the candidate you favor is the one they should hire. Your evidence—the reasons you provide to the committee for hiring your candidate—should be based on what you know about that person now.

For example, suppose you want to recommend your college roommate or next-door neighbor to the hiring committee. Consider what you already know about how your roommate or neighbor fits the job description, and then consider what specific examples of his or her talents or behavior you might provide to support your claims.

Rhetorical Considerations for Persuasive Writing

Audience: While your instructor and classmates are your initial audience for this assignment, you should also consider other audiences for your persuasive writing, depending on the scenario you have chosen.

What would you like them to believe or do? How might they respond to your argument? How might you best convince them?

Purpose: Your main purpose is to make your audience aware of the issue and convince them it is significant and that your position is the most reasonable one. You might also want to convince them to do something about it.

Voice, Tone, and Point of View: Why are you interested in the issue? What are your attitudes toward the issue and the audience? How will you convey those attitudes to your audience? Consider Maureen Dowd's tone (see "Our Own Warrior Princess," p. 337), which is conversational, and then compare it to Brian Pereira's tone (in his response to Dowd's column), which is all facts and figures. Both approaches are persuasive in different ways.

Context, Medium, and Genre: Although you are writing this persuasive paper to fulfill a college assignment, most issues worth writing about are important beyond the classroom. How might your views make a difference to your community? Keeping the context of the assignment in mind, decide on the most appropriate medium and genre for your writing. How will your writing be used? Obviously, your instructor will use your writing to help determine your grade for the course, so you should follow his or her instructions carefully. If you are writing for an audience beyond the classroom, however, consider what will be the most effective way to present your argument to this audience. You might write an e-mail message to a friend, prepare a memo for colleagues at work, or write a brochure or op-ed article for members of your community.

For more on choosing a medium and genre, see Chapter 17 and Appendix C.

 # Critical Thinking, Reading, and Writing

As we have seen, effective persuasive writing focuses on an issue and provides sufficient and compelling evidence to convince readers that the writer's position on that issue is correct, or at least worthy of respect. Before you begin to write your own persuasive paper, you need to consider the qualities of successful persuasive writing. It also helps to read one or more persuasive essays to get a feel for this kind of writing. Finally, you might consider how visuals could make your writing more convincing, as well as the kinds of sources you will need to consult.

When you write to convince, you will often need to draw on material from other sources by conducting research. To use your research effectively, you must read the material critically and evaluate it carefully, to make certain that the evidence you are offering as proof really does support your claims. Of course, thinking critically also means that you need to consider other points of view about your issue and decide whether those views are compatible or in conflict with your view.

For more on gathering and evaluating information from sources, see Chapter 19.

Learning the Qualities of Effective Persuasive Writing

Much of the writing that you do is intended to convince someone to agree with you about something, typically about an issue. An **issue** is a subject or problem area that people care about and about which they hold differing views. Issues of current concern in the United States include tax cuts, campaign finance reform, and school vouchers. Subjects about which people tend to agree—for example, the importance of education in general—are not usually worth writing arguments about.

Persuasive writing that achieves the goal of convincing readers has the following qualities:

- **Presentation of the issue.** You need to present your issue in a way that will grab your readers' attention and help them understand that an issue exists and that they should be concerned about it. For example, if you are attempting to convince buyers to purchase cellular phones with antivirus protection, you first need to demonstrate the existence and danger of viruses. One way to present an issue is to share an anecdote about it. You might tell your readers that in Japan, for example, a virus caused cell phones to randomly call emergency numbers. You might also offer some statistics that clearly demonstrate the prevalence of cell phone viruses.

- **A clearly stated, arguable claim.** A **claim** is the assertion that you are making about the issue. Your claim should be clear, of course; a confusing claim will not convince readers. Any claim worth writing about also needs to be arguable: a statement about which reasonable people may disagree. For example, "All cell phone users should purchase antivirus software" is an arguable claim; a reader could disagree by saying, "Cell phone viruses are not a major threat." However, no one would disagree with the statement "Computer viruses can be annoying and disruptive." Therefore, it is not arguable and not an effective claim for a piece of persuasive writing.

- **An awareness of audience.** Because your task as a writer is to convince other people, it is crucial to be aware of the needs, situations, and perspectives of your audience. For example, if you are a lawyer from the American Civil Liberties Union addressing the members of a victim's rights organization, you would have to consider their concerns about what they might see as your organization's overemphasis on the rights of criminals. In any audience, you can expect some members to be more open to your claim than others:

  - If someone already agrees with you, persuasion is unnecessary.

  - If someone mildly disagrees with you or is undecided, persuasion has a good chance of working.

TechNote One way to see argumentation and persuasion in action is to look at the political discussion boards on various Web sites, blogs, and online bulletin boards. Choose a topic thread, and as you skim or read the posts, ask yourself three questions about each post you see: 1) How much credibility does the writer seem to have as a person (*ethos*)? 2) How does the writer use reason and logic to make his or her points (*logos*)? 3) What is your emotional reaction to the writer's remarks (*pathos*)? You can determine the weight a writer's comments probably carry with others by assessing your impressions of that writer's credibility, reasoning, and emotional integrity.

- If someone strongly disagrees with you, there is little chance that persuasion will work.

- **Convincing reasons.** Writers of convincing arguments offer support for what they are asking their reader to believe or to do. For example, a reason to support lowering the property tax rate in a town is to attract new businesses ("businesses tend to move to places that have lower taxes, so if we lower our city taxes, more business will move here"). Think of the reasons you use to support your point as the other part of a *because* statement, with the claim being the first part. ("Animal fur should not be used in clothing *because* synthetic fur is available and looks like real fur.")

- **Sufficient evidence for each reason.** After considering the degree to which the audience agrees or disagrees with your claim, you need to provide enough evidence, and the kind(s) of evidence, that will convince your readers and, if applicable, persuade them to act accordingly. Evidence includes statistics, expert opinion, examples, and anecdotes (stories). If one of your reasons for lowering the property tax is to attract new businesses, you might include a graph showing increased revenues from new businesses in a town similar to yours that lowered its tax rate, as well as quotations from civic leaders in that town.

- **Appeals based on logic, emotion, and the writer's character.** Effective persuasive writers carefully decide when to use three kinds of appeals—*logos* (appeals based on logic), *pathos* (appeals to the audience's emotions), and *ethos* (appeals based on the writer's character or credibility). Appeals based on logic are generally the most effective. Emotional appeals can be effective with audience members who are predisposed to accept your claims. Appealing to an audience's emotions is risky, however, because critical thinkers will reject this type of appeal unless it is accompanied by logical and ethical appeals. Appeals based on the writer's authority and credibility—ethical appeals—can be powerful, especially when coupled with logical appeals.

- **An honest discussion of other views.** For any arguable claim or thesis, there will be at least one other point of view besides yours. To be effective, the writer of a persuasive text needs to acknowledge and deal with possible objections from the other side. You already make this kind of **counterargument** naturally. For example, when you are told that you "cannot register for this course because you have not completed the prerequisite," you probably already have an answer to that objection such as, "You're right, but I received approval from the dean because of my prior professional experience."

  If you think that another perspective has merit, you should certainly **acknowledge** it and even **concede** that it is valid. Another possibility is a Rogerian approach (see Chapter 14), in which both sides negotiate a compromise position. Perhaps you can offer a compromise

For more on strategies for argument, including dealing with opposing views, see Chapter 14.

by incorporating aspects of the other perspective into your thesis. For instance, instead of simply asserting, "Puerto Rico should become the fifty-first state," you could qualify the assertion by saying, "Puerto Rico should become the fifty-first state, but only if there can be some provision to protect the commonwealth's cultural heritage." Of course, if other perspectives on your issue are without merit, you will need to **refute** them by indicating how they are inappropriate, inadequate, or ineffective.

For example, suppose your family is planning a trip to visit relatives and a major theme park. You would prefer to spend as much time at the theme park as possible (and thus as little time as possible with your relatives). When you make your case, you need to acknowledge everyone's preferences, yet make it clear why the trip should focus more on the park. You might suggest extending the vacation, which would give you more time for both endeavors.

At times, though, the best strategy is to refute counterarguments directly. For instance, you might simply have to say, "We need to focus on the immediate family right now because we haven't done anything fun together in a long time. We owe it to ourselves to spend all of our time at the park. We can visit our relatives another time."

- **A desired result.** The goal of persuasive writing is convincing readers to change their minds about an issue or at least to give your view serious consideration. Often the goal is to get your reader to act in some way—vote for a candidate, write a letter to the school board, or buy some product.

For more on writing effective arguments, including claims, evidence, types of appeal, and counterarguments, see Chapter 14.

In a computer file, put the above qualities of effective persuasive writing into your own words, and then refer to those notes as you conduct research and write your paper.

A WRITER'S RESPONSIBILITY

Establishing and Maintaining Credibility

Dealing Fairly with Opposing Views

An ethical writer must deal with opposing views fairly and honestly. If you ignore or distort opposing views, readers will think you are either ignorant, unaware, or dishonest, which will quickly weaken or destroy your ethos—your credibility.

It is perhaps only natural to tend to ignore what those who disagree with you have to say about your topic—after all, if you just ignore their views, your view will be stronger, right? However, ignoring the other side of an issue, the objections that others might have to your point of view, actually weakens your position, as your readers will most likely know of the objections and wonder why you did not deal with them.

And if you are going to be honest with your readers, you have an ethical obligation to note that there are arguments against your position. You don't necessarily have to write, "Here is another position that you may think is stronger than mine," but, you do need to acknowledge that "other sides to this issue include XXX," and then explain why your position is still the stronger one.

Avoiding Logical Fallacies

Using faulty logic intentionally will weaken your credibility and annoy your audience. Using faulty logic unintentionally will indicate that you are not a critical thinker. If you include logical fallacies such as *stacking the deck*, in which you provide only one point of view, or use *red herrings*, in which you use misleading evidence that serves only to distract your readers, you are not presenting an ethical text. That is, instead of writing to persuade you are writing to mislead.

Unfortunately, today many writers also use unethical approaches designed to attack the character of the person who is arguing against the writer, instead of discrediting the other person's argument. For example, sometimes writers will use the logical fallacy of *guilt by association,* which attacks the character of someone who holds an opposing position. This logical fallacy asserts that an individual's character is determined by the people with whom he or she associates: "She cannot be an ethical person because she once had dinner with a person who was convicted of tax evasion." Or writers use an *ad hominem* attack—a attack on the person rather than his position, even though his argument might be sound: "Don't believe him because he is always gambling in Las Vegas."

See Chapter 14, pages 742–47, for a more detailed treatment of logical fallacies.

Reading, Inquiry, and Research: Learning from Texts That Persuade

The readings that follow are examples of persuasive writing. As you read the persuasive selections your instructor assigns, consider the following questions:

- What makes this selection convincing?
- To what extent am I convinced by the writer's reasons and evidence? Why?
- What parts of the selection could be improved? In what ways?
- How can I use the techniques of persuasive writing exemplified here in my own writing?

As you read an essay and respond to the questions that follow it, take notes, jot down questions, and make observations about the essay in a journal, preferably in a computer file. Then, if you want to use that information in your writing, you will already have the main points in a digital format.

ANNE APPLEBAUM

When Women Go to War

Anne Applebaum, a member of the *Washington Post* editorial board, writes a column that usually appears each Wednesday. Applebaum was born in Washington, D.C. She has a degree from Yale University and was a Marshall Scholar at the London School of Economics and St. Antony's College, Oxford. She was awarded the Charles Douglas-Home Memorial Trust award for journalism in the ex-Soviet Union in 1992. In 1996, her book *Between East and West* was given an Adolph Bentinck prize for European nonfiction. This essay first appeared as a column in the *Post* in 2003.

The argument about women in combat is over. In fact, it was over three years ago, when two female sailors were among the victims of the bombing of the USS Cole. Women had been serving aboard U.S. combat ships only since 1994, yet these deaths—the first time any female sailor had been killed in hostile action onboard—did not lead to a reversal of policy. No special outrage accompanied the sight of "women in body bags" being brought home for burial, as many had predicted, either then or during the 1991 Persian Gulf War. Now, as we fight a new Gulf war, women constitute nearly a sixth of the armed forces. More than 90 percent of service positions, including most combat positions, are open to women. Although these facts have been noted once or twice in recent days, they have provoked no special angst. Right now, women are flying helicopters, launching missiles and dropping bombs on Iraqi cities, and American civilization has not collapsed as a result.

But if the argument about women in combat is over, the conversation about women in the military should not be—just as the conversation about women in the law, or in business, or in factories did not end when more women took those jobs. To see why, look no further than this week's front pages, some of which feature the face of Army Spec. Shoshana Johnson, a POW in Iraq and the single mother of a 2-year-old. Johnson's fate is heartbreaking, but it is not entirely unique. Johnson's child is one of tens of thousands who have been left behind while their mothers—or their mothers *and* their fathers—go off to war.

Is there anything wrong with that? That is, is there anything wrong with the fact that Johnson was where she was when she was, "in harm's way," as the Army puts it? Some think not. Carolyn Becraft, assistant secretary of the Navy in the Clinton administration, puts the case like this: "This is a volunteer military. Everyone who stays is there of their own free will. This is their job. These are the conditions of their employment. If they have children, they still have to be available for worldwide deployment." Official policy is no different, and no wonder. After the long struggle for acceptance, higher-ranking women in particular loathe the idea of treating mothers and fathers differently.

Dig a little deeper, though, and the angst is palpable. Very far off the record, one high-ranking Pentagon official admits to being deeply disturbed by photographs of women hugging their babies before leaving for war. "We're the United States of America. How can we ask a young woman to leave her infant?" A military women's Web site burns with acrimony. "My husband is on a ship already and we are overseas. I have no one to care for my child if we are both underway," writes one. Another has no sympathy: "As a childless single woman working hard to cover up the slack that foolish pregnant women like you give the military, I and others have every right to be mad." The awareness of a stereotype—that women get pregnant on ships in order to be sent home—leads another to describe the "shame" she felt after a planned pregnancy led to her discharge from the Navy and to write of how she longs, once again, "to serve my country with pride."

Should she be able to? In civilian life, it would be easy. Whereas many among the first generation of female lawyers, like the first generation of female fighter pilots, took two-week maternity leaves or refused to have children at all, those in the second generation—my generation—happily take off a year, or five years, or work three days a week indefinitely. This isn't because younger women have sold out, but because they, and the working world, have made a series of imperfect compromises. Women give up some seniority, and sometimes some money. In exchange, they get some time. Many, if not all, find this a fair compromise.

It is in this sense that the military now needs to catch up to the civilian world, to make that same generational shift. The American military offers its enlisted men and women enormous choices of training and education. Why shouldn't they also be offered the chance to take a few years off, and then to reenlist, with no stigma attached? The military takes dozens of factors into consideration when it deploys people. Why shouldn't single mothers be deliberately kept out of harm's way? Military traditions make some of these questions starker and harder than they would be in civilian life, but it doesn't make them illegitimate. In fact, it is only when the armed forces are comfortable enough with women to treat them differently, and only when military mothers are comfortable enough to be treated differently, that we will know they have truly arrived.

QUESTIONS FOR WRITING AND DISCUSSION

Rhetorical Knowledge: The Writer's Situation and Rhetoric

1. **Audience:** Who is Applebaum's audience?

2. **Purpose:** What is Applebaum's purpose in writing this column? What does she want her readers to believe or to do?

3. **Voice and tone:** What is Applebaum's tone in this essay? How effective is it as a way of addressing her readers? Why?

4. **Responsibility:** How has Applebaum written responsibly?

5. **Context and format:** Applebaum is writing as a newspaper columnist. How does this context affect her writing? If she were writing in a different context, how might her essay change?

Critical Thinking: Your Personal Response

1. What is your initial response to Applebaum's column?

2. What do you think about sending single mothers into combat?

3. How much should the military's personnel practices be like those in civilian life?

Critical Thinking: The Writer's Ideas

1. What is Applebaum's claim?

2. To what extent do you agree with Applebaum—that is, how much has she convinced you? Why?

3. Applebaum notes that "The argument about women in combat is over" (paragraph 1) while "the conversation about women in the military should not be—just as the conversation about women in the law, or in business, or in factories did not end when more women took those jobs" (paragraph 2). What does Applebaum mean by these statements?

4. What parallels can you make between Applebaum's ideas and Santi De-Rosa's in his essay "The Objectification of Women: Whose Fault Is It?" (pp. 380–83)?

Composing Processes and Knowledge of Conventions: The Writer's Strategies

1. What aspect of "When Women Go to War" is an example of effective persuasive writing? Why is it effective?

2. How successfully has Applebaum used logos, pathos, and ethos? How might she have used any of these three appeals more convincingly?

3. Where does Applebaum address counterarguments, and how does she do so? How effective is she in doing this?

Inquiry and Research: Ideas for Further Exploration

1. Search for "women in war" at your college library or by using an Internet search engine. In no more than two pages, outline the most persuasive arguments you found both in favor of and against women going to war.

2. From what you have now learned through your reading on this subject, which argument do you find the most effective? Why?

3. What questions do you still have about women going to war?

MAUREEN DOWD

Our Own Warrior Princess

Maureen Dowd won the Pulitzer Prize for Commentary in 1999. In 1992, she received the Breakthrough Award from Women, Men and Media at Columbia University. She won the Matrix Award from New York Women in Communications in 1994. In 1996, she was named one of *Glamour*'s Women of the Year. In 1992, she was also a Pulitzer Prize finalist for national reporting.

In the following column, which first appeared in the *New York Times* on June 1, 2003, Dowd writes in a personal way about organ donation—telling the story of what her niece, Jennifer, did to help her brother, Michael. Although persuasive writing most often uses facts, statistics, and hard evidence to make its case, as you read Dowd's column consider how effective she is in using emotional appeals to persuade you.

Jennifer showed me her scar Friday. It's the most beautiful scar I've ever seen. A huge stapled gash on her stomach, shaped like the Mercedes logo. A red badge of courage. Jennifer is my niece, a 33-year-old lawyer. On Wednesday, she had half her liver taken out at Georgetown University Hospital to save the life of her uncle (my brother Michael), who had gotten hepatitis years ago from a tainted blood transfusion.

The complicated and risky operation for the two, side by side, went from 7:30 am. until after 10 pm. Then, when a Medivac helicopter arrived with a matching liver for another patient, the same team of doctors had to start on another emergency six-hour liver transplant.

The night nurse told Jennifer she was an oddity. "We don't see many live donors," she said. "Not many people are that generous."

Or brave. Jennifer's morphine drip wasn't attached properly the first night after the operation, and no one knew it. She felt pain, but didn't want to be a wimp by complaining too loudly. Instead, she was Reaganesque, cracking jokes and wondering where the cute doctors were.

She survived the first night after this excruciating operation au naturel, like Xena the Warrior Princess. If all goes well, her liver will grow whole again in several weeks, as will Michael's half.   5

Unlike her father, who charged people a nickel to see his appendix scar when he was 10, she let me look for free. As we sat in her room, watching Mariah Carey singing with a bare midriff on the "Today" show, I worried a little how she would take the disfigurement.   6

She's a fitness fanatic, who works as a personal trainer in her spare time. She's single, out in the cruel dating world. And we live in an airbrush culture, where women erase lines with Botox, wrinkles with lasers, and fat with liposuction. I told Jen scars are sexy; consider that great love scene in "Lethal Weapon 3" when Mel Gibson and Rene Russo, as police officers, compare scars.   7

Jennifer has every quality of heart, spirit, mind and body a woman could want. She's smart, funny, generous, loyal, principled, great looking and, obviously, adventurous.   8

"Write a column about me," she smiled, tubes coming out of every part of her body, as I left her room.   9

I knew what she meant. She didn't want me to write about her guts, but to encourage others to have the guts to donate organs. When she came to, she asked for the green ribbon pin that encourages organ donation. Her exquisite doll-like transplant surgeon, Dr. Amy Lu, in white coat and black high-heeled mules, still on the job after 21 hours in the operating room, removed her pin and gave it to Jennifer.   10

As Neal Conan said on NPR Thursday: "More than 80,000 Americans are on waiting lists for organ donations, and most will never get them. Thousands on those lists die every year. One big reason for the shortage is that families are reluctant to give up their relatives' organs. Even when people filled out a donor card or checked the organ donor box on their driver's license, family members often refuse. The need is so acute and so frustrating that more and more doctors are wondering whether financial incentives might persuade some families to change their minds and save lives." (Iran has wiped out its kidney transplant wait by offering rewards.)   11

As the New York Organ Donor Network Web site notes: "One donor can save up to eight lives through organ donation and improve dozens of lives through corneal, bone, skin and other tissue transplants. Across the U.S., 17 men, women and children of all races and ethnic backgrounds die every day for lack of a donated organ."   12

I'm one of the scaredy-cats who never checked the organ donation box or filled out the organ and tissue donor card.   13

Some people don't do it because they have irrational fears that doctors will be so eager to harvest their organs, they'll receive subpar care after an accident.   14

I had nutty fears, too, straight out of a Robin Cook medical thriller, that they might come and pluck out my eyes or grab my kidney before I was through with them.   15

On Friday, Michael's birthday, I got the card online, filled it out and stuck it in my wallet. If Jennifer is brave enough to do it alive, how can I be scared of doing it dead?   16

BRIAN J. G. PEREIRA, M.D.

Letter Responding to Dowd

Brian Pereira is a Professor of Medicine at the Tufts University School of Medicine. Dr. Pereira is a nationally recognized expert on kidney disease and nephrology. He is the President of the National Kidney Foundation, Chairman of the International Nephrology Network, and has served on the editorial board of many scientific journals. Dr. Pereira also serves as a director of Kidney Care Partners, Wellbound Inc., and Satellite Health Care Inc.

This letter, in response to Dowd's essay, appeared in the *New York Times* a few days after Dowd's column was published.

To the Editor:
Re "Our Own Warrior Princess" (column, June 1):

Maureen Dowd's inspiring story of her niece's live liver donation points to an emerging trend in transplantation.   1

The year 2001 was the first in which there were more living donors than nonliving donors in the United States. Because of new techniques for kidney removal and the medical success of live liver transplantation, more people are considering saving lives through organ donation while they are alive.   2

A recent survey by the National Kidney Foundation found that one in four Americans would consider donating a kidney or a piece of their liver or lung to a complete stranger.   3

This is not just talk. The real numbers are encouraging. In 2002, 353   4
people became living liver donors, and 6,234 were live kidney donors.

While the need for organ donors continues to grow, people like Ms.   5
Dowd's niece represent hope for a future when the transplant waiting
list will cease to exist.

BRIAN J. G. PEREIRA, M.D.
Pres., National Kidney Foundation
Boston, June 2, 2003
New York Times

QUESTIONS FOR WRITING AND DISCUSSION

Rhetorical Knowledge: The Writer's Situation and Rhetoric

1. **Audience:** How effective is Dowd in reaching the audience for whom this information is intended—someone reading the *New York Times* and perhaps interested in organ donation? What can you point to in Dowd's column to demonstrate what you mean?

2. **Purpose:** In what area of lite (academic, professional, civic, personal) does "Our Own Warrior Princess" best fit? What is Dowd trying to convince the reader to believe or do? What can you point to in the column to support your opinion?

3. **Voice and Tone:** What is Dowd's attitude toward people who don't offer to donate organs? How does she attempt to reach them?

4. **Responsibility:** Dowd's primary evidence consists of the story of her niece's sacrifice, which is an emotional appeal to her readers. How justified is Dowd's use of pathos—an appeal to readers' emotions? How effective is it? Why?

5. **Context and Format:** Newspaper columns such as Dowd's have specific length limits (as compared to, say, an essay that might appear in a book). How might such a form constrain Dowd? How might it benefit her?

Critical Thinking: Your Personal Response

1. What is your immediate reaction to Dowd's comments?

2. What is your response to Dr. Periera's comment that "[t]he year 2001 was the first in which there were more living donors than nonliving donors in the United States" (paragraph 2)?

3. To what extent are you a "scaredy-cat" when it comes to organ donation? Why?

4. What was the most interesting piece of information you learned from Dowd's column and Dr. Pereira's letter? Why?

5. Has Dowd's column affected your views about becoming an organ donor? If so, how?

Critical Thinking: The Writer's Ideas

1. What idea or ideas in Dowd's column seem the most important to you? Why?

2. Consider other persuasive writing that you have read in this chapter. In what way(s) are they similar to or different from Dowd's column?

3. Dowd's column includes an implicit definition of bravery. What is this definition? How does Dowd use it to convince her readers?

Composing Processes and Knowledge of Conventions: The Writer's Strategies

1. To what extent do you believe the information Dowd presents in her article? Why?

2. How does Dowd establish her ethos in this article? How does Pereira establish his ethos in his letter?

3. Dowd uses a personal story to make her point. How effective is this writing strategy? Why?

4. What is your response to Dowd's observation that her niece, Jennifer, is a "Warrior Princess"? Why? (Note that "Warrior Princess" refers to the main character in the television series *Xena, Warrior Princess*, starring Lucy Lawless in the title role.)

5. Dowd ends with this sentence: "If Jennifer is brave enough to do it alive, how can I be scared of doing it dead?" Is this a convincing conclusion for her column? Why?

Inquiry and Research: Ideas for Further Exploration

1. What questions do you still have about organ donation? Where can you go to get answers to those questions?

2. Would you consider donating your organs to someone after you die? Why? Would you consider donating part of one of your organs, as Jennifer did for her uncle, while you are still alive? Why?

ARTHUR LEVINE and JEANETTE S. CURETON

Collegiate Life: An Obituary

Dr. Arthur Levine is a professor at Harvard University and is the author of many articles and reviews, including the text *When Hope and Fear Collide: A Portrait of Today's College Student* (with Jeanette S. Cureton), published in 1998. Among other volumes are *Beating the Odds: How the Poor Get to College, Higher Learning in America; Shaping Higher Education's Future; When Dreams and Heroes Died: A Portrait of Today's College Students; Handbook on Undergraduate Curriculum; Quest for Common Learning* (with Ernest Boyer); *Opportunity in Adversity* (with Janice Green), and *Why Innovation Fails.*

Jeannette Cureton is a researcher at Elmhurst College in Elmhurst, Illinois. With Dr. Levine, Cureton was awarded the "Outstanding Research Award" in honor of their book, *When Hope and Fear Collide: A Portrait of Today's College Student* by the College Student Personnel Association of New York State (CSPANYS).

   "Collegiate Life: An Obituary" is an excerpt from their book *When Hope and Fear Collide: A Portrait of Today's College Student* (Jossey-Bass, 1998); it originally appeared in the magazine *Change* (May–June 1998: 12–18).

As you read, consider how your college or university experience compares with the comments in this essay. What can you understand and relate to?

In 1858, John Henry Cardinal Newman wrote *The Idea of a University*. His ideal was a residential community of students and teachers devoted to the intellect. To him, a college was "an alma mater, knowing her children one by one, not a foundry, or a mint, or a treadmill." Given a choice between an institution that dispensed with "residence and tutorial superintendence and gave its degrees to any person who passed an examination in a wide range of subjects" or "a university which . . . merely brought a number of young men together for three or four years," he chose the latter.

   Newman's ideal was so appealing that it has been embraced regularly over the years by higher education luminaries from Robert Hutchins and Paul Goodman to Alexander Meiklejohn and Mortimer Adler. Belief in it remains a staple of nearly every college curriculum committee in the country.

   But that ideal is moribund today. Except for a relatively small number of residential liberal arts colleges, institutions of higher education and their students are moving away from it at an accelerating pace. The notion of a living-learning community is dead or dying on most campuses today.

This is a principal finding of several studies we conducted between 1992 and 1997, which involved our surveying a representative sample of 9,100 undergraduate students and 270 chief student affairs officers, as well as holding focus groups on 28 campuses. The details of the studies can be found [at the end of this article], along with information about earlier surveys undertaken by Arthur Levine for the Carnegie Council on Policy Studies in Higher Education, which we use for the sake of comparison. Unless otherwise indicated, all findings we report in this article come from the surveys outlined. While much of this article focuses on students of traditional age, the current student generation is, in fact, multigenerational.

Demographics

A major reason for the changes we describe is simply demographic. In comparison with their counterparts of the 1960s and 1970s, undergraduates today are more racially diverse and, on average, considerably older. In fact, since 1980, the lion's share of college enrollment growth has come from students who might be described as nontraditional. By 1993, 24 percent of all college students were working full-time, according to our Undergraduate Survey; at two-year colleges, this figure had reached 39 percent.

By 1995, 44 percent of all college students were over 25 years old; 54 percent were working; 56 percent were female; and 43 percent were attending part-time. Currently, fewer than one in six of all undergraduates fit the traditional stereotype of the American college student attending full-time, being 18 to 22 years of age, and living on campus (see U.S. Department of Education, in Resources).

What this means is that higher education is not as central to the lives of today's undergraduates as it was to previous generations. Increasingly, college is just one of a multiplicity of activities in which they are engaged every day. For many, it is not even the most important of these activities; work and family often overshadow it.

As a consequence, older, part-time, and working students—especially those with children—often told us in our surveys that they wanted a different type of relationship with their colleges from the one undergraduates historically have had. They preferred a relationship like those they already enjoyed with their bank, the telephone company, and the supermarket.

What Students Want

Think about what you want from your bank. We know what we want: an ATM on every corner. And when we get to the ATM, we want there to be no line. We also would like a parking spot right in front of the ATM, and to have our checks deposited the moment they arrive at the bank, or perhaps the day before! And we want no mistakes in processing—unless they are in our favor. We also know what we do not want from our banks. We do not want them to provide us with softball leagues, religious counseling, or health services. We can arrange all of these things for ourselves and don't wish to pay extra fees for the bank to offer them.   9

Students are asking roughly the same thing from their colleges. They want their colleges to be nearby and to operate at the hours most useful to them—preferably around the clock. They want convenience: easy, accessible parking (at the classroom door would not be bad); no lines; and a polite, helpful, efficient staff. They also want high-quality education but are eager for low costs. For the most part, they are willing to comparison shop, and they place a premium on time and money. They do not want to pay for activities and programs they do not use.   10

In short, students increasingly are bringing to higher education exactly the same consumer expectations they have for every other commercial establishment with which they deal. Their focus is on convenience, quality, service, and cost.   11

They believe that since they are paying for their education, faculty should give them the education they want; they make larger demands on faculty than past students ever have. They are also the target audience for alternatives to traditional higher education. They are likely to be drawn to distance education, which offers the convenience of instruction at home or the office. They are prime candidates for stripped-down versions of college, located in the suburbs and business districts of our cities, that offer low-cost instruction made possible by heavy faculty teaching loads, mostly part-time faculties, limited selections of majors, and few electives. Proprietary institutions of this type are springing up around the country.   12

On campus, students are behaving like consumers, too. More than nine out of 10 chief student affairs officers told us in last year's Student Affairs Survey that student power in college governance has increased during the 1990s (or at least has remained the same), but that undergraduates are less interested in being involved in campus governance than in the past.   13

A small minority of undergraduates continue to want voting power or control over admissions decisions, faculty appointments, bachelor's   14 degree requirements, and the content of courses; however, a decreasing percentage desire similar roles in residential regulations and undergraduate discipline, areas in which students would seem most likely to want control. Overall, the proportion of students who want voting or controlling roles in institutional governance is at its lowest level in a quarter century, according to comparisons between our 1993 Undergraduate Survey and the 1969 and 1976 Carnegie Council surveys.

This is precisely the same attitude most of us hold with regard to the commercial enterprises we patronize. We don't want to be bothered with running the bank or the supermarket; we simply want them to do their jobs and do them well—to give us what we need without hassles or headaches. That is, help the consumers and don't get in their way. Students today are saying precisely the same things about their colleges. 15

Social Life

From a personal perspective, students are coming to college overwhelmed and more damaged than in the past. Chief student affairs officers in 1997 reported rises in eating disorders (on 58 percent of campuses), classroom disruption (on 44 percent), drug abuse (on 42 percent), alcohol abuse (on 35 percent), gambling (on 25 percent), and suicide attempts (on 23 percent). 16

As a consequence, academic institutions are being forced to expand their psychological counseling services. Three out of five colleges and universities reported last year that the use of counseling services had increased. Not only are counselors seeing students in record numbers, but the severity of the students' problems and the length of time needed to treat them are greater than in the past. 17

Students tell us they are frightened. They're afraid of deteriorating social and environmental conditions, international conflicts and terrorism, multiculturalism and their personal relationships, financing their education and getting jobs, and the future they will face. Nearly one-third of all college freshmen (30 percent) grew up with one or no parent (see Sax et al., in Resources). As one dean of students we talked with concluded, "Students expect the [college] community to respond to their needs to make right their personal problems and those of society at large." 18

The effect of these accumulated fears and hurts is to divide students and isolate them from one another. Students also fear intimacy in relationships; withdrawal is easier and less dangerous than engagement. 19

Traditional dating is largely dead on college campuses. At institutions all over the country, students told us, in the words of a University 20 of Colorado undergraduate, "There is no such thing as dating here." Two-person dating has been replaced by group dating, in which men and women travel in unpartnered packs.

It's a practice that provides protection from deeper involvement and intimacy for a generation that regularly told us in focus group interviews that they had never witnessed a successful adult romantic relationship. Romantic relationships are seen as a burden, as a drag or potential anchor in a difficult world. Yet sexual relationships have not declined, even in the age of AIDS. Student descriptions of sexual activity are devoid of emotional content; they use words such as "scoping," "clocking," "hooking," "scamming," "scrumping," "mashing," and "shacking" to describe intimate relations. 21

In general, with increasing pressures on students, collegiate social life occupies a smaller part of their lives. In the words of an undergraduate at the University of the District of Columbia, "Life is just work, school, and home." In fact, one-fifth of those queried on our campus site visits (21 percent) defined their social lives in terms of studying; for another 11 percent, sleeping was all they cared about. When we asked students at the University of Colorado for the best adjective to describe this generation, the most common choice was "tired." 22

But not all of the retreat from social life is time-based. Chief student affairs officers describe students as loners more often now than in the past. Requests for single rooms in residence halls have skyrocketed. The thought of having a roommate is less appealing than it once was. 23

Similarly, group activities that once connected students on college campuses are losing their appeal and are becoming more individualized. For instance, the venue for television watching has moved from the lounge to the dorm room. Film viewing has shifted from the theater to the home VCR. With student rooms a virtual menagerie of electronic and food-preparation equipment, students are living their lives in ways that allow them to avoid venturing out if they so choose. 24

Student Organizational Mitosis

None of this is to say that collegiate social life is dead, but its profile and location have changed. On campus, there is probably a greater diversity of activities available than ever before, but each activity—in the words of the chief student affairs officer of the University of Southern Mississippi—"appeals to smaller pockets of students." This is, in many respects, the consequence of student organizational mitosis and the proliferation of the divides between undergraduates. For instance, the business club on one college campus divided into more than a dozen 25 groups including women's; black; Hispanic; gay, lesbian, and bisexual; and Asian and Filipino business clubs.

Deans of students regularly told us last year that "there is less larger-group socializing" and that "more people are doing things individually and in separate groups than campus-wide." In contrast to the Carnegie Council's 1979 study, current students describe themselves in terms of their differences, not their commonalities. Increasingly, they say they associate with people who are like themselves rather than different.   26

In the main, when students do take time to have fun, they are leaving campus to do so. Our Campus Site Visits study indicated that drinking is the primary form of recreation for 63 percent of students, followed closely by going to clubs and bars (59 percent) and simply getting off campus (52 percent). By contrast, the latter two activities were not mentioned in the Carnegie Council's 1979 study.   27

Drinking was not a surprise. It was the first choice in our earlier study, but there is more binge drinking today. Drinking to get drunk has become the great escape for undergraduates.   28

Escaping from campus is a trend that goes hand in hand with the high numbers of students living in off-campus housing—more than triple the percentage in the late 1960s. Only 30 percent of students we surveyed reported living on campus. Add to this the fact that students are also spending less time on campus because of jobs and part-time attendance, and the result is that increasingly campuses are places in which instruction is the principal activity. Living and social life occur elsewhere.   29

Multiculturalism

Campuses are more deeply divided along lines of race, gender, ethnicity, sexuality, and other differences today than in the past. A majority of deans at four-year colleges told us last year that the climate on campus can be described as politically correct (60 percent), civility has declined (57 percent), students of different racial and ethnic groups often do not socialize together (56 percent), reports of sexual harassment have increased (55 percent), and students feel uncomfortable expressing unpopular or controversial opinions (54 percent).   30

Multiculturalism is a painful topic for many students. The dirty words on college campuses now are no longer four letters: they are six-letter words like "racist" and "sexist"—and "homophobic," which is even longer. Students don't want to discuss the topic. In focus group interviews, students were more willing to tell us intimate details of their sex lives than to discuss diversity on campus.   31

Tension regarding diversity and difference runs high all across college life. Students talked about friction in the classroom; in the residence halls; in reactions to posters placed on campus or to visiting speakers; in campus activities and the social pursuits of the day; in hiring practices; in testing; in the dining room, library, bookstore, and sports facilities; in every aspect of their campus lives. In this sense, the campus in the 1990s is a less hospitable place for all undergraduates, regardless of background, than it once was.   32

Academics

Although instruction remains the principal on-campus activity that brings undergraduates together, the academic arena is experiencing its own form of student disengagement. Pursuit of academic goals is clearly utilitarian. It's as if students have struck a bargain with their colleges. They're going to class all right, but they're going by the book—they're doing what's necessary to fulfill degree requirements and gain skills for a job, but then they're out the door. They're focused and career oriented, and see college as instrumental in leading to a lucrative career. "Task oriented students who focus on jobs" is how a Georgia Tech student affairs official labeled them.   33

Although students do not believe that a college education provides a money back guarantee of future success, they feel that without one, a good job—much less a lucrative or prestigious job—is impossible to obtain. At the very least, it's a kind of insurance policy to hedge bets against the future. As a student at Portland (Oregon) Community College put it, "College is the difference between white-collar and blue-collar work." Fifty-seven percent of undergraduates we surveyed in 1993 believed that the chief benefit of a college education is increasing one's earning power—an 11 percentage-point increase since 1976.   34

By contrast, the value placed on nonmaterial goals (that is, learning to get along with people and formulating the values and goals of one's life) has plummeted since the late 1960s, dropping from 71 and 76 percent respectively to 50 and 47 percent. Whereas in 1969 these personal and philosophic goals were cited by students as the primary reasons for attending college, in 1993, students placed them at the bottom of the list. Although a great number of students are focused and intent on pursuing career goals, many also face a variety of academic hurdles. They are coming to college less well prepared academically. Nearly three-fourths (73 percent) of deans in 1997 reported an increase within the last decade in the proportion of students requiring remedial   35 or developmental education at two-year (81 percent) and four-year (64 percent) colleges. Nearly one-third (32 percent) of all undergraduates surveyed reported having taken a basic skills or remedial course in reading, writing, or math, up from 29 percent in 1976. Despite high aspirations, a rising percentage of students simply are not prepared for the rigors of academe. Another academic hurdle for students is a growing gap between how students learn best and how faculty teach. According to research by Charles Schroeder of the University of Missouri-Columbia, published in the September/October 1993 *Change*, more than half of today's students perform best in a learning situation characterized by "direct, concrete experience, moderate-to-high degrees of structure, and a linear approach to learning. They value the practical and the immediate, and the focus of their perception is primarily on the physical world." According to Schroeder, three-quarters of faculty, on the other hand, "prefer the global to the particular; are stimulated by the realm of concepts, ideas, and abstractions; and assume that students, like themselves, need a high degree of autonomy in their work."

Small wonder, then, that frustration results and that every year   36
faculty believe students are less well prepared, while students increasingly think their classes are incomprehensible. On the faculty side, this is certainly the case. The 1997 Student Affairs Survey revealed that at 74 percent of campuses, faculty complaints about students are on the rise. One result is that students and faculty are spending less time on campus together. With work and part-time attendance, students increasingly are coming to campus just for their classes. This explains, in part, why students are taking longer to complete college. Fewer than two out of five are able to graduate in four years (see Astin et al., in Resources). Twenty-eight percent now require a fifth year to earn a baccalaureate, according to U.S. Department of Education statistics from 1996. In reality, obtaining the baccalaureate degree in four years is an anomaly today, particularly at public and less selective institutions.

The Future

The overwhelming majority of college students believe they will be suc-   37
cessful. But their fears about relationships, romance, and their future happiness were continuing themes in every focus group. Their concerns about finances were overwhelming. There was not one focus group in which students did not ask whether they would be able to repay their student loans, afford to complete college, get a good job, or avoid moving home with Mom and Dad.

The college graduate driving a cab or working at the Gap was a universal anecdote. There was more mythology here than there were concrete examples, however. College graduates being forced to drive taxis is one of the great American legends, rivaled only by the tale of George Washington and the cherry tree. Finances were a constant topic of discussion. Students told us of the need to drop out, stop out, and attend college part-time because of tuition costs. They told us of the lengths they had to go to pay tuition—even giving blood. More than one in five (21 percent) who participated in the Undergraduate Survey said that someone who helped pay their tuition had been out of work while they attended college.   38

At heart, undergraduates are worried about whether we can make it as a society, and whether they can actually make it personally. In our surveys, the majority did say they expected to do better than their parents. But in our focus groups, students regularly told us, "We're going to be the first generation that doesn't surpass our parents in making more money." "How will I buy a house?" "How will I send my kids to college?"   39

This is a generation of students desperately clinging to the American Dream. Nearly nine out of 10 (88 percent) students are optimistic about their personal futures, but their hope, though broadly professed, is fragile and gossamer-like. Their lives are being challenged at every turn: in their families, their communities, their nation, and their world. This is a generation where hope and fear collide.

Conclusion

In sum, these changes in America's undergraduates add up to a requiem for historic notions of collegiate life—the ivory tower, the living-learning community, the residential college, and all the rest. But the changes are not sudden; they began even before Cardinal Newman wrote his classic. Most are a natural consequence of the democratization of higher education. This is what happens when 65 percent of all high school graduates go on to college and higher education is open to the nation's population across the lifespan. Four years of living in residence becomes a luxury few can afford.   40

So how should higher education respond? Dismissing the present or recalling a golden era lost are not particularly helpful—for the most part the changes are permanent. But there are a few things colleges can do.   41

The first is to focus. Most colleges have less time with their students on campus than in the past. They need to be very clear about what they want to accomplish with students and dramatically reduce the laundry lists of values and goals that constitute the typical mission statement.   42

The second is to use all opportunities available to educate students. 43
Required events, such as orientation, should be used to educate rather
than to deal with logistics. The awards a college gives should represent
the values it most wants to teach. The same is true for speakers. The
in-house newsletter can be used to educate. And of course, maybe the
best advice is that almost any event can be used for educational purposes if the food and music are good enough.

Third, build on the strengths unique to every generation of students. 44
For instance, current undergraduates, as part of their off-campus activities, are involved in public service—an astounding 64 percent of them,
according to the Undergraduate Survey. Service learning, then, becomes
an excellent vehicle to build into the curriculum and co-curriculum of
most colleges.

Fourth, work to eliminate the forces that push students off campus 45
unnecessarily. For example, most colleges talk a great deal about multiculturalism, but in general have not translated the rhetoric into a climate that will make the campus more hospitable to current students.

In like manner, using financial aid more to meet need than to reward 46
merit would lessen the necessity for students to work while attending
college. These are steps any college with the will and commitment can
take. Both campus life and our students would benefit greatly.

Resources

- Astin, A. W., L. Tsui, and J. Avalos. *Degree Attainment Rates at American Colleges and Universities. Effects of Race, Gender and Institutional Type.* Los Angeles: Higher Education Research Institute, UCLA, 1996.
- Sax, L. J., A.W. Astin, W. S. Korn, and K. M. Mahoney. *The American Freshman: National Norms for Fall 1997.* Los Angeles: Higher Education Research Institute, UCLA, 1997.
- U.S. Department of Education. National Center for Education Statistics. *Condition of Education,* 1996 (NCES 96304). Washington, DC: U.S. Government Printing Office, 1996.
- National Center for Education Statistics. *Digest of Education Statistics, 1997* (NCES 98-015). Washington, DC: U.S. Government Printing Office, 1997.

Studies Used in This Article

The studies of undergraduate student life that form the basis of this
article and of the book *When Hope and Fear Collide: A Portrait of Today's
College Student* were conducted by the authors between 1992 and 1997 at

the Harvard Graduate School of Education. The first—the Undergraduate Survey—included a 1993 questionnaire sent to a random sample of 9,100 students at institutions stratified by Carnegie type.

The second—the Student Affairs Survey—consisted of questionnaires sent in 1992 and again in 1997 to a random sample of 270 student affairs officers at institutions also stratified by Carnegie type. The third—Campus Site Visits—involved interviews conducted between 1993 and 1995 with nearly 50 student affairs officers and 300 students, both individually and in focus groups, at 28 diverse campuses across the country. The data from the completed questionnaires were weighted by Carnegie category to reflect the composition of American higher education.

In this article, the authors use for comparison with the above-listed surveys similar ones conducted in the 1960s and 1970s by Arthur Levine for the Carnegie Council on Policy Studies in Higher Education. All of these studies targeted students of both traditional and nontraditional age in two- and four-year institutions varying in control (public versus private), mission, size, selectivity, gender distribution, racial and ethnic mix, religious orientation, residential status, and regional location.

QUESTIONS FOR WRITING AND DISCUSSION

Rhetorical Knowledge: The Writer's Situation and Rhetoric

1. **Audience:** Who is the intended audience for this essay? How effectively do Levine and Cureton address that audience?

2. **Purpose:** What do you think Levine and Cureton are trying to accomplish with this essay? What can you point to in the essay that supports your position?

3. **Voice and Tone:** What is Levine and Cureton's attitude toward the students and educators who participated in their survey? What is their attitude toward the ideal that John Henry Cardinal Newman articulated, which they cite in paragraph 1?

4. **Responsibility:** What have Levine and Cureton done to write responsibly in this essay?

5. **Content and Format:** What is the effect of Levine and Cureton's use of headings?

Critical Thinking: Your Personal Response

1. Levine and Cureton have added a subtitle to their essay: "An Obituary." To what extent do you agree or disagree with this view of higher education?

2. What is your initial response to Levine and Cureton's report, which was published in 1998? How much are the trends that they found through their surveying still part of academic life? How much are you affected by the changes in academic life that they suggest are happening? How important are these changes to you? Why?

3. What section of "Collegiate Life: An Obituary" (for example, "Demographics," "What Students Want," "Social Life") is the most interesting to you? Why?

Critical Thinking: The Writer's Ideas

1. To what extent do you accept the accuracy of Levine and Cureton's conclusions? Why? What can you cite from their essay that supports your view?

2. What ideas in this essay do you disagree with? Why?

3. Levine and Cureton talk about students as consumers, and compare attending college to accessing an ATM or shopping in a supermarket. What do you think of this metaphor?

4. Levine and Cureton note that students no longer value nonmaterial goals such as "learning to get along with people and formulating the values and goals of one's life" (paragraph 35). What is your opinion of these nonmaterial goals? How important are they? How appropriate is it to pursue them in college?

5. Levine and Cureton suggest several ways that "higher education [should] respond" to their findings (paragraph 41). To what extent do you agree or disagree? Why?

Composing Processes and Knowledge of Conventions: The Writer's Strategies

1. Comment on the research that Levine and Cureton draw on. How convincing is it? Why? How convincing are the statistics and examples that Levine and Cureton provide? Why?

2. How effective is Levine and Cureton's presentation of their research findings? Why do you think that?

3. What are some of the strategies that Levine and Cureton use to convince their readers? What other strategies might they have used?

4. How effectively have Levine and Cureton used logos, pathos, and ethos? Point to some specific examples of each.

Inquiry and Research: Ideas for Further Exploration

1. Read other views on how college life has changed or is changing. In no more than two pages, explain how they support or contradict what Levine and Cureton have to say.

2. Interview several of your classmates about each of the main subtopics Levine and Cureton focus on ("Demographics," "What Students Want," "Social Life," and so on). To what extent do they agree or disagree with Levine and Cureton? Why?

3. If one or both of your parents or some other relative of their generation went to college, what differences are there between your experience of college life and theirs? You may need to interview your parents or relative to answer this question.

Thinking about Visuals That Persuade

Photographs can be extremely persuasive; their appeal to a viewer's emotions is immediate. Suppose you are reading a paper whose author is trying to persuade you that there have been problems at a particular intersection, with drivers continually running red lights and causing accidents. Would the photograph shown in Figure 8.4 get your attention?

Consider, for example, how you could use a photograph such as this one—depicting a recent accident on the road that leads into your campus from a nearby neighborhood—to illustrate the editorial written in response to Scenario 3 on page 326 (a campus–community problem).

Or perhaps you are writing to persuade your neighbors that allowing a wind farm to be built on a nearby hill is not a good idea for your community. You plan to argue that the devices are unsightly and perhaps even dangerous. Would the photograph shown in Figure 8.5 on page 356 help make your point?

As you think about the use of both of these photographs as part of arguments to persuade, consider the following questions:

• How does each photograph connect to the main point the writer is trying to make?

• How does the photograph serve to support that point?

• In what way(s) does the picture help convince the reader?

**FIGURE 8.4
An Accident Scene**

- Each photograph obviously makes an appeal to a viewer's emotions. Is the appeal fair in each case? Why or why not?
- What other type of visual might you use for each of these arguments?

Drawing On Research to Persuade Your Reader

Research is critical to any persuasive text, for if you cannot provide evidence to support your position, you probably will not convince your reading audience. You can research an issue for a persuasive essay by reading books and articles, conducting searches online, interviewing those who may know more about the issue than you do, and employing other means of gathering information.

The subject you focus on and the kind of essay you are constructing help determine the kind of research you conduct. For the scenarios in this chapter, you could conduct several kinds of research:

- For Scenario 1 (p. 324), which asks you to focus on a controversial issue, assume that you have decided to write about whether the threat of criminal punishment helps prevent the insider trading of stocks. What kinds of research might you conduct? At your library, a search of business publications such as the *Wall Street Journal, BusinessWeek,* and *Forbes* would be a good place to start. But, in addition, you could

**FIGURE 8.5
A Wind Farm**

*For more on conducting
research and citing your
sources properly, see
Chapters 19 and 20.*

interview some local business executives to get their perspectives for your paper. You could interview law enforcement officials and attorneys to get their take on whether the threat of punishment helps stop insider trading.

- For Scenario 2 (p. 325), where you focus on some controversial issue that you are interested or involved in, that same kind of local research—interviewing your classmates, for example—will provide useful information for your paper. Consider all of the comments you could get, for instance, if you were writing about an issue involving your classrooms, such as the condition of the building or the time the classes are scheduled, or a campus issue, such as campus safety, student fees, or athletics. Speaking with campus officials and administrators will also give you useful information for your paper. In addition, a search of the campus newspaper archives in your college's library may provide good background information on the issue you are writing about.

- One way to learn about other perspectives on your subject is to read online blogs or join Listservs that focus on the topic of your essay. These ongoing electronic conversations can often provide multiple perspectives and ideas on the issue you are writing about—which can then help you with your own thinking and research.

Writing Processes

As you work on the assignment that you have chosen, remember the qualities of an effective and convincing persuasive paper, listed on pages 330–32. Also remember that writing is recursive—you might start with an invention activity or two and then conduct some research, which leads to more invention work and then a first draft; but then you might need to do more invention work to come up with additional reasons and conduct more research to add more support or refute an opposing argument; and then you'll revise your draft and possibly find another gap or two. . . . Writing, in other words, is more a circular than a linear process. So while the activities listed below imply that writers proceed step-by-step, the actual process of writing is usually more messy: you will keep coming back to your earlier work, adding to it, modifying the information to be more accurate as you conduct additional research and become more familiar with your issue.

If you are considering several issues for your persuasive text, put your notes into a separate computer document for each one. Once you determine the focus of your paper, it will be easy to access and use the notes on that issue. Also, as you work on your project, make sure that you save your computer files frequently because any work that you don't save could be lost. Many experienced writers save their files every fifteen minutes or so. Also, savvy writers back up their computer files in two or more places—on an internal or external hard drive of the computer, on a USB flash drive, and/or on a rewritable CD or DVD.

For a tip on organizing your computer files, see page 97.

Invention: Getting Started

The invention activities below are strategies that you can use to help you get some sense of what you already know about the issue you have chosen. These activities can lead to all sorts of questions that will help guide your research on your issue. You may find it effective to use one or more of these approaches to start exploring your issue. Whatever invention method(s) you use (or that your teacher asks you to use), try to answer questions such as these:

- What do I already know about this issue?
- What is my point of view on this issue?
- Where might I learn more about this issue? What verifiable information is available?
- What might my audience already know? What might their point of view be?
- What do I know about my audience? What don't I know that I should know?

- What questions do I have about the issue?
- What are some other views on this issue?

Doing your invention work in electronic form, rather than on paper, lets you easily use your invention work as you construct a draft.

WRITING ACTIVITY

Listing, Questioning, and Freewriting

For more on listing, questioning, freewriting, and other strategies for discovery and learning, see Chapter 3.

Listing, questioning, and freewriting are three useful techniques to help you generate ideas about an issue. When you list, you jot down keywords and ideas that come to mind about your issue. You might generate a list of ideas and details without trying to organize them in any way, or you might find it effective to establish categories to help jog your thinking.

You might also spend a few minutes jotting down answers to the reporter's questions about your issue: *who, what, where, when, why,* and *how.* You may find that your answers lead to still more questions.

Finally, using the questions above, try freewriting about your issue. During the time frame allowed, just keep writing because the very act of putting words down will help you generate more ideas.

While we present various invention strategies in a particular order here, you should always remember that every writing project is different, and you may find yourself using invention techniques in a different order, depending on the requirements of your particular project.

Santi DeRosa's Initial Listing

Student writer Santi DeRosa read an article in his college paper about how female students help to recruit male athletes for his school. According to the article, women serve as campus guides when potential athletes visit the school, a widespread practice. DeRosa had concerns about the ethics of this practice, so he decided to respond to Scenario 2 by writing an essay on the issue. Here is DeRosa's initial list on this issue:

Recruiting college (male) athletes
How women are treated/used
"Objectification"—means what?
My own family views of women
Who cares? Important!

Treat everyone as people
College guys, athletes
Do males recruit female athletes?
What's wrong with this picture?

Santi DeRosa's Answers to the Reporter's Questions

Santi DeRosa might ask—and answer—the reporter's questions as follows:

- Who is involved? Whom do they affect, and how are they affected? Who has control over recruiting practices? Who might change the situation?

  - Female students volunteer, and I wonder how people perceive this. How do the women feel about doing this? Who decides who gets to "volunteer"? What d**oes the president of the university think about this?**

- What do they do?

  - They act as guides and escorts. Nothing sexual—or is there? I wonder how their boyfriends feel about their participation.

- Where does the recruiting occur?

  - Taking someone to a local fast-food restaurant seems pretty harmless, while visiting other places may not.

- When does the recruiting happen? What sequence of events is involved?

  - I think that recruiting is in the fall, but I'm not certain. How do the people get matched up? Do they work (escort) in groups and if not, is there a chaperone?

- Why does this happen? Why are these particular students involved?

  - How well does this form of "recruiting" really work? Some young men might be influenced if attractive young women showed them around the campus and the city. Why do the young women volunteer? They must get some satisfaction—a sense of civic responsibility and pride in the school, which is a good thing.

- How do the female students act when they are with the athletes? React?

  - I need to find out more about the logistics of these recruiting visits. Do NCAA rules and regulations apply? How are the female students trained for this work?

Santi DeRosa's Freewriting

DeRosa also used freewriting to explore his ideas. A portion of his freewriting appears here:

> Interesting that women are used to recruit male athletes here, and that they volunteer. Is this a good idea? Are the women being used and objectified? What if they want to do it? What if the whole process is pretty innocent? The newspaper sensationalized it, which bothers me. I can't think of what to write, I can't think—hey, do they use males to recruit female athletes? I need to find out about that. . . .

Santi DeRosa's Expanding List

After doing his freewriting, DeRosa did some more listing to think further about his topic:

Objections to Program
- Manipulation
- Program that turns women into objects and reinforces sexism
- Stereotypes about young attractive women
- In the guise of school spirit?
- Is this sexist? What criteria are used to determine whether something is sexist?
- I am arguing that this program turns women into objects.
- I need to deal with opposing views—that this is simply a matter of school spirit.

Exploring Your Ideas with Research

Although you may be able to use information from your own experience as evidence, you will usually need to offer verifiable information from sources, such as facts, statistics, expert testimony, and examples. If you are writing about a local issue, for instance, a local official such as a member of the town council or a state senator might be a useful person to interview. His or her views on your issue could add ethos to your paper—if your audience will consider the official to be fair, knowledgeable, and honest.

To find evidence outside of your experience that you need to support your claim, look for answers to the following questions:

For help with locating sources of information, see Chapter 19; for help with documenting your sources, see Chapter 20.

- What facts or other verifiable information can I find that will provide solid evidence to convince my readers to agree with my position?
- What expert testimony can I provide to support my claim? What authorities on my issue might I interview?

- What statistical data support my position?
- What are other people doing in response to this issue or problem?

WRITING ACTIVITY

Conducting Research

Using the list of qualities of effective persuasive writing on pages 330–32, go through your invention writing and note what you already know about your issue. Next, determine whether you need to do research to come up with additional reasons or evidence, strengthen your appeals, or muster stronger counterarguments.

You also will find it useful to consider the issue you are writing about and, in no more than two pages, outline a research plan. In your plan, indicate the following:

- What you already know about your issue
- What questions you still have
- Who or what sources might be able to answer your questions
- Who (roommates, friends, college staff, professors) might be able to provide other perspectives on your issue
- Where you might look for further information (library, Web, primary documents, other sources)
- When you plan to conduct your research

Gather, read, and take notes on your issue from these outside sources. Use an electronic journal to record images, URLs, and other electronic pieces of information that you find as you are conducting your research. Such an e-journal makes it easy for you to add those e-documents once you start drafting your paper.

Student Example: An Excerpt from Santi DeRosa's Research

For my presentation, I can use some of the details from the State Press articles. Those articles offer a clear narrative account of recruiting activities. They also help to demonstrate that there is an issue.

I also found some information about the same kind of thing at Colorado State University (Lambert article).

I will need to research how to define the concept of "objectification," a term I've read about. I need to be clearer on this concept. I did check the American Heritage Dictionary through Dictionary.com and they had this great quotation under the word's definition that I could include in my paper:

> To present or regard as an object: "Because we have objectified animals, we are able to treat them impersonally" (Barry Lopez).

I like how that really connects to the point I'm trying to make in my paper.

Reviewing Your Invention and Research

After you have conducted your research, you need to review your invention work and notes and the information you have collected from outside sources. Once you have a general idea of the conclusion your research is leading you to, you can develop a working thesis statement: if you had to make a point now, based on what you have learned, what would it be? It is called *For more on deciding on a* a working thesis because your main point or thesis will inevitably change *thesis, see Chapter 13.* as you continue to conduct research and learn more. And, as you know, through the process of writing itself, you will learn about your topic, so give yourself permission to modify and develop this initial thesis statement as you draft and revise your text. Once you have written several drafts, have received feedback on them, and have revised them, you will be better able to determine what your final thesis statement should be.

WRITING ACTIVITY

Considering Your Research and Focusing Your Ideas

Examine the notes you have taken from your research. Then, using the *who, what, where, when, why,* and *how* questions as a starting point, see what information you have. For example, if you are trying to persuade your readers of the existence of a campus–community problem (see Scenario 2 on p. 325), some of your research notes might look like this:

who: students and neighbors alike are affected when lots of student cars are going through the neighborhood as they come to campus to attend classes and, of course, when they leave campus
what: the biggest issues seem to be too many cars on neighborhood streets, too many of them speeding, and too many of them parking where they should not
when: all the time but especially when classes change during the day . . .

WRITER'S WORKSHOP

Reacting to Your Classmates' Invention Work and Research

With any writing assignment, your invention materials and research can improve with peer feedback and suggestions. This is especially true for persuasive writing. Get together with several of your classmates and share your invention work and a summary of the results of your research, along with your working thesis statement. Provide comments and suggestions and ask one another questions, with the overall goal of helping one another to understand your rhetorical situation more clearly and to generate stronger reasons and evidence to support your claim. Be sure to bring up opposing views so that writers will have an opportunity to formulate their counterarguments.

Comments

- I understand _____ about what you have generated thus far.

- I agree with/disagree with _____.

- _____ in what you have so far is familiar/unfamiliar to me, so you might _____.

- I like _____ in what you've generated so far.

- I don't see how _____ is very persuasive.

- I'm confused when you write about _____.

- These aspects of your argument— _____ and _____—don't seem related, so I'm not sure why you've included them.

- The part about _____ seems promising, but the part about _____ seems underdeveloped.

- I'm not convinced when you write about _____.

- I'd suggest that you include these ideas or this information to strengthen your argument: _____

  _____

  _____

  _____

Questions

- What is _____ ? (Ask this kind of question when something is unclear.)

- I still have questions about _____.

- How would you describe the purpose of the _____ that you mention?

(cont'd)

(continued)

- How do _____ and _____ work together?

- Why you think this is an important issue?

- What are the larger implications of this issue?

- What are the other perspectives on this issue?

- Have you thought about this perspective on your issue: _____?

As your classmates respond to your invention work and research, listen carefully—and with an open mind—to what they are saying, and take notes so that you do not forget their questions, comments, and suggestions. Your classmates' responses to your writing will help you anticipate the responses of your audience. In persuasion, your biggest challenge is to understand the views of others and to address them adequately, so you should solicit readers' responses as early and as often as feasible. You can get responses to your work in class, but you can also do so online, at the campus writing center, or even in your local coffee shop.

Organizing Your Information

Because the purpose of writing a persuasive text is to convince your readers to accept your point of view, you will need to organize your reasons and evidence strategically. The questions that you need to ask yourself when deciding on your organization are all rhetorical:

- Who is your audience? What is your readers' position on your issue likely to be? If they are undecided, you might try a classical or an inductive approach, both of which are discussed below. If they are likely to hold an opposing view, then a refutation approach, also discussed below, may be the better choice.

- Why might they be interested in your persuasive writing, or how can you make them interested in it? One way to emphasize the importance of your issue to your audience is to show them why your subject is important, as Maureen Dowd does by opening with the example of her niece's operation (see p. 337).

- What is your purpose for writing—that is, why do you need to convince readers of this position?

When you construct a persuasive paper, you have to determine the most effective organizational approach for your purpose and audience. One method of organizing an argument, called the *classical scheme*, was first outlined by Aristotle nearly 2,400 years ago. Aristotle listened to the effective public speakers of his day, determined how their best speeches were organized, and suggested that persuasive writing be organized the same way. If you are using the classical scheme, this is the sequence you will follow:

introduction → main claim → evidence supporting claim →
discussion of other perspectives (acknowledging, conceding,
and/or refuting them) → conclusion.

Aristotle's approach is also called the **deductive method** because you
state your claim and then help the reader understand, or deduce, how the
evidence supports your claim. The advantage of this method is that you state
your position and make your case early, before your reader starts thinking
about other perspectives.

Another organizational approach is commonly known as the **inductive
method.** When using this approach, you first present and explain all of your
reasons and evidence, then draw your conclusion—your main claim. The
advantage is that your reader may come to the same conclusion before you
explicitly state your position and will therefore be more inclined to agree
with your point of view.

Because persuasive writing must usually acknowledge and incorporate or
refute opposing viewpoints, a third organizational method starts by presenting the views of the other side. In this method, you first deal with objections
to your claim and then state your position and provide reasons and evidence
to support it. The advantage of this approach is that you place the opposing
views immediately on the table, an especially effective strategy if the opposing view or views are widely held.

Here are the three organizational structures that you might consider for
your persuasive paper.

Options for Organization

The Classical (Deductive) Approach	The Inductive Approach	Refutation Approach
• Introduce the issue. ↓ • Explain the importance of the issue. ↓ • Present your reasons and evidence—why readers should agree with you. ↓ • Answer objections—either incorporate or refute other points of view. ↓ • Conclude—often with a call to action.	• Introduce the issue. ↓ • Offer reasons and evidence for your claim. ↓ • Draw your conclusion—your main claim. ↓ • Deal with other viewpoints either before or after pre-senting your claim. ↓ • Conclude—often with a call to action.	• Introduce the issue. ↓ • List opposing views. ↓ • Deal with each objection in turn. ↓ • Introduce your position and explain why it makes sense, offering reasons and evidence. ↓ • Conclude—often with a call to action.

WRITING ACTIVITY

Deciding on an Organizational Approach

Before you construct a full draft, consider which organizational approach will best serve your writing purpose, given your audience's views. It is sometimes useful to try several organizational approaches to determine which is most effective for your specific purpose, audience, and rhetorical situation. Try out several organizational approaches on the computer before deciding on one—and be sure to save each first attempt with a different file name. That strategy makes it easy to recall the one that seems best. You can then start to develop your draft using that organization.

Student writer Santi DeRosa (a draft of his paper is on pp. 371–73) decided to organize his paper by first asking a controversial question, which leads to his thesis: women are objectified. He then provides specific, local examples as evidence.

 ## Constructing a Complete Draft

Once you have chosen the best organizational approach for your audience and purpose, you are ready to construct your draft. After you have reviewed your invention writing and research notes, developed a working thesis, and carefully considered all of the reasons and evidence you have generated, construct a complete first draft. Remember that your thinking about your issue and claim will evolve as you write, so your ideas will most likely change as you compose the first draft.

As you work, keep the following in mind:

- You may discover you need to do more invention work and/or more research as you write.

- As you try out tentative claims and reasons, ask your classmates and other readers about the kinds of supporting evidence they consider convincing.

For more on choosing visuals, see Chapter 18.

- Consider whether photographs or other visuals might help support your thesis.

- If you become tired and the quality of your thinking or your productivity is affected, take a break.

As you write your first draft, remember the main point that you are trying to make. In a piece of persuasive writing, you will want to make sure that you provide enough evidence to convince your readers to agree with you.

Introduction: Regardless of your organizational approach, you need to have a strong **introduction** to capture your readers' attention and introduce the issue. To accomplish these two goals in an introduction, you might do one or more of the following:

- *Provide a brief history of the issue.* Arthur S. Levine and Jeannette Cureton open "Collegiate Life: An Obituary" (p. 342) with a brief overview of the concept of the ideal university, dating from the time of John Henry Cardinal Newman in the middle of the nineteenth century. They go on to demonstrate how the students they studied view colleges and universities in an entirely different light.

- *Share an anecdote that clearly exemplifies the issue.* Maureen Dowd begins her column on organ donation (p. 337) with the story of her niece's bravery in choosing to donate part of her liver to her uncle:

  > Jennifer showed me her scar Friday. It's the most beautiful scar I've ever seen. A huge stapled gash on her stomach, shaped like the Mercedes logo. A red badge of courage.

- *Provide a fact or statistic about the issue that will surprise—and possibly concern—readers.* In her article about women in combat (p. 334), Anne Applebaum begins by informing readers of something they may not realize:

  > The argument about women in combat is over. In fact, it was over three years ago, when two female sailors were among the victims of the bombing of the USS Cole.

- *Ask an intriguing question about your subject.* Santi DeRosa opens his paper (p. 380) by asking this key question:

  > Are women at Arizona State University being treated as objects by the very university that has a responsibility to treat them with equality and dignity and not as second-class citizens?

- *Explain (briefly) why your persuasive text is important.* One way to establish the importance of your persuasive writing is to explain, right at the start, how the issue you will focus on affects the reader. In Santi DeRosa's essay (p. 380), he could have asked, "How would you like your sister or daughter to be treated as an object to be used to tempt a male athlete to attend a certain college?"

Body: You can use various writing strategies, including defining all terms your reader might not understand, within the body of your text to effectively persuade your reader:

- *Provide supporting examples or evidence for each reason you offer.* Such evidence shows your reader that your position is correct. The more relevant, reliable supporting evidence that you can provide, the stronger your case will be.

- *Use visual aids (photographs, charts, tables) to support your position.* Visuals can provide evidence for your thesis, and you can use them in a

For more on rhetorical appeals and argument strategies, see Chapter 14.

number of ways. See pages 369 and 370 for examples of ways to use visuals in arguments.

- *Use rhetorical appeals—ethos, logos, pathos (p. 331)—to help convince your readers.* For example, Maureen Dowd in "Our Own Warrior Princess" (p. 337) uses her niece's story throughout her article to create an emotional response in her readers. Arthur Levine and Jeanette Cureton (p. 342), however, rely on the results of their research— logos—to convince readers of their main points about college life and student attitudes.

Conclusion: In your conclusion you need to restate or allude to your thesis and let your readers know what you would like them to do with the information they learned from your essay. Conclusions in persuasive writing often do the following:

- *Explain your main thesis or point—what you want to persuade your reader about.* Anne Applebaum states her main point in her final paragraph (p. 335), a point that she has led up to: "the military now needs to catch up to the civilian world"; in other examples of persuasive writing, the writer may conclude by reiterating a point made at the beginning.

- *Summarize how each supporting point adds evidence to support your main point.* In a long, involved argument, a summary can help readers recall the main points that you are making.

- *Reach out to the audience.* An appeal to the audience is an especially effective way to end a piece of persuasive writing. As noted above, one way to do this is to relate the subject of your essay specifically to your readers.

- *Include a "call to action" in your conclusion.* Maureen Dowd ends "Our Own Warrior Princess" with a description of herself filling out an organ donor card and the strong implication that readers should do so as well: "If Jennifer is brave enough to do it alive, how can I be scared of doing it dead?"

Title: As you compose your persuasive writing, a title should emerge at some point—perhaps late in the process. The title should reflect the point you are trying to make, and it should catch your readers' attention and make them want to read your essay. "Our Own Warrior Princess" suggests the topic of Maureen Dowd's essay without stating it in an obvious way. "Collegiate Life: An Obituary" should catch the interest of anyone interested in college life. However, it may be risky to state your major claim in the title. If you are making a controversial claim, you may want to withhold it from your readers until you have introduced the issue to them. If you state a controversial claim in your title, you take the chance that some readers will choose not to read your argument. On the other hand, there are times when stating a bold claim in the title is appropriate—especially if readers may not even have considered the topic.

VISUALIZING VARIATIONS

Using Charts and Other Visuals to Support Your Claim

If you were writing in response to Scenario 2, which asks you to focus on a controversial issue, you might choose to write about global warming. Here is a dramatic image that you could use at the beginning of your paper:

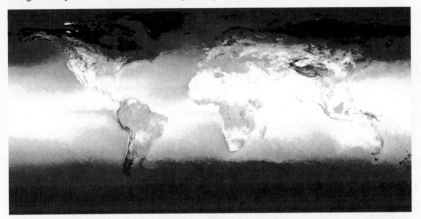

But while you could focus on an image like this one as a way to help make your points, you could also use charts and graphs to convince your reader, as they can provide useful information. This chart shows the global variation in temperatures from 1860 to 2000:

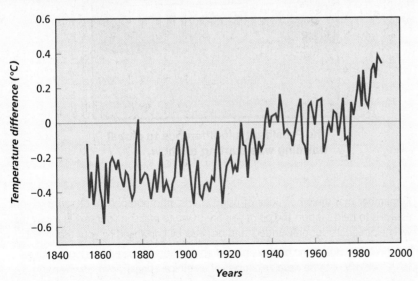

If you were to combine this chart with the following information from the same source, you would be providing your reader with a useful chart along with some specific data to explain it.

(cont'd)

(continued)

The temperature values in the data set are provided as **differences** from a mean of 15 degrees C. These data have been analyzed by scientists to show a 0.5 degrees C increase in global temperatures. However, this finding is under dispute because some claim that the amount of error in the data is too large to justify the conclusion. This data set has been created using the follwing steps:

- Data was collected from land based stations, from ocean buoys, and from ships.
- For each year data has been averaged to come up with a yearly average.
- Data is smoothed to accommodate historical changes that skew the data (e.g., weather stations near cities record artificially high temperatures because [cities] create what is called an "urban heat island effect").

If it were appropriate to put a political spin into your essay, you could use a cartoon like this one to make your point.

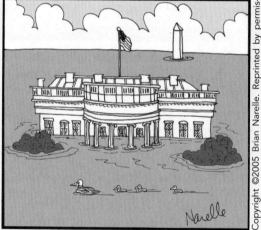

The President's indifference to global warming was starting to show.

Remember that the whole idea of using charts, photographs, or cartoons in your essays is to help support the point you are trying to make in your text in a way that will help readers not only understand but also be convinced by your argument.

- Which visual is the best example of an emotional appeal? Of a logical appeal? Are any of these visuals examples of an ethical appeal? Why or why not?
- Comment on the effectiveness of each visual as support for an argument on the danger of global warming.
- How might someone opposed to the claim that global warming is a current danger argue against the appeals presented by these three visuals?

WRITING ACTIVITY

Constructing a Full Draft

After reviewing your notes, invention activities, and research and carefully considering all of the information that you have generated and the comments you have received, construct a complete first draft of your persuasive paper, using the organizational approach that you have decided on. Remember that your argument will evolve as you write, so your ideas will most likely change as you compose this first draft.

Santi DeRosa's First Draft

In this brief draft, note how Santi DeRosa incorporates information and examples from his own life as well as from outside sources. As he wrote, DeRosa did not worry about grammar, punctuation, and mechanics; instead, he concentrated on getting his main ideas on paper.

> The Objectification of Woman. Who's Fault Is it?
>
> Are women at ASU being objectified by the very university that has a responsibility to treat women with equality and not as second class citizens?
>
> I say yes. All you need to do is look at the athletics department to see the way women are treated. What I don't understand is that in the year 2003, women are still allowing themselves to be used in such a way
>
> In the past week I have read a couple of news articles from the State Press that got me a little perplexed. Maybe it's the fact that I have a son the age of the female students in the articles. Or, maybe it's the fact that I have a wife, a sister, a mother and nieces that I respect as people and as women. The articles upset my sense of right and wrong.
>
> Joe Watson wrote the first article, "Risky behavior not policed in ASU recruiting" and explains how high school football players that visit ASU for the purpose of being recruited are met by coeds from the "ASU Sun Devil Recruiters" of which, thirty-five of the thirty-seven are females. Is

this just a coincidence? No, I don't think so. It is no coincidence when schools from all over the country use the same practices to recruit high school players. The reporter took an informal survey of 117 Division 1-A football programs nationwide and found many with the same recruiter make-up. Louisiana State has 55 females; Alabama leads the way with 100 females. ASU advertises every spring for new recruiters. Most come from sororities. The football coaches say they prefer using females because that's the way the other schools do it and the players coming ASU to be recruited would be uncomfortable if they were greeted by males, because they are used to female recruiters. I think that this is just an excuse to turn a blind eye to a potential problem. Most of the players who come to ASU to be recruited are 17 and 18 years old. There have been many reports of under-age drinking at local clubs and parties and sometimes sex according to some senior recruiters. The people interviewed for the article who are in support of the "hostess" program defend it by saying that "the recruiters perform respectable duties during high school recruits' campus visits." Does the responsibility of "performing respectable duties" end when they leave the campus for a party? I believe that Becky Stoltz, a forth year recruiter at ASU said it best when interviewed, "It's a disaster waiting to happen."

The second news article I read was by Megan Rudebeck. The story titled "'Hot' recruiters draw prospects" seems to be defending the program. Ms. Rudebeck not only talked to the coaches that run the program; she spoke with recruiters and players as well. She almost had me convinced that I might have been over reacting. I started to think that here is a woman writing a story that seems to be in defense of the way the recruiting program works. Maybe I am reacting wrongly. That is until the last line of the story when she quotes Zach Krula, a freshman offensive lineman. Zach says, "We've got a lot of hot girls, we might as well utilize them." After a few minutes I started to think to myself, why isn't Ms. Rudebeck insulted by that comment? Is she, as well as the women that are part of the program, so brain-washed with the need to get quality players into the football program that they are willing to overlook the fact that they are being "utilized."

As ideas for further development, Santi made these notes at the end of his initial draft:

> Short history of women's struggle for equality.
>
> Use family stories to tell history of strong women?
>
> Define the objectification of women.
>
> Conclusion.

 ## Revising

Once you have a full draft of your persuasive text, you still have much to do. First, however, you should set the draft aside so that you can gain some critical distance. You should then read it with fresh eyes. When you approach your work this way, you will find it easier to notice reasons that are irrelevant, evidence that is not fully developed, or places where a compelling photograph might add to the impact of your argument.

As you work to revise your early drafts, do not be concerned about doing a great deal of heavy editing. When you revise you will probably change the content and structure of your paper, so time spent fixing problems with sentence style or grammar, punctuation, or mechanics at this stage is often wasted.

Think of revision as re-envisioning your work, reconsidering what you mean to say, not just editing for surface features. When you reread the first draft of your persuasive writing, here are some questions to ask yourself:

- How clearly and persuasively am I making my point? Am I sure my readers can understand it? How easily will they be able to restate the thesis?
- How effectively does all of my evidence support that main point? (Sometimes it is easy to include evidence that seems persuasive but that does not support the point you are arguing for.)
- Are there other photographs, charts, or graphs that might help make my point?
- Are there parts of my paper that might confuse a reader? If so, how might I clarify them?
- Do I restate or allude to my main point at the end of my paper and also explain to the reader what I would like him or her to do (to vote, to write a letter to the editor, to *do* what I have been arguing for)?

Technology can help you revise and edit your writing more easily. Use your word processor's track-changes tool to try out revisions and editing changes. After you have had time to think about the possible changes, you can "accept" or "reject" them. Also, you can use your word processor's comment tool to write reminders to yourself when you get stuck with a revision or some editing task. If your classmates are offering feedback on your draft, they can also use track changes, the comment tool, or the peer-commenting feature of the software.

Because it is so difficult even for experienced writers to see their emerging writing with a fresh eye, it is almost always useful to ask classmates, friends, or family members to read and comment on drafts of your persuasive writing.

WRITER'S WORKSHOP

Responding to Full Drafts

Working with one or two classmates, read each paper and offer comments and questions that will help each of you see your papers' strengths and weaknesses. You might share your comments and questions in a conversation, or you may have each reader write comments and questions (either with pen or pencil or electronically) on the writer's draft. Consider the following guidelines and questions as you do:

- Write a brief narrative comment outlining your first impression of this draft. How effective is the title at drawing you in? Why? What are your overall suggestions for improvement? What part(s) of the text are especially persuasive? What reasons could use more support? Indicate what you like about the draft, and provide positive and encouraging feedback to the writer.

- Comment on the writer's focus. Does the paper wander a bit? If so, indicate where.

- Comment on how convincing you found the paper. Explain, in a brief paragraph, how much you were persuaded by the paper.

- Comment on the effectiveness of the introduction. What suggestions can you make to improve it?

- What is the author's thesis or main claim? Could it be expressed or supported more effectively? If so, how?

- Are there parts that are confusing? Where would you like more details or examples to help clarify the writer's meaning?

- How accurate and appropriate is the supporting evidence? Has the writer included questionable statistics or concepts? How clearly does the author indicate the sources of statistics and other supporting evidence that may not be common knowledge?

- Might visuals such as charts, tables, photographs, or cartoons strengthen the writer's case and make the text more convincing?

- How clearly and effectively does the writer present any opposing points of view? How might this presentation be improved? How effectively does the writer answer opposing viewpoints? How might the writer acknowledge, concede, and/or refute them more effectively?

- How well has the writer demonstrated an awareness of readers' knowledge, needs, and/or expectations? How might the writer demonstrate greater awareness?

- How carefully has the writer avoided logical fallacies? Point out any that you have found.

- Reread the conclusion. What could be added or changed to make it more effective? How well does it tie everything together? If action is called for, to what extent does it make you want to take action?

- In a brief paragraph, explain what you see as the paper's strengths. In another paragraph, outline what you see as the paper's weaknesses—and suggest improvements.

Notes on Santi DeRosa's First Draft, from a Conference with His Instructor

After writing his first draft, DeRosa met with his instructor, who thought his topic was promising but indicated that he needed more support on recruiting practices at his school and at other campuses. Together they brainstormed more ideas to develop his paper in more depth. The practice of using female students to help recruit male athletes led to these objections, which are more completely developed in DeRosa's final draft (see pp. 380–83):

1. Using women for their bodies
2. Manipulation
3. A program that reinforces age-old notions of prostitution
4. Limits and defines women's roles
5. Under the guise of school spirit
6. I'd better add some more extensive research info—mine is all from ASU

Responding to Readers' Comments

Once they have received feedback on their writing from peers, instructors, friends, and others, all writers have to figure out what to do with that feedback. Since your text is *your* responsibility, you must determine how to deal with reader responses to your work.

The first thing to do with any feedback is to consider carefully what your readers have said about your text. In his case, DeRosa arranged a conference with his writing teacher, who helped him brainstorm some specific objections to the recruiting program at his school to give his argument more depth.

As with all feedback, it is important to really listen to it and consider what your reader has to say. Then it is up to you, as the author, to decide how to come to terms with these suggestions. You may decide to reject some comments, of course; other comments, though, deserve your attention, as they are the words of real readers speaking to you about how to improve your text. It is especially important to deal with comments from readers that indicate that they are unconvinced by your argument. You sometimes may find that comments from more than one reader contradict each other. In that case, you need to use your own judgment to decide which reader's comments are on the right track.

In the final version of his paper on pages 380–83, you can see how Santi DeRosa responded to his instructor's comments, as well as to his own review of his first draft.

Knowledge of Conventions

When effective writers edit their work, they attend to the conventions that will help readers process their work. These include genre conventions, documentation, format, usage, grammar, and mechanics. By attending to these conventions in your writing, you make reading a more pleasant experience for readers.

Editing

See Chapter 20 for more on documenting sources using MLA or APA style.

The last task in any writing project is editing—the final polishing of your document. When you edit and polish your writing, you make changes to your sentence structure and word choice to improve your style and to make your writing clearer and more concise. You also check your work to make sure it adheres to conventions of grammar, usage, punctuation, mechanics, and spelling. Use the spell-check function of your word-processing program, but be sure to double-check your spelling personally. If you have used sources in your paper, make sure you are following the documentation style your instructor requires.

As with overall revision of your work, this final editing and polishing is most effective if you can put your text aside for a few days and come back to it with fresh eyes. Because checking conventions is easier said than done, though, we strongly recommend that you ask classmates, friends, and tutors to read your work to find editing problems that you cannot see. Another option is to post your paper on a course Web site and invite everyone in class to read it. You may get only one or two takers, but one or two is better than none.

To assist you with editing, we offer here a round-robin editing activity focused on citing sources correctly.

Round-Robin Editing with a Focus on Citing Sources

Focus in this workshop on the conventions for citing sources. Look over both the in-text citations and the works-cited or references lists in your papers. For example, you might notice a problem with an in-text citation that is supposed to be in MLA style, such as this one:

INCORRECT In the last line of the story, however, Rudebeck quotes Zach Krula, a freshman offensive lineman. Zach says, "We've got a lot of hot girls, we might as well utilize them" (Rudebeck 1).

In MLA style, it is not necessary to include the source's name in parentheses if the name has been given within the text, so this citation needs to be corrected.

CORRECT In the last line of the story, however, Rudebeck quotes Zach Krula, a freshman offensive lineman. Zach says, "We've got a lot of hot girls, we might as well utilize them" (~~Rudebeck~~ 1).

As you work with your peers, consult Chapter 20 of this text, which provides guidelines for using MLA or APA style when citing sources.

Genres, Documentation, and Format

If you are writing an academic paper in response to Scenario 1 or 2, you will need to follow the conventions for the discipline in which you are writing and the requirements of your instructor. If you are writing an editorial for your college newspaper (Scenario 3), you should check the newspaper's editorial page or its Web site to see what the requirements are for length and format and what information you need to include when you submit the editorial. If you are writing a reference for a job application (Scenario 5), consult the example in Appendix C to follow the conventions of a business letter.

Convention in Genre and Design

University of Georgia student Phillip Kisubika provides a somewhat humorous but still thoughtful persuasive essay in the following newspaper opinion piece. His thesis is that many college-age students are not ready for marriage. Do you find his argument convincing?

(cont'd)

(continued)

MUCH TO DO BEFORE TYING THE KNOT

by Phillip Kisubika

We're living in strange times.

No, I don't mean the random wars, the crazy technology or the neglected disease pandemics and natural disasters. I mean that in this time of individualism, free thought and experimentation, so many of us contemplate and go through with tying the knot at a young age.

According to a CNN poll in 2002, 63 percent of people between the ages of 17 and 23 were seriously considering, or in favor of young marriage. In November 2004, MS-NBC reported a 17 percent increase in young marriages in the United States.

Not that there's anything wrong with that. In fact, I'm probably one of those people.

I've definitely thought a lot about marriage recently, especially after I was asked to write this column.

As nice as it would be to have a companion to come home to after a long day of class, I think a steady girlfriend is more my speed right now.

Especially since I've never had one.

Most of us aren't ready for a lifelong commitment like marriage.

Yeah, that's right.

Contrary to what society may tell you, you're not joking at the altar when you look into your partner's eyes and agree to "for as long as we both shall live."

According to the U.S. Census Bureau, two out of three marriages taking place under 30 years of age end in divorce.

Surprised? Don't be.

The trends of today's relationships sometimes make me wonder how any couple stays together.

In the past, couples did marry young, but it was more an arrangement of convenience instead of passion. Men chose women who they cared for and who could run a household and raise children. Divorces happened, but they weren't as common, probably because women were limited financially and had trouble making it on their own.

Times have definitely changed.

Women no longer come to college to find a husband or acquire skills needed to help support the household. Women now come to college to learn and establish themselves as individuals who are often working toward a successful career of their own. Now, women are more independent, and marriages occur out of feelings rather than necessity.

It's just my feeling that most college students can't really make the best decision in terms of selecting a life companion right now. I mean, some of us can't even dress ourselves. Have you seen some of the stuff we walk out wearing in the morning?

Personally, I'd like to graduate and establish a good, well-paying career before I get married. That's not just for my own benefit—I'm doing it for my future wife, too. A lot of young marriages struggle financially, and a good job cuts down on the potential hardship.

We, as young people, sometimes get so wrapped up in the ideals of romance and passion that our thoughts totally lack practicality. There are real challenges, and love alone won't make a marriage last. Sure, every marriage struggles, but at our age, I don't think we have the emotional tools to really work at solving the problems that arise in marriage.

I know there are a lot of married students who might think I don't know what I'm talking about.

I would ask those couples to contact me in 20 years if they're still together, and I wouldn't be surprised if they were all divorced.

That's just the society we live in.

My beliefs about marriage won't stop my heart from doing what it always does.

I've met a few girls that I thought I could marry, but that's mainly because they're what I want now, not what I need forever.

More than likely, I'll be a groomsman at a few weddings before I'm the groom.

Not that there's anything wrong with that.

Considering Genre and Design

Consider these questions about Kisubika's essay:

1. How convincing is Kisubika? Why?

2. Kisubika's essay is typical of a newspaper article in that many of the paragraphs within it are short. Do the short paragraphs make his essay seem more, or less, effective to you?

3. How effectively does the title catch your interest? Does Kisubika's one-sentence introduction make you want to read more?

4. How closely do you relate to his position?

5. How do your experiences and those of your friends match Kisubika's?

6. Kisubika's essay was written for his college newspaper. How well does his text seem to fit that genre? Would Kisubika's essay be appropriate for your college newspaper?

7. How effective is Kisubika's use of statistics? Did any of them surprise you?

8. With one or two classmates, look again at the qualities of an effective persuasive essay (pp. 330–32). In what ways does this one fulfill the requirements of this genre?

A Writer Shares His Persuasive Writing: Santi DeRosa's Final Draft

Santi DeRosa continued to revise and edit his paper and constructed a finished draft, which follows. As you read the essay, think about what makes it effective. Following the essay, you'll find some specific questions to consider.

SANTI DEROSA

The Objectification of Women: Whose Fault Is It?

Santi DeRosa and his instructor brainstormed a number of objections to the recruiting practices for him to develop in his revised draft, including this one:

I need to develop the idea that these practices use women for their bodies.

Note how DeRosa develops this objection.

Are women at Arizona State University being treated as objects by the very university that has a responsibility to treat them with equality and dignity and not as second-class citizens? All anyone needs to do is look at the athletics department to see the way women are treated here at ASU. What I don't understand is why in the year 2003 women are still allowing themselves to be used in such a way.

In the past week I have read two news articles in the State Press about recruiting practices at ASU that made me a little perplexed. Maybe it's because I have a son the age of the female students in the articles, or maybe it's because I have a wife, a sister, a mother, and nieces whom I respect as people and as women, but these articles upset my sense of right and wrong. Objectification of women, sexual or otherwise, should never be allowed or condoned.

In the first article I read, "Risky Behavior Not Policed in ASU Recruiting," reporter Joe Watson explains how high school football players who visit ASU for the purpose of being recruited are met by coeds from the "ASU Sun Devil Recruiters." Thirty-five of thirty-seven student recruiters are females. Is this just a coincidence? I don't think so. Schools from all over the country use the same practices to recruit high school players. Watson conducted an informal survey of 117 Division 1-A football programs nationwide and found many with similar proportions of female to male recruiters. Louisiana State has 55 females; Alabama leads the way with 100 females (1).

As Watson reports, ASU advertises every spring for new recruiters. Most come from sororities. The football coaches say they prefer using women because that's the way the other schools do it. They maintain that the players coming to ASU to be recruited would be uncomfortable if they were greeted by men because they are used to female recruiters.

This justification is just an excuse to ignore a potential problem. Most of the players who come to ASU to be recruited are 17 and 18 years

1

2

3

4

5

old. There have been many reports of under-age drinking at local clubs and parties and sometimes sex, according to some senior recruiters. The people interviewed for the article who support the "hostess" program defend it by saying that "the recruiters perform respectable duties during high school recruits' campus visits" (Watson 2). Does the responsibility of "performing respectable duties" end when they leave the campus for a party? I believe that Becky Stoltz, a fourth-year recruiter at ASU who was interviewed for the article said it best: "It's a disaster waiting to happen." Big problems have in fact already happened at the University of Colorado, where a recruiting aide was indicted for improper conduct after a three-month grand-jury investigation of illegal recruiting practices, including allegations of sexual assault (Lambert).

Over the last hundred years, women have traveled a rocky road to greater equality. At the turn of the twentieth century women didn't have many of the rights we take for granted today, such as the right to own property and the right to vote. By staying strong, working together, and maintaining their dignity, women eventually gained these rights for themselves and their daughters and granddaughters. 6

In my own family, my grandmother and great-grandmother took care of their family in Italy while my grandfather came to America to set up a decent life for them. My grandmother held things together for six years until her husband was able to go back and get her. Although she did not have the same rights as a man of that time, she never gave up hope and never lost her pride. In this country she worked as a seamstress, as so many Italian women did, in order to help the family make it through bad times and to provide a better life for her children. My mother also worked a full-time job as a seamstress in a factory while taking care of her home and family, as women did in the 1950s and 1960s. However, women of that time were being taken for granted, and their roles had to change. Women wanted more, and through their strength of conviction, they got it—more equitable pay for their work. However, over the last forty years, the great strides women have made have been somewhat squandered. Women have made impressive gains in their professional lives, but they have also come to be seen, more and more, as objects. 7

The objectification of women in popular culture and sports is not new. During the 1950s and 1960s, the advertising industry started to portray women in roles outside the kitchen, but it also created a perspective on women that objectified them. To consider women in terms of the way they look is objectification. Examples of this are common: (1) Female newscasters chosen for their appearance, (2) the Dallas Cowboy cheerleaders—and cheerleading squads for other teams, and (3) beautiful women appearing in advertisements for beer and automobiles. 8

DeRosa and his instructor also came up with the following objection for him to develop:

The program reinforces age-old notions of prostitution.

Note how he adds details and specific examples to support this part of his persuasive text.

Amanda Bonzo, in an opinion piece in the online journal The Digital   9
Collegian, writes the following about this process of objectification:

> In our society, a woman's body is objectified daily on television, music videos, advertisements. What do we do with objects? We buy, sell, trade them. . . . We tame them through rape and domestic abuse. Finally, we destroy them.

And Casey Jacketta, writing for the University of New Mexico's Daily Lobo, notes the following:

> I was pleased that my favorite show, "Law and Order," was on. Then,   10
as I kept watching, I realized that the assistant district attorney, played by Angie Harmon — a woman — didn't say a word in court. This troubled me, so I changed the channel to MTV. This upset me even more! All I saw was a bunch of barely clothed women shaking their bodies for the male singer's pleasure. (1)

We see what these writers are talking about daily in advertising   11
and in other media such as television, movies, and music. It is unfortunate that the sexual objectification of women sells products, and unless women understand that advertisers, filmmakers, college athletic departments, and others are taking advantage of them, this exploitation will never change. Barbara Fredrickson and her colleagues explain that this process causes women to start to view themselves the way others view them; as a consequence, "[a] woman views her own body as an object (or each piece as a separate object)" (274).

Objectification is often disguised as free speech and free expression,   12
which are both noble principles, although they are often misused. What I don't understand is how any woman would allow herself to be used in this way. In the case of ASU recruiters, objectification is disguised as school spirit.

In the second news article I read, "'Hot' Recruiters Draw Prospects,"   13
Megan Rudebeck seems to be defending the program. Ms. Rudebeck not only talked to the coaches that run the program; she spoke with recruiters and players as well. She almost had me convinced that I might be overreacting. After all, here is a woman who is defending the way the recruiting program works. In the last line of the story, however, Rudebeck quotes Zach Krula, a freshman offensive lineman. Zach says, "We've got a lot of hot girls, we might as well utilize them" (1). That quotation made me wonder why Ms. Rudebeck wasn't insulted by that comment. Is she, as well as the women who are part of the program, so brainwashed by the need to get quality players onto the football team that they are willing to overlook the fact that they are being "utilize[d]"?

The use of women as sexual objects in mass media advertising, tele-   14
vision, and music has made the practice so commonplace that we fail

---

DeRosa also needed to develop this objection to the recruiting program:

It operates under the guise of school spirit.

He added information from another article (by Megan Rudebeck) that puts a positive spin on the practice DeRosa is criticizing and provides a defense of the program; he then refutes Rudebeck's argument.

to see that it degrades our society. It amazes me that the women of the ASU recruiting staff have not made the connection. It amazes me that Ms. Rudebeck and the ASU coaching staff say they don't see what's going on, and that students, faculty, the alumni, and the administration buy into this degrading and potentially dangerous practice. I hope that a copy of Joe Watson's article makes it into the hands of each of the recruiter's parents and the Board of Regents. This practice is an insult to the women of ASU, as well as to every woman in the last century who has sacrificed in order to achieve social equality.

Works Cited

Bonzo, Amanda. Letter. The Digital Collegian. 20 Nov. 2000. 4 Feb. 2003 <http://www.collegian.psu.edu/archive/2000/11/11-20-00tdc/11-20-00dops-letter-1.asp>.

Fredrickson, Barbara L., Tomi-Ann Roberts, Stephanie M. Noll, Diane M. Quinn, and Jean M. Twenge. "That Swimsuit Becomes You: Sex Differences in Self-Objectification, Restrained Eating, and Math Performance." Journal of Personality and Social Psychology, 75 (1998): 269–84.

Jacketta, Casey. "Women's Lib Has Not Ended Objectification." Daily Lobo. 25 Nov. 2002. 3 Feb. 2003 <http://www.dailylobo.com/news/2002/11/25/Opinion/Column. Womens.Lib.Has.Not.Ended.Objectification-332561.shtml.>

Lambert, Liz. "Maxcey Indicted in CU Grand Jury Probe." 6 Sept. 2004. <http://9news.com/cu/>.

Rudebeck, Megan. "'Hot' Recruiters Draw Prospects." The State Press. 18 Oct. 2002: 1–2. 3 Feb 2003 <http://www.asuwebdevil.com/main.cfm?include=detail&storyid= 300645>.

Watson, Joe. "Risky Behavior Not Policed in ASU Football Recruiting." The State Press. 9 Dec. 2002: 1–2. 3 Feb. 2003 <http://www.asuwebdevil.com/main.cfm?include=detail&storyid= 339775>.

QUESTIONS FOR WRITING AND DISCUSSION

Rhetorical Knowledge: The Writer's Situation and Rhetoric

1. **Audience:** What audience does DeRosa have in mind for this essay? How can you tell?

2. **Purpose:** What purpose(s) does DeRosa have for writing this essay? How well does he achieve his purpose(s)?

3. **Voice and tone:** How does DeRosa's voice and tone help to establish his ethos? Is his tone appropriate? Why or why not?

4. **Responsibility:** How effectively does DeRosa represent opposing views on the issue of using female students as recruiters? In what ways, if any, could he represent their views more fairly?

5. **Context and format:** DeRosa is writing as an ASU student but also as a husband and father. How does this context affect his use of language, appeals, and evidence?

Critical Thinking: Your Personal Response

1. What is your initial response to DeRosa's essay? What can you point to in the text that causes you to respond in this way?

2. To what extent does DeRosa's text appeal to your emotions? In what way(s)?

3. If your college or university has the type of recruiting program DeRosa describes, what is your opinion of it? Why?

4. Would you try to do anything about such a program? If so, what would you do?

Critical Thinking: The Writer's Ideas

1. What is DeRosa's main point, or claim? To what extent do you agree with it? Why?

2. If the ASU Sun Devil Recruiters included an equal number of male and female students, how do you think that would change DeRosa's views? Why?

3. DeRosa deplores the objectification of women in advertising and in media products. Are there ways in which men are objectified? How?

4. To what extent do you agree with DeRosa that the objectification of women is a fairly recent phenomenon (since the 1950s and 1960s)?

Composing Processes and Knowledge of Conventions: The Writer's Strategies

1. How convincing is the evidence DeRosa supplies? What other evidence might he have used?

2. What passages can you point to in the text that help demonstrate DeRosa's credibility on this issue? How does his use of his family's history as evidence affect his ethos?

3. How effectively does DeRosa use his family stories? What can you cite to show what you mean?

4. What in DeRosa's essay was most convincing to you? What was least convincing?

5. What organizational method does DeRosa use? How effective is it? What other method(s) might he have used?

Inquiry and Research: Ideas for Further Exploration

1. What questions do you have after reading DeRosa's text? In ten minutes, write down as many as you can think of.

2. Conduct a search (at your school library or on the Web), focusing on the events that DeRosa describes in his family history (paragraph 7). What similarities can you find to the family story that DeRosa relates in his text?

3. Interview several friends about the recruiting practice DeRosa writes about, and record their comments. Share them with several classmates. In no more than two pages, write about the similarities and differences in their views that you have discovered.

 # Self-Assessment: Reflecting on Your Learning Goals

Now that you have constructed a piece of writing designed to convince your readers, go back and consider your learning goals, which you and your classmates may have considered at the beginning of this chapter (pp. 318–19). Then, reflect on all the thinking and writing that you have done in constructing your persuasive paper. To help reflect on the learning goals that you have achieved, respond in writing to the following questions:

Rhetorical Knowledge

- *Audience:* What have you learned about addressing an audience in persuasive writing?

- *Purpose:* What have you learned about the purposes for constructing an effective persuasive text?

- *Rhetorical situation:* Consider some of the aspects that you have to think about, as a writer: How did the writing context affect your persuasive text? How did your choice of topic affect the research you conducted and how you presented your position to your readers?

- *Voice and tone:* How would you describe your voice in this essay? Your tone? How do they contribute to the effectiveness of your persuasive essay?

- *Context, medium, and genre:* How did your context determine the medium and genre you chose, and how did those decisions affect your writing?

Critical Thinking, Reading, and Writing

- *Learning/inquiry:* How did you decide what to focus on for your persuasive text? Describe the process you went through to focus on a main idea, or thesis. How did you judge what was most and least important in explaining your position to your readers?

- *Responsibility:* How did you fulfill your responsibilities to your readers?

- *Reading and research:* What did you learn about persuasive writing from the reading selections you read for this chapter? What research did you conduct? How sufficient was the research you did? Why? What additional research might you have done?

- As a result of writing this persuasive paper, how have you become a more critical thinker, reader, and writer? What critical thinking, reading, and writing skills do you hope to develop further in your next writing project? How will you work on them?

Composing Processes

- *Invention:* What invention strategies were most useful to you?

- *Organizing your ideas and details:* What organizational approach did you use? How successful was it?

- *Revising:* What one revision did you make that you are most satisfied with? What are the strongest and the weakest parts of the essay or other piece of writing you wrote for this chapter? Why? If you could go back and make an additional revision, what would it be?

- *Working with peers:* How did your instructor and peer readers help you by making comments and suggestions about your writing? List some examples of useful comments that you received. List some examples of how you revised your persuasive text based on those comments and suggestions. How could you have made better use of the comments and suggestions you received? How could your peer readers help you more on your next assignment? How might you help them more, in the future, with the comments and suggestions you make on their texts?

- Did you use photographs, charts, graphs, or other visuals to help you convince your readers? If so, what did you learn about incorporating these elements?

- What "writerly habits" have you developed, modified, or improved on as you constructed the writing assignment for this chapter? How will you change your future writing activities based on what you have learned about yourself?

Conventions

- *Editing:* What sentence problem did you find most frequently in your writing? How will you avoid that problem in future assignments?

- *Genre:* What conventions of the genre you were using, if any, gave you problems?
- *Documentation:* Did you use sources for your paper? If so, what documentation style did you use? What problems, if any, did you have with it?

If you are constructing a course portfolio, file your written reflections so that you can return to them when you next work on your portfolio.

Santi DeRosa Reflects on His Writing

Notice how this excerpt from Santi DeRosa's reflection addresses his knowledge and skills, as well as some connections between the academic and personal arenas of his life:

> I could be more passionate about this paper than the previous paper I wrote. Then, I wanted to kind of distance myself from the topics that were assigned to us, but this time, I was really involved. This topic made me upset (and my readers can probably tell!).
>
> When I started defining the issue, I was more involved in the topic. However, this paper was more difficult to organize than the first one. When I read the article about what happens during recruiting at ASU, I was surprised and angry. Having these emotions made it easier to write the paper—I guess that they'd add to what my teacher called an "emotional appeal." During my research, I found that there are many ways in which women are objectified, and there are many ways to define "objectification."
>
> I enjoyed writing this paper because it allowed me to explore my own feelings as well. Each time I revised the paper, I found that I had more to say. Because of peer review and input—as well as input from my wife (who is my best critic), I was able to organize the paper and develop the ideas more fully. I hope that it reads well.
>
> My skills are getting better, but I feel that I still have much to do. Writing this paper also allowed me to consider the women in my life and get a better understanding of what makes them the way they are.
>
> I also think that this persuasive essay might make a real difference to people, at colleges, if they read it and understand my point and then see if their school has a similar program. . . .

Rhetorical Knowledge

- *Audience:* When you are writing an evaluation, determine who will benefit from your evaluation. Who needs to make decisions about the subject of your evaluation? What do the audience members probably already know about your subject? What will you need to tell them? How can you best explain the criteria on which you will base your evaluation?

- *Purpose:* When you evaluate, you make a judgment based on specific criteria. Your purpose is not to say just "I think the Toyota truck is better than the Chevy," but to convince your reader to agree with your judgment.

- *Rhetorical situation:* Consider the many factors that affect where you stand in relation to your subject. If you have some personal interest in your evaluation (you love Ford automobiles, for example) you will have a different stance about evaluating the new Mustang than a more neutral party might.

- *Writer's voice and tone:* When you construct an evaluation, you are trying to explain your reasoned judgment. If you come across as a know-it-all, rather than as someone trying to explain how you came to your evaluative judgment, your readers may lose interest or suspect your judgment.

- *Context, medium, and genre:* You will need to decide on the best medium and genre to use to present your evaluation to the audience you want to reach. Often, you can use tables, charts, and graphs as well as words to help show how the subject you are evaluating compares to other similar items.

Critical Thinking, Reading, and Writing

- *Learning/inquiry:* By observing, listening to, and/or reading about the subject of your evaluation, and then by writing about it, you gain a deeper understanding of its qualities and the ability to make more informed judgments about it. This kind of thinking will help you make more informed decisions throughout your college and professional careers.

- *Responsibility:* Effective evaluative writing leads naturally to critical thinking. When you engage in evaluating something, you have consider all aspects of that item, not only to determine the criteria on which you will base your evaluation, but also to construct a reasoned argument for your evaluation.

- *Reading and research:* To evaluate a subject, you not only need to examine it in detail (which means you need to conduct research), but you also need to examine similar items (which means you need to research them, too).

 ## Writing Processes

- *Invention:* Various invention activities—brainstorming, listing, clustering—can help you consider all aspects of the subject you are evaluating.

- *Organizing your ideas and details:* The act of evaluating necessarily means that you think about the various aspects of your subject. That process can help you organize your thinking, and later your writing, into categories, based on your criteria.

- *Revising:* You will need to read your work with a critical eye, to make certain that it fulfills the assignment and displays the qualities of effective evaluative writing.

- *Working with peers:* Listen to your classmates to make sure that they understand your evaluation. What do they say about how well your details justify your conclusion?

 ## Conventions

- *Editing:* Effective evaluations usually require careful word choice. The round-robin activity on page 446 will help you improve your word choice.

- *Genres for analytical writing:* In many situations your evaluation will be a formal report or an academic paper. Evaluations written about movies, restaurants, or other products or services are not quite as formal as college assignments, however. Evaluations, especially of fellow employees, are also a common type of writing for employees in many businesses.

- *Documentation:* If you have relied on sources outside of your experience, you will need to cite them using the appropriate documentation style.

Chapter 9

Writing to Evaluate

In 1997, the American Film Institute (AFI) announced a list of 100 greatest American films. The list was chosen by a panel of "leaders from across the film community." In 2007, the AFI updated this list, which now includes one film released since 2000: *Lord of the Rings: The Fellowship of the Ring. Citizen Kane,* however, retained its spot at the top of list.

American Film Institute's Greatest Movies

1. *Citizen Kane* (1941)
2. *The Godfather* (1972)
3. *Casablanca* (1942)
4. *Raging Bull* (1980)
5. *Singin' in the Rain* (1952)
6. *Gone With the Wind* (1939)
7. *Lawrence of Arabia* (1962)
8. *Schindler's List* (1993)
9. *Vertigo* (1958)
10. *The Wizard of Oz* (1939)
11. *City Lights* (1931)
12. *The Searchers* (1956)
13. *Star Wars* (1977)
14. *Psycho* (1960)
15. *2001: A Space Odyssey* (1968)
16. *Sunset Boulevard* (1950)
17. *The Graduate* (1967)
18. *The General* (1927)
19. *On the Waterfront* (1954)
20. *It's a Wonderful Life* (1946)
21. *Chinatown* (1974)
22. *Some Like It Hot* (1959)
23. *The Grapes of Wrath* (1940)
24. *E.T. – The Extra-Terrestrial* (1982)
25. *To Kill a Mockingbird* (1962)
26. *Mr. Smith Goes to Washington* (1939)
27. *High Noon* (1952)
28. *All about Eve* (1950)
29. *Double Indemnity* (1944)
30. *Apocalypse Now* (1979)
31. *The Maltese Falcon* (1941)
32. *The Godfather, Part II* (1974)
33. *One Flew over the Cuckoo's Nest* (1975)
34. *Snow White and the Seven Dwarfs* (1937)

35. *Annie Hall* (1977)

36. *The Bridge on the River Kwai* (1957)

37. *The Best Years of Our Lives* (1946)

38. *The Treasure of the Sierra Madre* (1948)

39. *Dr. Strangelove* (1964)

40. *The Sound of Music* (1965)

41. *King Kong* (1933)

42. *Bonnie and Clyde* (1967)

43. *Midnight Cowboy* (1969)

44. *The Philadelphia Story* (1940)

45. *Shane* (1953)

46. *It Happened One Night* (1934)

47. *A Streetcar Named Desire* (1951)

48. *Rear Window* (1954)

49. *Intolerance* (1916)

50. *Lord of the Rings: The Fellowship of the Ring* (2001)

51. *West Side Story* (1961)

52. *Taxi Driver* (1976)

53. *The Deer Hunter* (1978)

54. *M*A*S*H* (1970)

55. *North by Northwest* (1959)

56. *Jaws* (1975)

57. *Rocky* (1976)

58. *The Gold Rush* (1925)

59. *Nashville* (1975)

60. *Duck Soup* (1933)

61. *Sullivan's Travels* (1941)

62. *American Graffiti* (1973)

63. *Cabaret* (1972)

64. *Network* (1976)

65. *The African Queen* (1951)

66. *Raiders of the Lost Ark* (1981)

67. *Who's Afraid of Virginia Woolf?* (1966)

68. *Unforgiven* (1992)

69. *Tootsie* (1982)

70. *A Clockwork Orange* (1971)

71. *Saving Private Ryan* (1998)

72. *The Shawshank Redemption* (1994)

73. *Butch Cassidy and the Sundance Kid* (1969)

74. *The Silence of the Lambs* (1991)

75. *In the Heat of the Night* (1967)

76. *Forrest Gump* (1994)

77. *All the President's Men* (1976)

78. *Modern Times* (1936)

79. *The Wild Bunch* (1969)

80. *The Apartment* (1960)

81. *Spartacus* (1960)

82. *Sunrise* (1927)

83. *Titanic* (1997)

84. *Easy Rider* (1969)

85. *A Night at the Opera* (1935)

86. *Platoon* (1986)

87. *12 Angry Men* (1957)

88. *Bringing up Baby* (1938)

89. *The Sixth Sense* (1999)

90. *Swing Time* (1936)

91. *Sophie's Choice* (1982)

92. *Goodfellas* (1990)

93. *The French Connection* (1971)

94. *Pulp Fiction* (1994)

95. *The Last Picture Show* (1971)

96. *Do the Right Thing* (1989)

97. *Blade Runner* (1982)

98. *Yankee Doodle Dandy* (1942)

99. *Toy Story* (1995)

100. *Ben-Hur* (1959)

Evaluations are part of everyday life. When you decide which classes to take, what to eat for breakfast, or which candidate to support, you decide which choice is best for you and act accordingly. As you think about all the choices you confront in your life, consider why you make the ones that you do. How do you decide which items to buy at the grocery store, what radio station to listen to, what song to download, or what book to read next?

You make such decisions by evaluating your available choices based on certain **criteria,** or standards. For example, if you are evaluating a product, you may consider factors such as price, brand name, location, and size. Usually, you will base your evaluation on a combination of criteria—and you will inevitably weight some criteria more heavily than others. The price of a new washing machine may matter more to one person while the brand may be more important to another.

Whether you realize it or not, you have years of practice in judging the trustworthiness of others' evaluations and the relevance of the criteria they use. When a newspaper endorses a political candidate, your familiarity with the newspaper and its editorial policy influences your view of that endorsement. When your friend recommends a coffee shop, you decide whether you want to go there based on what she says about it and your judgment of both her criteria and past recommendations. If you are a movie fan, you have probably already come to some conclusions about the American Film Institute's evaluation of the "Greatest Movies" (shown on the opening pages of this chapter) based on your agreement or disagreement with its list of films. Your experience with everyday evaluations will help you determine the criteria for the evaluations you write in the different situations you will encounter in your life?

Rhetorical Knowledge

When you write an evaluation, you need to consider the criteria on which you will base your evaluation as well as how you will come up with that criteria. How do you determine evaluative criteria? What aspects of the work, product, service, or idea should you examine for your evaluation? How can you best make an evaluative judgment about it? You will also need to decide what medium and genre will help you get your evaluation across to your audience most effectively?

Writing to Evaluate in Your College Classes

As a college student, you will be expected to read evaluations in most of your classes. While you may think most academic writing consists of logical arguments or the presentation of information or new theories or perspectives, you will also be asked to write evaluations in many of your college courses:

- Your psychology instructor may ask you to read brief summaries of experiments and evaluate how well the experiment's design served to answer the research question.
- Your political science instructor might ask you to rate the effectiveness of a political campaign.
- Your business and marketing instructor might ask you to evaluate several potential store locations.
- Your art instructor might ask you to evaluate several oil paintings.
- In a journalism course, you may be asked to evaluate coverage of a local news story.

In your college courses, you will also be asked at the end of the term to evaluate the course and the instructor, according to specific criteria. Finally, in much of your academic writing, you will have to evaluate the sources and evidence you select to support your thesis statements.

Writing to Evaluate for Life

In addition to the evaluations you will consider and write while in college, you no doubt make evaluations every day in the professional, civic, and personal areas of your life.

In your **professional life,** your writing may often have an evaluative purpose. For example, if you have employees reporting to you, you will probably be asked to evaluate their job performances. Constructing a performance review requires you to make evaluations that range from empirically verifiable judgments supported by quantitative evidence to highly controversial recommendations—that your company fire someone who once was a "star employee," for example. You may consider criteria that include both verifiable information (does your employee arrive at work on time?) and opinions (is he or she an effective leader?). You will need to provide facts to support your judgments while sufficiently explaining your opinions.

In your **civic life,** you will often evaluate people and proposals and then make decisions or recommendations. Suppose that a local power company is planning to expand a power generation plant in your neighborhood and, as a member of your homeowners' or tenants' association, you are a member of a committee that is evaluating the impact of the power plant expansion. Before drafting its report, the members of your committee will need to establish appropriate criteria for evaluating the plant, including the impact that the plant will have on property values and rents and the change it will cause in the local landscape, and then determine which criteria are most important. To provide a responsible, credible perspective, your committee will need to make your criteria explicit.

Without even realizing it, we often make evaluations when writing in our **personal life.** Even a piece of writing as simple as a grocery list includes judgments about brand names of food products. An e-mail to a relative may include comments about favorite restaurants, teachers, or newfound friends. On the one hand, we might feel more comfortable making evaluations for our friends and family. On the other, we may feel especially obligated to provide a useful evaluation because we care about the relationship. You can see these considerations at work in the following e-mail to a friend suggesting a contractor:

> You mentioned that you and Jim might be replacing your carpeting with floor tile. Last year when we had ceramic tile installed in our entry area, the CK Company was terrific. Cal, the owner, gave us a discount on the tile. The crew was good and did an outstanding job. Their workmanship was great (every tile lines up) and they always cleaned up after themselves. They did all the tile sawing outside, so we didn't get a lot of dust in the house. I think they'd do a good job for you, too. Want their phone number?

This short e-mail contains a number of evaluative statements. The first is the recommendation itself, which the writer then supports with evidence based on several criteria: price, quality of the workmanship, and cleanliness of the work site during the project.

WRITER'S WORKSHOP

Applying Learning Goals to Evaluative Writing

As we have seen, constructing an evaluative text involves, not only determining your criteria, but also explaining how you used that criteria to make your evaluative judgment.

As a group, think of a writing situation in which you need to evaluate a particular subject—a work of art, a product, a service, a performance, or an idea—and persuade an audience to agree with your evaluation. Perhaps the situation is a college assignment, a piece of workplace writing, a piece of writing for a civic group or organization, or a personal circumstance. With several of your classmates, discuss your writing situation in terms of the learning goals listed on pages 388–89. How would you address these goals? In what ways does it matter who your reader might be?

 ## Scenarios for Writing: Assignment Options

Your instructor may ask you to complete one or more of the following writing assignments that call for evaluation. Each of these assignments is in the form of a scenario, which gives you a sense of who your audience is and what you need to accomplish with your evaluative writing. The list of rhetorical considerations on page 400 encourages you to think about your audience; purpose; voice, tone, and point of view; and context, medium, and genre for the scenario you have chosen.

As in the other chapters in this text, we have provided two scenarios focused on academic writing and three scenarios that you might encounter outside of college. Starting on page 425, you will find guidelines for completing whatever assignment option you decide—or are asked to—complete.

Writing for College

SCENARIO 1   What Are the Rules? An Academic Evaluation

You may currently live (or may previously have lived) in a communal setting such as a dormitory, a military barracks, a summer camp, or a house or apartment with roommates. In that setting you are probably aware of rules and regulations (if you were in the military, you were definitely aware of them), yet you may not have thought about whether they are fair or not, or even if there are punishments for not obeying the rules. Or you may be living with one or both of your parents, who probably insist on certain rules (for example, rules about guests, cleanliness, a curfew, music level, what you can hang on the walls). Your audience will be your instructor and your classmates.

Consider questions such as these:

- Who controls what happens in the living quarters?
- What are the rules for living in the particular setting (communal or parental)? Are they fair and reasonable?
- Who is paying for the living quarters? Do they (should they) have total control of what happens in them? What, if any, restrictions are there?
- Should parents be allowed to place restrictions on college-age students who live at home? What rules would be reasonable? How would the parents or student decide?
- If an organization such as a college or the government controls the living quarters, can they monitor e-mail? Internet access? Are there restrictions as to what residents can view on the Internet in their rooms? Should there be?

Writing Assignment: Write an evaluation of the rules of the communal setting in which you currently live or once lived (for example, a dorm room such as that shown in Figure 9.1 or an apartment with others), or of your parent's or parents' rules. You will need to do some research on what the rules are and consider what you might use as criteria for evaluating them.

**FIGURE 9.1
A College
Dormitory Room**

SCENARIO 2   An Evaluation of a Subject You Are Curious About

For this scenario, select a work of art, a film, a television program, a product, a service, an event, or a place to evaluate—something you are interested in and would like to know more about. Your audience will be your instructor and your fellow classmates.

Writing Assignment: Choose a subject whose value you would like to consider. You may value it highly and want others to know about it, or you may think that it is highly overrated and want others to see why. Construct an evaluation in which you make your judgment known. Be sure to explain clearly the criteria on which you will make your evaluation, and then show how your subject meets—or does not meet—those criteria.

Writing for Life

SCENARIO 3   Professional Writing: A Formal Report
Evaluating Advertisements

Almost every enterprise advertises in one form or another: in newspapers, in the Yellow Pages, online, on radio, on television, in movie theaters, in magazines—the list is large and growing. Even the U.S. Post Office advertises; the U.S. military advertises; and many nonprofit organizations such as hospitals advertise. For this assignment, assume that you work for the type of company or organization you hope one day actually to work for. (If you already are employed, you can write this assignment as an employee of your current employer or another organization.) One of your duties is to evaluate possible advertisements that are appropriate for this organization.

FIGURE 9.2 How might you evaluate this outdoor sign for a sandwich shop?

Writing Assignment: For this assignment, locate several newspapers, magazines, or online publications in which your organization might actually advertise. Find at least two examples of advertisements—one that you consider effective and another that seems much less effective. You will need to come up with criteria to evaluate these advertisements. What makes an advertisement effective in presenting the benefits of the type of product or service your organization offers?

SCENARIO 4 Civic Writing: An Opinion Column in Your Local Newspaper

Recently in your political science class, your professor focused on the notion of bias and made the following provocative statement: "Even many news organizations are biased in some manner, just like everyone and everything else." After the discussion that followed, during which some students objected that publications such as the *New York Times,* the *Wall Street Journal,* or *Time* magazine, while they have editorials like other newspapers and magazines, present the news as the news, your professor suggested that the class should investigate the issue of media bias more closely. You are intrigued by the discussion and decide to look at your local newspaper on your own to determine if it is in fact biased. Are newspapers supposed to print just the news? Are editorial statements always clearly presented as editorials and not as the news? How can you tell?

Writing Assignment: Choose one of your local newspapers, evaluate it for bias, and prepare an essay for your local newspaper's "Opinions" page. For this assignment assume your local paper prints not only letters to the editor, but also asks for longer essays for a "Your Opinion, Please" section. You will

FIGURE 9.3 How might you evaluate New York's Guggenheim Museum?

need to determine the criteria you will focus on, such as the newspaper's treatment of issues related to gender, race, and age; the language used to give a particular impression of a story or public figure; or the variety of views presented in the editorial page. How can you determine bias? Can you spot any possible source of bias in the advertising the newspaper carries? That is, do you see a large amount of advertising for a product or service and at the same time find nothing critical about that item in the paper?

You will need to examine at least six issues of the paper to see how its articles, photographs, and advertisements match up to the criteria you select. The essay that you write will outline the problem of determining media bias, explain the criteria you are using, and judge whether (and, if so, in what ways) the local paper is biased.

SCENARIO 5   Personal Writing: An Opinion Essay
Evaluating a Cultural Subject

Is there a cultural event taking place on your campus or in your community that you have a personal connection to and would like to evaluate? Or is there a place, such as a museum (Figure 9.3) or theater, where you would like to spend some time in a cultural pursuit: listening to music, watching a film, examining works of art? This assignment gives you an opportunity to evaluate a subject that matters to you personally.

Writing Assignment: Construct an evaluation of a cultural artifact, event, or place, explaining in detail the criteria on which you base your evaluation as well as how the cultural event or place fits your criteria. For this assignment—which asks for a personal evaluation—focus on a subject that matters to you, and then develop criteria based on your personal ideas. That is, decide how your subject—the book, play, building, work of art, or other cultural artifact, event, or place—makes you feel, what it brings to your mind, how it inspires a reaction within you.

This kind of personal evaluation is different from the evaluations that you are probably accustomed to making because they often focus on public issues or situations, and you must establish criteria that most members of your audience will agree with. For this more personal evaluation, we suggest that you look inward for your own ideas and criteria; it is a useful exercise, not only to explain such criteria to others, but also to then outline how your subject matches it.

Rhetorical Considerations in Evaluative Writing

Audience: While your instructor and classmates are your initial audience for this assignment, you should also consider other audiences for your evaluative writing, depending on the scenario you have chosen. You need to consider whether the members of your audience will agree with you about the criteria for evaluating your subject, or whether you will need to convince them to accept your criteria.

Purpose: Your purpose is to evaluate your subject in terms of the criteria you decide on and persuade your audience to accept your judgment of it.

Voice, Tone, and Point of View: You have probably chosen your subject because you have a personal interest in it. What preconceptions about it do you have? How can you avoid letting them color your evaluation, perhaps leading you to a simplistic judgment? How can you use voice and tone to establish credibility, so your readers believe your evaluation and judgment? Put another way, how will your evaluation be most effective: if you write in a shrill or sarcastic tone, or a more professional, even-tempered tone?

Context, Medium, and Genre: Keeping the context of the assignment in mind, decide on a medium and genre for your evaluation. How will your evaluation be used? Obviously, your instructor will use your writing to help determine your grade for the course, so follow his or her instructions carefully. If you are writing for an audience beyond the classroom, consider what will be the most effective way to present your evaluation to this audience. You might write an e-mail message to a friend, prepare a report for colleagues at work, or construct a Web site for members of your community.

For more on choosing a medium and genre, see Chapter 15 and Appendix C.

Critical Thinking, Reading, and Writing

Before you begin to write your own evaluation, you need to consider the qualities of a successful evaluation. It also helps to read one or more evaluations to get a feel for this kind of writing. Finally, you might consider how visuals could enhance your evaluative writing, as well as the kinds of sources you may need to consult.

To write an effective, responsible evaluation, you need to understand your subject and the reasons for your evaluation of it, and then use your understanding responsibly and accurately in your writing. You will need to choose valid criteria, organize your writing logically, and present your evaluation in a way that fulfills your responsibility to your readers. To do this, you need to think critically about your own views as well as those of any outside sources. Thinking critically does not necessarily mean that you will criticize, but rather that you will carefully consider which criteria are most and least important and how different aspects of your subject relate to each other. This critical evaluation will help you determine the strongest evidence for your judgment.

Learning the Qualities of Effective Evaluative Writing

As we have seen, most writing is purposeful—you want to accomplish something. Focusing on the outcome should be the starting point for everything you write, and for an evaluation you want to make a reasoned, thoughtful, and justifiable judgment. You need to outline the criteria on which you will base your evaluation and then explain, in terms your readers can understand, how the subject of your evaluation fits the criteria.

Evaluative writing that achieves its goal has the following qualities:

- **Clearly defined and explained criteria.** Readers expect an evaluation to be based on specific criteria that are germane to the item being evaluated. You would evaluate an array of backpacks in a sporting-goods store using different criteria from what you would use to evaluate, say, a television news program. Readers deserve to have the criteria on which you are basing your evaluation spelled out and defined, in detail, so they can understand your reasoning. Any terms you use in explaining your criteria that your reader may not understand should be defined. Even familiar terms may need to be defined if readers need to understand how you are using them in your evaluation. If you are comparing new cars, for example, you can assume that most readers will understand "gas mileage," but how you are defining "quality" might be more nebulous and, if so, should be explained.

    If you are evaluating a work of art, you would use—and explain—criteria appropriate for evaluating art: for example, aesthetic appeal, the impact the work has on the viewer, and how well it represents a specific genre. If you are evaluating a current television program, you probably do not need to explain the criterion "entertaining the audience," as this is usually the function of a TV show, unless it is a news show, although news shows can also be entertaining at times.

Here is how *Consumer Reports* magazine explains its criteria for judging hand mixers. Note that the magazine focuses on size, wattage, mixing speed, weight, and beater style and motion.

HOW TO CHOOSE: STAND & HAND MIXERS

Decide how much mixer you need. Just about any stand or hand mixer will do for simple mixing and whipping. But if you're a dedicated baker, you'll probably want to invest in a heavy, powerful stand mixer. They can knead even two loaves' worth of bread dough with ease.

Downplay wattage. Manufacturers stress wattage, but it doesn't always translate into better performance.

Be savvy about speeds. Some stand mixers have as many as 16 speeds; some hand mixers have 9. We think three well-differentiated speeds are sufficient. The slower the lowest speed, the better; slow speeds prevent spattering.

Speeds should be clearly indicated. With some of the inexpensive hand mixers we tested (from GE, Hamilton Beach, and Proctor-Silex), the switch you use to select speeds didn't line up well with the speed markings.

Consider size and weight. Hand mixers should feel well balanced and comfortable to hold; most that we tested did. Size and weight can be a concern with stand mixers–some weigh more than 20 pounds–but their heft gives them the stability to handle tough jobs.

All the stand mixers that we tested have heads that tilt up. Make sure that you will have enough clearance if you plan to keep the mixer on a counter below a cupboard.

Consider beater style and motion. Most of the top-performing hand mixers have wire beaters without the thick center post found on traditional-style beaters. The wire beaters performed well and were easier to clean.

Light-duty stand mixers typically have stationary beaters and a bowl that sits on a revolving turntable. The bowl sometimes needs a push to keep spinning. There's no such problem with the heavy-duty KitchenAid or DeLonghi stand mixers, which have a single flat beater that moves around inside the stationary bowl.

- **Comparisons based on the criteria.** Especially when you are evaluating products or services, you will need to show how your subject can be measured against other, similar, subjects and then explain this basis of comparison. You will compare like with like, showing how each aspect of the item you are evaluating rates in comparison with the same (or a similar) aspect of a similar item. Readers also need to see how you use the criteria to determine your evaluation.

You can make comparisons based on numerical information ("Tire brand C has a 50 percent longer tread life rating than Brand B, and twice as long as Brand A"). A table can help your readers see the basis of your claim.

Tire Brand	Tread Life Rating
Brand A	30,000 miles
Brand B	40,000 miles
Brand C	60,000 miles

Because this numerical information is verifiable and is not a matter of opinion, it can be persuasive evidence for your overall evaluation.

You can also make comparisons based on other verifiable criteria, such as facts about the subject's longevity: a business that stays in business for a long time is generally successful ("Company X has been in business for 50 years, whereas Company Y has been in business for only 10 years"). Or you can compare guarantees ("This refrigerator has a five-year warranty, whereas the other warranty is only for two years").

Finally, you can make comparisons based on more subjective criteria, such as your definition of "quality": you might note that a backpack "should have this kind of fabric, this type of zipper, a lifetime warranty, and straps made out of this material." Then you would go on to outline how each backpack matches (or perhaps doesn't match) each of your criteria.

When you compare, it is important not to slant your evaluation by leaving out negative information or highlighting only those details that make the product, service, or work you favor seem to be the best. Instead, explain and compare honestly so your readers can reach their own conclusions about the effectiveness of your evaluation. You may find that the item you judge to be best is weak when measured on the basis of one or more of your criteria. It is vital to your overall credibility to account for such shortcomings. Just because something is comparatively weak in one or more areas does not mean that it can't still come out on top in your evaluation.

Consider Matthew Power's essay "Immersion Journalism" (p. 414) in which he compares the national broadcast media's and a local paper's coverage of Hurricane Katrina, adding an emotional appeal as part of his criteria.

- **Evidence that supports your claims.** To accept your evaluation, your reader needs to understand that you are not just making assertions about your subject, but that you actually have evidence to support your claims. Evidence can include the following:

FIGURE 9.4 How safe are worn tires?

- Testimony: "I've owned Ford automobiles for twenty years, and they've never let me down."

- Statistical information: "A recent study by the National Highway Traffic Safety Administration found that nearly 50 percent of the 11,500 cars, pickup trucks, vans, and sport-utility vehicles the agency checked had at least one tire with half-worn tread. Another 10 percent had at least one bald tire." (*Consumer Reports*)

- Detailed description: the more details you can provide, the easier it will be for a reader to understand what you mean. Consider the excerpt shown in Figure 9.4 from an article in *Consumer Reports* magazine describing tire wear—note how thorough this description is, and how the illustration and caption help show what the article is about.

- **An analysis and explanation of how any visual elements affect your evaluation.** When they evaluate textbooks, teachers often consider how the visual elements in the books might help students learn more effectively. If you were a science teacher, for example, and you were part of a team working to determine which textbook(s) to use for a specific course, you might focus on the photographs or drawings in the various books under consideration and cite examples from the texts in your evaluative comments.

- **A clearly-stated judgment.** Readers can either agree or disagree with your conclusions, but if you have written a successful evaluation, at least they will understand how you arrived at your judgment and respect you for the care and thoughtfulness you have demonstrated.

In a computer document, put the above qualities of effective writing into your own words, and then refer to those notes as you conduct research and write your paper.

A WRITER'S RESPONSIBILITY

Constructing Ethical Evaluations

As humans, we all make judgments, yet we rarely analyze the process that we use to make those judgments. When we take time to think about our snap decisions, we can see that even those judgments are based on some kind of criteria or standards. In some instances we use valid, useful criteria while in other cases our criteria are neither appropriate nor helpful. And sometimes there may be an overriding issue that supersedes all of our carefully chosen criteria.

Whenever you make an evaluation, your judgments will have an impact, and because of that impact, you have certain responsibilities. When you make an evaluation in a civic writing situation, such as a report on whether a local power plant should be expanded, you have a responsibility to all who will be affected by the decision that will eventually be made. Remember, too, that the audience for a civic evaluation will include some who will disagree, and that potential for disagreement makes your honesty and sense of responsibility even more important. If you misrepresent some aspect of your evaluation, someone can use that distortion to discredit your entire evaluation. Writing an ethical evaluation means you must present statistics and other data accurately, without skewing them in your favor. If you have asked only a few of your classmates about the effectiveness of your campus recycling program, for example, you cannot say, "The majority of students who attend my college think that campus recycling is effective."

Another common task in professional writing is to prepare evaluations of people you supervise. In these situations, writers need to balance many ethical responsibilities. First, they need to consider that an evaluation can have important consequences for an employee's career. A negative evaluation can dash an employee's hopes for a salary increase and lead to probation or even termination. Second, supervisors need to be fair to everyone they are evaluating, applying identical or comparable criteria to each employee's evaluation. When employees feel they are being evaluated unfairly, their morale can plummet, which can lead to low morale and lower productivity. Of course, lower productivity can harm the organization and the people who depend on it, including customers and shareholders. Third, writers of professional evaluations need to be responsible to those affected by each employee's performance. For example, if an employee sometimes fails to follow safety procedures and his or her supervisor does not bring that problem to the employee's attention in an evaluation, co-workers or customers could be injured.

Reading, Inquiry, and Research: Learning from Texts That Evaluate

The reading selections that follow are examples of evaluative writing. As you read through the selections that your instructor assigns, consider the following questions:

- How clearly are the evaluative criteria explained?
- To what extent do I agree with the evaluation? Why?
- How well do I understand why the writer evaluated this subject as he did? That is, how clearly has the writer explained his judgment?
- How familiar am I with the subject that is being evaluated? What does my knowledge add to my reading of this text?
- What else would I like to know about the subject being evaluated? How can I learn more about it?
- How can I use the techniques of evaluative writing, as demonstrated here, in my own writing?

As you read an essay, take notes, jot down questions, and make observations about the essay, preferably in a computer file. If you want to use the information in your own writing, you will already have the main points in a digital format.

ROGER EBERT

Harry Potter and the Sorcerer's Stone

Roger Ebert has been the film critic for the *Chicago Sun-Times* since 1967. He is probably best known for his partnership with the late Gene Siskel in the television show "Siskel and Ebert at the Movies," which popularized the simple thumbs-up, thumbs-down critique of films. Today, Ebert's show with co-host Richard Roeper is seen in over 200 television markets across the country. Ebert was born in Urbana, Illinois, in 1942, and every year the city hosts the Roger Ebert Overlooked Film Festival, which Ebert founded in 1999. He is also the author of fifteen books including *The Great Movies; I Hated, Hated, HATED This Movie*; and *Roger Ebert's Book of Film*. You can read Ebert's weekly film reviews at rogerebert.suntimes.com. Ebert's review of *Harry Potter and the Sorcerer's Stone* originally appeared in the *Chicago Sun-Times* on November 16, 2001.

Ebert likes *Harry Potter and the Sorcerer's Stone* much more than does fellow reviewer Elvis Mitchell, whose review appears on pages 409–12. If you have seen this film, whom do you agree with?

Harry Potter and the Sorcerer's Stone is a red-blooded adventure movie, dripping with atmosphere, filled with the gruesome and the sublime,   1 and surprisingly faithful to the novel. A lot of things could have gone wrong, and none of them have: Chris Columbus' movie is an enchanting classic that does full justice to a story that was a daunting challenge. The novel by J. K. Rowling was muscular and vivid, and the danger was that the movie would make things too cute and cuddly. It doesn't. Like an Indiana Jones for younger viewers, it tells a rip-roaring tale of supernatural adventure, where colorful and eccentric characters alternate with scary stuff like a three-headed dog, a pit of tendrils known as the Devil's Snare and a two-faced immortal who drinks unicorn blood. Scary, yes, but not too scary—just scary enough.

Three high-spirited, clear-eyed kids populate the center of the movie. Daniel Radcliffe plays Harry Potter, he with the round glasses, and like all of the young characters he looks much as I imagined him, but a little older. He once played David Copperfield on the BBC, and whether Harry will be the hero of his own life in this story is much in doubt at the beginning. 2

Deposited as a foundling on a suburban doorstep, Harry is raised by his aunt and uncle as a poor relation, then summoned by a blizzard of letters to become a student at Hogwarts School, an Oxbridge[1] for magicians. Our first glimpse of Hogwarts sets the tone for the movie's special effects. Although computers can make anything look realistic, too much realism would be the wrong choice for Harry Potter, which is a story in which everything, including the sets and locations, should look a little made up. The school, rising on ominous Gothic battlements from a moonlit lake, looks about as real as Xanadu[2] in *Citizen Kane,* and its corridors, cellars and great hall, although in some cases making use of real buildings, continue the feeling of an atmospheric book illustration. 3

At Hogwarts, Harry makes two friends and an enemy. The friends are Hermione Granger (Emma Watson), whose merry face and tangled curls give Harry nudges in the direction of lightening up a little, and Ron Weasley (Rupert Grint), all pluck, luck and untamed talents. The enemy is Draco Malfoy (Tom Felton), who will do anything, and plenty besides, to be sure his house places first at the end of the year. 4

The story you either already know, or do not want to know. What is good to know is that the adult cast, a who's who of British actors, play their roles more or less as if they believed them. There is a broad style of British acting, developed in Christmas pantomimes, which would have been fatal to this material; these actors know that, and dial down 5

---

[1] an academic program run jointly by Oxford and Cambridge universities
[2] newspaper magnate Charles Foster Kane's "castle" in the film *Citizen Kane*

to just this side of too much. Watch Alan Rickman drawing out his words until they seem ready to snap, yet somehow staying in character. Maggie Smith, still in the prime of Miss Jean Brodie[3] is Prof. Minerva McGonagall, who assigns newcomers like Harry to one of the school's four houses. Richard Harris is headmaster Dumbledore, his beard so long that in an Edward Lear[4] poem, birds would nest in it. Robbie Coltrane is the gamekeeper, Hagrid, who has a record of misbehavior and a way of saying very important things and then not believing that he said them.

Computers are used, exuberantly, to create a plausible look in the gravity-defying action scenes. Readers of the book will wonder how the movie visualizes the crucial game of Quidditch. The game, like so much else in the movie, is more or less as I visualized it, and I was reminded of Stephen King's theory that writers practice a form of telepathy, placing ideas and images in the heads of their readers. (The reason some movies don't look like their books may be that some producers don't read them.)   6

If Quidditch is a virtuoso sequence, there are other set pieces of almost equal wizardry. A chess game with life-size, deadly pieces. A room filled with flying keys. The pit of tendrils, already mentioned, and a dark forest where a loathsome creature threatens Harry but is scared away by a centaur. And the dark shadows of Hogwarts library, cellars, hidden passages and dungeons, where an invisibility cloak can keep you out of sight but not out of trouble.   7

During *Harry Potter and the Sorcerer's Stone*, I was pretty sure I was watching a classic, one that will be around for a long time, and make many generations of fans. It takes the time to be good. It doesn't hammer the audience with easy thrills, but cares to tell a story, and to create its characters carefully. Like *The Wizard of Oz, Willy Wonka and the Chocolate Factory, Star Wars* and *E.T.*, it isn't just a movie but a world with its own magical rules. And some excellent Quidditch players.   8

---

[3] an unorthodox teacher, played by Maggie Smith, who had an unusual—and risky—relationship with some of her students
[4] writer of "nonsense" poetry

ELVIS MITCHELL

The Sorcerer's Apprentice

Elvis Mitchell began doing film reviews on public radio as an undergraduate at Wayne State University in Detroit. He has worked as a film critic for National Public Radio "Weekend Edition," the *Detroit Free Press*, the *Village Voice*, the *Fort Worth Star-Telegram*, *Spin* magazine, and the Independent Film Channel. From 1999 until 2004 Mitchell was a film critic for the *New York Times*. More recently he has been a visiting professor at Harvard, teaching film criticism and African-American film, and became a production consultant for Columbia Pictures. His review originally appeared in the *New York Times* on November 16, 2001.

Mitchell does not seem to like *Harry Potter and the Sorcerer's Stone*. If you have seen the film, do you agree with his comments?

The world may not be ready yet for the film equivalent of books on tape, but this peculiar phenomenon has arrived in the form of the film adaptation of J. K. Rowling's *Harry Potter and the Sorcerer's Stone*. The most highly awaited movie of the year has a dreary, literal-minded competence, following the letter of the law as laid down by the author. But it's all muted flourish, with momentary pleasures, like Gringott's, the bank staffed by trolls that looks like a Gaudí[1] throwaway. The picture is so careful that even the tape wrapped around the bridge of Harry's glasses seems to have come out of the set design. (It never occurred to anyone to show him taping the frame together.)

The movie comes across as a covers act by an extremely competent tribute band—not the real thing but an incredible simulation—and there's an audience for this sort of thing. But watching *Harry Potter* is like seeing *Beatlemania* staged in the Hollywood Bowl, where the cheers and screams will drown out whatever's unfolding onstage.

To call this movie shameless is beside the point. It would probably be just as misguided to complain about the film's unoriginality because (a) it has assumed that the target audience doesn't want anything new and (b) Ms. Rowling's books cannibalize and synthesize pop culture mythology, proof of the nothing-will-ever-go-away ethic. She has come up with something like *Star Wars* for a generation that never had a chance to thrill to its grandeur, but this is *Young Sherlock Holmes* as written by C. S. Lewis from a story by Roald Dahl.

---

[1] Antoni Gaudí is a Spanish architect, famous for his unusual designs.

The director, Chris Columbus, is as adept as Ms. Rowling at cobbling free-floating cultural myths into a wobbly whole. The first film from a Columbus script, *Gremlins*, had the cheeky cheesiness of an urban legend written for Marvel Comics. Mr. Columbus probably felt like the right choice for *Harry Potter* because he has often used the same circuit boards as Ms. Rowling to design his fables. His *Home Alone* movies, *Mrs. Doubtfire* and *Stepmom* employ the theme of abandonment by parents as if it were a brand name. And like Mr. Columbus's films, Ms. Rowling's novels pull together archetypes that others have long exploited. This movie begins with a shot of a street sign that will cause happy young audiences to erupt in recognition, as the dry-witted giant Hagrid (Robbie Coltrane) and Professor McGonagall (Maggie Smith) drop a baby at the Doorstep of Destiny.   4

Years later Harry (Daniel Radcliffe), sporting the jagged thunderbolt scar across his forehead, is living there with his terrors of an aunt (Fiona Shaw) and uncle (Richard Griffiths).   5

Harry is the kid all kids dream they are. His special abilities are recognized by people other than the ones who have raised him. Hagrid returns to rescue him from his tiny room under the stairs and clues Harry in about the boy's inner force, which is why he doesn't fit into the world of Muggles, the nonmagical and nonbelievers.   6

Harry is shown the way to Hogwarts, an English boarding school for wizards run by Professor Dumbledore (Richard Harris), where Harry pals up with the gawky but decent Ron (Rupert Grint) and the bossy, precocious Hermione (Emma Watson). The instructors, who rule the classrooms with varying degrees of imperiousness, include the acid Snape (Alan Rickman) and the mousy stutterer Quirrell (Ian Hart).   7

The casting is the standout, from the smaller roles up; it seems that every working British actor of the last 20 years makes an appearance. John Hurt blows through as an overly intense dealer in magic equipment, schooling Harry on selecting his tools. While shopping for his magic equipment, Harry comes across the Sorcerer's Stone, a bedeviled jewel whose power affects his first year at the enchanted school.   8

Mr. Radcliffe has an unthinkably difficult role for a child actor; all he gets to do is look sheepish when everyone turns to him and intones that he may be the greatest wizard ever. He could have been hobbled by being cast because he resembles the Harry of the book cover illustrations. It's a horrible burden to place on a kid, but it helps that Mr. Radcliffe does have the long-faced mournfulness of a 60's pop star. He also possesses a watchful gravity and, shockingly, the large, authoritative hands of a real wizard.   9

The other child actors shine, too. Ms. Watson has the sass and smarts to suggest she might cast a spell of her own on Harry in the coming years   10 and, one supposes, sequels. Mr. Grint has a surprising everyman quality, but the showstopper is Tom Felton as Draco Malfoy. This drolly menacing blond with a widow's peak is Harry's plotting foe, and he has the rotted self-confidence of one of the upperclassmen from Lindsay Anderson's "If." There has never been a kid who got so much joy from speaking his oddball name.

Ms. Shaw and Mr. Griffiths are enjoyably swinish, the most resolute of Muggles. Mr. Rickman, whose licorice-black pageboy has the bounce of a coiffure from a hair products ad, is a threatening schoolroom don who delivers his monologues with a hint of mint; his nostrils flare so athletically that he seems to be doing tantric yoga with his sinuses. The mountainously lovable Mr. Coltrane really is a fairy-tale figure that kids dream about. 11

The movie's most consistently entertaining scene features a talking hat, and that's not meant as an insult. The Sorting Hat, which has more personality than anything else in the movie, assigns the students to the various dormitories; it puts Harry, Ron and Hermione together. 12

But the other big set pieces are a letdown. The Quidditch match—the school sport that's part polo, part cricket and part Rollerball, played on flying brooms—has all the second-rate sloppiness of the race in *Stars Wars—Episode 1: The Phantom Menace*. It's a blur of mortifyingly ordinary computer-generated effects. 13

Given that movies can now show us everything, the manifestations that Ms. Rowling described could be less magical only if they were delivered at a news conference. And the entrance that may be as eagerly awaited as Harry's appearance—the arrival of Voldemort (Richard Bremmer), the archvillain—is a disappointment, a special effect that serves as a reminder of how much he stands in Darth Vader's shadow. 14

This overly familiar movie is like a theme park that's a few years past its prime; the rides clatter and groan with metal fatigue every time they take a curve. The picture's very raggedness makes it spooky, which is not the same thing as saying the movie is intentionally unsettling. 15

No one has given Harry a pair of Hogwarts-edition Nikes, nor do he, Hermione and Ron stop off to super-size it at the campus McDonald's: exclusions that seem like integrity these days. (There's no need for product placement. The Internet is likely to have a systems crash from all the kids going online to order maroon-and-gold scarves, which Harry and his dorm mates wear.) 16

Another kind of exclusion seems bothersome, though. At a time when London is filled with faces of color, the fleeting appearances by minority kids is scarier than Voldemort. (Harry's gorgeous owl, snow white with sunken dark eyes and feather tails dappled with black, gets more screen time than they do.) 17

Mr. Columbus does go out of his way to give a couple of lines to a little boy with a well-groomed head of dreadlocks. This movie may not be whiter than most, but the peering-from-the-sidelines status accorded to minorities seems particularly offensive in a picture aimed at kids. It's no different in the books, really, but young imaginations automatically correct for this paucity. 18

A lack of imagination pervades the movie because it so slavishly follows the book. The filmmakers, the producers and the studio seem panicked by anything that might feel like a departure from the book—which already feels film-ready—so *Harry Potter and the Sorcerer's Stone* never takes on a life of its own. 19

Someone has cast a sleepwalker's spell over the proceedings, and at nearly two and a half hours you may go under, too. Its literal-mindedness makes the film seem cowed by the chilling omnipresence of its own Voldemort, Ms. Rowling, who hovered around the production. 20

The movie is so timid it's like someone who flinches when you extend a hand to shake. This film is capable of a certain brand of magic: it may turn the faithful into Muggles. 21

Harry Potter and the Sorcerer's Stone is rated PG (Parental Guidance suggested), probably so that kids older than 12 won't think it's baby stuff. It includes scenes of magic someone must have found intense and threatening and a soupçon of strong language. 22

QUESTIONS FOR WRITING AND DISCUSSION

Rhetorical Knowledge: The Writer's Situation and Rhetoric

1. **Audience:** Before the film was released, many people had read *Harry Potter and the Sorcerer's Stone*. As a result, critics Mitchell and Ebert are aware that many readers will know what will happen in the movie while others will not want to have the plot spoiled for them. How adequately do these reviewers present information for both audiences?

2. **Purpose:** Film reviewers have one main task: to explain what they see as the strengths and weaknesses of the film being reviewed. How well do these two reviewers fulfill that task here? What can you point to in their reviews to illustrate your comments?

3. **Voice and tone:** Ebert seems to take a kinder, gentler stance toward the film than does Mitchell. What can you quote from the text to show this contrast?

4. **Responsibility:** As critics for major American newspapers—the *Chicago Sun-Times* (Ebert) and the *New York Times* (Mitchell)—both reviewers

have responsibilities to their readers. If you were such a critic, what might you see as your responsibilities to your readers?

5. **Context and format:** Consider the way this film had been highly anticipated by a huge audience. How does that anticipation seem to affect both reviews?

Critical Thinking: Your Personal Response

1. What is your initial reaction to Ebert's review? To Mitchell's review?

2. If you have seen this film and subsequent Harry Potter films, how do the films compare?

3. Mitchell says the film is filled with "dreary, literal-minded competence" (paragraph 1). How much do you agree? Why?

4. What did you learn from Ebert's review? What was surprising to you? Why? What was the most interesting comment in his review? Why?

5. Ebert writes that "Chris Columbus' movie is an enchanting classic that does full justice to a story that was a daunting challenge" (paragraph 1). Mitchell argues, though, that "Someone has cast a sleepwalker's spell over the proceedings, and at nearly two and a half hours you may go under, too" (paragraph 20). Whom you agree with more? Why?

Critical Thinking: The Writer's Ideas

1. Make a list of the evaluative criteria that Ebert uses to judge this film. How fair is the evaluation that he makes? Why?

2. Do the same with Mitchell's review: list his evaluative criteria. How fair is Mitchell's evaluation? Why?

3. Of the two reviewers, which one do you see as being fairer in his review? Why?

Composing Processes and Knowledge of Conventions: The Writer's Strategies

1. What is the strongest part of Ebert's review? Why? Of Mitchell's review? Why? What do you consider to be the least effective part of each review? Why?

2. One criterion for an effective evaluation is that the writer explains the criteria on which he or she bases the evaluation. In what ways does Ebert do this? In what ways does Mitchell?

3. In addition to its evaluative features, in what way(s) are Ebert's and Mitchell's essays also persuasive?

4. Which reviewer do you find more convincing? Why?

5. Ebert uses many examples from Rowling's novel in his own text. How helpful are they for purposes of constructing a film review? Why?

Inquiry and Research: Ideas for Further Exploration

1. Mitchell writes that "A lack of imagination pervades the movie because it so slavishly follows the book. The filmmakers, the producers and the studio seem panicked by anything that might feel like a departure from the book—which already feels film-ready—so *Harry Potter and the Sorcerer's Stone* never takes on a life of its own" (paragraph 19). Can you think of another movie that you have seen that closely follows the book it was based on? How did being faithful to the text affect that other film? How much? In what ways?

2. In your library or on the Internet, find reviews of some of the other films that Ebert mentions—the *Indiana Jones* movies, *Citizen Kane*, *Star Wars*—and compare those reviews to Ebert's review of the Harry Potter movie. How effective are they as evaluations, compared to Ebert's comments?

3. What questions do you have about the film, after reading these reviews? Make a list of all that you can think of.

4. Select the most interesting question you generated in 3. above and conduct a search (at your school library or on the Web) to find answers to that question. In no more than two pages, explain what you learn from this search.

MATTHEW POWER

Immersion Journalism

Journalist Matthew Power earned an undergraduate degree in English literature at Middlebury College and a Master of Fine Arts degree in writing and photography at Columbia University. He is a contributing editor for *Harper's Magazine*. His work has appeared on National Public Radio (http://matthewpower.net/radio.html), and in magazines and newspapers such as *Discover, the New York Times, GQ, Christian Science Monitor, Popular Science, National Geographic Adventure,* and *Spin*. He has served as a contributing producer for Public Radio International's "The Next Big Thing." This essay was originally published in *Harper's Magazine* in 2005.

A week after the levees broke in New Orleans and the last busloads of refugees had been moved from the Morial Convention Center and the Superdome into a nationwide diaspora, the P.R. divisions of the disaster-industrial complex were at last fully deployed.

The entrance of Harrah's Casino had become a staging area for thousands of law-enforcement personnel, FEMA flacks, EMTs, insurance claims adjusters, construction contractors, and the hordes of media whose satellite trucks bloomed like a row of poppies for four blocks down Canal Street. Scientology Volunteer Ministers doled out backrubs, chewing tobacco, and cartons of cigarettes. Anderson Cooper was interviewing Dr. Phil interviewing Anderson Cooper, both men's camera crews recording the scene for posterity, rivulets of sweat running down Dr. Phil's face in the subtropical heat.

Only a week earlier, Harrah's had been the site of an encampment of hundreds of desperate evacuees who were later prevented, at gunpoint, by Gretna sheriff's deputies from escaping the city across the Crescent City Connection, a bridge over the Mississippi. Now soldiers of the 82nd Airborne in rakish berets stood in a block-long line with security contractors from Blackwater ("It's our first stateside op!"), CNN boom-mic operators, SWAT teams from Oregon, and the FDNY to get burgers and sausages doled out by the thousands by the staff of the USS *Iwo Jima*. There was enough firepower in line to atomize any looter who showed his face, but there were precious few bad guys left in town. The disorder that followed the flooding had visited upon the city a show of force unprecedented in modern American history. An Abrams tank rattled through the empty quarters of the Ninth Ward. The state's monopoly on violence was utterly reasserted.

Smoke billowed up from barbecue grills placed directly in front of New Orleans' World Trade Center. That it happened to be September 11 lent the scene an air of exquisite surreality. Two blocks away, the Morial Convention Center still smelled like an empty slave ship moored at a wharf. In flooded sections of the city, helicopters with buckets had been using forest-fire-fighting techniques to control blazes. The riverfront was a sealed security zone, but the *Iwo Jima*'s radar tower could be seen spinning lazily above the shattered glass facades of the Riverwalk mall.

The conversion of New Orleans' central business district from humanitarian crisis to full-blown media circus was near completion; it is a natural progression in the arc of any big story, an inevitable step toward national healing and reconciliation. That all present were presiding over a city of ghosts only heightened the sense, carried on the breeze from the septic and desolate precincts of Lakeview and Bywater, that those at the cookout were inside the most exclusive velvet rope in America.

I should have realized, driving into New Orleans from Baton Rouge at midnight a few days earlier, that whatever historical truth was made manifest in the destruction of New Orleans was quickly being combed over and tarted up for the cameras, and that the flashes of reality that had been broadcast to the world were already being transformed into media spectacle and political theater. At a Louisiana State Police checkpoint on I-10 just outside the city, a trooper, after seeing my credentials, walked over to her cruiser and came back with a highway vest and a Sharpie. She was collecting autographs. My voicemail filled up with military public-affairs officers who really wanted to get the press up in a Black Hawk to show just how assiduous was their response. The National Guard took news crews in the back of HEMIT missile carriers through flooded neighborhoods, which in the absence of almost anyone left to rescue seemed like a combination of Disney's Jungle Cruise and a fifth-grade field trip.

As happens in these situations, tragedy quickly devolved into parody. The satellite trucks cost money, news budgets were stretched tight, and there was already whispered speculation concerning the point at which the story would recede from its high-water mark like the filthy water being pumped back out of the city.

I spoke with Anderson Cooper outside Harrah's, commenting on the scrum of press that was casting about for stories in the wreckage. Cooper had earlier scolded Louisiana Senator Mary Landrieu on live television, tearfully berating the self-congratulation of politicians while a rat-gnawed body lay in the street he was reporting from in Waveland, Mississippi. After that, and the quadrupling of CNN's post-Katrina ratings, theatrical advocacy became the order of the day. Network correspondents paced about in the heat in shorts and blazers, rehearsing their lines as though they were trying out for the school play. Cooper had covered the tsunami from Sri Lanka, and I had reported on it from Thailand, and we discussed the cynical nature of round-the-clock disaster coverage. As Cooper put it: "When Ricky Martin shows up, it's jumped the shark."

Martin hadn't made his appearance at the casino yet (as he had in Phuket, Thailand, a few weeks after the tsunami), but Sean Penn had come to rescue people from rooftops, John Travolta had flown in relief supplies, and Oprah Winfrey did a flyover in a helicopter. It was the hottest ticket in America, no different than the backstage passes that had been handed out at Ground Zero four years earlier, when Brooke Shields, Don King, Muhammad Ali, and Bette Midler got publicity tours of the recovery operation.

In New Orleans everyone wanted a piece of the action, and here was a humanitarian tragedy without the hassle of jet lag. The hurricane clip goes on top of the résumé. There were careers to be made and theme songs to be composed, pieces in a genre that includes what Peter Fish, a composer for *CBS Evening News*, has called "dead Pope music." What key will best express the sorrow of Biloxi or Banda Aceh?

Television, for all its immediacy and drama, is hardwired for illusion and was all too willing to make of the disaster a soap opera, with "stars" like nine-year-old Charles Evans, discovered outside the Convention Center and suited up for Katie Couric and the Emmys. The TV people inevitably reduce history to a series of bathetic tropes: the flag waving in slow motion, the rescued puppy, the evacuee given the star treatment of *American Idol. And next on* Larry King Live, *Deepak Chopra on healing shattered spirits.*   11

Consider the following scene, which I witnessed after the tsunami in Thailand, in the crushed remains of the Emerald Beach Resort in Khao Lak. Stuart Breisch, a doctor from Salt Lake City whose fifteen-year-old daughter had been missing since the waves had wiped out the resort, stood in the tropical sun being interviewed by a crew from *Good Morning America*. They stood with the man whose daughter was missing and had him do multiple takes of his story. They asked him to switch angles for the light. They told him, Thank you, I think we have enough narrative. How does this all make you feel? The producer stopped the shot for a moment, hoping aloud amid the destroyed landscape that whatever he had in his eye was only sunblock. They followed Dr. Breisch and his surviving daughter from temple to temple (which had all become way stations for thousands of bodies) as he searched for his daughter. There were boards set up with snapshots of the dead to aid in identification. Breisch's daughter spotted her sister's photograph among the hundreds of mangled bodies, and *Good Morning America* was there to capture the family's moment of private horror for all the world to see. Money shot. Mission accomplished. Our work here is done. And now a word from our sponsors.   12

In the first days after the storm hit, it was different in New Orleans. For once at a major news event, the self-interest of the media—ratings, careers, scoops, the great television of terrible news—seamlessly converged with the larger public interest. And only in those hours when the story was so wildly out of control, when the complete failure of government to help its citizens was most apparent, did the images scream for some actual justice to be done. Geraldo and Shepard Smith and Anderson Cooper melting down on live TV was theater, yet it was in the service of a public good. But the brief reanimation of journalistic responsibility could not last: they would not stay off-script for long. The national press found its integrity, briefly, in the muck of New Orleans, but that soon led to little more than an   13 orgy of back-patting. The veil dropped down again, and broadcast news returned to its default setting as the pornography of disaster.

What those who get their news from CNN and Fox were missing was the perspective of reporters with an intimate knowledge of what had been washed away in the tidal surge, who had more than their highlight reels at stake. Those best suited to tell the story in New Orleans were in the first days of the storm and flood in an almost impossible position to do so. About 240 staffers of the New Orleans *Times-Picayune*, many with their families in tow, had ridden out the hurricane in the paper's Mid-City offices—which also held the paper's presses. When the levees were breached and the water started rising, most of the staff, carrying garbage bags filled with files, climbed into newspaper delivery trucks and fled the city. They would not get the paper out on newsprint for four days, but beginning almost immediately they set up shop in Houma, Louisiana, and then Baton Rouge, and converted the paper's website into a blog, a tenuous lifeline to a scattered city that was publishing the most vital reports from the ground. On Monday night, when most national news outlets were tying a ribbon on their storm coverage and New Orleans' close call, the *Picayune*'s environmental reporter, Mark Schleifstein, had put out the first word that the levees had been breached. As many as half of the staff had lost their homes, and still they worked to put out the news. But as Jim Amoss, the *Times-Picayune* editor, later recalled, "It was very frustrating to know what we knew, and see that the story wasn't getting told to the nation and to the world." 14

By the time I arrived in New Orleans, a dozen reporters had set up shop in a *Picayune* staffer's house on Laurel Street in Uptown. The neighborhood was empty, with downed power lines and trees across the streets. While the national networks had portable studios set up on Canal Street in Winnebagos, they ran the lights of the house off a temperamental gasoline generator, and filed their dispatches and photographs over a single dial-up connection. The house had the curious honor of being, for the moment, the New Orleans bureau of the New Orleans *Times-Picayune*. The reporters and photographers bathed in a neighbor's swimming pool and ate military MRE rations liberated from the staging area at Harrah's. They slept on couches and floors, a shotgun leaning up against the wall in a corner. The neighborhood was desolate, except for stray dogs wandering past in the flickering light of a gas lamp that, strangely, still worked. A body lay on a porch under a sheet a few blocks away, and even after two weeks was still lying there, a grim barometer of the recovery's pace. The *Picayune*'s staff had accepted the bizarre circumstance of being war reporters in their own city. 15

The reporters had been out in what remained of New Orleans all day, navigating the landscape that *Picayune* columnist Chris Rose called a "city of melted clocks." They were being bigfooted for access by the media superstars that had parachuted into the city: Koppel strolling through the crowd by Dick Cheney's side, Ed Bradley getting a private tour with the superintendent of police. Sean Penn, a reporter was told by his handlers, was permitted to talk only to the reporter from *Rolling Stone*. Perhaps they were afraid someone might question the premise of Penn's visit. 16

In the evening, after filing, after the next day's news budget meeting, which had DEATH as the first item on a dry erase board, the mosquitoes came out and there was no sound in the darkened neighborhood but an occasional barking dog and the thwack-thwack of Black Hawks flying low over the city with thermal sensing devices, looking for looters or survivors. The little group of reporters smoked cigarettes on the porch and drank warm brown liquor and talked long into the night about what exactly it meant to file dispatches from the apocalypse. 17

The risks of staying were real. Reporter Jim Varney had spent two days after the storm with a photographer, filing from a grocery store in the French Quarter, with looters running amok outside in what he called a "Stalingrad pocket." Gordon Russell, a staff writer, had been traveling with a photographer the previous week near the convention center when they stopped to take pictures of a man who had just been shot dead by the New Orleans police. When they were spotted, the police grabbed them, held them at gunpoint, and threw their camera and notebooks across the street. When they showed credentials and had the camera returned, one of the memory chips was missing. Not, luckily, the one that contained the photos of the dead man. 18

Publishing online, the paper set up an exhaustive clearinghouse for essential reports from the city, recruiting volunteers, creating a missing-persons forum, and calling angrily on the federal government to come to New Orleans' aid. Their efforts were a pointed reminder of the indispensability of good local media in an era when that is neither economic nor fashionable. Running the *Picayune* was a de facto volunteer operation: the staff were told they would be paid whether they worked or not, but they stayed anyway. Mark Schleifstein, who first reported the breached levees, took little satisfaction from being Katrina's Cassandra; in a series of frighteningly proleptic articles that ran in 2002, he and John McQuaid predicted exactly why and how the levees could fail, and how many people would be left behind. And it was the *Times-Picayune*—weeks after the anchormen had gone chasing after Rita and were again tying themselves to telephone poles in the wind—that 19 methodically debunked the rumor-mongering and speculation of wide-spread murder, rape, and anarchic violence that had colored much of the early television coverage with shades of racial hysteria and served to slow the pace of relief efforts. The television networks that echoed and amplified that story didn't have to stay behind and sort out the truth from the legends; their ultimate accountability was to the bottom line of ratings and advertisers.

The business of news—print and broadcast—is filled with many such ugly economic realities, and whether the *Picayune* will be able to survive in a city with a decimated readership and advertising base remains to be seen. Television, lurid and amnesiac, may drive public discourse, but this is rarely to the public's benefit. In New Orleans' loss, the local newspaper's value to the people it serves has never been more manifest.

20

QUESTIONS FOR WRITING AND DISCUSSION

Rhetorical Knowledge: The Writer's Situation and Rhetoric

1. **Audience:** Who is the audience for Power's evaluative essay? Would you consider yourself as part of his target audience? Why?

2. **Purpose:** In no more than one paragraph, indicate what you see as Power's purpose in writing this essay. How well does Power achieve this purpose? Why?

3. **Voice and tone:** How does Power come across to you as a writer? Does his tone ever seem overly cautious or too strident? If so, what can you cite from the text to show what you mean?

4. **Responsibility:** How responsible does Power's essay seem to you? How does he treat major news media and celebrities?

5. **Context and format:** Power's essay appeared in *Harper's Magazine*, a magazine known for thoughtful essay writing. How well does Power's essay fit that description?

Critical Thinking: Your Personal Response

1. What is your initial reaction to Power's evaluation of how the news media (and some celebrities) dealt with the New Orleans hurricane disaster?

2. What parts of Power's essay surprised you? Why?

3. What aspects of Power's essay did not surprise you? Why?

4. To what extent do you agree with Power's conclusion that the New Orleans *Times-Picayune* reporters and staff handled the situation better and reported more accurately than did the national news media? Why?

Critical Thinking: The Writer's Ideas

1. Make a list of the evaluative criteria that Power uses to judge the national news media. How fair is the evaluation that he makes? Why?

2. How difficult was it to list Power's evaluative criteria? He does not explicitly spell out his criteria, but do you, as a reader, understand on what basis he makes his evaluative comments?

3. To what extent does Power seem to apply the same criteria to the New Orleans *Times-Picayune* reporters and staff as he does to the national media?

4. In what ways does Power portray film and television celebrities in his essay? How fair does this portrayal seem to you? Why?

5. In his essay, Power mentions a number of celebrities. How does this "name dropping" affect his critique?

Composing Processes and Knowledge of Conventions: The Writer's Strategies

1. What is the strongest part of Power's evaluation? Why? What do you consider to be the least effective part of his essay? Why?

2. Power does not explicitly state the evaluative criteria he is focusing on. In what ways does that affect his review?

3. In addition to its evaluative features, in what way(s) is Power's essay also persuasive?

Inquiry and Research: Ideas for Further Exploration

1. In your library or on the Web, find several other essays about the media's coverage of Hurricane Katrina and its aftermath. How effective are they as evaluations, compared to Power's comments?

2. What questions do you have about the way the national media handled its coverage of the hurricane after reading Power's essay? Make a list of all that you can think of.

3. Select the most interesting question you generated in response to 2 above and conduct a search (at your school library or on the Web), to find answers to your question. In no more than two pages, explain what you learn from this search.

FIGURE 9.5
A Checklist of Criteria for Evaluating Small Businesses

Evaluation criteria checklist

- Product/service delivered on time and within budget

- Experienced project management staff

- Excellent customer services

- Product met or exceeded needs

- Would recommend to others

Thinking about Visuals That Evaluate

We have already seen how a simple list of great films can help explain an evaluation in the American Film Institute's list of the Greatest 100 Films at the beginning of this chapter (pp. 391–92), and we have also seen how a simple table can help a writer make evaluative comparisons clear for readers, as in tire tread rating on page 403. How else might you as a writer use a visual aid to help explain your evaluation?

Figure 9.5 is an evaluation checklist of criteria from the federal government's Small Business Administration used to evaluate how well a business does its job. While the checklist is simple and brief, it could serve at least as a starting point for developing specific criteria for each item in more detail. How might you construct criteria, for example, for the first item: "product/service delivered on time and within budget"? What evidence would you look for in a company's past history to demonstrate how effectively it met that criteria?

Notice how the photographs of the tires in Figure 9.6 add to this excerpt from *Consumer Reports* on how to evaluate tire conditions:

> Worn tires—especially bald ones—can be deadly on wet roads, where the grooves aren't deep enough to channel water out from beneath the tread. The result is hydroplaning, where the tread skims the water's surface and the vehicle no longer responds to the steering wheel. Wet-weather braking and snow traction also decrease as tires wear.
>
> Tires are considered bald when one or more of their grooves reaches 2/32 of an inch deep, compared with about 10/32 of an inch for new tires (tread wear is usually measured in 1/32-inch increments). Manufacturers have made bald tires easier to spot by placing a series of molded horizontal bars at the base of the grooves. The bars become flush with

FIGURE 9.6
Examining Tire Treads

PINCHING PENNIES
Grooves reveal more of Lincoln's head as tires wear; wet-weather grip declines long before the top is visible.

GAUGING WEAR A tread-depth gauge shows wear more precisely. Wear bars approach the tread surface as grooves get shallow.

surrounding tread when wear reduces a groove's depth to 2/32 of an inch. That's also the point where tires will flunk a state safety inspection—and where tread must be worn for you to collect on a tire's tread-wear warranty.

Unfortunately, 2/32 of an inch may be too late if you drive in rain or snow. Based on our tests of new and half-tread-depth tires, you may want to consider replacing the ones on your car or truck closer to the 5/32-inch groove depth that marks the half-tread point on many tires.

Consider how each of these visual aids makes an evaluation more effective as well as more interesting to a reader.

- How does each visual serve the writer's evaluative purpose?
- How effectively does the visual help the reader understand the point of the evaluation?
- What other type of visual might be used in each situation?
- Besides lists of criteria and photographs, what other visuals can help writers explain an evaluation to readers?
- What other types of visual aids might help the reader better understand and agree with the evaluation?

Drawing On Research for Your Evaluation

Although evidence you gather from your subject is sometimes sufficient for an evaluation, in more formal settings you will need to support your claims with outside research. One advantage of conducting research is that the information you find will help you form your judgment about your subject. It is important not to make that judgment too soon—often you won't know what you really think until you have done a lot of invention work, conducted much of your research, and have even written a draft or two.

For example, suppose you want to buy a particular mountain bike, but you need to explain and justify your decision. Wouldn't it be more useful, and give you more credibility, to cite information from a magazine report—especially one that is balanced and presumably unbiased, such as an article in *Consumer Reports* or a bicycle magazine—to explain and justify your choice, rather than basing it on a more subjective opinion?

Research, then, can give you solid evidence—verifiable information, such as figures, statistics, data, or expert testimony—to support your final evaluation. The kind and amount of research you will need to do will vary according to the rhetorical situation: who your audience is and what you are trying to accomplish.

The subject you focus on, and the kind of essay you are constructing, help to determine the kind of research you conduct. For example, for the scenarios on pages 396–400, you could conduct several kinds of research:

- For Scenario 1, you could ask others who live under similar circumstances (at home, in a dorm, in the military) what rules they have to live by and how they react to those rules.

- Scenario 2 asks you to choose a subject that you are interested in and would like to learn more about. You might have a good opinion of it, or you might think it is overrated. In addition to presenting your point of view on the subject, citing library or online research on it would help you show that others see it the same way. Asking others for their evaluation of your subject—their own evaluative comments—gives you more research to use in your evaluation.

- Scenario 4 asks you to evaluate your local newspaper for bias. Conducting library research, not only to find instances of bias, but also to cite other newspapers that reported on the same stories but in a more, or less, neutral manner than the paper you are evaluating could provide you with evidence of biased or objective reporting.

As you review your notes, look for information that will help you show how your subject does, or does not, meet a given criterion. Look as well for any conclusions that others have drawn about the subject of your evaluation—and consider if and how your evaluation differs from theirs. While you can use others' opinions in support of your conclusion, hearing and reading what others have said will often provide new ideas and suggest additional avenues for research.

For more on conducting research and citing your sources properly, see Chapters 19 and 20. For more on counterargument, see Chapter 14.

As you research, you may find that other writers have reached judgments that differ from yours. You will want to address—and counter—their opinions in your own comments, since doing so will strengthen your evaluation.

Writing Processes

As you work on the assignment that you have chosen, remember the qualities of an effective and convincing evaluative paper, which are listed on pages 401–5. Also remember that writing is recursive—you might start with an invention activity or two and then conduct some research, which leads to more invention work and then a first draft; but then you might need to do more invention work to help flesh out your evaluation and conduct more research to add more criteria or more support; and then you'll revise your draft and possibly find another gap or two. . . . Writing, in other words, is more a circular than a linear process. So while the activities listed below imply that writers proceed step-by-step, as you actually write you will keep coming back to your earlier work, modifying the criteria and strengthening the support as you conduct additional research and become more familiar with your topic.

As you work on your project, make certain that you save your computer files frequently because any work that you don't save could be lost. Many experienced writers save their files every fifteen minutes or so. Also, savvy writers back up their computer files in two or more places—on an internal or external hard drive of the computer, on a USB flash drive, and/or on a rewritable CD or DVD, for example.

Invention: Getting Started

Invention activities can help you decide what you might want to evaluate and then make your evaluation. Writers often find it useful to work through several invention activities for any particular writing task. Regardless of the invention activities you do, try to answer these questions while you work:

- What do I already know about the subject (film, TV program, performance, place, product, service, or other subject) that I am thinking about evaluating?
- What makes each potential subject suitable for evaluation?
- What criteria can I establish for my evaluation? On what basis should I make my judgment? How can I compare it with other, similar, items?
- What kinds of details and explanation can I provide about each of my criteria?
- Where might I learn more about the subject (in the library, on the Web, by interviewing people)?
- What verifiable information about my subject is available (warranty period, price, size, weight, cast list, production information, historical information)?

- Are any of my criteria potentially just a matter of opinion and, if so, how might I explain them? How can I define criteria such as "quality" or "comfort" or "more reasonable" or "fairness"?
- What might my audience already know about my subject? What do I know about my audience? What don't I know that I should know?

Doing your invention work in electronic form, rather than on paper, lets you easily use your invention work as you construct a draft.

WRITING ACTIVITY

Brainstorming, Freewriting, Clustering, and Listing

Brainstorming, freewriting, clustering, and listing are invention techniques that can help you focus on a subject to evaluate and come up with criteria for your evaluation. Working with the questions above, spend a few minutes jotting down everything you can think of about the subject or subjects you want to evaluate or discussing them with classmates. Don't worry about putting this information into sentences or paragraphs; simply record it using any words that come to mind. Or try freewriting, which involves writing continuously. Using the questions above, jot down everything you can think of about the subject of your evaluation for the specified amount of time.

Once you have some ideas, you can then use clustering to see relationships between or among them. Put the subject you are focusing on into a circle in the center of a piece of paper, and spend a few minutes creating a cluster of your ideas about the subject. Or use listing to put them into a sequence.

For more on brainstorming, freewriting, clustering, listing, and other strategies for discovery and learning, see Chapter 3.

Student Writer Annlee Lawrence's Brainstorming

In response to Scenario 2, student writer Annlee Lawrence decided to write an evaluation of the meals available at some local fast-food restaurants. To get started, Lawrence brainstormed her initial thoughts, which turned out to be a series of questions:

Hamburgers—something all of us eat—can they ever be healthy?
Is one is better than another, or at least less unhealthy than some others?
And what about fries? They have to be really full of fat or something.
What makes an unhealthy burger, or at least makes one less-unhealthy than some others?
Fat? Calories? What?

Annlee Lawrence's Freewriting

Annlee Lawrence continued her invention work for her evaluative paper by doing some freewriting. This brief excerpt will give you a sense of what freewriting on this topic might look like:

> I know I'm supposed to just start writing, but I'm not sure what to focus on for my evaluation of burgers. I could do taste or cost but I think I'm more interested in health. Or which burger from what company might be less unhealthy. Or can you eat a burger only now and then and then the health aspect doesn't matter? And what's important? Fat or calories or something else (like transfat, whatever that is) I've never even heard of?
>
> How would I learn about that sort of data? Does taste matter and how could I ever measure that and make a comparison for my evaluation?

An Example of Clustering

Below is an example of a cluster Annlee Lawrence might have done for her evaluation of fast-food restaurants.

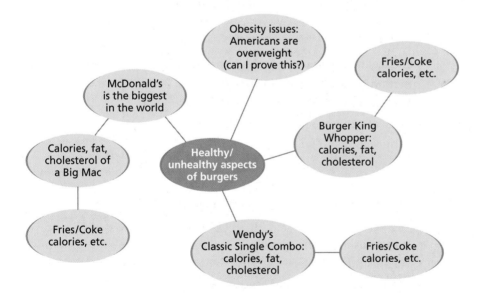

Constructing and Supporting Evaluative Criteria

To evaluate any subject, you need to begin by considering the basis on which you will make your evaluation, as well as how you might support your criteria.

You evaluate a consumer product like a backpack differently than you evaluate a potential job, a work of art, a film, a CD, a computer game, or an evening news broadcast, so consider the various aspects of the subject on which you might base your evaluation. Here are just a few possibilities:

- Physical aspects (think about what measurements would demonstrate this aspect of your evaluation):
  - size
  - weight
  - shape
  - taste
  - smell
  - sound
- Quality aspects:
  - warranty period
  - type of warranty offered (limited or full)
  - component quality (steel vs. plastic, for example)
  - power aspects (size of amplifier; horsepower; lack of exhaust emissions)
- Aesthetic aspects:
  - how it feels to use (drive, listen to, sit in, wear) the item
  - color
  - proportion
  - the feeling it gives you (using it, listening to it, or viewing it)
- Entertainment-value aspects (what will you use this product for?):
  - Why would you listen to this CD?
  - Why would you read this book?
  - Why would you go to see this film?
- Comparative aspects:
  - Which film is better? Why?
  - Why might this stock be a good investment?
  - Which career would give me the greatest satisfaction? Why?
  - Which airline is the safest?
  - What is the best place to study? Why?
  - Which employee should I promote to manager?
  - Which political candidate should get my vote?

In most evaluations, you will need to show how your subject can be measured against other, similar, subjects and explain the basis of your comparison. Always compare like with like, showing how each relevant aspect of the item you are evaluating rates in comparison with the same, or a similar, aspect of a similar item. If you are comparing two automobiles, for example, you would probably compare both cars in terms of price, gas mileage, and maintenance, among other criteria.

For more on making comparisons, see Chapter 13.

Once you have a basis for comparison, the first step in deciding the criteria for your evaluation is to look over your invention work and consider what you have learned so far about your subject. Try to answer these questions:

- What do you consider the most important aspect of your subject? Would most people agree that this aspect is most important?

- What other features or qualities, either positive or negative, does this subject have? Which are more important to you, and which are less important?

- If you are evaluating a subject for its usefulness, what must it do? How can you determine that your subject will do what you want or need it to?

- If you are evaluating a product or service, think about what you will use it for. If you are evaluating a child's car seat, for example, the most important criterion will probably be safety. What do you mean by the term *safe*, and how can you tell if a particular car seat is safe?

- If a product or service needs to be reliable, what do you mean by that term, and how can you determine reliability?

- What criteria are absolutely necessary for the subject to possess? What must it have? What criteria are important, but perhaps not as necessary? How can you assign a value or weight to each criterion?

- What research might help you to make your evaluation? What can you learn at the library? Will a search of the World Wide Web help? What would you gain from talking with your friends or relatives or conducting a survey of some kind?

WRITING ACTIVITY

Constructing and Supporting Criteria

Construct a list of possible criteria for your evaluation. For each of your criteria, explain, in no more than one sentence, why it is important in evaluating your subject. Also, in no more than one sentence, outline what kind of evidence you might use to support each criterion.

Annlee Lawrence's Criteria

After Annlee Lawrence completed some brainstorming and freewriting about her subject, she made a list of the criteria for evaluating fast-food restaurants and did some additional freewriting to discover what they meant and what she thought about each one. Here is an excerpt:

- Why should anyone care about eating a burger?
- What does "obesity" mean? Who says it's important?
- Why is "fat" bad and are there different kinds of fat?
- How does cholesterol hurt people? And I read somewhere that there is both good and bad cholesterol—I wonder if any of each is in a burger?
- And everyone knows that we want to consume less calories, right?
- Does any of this affect taste?
- What about the other stuff we usually eat with a burger? Fries? A Coke?

I guess I know it's important to not be overweight and all, but I wonder if eating a burger now and then really matters. Aren't there some people who eat them all the time, though? I mean, with fries and all? How bad could that be? I need to learn more about fat and calories and things, so I can point to what is bad (and if anything is good) about America's burgers.

Once I learn some stuff—now, where can I learn the fat content, etc. of burgers? Does McDonald's and Wendy's and Burger King post them somewhere? Online? It'd be kind of funny if I had to go and buy a burger at each place, just to find out how unhealthy it might be!

And once I have some information, how can I present it so readers can understand and make a wise choice, based on my evaluation?

WRITER'S WORKSHOP

Reacting to Your Classmates' Criteria

Working with several of your classmates, compare your lists and reach a consensus of what your group considers to be the best criteria to apply to each subject. Use the following questions to guide your discussion:

- The criterion about _____ seems promising and could be developed more.

- Isn't _____ a more important criterion than _____?

- How about adding a criterion that deals with _____?

Exploring Your Ideas with Research

Before you begin your research, consider how you plan to focus your evaluation. For example, before you purchase or lease a new cell phone, you might want to do research on various brands, the features that you think are important, how many "free" minutes you get every month, cost information, and other criteria. The object is to narrow down your list to the criteria you think are most important and then compare plans and phones offered by the wireless carriers in your area.

You can see that Annlee Lawrence is engaged in this kind of focusing activity above. Look over your own invention work to remind yourself of the information you have gathered about your subject so far, and the questions you have come up with about it. Use the reporter's questions of *who*, *what*, *where*, *when*, *why*, and *how* to get started on your research. After you have determined the information you need, decide what kind of research you need to conduct in order to gather that information, and conduct research in the library and on the Web. You may also find it necessary to do field research.

For help with locating sources of information and with field research, see Chapter 19; for help with taking notes and documenting your sources, see Chapter 20.

WRITING ACTIVITY

Conducting Research

Using the list of qualities of effective evaluative writing on pages 401–5, go through your invention writing and your list of criteria and note what you already know about your issue. Next, determine whether you need to do research to come up with additional criteria or evidence, learn more about similar subjects, or muster stronger counterarguments.

You will also find it useful to consider the subject you are writing about and, in no more than two pages, outline a research plan. In your plan, indicate the following:

- What you already know about your subject
- What questions you still have
- Who or what sources might answer your questions
- Who might provide other perspectives on your subject
- Where you might look for further information (library, Web, consumer magazines, other sources)
- When you plan to conduct your research

Gather, read, and take notes on your subject from these outside sources. Use an electronic journal to record images, URLs, and other electronic pieces of information that you find as you are conducting your research. Such an e-journal makes it easy for you to add these e-documents once you start drafting your paper.

Annlee Lawrence's Research Strategy

Annlee Lawrence needed to research the nutritional content of typical meals available from the three restaurants she was evaluating. She came up with the following research plan:

- I'll check both online and at the stores themselves, to see if the information is provided.

- I need to try to compare apples-to-apples as much as I can—that is, I want to compare similar-size hamburgers, and similar-size fries and drinks (otherwise it would be an unfair evaluation and my readers would not benefit and probably wouldn't believe me).
- I should check in the library for information on why these things (calories, fat, cholesterol) are bad for people.
- I may also find in the library some useful information about the companies I'm focusing on (McDonald's, Wendy's, Burger King). I know there are others (Sonic, A&W), but I want to concentrate on the big three, as they're everywhere.

 ## Reviewing Your Invention and Research

After you have conducted your research, you need to review your invention work and notes and think about the information you have collected from outside sources and how that information matches the criteria you have for your evaluation. You may be ready to decide on a working thesis statement—a statement that summarizes the main point of your evaluation—at this point. Even though you might already have a general idea of the conclusion your evaluation is leading you to, until you get some of your ideas and research down on paper, it is often hard to know for certain what your thesis will be. Your thesis should come from your complete evaluation. It is best to decide on your thesis when you have done a lot of invention work (listing, brainstorming, clustering, and other strategies) and research. You might even wait after you construct your first draft.

WRITING ACTIVITY

Considering Your Research and Focusing Your Ideas

Examine the notes you have taken from your research. Then, using your criteria as a starting point, see how your information matches the criteria you have established. For example, if you were evaluating an advertisement in response to Scenario 3, you might have criteria such as *eye-catching* and *easy to see the product advertised,* along with notes about the specific advertisement.

WRITERS' WORKSHOP

Reacting to Your Classmates' Invention Work and Research

With any writing assignment, your invention materials and research can improve with peer feedback and suggestions. Working with several of your classmates, provide comments and suggestions and ask one another questions, with the overall goal of helping one another to understand your rhetorical situation more clearly and to generate more useful information:

Comments

- I understand _____ about what you've generated so far.

- _____ in what you have so far is familiar/unfamiliar to me, so you might _____.

- I like _____ in what you've generated so far.

- I don't see how _____ fits as part of your evaluation.

- I'm confused when you write about _____.

- These aspects of your subject— _____ and _____—don't seem related, so I'm not sure why you're thinking of including them.

- The part about _____ seems promising, but the part about _____ seems underdeveloped.

- I'd suggest that you include these ideas or this information:

  _____   _____

  _____   _____

Questions

- Why you think this is an important subject to evaluate?

- What is a _____ ? (Ask this kind of question when something is unclear.)

- I still have questions about _____.

- How would you describe the purpose of the _____ that you mention?

- How do _____ and _____ work together?

- Why don't you compare _____ with your subject?

As your classmates respond to your invention work and research, listen carefully—and with an open mind—to what they are saying and take notes so that you do not forget their questions, comments, and suggestions. Your classmates' responses to your writing will help you anticipate the responses of your audience. In evaluation, your biggest challenge is to understand how others view your subject so that you can convince them to accept your judgment of it, so you should solicit readers' responses as early and as often as feasible. You can get responses to your work in class, but you can also do so online, at the campus writing center, or even in your local coffee shop.

Organizing Your Evaluation

Once you have some sense of the criteria you will use and how your subject matches those criteria, you need to consider how you might organize your evaluation. The questions that you need to ask yourself when deciding on your organization are all rhetorical:

- Who is the audience for your evaluation?

- Why might they be interested in your evaluation, or how you can make them interested in it? (One way to emphasize the importance of your evaluation to your audience is to show them why they need to understand your subject.)

- What is your purpose for writing—that is, why do your readers need this evaluation? What will your readers learn about your subject by reading your evaluation? How will that knowledge help them with their evaluation?

The answers to these questions can help you decide what you need to emphasize, which in turn will help you choose an organization.

For more on design and visuals, including examples of different kinds of graphics, see Chapter 18.

TechNote

If there's one thing computers are good at, it's establishing hierarchies (systems of ranking, prioritizing, and organizing things). When you're writing an essay that evaluates something, the computer screen can serve as a kind of workshop space, where you can move around ideas, concepts, criteria, issues, and controversies.

You can use different programs—and sometimes different windows within the same software application—to design charts, outlines, tables, Venn diagrams, timelines, and other visual space-holders for your information. Use color, line, shape, and space to move information around on the plane of the computer screen, looking for categories and interesting interrelations among your ideas and segments of information.

For more on the inductive and deductive methods, see Chapter 8, page 365.

Here is a brief outline of three possible organizational approaches for writing an evaluation.

Options for Organization

First Inductive Approach	Second Inductive Approach	Deductive Approach
• Outline why you are making the evaluation. • Discuss/explain the criteria.	• Begin with a discussion of the subject or subjects that you are evaluating. • Explain it or their strengths and weaknesses.	• At the beginning, outline the conclusion that you have reached about the subject or subjects (your thesis statement)

First Inductive Approach	Second Inductive Approach	Deductive Approach
• Explain how well your subject or subjects match (or fail to) the various criteria. • Discuss and explain which subject or subjects are "best," according to the evaluative criteria you have established. Your thesis statement is explained, then, at your conclusion.	• Outline how the positive and negative points match each of your criteria. • Explain how the subject or subjects you are evaluating fulfill those criteria (this, then, is your thesis statement)	• Explain why and how you reached that conclusion using a compare-and-contrast format: compare and contrast each aspect of what you are evaluating in relation to the criteria.

WRITING ACTIVITY

Deciding on an Organizational Approach

Before you construct a full draft of your evaluation, consider which organizational approach will best serve your writing purpose. It is sometimes useful to try several organizational approaches to see what seems most effective for your specific purpose, audience, and rhetorical situation. Try writing a page or two using at least two organizational approaches before you decide, and be sure to save each attempt with a different file name. That strategy makes it easy to recall the one that seems best. You can then start to develop your draft using that organization.

Constructing a Complete Draft

Once you have generated some initial thoughts and ideas, selected the criteria for judging your subject, and reviewed your notes from the reading and research you have done, your next step is to write a first draft, which is often called a working draft. For this first draft of your evaluation, concentrate on organizing your work in a coherent form. Your first draft is your opportunity to expand, explain, and develop your ideas. In this draft, you are exploring a number of areas: how much you already know, what you might want to say about it, the research you have already done, and the research that might still be necessary. At this point, do not worry about editing your work—that step can come later.

Before beginning your draft, review the writing you have done so far. What are the relative advantages of evaluating several items or of concentrating on just one? Why? Review the criteria that you have developed and decide which you want to emphasize. If your instructor and/or peers have given you suggestions, consider how you will incorporate their advice into your evaluation (you, after all, are the writer, so you decide what feedback to accept and use and what to ignore). As you prepare to write, ask yourself the following questions:

- What is the most effective way to explain my criteria?
- In what ways does the subject of my evaluation match up with (or fail to match up with) the criteria I have selected?
- What is my final evaluation?
- How can I express my main point effectively as a thesis statement?

As you work, you should be aware of the strategies you can use to explain your evaluation:

- You can compare different products, services, or other items using the criteria you have developed as your basis for comparison.
- You can define each aspect of your subject, and then explain how each item fits (or does not fit) those definitions.
- You can describe each item you are evaluating in detail, using the details to establish your evaluative criteria.

For more on comparison, definition, and description, see Chapter 13.

As you draft your evaluation, stop occasionally to read your work, imagining that you are reading it for the first time. Because your draft is an exploratory text, ask yourself the following questions:

- How clearly have I explained the criteria I am using to evaluate my subject?
- How have I compared my subject with other, similar items?
- How effectively have I added details demonstrating how well the subject matches my criteria?
- What visual information might I use to explain my evaluation?
- How clear is my final judgment?

Introduction: One of the qualities of a successful evaluation is that it grabs and holds readers' attention. Some strategies that will help you hook your readers include the following:

- *Begin by explaining why you are making the evaluation—your rhetorical purpose—followed by a discussion of your criteria.* It is also often helpful to include an explanation of why you selected these criteria. This is usually the approach taken by articles in consumer magazines such as *Consumer Reports.*
- *Indicate your conclusion at the beginning.* You will then explain in the body of your text why and how you reached that conclusion. Both of the reviews of *Harry Potter and the Sorcerer's Stone* reprinted in this chapter

begin with the critic's judgment. Elvis Mitchell, for example, begins his review with this assessment (p. 409):

> The most highly awaited movie of the year has a dreary, literal-minded competence, following the letter of the law as laid down by the author.

- *Set the scene for your evaluation.* Depending on your topic, you might open your evaluation with a description of your subject. Matthew Power opens with a description of the national news media's coverage of the Katrina disaster (p. 415):

> A week after the levees broke in New Orleans and the last busloads of refugees had been moved from the Morial Convention Center and the Superdome into a nationwide diaspora, the P.R. divisions of the disaster-industrial complex were at last fully deployed.

Body: The first introduction listed above leads to an organizational scheme using an inductive method: you indicate what you want to evaluate and on what basis at the beginning, and as you work through the process, you answer as you go. This is the approach Annlee Lawrence uses in "Who Has the Better Burger?" (p. 448). A third approach to organizing an evaluation uses what is called the deductive method. If you use this approach, you begin by stating your judgment, and then use the body of your paper to support it, often by comparing and contrasting your subject with other subjects of the same type. Elvis Mitchell compares *Harry Potter and the Sorcerer's Stone* to other children's films by the same director (paragraph 4), for example.

Conclusion: Regardless of the organizational method you decide to employ, you need to make sure that your judgment of your subject—your evaluation—is clearly stated. Remember that in an evaluation, your ultimate conclusion is usually your thesis statement, or main point, but your conclusion also can serve other purposes. A conclusion in evaluative writing often does the following:

- *Summarizes how each supporting piece of evidence helps support your main point.* In a lengthy, detailed evaluation, a summary of your findings can help readers recall the main points that you are making.

- *Reaches out to your audience.* An appeal to the audience is an especially effective way to end an evaluation, as often you want them to not only agree with your evaluation but also to do something with what they have learned. For example, Annlee Lawrence probably hopes her readers will be more careful about their eating habits once they read her evaluation.

Title: As you compose your evaluative writing, a title should emerge at some point—perhaps late in the process. The title should reflect your judgment of your subject, and it should catch your readers' attention and make them want to read your essay. Many newspapers simply give the title of the film as the headline for an evaluation by their movie critic, as is done for the review of *Harry Potter and the Sorcerer's Stone* by Roger Ebert, but other newspapers are more creative. The title of Elvis Mitchell's review, which appeared in the *New York Times*, is "The Sorcerer's Apprentice." Matthew Power suggests the subject of his evaluation in his title, "Immersion Journalism." Annlee Lawrence expresses hers more directly: "Who Has the Better Burger?"

VISUALIZING VARIATIONS

Using Visuals to Support Your Evaluation

If you decided to respond to Scenario 5, which asks that you evaluate a cultural subject, you might include photographs to illustrate what you are evaluating.

It is usually fairly easy to find photographs of most cultural subjects, but it can be more difficult to find photographs that help tell the story of what you are evaluating. For instance, the three authors of this text live in Arizona—part of what is called the Old West. We still have cowboys and cowgirls, and rodeos and parades are part of our tradition.

If we were evaluating the local rodeo or a Fourth of July parade, we could find any number of photographs that would illustrate the event. What if our criteria for evaluating this cultural event included *plenty of activities, tradition*, and *audience involvement?* Consider what this photograph would illustrate.

Think about what this photograph shows and what it might suggest to a reader of our rodeo evaluation:

- Part of American history; part of a long-standing tradition

- Movement; action

- The involvement of animals; this horse is decorated with fancy hardware

- Lots of people watching in the audience

What do you think this picture would add to our evaluation of a local rodeo?

Now suppose you were evaluating your local art museum. You could probably find a generic photograph of the museum or some exhibits within its galleries, but ask yourself if you might support your evaluation more effectively by including a photograph that illustrates something about your evaluative criteria. For example, suppose one of your criteria is *artists available to explain their work*. Consider this photograph—what would it add to your evaluation?

For any photograph you are considering, then, ask yourself the following questions:

- What might this photograph show about my subject?

- How can I select a photograph that will support a point I want to make and help me justify my overall judgment about my subject?

TechNotes It is always a good idea to store the photographs you find in your research in a separate computer file, so you will have easy access to them when you start constructing your evaluation. Charts and graphs are also useful visuals for evaluations—Annlee Lawrence uses three bar graphs in her evaluation of fast-food burgers, for example (pp. 448–51). If you find that you need to include numbers and statistical information in your evaluation, consider putting them into an Excel document. The Excel program has a function that allows you easily to convert your numerical data into a table or graph.

For more on using visuals, see Chapter 18.

WRITING ACTIVITY

Constructing a Full Draft

After reviewing your notes, invention activities, and research and carefully considering all of the information that you have generated and the comments you have received, construct a complete first draft of your evaluation, using the organizational approach that you have decided on. Remember that your evaluation will evolve as you write, so your ideas will most likely change as you compose this first draft. Remember also that you will be learning as you write. While you may have some sense of whether your subject fits your criteria, expect to modify your position as you develop your evaluation essay.

Annlee Lawrence's First Draft

After deciding on an organizational approach and a tentative thesis, Annlee Lawrence was ready to begin her first, or working, draft. She did not worry about errors and instead concentrated on getting her main ideas on paper. Note that she started her paper by outlining what she was going to do, without revealing her conclusions. This inductive approach is one of the possible organizational methods described on pages 434–35. As she wrote, Lawrence did not worry about grammar, punctuation, and mechanics; instead, she concentrated on getting her main ideas into her draft. (The numbers in circles refer to peer comments—see page 444.)

Who Has the Better Burger?

Did you know that McDonald's operates more than thirty thousand restaurants in more than one hundred countries on six continents? In the United States, McDonald's represents 43% of the total fast-food market. McDonald's feeds more than forty-six million people a day—more than the entire population of Spain! Surgeon General David Satcher comments, "Fast food is a major contributor to the obesity epidemic." It's no wonder that sixty percent of America is overweight or obese. Obesity, if left unabated, will surpass smoking as the leading cause of preventable death in America. So why is it that we can't seem to stay away from our beloved Big Macs or Whoppers? Probably because our lives demand it at times. We don't have time to prepare a full-blown meal, so we have created fast food to fit with our fast-paced lives. So unfortunately, obesity can't be helped in today's society, but can be avoided through moderation of consumption. Generally speaking, most fast food is unhealthy. But if you had to pick one that was the healthiest, which would it be? I felt that for this evaluation, the most important criteria for determining a "healthy" burger should be calories, total fat, and cholesterol. I chose some of the favorite meals to evaluate: the Whopper Combo from Burger King, Wendy's Classic Single Combo, and McDonald's Quarter Pounder Combo. ❶

The Whopper Combo from Burger King has been a favorite of Americans for generations. But is it as good to your body as it is to your taste buds? When I researched the nutritional information, I discovered that the sandwich itself has seven hundred calories, eighty-five milligrams of cholesterol, and forty-two grams of total fat. A medium fry has 360 calories and eighteen grams of fat. Not to mention the medium Coke that contains two hundred calories. All this adds up to be a grand total of 1260 calories, fifty-eight grams of fat, and eighty-five milligrams of cholesterol. ❷

Because I used the Burger King Whopper, I picked a similar sandwich from Wendy's, the Classic Single Combo. The burger has 430 calories, twenty grams of total fat, and sixty-five milligrams of cholesterol. A medium fry has 440 calories, twenty-one grams of fat, and a medium coke has 120 calories. This all adds up to 990 calories, forty-one grams of total fat, and 65 milligrams of cholesterol.

Last but not least, there is the McDonald's Quarter Pounder Combo. Despite popular opinion, this burger is the best for you. It has 420 calories, eighteen grams of fat, and seventy milligrams of cholesterol. A medium fry has 350 calories, sixteen grams of fat, and a medium Coke has 210 calories. The total calories would be 980, total fat thirty-four, and total cholesterol is seventy milligrams.

So if you do get caught up in a hurry and feel like grabbing a burger, then get the McDonald's Quarter Pounder. The McDonald's Quarter Pounder has seven fewer grams of fat than the Wendy's Classic Single and twenty-four fewer grams of fat less than the Burger King Whopper. Even their fries have five fewer grams of fat than Wendy's and two fewer than Burger King. This doesn't mean that you should go and buy out McDonald's. Obviously, as the movie <u>Super-Size Me</u> proved, even the "healthy" fast food isn't good for you. But if eaten in moderation, fast food is one of the best things to happen to America. ❸

Works Cited

Wendy's U.S. Nutrition Information. Apr. 3 2005. <http://www.wendys
.com/food/US_Nutrition_2003.pdf>

Burger King Nutritional Information. 18 Aug. 2004

McDonald's USA Nutrition Facts for Popular Menu Items. Apr. 3 2005.
<http://www.mcdonalds.com/app_controller.nutrition.index1.html>

Revising

Once you have a full draft of your evaluation, you still have much to do.
First, however, you should set the draft aside so that you can gain some
critical distance. You should then read it with fresh eyes. When you approach
your work this way, you will find it easier to notice criteria that are irrelevant,
support that is not fully developed, or places where a compelling photograph or other visual might add to the impact of your argument.

As you work to revise your early drafts, hold off on doing a great deal
of heavy editing. When you revise you will probably change the content
and structure of your paper, so time spent working to fix problems with
sentence style or grammar, punctuation, or mechanics at this stage is
often wasted.

Think of revision as reenvisioning your evaluation, reconsidering what
you mean to say, not just editing for surface features. When you reread the
first draft of your evaluation, be sure to begin at the beginning. Here are
some questions to ask yourself:

- Have I effectively explained or indicated my criteria, so the reader
  knows on what basis I am making my evaluation?

- What else might my audience want or need to know about my subject?

- How else might I interest my audience in my evaluation of this subject?

- What did I find out about my subject that I did not include in my
  evaluation? (Effective research always results in more information
  than you can include, so consider what you left out that you might
  include in your next draft.)

- How clearly have I explained and defined any terms my readers might
  not know?

- Could some aspects of my evaluation be better presented as a graph or
  chart?

Technology can help you revise and edit your writing more easily. Use
your word processor's track-changes tool to try out revisions and editing
changes. After you have had time to think about the possible changes, you can
"accept" or "reject" them. Also, you can use your word processor's comment

tool to write reminders to yourself when you get stuck with a revision or some editing task. If your classmates are offering feedback on your draft, they also can use track changes, the comment tool, or the peer-commenting feature of the software.

Because it is so difficult even for experienced writers to see their emerging writing with a fresh eye, it is almost always useful to ask classmates, friends, or family members to read drafts of your persuasive writing.

WRITER'S WORKSHOP

Responding to Full Drafts

Working with one or two other classmates, read each evaluation and offer comments and questions that will help each of you see your papers' strengths and weaknesses. You might share your comments and questions in a conversation, or you may have each reader write comments and questions (either with pen or pencil or electronically) on the writer's draft. Consider the following guidelines and questions as you do:

- Write a brief narrative comment outlining your first impression of this draft. How effective is the title at drawing you in? Why? What are your overall suggestions for improvement? What part(s) of the text are especially strong? What criteria could use more support? Indicate what you like about the draft, and provide positive and encouraging feedback to the writer.

- How clear and understandable is the point of the evaluation?

- How has the writer explained the subject of the evaluation? How might the writer develop the explanation further to make it more effective?

- How clearly and thoroughly has the writer explained and justified the criteria? What details need to be added or clarified?

- How effectively has the writer applied his or her criteria?

- How adequately are all assertions supported with evidence?

- If the writer makes comparisons, how clear are they? Where might additional comparisons be called for?

- How could the writer more clearly match the criteria to the subject? Are there any criteria that the writer discusses but never applies to the subject, or is there an aspect of the subject that you think should be matched to criteria but isn't?

- What terms need to be defined?

(cont'd)

(continued)

- How effective is the organization of this evaluation? How logically are the points connected to the writer's thesis? Point out any gaps that you notice. What evidence is provided in support of each contention?

- How might visuals such as charts, tables, graphs, or photographs help the writer explain or support his or her criteria more effectively?

- How clearly and effectively does the writer present any opposing points of view on this subject? If so, how might this presentation be improved? How effectively does the writer answer opposing viewpoints? How might the writer acknowledge, concede, and/or refute them more effectively?

- How adequately is the writer's overall evaluation supported by the evidence he or she has presented? Would you, the reader, reach the same conclusion? Why or why not?

Student Comments on Annlee Lawrence's First Draft

Using the questions above, Annlee Lawrence's classmates made some suggestions on her first draft. Below are comments she received, keyed to the first draft on pages 440–42.

❶ These seem like good criteria, but why did you choose them? Do you need a stronger reason for your criteria here?

❷ These are a lot of statistics to digest at once (sorry!). I got lost. Can you give all this in a table or chart?

❸ Seems like the ending contradicts the rest of your essay. Why is fast food good for America? The ending seems wrong here.

❹ You should check your formatting here. I think the dates might be wrong. Also, don't you have a quote in the first paragraph from the Surgeon General? There's no citation for it here.

Responding to Readers' Comments

Once they have received feedback on their writing from peers, instructors, friends, and others, all writers have to figure out what to do with that feedback. Since your writing is your responsibility, you must determine how to deal with reader responses to your work.

The first thing to do with any feedback is to consider carefully what your readers have to say about your text. For example, Annlee Lawrence's readers indicate that they have the following reactions:

- One reader wonders why she chose the criteria she did. Lawrence needs to think about whether she needs to justify her criteria for her readers.

- Another reader felt overwhelmed by all of the statistical information in the paper and suggested a chart. Lawrence needs to think about what one or more charts might add to her paper, and what type of chart or graph she might use.

- A reader felt dissatisfied with her ending. How might Lawrence improve her conclusion?

- A reader pointed out problems with Lawrence's documentation, which affects the credibility of her evaluation.

As with all feedback, it is important to listen carefully to it and consider what your reader has to say. Then it is up to you, as the author, to decide how to come to terms with these suggestions. You may decide to reject some comments, of course; other comments, though, deserve your attention. You may find that comments from more than one reader contradict each other. In that case, use your own judgment to decide which reader's comments are on the right track.

In the final version of her paper on pages 448–51, you can see how Annlee Lawrence responded to her reader's comments, as well as read her review of her first draft.

 ## Knowledge of Conventions

When effective writers edit their work, they attend to the conventions that will help readers understand their writing. These include genre conventions, documentation, format, usage, grammar, and mechanics. By attending to these conventions in your writing, you make reading a more pleasant experience for readers.

 ### Editing

After you revise, you have one more important step—editing and polishing. When you edit and polish, you make changes to your sentence structure and word choice to improve your style and to make your writing clearer and more concise. You also check your work to make sure it adheres to conventions of grammar, usage, punctuation, mechanics, and spelling. Use the spell-check function of your word-processing program, but be sure to double-check your spelling personally. If you have used sources in your paper, you should make sure you are following the documentation style your instructor requires.

See Chapter 20 for more
on documenting sources
using MLA or APA style.

Because it is sometimes difficult to identify small problems in a familiar text, it often helps to distance yourself so that you can approach your draft with fresh eyes. Some people read from the last sentence to the first so that the content, and their familiarity with it, doesn't cause them to overlook an error. We strongly recommend that you ask classmates, friends, and tutors to read your work to help you find editing problems that you may not see. Another option is to post your paper on a course Web site and invite everyone in class to read your paper.

To assist you with editing, we offer here a round-robin editing activity focused on careful word choice, which is a common concern in writing to evaluate.

WRITER'S WORKSHOP

Round-Robin Editing with a Focus on Careful Word Choice

Because evaluative writing often requires careful word choice (diction), the focus in this workshop is on word choice—especially in those sections of the paper where the writer is using words that seem evaluative or judgmental. As Mark Twain said, "[t]he difference between the right word and the almost-right word is the difference between the lightning and the lightning-bug," so it is critical to select words that clearly represent what you intend to say. For example, notice how the revision to this word choice problem improves the clarity of this sentence:

                                           rely on

We don't have time to prepare a full-blown meal, so we ᴧ have ~~created~~ fast food to fit with our fast-paced lives.

    People in general have not "created" fast food, but they have come to rely on the convenience that it provides.

As you work with your peers, consult a good college dictionary and the portion of a handbook or other writing text that covers word choice. If you are uncertain about a specific word choice, underline it and put a question mark in the margin.

Genres, Documentation, and Format

If you are writing an academic paper in response to Scenarios 1 or 2, you will need to follow the conventions for the discipline in which you are writing and the requirements of your instructor. If you are writing a formal report in response to Scenario 3, you should follow the conventions for that business genre. Personal opinion essays, such as the one called for in Scenario 4, are generally of moderate length and provide thoughtful commentary. If you are working on Scenario 5, which asks for an opinion essay but in response to a personal writing situation, you can be somewhat more informal than you would be for an academic paper.

For advice on writing
in different genres, see
Appendix C. For guidelines
for formatting and
documenting papers in
MLA or APA style, see
Chapter 20.

If you have used material from outside sources, including visuals, you will need to give credit to those sources, using the documentation style required by the discipline you are working in and by your instructor.

WRITING IN ACTION

Convention in Genre and Design

While many of us read published film reviews and decide which films to attend based on them, the Internet allows readers to respond to such reviews and to post their own comments. The comments below focus on the film *The Matrix Revolutions*, and the review of it by *New York Times* reviewer A. O. Scott. In this example, from a blog available at the *New York Times Online*, a viewer writes his own film review. Note that at the end of the review, readers are asked to indicate whether or not they found the review helpful—essentially, evaluating the review. These comments come as a response from a reader using the reviewer name of jhassenger.

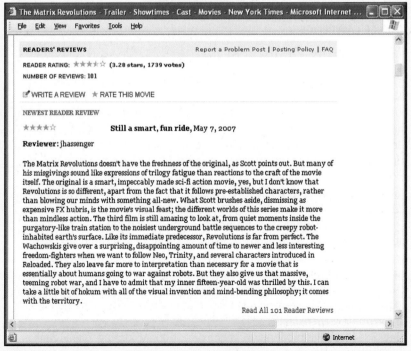

The Matrix Revolutions - Trailer - Showtimes - Cast - Movies - New York Times - Microsoft Internet ...

File   Edit   View   Favorites   Tools   Help

READERS' REVIEWS   Report a Problem Post | Posting Policy | FAQ

READER RATING: ★★★★☆ **(3.28 stars, 1739 votes)**

NUMBER OF REVIEWS: **101**

✍ WRITE A REVIEW   ★ RATE THIS MOVIE

NEWEST READER REVIEW

★★★★☆   **Still a smart, fun ride,** May 7, 2007

Reviewer: jhassenger

The Matrix Revolutions doesn't have the freshness of the original, as Scott points out. But many of his misgivings sound like expressions of trilogy fatigue than reactions to the craft of the movie itself. The original is a smart, impeccably made sci-fi action movie, yes, but I don't know that Revolutions is so different, apart from the fact that it follows pre-established characters, rather than blowing our minds with something all-new. What Scott brushes aside, dismissing as expensive FX hubris, is the movie's visual feast; the different worlds of this series make it more than mindless action. The third film is still amazing to look at, from quiet moments inside the purgatory-like train station to the noisiest underground battle sequences to the creepy robot-inhabited earth's surface. Like its immediate predecessor, Revolutions is far from perfect. The Wachowskis give over a surprising, disappointing amount of time to newer and less interesting freedom-fighters when we want to follow Neo, Trinity, and several characters introduced in Reloaded. They also leave far more to interpretation than necessary for a movie that is essentially about humans going to war against robots. But they also give us that massive, teeming robot war, and I have to admit that my inner fifteen-year-old was thrilled by this. I can take a little bit of hokum with all of the visual invention and mind-bending philosophy; it comes with the territory.

Read All 101 Reader Reviews

🕮 Internet

(cont'd)

(continued)

Considering Genre and Design

1. How effective is the overall visual layout of this Web review? Does the layout make you want to read more? Why?
2. What would make the review more visually appealing?
3. The original review was surrounded by other reviews of *The Matrix Revolutions*. If you can, visit the *New York Times Online* site (www.nytimes.com) and read a few of the reviews that surround jhorst's review. How do the other reviews change your response to this one?

A Writer Shares Her Evaluation: Annlee Lawrence's Final Draft

Here is Annlee Lawrence's final draft. Note that she has addressed the questions and concerns that her classmates had, adding information and examples based on their suggestions.

ANNLEE LAWRENCE

Who Has the Healthiest Burger?

Did you know that McDonald's Corporation operates more than thirty thousand restaurants in more than one hundred countries on six continents? In the United States, McDonald's represents 43% of the total fast-food market (Super-Size Me). Restaurants that are part of the McDonald's organization feed more than forty-six million people a day—more than the entire population of Spain. While the global reach of McDonald's and other fast-food chains is impressive, it is also dangerous. As Surgeon General David Satcher comments, "Fast food is a major contributor to the obesity epidemic" (Super-Size Me).

It's no wonder that 60% of Americans are overweight or obese. Obesity, if left unchecked, will soon surpass smoking as the leading cause of preventable death in America. So why can't we seem to stay away from our beloved Big Macs or Whoppers? Probably because our lives demand it at times. Busy Americans often don't have time to prepare a home-cooked meal, so they rely on fast food to fit in with their fast-paced lives. Unfortunately, then, fast food is a part of today's society, but obesity can be avoided through moderation of consumption. According to guidelines published by the Office of the Surgeon General, most fast food contains high—and therefore unhealthy—levels of calories, fat, and cholesterol, three dangerous aspects of an unhealthy lifestyle. But some fast-food meals are not as bad for you as others. For this evaluation, I chose three popular meals: the Whopper Combo from Burger King, Wendy's Classic Single Combo, and McDonald's Quarter Pounder Combo.

When I researched the nutritional content of these three meals, I found that all three have high calorie content (see Fig. 1). The Whopper Combo from Burger King has been a favorite of Americans for generations. But is it as good for your body as it is to your taste buds? When I researched the nutritional information, I discovered that this meal has a grand total of 1260 calories. By contrast, Wendy's Classic Single Combo has 990 calories, and McDonald's Quarter Pounder Combo has 980. The Burger King Whopper meal not only has the highest calorie count, it also has the highest fat content at 58 grams of total fat (see Fig. 2). The next lowest is Wendy's Combo meal at 41 grams of total fat. The lowest of the three is McDonald's Quarter Pounder Combo at 34 grams of fat.

Last but not least is the cholesterol content (see Fig. 3). A high level of cholesterol in the blood can increase the risk of heart disease. Once again, the Burger King Whopper meal has the highest level at 85 milligrams. McDonald's Quarter Pounder Combo has the next highest

3

4

One of Lawrence's classmates commented on her criteria:

These seem like good criteria, but why did you choose them? Do you need a stronger reason for your criteria here?

Notice how Lawrence has added support for her criteria: information from the Surgeon General's guidelines.

One peer reviewer had this comment:

This is a lot of statistics . . . Can you maybe give all this in a table or chart?

Note how Lawrence put that data into three charts.

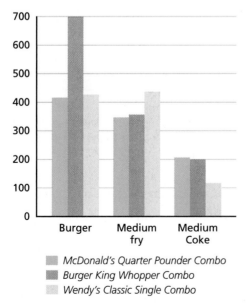

Fig. 1 Total calories in three fast-food meals.

Legend:
- McDonald's Quarter Pounder Combo
- Burger King Whopper Combo
- Wendy's Classic Single Combo

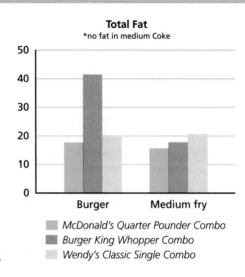

Fig. 2   Total fat in three fast-food meals.

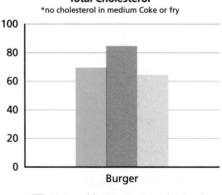

Fig. 3   Total cholesterol in three fast-food meals.

Lawrence's classmate felt the ending of her first draft had problems:

Seems like the ending contradicts the rest of your essay. Why is fast food good for America? The ending seems wrong here.

She has made a slight change here to address this comment.

level at 70 milligrams, and this time Wendy's meal has the lowest level of cholesterol at 65 milligrams.

So if you are in a hurry and feel like grabbing a burger, you are prob-   5
ably better off getting the McDonald's Quarter Pounder meal, which has fewer calories and lower fat content than the other two meals. This doesn't mean, however, that you should make a habit of eating at McDonald's or any other fast-food restaurant chain, especially if you

have a genetic predisposition to high cholesterol levels. Obviously, as the movie <u>Super-Size Me</u> proved, even the "healthy" fast food isn't good for you when consumed on a regular basis. But if eaten in moderation, fast food is one of the best things to happen to busy Americans.

Works Cited

AOA Fact Sheets. American Obesity Association. 2 May 2005. 14 Oct. 2005. <http://www.obesity.org/subs/fastfacts/obesity_US.shtml>.

<u>Burger King Nutritional Information</u>. 18 Aug. 2004. <http://www.bk.com/ Nutrition/PDFs/brochure.pdf>.

<u>McDonald's USA Nutrition Facts for Popular Menu Items</u>. 3 Apr. 2005. <http://www.mcdonalds.com/app_controller.nutrition.index1 .html>.

<u>McDonald's Investor Fact Sheet 2006</u>. 14 Oct. 2005. <http://mcd.mobular .net/mcd/90/8/26/>.

<u>Super-Size Me</u>. Dir. Morgan Spurlock. Hart Sharp Video. 2004.

United States. Office of the Surgeon General. <u>Dietary Guidelines for Americans</u> 2005. 12 Jan. 2005. 10 Apr. 2005. <http://www.healthierus.gov/ dietaryguidelines/index.html>.

<u>Wendy's U.S. Nutrition Information</u>. 3 Apr. 2005. <http://www.wendys .com/food/US_Nutrition_2003.pdf>.

One of Lawrence's classmates pointed out that she had problems with her documentation:

Don't you have a quote in the first paragraph from the Surgeon General? There's no citation for it here.

Her revised list includes a citation for the Surgeon General's *Dietary Guidelines*.

QUESTIONS FOR WRITING AND DISCUSSION

Rhetorical Knowledge: The Writer's Situation and Rhetoric

1. **Audience:** Who do you see as Lawrence's audience? What can you point to in the text that supports your claim?

2. **Purpose:** Lawrence seems to have another purpose for her evaluation, in addition to writing this paper for a class assignment: to help her classmates. How well does she fulfill that larger purpose?

3. **Voice and tone:** What voice/tone strategies does Lawrence use to establish her ethos? What passages can you point to in the text that help demonstrate her credibility on this issue? How could she have increased her credibility?

4. **Responsibility:** How effectively does Lawrence represent the facts about calories, and other nutritional data. in her evaluation?

5. **Context and format:** Lawrence is writing as a college student who eats fast food. How does that affect her credibility in this evaluation?

Critical Thinking: Your Personal Response

1. What is your initial response to Lawrence's essay? How much do you agree with her evaluation? Why?

2. What is the strongest part of Lawrence's evaluation? Why?

3. Has your thinking about eating fast-food hamburgers changed, now that you have read Lawrence's evaluation? In what ways?

Critical Thinking: The Writer's Ideas

1. Lawrence focuses on only three criteria for her evaluation. How sufficient is that, do you think, for her to construct an effective evaluation? Why?

2. Examine how Lawrence uses evidence and information about fast-food hamburgers. How well can you understand what she means?

Composing Processes and Knowledge of Conventions: The Writer's Strategies

1. How effective is the evidence that Lawrence provides? What other evidence might she have used?

2. How effectively does Lawrence use the quotation and information from the Surgeon General?

3. What in Lawrence's essay was most persuasive to you? What was least persuasive? Why?

Inquiry and Research: Ideas for Further Exploration

1. What other criteria might have been more useful to Lawrence in her evaluation of fast-food hamburgers? Why?

2. In no more than five pages, evaluate another fast-food item: salads offered by several major fast-food chains.

3. Interview several of your classmates, explaining Lawrence's conclusions. What is their reaction to her evaluation? Might it influence their dining decisions in the future?

Self-Assessment: Reflecting on Your Learning Goals

Now that you have constructed a piece of evaluative writing, go back and reconsider your learning goals, which you and your classmates considered at the beginning of this chapter (see pp. 388–89). Then, reflect on all the thinking and writing that you have done in constructing your evaluative paper. To help reflect on the learning goals that you have achieved, respond in writing to the following questions:

Rhetorical Knowledge

- *Audience:* What have you learned about addressing an audience in evaluative writing?

- *Purpose:* What have you learned about the purposes for constructing an evaluation?

- *Rhetorical situation:* Consider some of the aspects of the writing situation that you have to think about, as a writer: How did the writing context affect your evaluative text? How did your choice of subject affect the research you conducted and how you presented your evaluation to your readers?

- *Voice and tone:* How would you describe your voice in this essay? Your tone? How do they contribute to the effectiveness of your evaluation?

- *Context, medium, and genre:* How did your context determine the medium and genre you chose, and how did those decisions affect your writing?

Critical Thinking, Reading, and Writing

- *Learning/inquiry:* How did you decide what to focus on in your evaluation? Describe the process you went through to focus on a main idea, or thesis. How did you judge what was most and least important in your evaluation?

- *Responsibility:* How did you fulfill your responsibility to your readers?

- *Reading and research:* What did you learn about evaluative writing from the reading selections in this chapter? What research did you conduct? How sufficient was the research you did? Why? What additional research might you have done?

- As a result of writing this evaluation, how have you become a more critical thinker, reader, and writer? What critical thinking, reading, and writing skills do you hope to develop further in your next writing project? How will you work on them?

Composing Processes

- *Invention:* What invention strategies were most useful to you?

- *Organizing your ideas and details:* What organization did you use? How successful was it?

- *Revising:* What one revision did you make that you are most satisfied with? What are the strongest and the weakest parts of the paper or other piece of writing you wrote for this chapter? Why? If you could go back and make an additional revision, what would it be?

- *Working with peers:* How did your instructor or peer readers help you by making comments and suggestions about your writing? List some examples of useful comments that you received. List some examples of how you revised your evaluation based on those comments and suggestions. How could you have made better use of the comments and suggestions you received? How could your peer readers help you more on your next assignment? How might you help them more, in the future, with the comments and suggestions you make on their texts?

- Did you use photographs or other visuals to help explain your evaluation to readers? If so, what did you learn about incorporating these elements?

- What "writerly habits" have you developed, modified, or improved on as you constructed the writing assignment for this chapter? How will you change your future writing activities, based on what you have learned about yourself?

Conventions

- *Editing:* What sentence problem did you find most frequently in your writing? How will you avoid that problem in future assignments?

- *Genre:* What conventions of the genre you were using, if any, gave you problems?

- *Documentation:* Did you use sources for your paper? If so, what documentation style did you use? What problems, if any, did you have with it?

If you are preparing a course portfolio, file your written reflections so that you can return to them when you next work on your portfolio.

Annlee Lawrence Reflects on Her Writing

In this brief excerpt from her reflective writing, notice how Annlee Lawrence addresses her knowledge and skills, as well as some connections between the academic and personal areas of her life:

Evaluations are always based on a set of criteria, and the item is then "tested" or compared to the list of criteria. Now that I look back over this writing assignment, I think I could have defined my criteria more effectively—with more details and examples. And maybe I should have used more than the three criteria—calories, fat, and cholesterol—than I did. I expect I also could have done more research, too, to better explain even those three criteria to my classmates.

I could have spent more time finding things out from other fast-food chains—more research would have helped. But I also learned a lot about how to effectively conduct research, and what to do with that information I found for my evaluation paper. I learned how to keep separate computer files for all sorts of stuff, which really helped when I had to put it all together in the paper.

I also should have started the project much sooner—I waited until a couple of days before the draft was due to begin my work. I'd been able to get away with that in the past, but I can't at this level!

I did get a lot of useful comments from my classmates—they asked a lot of good questions and the one about my confusing facts really helped. I had to put that data into some charts and I'd never done that before, so that was useful. That will make it easier for me when I have to make charts and graphs for a future assignment. And those charts added a useful visual element to my paper, too.

Then again, I should have started to revise the day after we had that in-class peer review session, as then their comments and suggestions would have been fresh in my mind. Instead, I again procrastinated. I'll know better next time. I also learned that the better comments I make during peer review, the more help my classmates offer to me. It's kind of a reciprocal thing, I guess.

I also learned a lot about what it means to really logically and fairly evaluate something. I mean, I'd always evaluated things like movies or restaurants, to some extent. We all do that kind of thing. But I'd never evaluated anything like this, which focused on data and other information.

Rhetorical Knowledge

- *Audience:* Your success will partially depend on how accurately you have analyzed your audience. Consider what they already know about your topic, as well as their attitudes toward it. How can you make your audience interested in this cause-and-effect relationship? What might this audience already know or believe about this relationship? How will your audience benefit from what you have to say? What evidence will convince this audience that this cause-and-effect relationship exists?

- *Purpose:* Your main purpose is argumentative: to convince readers that a cause-and-effect relationship exists. Your purpose may be first to identify a cause and then determine its effect(s). Or your purpose may be to determine a series of causes and effects—often called a *causal chain*—where one cause leads to an effect, which then causes a second effect, and so on.

- *Rhetorical situation:* Think about all of the factors that affect where you stand in relation to your subject—what is compelling you to write your causal analysis essay?

- *Writer's voice and tone:* You will need to present yourself as a logical writer who provides reliable information. If readers perceive you as uninformed, illogical, or inflexible, you will lose credibility.

- *Context, medium, and genre:* You will need to decide on the best medium and genre to use to present your causal analysis to the audience you want to reach. Since cause and effect shows relationships between events, visuals such as flowcharts are often an effective way of helping audiences understand the relationships.

Critical Thinking, Reading, and Writing

- *Learning/inquiry:* When you write about causes and effects, you must think critically about whether an actual cause-and-effect relationship exists. It may be coincidental that one event happens right after another or that two phenomena often occur together; the events or phenomena may not have a causal relationship.

- *Responsibility:* You have a responsibility to recognize that causes and effects may be more complex than you first realize. Any given phenomenon or event is likely to have many causes and to produce many effects. Determining what is and is not a cause (or an effect), or determining which of several causes (or effects) is most important, may require considerable time and thought.

- *Reading and research*: As you conduct research about a causal relationship, make sure you understand the nature of the relationship well enough to be able to document the causality. Also, as you conduct research, always ask, "How could X cause Y, specifically?" This question forces you to look for real evidence that one thing causes the other.

Writing Processes

- *Invention*: Begin by recording possible answers to the question you are considering (for example, why do gasoline prices fluctuate?), using an invention strategy such as brainstorming or listing. As you write, you will undoubtedly come up with more questions about a possible cause-and-effect relationship.

- *Organizing your ideas and details*: Once you have recorded some ideas, you can think about how to organize your main points and what supporting evidence you need to provide.

- *Revising*: You will need to read your work with a critical eye, to make certain that it fulfills the assignment and displays the qualities of a good causal analysis.

- *Working with peers*: Peer review is a crucial part of the process of writing a causal analysis because it enables you to get a sense of how an audience will respond to your claim that a cause-and-effect relationship exists. Peers can be especially useful in helping you think critically about possible causes for an effect or possible effects of a cause.

Conventions

- *Editing*: When you edit a causal analysis—or anything that you write—make sure that the subordinate clauses in your paper are attached to independent clauses and are therefore part of complete sentences. The round-robin activity in this chapter will help you look for and correct this type of sentence fragment (p. 513).

- *Genres for cause-and-effect writing*: In your college classes, writing about cause-and-effect relationships is usually academic writing, so you will be required to follow the conventions for an academic essay. Other, nonacademic, writing situations may call for a variety of genres, including memos, essays, Web log (blog) postings, letters to the editor, and even formal position papers.

- *Documentation*: You will probably need to rely on sources outside of your experience, and if you are writing an academic essay, you will be required to cite them using the appropriate documentation style.

Writing to Explain
Causes and Effects

Here is the space weather report from NASA for one day in October 2003:

> Giant sunspots 484 and 486 remain visible on the sun, posing a continued threat for X-class solar explosions. Indeed, on Sunday, Oct. 26, 2003, there were two such blasts—one from each sunspot. The explosions hurled coronal mass ejections (CMEs) into space and somewhat toward Earth.
>
> Because of these events, sky watchers should be alert for auroras during the nights ahead. High-latitude sites such as Alaska, Canada, and U.S. northern border states from Maine to Washington are favored, as usual, but auroras could descend to lower latitudes as well. Forecasters estimate a 25 percent chance of severe geomagnetic storming when the incoming CMEs sweep past Earth and deliver (probably glancing) blows to our planet's magnetic field.

Things happen, and we are often curious about how and why. We wonder what causes natural phenomena such as the northern lights (aurora borealis), lightning, or the seasons. We want to know what caused the extinction of species such as mammoths, Neanderthals, or passenger pigeons. We have a vested interest in knowing the causes of diseases such as cancer, Alzheimer's, or schizophrenia. In some cases, we simply want to understand how the world works—how can an event in another part of the world send the Dow Jones Industrial Average up or down?

Consider the events that take place in your life: Why does your rent increase every year? Why did your favorite bookstore close? Why do businesses in certain areas of your city shut down? Why is your old high school looking run-down? Why do some of your classmates seem to be uninterested in school? You are always surrounded by *changes* that occur, *trends* you can observe (and wonder why they happen), *behavior* that is unusual or surprising. All have *causes*, reasons why they happened. In fact *why* is probably the best question you can ask (and continue to ask) as you explore any cause-and-effect relationship. The answers to your "why?" questions will provide the causes of the effect you are examining.

In some cases, discovering the cause is an end in itself. For instance, we may one day know precisely why the dinosaurs became extinct about sixty million years ago, but we may not be able to use that information to change life as it is currently lived on Earth. In other cases, though, we can use information gained from causal analysis to eliminate or avoid the causes of certain effects. For instance, in recent years scientists have come to understand—and share with the public—the strong cause-and-effect relationship between tobacco use and certain kinds of cancer.

In other cases, causes can be difficult to determine and understand. Consider, for example, the following pop culture phenomena:

- Why was Madonna so popular in the 1980s and 1990s (and even in the 2000s)?

- What made the *Lord of the Rings* film trilogy so interesting to so many age groups?

- What made *The DaVinci Code* such a best seller?

 ## Rhetorical Knowledge

When you write about causes and effects, you need to have a specific purpose in mind, some sense of your audience, and an idea of what might be an effective way to substantiate the cause-and-effect relationships you are considering. What details, statistics, charts, or tables might you include to demonstrate that a cause-and-effect relationship exists? How can you prove your claim that a cause-and-effect relationship exists?

 ### Writing about Causes and Effects in Your College Classes

Many of the assignments for your college classes will ask you to determine the causes of an event, a trend, or a phenomenon. Most college disciplines are about asking "why," so your work in determining and explaining causes in this class will help you in your other college courses. Many of your science classes, especially, will focus on why things happen (why nature acts in specific ways, for example). Here are some examples:

- Your political science teacher may ask you to determine the reasons why a particular election turned out the way it did.

- Your dance instructor may ask you to explain why and how dance steps and movement have evolved over time.

- Your business communications teacher may ask you to explain why one restaurant chain produces more revenue than another.

- Your biology instructor may ask you to explain what causes leaves to turn color and drop from trees in certain parts of the world in the fall.

- In a sociology course, you might investigate the possible effects of anti-poverty programs on the crime rate in low-income neighborhoods.

- For a psychology class, you may try to explain why many teenagers post Web logs (blogs), or why so many people feel that they *must* use their cell phones in public places.

Writing about Causes and Effects for Life

Much of the writing constructed in **professional settings** is designed to solve problems. The first step in solving any problem is determining why the problem exists:

- *Why* is quality control so much better at our Pittsburgh plant than it is at the others?

- *Why* can't we increase sales to the level we need to become profitable?

- *Why* are there fewer break-ins in this neighborhood than in that one?

Many professionals in the work world spend a good deal of their time determining causes and effects:

- An attorney asks an expert witness to prepare testimony explaining that road conditions, rather than reckless driving, caused an automobile accident.

- A team of medical researchers writes a paper reporting on a study that reveals a cause-and-effect relationship between Vitamin C deficiency and osteoporosis.

- A teacher wonders why some students have difficulty reading and studies them to find out the causes of their problems.

When writers focus on **community issues,** they often need to find answers to *why* questions: why did one school bond issue pass but another did not, or why did the city council vote the way it did?

Other examples of cause-and-effect writing in civic situations include the following:

- A dog lover writes to the city council to explain that leash laws lead to a decrease in accidental deaths of dogs, as well as a decrease in the number of dogs who bite people.

- A citizens' group submits a written report to the county health board arguing that more restaurant inspections lead to fewer incidences of *E. coli* food poisoning.

- A homeowner writes a letter to the editor of a county newspaper arguing that a nearby golf course is the source of the chemical residue recently discovered in local well water.

You will also encounter many occasions for thinking and writing about causes and effects in **personal settings.** It is critical to understand why things happen. If you can understand why your last relationship was difficult, you may not make the same mistakes in the next one. Journals are an excellent place to explore such cause-and-effect relationships. For example, a young couple might keep a daily journal on the activities of their infant daughter. After a few weeks, when they reread their entries, they might notice a pattern suggesting that when they feed their daughter one kind of formula, she sleeps fewer hours at night.

WRITER'S WORKSHOP

Applying Learning Goals to Cause-and-Effect Writing

As we have seen, writing about causes and effects involves not only determining a question to write about ("Why has the AIDS virus spread so rapidly in Africa?" "Why are there increasing numbers of homeless people in the downtown area?"), but also how you will convince a particular audience that your answer to the question is plausible.

As a group, think of a writing situation in which you need to convince a particular audience to agree with you about the cause-and-effect relationship you have chosen as your subject. Perhaps the situation is a college assignment, a piece of workplace writing, a piece of writing for a civic group or organization, or a personal circumstance. With several of your classmates, discuss your writing situation in terms of the learning goals listed on pages 456–57. How would you address these goals? In what ways does it matter who your reader might be?

Scenarios for Writing: Assignment Options

Your instructor may ask you to complete one or more of the following assignments that call for writing about causes or effects. Each of these assignments is in the form of a scenario, which gives you a sense of who your audience is and what you need to accomplish with your causal analysis. The list of rhetorical considerations on page 468 encourages you to think about your audience; purpose; voice, tone, and point of view; and context, medium, and genre for the scenario you have chosen.

As with the other chapters in this text, we have provided two scenarios focused on academic writing and three scenarios that you might encounter outside of college. Starting on page 492, you will find guidelines for completing whatever assignment option you decide—or are asked to—complete.

Writing for College

In your college courses you will write many kinds of papers. In some, you will consider the causes of effects; in others you will consider the effects of some causes; in still others you will write about series of causes and effects.

SCENARIO 1 An Academic Paper on Causes and Effects in One of Your Other College Courses

Consider the topics that you are studying in your courses this semester that involve causes and effects. To complete this assignment, you must first decide which of those topics interests you and then come up with a question about that topic that will lead you to investigate causes and/or effects. Here are some possibilities:

- **Geology:** What causes an earthquake? What are the effects of continental drift?
- **Music:** How did hip-hop change popular music? What led to the development of jazz (Figure 10.1)?
- **Art:** How did the invention of the camera affect the kinds of painting that artists did in the nineteenth century?
- **Physics:** What causes the lift that makes it possible for airplanes to fly?

FIGURE 10.1 A Musician Playing Jazz on a Clarinet

Alternatively, you might consider some general cause-and-effect relationships that you have noticed in your college community, in a class, in a department, or on campus. For example,

- **College:** Why does the cost of attending college always seem to increase?
- **Community:** Why do some neighbors around the college resent having students rent homes nearby?
- **Classroom:** Why do some students take so long to finish college?

Writing Assignment: For this assignment, you can choose among several options. One possibility is to select an effect and then write about its causes. Another possibility is to select a cause and then write about its effects. Your goal is to convince an audience of instructors and students in the discipline your topic belongs to that your causal analysis is credible.

SCENARIO 2   An Academic Paper about a Personal Interest

This assignment asks you to write about a cause-and-effect relationship from any area of your life for an audience of your classmates. Choose a topic that interests you, raises your curiosity, and that you would like to explore for any reason.

Writing Assignment: Here are some questions about cause-and-effect relationships that interest many people. Even if these particular topics do not interest you, they should get you thinking about other questions—and cause-and-effect relationships—that may intrigue you:

- What caused the Boston Red Sox finally to win a World Series Championship in 2004?
- Why do some entertainment or sports figures engage in self-destructive activities?
- Why are you attending college?
- Why do some of your college classes seem more useful than others?
- What caused you to choose your particular college or university?
- What caused your family to live where they did when you were growing up? What were the effects on you of where you grew up? What caused you to live where you are now?

Writing for Life

In the professional, civic, and personal areas of your life there are many opportunities to write about cause-and-effect relationships because every civic action—a vote, a decision to allow a business to develop a specific piece of property, a new tax—is *caused* by something and has definite, and often unforeseen, *effects*. The same is true for the other two areas of your life.

SCENARIO 3 Civic Writing: A Newsletter to Inform Students and the Administration about a Situation on Campus or in Your Community

Focusing on either your college campus or the community in which your campus is located, consider some civic or public event, phenomenon, trend, or activity that interests you and that will interest your fellow students. You may explore a cause, an effect, or a chain of causes and effects. Here are some possible questions to consider:

- What causes the conflicts between or among certain groups on campus?
- What are the major causes of bicycle-pedestrian collisions on campus or in the community?
- How does the accessibility of campus buildings and facilities affect the lives of students with particular disabilities (Figure 10.2)?
- What has caused the recent growth (or lack of growth) in charitable organizations in your community?

Writing Assignment: Construct a newsletter in which you identify a campus or community problem or other situation and then persuade your readers of

FIGURE 10.2 Accessibility is an Issue for People with Disabilities

the causes of that problem or situation or of its effects. Your goal is to convince your readers that your analysis of the causes and/or effects of this problem or situation is accurate.

Remember that a newsletter can include more than just text—it can include photographs illustrating the issue you are focusing on, tables, charts and graphs, boxes with related information and photographs of people you interview.

SCENARIO 4   Professional Writing: A Report on Causes and/or Effects That Affect Your Employer

Think about the kinds of causes and effects that you encounter on your current job or that you expect to encounter in your future profession. Here are some possibilities to get you thinking:

- What causes a business to succeed or to fail?
- What causes customers to choose one product over similar products that competitors offer?
- What causes employees to remain loyal to an organization?
- What causes a company or an organization to treat its workers well or poorly? What are the effects of the way a manager treats employees?

FIGURE 10.3   What causes or effects do people encounter in the workplace?

- What causes employees to leave a company or other type of organization voluntarily? What are the effects of employees leaving an organization?
- What are the effects of rudeness at work?
- What causes high or low morale in the workplace? What are the effects of high or low morale?

Writing Assignment: Write a report for your supervisor—along with a cover memo—in which you identify a cause-and-effect question important to your organization and write a causal analysis in response to that question. If you are writing about a problem, you need to do more than simply provide information about it (that is an informative paper, covered in Chapter 6), but you do not need to suggest detailed solutions to the problem (that is a proposal, covered in Chapter 11). Your goal is to convince your readers that the causes or effects that you are proposing are plausible.

SCENARIO 5   Personal Writing: A Letter to a Friend or Family Member about the Causes and/or Effects of a Hobby, Habit, Decision, or Behavior

Are you curious about any hobbies, habits, decisions, or behaviors that friends of yours and/or members of your family have or have made? Think about what might cause the hobby, habit, decisions, or behavior and/or what the effects of it (or them) might be. Here are the kinds of questions that you might ask to get started:

- Why does my family love football (or baseball or basketball) so much?
- Why does my family always buy a certain brand of cars or trucks?
- How does a relative's or friend's behavior affect me?
- What are the possible consequences of my aunt's (or uncle's or cousin's) decision not to wear seatbelts?
- What are the possible consequences of a harmful habit that a friend or relative has?
- What have been the effects of a major personal decision I made? What might have been the effects if I had decided differently?
- What causes my friends and me to choose one kind of music over another, one television show or movie over another, or one form of entertainment over another? What are the effects of those choices?

Writing Assignment: Craft a letter to your family member or friend to make him or her aware of a cause-and-effect relationship that touches that person's life in some way. Your topic could be suggested by one of the questions listed above, or you may think of a different question. As you research and write about your topic, your purpose is not to persuade your friend or relative to change some behavior, although that may happen. Your purpose is simply to determine whether a cause-and-effect relationship exists and then to provide evidence for it.

Rhetorical Considerations in Cause-and-Effect Writing

Audience: While your instructor and classmates are your initial audience, you should also consider other audiences for your causal analysis, depending on the scenario you have chosen. What evidence will convince your readers that you are making a valid claim about a cause-and-effect relationship?

Purpose: Your general purpose is to convince readers that a cause-and-effect relationship exists. Beyond that, your purpose is either to establish the causes of something (an effect), to establish the effects of something (a cause), or to show how a series of causes and effects are related. It is critical to provide sufficient evidence to show that a cause-and-effect relationship actually exists.

Voice, Tone, and Point of View: Why are you interested in the cause-and-effect relationship that you have chosen to write about? What preconceptions about it do you have? What are your attitudes toward the topic and the audience? How will you convey those attitudes? Note Juan Williams' reasoned, thoughtful tone in "Brown vs. Board of Education" (p. 473). How does his tone affect whether or not you agree with his reasoning?

Context, Medium, and Genre: Keeping the context of the assignment in mind, decide on a medium and a genre for your writing. How will your writing be used? Obviously, your instructor will use your writing to help determine your grade for the course, so follow his or her instructions carefully. If you are writing for an audience beyond the classroom, consider what will be the most effective way to present your information to this audience. You might write an e-mail message to a friend, prepare a report for colleagues at work, or construct a Web site for members of your community.

For more on choosing a medium and genre, see Chapter 15 and Appendix C.

Critical Thinking, Reading, and Writing

Before you begin to write your causal analysis, you need to consider the qualities of a successful paper of this type. It also helps to read one or more examples of writing about causes and effects to get a feel for this kind of writing. Finally, you might consider how visuals could enhance your causal analysis, as well as the kinds of sources you will need to consult.

The qualities of writing about causes and/or effects include a focused presentation of the effect(s) or cause(s), a clearly stated claim that a cause-and-effect relationship exists, and sufficient evidence to support the claim. The writer also has the responsibility to employ logical thinking and to avoid logical fallacies in making his or her case. These qualities and responsibilities are discussed in the section that follows.

When you write about causes and effects, especially in academic situations, you will almost always need to draw on material from other sources by conducting research. You might consult secondary sources or conduct research in the field. To use your research effectively, read the material critically and evaluate it carefully to make certain that the evidence you are offering as proof really does support your claims. Of course, thinking critically also means that you need to consider other points of view about the cause-and-effect relationship you are writing about and decide whether those views are compatible or in conflict with your views.

Learning the Qualities of Effective Writing about Causes and Effects

When you consider what causes what, or what the effects of something are, you need to build a case in order to convince others that the relationship you see in fact exists. Here are the qualities of writing that analyzes causes and/or effects successfully:

- **Presentation of focused cause(s) or effect(s).** At the beginning of your essay, you need to introduce the event, activity, or phenomenon for which you wish to establish cause(s), or effect(s), or both. To focus the causes or effects, you should limit the time period that you are considering. For instance, in his book *Connections*, James Burke analyzes a series of events that led to the invention of the atomic bomb, beginning with the invention of the stirrup. To cover a series of events in that large a time period, Burke had to write a fairly long book chapter. This does not mean you cannot write about long periods of time (for a geology paper, you almost have to do so), but rather that you always keep the time period in mind as you determine exactly what to focus on. If you were writing a paper for your geology class, for example, and you needed to cover a 1 million-year period, you would not write about what happened every year (!) or even every thousand years, as those time increments are too numerous for such a short paper. Instead, you would probably focus on events that occurred every 100,000 years. The point is that you need to focus on a topic that you can reasonably cover given the limits of your assignment.

- **A clearly stated claim that a cause-and-effect relationship exists.** After you have done enough research to be certain that a cause-and-effect relationship exists, you will be prepared to state the nature of that relationship. State the claim so that readers understand it, especially since they may know little or nothing about your topic. For example, if you were writing about why jazz became popular in the 1920s, you might write that "Jazz grew in popularity in the 1920s because musicians from New Orleans traveled to northern cities, and bands took advantage of the new technology of recorded music to reach a mass audience."

- **Sufficient evidence to support your claim.** To support your claim, present evidence that readers will consider persuasive. Such evidence may consist of the following:

  - The results of empirical studies or historical research found in scholarly and popular books, in journals, and on Web sites.
  - Your own observations, experience, or reading.
  - Testimony from interested or affected parties ("Interviews with other students indicate that . . .") or experts ("Professor X, a noted authority, asserts that . . .").
  - The use of examples that demonstrate that your suggested cause or causes actually do cause the effect.

- **Clear, logical thinking.** It is easy to think illogically about possible cause-and-effect relationships: people often jump to conclusions when they see two events happening at the same time and assume there is a cause-and-effect relationship (see the discussion of *post hoc, ergo propter hoc* in the box on pages 471–72). You will need to think critically when evaluating your proof to make certain you have chosen relevant evidence that comes from reliable sources. Be aware that there are several issues to consider as you search for cause-and-effect relationships:

  - **Does the effect have a single cause, or multiple causes?** Things are rarely as simple as they may first appear to be. More often than not, an effect will have multiple causes. Carefully analyze and thoroughly research all the causes that may contribute to some particular effect.

  - **What are the contributing causes, and do they lead to a precipitating cause?** Often, a number of causes together contribute to what might be called a *precipitating* cause, the final cause that sets the effect in motion. Several contributing causes might set up a single precipitating cause. For example, while the football fan might blame the kicker who missed a last-second field goal for the team's loss of the important game, there surely were many other reasons that contributed to the loss (dropped passes, poor execution of running plays, and other missed opportunities).

  - **Is a particular cause remote or immediate?** It is sometimes useful to examine a chain of causes so that you understand what came first, what happened next, and so on. An event that you might think caused an effect may in fact be removed from it—it may be the cause of an effect that in turn caused the event you are concerned about. Writing down the sequence of causes and effects will help you see the events in the **causal chain** as they happened over time.

- **Is a particular cause necessary or sufficient?** A **necessary cause** is one that must be present for the effect to occur. A **sufficient cause** is one that, if present, always triggers a particular effect. For example, for a teenager to be able to borrow the family car, his or her family must have a car—that cause is *necessary* to the effect of the teenager being able to borrow it. The teenager's forgetting to put gas into the family car before bringing it back, however, is a sufficient cause for the parents to refuse to lend it again; other causes would be *sufficient* as well (bringing the car home dirty or after running into a utility pole and denting the fender are also possible causes for the parents' decision), so forgetfulness is not a necessary cause.

- **Anticipation of possible objections or alternative explanations.** While your causal analysis may be highly plausible, there are almost always other possible causes for the same effect or other possible effects of the cause that you are considering. Be prepared to acknowledge those other potential causes or effects and to show why your causes or effects are more likely. For example, you might argue that the third *Lord of the Rings* film, *Return of the King*, caused more interest in Tolkien's work than the other two films in the series. Others might suggest that you are wrong, that the first film in the series, *The Fellowship of the Ring*, caused more interest, citing total film revenues to prove their point. How might you refute this claim? One way to do so would be to acknowledge it and then provide other examples that prove your point. You might note an increase in total book sales following release of the third film as well as other data such as an increase in DVD and video rentals and sales.

For more on writing effective arguments, including claims, evidence, types of appeals, and counterarguments, see Chapter 14.

In a computer file, put the above qualities of effective writing into your own words, and then refer to those notes as you conduct research and write your paper.

A WRITER'S RESPONSIBILITY

Determining True Causes and Effects

Events that happen at the same time may or may not be related causally—you need to take care to be sure you are not asserting a relationship that does not in fact exist, or mistaking a cause for an effect, or vice versa. An ethical writer works diligently to avoid the logical fallacy of *post hoc, ergo propter hoc*, a Latin phrase meaning "after this, therefore because of this." If you argue that X caused Y simply because X preceded Y, you are guilty of this logical fallacy. Here are some examples:

(cont'd)

(continued)

- Christopher reads about an explosion at a local power plant and notes that he has recently developed a rash. He assumes that contamination from the explosion is causing his rash. However, there is no evidence that the explosion is related to the rash.
- After receiving a vaccination against whooping cough, an infant develops a high fever, which her parents attribute to the vaccine. However, the child has actually caught a virus from her older sister; the timing of the fever was coincidental.

What are some other examples of *post hoc, ergo propter hoc* thinking that you have recently witnessed?

Often in cases where two events happen at the same time and are probably causally related, it still may not be obvious which is the cause and which is the effect. For instance, educational experts have observed that students with low self-esteem often underperform in school. But do people who have low self-esteem perform poorly in school because they have low self-esteem, as has been assumed in the past? Or do they have low self-esteem because they perform poorly in school, as some psychologists now believe? A responsible writer needs to consider both of these possibilities.

Reading, Inquiry, and Research: Learning from Texts That Explain Cause-and-Effect Relationships

The readings that follow are examples of writing about causes and effects. As you read them, consider the following questions.

- To what extent is the writer focused on causes, on effects, or on both causes and effects? What specific elements of the selection support your judgment?
- What parts of the selection seem the strongest? Why do you think so?
- How can you use the techniques of cause-and-effect writing exemplified here in your writing?

As you read an essay, take notes, jot down questions, and make observations about the essay, preferably in a computer file. Then, if you want to use the information in your writing, you will already have the main points in a digital format.

JUAN WILLIAMS

The Ruling That Changed America

Juan Williams is the author of *Thurgood Marshall: American Revolutionary*, the non-fiction bestseller *Eyes on the Prize: America's Civil Rights Years, 1954–1965*, and *This Far by Faith: Stories from the African American Religious Experience*. He was born in Colon, Panama, but moved to Brooklyn, New York, in 1958. In an interview for the Web site *Tolerance.org*, Williams said, "Since I was born in 1954 my whole education is tied to the Brown case. I attended public schools in Brooklyn, New York, during the 1960s [and] those schools were very integrated. . . . I went to schools with Jewish children, Irish children, Italian children, and a stunning range of immigrant children from around the world."

Williams attended Haverford College and graduated with a degree in philosophy in 1976. For more than 20 years, Williams was an editorial writer, op-ed contributor, and White House reporter for the *Washington Post*. His work has appeared in *Newsweek, Fortune, Atlantic Monthly, Ebony, Gentlemen's Quarterly*, and the *New Republic*. Williams is currently a senior correspondent for National Public Radio.

This essay originally appeared in the April 2004 issue of the *American School Board Journal*.

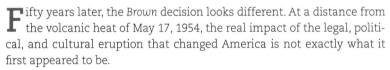

Fifty years later, the *Brown* decision looks different. At a distance from the volcanic heat of May 17, 1954, the real impact of the legal, political, and cultural eruption that changed America is not exactly what it first appeared to be.

On that Monday in May, the high court's ruling outlawing school segregation in the United States generated urgent news flashes on the radio and frenzied black headlines in special editions of afternoon newspapers. One swift and unanimous decision by the top judges in the land was going to end segregation in public schools. Southern politicians reacted with such fury and fear that they immediately called the day "Black Monday."

South Carolina Gov. James Byrnes, who rose to political power with passionate advocacy of segregation, said the decision was "the end of civilization in the South as we have known it." Georgia Gov. Herman Talmadge struck an angry tone. He said Georgia had no intention of allowing "mixed race" schools as long as he was governor. And he touched on Confederate pride from the days when the South went to war with the federal government over slavery by telling supporters that the Supreme Court's ruling was not law in his state; he said it was "the first step toward national suicide." The Brown decision should be regarded, he said, as nothing but a "mere scrap of paper."

Meanwhile, newspapers for black readers reacted with exultation. 4
"The Supreme Court decision is the greatest victory for the Negro people
since the Emancipation Proclamation," said Harlem's *Amsterdam News*. A
writer in the *Chicago Defender* explained, "neither the atomic bomb nor
the hydrogen bomb will ever be as meaningful to our democracy." And
Thurgood Marshall, the NAACP lawyer who directed the legal fight that
led to *Brown*, predicted the end of segregation in all American public
schools by the fall of 1955.

Slow Progress, Backward Steps

Ten years later, however, very little school integration had taken place. 5
True to the defiant words of segregationist governors, the Southern states
had hunkered down in a massive resistance campaign against school
integration. Some Southern counties closed their schools instead of
allowing blacks and whites into the same classrooms. In other towns,
segregationist academies opened, and most if not all of the white children left the public schools for the racially exclusive alternatives. And in
most places, the governors, mayors, and school boards found it easy
enough to just ask for more time before integrating schools.

That slow-as-molasses approach worked. In 1957, President Eisen- 6
hower had to send troops from the 101st Airborne into Little Rock just to
get nine black children safely into Central High School. Only in the late
'60s, under the threat of losing federal funding, did large-scale school
integration begin in Southern public schools. And in many places, in both
the North and the South, black and white students did not go to school
together until a federal court ordered schoolchildren to ride buses
across town to bring the races together.

Today, 50 years later, a study by the Civil Rights Project at Harvard 7
University finds that the percentage of white students attending public
schools with Hispanic or black students has steadily declined since 1988.
In fact, the report concludes that school integration in the United States
is "lower in 2000 than in 1970, before busing for racial balance began." In
the South, home to the majority of America's black population, there is
now less school integration than there was in 1970. The Harvard report
concluded, "At the beginning of the 21st century, American schools are
now 12 years into the process of continuous resegregation."

Today, America's schools are so heavily segregated that more than 8
two-thirds of black and Hispanic students are in schools where a majority of the students are not white. And today, most of the nation's white
children attend a school that is almost 80 percent white. Hispanics are
now the most segregated group of students in the nation because they
live in highly concentrated clusters.

At the start of the new century, 50 years after Brown shook the nation, segregated housing patterns and an increase in the number of black and brown immigrants have concentrated minorities in impoverished big cities and created a new reality of public schools segregated by race and class.

The Real Impact of Brown

So, if *Brown* didn't break apart school segregation, was it really the earthquake that it first appeared to be?

Yes. Today, it is hard to even remember America before *Brown* because the ruling completely changed the nation. It still stands as the laser beam that first signaled that the federal government no longer gave its support to racial segregation among Americans.

Before Brown, the federal government lent its power to enforcing the laws of segregation under an 1896 Supreme Court ruling that permitted "separate but equal" treatment of blacks and whites. Blacks and whites who tried to integrate factories, unions, public buses and trains, parks, the military, restaurants, department stores, and more found that the power of the federal government was with the segregationists.

Before Brown, the federal government had struggled even to pass a law banning lynching.

But after the Supreme Court ruled that segregation in public schools was a violation of the Constitution, the federal attitude toward enforcing second-class citizenship for blacks shifted on the scale of a change in the ocean's tide or a movement in the plates of the continents. Once the highest court in the land said equal treatment for all did not allow for segregation, then the lower courts, the Justice Department, and federal prosecutors, as well as the FBI, all switched sides. They didn't always act to promote integration, but they no longer used their power to stop it.

An irreversible shift had begun, and it was the direct result of the *Brown* decision.

The change in the attitude of federal officials created a wave of anticipation among black people, who became alert to the possibility of achieving the long-desired goal of racial equality. There is no way to offer a hard measure of a change in attitude. But the year after *Brown*, Rosa Parks refused to give up her seat to a white man on a racially segregated bus in Montgomery, Ala. That led to a yearlong bus boycott and the emergence of massive, nonviolent protests for equal rights. That same year, Martin Luther King Jr. emerged as the nation's prophet of civil rights for all Americans.

Even when a black 14-year-old, Emmit Till, was killed in Mississippi for supposedly whistling at a white woman, there was a new reaction to old racial brutality. One of Till's elderly relatives broke with small-town Southern tradition and dared to take the witness stand and testify against the white men he saw abduct the boy. Until Brown, the simple act of a black man standing up to speak against a white man in Mississippi was viewed as futile and likely to result in more white-on-black violence.

The sense among black people—and many whites as well—that a new era had opened created a new boldness. Most black parents in Little Rock did not want to risk harm to their children by allowing them to join in efforts to integrate Central High. But working with local NAACP officials, the parents of nine children decided it was a new day and time to make history. That same spirit of new horizons was at work in 1962 when James Meredith became the first black student to enroll at the University of Mississippi. And in another lurch away from the traditional support of segregation, the federal government sent troops as well as Justice Department officials to the university to protect Meredith's rights.   18

The next year, when Alabama Gov. George Wallace felt the political necessity of making a public stand against integration at the University of Alabama, he stood only briefly in the door to block black students and then stepped aside in the face of federal authority. That was another shift toward a world of high hopes for racial equality; again, from the perspective of the 21st century, it looks like another aftershock of the *Brown* decision.   19

The same psychology of hope infected young people, black and white, nationwide in the early '60s. The Freedom Rides, lunch-counter sit-ins, and protest marches for voting rights all find their roots in Brown. So, too, did the racially integrated 1963 March on Washington at which Martin Luther King Jr. famously said he had a vision of a promised land where the sons of slaves and the sons of slave owners could finally join together in peace. The desire for change became a demand for change in the impatient voice of Malcolm X, the militant Black Muslim who called for immediate change by violent means if necessary.   20

In 1964, a decade after *Brown*, the Civil Rights Act was passed by a Congress beginning to respond to the changing politics brought about by the landmark decision. The next year, 1965, the wave of change had swelled to the point that Congress passed the Voting Rights Act.   21

Closer to the Mountaintop

This sea change in black and white attitudes toward race also had an impact on culture. Churches began to grapple with the Christian and Jewish principles of loving thy neighbor, even if thy neighbor had a different color skin. Major league baseball teams no longer feared a fan revolt if they allowed more than one black player on a team. Black writers,   22 actors, athletes, and musicians—ranging from James Baldwin to the Supremes and Muhammad Ali—began to cross over into the mainstream of American culture.

The other side of the change in racial attitudes was white support for equal rights. College-educated young white people in the '60s often defined themselves by their willingness to embrace racial equality. Bob Dylan sang about the changing times as answers "blowing in the wind." Movies like "Guess Who's Coming to Dinner" found major audiences among all races. And previously all-white private colleges and universities began opening their doors to black students. The resulting arguments over affirmative action in college admissions led to the Supreme Court's 1978 decision in the *Bakke* case, which outlawed the use of quotas, and its recent ruling that the University of Michigan can take race into account as one factor in admitting students to its law school. The court has also had to deal with affirmative action in the business world, in both hiring and contracts—again as a result of questions of equality under the Constitution raised by *Brown*.

But the most important legacy of the *Brown* decision, by far, is the growth of an educated black middle class. The number of black people graduating from high school and college has soared since *Brown*, and the incomes of blacks have climbed steadily as a result. Home ownership and investment in the stock market among black Americans have rocketed since the 1980s. The political and economic clout of that black middle class continues to bring America closer to the mountaintop vision of racial equality that Dr. King might have dreamed of 50 years ago.

The Supreme Court's May 17, 1954, ruling in *Brown* remains a landmark legal decision. But it is much more than that. It is the "Big Bang" of all American history in the 20th century.

QUESTIONS FOR WRITING AND DISCUSSION

Rhetorical Knowledge: The Writer's Situation and Rhetoric

1. **Audience:** Williams is writing for an audience that, more likely than not, takes the decision in *Brown vs. Board of Education* for granted. How does he show his audience the real importance of the decision?

2. **Purpose:** Williams wants readers to understand that even if U.S. public schools are still largely segregated, *Brown vs. Board of Education* was perhaps the most important Supreme Court decision of the twentieth century. How successful is he in convincing you?

3. **Voice and tone:** Williams begins his article with measured language, much as you'd expect from a newspaper reporter. He then intersperses

his reporting with several short, one-sentence paragraphs of commentary (for example, see paragraphs 13, 15). How does this tone affect your response to what you read?

4. **Responsibility:** Part of what Williams needs to do is to make sure his readers understand the social situation in the United States in 1954. How effectively does he do that?

5. **Context and format:** This essay is written as a retrospective, looking back over U.S. history in the fifty years since the Supreme Court decision. How sufficiently does Williams provide the historical background for you as readers today? How well does he establish the appropriate context?

Critical Thinking: Your Personal Response

1. Before reading Williams's article, how aware were you of the wide impact of *Brown vs. Board of Education*? Can you think of another Supreme Court ruling that has had as significant an impact? What was it and what was the impact?

2. If Williams is right, and *Brown vs. Board of Education* had such a far-reaching effect, why do you think the public schools are now more segregated than they were in 1970?

3. What impact has *Brown vs. Board of Education* had on you, on one of your family members, or on your close friends?

Critical Thinking: The Writer's Ideas

1. Williams tries to show that the impact of *Brown vs. Board of Education* went beyond education. To what extent was the decision a sign of the times—an effect? To what extent was the Supreme Court caught up in the mood of the country? To what extent did the decision itself cause other effects?

2. At the end, Williams asserts that *Brown vs. Board of Education* was instrumental in helping to establish the emerging black middle class. Given this observation, and given that school enrollment patterns are determined by housing patterns that depend on economic status, why are schools more segregated today?

3. Once the Court ruled in *Brown vs. Board of Education*, Williams asserts that the attitude of the whole federal government changed. How might a change in the attitude and actions of federal agencies—even if that change means they become neutral—lead to inevitable social change?

Composing Processes and Knowledge of Conventions: The Writer's Strategies

1. Because for many people, fifty years after the fact, *Brown vs. Board of Education* is simply an entry in history books, how does Williams make the decision real for his current readers?

2. Williams structures his argument to show that *Brown vs. Board of Education* did not accomplish what it intended, but that it eventually did more. How effective is his argument? Why?

3. Williams mentions quite a few names: Talmadge, Wallace, Marshall, Meredith, and others. How familiar are you with those names? How does including them help Williams make his point?

Inquiry and Research: Ideas for Further Exploration

1. Investigate other Supreme Court decisions. Which seem to have had greater impact than expected at the time they were made? What was the impact?

2. Conduct a search at your library that focuses on recent appointments to the Supreme Court. What effect have these appointments had on the Court's decisions?

BRUCE NUSSBAUM

Where Are the Jobs?

Bruce Nussbaum is the editorial page editor at *BusinessWeek*, and author of the book *Good Intentions: How Big Business and the Medical Establishment Are Corrupting the Fight against AIDS*. In 2005, Nussbaum was honored with a place on the "I.D. Forty," which is the *International Design* magazine's list of the forty most influential people in the world of design. This essay originally appeared in *BusinessWeek* in 2004.

Americans live in a faith-based economy. We believe deeply in educa- 1 tion, innovation, risk-taking, and plain hard work as the way to a better life. But that faith is being eroded. The link between strong growth and job creation appears to be broken, and we don't know what's wrong with it.

Profits are soaring, yet no one is hiring. Angry voices are blaming Benedict Arnold CEOs who send jobs to India and China. If highly educated "knowledge" workers in Silicon Valley are losing their jobs, who is really safe?

The truth is that we are living through a moment of maximum uncertainty. The economy is at an inflection point as new forces act upon it. Yet the shape and impact of these forces remains unknown. Outsourcing looms large as a potential threat because no one knows how many jobs and which industries are vulnerable. And productivity seems problematic because it's hard to see where the rewards for all the cost-cutting and hard work are going. Meanwhile, the Next Big Thing that is supposed to propel the economy and job growth forward after the Internet boom isn't obvious. As a result, CEOs are reluctant to place big bets on the future. Workers hunker down. And those laid off are at a loss trying to retrain. How can they, when they don't know where the new jobs will be and who will be hiring? It's not even clear what college students should major in anymore. No wonder this feels like a new age of uncertainty.

The Real Culprit

Yet there are things we do know. The real culprit in this jobless recovery is productivity, not offshoring. Unlike most previous business cycles, productivity has continued to grow at a fast pace right through the downturn and into recovery. One percentage point of productivity growth can eliminate up to 1.3 million jobs a year. With productivity growing at an annual rate of 3 percent to 3.5 percent rather than the expected 2 percent to 2.5 percent, the reason for the jobs shortfall becomes clear: Companies are using information technology to cut costs—and that means less labor is needed. Of the 2.7 million jobs lost over the past three years, only 300,000 have been from outsourcing, according to Forrester Research Inc. People rightly fear that jobs in high tech and services will disappear just as manufacturing jobs did. Perhaps so. But odds are it will be productivity rather than outsourcing that does them in.

We know also where the benefits of rising productivity are going: higher profits, lower inflation, rising stocks, and, ultimately, loftier prices for houses. In short, productivity is generating wealth, not employment. Corporate profits as a share of national income are at an all-time high. So is net worth for many individuals. Consumer net worth hit a new peak, at $45 trillion—up 75 percent since 1995—and consumers have more than recouped their losses from the bust.

We know, too, that outsourcing isn't altogether a bad thing. In the '90s, high-tech companies farmed out the manufacture of memory chips, computers, and telecom equipment to Asia. This lowered the cost of tech gear, raising demand and spreading the IT revolution. The same will probably happen with software. Outsourcing will cut prices and make the next generation of IT cheaper and more available. This will generate greater productivity and growth. In fact, as venture capitalists increasingly insist that all IT startups have an offshore component, the cost of innovation should fall sharply, perhaps by half.

We know something about the kinds of jobs that could migrate to Asia and those that will stay home. In the '90s, the making of customized chips and gear that required close contact with clients remained in the U.S., while production of commodity products was outsourced. Today, the Internet and cheaper telecom permit routine service work to be done in Bangalore. But specialized jobs that require close contact with clients, plus an understanding of U.S. culture, will likely remain. 6

America has been at economic inflection points many times in the past. These periods of high job anxiety were eventually followed by years of surging job creation. The faith Americans have in innovation, risk-taking, education, and hard work has been sustained again and again by strong economic performance. 7

There's no question that today's jobless recovery is causing many people real pain. The number of discouraged workers leaving the workforce is unprecedented. Labor-force participation is down among precisely the most vulnerable parts of the workforce—younger and nonwhite workers. Some are going back to school, but many are simply giving up after fruitless searches for decent jobs. If the participation rate were at its March 2001 level, there would be 2.7 million more workers in the labor force looking for jobs. This would push the unemployment rate up to 7.4 percent, not the current 5.6 percent. 8

History has shown time and again that jobs follow growth, but not necessarily in a simple, linear fashion. America has a dynamic, fast-changing economy that embodies Joseph A. Schumpeter's ideal of creative destruction. We are now experiencing the maximum pain from the wreckage of outmoded jobs while still awaiting the innovations that will generate the work of the future. While America's faith in its innovation economy has often been tested, it has never been betrayed. Given the chance, the economy will deliver the jobs and prosperity that it has in the past. 9

QUESTIONS FOR WRITING AND DISCUSSION

Rhetorical Knowledge: The Writer's Situation and Rhetoric

1. **Audience:** Nussbaum wrote this piece for the readers of *BusinessWeek*. What does he do to appeal to that audience? How might this particular

audience feel more comfortable about Nussbaum's views than other audiences?

2. **Purpose:** Nussbaum is trying to allay fears that outsourcing is causing significant harm to the American economy. How successfully does he fulfill his purpose? Why?

3. **Voice and tone:** How would you describe Nussbaum's tone? What can you cite from his essay to illustrate what you mean?

4. **Responsibility:** As a writer, Nussbaum has a responsibility to his readers when he presents a causal argument to make sure his facts are right—that X really caused Y. How responsibly has he done that? What does he do to convince you that the real problem with the job market is that Americans are more productive than ever?

5. **Context and format:** This piece originally appeared as an article in a weekly magazine. As a result, it is necessarily tied to the time frame in which it was written and the form expected by the magazine. How timely is Nussbaum's argument? Why? How effective would Nussbaum's argument have been if he had chosen a different format such as a blog? Why?

Critical Thinking: Your Personal Response

1. As college students, you will be entering the job market in the next several years. What does Nussbaum say either to encourage or discourage you about your prospects?

2. Based on your interpretation of Nussbaum's analysis, what specific kinds of jobs do you think will remain in the United States? On what do you base your prediction?

3. What factors besides worker productivity and outsourcing do you think will influence the job market in the future?

Critical Thinking: The Writer's Ideas

1. Nussbaum's central idea is that increased worker productivity in the United States, not outsourcing, is the primary cause for the reduction in job growth. How believable is he? Why?

2. Nussbaum wrote this article in 2004. You now have the advantage of looking back to see if he was right. What do you think?

3. Ultimately, Nussbaum asserts that since the U.S. economy has shown resilience in the past, it will do so in the future. How believable is he? What proof does he offer? What additional proof would you like to see?

Composing Processes and Knowledge of Conventions: The Writer's Strategies

1. Nussbaum's first sentence uses the phrase "faith-based economy." His closing paragraph returns to the notion that we need to have faith that our economy will rebound—even if it takes some time. How effective do you find the strategy of ending an essay with an echo of where it began? Why?

2. The basic argument that Nussbaum presents is that the cause of the downturn in job creation is a significant increase in worker productivity. How effectively has he presented evidence to make a convincing case? Why?

3. The title of this article is "Where Are the Jobs?" How directly does the article address that question? What evidence can you offer to support your judgment?

Inquiry and Research: Ideas for Further Exploration

1. What factors besides productivity and outsourcing might have an impact on job creation?

2. Nussbaum suggests that we all just need to have faith in the resiliency of the American economy. What examples might justify his view? What examples might contradict his view?

3. In your college library, search for other essays on Nussbaum's topic. In no more than two pages, explain how their comments relate to Nussbaum's ideas.

NEAL GABLER

How Urban Myths Reveal Society's Fears

A well-known film critic and television personality, Neal Gabler has written articles for a number of publications, including the *New York Times, Esquire, New York Magazine, Vogue, Salon, Us,* and *Playboy.* His books include *An Empire of Their Own: How the Jews Invented Hollywood* (1988), *Winchell: Gossip, Power and the Culture of Celebrity* (1994), *Life the Movie: How Entertainment Conquered Reality* (1998), and *Walt Disney: The Triumph of American Imagination* (2006). The following essay was originally published in the *Los Angeles Times* in 1995.

The story goes like this: During dinner at an opulent wedding reception, the groom rises from the head table and shushes the crowd. Everyone naturally assumes he is about to toast his bride and thank his guests. Instead, he solemnly announces that there has been a change of plan. He and his bride will be taking separate honeymoons and, when they return, the marriage will be annulled. The reason for this sudden turn of events, he says, is taped to the bottom of everyone's plate. The stunned guests quickly flip their dinnerware to discover a photo—of the bride *in flagrante*[1] with the best man.

At least that is the story that has been recently making the rounds up and down the Eastern seaboard and as far west as Chicago. Did this really happen? A *Washington Post* reporter who tracked the story was told by one source that it happened at a New Hampshire hotel. But then another source swears it happened in Medford, Mass. Then again another suggests a banquet hall outside Schenectady, N.Y. Meanwhile, a sophisticated couple in Manhattan has heard it happened at the Pierre.

In short, the whole thing appears to be another urban myth, one of those weird tales that periodically catch the public imagination. Alligators swarming the sewers after people have flushed the baby reptiles down the toilet. The baby-sitter who gets threatening phone calls that turn out to be coming from inside the house. The woman who turns out to have a nest of black-widow spiders in her beehive hairdo. The man who falls asleep and awakens to find his kidney has been removed. The rat that gets deep-fried and served by a fast-food outlet. Or, in a variation, the mouse that has somehow drowned in a closed Coca-Cola bottle.

These tales are preposterous, but in a mass society like ours, where stories are usually manufactured by Hollywood, they just may be the most genuine form of folklore we have. Like traditional folklore, they are narratives crafted by the collective consciousness. Like traditional folklore, they give expression to the national mind. And like traditional folklore, they blend the fantastic with the routine, if only to demonstrate, in the words of University of Utah folklorist Jan Harold Brunvand, the nation's leading expert on urban legends, "that the prosaic contemporary scene is capable of producing shocking or amazing occurrences."

Shocking and amazing, yes. But in these stories, anything can happen not because the world is a magical place rich with wonder—as in folk tales of yore—but because our world is so utterly terrifying. Here, nothing is reliable and no laws of morality govern. The alligators in the sewers present an image of an urban hell inhabited by beasts—an image that might have come directly from Hades and the River Styx in Greek mythology. The baby-sitter and the man upstairs exploits fears that we are not even safe in our own homes these days. The spider in the hairdo says that even on our own persons, dangers lurk. The man who loses his kidney plays to our fears of

2

3

4

5

---

[1] caught in the act of being unfaithful

the night and the real bogymen who prowl them. The mouse in the soda warns us of the perils of an impersonal mass-production society.

As for the wedding-reception tale, which one hacker on the Internet has dubbed "Wedding Revenge," it may address the greatest terror of all: that love and commitment are chimerical and even friendship is meaningless. These are timeless issues, but the sudden promulgation of the tale suggests its special relevance in the age of AIDS, when commitment means even more than it used to, and in the age of feminism, when some men are feeling increasingly threatened by women's freedom. Thus, the groom not only suffers betrayal and humiliation; his plight carries the hint of danger and emasculation, too. Surely, a legend for our time.

Of course, folklore and fairy tales have long subsisted on terror, and even the treacly cartoons of Walt Disney are actually, when you parse them, dark and complex expressions of fear—from Snow White racing through the treacherous forest to Pinnochio gobbled by the whale to Dumbo being separated from his mother. But these crystallize the fears of childhood, the fears one must overcome to make the difficult transition to adulthood. Thus, the haunted forest of the fairy tales is a trope for haunted adolescence; the witch or crone, a trope for the spent generation one must vanquish to claim one's place in the world, and the prince who comes to the rescue, a trope for the adult responsibilities that the heroine must now assume.

Though urban legends frequently originate with college students about to enter the real world, they are different from traditional fairy tales because their terrors are not really obstacles on the road to understanding, and they are different from folklore because they cannot even be interpreted as cautionary. In urban legends, obstacles aren't overcome, perhaps can't be overcome, and there is nothing we can do differently to avoid the consequences. The woman, not knowing any better, eats the fried rat. The baby-sitter is terrorized by the stranger hiding in the house. The black widow bites the woman with the beehive hairdo. The alligators prowl the sewers. The marriage in Wedding Revenge breaks up.

It is not just our fears, then, that these stories exploit. Like so much else in modern life—tabloids, exploitalk programs, real-life crime bestsellers—urban legends testify to an overwhelming condition of fear and to a sense of our own impotence within it. That is why there is no accommodation in these stories, no lesson or wisdom imparted. What there is, is the stark impression that our world is anomic. We live in a haunted forest of skyscrapers or of suburban lawns and ranch houses, but there is no one to exorcise the evil and no prince to break the spell.

Given the pressures of modern life, it isn't surprising that we have created myths to express our malaise. But what is surprising is how many people seem committed to these myths. The *Post* reporter found people insisting they personally knew someone who had attended the doomed wedding reception. Others went further: They maintained they had actually attended the reception—though no such reception ever took place. Yet even those who didn't claim to have been personally involved seemed to feel duty bound to assert the tale's plausibility.

Why this insistence? Perhaps the short answer is that people want 11 to believe in a cosmology of dysfunction because it is the best way of explaining the inexplicable in our lives. A world in which alligators roam sewers and wedding receptions end in shock is at once terrifying and soothing—terrifying because these things happen, soothing because we are absolved of any responsibility for them. It is just the way it is.

But there may be an additional reason why some people seem so will- 12 ing to suspend their disbelief in the face of logic. This one has less to do with the content of these tales than with their creation. However they start, urban legends rapidly enter a national conversation in which they are embellished, heightened, reconfigured. Everyone can participate—from the people who spread the tale on talk radio to the people who discuss it on the Internet to the people who tell it to their neighbors. In effect, these legends are the product of a giant campfire around which we trade tales of terror.

If this makes each of us a co-creator of the tales, it also provides us with a certain pride of authorship. Like all authors, we don't want to see 13 the spell of our creation broken—especially when we have formed a little community around it. It doesn't matter whether these tales are true or not. What matters is that they plausibly reflect our world, that they have been generated from the grass roots and that we can pass them along.

In a way, then, these tales of powerlessness ultimately assert a kind 14 of authority. Urban legends permit us to become our own Stephen Kings, terrorizing ourselves to confirm one of the few powers we still possess: the power to tell stories about our world.

QUESTIONS FOR WRITING AND DISCUSSION

Rhetorical Knowledge: The Writer's Situation and Rhetoric

1. **Audience:** When we selected Gabler's essay for this textbook, we thought it was about a topic that college students would be interested in. To what extent do you agree or disagree? Why? Why might college students be interested in urban legends?

2. **Purpose:** What do you see as Gabler's purpose in writing this essay? In what ways is he trying to affect his audience?

3. **Voice and tone:** How would you describe Gabler's tone in this essay? Are there places where he seems to be poking fun at the whole idea of urban myths? Where?

4. **Responsibility:** How does Gabler's use of Disney characters (paragraph 7) help or hurt his credibility?

5. **Context and format:** Because Gabler's essay was originally published in a newspaper, it is fairly brief, as most newspaper articles are. How does that conciseness affect how Gabler presents his information? What additional information would you like to have? Why?

Critical Thinking: Your Personal Response

1. How would you describe your initial personal reaction to Gabler's essay?

2. Do you agree with Gabler that urban myths are the current version of "the most genuine form of folklore [traditional beliefs, myths, legends, and tales that are shared orally] we have" (paragraph 4)? Why?

3. What "folklore" do you know well enough to explain to your classmates?

Critical Thinking: The Writer's Ideas

1. What is your response to Gabler's argument that urban myths in some way terrorize American society? List some other urban myths and explain how much they terrorize society.

2. Gabler writes that urban myths "testify to an overwhelming condition of fear and to a sense of our own impotence within it" (paragraph 9). How do you interpret this statement?

3. Gabler argues that urban myths require us to "suspend . . . disbelief in the face of logic" (paragraph 12). What instances can you think of in your life where you have suspended your disbelief? How willingly do you suspend disbelief? Why?

4. What are the differences between the way Gabler characterizes how urban myths affect you—today's audience—and how more traditional myths probably affected their audience?

Composing Processes and Knowledge of Conventions: The Writer's Strategies

1. What kind of evidence in Gabler's essay do you find the most convincing? The least?

2. Gabler says that urban myths allow us each to become "a co-creator of the tales" (paragraph 13) and that they "permit us to become our own Stephen Kings, terrorizing ourselves . . ." (paragraph 14). How effective is this cause-and-effect argument?

Inquiry and Research: Ideas for Further Exploration

1. Conduct an Internet search for "urban myth" and see how many myths you can find that you, personally, know of. Which myths are new to you?

2. Search in your college library for a copy of *The Vanishing Hitchhiker* or *The Choking Doberman*, books that focus on cultural myths. How do author Jan Harold Brunvand's myths compare to some of Gabler's?

3. Interview several of your friends about myths they are familiar with. Outline them and make a brief report to your class.

TechNote

Graphics, and even video, can help you explain complex cause-and-effect relationships. If your instructor allows, see if you can find a short video clip (one to three minutes long) that shows the causal relationship you are explaining. Many Web search engines include video searches. Or you might explore a large video site such as YouTube (http://youtube.com). If you have access to a digital video camera, or if you own a video-capable cell phone or smart phone, you can create a short video clip yourself. For example, if you are writing about the effects of proper stance and follow-through on curveball execution in baseball, you could ask a campus baseball player to demonstrate while you record video of various techniques. Consider recording a voice-over that explains the movements involved.

Thinking about Visuals That Indicate Cause-and-Effect Relationships

Visuals can often explain the effect of an event better than words can. The map in Figure 10.4 shows that some aftershocks of an earthquake that occurred in 1895 and was centered near Charleston in southeastern Missouri were felt as far away as the Atlantic seaboard, the Gulf Coast, and even north of Green Bay, Wisconsin.

Consider the photograph in Figure 10.5 on page 490, which shows the effects of an earthquake, as shown on a seismograph. If you were writing a paper about earthquakes, how would such a photograph, or a map like the one in Figure 10.4, help illustrate a cause-effect relationship? And how would a photo like the one shown in Figure 10.6 on page 491 also help illustrate the damages caused by an earthquake?

As you look at these visual aids, consider these questions about the effective use of visuals in showing a cause-effect relationship:

- How does each visual provide information about the cause-and-effect relationship?

- What does the visual illustrate for a reader that it would be hard to show with text alone?

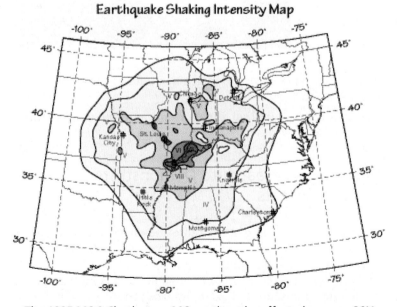

The 1895 M6.0 Charleston, MO earthquake affected an area 20X greater than an equivalent magnitude quake in California

FIGURE 10.4   Map Showing the Intensity of the 1895 Earthquake

**FIGURE 10.5
Seismograph
Registering
an Earthquake**

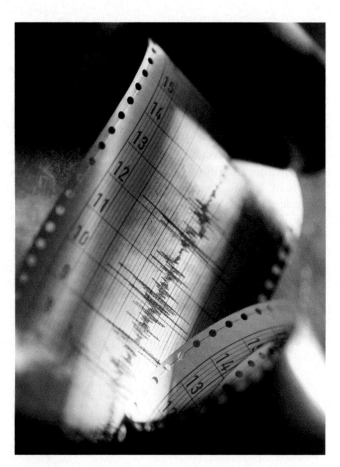

- What other types of visuals might be useful in illustrating cause-and-effect relationships?
- How might visuals mislead readers about cause-and-effect relationships?

Drawing on Research to Demonstrate Causes or Effects

Usually when you are writing about cause-and-effect relationships, you will need to provide evidence to support your claims. Although you may be able to draw on your experience and common sense or on anecdotes to provide some evidence, you will also need to offer verifiable facts, statistics, expert testimony, experimental results, and examples. For instance, if you were writing about cause-and-effect relationships in the areas of health or safety, two good sources are the Centers for Disease Control or the U.S. Department of Transportation, both of which have Web sites filled with reliable information.

FIGURE 10.6
A Road Damaged by an Earthquake

To find evidence outside your experience, do research to answer questions such as the following:

- What verifiable information will provide solid evidence that a cause-and-effect relationship actually exists? Where can I find this information? What sources will be most reliable and credible?

- What expert testimony can I provide to support my thesis about causes or effects or both? What authorities might I interview?

- What statistical data support my contention that a cause-and-effect relationship exists?

- How can I best explain the data to my readers so that (1) they can easily understand it and (2) the evidence I provide supports my conclusions?

The subject you focus on and the kind of essay you are constructing help to determine the kind of research you conduct. For example, for the scenarios in this chapter (pp. 462–67), you could conduct several kinds of research:

- For Scenario 1, in which you focus on a cause-and-effect relationship having to do with a topic in one of your courses, interviewing class-mates, professors, staff members, and/or administrators is a useful way to discover different perspectives on the relationship you are focusing on.
- For Scenario 4, which asks you to examine an issue in the company you work for, a search through past business memos and other records often will provide historical information that might help you see cause-and-effect relationships.

Writing Processes

As you work on your assignment, remember the qualities of an effective cause-and-effect paper (see pp. 469–71). The pages that follow will demon-strate to you how one student worked through her writing process as she focused her ideas and drafted, revised, and edited her work. As you will continue to notice, all of these processes are recursive—that is, writers move back and forth among all of the steps. After you engage in invention strate-gies and conduct some research, you may start writing, or you may decide to do some more research. In fact, the more writing experience you get, the more you will realize that no piece of writing is ever finished until your final draft.

For a tip on organizing your computer files, see page 97.

If you are considering several topics for your causal analysis, put your notes into a separate computer document for each subject. Once you deter-mine the focus of your analysis, it will be easy to access and use those notes. Also, as you work on your project, make sure that you save your computer files frequently because any work that you don't save could be lost. Many experienced writers save their files every fifteen minutes or so. Also, savvy writers back up their computer files in two or more places—on an internal or external hard drive of the computer, on a USB flash drive, and/or on a rewrit-able CD or DVD, for example.

Invention: Getting Started

The more invention activities that you use, the more effective your causal analysis will be. As you work, try to answer these questions:

- What do I already know about this event, phenomenon, trend, or activity?
- What do I know about its cause(s) or effect(s)?
- Where can I learn more about the causal relationships involved? What relevant personal experiences or observations can I contribute?

- What might my audience already know about the cause-and-effect relationship I am exploring?
- What do I know about my audience? What don't I know that I should know?
- What might my audience's point of view be?
- What questions do I have? What do I want and need to find out?

WRITING ACTIVITY

Brainstorming, Listing, and Clustering

Brainstorming, listing, and clustering are invention techniques that can help you focus your causal analysis and come up with possible causes and/or effects. Working with the questions above, spend a few minutes writing everything you can think of about the causal relationship you plan to discuss. Don't worry about putting this information into sentences or paragraphs; simply record it using any words that come to mind.

To explore your ideas further, list keywords that will remind you of ideas later, when you construct the first draft of your text. You might find it effective to establish categories for your lists to help jog your memory. If you are exploring causes of a phenomenon, for instance, you might organize your keywords under different types of causes.

Clustering is especially useful for figuring out possible cause-and-effect relationships. For your potential cause-and-effect paper, create a cluster of what you already know about the relationship you are exploring.

For more on brainstorming, listing, clustering, and other strategies for discovery and learning, see Chapter 3.

Deborah Schlegel's Brainstorming

Deborah Schlegel became interested in the topic of global warming in her environmental studies class. She decided to write a cause-and-effect essay about global warming in response to Scenario 1 (see p. 463). Schlegel began by brainstorming to focus her topic and to choose whether to look at the causes of global warming, its effects, or both.

- Could global warming be caused by too much heat on the planet, whether that comes from the sun or from humans or animals?
- There was something a few years ago about the stuff they used for air conditioning in homes and cars and buildings—Freon?—that ruined the

ozone layer, the part of our atmosphere that keeps some of the warming things away from Earth.
- NASA had some reports showing how the ozone layer was changing, shrinking. There's also something like higher greenhouse gas production.
- I wonder what governments might do about global warming?
- What can the average person do?
- How does global warming affect people, ecosystems, etc.?
- Are there any positive effects from global warming, or are all of its effects negative?
- It seems to me that someone thinks that global warming is a good idea, but only if your community isn't on the ocean, where it will be flooded!

Deborah Schlegel's Listing

After discovering that some experts believe global warming could lead to an unexpected effect—an ice age—Deborah Schlegel decided to make an additional list of ideas by considering the other side of the global warming issue: people who are skeptical about this phenomenon. Here is a portion of the list she came up with.

Theories on causes of ice ages:

- Massive volcanic eruptions
- Amount of space dust in the atmosphere
- Variations in Earth's orbit
- Amount of sunlight hitting continents
- Changes in atmospheric and oceanic circulation patterns

What the skeptics think:

- Climate is too complicated to be predicted by a single parameter
- Details and the long-term results (100 years) of these changes have been explored by very few studies
- We haven't had computer climate models long enough to predict long-term (100 years) future
- Credibility rests on the validity of the models

 ## Exploring Your Ideas with Research

As we have seen, Deborah Schlegel already had an interest in global warming when she began her cause-and-effect assignment. She wanted to explore this topic in more depth and detail. At her college library, she searched the library's newspaper index for sources using the keywords "global warming" and "ice age" and found some newspaper articles that might be helpful. Sources she located included the following newspaper article:

"Atlantic Surf Seekers Get Big Chill." Arizona Republic. 4 November 2003.
          B10.

She also conducted a Web search using the search engine *Google* and found more information. Her sources included news organizations like the Cable News Network (CNN):

"Study Hints at Extreme Climate Change." CNN. 28 October 1999. 1 November
          2003 <http://www.cnn.com/NATURE/9910/28/climate.change.enn/>.

After researching, Schlegel had information that she could use to formulate a thesis, or main idea, about what causes global warming and what its effects might be.

WRITING ACTIVITY

Conducting Research

Consider your topic for your causal analysis. What sources could help you answer the questions you have about your topic and formulate a working thesis? The following questions will help you focus your research:

- What do you already know about the subject from your invention work?
- What cause-and-effect connections can you make, based on your knowledge or experience?
- For what cause-and-effect connections do you need to provide some evidence?
- Whom might you quote as an expert to help you prove your claim?
- Where can you find statistics that will support your claim?
- Where do you think you might look for more information and evidence?
- Who is an expert you might interview about your subject?

Reviewing Your Invention and Research

After you have conducted your research, review your invention work and notes and the information you have collected from outside sources. Once you have a general idea of the cause(s) and/or effect(s) your research is leading you to, try to develop what is called a *working thesis statement:* If you had to explain the cause-and-effect relationship now, based on what you have learned, what would it be? This statement is called a working thesis because your thesis or main point will inevitably be subject to change as you continue to conduct research and learn more. And, as you know, through the process of writing itself, you will learn more about your topic and possible cause-and-effect relationships, so you will modify and develop the working thesis statement as you draft and revise your text. Once you have written several drafts, have received feedback on those drafts, and have revised them, you will be better able to determine what your final thesis statement should be.

WRITING ACTIVITY

Concept Mapping

Concept mapping takes clustering a step further and is especially useful for cause-and-effect papers because it helps you see the relationships between causes and their possible effects. Concept mapping asks you to show connections or relationships, so constructing such a map is an especially a useful invention activity for a cause-and-effect paper.

For more on concept mapping, see Chapter 3.

Deborah Schlegel's Concept Mapping

To clarify for herself—and perhaps for readers—the causal chain leading from global warming to an ice age, Deborah Schlegel looked over the research she had conducted and constructed the following concept map, based on her working thesis that global warming will eventually lead to an ice age.

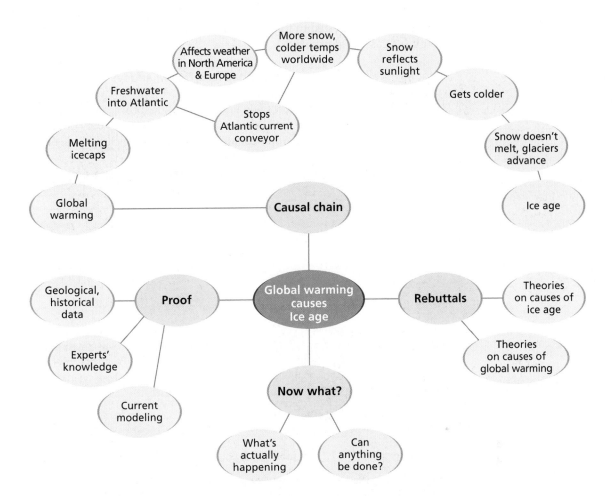

WRITING ACTIVITY

Considering Your Research and Focusing Your Ideas

Examine the notes you have made based on your research. Then, using the *who, what, where, when, why,* and *how* questions as a starting point, see what information you have. For example, if you were working on Scenario 5 (p. 467) and were trying to explain to your readers why your family was so interested in football, here are the kinds of questions that you might ask to get started:

who: My two brothers are true football fans, but what does that mean?
what: What do they do to show their allegiance to the local team? What do they wear? How do they act? What do they say? Where do they go and what do they do there? (Your research answers might include wearing team colors, tailgating picnics before the game, and so on.)
when: All the time but especially on Saturday when the college team plays.

WRITER'S WORKSHOP

Reacting to Your Classmates' Invention Work and Research

With any writing assignment, your invention materials and research can improve with peer feedback and suggestions. Working with several of your classmates, provide comments and suggestions and ask one another questions, with the overall goal of helping each of you to understand your rhetorical situation more clearly and to generate more useful information for your causal analysis:

Comments

- I understand _____ about what you've generated so far.

- I especially like _____ in what you've generated so far.

- I agree with/disagree with _____.

- I'm confused when you write about _____.

- I'm not convinced yet about _____.

- These causes you provide—_____ and _____—don't seem to cause the effect you suggest, so I'm not sure why you've included them. Can you explain in more detail?

- The part about _____ seems promising, but the part about _____ seems underdeveloped.

- I'd suggest that you include these ideas or this information:

    _____   _____

    _____   _____

Questions

- What is a _____? (Ask this kind of question when something is unclear.)

- Why do you think this causal relationship is important?

- What alternative explanations have been proposed instead of the cause(s)/effect(s) you are focusing on?

- How can you be certain that the cause-and-effect relationship you are writing about really exists?

- What are the other perspectives on this causal relationship?

As your classmates respond to your invention work and research, listen carefully—and with an open mind—to what they are saying, and take notes so that you do not forget their questions, comments, and suggestions. Your classmates' responses to your writing will help you anticipate the responses of your audience. In causal analysis, your biggest challenge is to establish the plausibility of the cause-and-effect relationship for your readers, so solicit readers' responses as early and as often as feasible. You can get responses to your work in class, but you can also do so online, at the campus writing center, or even your local coffee shop.

 ## Organizing Your Cause-and-Effect Paper

Once you have some sense of the thesis and supporting evidence for your cause-and-effect paper, you need to consider how you might organize your text. The questions to ask yourself when deciding on your organization are all rhetorical:

- Who is the audience for your paper?
- Why might they be interested in your reasoning about causes and/or effects, or how can you make them interested in it? (One way to emphasize the importance of your ideas to your audience is to show them why they need to understand your subject.)
- What is your purpose for writing—that is, why do your readers need to understand this cause-and-effect relationship? What will your readers learn about your subject by reading your paper? How will that help them to determine cause-and-effect relationships of their own?

Once you have determined your purpose, you can choose the organizational approach that is best suited to it. Here are three possible organizational approaches that you might choose for your paper. Note that each is related to one of the purposes described earlier in this chapter.

Options for Organization

Identify an Effect and Then Determine Its Cause(s)	Identify a Cause and Then Determine Its Effect(s)	Determine a Series of Causes and Effects
• Introduce the effect. • Explain the importance of the effect. • List possible causes. • Assert probable cause-and-effect relationship(s). • There may be several causes. • Provide evidence to support your claim about cause-and-effect relationship(s). • Address skeptics' doubts—others might say these causes do not cause the effect, so address those objections. • Conclusion.	• Introduce the cause. • Explain the importance of the cause. • List possible effects. • Assert probable cause-and-effect relationship(s). • There may be several effects. • Provide evidence to support your claim about cause-and-effect relationship(s). • If others might see different effects from your cause, address their objections. • Conclusion.	• Introduce one of the causes or one of the effects. • Explain the importance of the cause or the effect that you have identified. • List possible causes and effects. • Assert probable chain of causes and effects. • Provide evidence to support your claim about series of causes and effects. • Address skeptics' doubts. • Conclusion.

WRITING ACTIVITY

Deciding on an Organizational Approach

Before you construct a full draft, consider which organizational approach will best serve your writing purpose. It is sometimes useful to try several organizational approaches to see which seems most effective for your specific purpose, audience, and rhetorical situation. Note that these approaches are not meant to be rigid; you may decide to adapt one to work better for your particular rhetorical situation. You might try out several organizational approaches on the computer before deciding on one. Be sure to save each first attempt with a different file name. That makes it easy to recall the one that seems best and start to develop your draft using that organization.

 ## Constructing a Complete Draft

Once you have chosen the organizational approach that works best given your audience and purpose, you are ready to construct the rest of your draft. As you work, keep the following in mind:

- Draw on your invention work and your research. If necessary, do more invention work and/or more research.

- As you try out tentative ideas about possible causes and/or possible effects, ask peers about what they consider necessary to support your ideas.

For more on constructing visuals, see Chapter 18.

- Ask yourself and peers whether visuals might help make your case.

Introduction: When writing about causes and effects, writers often begin with a statement that announces the causal relationship. In order to write an introduction that captures readers' attention, however, you might want to try one of the following strategies:

- *Make a statement that suggests the unexpected.* Juan Williams uses this strategy in "The Ruling That Changed America" (p. 473):

    Fifty years later, the *Brown* decision looks different. At a distance from the volcanic heat of May 17, 1954, the real impact of the legal, political, and cultural eruption that changed America is not exactly what it first appeared to be.

- *Give your audience a reason for being interested by vividly portraying how this topic makes a difference in their lives.* In her final draft (p. 515), Deborah Schlegel uses this approach to establish the impact global warming could have on her readers' lives:

    Climate researchers have recently come up with good and bad news about the global warming crisis. The good news first—maybe it wasn't such a bad idea to move to hot Phoenix after all, and we may not have to worry about global warming. The bad news? Teenagers may have spent too much money on summer clothes. A growing number of scientists are warning that global warming may cause really big-time global cooling—an ice age.

- *Examining a surprising or unexpected causal relationship that you can substantiate is one way to hold an audience's interest.* In "Where Are the Jobs?" Bruce Nussbaum (p. 479) makes several surprising statements in an attempt to capture his readers' attention.

    Americans live in a faith-based economy. We believe deeply in education, innovation, risk-taking, and plain hard work as the way to a better life. But that faith is being eroded. The link between strong growth and job creation appears to be broken, and we don't know what's wrong with it. Profits are soaring, yet no one is hiring. Angry voices are blaming Benedict Arnold CEOs who send jobs to India and China. If highly educated "knowledge" workers in Silicon Valley are losing their jobs, who is really safe?

Body: There are many strategies you can use to show cause and effect, including the following:

- *List possible causes.* Bruce Nussbaum mentions several possible causes of the reduction in job growth and then asserts that increased productivity is the real cause.

- *List possible effects.* In "The Ruling That Changed America," Juan Williams lists a variety of far-reaching effects that he claims were an unforeseen result of the 1954 Supreme Court ruling.
- *Refute skeptics' claims.* For example, in a causal analysis on the dangers of smoking, you might note that while many smokers may feel their habit endangers only themselves, research data indicates the harmful effects of second-hand smoke. You could then present the data as evidence.

Conclusion: In your conclusion you need to reinforce the connections between the causes and effects that you have established. Do not assume your reader will make the same connections you have. Ask yourself the following questions:

- Have you shown that the effect was truly a result of the cause?
- How well have you tied together all of the different ideas you have been working with?
- How clearly have you articulated your perspective so your audience has no doubt about what you have been trying to prove?
- Have you given your reader a sense of closure?

Note how Juan Williams accomplishes these goals in the last two paragraphs of "The Ruling That Changed America."

> But the most important legacy of the *Brown* decision, by far, is the growth of an educated black middle class. The number of black people graduating from high school and college has soared since *Brown*, and the incomes of blacks have climbed steadily as a result. Home ownership and investment in the stock market among black Americans have rocketed since the 1980s. The political and economic clout of that black middle class continues to bring America closer to the mountaintop vision of racial equality that Dr. King might have dreamed of 50 years ago.
>
> The Supreme Court's May 17, 1954, ruling in *Brown* remains a landmark legal decision. But it is much more than that. It is the "Big Bang" of all American history in the 20th century.

Title: As you construct your cause-and-effect paper, a title should emerge at some point—often late in the process. The title should reflect the cause-and-effect claim that you are considering. Putting that claim in the form of a question is often a useful way to interest readers. For instance, Deborah Schlegel might consider titles such as the following:

- Are Humans Warming Themselves to Death?
- A New Ice Age for Your Children?
- Will Our Hot Climate Freeze Us to Death?
- Warm but Not Comfortable?

VISUALIZING VARIATIONS

Choosing Visuals That Illustrate Cause-and-Effect Relationships

If you have prepared a causal analysis for a civic or professional writing situation, you will often need to present the results of your analysis to a group. If, as part of your response to Scenario 3 or 4 (pp. 465–67), you were to prepare an oral presentation using either PowerPoint slides or transparencies and an overhead projector, what content would you need to include on your slides or transparencies, and how would you format them? Here are some aspects of PowerPoint slides or transparencies that you would need to keep in mind:

- Slides allow you to "show" as well as "tell." What information will you "show" and what will you "tell"?

- How can you use graphics (charts, graphs, photographs) most effectively as part of your presentation?

- When you prepare presentation slides, your writing becomes very visible. Make sure to edit your slides carefully.

- Programs for creating presentation slides often provide options for background templates. How can you pick a background that will complement your slides?

For example, for a presentation to members of a civic association, consider the text font and color you might use to make an overhead transparency showing an increase in the number of bicycle/pedestrian accidents during the past year. You might start with plain black type.

In the past year, bicycle/pedestrian accidents have increased 70%

You also could add some shading, to highlight the most important part of the sentence.

In the past year, bicycle/pedestrian accidents have increased 70%

You could include a slide with a bar graph to illustrate the problem.

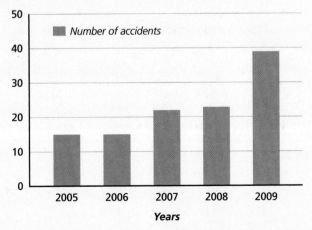

(cont'd)

(continued)

And if you were using PowerPoint for your slides, you could apply a background template to your bar graph.

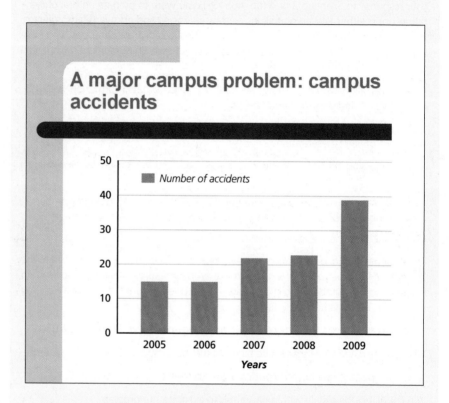

For any photograph or illustration that you are considering, then, ask yourself the following questions:

- What might this photograph show about the cause-and-effect relationship I am arguing for?

- How do I select a chart or graph that will support a point I want to make and help me justify my overall judgment?

- What other kind of illustration (drawing, table) might help show that a cause-and-effect relationship exists?

For more on oral presentations, including the use of PowerPoint, see Chapter 16.

WRITING ACTIVITY

Constructing a Full Draft

After reviewing your notes and research and invention activities and carefully considering all of the information that you have generated, you are ready to construct a first complete draft, using the organizational approach that you have decided on. Remember that your thinking about the nature of the cause-and-effect relationship may evolve as you draft your paper so your ideas will most likely change as you compose the first draft of your essay.

As you draft, keep in mind that you are proving that something occurred as a direct result of something else. Make sure you have support for your claims about cause-and-effect relationships.

There is no one right way to start composing. However, if you have an organizational plan that you are comfortable with, you might begin by filling in parts of the sections that you feel best about or those where you feel you have the best information. You can always put everything together later.

An Excerpt from Deborah Schlegel's First Draft

In this excerpt from her first draft, note how Deborah Schlegel incorporates evidence from a variety of sources to prove her claim. As she wrote, Schlegel did not worry about grammar, punctuation, and mechanics; instead, she concentrated on getting her main ideas onto paper. (The numbers in circles refer to peer comments—see page 511.)

(The numbers in circles refer to peer comments—see page 511.)

Global Warming

The arguments are endless over what is causing our global temperatures to rise. Is it higher amounts of green house gases such as CO_2 and aerosols in the atmosphere caused by man? Is it higher amounts of green house gases like methane that we humans are "pumping" into the atmosphere by the incredibly large numbers of cows living on this planet? Or is it something totally unavoidable such as where we are in the sunspot cycle or the increased solar output of our Sun? How does this affect all of us? ❶

The Earth's oceans are ringed by several ocean currents linked together forming what is called the Global Ocean Conveyor. Like the conveyor belt this brings to mind, these currents move water around the globe cooling the atmosphere above them when they're carrying cold water on the surface and warming the atmosphere when they carry warm surface water. This giant conveyor belt is driven by very cold, very salty water that sinks to the bottom of the ocean and creeps along slowly—moving also the water above it. . . .

Stopping the Global Ocean Conveyer means there will no longer be warm surface water arriving from the equatorial regions and the Caribbean. The jet stream will no longer be able to pick up warm air to distribute over Europe, causing that area to become colder. The jet stream will be delivering colder air to each point east of Europe—Northern Asia and the Northern Pacific. Onshore winds will no longer be warming the East Coast of North America—that area will become colder. In a snowballing effect, because the jet stream will be passing over colder water and colder landmasses, the weather everywhere will be affected. Any place that currently depends on warming from ocean currents, directly or indirectly, will become colder.❷

So now we have colder temperatures and winter's coming. The North Atlantic regions, the English Isles, Europe, Japan and the Pacific Northwest normally receive heavy rains in the winter. When their winter temperatures are colder, this will fall instead as snow. Snow will fall in many places that never or rarely saw it in the good old days of global warming.

Those who've lived in northern climates where it snows all winter know once it snows, the temperatures go down further and stay down. With no warm winds coming, the same thing will happen in our story. To make matters worse, the snow that stays on the ground will reflect sunlight back up making the temperatures even colder. This surface reflection of incoming solar radiation is called albedo. NASA's Earth Observing System satellites have measured the albedo value of non-melting snow-covered surfaces at 80% to 90% (Goddard Space Center 264). This means that 80% to 90% of the sunlight falling on these snow-covered areas will reflect back into space, leaving only 10% to 20% of the heat. And remember that we now have many more regions of the Earth covered with snow than we used to. The reflection of sunlight causes temperatures to fall even further—it's called a vicious cycle.

Snow and ice also act as an insulating blanket to keep ground temperatures cold. It takes a large amount of energy to warm up this insulated blanket and . . . you know it by now. We don't have that energy anymore.

Now we get to the ice age part. When snow keeps falling, it packs down, becoming ice. The more snow, the more the ice thickens. As the ice thickens, more stress is put on the deep ice. When enough stress is placed on it, the ice will begin to move or flow—it will advance. In fact, this is the definition of a glacier—an ice sheet that advances. An ice age is declared when widespread glaciers advance. In our story, we are now in an ice age. . . .

The first group of disbelievers falls into the "it isn't what we've traditionally thought causes ice ages, so this new theory can't be trusted" category. Every new theory in science since Galileo announced the sun didn't travel around the Earth has had to deal with this group. ❸ Past theories of ice age causes include events that put a lot of dust and particles into the atmosphere thus blocking out the sun (massive volcanic eruptions or increased space dust from meteors and/or comets), less energy from the sun reaching the earth (from variations in the Earth's orbit, lessened solar output, or changes in the Earth's tilt), or events that block ocean and air currents such as the shifting of the continental plates or massive mountain ranges like the Himalayas lifting up. These all have problems in that every time one of these events occurs an ice age does not follow and some ice ages have occurred without any of these events happening. If any of these theories are valid, they must be only a part of the picture, not the main contributing factor.

The other group of critics questions whether the specific models used in predicting the events in our story will in fact lead to an ice age or questions whether any model could predict such a complex event that is in the future. It is true that computer models are only as good as the data being used in them. So there are several points we want to make sure are present in any model we consider the validity of. Was the research done by a scientifically reputable institution? Was it published in a scientifically reputable journal? Were the results of the model replicated by other reputable institutions? . . .

Dr. Richard Alley, a professor of geosciences at Pennsylvania State University says that Global Ocean Conveyer disruptions and sudden climate changes are ". . . nothing new—only the realization that they have occurred"

(Wood). He states that while we used to think climate changes, like aging, happened gradually, recent studies of ice cores dating back 100,000 years ago show sudden shifts. "Large, abrupt and widespread climate changes occurred repeatedly in the past across most of the Earth, and followed closely after freshening of the North Atlantic" (Wood).

It is true we can't predict the future with absolute certainty, but we can look at past trends and see where we might be going. Where are we now? The Gulf Stream and Global Ocean Conveyor are still running, although one climate scientist, Dr. Andrew Weaver at the University of Victoria in British Columbia suspects they might be slowing down. His work shows that the Scandinavian Glacier is growing and suggests this may be the result of less warm air reaching that far corner of the North Atlantic (Wood). Records of past climates suggest that when the Gulf Stream stops, it is within a few decades of its first sign of slowing down ("Climate Impact").

And we continue to see increases in those factors that may cause the currents to stop. The Geophysical Fluid Dynamics Lab found CO_2 levels are continuing to rise 0.4% per year and have risen 28% since preindustrial times indicating continued global warming ("Climate Impact"). A Danish study from the University of Bremen found a decrease in the amount of Arctic sea ice each year since 1978, with 2002 seeing the smallest amount of ice observed for at least 100 years (Kaleschke). The melting of this sea ice is a continuing source of fresh water for the North Atlantic.

All of this means that we—all human beings, everywhere on earth—may be in for some serious climate changes, and that those changes will be more negative than positive. ④

◣ Revising

Once you have a draft, put it aside for a day or so. This break will give you the chance to come back to your text as a new reader might. Read through and revise your work, looking especially for ideas that are not explained completely, terms that are not defined, and other problem areas. As you revise your early drafts, hold off on doing a great deal of heavy editing. When you revise you will probably change the content and structure of your paper, so time spent working to fix problems with sentence style or grammar, usage, punctuation, or mechanics at this stage is often wasted.

Think of revision as reenvisioning your causal analysis, reconsidering what you mean to say, not just editing for surface features. When you reread the first draft of your paper, be sure to begin at the beginning. Here are some questions to ask yourself:

- How effectively have I explained or indicated my thesis so the reader knows my view of the cause-and-effect relationship and what I intend to prove about it?

- What else might my audience want or need to know about my subject?

- How else might I interest my audience in my causal analysis?

- What did I find out about my subject that I did not include in my causal analysis? (Effective research always results in more information than you can include, so consider what you left out that you might include in your next draft.)

- Have I clearly explained and defined any terms my readers might not know?

- Could some aspects of my causal analysis be better presented as a graph or chart?

Technology can help you revise and edit your writing more easily. Use your word processor's track-changes tool to try out revisions and editing changes. After you've had time to think about the possible changes, you can "accept" or "reject" them. Also, you can use your word processor's comment tool to write reminders to yourself when you get stuck with a revision or some editing task. If your classmates are offering feedback on your draft, they can also use track changes, the comment tool, or the peer-commenting feature of the software.

Your instructor may also ask you to share your work with your class-mates and ask them for suggestions and ideas. Friends or family members may also be willing to read your draft and offer useful suggestions.

WRITER'S WORKSHOP

Responding to Full Drafts

Working with one or two classmates, read each paper and offer comments and questions that will help each of you see your paper's strengths and weaknesses. You might share your comments and questions in a conversation, or you may have each reader write comments and questions (either with pen or pencil or electronically) on the writer's draft. Consider the following guidelines and questions as you do:

- Write a brief narrative comment that outlines your first impression of this draft. How effectively does the title draw you into the paper? Why? How might the title be improved? What part(s) of the text are especially effective

(cont'd)

(continued)

for showing a cause-and-effect relationship? What could use more explanation or definitions?

- What do you like about the draft? Provide positive and encouraging feedback to the writer.

- How well does the writer stay on track? How much does the paper wander? If it loses focus, indicate where.

- How logical is the paper? Explain, in a brief paragraph, the strengths and weaknesses you see in the writer's logic.

- How effective is the introduction? What suggestions can you make to improve the introduction?

- What do you think is the author's thesis or main point? How could it be expressed or supported more effectively?

- In the main part of the paper, are there parts that need more explanation? Where would you like more details or examples to help you see what the author means?

- How clear is the author's cause-and-effect writing? If it is unclear, how might the writer address those matters?

- How credible is the writer's case that a relationship exists? How credible are the writer's sources?

- Might visuals such as charts, tables, graphs, or photographs help the writer to explain or support his or her claims about causes and/or effects more simply and clearly?

- How clearly and effectively does the writer present any opposing points of view on this subject? If so, how might this presentation be improved? How effectively does the writer answer opposing viewpoints? How might the writer acknowledge, concede, and or refute them more effectively?

- What could be added or changed to make the conclusion more effective? To what extent does it make you want to learn more about this topic?

- In a brief paragraph, outline what you see as the main weaknesses of this paper—and suggest how the writer might improve the text.

Student Comments on Deborah Schlegel's First Draft

Using the questions above, Deborah Schlegel's classmates made some suggestions on her first draft. Below are comments she received, keyed to the first draft on pages 505–8.

❶ "I suggest that you provide more information after your first paragraph, to give us more background on how the climate works and how do we know that?"

❷ "This is pretty informal, especially the use of 'we.' I realize that you're trying to 'draw your readers in' to make them interested in your paper—how else might you do so?"

❸ "It was Copernicus, not Galileo, who first suggested the earth moves around the sun. Make sure your facts are right!"

❹ "Interesting and thoughtful first draft, with good quotations to support your claims. I'd like to read even more on the human causes of global warming and climate change. Are there any illustrations that you found in your research that might help readers *see* what you mean?"

Responding to Readers' Comments

Once they have received feedback on their writing from peers, teachers, friends, and others, writers have to figure out what to do with that feedback. Since your writing is your responsibility, you must determine how to deal with reader responses to your work. For example, how might you deal with this reader's comment that Deborah Schlegel received on her paper?

> Interesting and thoughtful first draft, with good quotations to support your claims. I'd like to read even more on the human causes of global warming and climate change. Are there any illustrations that you found in your research that might help readers *see* what you mean?

One way Schlegel could respond would be to do just what the reader suggests: to find and add some pictures, charts, or tables to *show* what she has in mind.

The first thing to do with any feedback, then, is to consider seriously what your reader has to say. The classmates who read Deborah Schlegel's paper have done the following:

• Asked for more information and background after the initial paragraph.

• Told the writer to get her facts right.

• Noted that the tone is fairly informal and wondered how else she might interest readers in the subject of the paper.

Schlegel needs to address all of these questions or concerns. As with any feedback, it is important to listen to it carefully and consider what your reader has to say. Then it is up to you, as the author, to decide *how* to come to terms with these suggestions. You may decide to reject some comments, of course; other comments, though, deserve your attention. You may find that comments from more than one reader contradict each other. In that case, use your own judgment to decide which reader's comments are on the right track.

In the final version of her paper on pages 515–21, you can see how Deborah Schlegel responded to her reader's comments, as well as to her own review of her first draft.

 # Knowledge of Conventions

In your college classes, writing about a cause-and-effect relationship is usually academic writing, so you will be required to follow the conventions for an academic essay. Other nonacademic writing situations may call for a variety of genres, including memos, essays, blog postings, letters to the editor, and even formal position papers. Such documents often include tables, charts, graphs, or photos. Be aware of the conventions for any genre you use.

 ## Editing

After you revise, you have one more important step—editing and polishing. At the editing stage, which comes at the end of your writing process, make changes to your sentence structure and word choice to improve your style and to make your writing clearer and more concise. Also check your work to make sure it adheres to conventions of grammar, usage, punctuation, mechanics, and spelling. Use the spell-check function of your word-processing program, but be sure to double-check your spelling personally (your computer cannot tell the difference between *compliment* and *complement*, but you can). If you have used sources in your paper, make sure you are following the documentation style your instructor requires.

See Chapter 20 for more on documenting sources using MLA or APA style.

As with overall revision of your work, this final editing and polishing is most effective if you can put your text aside for a few days and come back to it with fresh eyes. Because checking conventions is easier said than done, though, we strongly recommend that you ask classmates, friends, and tutors to read your work to find editing problems that you may not see. Another option is to post your paper on a course Web site and invite everyone in class to read it. You may get only one or two takers, but one or two is better than none.

To assist you with editing, we offer here a round-robin editing activity focused on making sure that subordinate clauses are attached to independent clauses.

Round-Robin Editing with a Focus on Subordinate Clauses

Writing about causes and effects benefits from the careful use of **subordinate clauses**. A subordinate clause has a subject and a verb, but it cannot stand on its own because it begins with a subordinating conjunction (such as *although*, *because*, *while*, *if*, or *since*). For instance, the following clause can stand on its own; it is a sentence:

SENTENCE   My car did not start this morning.

If the subordinating conjunction *because* is added, though, it cannot stand on its own and is a sentence fragment:

FRAGMENT   *Because my car did not start this morning.*

Because subordinate clauses cannot stand on their own, they need to be attached to an independent clause:

SENTENCE   *Because my car did not start this morning,* I was late for class.

or

SENTENCE   I was late for class *because my car did not start this morning.*

For this activity, look for the subordinate clauses in your papers, and make sure they are attached to independent clauses. If you are uncertain about a specific convention for using subordinate clauses, underline the sentence you are unsure about and put a question mark in the margin. To resolve such questions, consult a handbook or ask your instructor.

Genres, Documentation, and Format

If you are writing an academic paper in response to Scenarios 1 or 2, follow the conventions appropriate for the discipline in which you are writing and the requirements of your instructor. However, if you are responding to Scenario 4, you may decide to write a report with a cover memo. In that case, follow the acceptable format for memos required by the organization you are writing for. Also format your report so that it meets the needs and requirements of your intended audience. For example, determine what material should go into the body of the report and what supporting material is better presented in an appendix.

If you have used material from outside sources, including visuals, give credit to those sources, using the documentation style required by the discipline you are working in and by your instructor.

For advice on writing in different genres, see Appendix C. For guidelines for formatting and documenting papers in MLA or APA style, see Chapter 20.

WRITING IN ACTION

Convention in Genre and Design

In this introduction to a report by the Morrison Institute for Public Policy, the writer identifies six "keys" to success for Latino students in Arizona's public schools. The introduction is in effect a summary or abstract of the entire report, which can be seen at http://www.asu.edu/copp/morrison/LatinEd.pdf.

Considering Genre and Design

Consider these questions about the introduction:

1. How effective is the introduction? How does it make you want to read the full report?
2. How does the title catch your interest?
3. If you were writing a causal analysis on the topic of Latino achievement in public schools, how would this abstract help you determine whether the full report would be useful to you?
4. Comment on the design of the introduction. How is it inviting? What might make it more appealing to readers?

A Writer Shares Her Causal Analysis: Deborah Schlegel's Final Draft

Below is Deborah Schlegel's finished cause-and-effect paper. Note that she has addressed the questions and concerns that her classmates had, adding information and examples based on their suggestions.

DEBORAH SCHLEGEL

Weather Forecast: Bikinis or Parkas?

Climate researchers have recently come up with good and bad news about the global warming crisis. The good news first—maybe it wasn't such a bad idea to move to hot Phoenix after all, and we may not have to worry about global warming. The bad news? Teenagers may have spent too much money on summer clothes. A growing number of scientists are warning that global warming may cause really big-time global cooling—an ice age.

To understand how this seeming contradiction could happen, we'll follow a path that leads from the Arctic ice cap to the Atlantic Ocean and around the world on the same ocean current the turtles rode in <u>Finding Nemo</u>. But first we start with the current crisis, global warming. I also want to note that while some politicians do <u>not</u> believe that global warming is a real and serious problem, the majority of scientists—the great majority—are positive that the earth is warming up, and that humans are a primary cause of global warming.

The arguments are endless over what is causing our global temperatures to rise. Is it the higher amounts of greenhouse gases such as CO_2 and aerosols in the atmosphere caused by humans? Is it the higher amounts of greenhouse gases like methane being pumped into the atmosphere by the large numbers of cows living on this planet? Or is it something totally unavoidable, such as where we are in the sunspot cycle or the increased solar output of our sun? Whatever the causes are, temperatures are rising, and it is this increase that is the beginning of the story.

When temperatures heat up, increased amounts of fresh water enter the northern Atlantic Ocean. This effect happens for two reasons. First, the warmer temperatures cause the Arctic ice cap and the sea ice that surrounds it to melt. Second, runoff into the ocean increases, caused by increased rain and snow in the northern latitudes of North America. NASA's Earth Observing System (EOS) science report ("The Earth Observing System Science Plan") points to the models on global climate change,

1

2

3

4

One classmate wrote to Schlegel the following comment:

I suggest that you provide more information after your first paragraph, to give us more background on how the climate works and how do we know that?

In her revision, Schlegel provides significantly more background.

all showing that these are the two ways global warming will cause the amount of fresh water entering the Atlantic Ocean to increase. Clearly, increased global temperatures cause an increase in fresh water entering the Atlantic Ocean.

Earth's oceans are ringed by several ocean currents linked together, forming what is called the Global Ocean Conveyor. Like a conveyor belt, these currents move water around the globe, cooling the atmosphere above them when they're carrying cold water on the surface and warming the atmosphere when they carry warm surface water. This giant conveyor belt is driven by very cold, very salty water that sinks to the bottom of the ocean and creeps along slowly—also moving the water above it. The turtles in the film <u>Finding Nemo</u> rode a portion of the Global Ocean Conveyor that slides around Australia and down its east coast (not as quickly as shown in the movie, but then, that was fiction). The portion of this conveyor in the Atlantic, the Gulf Stream, is an important force in driving the whole system.

How fast the Gulf Stream moves is determined by thermohaline circulation—what the temperature of the water is (thermo-) and how salty it is (-haline). Ideally, the Gulf Stream brings warm, salty water from the equatorial and Caribbean regions up to the North Atlantic. There the winds of the jet stream, moving from west to east, take out a fair amount of the heat and move it to the North Atlantic regions and Europe. The journal <u>Natural Science</u> likens the amount of heat sent on via the jet stream ". . . to the total energy output of a million nuclear power plants" ("A New European Ice Age?"). That's why Europe has such balmy temperatures for its latitude. London is as far north as Moscow, the Aleutian Islands and Edmonton, Canada. Rome shares its latitude, but not its Mediterranean weather, with Upper Mongolia and northern Montana. The East Coast of the United States also benefits from warmer temperatures through this heat transfer.

As the surface water of the Gulf Stream cools, it becomes denser, sinks to a depth of about two kilometers, and begins its slow progress around the world. As the dense water leaves an area, it pulls in new water from the equatorial and Caribbean regions, and the cycle continues. That is, the cycle continues as long as the water traveling north becomes denser and sinks. However, an increase in cold, fresh water entering the North Atlantic cools the surface temperatures and, because it's fresh water, makes the ocean currents less salty. Cooler surface temperatures and less salty currents, in turn, cause a slowdown in the Gulf Stream. If there is a lot of cold, fresh water, the surface temperatures no longer have enough heat to transfer to the jet stream as it passes over, nor are the waters salty enough to sink and continue driving the Global

(margin notes)

One of Schlegel's peers wondered about using other strategies besides the word "We."

This is pretty informal, especially the use of 'we.' I realize that you're trying to draw your readers in to make them interested in your paper—how else might you do so?

While Schegel still sometimes uses the word *we*, she also engages her readers by asking questions.

(paragraph numbers in margin) 5   6   7

Ocean Conveyer. The Global Ocean Conveyer could stop. No more nice winters for London, Rome, and the rest of Europe. But that's not all.

The end of the Global Ocean Conveyer would mean an end to warm surface water arriving from the equatorial regions and the Caribbean. The jet stream would no longer be able to pick up warm air to distribute over Europe, causing that area to become colder. The jet stream would be delivering colder air to each point east of Europe—Northern Asia and the Northern Pacific. Onshore winds would no longer be warming the East Coast of North America—that area would become colder. Because the jet stream would be passing over colder water and colder landmasses, the weather everywhere would be affected. Any place that currently depends on warming from ocean currents, directly or indirectly, would become colder.

The results of these colder temperatures when winter comes would be devastating. The North Atlantic regions, the British Isles, Europe, Japan, and the Pacific Northwest normally receive heavy rains in the winter. If their winter temperatures were colder, this precipitation would fall instead as snow. Snow would fall in many places that had never or rarely seen it previously. Snow stays on the ground during the entire winter in the northern latitudes, waiting for the warm winds of spring (called chinooks in the northern United States and Canada) to melt it. But without a Global Ocean Conveyor, the system that transfers warm temperatures from the tropics to the northern climates via the ocean currents would no longer exist. So this snow would stay on the ground.

Those who've lived in northern climates, where it snows all winter, know that once it snows, the temperatures go down further and stay down. With no warm winds coming, the same effect would happen in the scenario just described. To make matters worse, the snow on the ground would reflect sunlight back up, making the temperatures even colder. This surface reflection of incoming solar radiation is called <u>albedo</u>. NASA's Earth Observing System satellites have measured the albedo value of non-melting snow-covered surfaces at 80% to 90% ("The Earth Observing System Science Plan"). This means that 80% to 90% of the sunlight falling on these snow-covered areas will reflect back into space, leaving only 10% to 20% of the heat. With many more regions of the Earth covered with snow, the reflection of sunlight would cause temperatures to fall even further in a vicious cycle. Snow and ice would also act as an insulating blanket to keep ground temperatures cold. It takes a large amount of energy to warm up this insulated blanket, but that energy would no longer be available.

When snow keeps falling, it packs down, becoming ice. The more snow, the thicker the ice. As the ice thickens, more stress is put on the deep ice. When enough stress is placed on it, the ice begins to move or flow—it advances. In fact, this is the definition of a glacier—an ice sheet that advances. An ice age occurs when widespread glaciers advance. In our scenario, we would now be in an ice age.

You shouldn't sell off your tank tops and shorts yet, though. Not everyone in the scientific community agrees with this scenario. In fact, scientists have never agreed on a cause for the ice ages that have occurred in the past. Because no one was recording and preserving data then, we have no record of the events leading up to the ice ages or the events that caused them to end. What scientists do have is physical evidence—clues they can put together and run through computer models to see how they relate to what's happening in our climate today.   12

One group of disbelievers argues that this new theory isn't what we've traditionally thought causes ice ages, so it can't be trusted. Every new theory in science since Copernicus announced that the sun doesn't travel around the Earth has confronted similar resistence. Past theories of the causes of ice ages include the occurrence of massive volcanic eruptions or increased amounts of space dust from meteors or comets, events that put large amounts of dust and particles into the atmosphere and block out the sun; decreases in the amount of the sun's energy reaching the earth caused by variations in Earth's orbit, lessened solar output, or changes in the Earth's tilt; or events that block ocean and air currents such as the shifting of the continental plates or the lifting up of massive mountain ranges like the Himalayas. These theories all have problems. An ice age has not followed every time one of these events has occurred, and some ice ages have occurred without any of these events happening first. If any of these theories are valid, they must be only a part of the picture, not the main contributing factor.   13

Another group of critics questions whether the specific models used to predict the events in our scenario indicate that our current situation will in fact lead to an ice age. These critics question whether any model could predict such a complex future event. Computer models are only as good as the data being used in them, so before accepting the results of these models we must consider the validity of the research. Was it done by a scientifically reputable institution? Was it published in a reputable, peer-reviewed journal? Were the results of the model replicated by other reputable institutions?   14

In considering possible causes of ice ages, we have good sources of computer modeling. Several studies looking at the effects of global warming have come up with models that support a global cooling. The government-funded Geophysical Fluid Dynamics Lab working with Princeton University has used a computer model to look at the effects on our climate of CO_2 increases. The global warming that resulted led to a shutdown of the Global Ocean Conveyor. The model indicated that this shutdown would occur within a decade and that the conveyor would   15

A student reader caught an error of fact:

It was Copernicus, not Galileo, who first suggested the earth moves around the sun. Make sure your facts are right!

Like any good researcher, Schlegel makes sure all her facts are correct in her final draft.

take several centuries to recover (Raphael). Scientists at the Physics Institute of the University of Bern in Switzerland duplicated these results using a different model (Stocker and Schmitter).

Researchers at Woods Hole Oceanographic Institute on Cape Cod looked at evidence gathered over the past ten or fifteen years and concluded that we may be heading for the colder climate predicated by our scenario. As the President and Director of the Institute, Dr. Robert B. Gagosian, puts it, ". . . we've seen ominous signs that we may be headed toward a potentially dangerous threshold. If we cross it, Earth's climate could switch gears and jump very rapidly—not gradually—into a completely different mode of operation."

Scientists at the Woods Hole Oceanographic Institute found that in the past decade, the North Atlantic waters have become dramatically fresher—they are losing their saltiness (Gagosian). If this trend continues, we may get to see firsthand whether or not the predictions of these models are accurate.

While computer climate models have not existed long enough for us to see if their long-term predictions will hold, we can look at evidence we have from past eras and see what happened before previous ice ages occurred. While studying fossilized remains of plankton algae drilled from the bottom of the mid-Atlantic, Scott Lehman and Julian Sachs, former University of Colorado–Boulder researchers now at Columbia University's Barnard College, found that the temperature of the Atlantic dropped prior to the beginning of ice ages and rose prior to their ending. These temperature changes were abrupt and "seem to be almost entirely ocean driven" (qtd. in "Study Hints at Extreme Climate Change"). These temperature changes seem to indicate changes in how the Gulf Stream was distributing warmer water. Lehman and Sachs also note that the "temperatures in the Sargasso Sea during the last ice age fluctuated up to 9 degrees Fahrenheit" (Fig. 1).

Dr. Richard Alley, a professor of geosciences at Pennsylvania State University, says that Global Ocean Conveyer disruptions and sudden climate changes are "nothing new—only the realization that they have occurred [is]" (qtd. in Wood). He states that while we used to think climate changes, like aging, happened gradually, recent studies of ice cores dating back 100,000 years show sudden shifts. Alley notes that "Large, abrupt and widespread climate changes occurred repeatedly in the past across most of the Earth, and followed closely after freshening of the North Atlantic" (qtd. in Wood).

While we can't predict the future with absolute certainty, we can look at past trends and see where we might be going. Where are we now? The Gulf Stream and Global Ocean Conveyor are still running, although one climate scientist, Dr. Andrew Weaver at the University of Victoria in

16

17

18

19

20

In response to Schlegel's first draft, one classmate had this comment:

Interesting and thoughtful first draft, with good quotations to support your claims. I'd like to read even more on the human causes of global warming and climate change. Are there any illustrations that you found in your research that might help readers *see* what you mean?

One of the ways that Schlegel responded was to include the illustration on the following page.

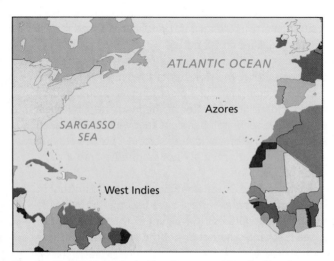

Fig. 1   Temperatures in the Sargasso Sea during the Last Ice Age. "Study Hints at Extreme Climate Change." CNN. 28 Oct. 1999. 1 Nov. 2003. <http://www.cnn.com/NATURE/9910/28/climate.change.enn/>.

British Columbia, suspects they might be slowing down. His work shows that the Scandinavian Glacier is growing and suggests this may be the result of less warm air reaching that far corner of the North Atlantic (Wood). Records of past climates suggest that when the Gulf Stream stops, it does so within a few decades of the first sign that it is slowing down (Raphael).

21   And we continue to see increases in those factors that may cause the currents to stop. The Geophysical Fluid Dynamics Lab found CO_2 levels are continuing to rise 0.4% per year and have risen 28% since pre-industrial times, indicating continued global warming. A Danish study from the University of Bremen found a decrease in the amount of Arctic sea ice each year since 1978, with 2002 seeing the smallest amount of ice observed for at least 100 years (Kaleschke). The melting of this sea ice is a continuing source of fresh water for the North Atlantic.

22   So what is happening now? Water temperatures off Atlantic City, New Jersey, were colder in 2003 than in any other year since 1911, when record keeping began ("Atlantic Surf" B10). These colder water temperatures were seen as far south as Florida. In fact, the water temperatures along the East Coast were almost three degrees Fahrenheit below normal. Next time you see a sale on parkas, take another look. And you might want to start selling those tank tops and shorts after all!

Works Cited

"A New European Ice Age?" <u>Natural Science</u>. 1 Nov. 1997. 24 Oct. 2003 <http://naturalscience.com/us/cover/ cover5.html>.

"Atlantic Surf Seekers Get Big Chill." <u>Arizona Republic</u>. 4 Nov. 2003. B10.

Gagosian, Robert B. "Triggering Abrupt Climate Change." <u>Argentinean Foundation for a Scientific Ecology Web site</u>. 24 Oct. 2003 <http://mitosyfraudes.8k.com/Calen/ TriggerIceAge.html>.

Kaleschke, Lars. "New Trend of Arctic Sea Ice Decrease?" Sept. 2002. University of Bremen, Denmark. 1 Nov. 2003 <http://iup.physik.uni-bremen.de:8084/decade.html>.

Raphael, Catherine. "Climate Impact of Quadrupling Atmospheric CO_2—An Overview of GFDL Climate Model Results." Geophysical Fluid Dynamics Lab. 24 Oct. 2003 <http://www.gfdl.gov/~tk/climate_dynamics/index.html>.

Stocker, T. F., and A. Schmittner. "Influence of CO_2 Emission Rates on the Stability of the Thermohaline Circulation." 1997 University of Bern, Switzerland. 24 Oct. 2003 <http://www.climate.unibe.ch/~stocker/abstracts/stocker97nat.html>.

"Study Hints at Extreme Climate Change." CNN. 28 Oct. 1999. 1 Nov. 2003 <http://www.cnn.com/NATURE/9910/28/climate.change.enn/>.

"The Earth Observing System Science Plan." Goddard Space Flight Center. 1999. 1 Nov. 2003 <http://eospso.gsfc.nasa.gov/science_plan/>.

"The Great Ice Age." US Department of the Interior/US Geological Survey. 1 Nov. 2003 <http://pubs.usgs.gov/gip/ice_age/ice_age.pdf>.

Weart, Spencer. "Past Cycles: Ice Age Speculations." <u>The Discovery of Global Warming</u>. 2003. American Institute of Physics. 24 Oct. 2003 <www.aip.org/history/climate/cycles.htm>.

Wood, Anthony R. "After Mild Winters, a Possible Sea Change." <u>Philadelphia Inquirer</u>. 8 Dec. 2002. 1 Nov. 2003 <http://www.philly.com/mld/inquirer/4689103.hrm?template+contentMdules/printstory.jsp>.

QUESTIONS FOR WRITING AND DISCUSSION

Rhetorical Knowledge: The Writer's Situation and Rhetoric

1. **Audience:** Who is the intended audience for this essay? What in the essay makes you think so?

2. **Purpose:** What is Schlegel's purpose in writing this essay? What does she want her readers to understand?

3. **Voice and tone:** What tone does Schlegel take in this essay? How does this tone affect her credibility?

4. **Responsibility:** How responsibly has Deborah Schlegel written? What can you cite from her essay to illustrate your conclusion? How effectively does she present and counter opposing viewpoints?

5. **Context and format:** Deborah Schlegel is writing as a student in a first-year writing course. How does this context affect her writing? If Schlegel were writing in a different context, how might her essay change?

Critical Thinking: Your Personal Response

1. What is your initial response to Deborah Schlegel's essay? What can you point to in the text that causes you to respond in this way?

2. To what extent does Schlegel increase your concerns about global warming? Why?

3. What questions do you still have about global warming?

Critical Thinking: The Writer's Ideas

1. Does Schlegel focus mainly on causes? Effects? A series of causes and effects?

2. How do Schlegel's ideas correspond to what you already knew about global warming? What ideas do you find most surprising?

3. Are any ideas confusing? Could any part of the paper use more explanation and development? If so, what part?

Composing Processes and Knowledge of Conventions: The Writer's Strategies

1. How well do you think Schlegel has researched her topic? How can you tell? What additional research might she have done?

2. How effective is the supporting evidence that Schlegel has provided? What other evidence might you find more convincing?

3. What part(s) of Schlegel's essay are the most convincing? Why? The least convincing? Why?

Inquiry and Research: Ideas for Further Exploration

1. What questions do you have after reading Schlegel's essay? In ten minutes, write down as many as you can.

2. Conduct a search at your school library or on the Web focusing on global warming. What similarities can you find between Schlegel's essay and the information that you find in the library or on the Web? What else might she have included? Why?

3. Interview several friends about the causes and/or effects of global warming, and record their comments. In no more than two pages, write about the similarities and differences that you discover in the comments you have received.

 # Self-Assessment: Reflecting on Your Learning Goals

Now that you have constructed a piece of writing that focuses on the cause(s) and/or effect(s) of something, go back and consider your learning goals, which you and your classmates may have considered at the beginning of this chapter (see pp. 456–57). Then, reflect on all the thinking and writing that you have done in constructing your evaluative paper. To help reflect on the learning goals that you have achieved, respond in writing to the following questions:

Rhetorical Knowledge

- *Audience:* What have you learned about addressing an audience in this kind of writing?
- *Purpose:* What have you learned about the purposes for writing about causes and effects?
- *Rhetorical situation:* Consider some of the aspects that you have to think about, as a writer: How did the writing context affect your writing about cause(s) and/or effect(s)? How did your choice of subject affect the research you conducted and how you presented your analysis of cause(s) and/or effect(s) to your readers?
- *Voice and tone:* How would you describe your voice in this essay? Your tone? How do they contribute to the effectiveness of your writing about cause(s) and/or effect(s)?
- *Context, medium, and genre:* How did your context determine the medium and genre you chose, and how did those decisions affect your writing?

Critical Thinking, Reading, and Writing

- *Learning/inquiry:* While working on your paper, did you learn anything you might be able to generalize about in the causal relationship you focused on? If so, what might that be?
- *Responsibility:* How did you show that the effect or effects you wrote about were really the result of the cause or causes you identified?

- *Reading and research:* What did you learn about writing about cause(s) and effect(s) from the reading selections you read for this chapter? What research did you conduct? How sufficient was the research you did? Why? What additional research might you have done?

- What critical thinking, reading, and writing skills have you learned while being engaged in this project? How do you hope to develop them further in your next writing project? How will you work on them?

Composing Processes

- *Invention:* What invention skills have you learned in writing about causes and effects? Which skills were most useful to you?

- *Organizing your ideas and details:* Describe the process you used to identify the causes and then the effects you wrote about. How helpful was this process? How would you do it next time? How did you decide to organize your paper, and how successful was your organization?

- *Revising:* What one revision did you make that you are most satisfied with? What are the strongest and the weakest parts of the paper or other piece of writing you wrote for this chapter? Why? If you could go back and make an additional revision, what would it be?

- *Working with peers:* How have you developed your skills in working with peers? What might you do differently for your next writing assignment? How did you make use of feedback you received from both your instructor and your peers? List some of the examples of the feedback you received. Comment on how you used the feedback or chose not to use it and why. How could your peer readers help you more with your next assignment? How might you help them more, in the future, with the comments and suggestions you make on their texts?

- Did you use photographs or other visuals to help explain your cause(s) or effect(s) to readers? If so, what did you learn about incorporating these elements?

- What "writerly habits" have you developed, modified, or improved on as you constructed the writing assignment for this chapter? How will you change your future writing activities, based on what you have learned about yourself?

Conventions

- *Editing:* What sentence problem did you find most frequently in your writing? How will you avoid that problem in future assignments?

- *Genre:* What conventions of the genre you were using, if any, gave you problems?

- *Documentation:* Did you use sources for your paper? If so, what documentation style did you use? What problems, if any, did you have with it?

If you are constructing a course portfolio, file your written reflections so that you can return to them when you next work on your portfolio.

Deborah Schlegel Reflects on Her Writing

In this brief excerpt from her reflective writing, student writer Deborah Schlegel considers how she used comments from her peer reviewers, as well as her use of source material and a visual.

I found this cause and effect topic interesting because it's kind of contradictory—global warming leads to an ice age. Yet, the more I researched it, the more interesting it became. It's kind of hard to think about—that the temperature of ocean currents can lead to an ice age. It was hard to stop doing research and start writing, since the reading was so interesting.

I learned a lot about writing a paper, or actually, getting started writing a paper: listing, mapping, and those sorts of things (my teacher called them invention activities, which makes sense). I learned that the more of them I do, the better the final paper is and also that it's a lot easier to write the paper if I have all of that invention work to start with. I just have <u>so much</u> more to work with.

While I thought the comments I got back on my draft were helpful, I have to admit I was a bit resistant in incorporating them. After all, it is my paper. I know it's supposed to be an academic paper, but, still, I didn't want to sound so dry that no one would ever want to read it. I hope I did that all right. And I guess it's normal to resist someone else's ideas about your own paper. But I learned that my classmates did offer some good suggestions. I especially liked the one that suggested that I give more background information on how climate works. That comment helped me know exactly what to add to my first draft.

I also learned to read things more closely. I think most of us read and skim, just trying to get the main idea, without really paying much attention to the details. For this assignment, I tried to read more critically and to think about what the writer was trying to get across. That helped me understand what a real cause-effect relationship was, which helped me explain my own cause-effect relationships in my own paper.

I found that organizing was relatively easy in a cause-and-effect paper. First of all, I had to define my cause and show how it works. Then, naturally, I could move on to the effect—at least, the effect the scientists' computer models are predicting. I also tried to use a small visual aid so my reader could better see what I was working to say. . . .

Rhetorical Knowledge

- *Audience:* To convince your audience to accept your solution, you need to pay careful attention to your readers' views on and attitudes toward the problem. Who will be interested in your solution? What are their needs, their values, their resources? What arguments are most likely to convince this audience?

- *Purpose:* One purpose of any proposal is to convince readers of the existence of a problem and the need for a solution. Another purpose is to convince readers that the solution(s) you propose is(are) the best one(s) possible. If your solution involves money, you will also have to convince your readers that implementing your solution is cost-effective.

- *Rhetorical situation:* Think about all of the factors that affect where you stand in relation to your subject. What is compelling you to write your proposal essay?

- *Writer's voice and tone:* When you write to solve problems, you will need to be persuasive. As a result, you will need to make sure your tone engages your readers and does not in any way threaten or offend them.

- *Context, medium, and genre:* You will need to decide on the best medium and genre to use to present your proposal to the audience you want to reach. Visuals such as charts, graphs, or photographs may help you make your case.

Critical Thinking, Reading, and Writing

- *Learning/inquiry:* When you propose a solution, you first need to think critically to determine whether the problem exists and needs to be solved and whether your proposed solution is viable. You will also need to think critically about the kind of evidence that will convince your readers. Further, you will need to evaluate a range of possible solutions to find one or more that are not only viable but also effective.

- *Responsibility:* As you read solutions proposed by others, you have the responsibility to consider their solutions fairly as well as critically. You cannot simply ignore other good ideas simply because you do not agree with them.

- *Reading and research:* Readers will find your solution more acceptable if you have carefully and critically examined the problem and the issues surrounding your solution, supporting it with strong evidence, not unproven assumptions and assertions.

Chapter 11

Writing Processes

- *Invention:* As with other kinds of writing, you should start by recording on paper or computer disk the ideas that you have about your problem, using an invention strategy such as brainstorming or listing. After recording your own initial ideas and findings, you will also need to conduct research to find information that will support your proposed solution.

- *Organizing your ideas and details:* Once you have some ideas down, you can then think of how you might want to organize your main points, what evidence you might need to provide to support those points, and how you might deal with competing solutions to the problem.

- *Revising:* As you write, you will undoubtedly learn what you think about your problem and solution, and you may even qualify or change your opinion about it. Once you have a draft, you will need to read your work with a critical eye to make certain that it fulfills the assignment and displays the qualities of an effective proposal.

- *Working with peers:* Make sure you "test" your solution on your classmates. If they have trouble accepting your idea, your readers will likely have the same problem.

 Conventions

- *Editing:* One of the hallmarks of effective proposals to solve problems is the use of inclusive language—language that makes diverse readers feel like part of the team that is solving the problem. The round-robin activity in this chapter (pp. 576–77) addresses the issue of inclusive language.

- *Genres for writing to solve problems:* In your college classes, proposing a solution usually involves academic writing, so you will probably be required to follow the conventions for an academic essay. Other, nonacademic writing situations may call for a variety of genres, including reports, Web sites, editorials, brochures, letters to the editor, newspaper columns, blog entries, and formal proposals.

- *Documentation:* When writing to solve problems, you will probably need to rely on sources outside of your own experience. Make sure you document them using the appropriate style.

http://www.accion.org/about_our_mission.asp

Home Español Français

ACCIÓN
INTERNATIONAL

Giving People the Tools They Need
to Work Their Way Out of Poverty

About ACCION   Meet our Partners   Get Involved   Our Services & Products   Microfinance Resources   Media Center

about ACCION

Our Mission
ACCION's Approach
Where We Work
Key Statistics
Annual Reports/Newsletters
Our History
Awards and Recognition
Board of Directors
Management Team
President's Council
Financial Information
FAQs
Contact Us

CHARITY
NAVIGATOR
★★★★
Four Star Charity

▸ Donate Now

▸ Invest Now

▸ Meet
Microentrepreneurs

▸ ACCION Publications

▸ Need a Loan in the US?

▸ **Helping Millions
Help Themselves
Campaign**

▸ CONFERENCE: Cracking
the Capital Markets

▸ HBS-ACCION Program
on Strategic Leadership
for Microfinance

sign up for e-News

Sign Up

SOCIAL
CAPITALIST
Awards
2007

our mission

The mission of ACCION International is to give people the tools they need to work their way out of poverty. By providing "micro" loans and business training to poor women and men who start their own businesses, ACCION's partner lending organizations help people work their own way up the economic ladder, with dignity and pride. With capital, people can grow their own businesses. They can earn enough to afford basics like running water, better food and schooling for their children.

In a world where three billion people live on less than $2 a day, it is not enough to help 1,000 or even 100,000 individuals. Our goal is to bring microfinance to tens of millions of people - enough to truly change the world. We know that there will never be enough donations to do this. That's why ACCION has created an anti-poverty strategy that is permanent and self-sustaining.

Learn More About Our Work

- Why Microfinance?
- How We Work
- Who Are Our Borrowers?
- The ACCION Lending Model

Why Microfinance?
Most of the world's three billion poor people cannot find work. Where they live, few jobs are available and those that are often don't pay a living wage.

To survive, they must create their own jobs by starting tiny businesses or "microenterprises." They make and sell tortillas, sew clothes or sell vegetables in the street - anything to put food on the table.

"Microentrepreneurs" work hard - sometimes 18 hours a day. Yet with no capital to grow their businesses, they remain trapped in a cycle of poverty. To open their businesses each day, they borrow from loan sharks, who charge as much as ten percent daily, or they pay higher prices to buy goods on credit. Any profit they earn goes to others, leaving them locked in a daily struggle for survival. What they need to break free is working capital - a loan as small as $100 at a fair rate of interest. But most banks will not lend to them. The loans they need are often considered too small for banks to justify the time and expense to administer them, and microentrepreneurs lack the collateral and credit history required by traditional lenders.

That's why ACCION began issuing microloans 40 years ago. A small loan can cut the cost of raw goods or buy a sewing machine. Sales grow, and so do profits. With a growing income, people can work their way out of poverty.

In the United States, microlending helps people leave welfare, rebuilds inner city neighborhoods and provides a valuable alternative for those left behind by factory closings and corporate downsizing.

Microlending is a smart strategy because it builds on the one asset found even in the poorest communities: the power and determination of the human spirit.

Writing to Solve Problems

You see, hear, and read about problems and possible solutions to those problems all the time. The seriousness of the problems varies significantly. In developing countries, governments and nongovernmental organizations struggle with problems like starving children, poverty, or high rates of disease. Closer to home, your community might experience a high dropout rate in your local school system or a shortage of affordable housing. Less serious problems might include the lack of good coffee or exercise facilities on your campus. When you write to **propose solutions,** you first identify an existing problem and then suggest one or more possible ways to solve it. In the Web site on the opposite page, ACCION International has identified world poverty as a problem and has proposed a possible solution. ACCION started its lending program more than forty years ago, providing loans to what it calls "Microentrepreneurs," so those business owners can grow their own small companies. In turn, the interest they pay provides funding for even more small business loans.

It is ideal—but rare—when those who identify problems and propose solutions, such as ACCION, also have the means to implement them. It is more often the case that one person or group proposes a solution such as microloans, and another group finds the proposal compelling enough to take action.

When you are faced with a smaller-scale problem than world poverty, perhaps one in your own life or your friends' lives, you will often propose your own solution to it. When you suggest counseling to an unhappy friend, you are proposing a solution—a known treatment—to an emotional problem: depression. When you recommend a heating and air conditioning repair company to a friend with a broken furnace, you are proposing a solution—the repair company—to a more practical problem: the faulty furnace.

When you propose any solution, however, you may be attempting to solve a problem that various people view in a number of legitimately different ways, and others may already have suggested different solutions to the same problem. Therefore, you must support your own proposal with convincing evidence—not just opinions—and demonstrate that the proposal has a reasonable chance of success. This requirement applies to proposals written in academic, professional, civic, or personal situations. Consider the solutions that you might propose in each of these three areas:

- In response to your organization's skyrocketing travel expenses, you propose that more meetings occur via telephone conference calls or Web conferences. Others, of course, might suggest that a videoconference system might be a better approach. You might have to defend your ideas and explain why your thinking makes more sense.

- In response to a reported 46 percent failure rate in first-year math courses in your school, you propose that the school take the following two steps: (1) institute a math placement test and (2) establish an online and walk-in math tutoring center.

- In response to the deterioration of historic homes in your city, you propose that the city offer residents grants and low-interest loans to restore buildings designated as local landmarks. Others may make alternative suggestions, so you need to be sure you have the evidence to show that your solution is the best available approach.

In each situation, you will follow the same pattern: You become aware of the problem, and you respond by proposing one or more possible solutions to it, demonstrating both how your solution can work and how other solutions will not work or will not work as well.

Rhetorical Knowledge

If you want to propose a solution that your audience will take seriously, you will need to pay careful attention to rhetorical issues. Readers of any proposal will ask themselves, "Why should I believe *you*?" Therefore, all successful proposals have one important aspect in common: the establishment of a credible *ethos*. In other words, you need to be taken seriously. The nature of your subject and your audience will help determine the balance between logical arguments and emotional appeals that you will need to maintain.

Writing to Solve Problems in Your College Classes

In many of your classes, your instructor may present you with a problem and ask you to propose a solution. Of course, when your professors ask you to solve these problems, they realize that you will need to solve similar problems throughout your career, so they are hoping you will learn from the problem-solving activity itself. In many of your classes, you can expect to be asked to construct academic proposals. Here are some examples:

- In a political science class, you might be asked to propose a solution for the problems that surround the role of the Electoral College in presidential elections.
- In a course in environmental studies, you might be asked to propose ways to reduce U.S. dependence on fossil fuels.
- In a sociology course, you might be asked to propose a range of solutions to the problem of homelessness in the United States.
- In a geology course, your instructor might ask you to write a research proposal to study the problem of erosion in a nearby gully or canyon.

Writing to Solve Problems for Life

As common as it is to propose solutions in academic settings, this kind of thinking and writing is even more prevalent in the other areas of your life. Many people feel that all they ever do in their **professional lives** is propose solutions to problems. For instance, the following examples all call for proposals:

- An employee writes to his organization's communications director to suggest a solution to the problem of rapidly rising telephone bills.
- An employee writes to her company's personnel director to propose a solution to the high turnover rate in her division.
- A new member of a company's product-development division writes to her supervisor to suggest ways to reduce the time and costs required to develop and test new products.

People who are active in their communities often find themselves proposing solutions as part of their **civic life.** Since problems continually emerge—and old problems often reemerge—every community constantly needs ideas to help solve its problems. Perhaps you live in an apartment complex where many of the tenants have dogs and where pet owners and nonowners feud over the use of common areas outdoors. You might be called on to serve on a committee whose goal is to propose a solution that will allow all tenants to enjoy the areas equally. Or you might write a letter to a local newspaper in which you propose a plan for raising funds for a non-profit organization, a food bank, or a homeless shelter.

In your **personal life,** you will also encounter problems that need to be solved. Many of them will be small, but some will no doubt be large and potentially life altering. Suppose your mother, who lives alone, is suffering from a worsening case of Alzheimer's disease. You might send an e-mail to your siblings, proposing several possible solutions that you will then discuss by phone in a conference call. Or suppose your child is having a problem at school. You might send a letter to your child's teacher, suggesting a possible solution.

WRITER'S WORKSHOP

Applying Learning Goals to Writing about Solving Problems

Proposing a solution to a problem involves first making sure that you have accurately identified the real problem and then coming up with a viable solution to it that your audience will accept.

As a group, brainstorm some potential problems that students regularly complain about on your campus or that people complain about in some other community. Once you have a list of problems make sure the problem that people complain about really *is* the problem rather than simply a symptom of the problem. Next, think of a writing situation in which you would need to propose a solution to this particular problem. Perhaps the situation is a college assignment, a piece of workplace writing, a piece of writing for a civic group or organization, or a personal circumstance. With several of your classmates, discuss your writing situation in terms of the learning goals listed on pages 526–27. How would you address these goals? In what ways does it matter who your reader might be?

 ## Scenarios for Writing: Assignment Options

Your instructor may ask you to complete one or more of the following assignments that call for a solution to a problem. Each of these assignments is in the form of a *scenario,* which gives you a sense of who your audience is and what you need to accomplish with your proposal. The list of rhetorical considerations on pages 537–38 encourages you to think about your audience; purpose; voice, tone, and point of view; and context, medium, and genre for the scenario you have chosen.

We have provided two scenarios focused on academic writing and three scenarios that you might encounter outside of college. Starting on page 558, you will find guidelines for completing whatever assignment option you decide—or are asked—to complete.

Writing for College

Although you will write a variety of papers in your college courses, many of them will involve solving problems. We have designed the following scenarios so that you will learn problem-solving strategies for this course as well as others.

SCENARIO 1 Solving a Social Problem from One of Your Courses

Think about a problem—local, national, or global—that you have learned about in another class you are taking this term. To complete this assignment, assume that the instructor for this class has asked you to choose a problem and propose a solution for it, which you will present to your classmates. You must first decide which problem you wish to address and then look at various options available for solving the problem. Here are some possible social problems to consider:

- **Education:** In some states, the high school dropout rate is relatively high compared to rates in other states.
- **Criminal Justice:** In some cities, motorists run red lights more frequently than they do in other communities (Figure 11.1).
- **Business Administration:** In many sectors of the U.S. economy, relatively few women have high-level management positions.

FIGURE 11.1 Red lights are no barrier to many motorists.

- **Health:** The incidence of diabetes is relatively high among some segments of the population in the United States.
- **Nutrition:** The incidence of obesity is relatively high in the United States.

Writing Assignment: Construct a paper that proposes a solution to the social problem that you have selected. Be sure to focus on solving one aspect of the problem, thus narrowing it down to a manageable size for a three-to five-page paper.

SCENARIO 2   An Academic Paper about a Problem That Matters to You

For this scenario, decide on a problem for which you would like to propose a solution. You may choose a problem from any area of your life that you are interested in and would like to solve. Here are some possibilities:

- Your campus lacks adequate services for students with various kinds of disabilities.
- Your college needs day-care facilities for students who have young children.
- Your city's public library has too few computers, which means that patrons must wait in long lines to use the ones that are available.
- The hourly pay rate for student workers on campus is relatively low.
- The number of arrests for driving under the influence rises dramatically in your city during major holidays.

Writing Assignment: Do you have a problem on your mind? What do you think should be done about it? Answering these two questions may lead you to a topic that you will want to write about. Your audience will be your classmates and members of the community that is affected by this problem.

Writing for Life

Although proposing a solution to a problem is a common assignment in college, you will probably have to do much more problem solving in your professional life simply because it could continue for as long as forty years or more after you have finished college. You will probably be called upon to solve problems throughout your civic and personal lives as well.

SCENARIO 3   Professional Writing: A Formal Proposal to Solve a Problem

Like many college students, you may also be working at a part- or full-time job. Think about a problem related to that job and how you might solve it. Here are some typical work-related problems:

- A problem between a supervisor and one or more employees

FIGURE 11.2 What problems could working in cubicles lead to? How could they be solved?

- A dissatisfied customer
- A problem with policies in the workplace
- Low morale, possibly caused by the working environment (See Figure 11.2)
- Inadequate benefits

Writing Assignment: Construct a formal report to a supervisor or employer in which you identify a work-related problem and propose a workable solution to that problem.

SCENARIO 4 Civic Writing: A Letter to an Official Proposing a Solution to a Community Problem

Think about some problem in your community that has affected you, your family, or someone you are close to. Perhaps you have been affected by a situation like one of these:

- Some in the community are convinced that a local factory, power plant, or other facility might be an attractive target for terrorists.

FIGURE 11.3   Local merchants can be threatened when big-box superstores open nearby.

- The community's only grocery store, laundromat, or hardware store is about to close.
- A new family in your neighborhood has decided to paint its house an ugly color, or decorate the front lawn with pink flamingos, or its members play loud music late at night.
- A major chain of big-box superstores wants to build an enormous new store on the outskirts of your town, threatening the livelihood of local merchants (Figure 11.3).
- A group of angry voters wants to oust a local politician who has recently been reelected.

As you consider possible topics, you will need first to figure out what the problem is so that you can define it—and prove its existence—to others.

Writing Assignment: Construct a letter to a local official outlining and explaining the problem in your community and then identifying and proposing a workable solution to that problem.

SCENARIO 5   Personal Writing: A Letter about Solving a Problem

For this scenario, assume that there is a problem that you need to have solved and that you want to write to someone who can help solve the problem:

- Your child or younger sibling is being taunted mercilessly by a group of students in his or her classroom.

- The trash disposal unit for your building is inadequate.

- You recently encountered a problem with a defective product that is not easy to return to a store, such as a sprinkler system or a wall-to-wall carpet.

- A waiter at a local restaurant was rude to you and your guests.

- Several repair technicians have worked on your car but cannot find the problem—yet they keep charging you for their time.

- You have noisy neighbors who shout and laugh at 3:00 a.m. When you complained to the police, they told you it was an issue for your homeowners' association.

Writing Assignment: Write a letter to a person who is in a position to help solve your problem—for example, your child's or sibling's teacher—in which you explain the problem and also propose a solution to it. How would you construct such a letter? What kind of evidence would you provide? How would you ask for the help you need?

Rhetorical Considerations

Audience: While your instructor and classmates will be the primary audience for this kind of assignment, you should also consider other audiences for your proposal, depending on the scenario you have chosen. You may be proposing a solution to a problem that affects a particular segment of society; if so, you should consider that group part of your audience as well. What will your audience know about this problem? Why should they be concerned about it? How can you make your solution(s) seem reasonable to them? What kinds of responses would you expect them to have to your proposal?

Purpose: Your purpose is to identify a particular problem, convince readers that it needs attention, and propose a viable solution.

Voice, Tone, and Point of View: You may choose to write about a problem that you have strong feelings about. How much has your view of the problem—or even your view that it *is* a problem—been determined by your own value system? How will you deal with your preconceptions about the problem, and how might these preconceptions affect your tone? What attitudes, if any, do you hold toward members of your audience, and how might that affect how you present your information? For example, Michelle Mise Pollard has an objective tone as she reports on the nursing crisis in the United States (p. 541). By contrast, Thomas Friedman, in his proposal "World War III," written in the aftermath of the attacks on the World Trade Center and the Pentagon, has a more impassioned tone (see p. 548). Each writer's choice of tone is determined by his or her audience, purpose, and context.

Context, Medium, and Genre: Keeping the context of the assignment in mind, decide on a medium and a genre for your writing. How will your writing be used? Of course, your instructor will use your writing to help determine your grade for the course, so you should follow his or her instructions carefully. If you are writing for an audience beyond the classroom, consider what will be the most effective way to present your proposal to this audience. You might write a letter, prepare a report for a supervisor at work, or construct a Web site for members of your community.

For more on choosing a medium and genre, see Chapter 15 and Appendix C.

 ## Critical Thinking, Reading, and Writing

Before you begin to write your own proposal, you need to consider the qualities of a successful proposal. It also helps to read one or more proposals to get a feel for this kind of writing. Finally, you might consider how visuals could enhance your proposal, as well as the kinds of sources you will need to consult.

Effective writing that solves problems contains a clearly defined problem and a well-articulated solution that is targeted for a specific audience. In addition, this kind of writing will include convincing evidence for the proposed solution's effectiveness as well as a well-documented review of alternative solutions. Finally, an effective piece of writing that proposes a solution will include a call to action. You will learn more about the qualities of successful proposals in the reading selections that follow the next section.

 ### Learning the Qualities of Effective Proposals

A piece of writing that proposes a solution to a problem should include the following qualities:

- **A clearly defined problem.** An effective proposal first establishes the existence of a problem that is both understandable and manageable within the scope of the assignment. One way to do so is to show the specific causes of a problem. Michelle Pollard, for instance, takes care to define the crisis in nursing by showing what she views as the causes of the problem (see p. 541).

For more information on cause and effect, see Chapter 10.

- **An awareness of the audience.** For your proposal to be effective with an audience, your readers need to believe that the problem you are writing about actually exists and that your proposed solution will work. Therefore, you should use what your audience already knows and believes to shape your proposal. For instance, if your audience readily accepts that there is a problem, you need not spend time and effort on establishing that; you can focus almost exclusively on the proposed solution. If, however, your readers may be unaware of the problem, or may not believe it *is* a problem, you will need to spend time making them aware of it and convincing them to be concerned about it.

- **A well-explained solution.** Your readers need both to understand your solution and to find it reasonable. One way to help any audience understand your proposal is to use language that the audience understands, and to provide definitions of unfamiliar terms.

- **Convincing evidence for the effectiveness of the solution.** You will need to prove that your solution is viable and the best answer to the problem by supporting your assertions with evidence such as expert testimony, case studies, experimental studies, and examples of similar solutions to similar problems. A solution needs to be feasible, affordable, and effective. For instance, if you are proposing that your neighborhood install "speed bumps" to slow down traffic, you should include information about how effectively these devices work in other places to slow down vehicles and make streets safer, as well as the estimated costs of installing them.

  In his essay on grade inflation (pp. 553–54), for example, Michael Bérubé compares his solution to a similar solution that many will be familiar with from sports competitions: "The principle is simple enough, and it's crucial to every diving competition: we would merely need to account for each course's degree of difficulty" (paragraph 5). You will also need to anticipate readers' objections to your proposed solutions so that you can address them. The cost of any solution almost always comes up as an objection, so you need to be prepared to deal with that objection ("While this solution is expensive in the near future, I will demonstrate how the costs will actually save us money in the long run.").

- **A well-documented review of alternative solutions.** While your proposed solution should be able to stand on its own merits, for your proposal to convince the most skeptical readers, you must also acknowledge alternative ways to solve the problem and then in a careful, detailed fashion show why the alternatives will not work, or work as well, thus demonstrating that your solution is the best option In "World War III," Thomas Friedman suggests that, based on his experience of and sources in the Middle East, it will be almost impossible for U.S. intelligence agencies to infiltrate terrorist cells: "The only people who can penetrate these shadowy and ever-mutating groups, and deter them, are their own societies" (paragraph 6).

- **A call to action.** There is little point to proposing a solution to a problem unless someone actually implements that solution. At the end of your proposal, you should urge those who can take action to solve the problem to do so. Michelle Mise Pollard issues just such a call to her fellow nurses at the end of her proposal on ways to solve the nursing crisis in the United States (see pp. 541–46):

Whether you are a bedside nurse or a top nursing executive, it is the responsibility of us all to make our voices heard throughout the halls of our hospitals, state legislatures, and this country. We must show why it is important to improve conditions and what a wonderful and rewarding career nursing is and can be to many individuals who have much to offer this outstanding and admirable profession. If we, ourselves, have immense pride and respect for what it is we do, we have to influence others to share this frame of mind in order to make a difference in the careers we have chosen. Be proud and speak loudly, letting everyone know what a noble and caring profession it is that we share.

If you keep a version of the qualities of an effective proposal in a computer file, you can easily refer to them as you work. Rewriting the qualities in your own words will help you better remember and understand them as you research your solution and develop your proposal.

A WRITER'S RESPONSIBILITIES

Constructing Writing to Solve Problems

When you propose a solution to a problem, you have multiple responsibilities. You have a responsibility to be honest about the scope and magnitude of the problem: Who is affected and how much are they affected? In addition, if there are costs associated with your proposal, it is your responsibility to provide an accurate estimate of those costs.

You also have a responsibility to consider a range of viable solutions and to evaluate carefully the effectiveness, affordability, and limitations of each. By doing so, you establish your credibility with your readers by demonstrating that you have looked at a number of solutions, that you have thoroughly investigated each one, and that you have made a carefully considered recommendation. By presenting each option fairly and by showing how *your* solution is the best, you also make your own position more credible and believable.

Proposal writers always have a responsibility to those constituencies involved in solving the problem at hand to be accurate and thorough in their presentation of the problem and possible solutions to it. Suppose you are working with your neighbors to solve a problem with speeding cars in your area, and you have learned that your idea of "speed bumps" is more expensive than other possible solutions. You still need to discuss the cost of your idea—even if those costs might potentially weaken your argument for some of your readers. Instead of suppressing evidence, it is better to provide *more* evidence in support of your position—perhaps speed bumps are less costly to maintain than other solutions, such as hiring additional police officers to patrol the area.

Reading, Inquiry, and Research: Learning from Texts That Propose Solutions

The following selections all propose solutions. As you read the selections your instructor assigns, consider the following questions:

- How effective is the writer at convincing you that there is a problem that needs to be addressed?
- To what extent has the writer offered a workable solution?
- How convincing is the evidence? Why? What other information would it take to convince you?
- How effectively does the writer anticipate opposing views, look at alternative solutions, and otherwise show that he or she has considered the problem in depth?
- What parts of the selection could be improved? How?
- How can you use the techniques of proposal writing exemplified here in your own writing?

As you read an essay, take notes, jot down questions, and make observations about the essay in a computer file. If you want to use the information in your own writing, you will already have the main points in a digital format.

MICHELLE MISE POLLARD

The Nursing Crisis: The Solution Lies Within

As a nursing student at the University of North Carolina, Charlotte, Michelle Pollard wrote this paper for the *Journal of Undergraduate Nursing Scholarship*. In it, she vividly describes the nursing shortage in the United States, as well as some ways to solve the shortage.

Abstract

The nursing crisis, in our country, has reached such epidemic proportions   1
that congressional testimony indicates a need for immediate action. Exploring the causes, finding clues to the attrition, and understanding the implications of this worsening shortage can help us to search for solutions.

This paper attempts to express how solutions may lie within the nursing profession itself to stop the outflow of nurses from the profession and to increase the inflow of new individuals to the profession.

Introduction

On September 25th 2001, a congressional hearing took place to address the problem of the current nursing shortage, which has reached critical proportions. Members of the House of Representatives met and heard nurses tell stories of poor working conditions that include inadequate staffing, heavy workloads, use of mandatory overtime, lack of sufficient support staff, and inadequate wages. One such nurse from a Washington area hospital said eliminating mandatory overtime, setting better nurse to patient ratios and giving staff nurses a voice in hospital policy were more important than higher pay. "Until you fix the working environment, the salary issue is kind of moot" (Romig, 2001, p. 733). The current nursing shortage, unlike those of the past, appears to be headed toward a path of rapid decline.

This unstable environment in the healthcare setting has been blamed on many issues that stem from changes in healthcare to societal attitudes about the nursing profession. Steps can be taken and words spoken that can lessen the declivity[1] of nursing professionals. This has become an issue that affects all Americans and immediate steps need to be taken to stop the worsening progression of this threat to healthcare as we know it.

Exploring the Causes

An aging population of patients that are often in need of more intense and specialized care from qualified medical professionals, of which nurses comprise the largest percentage, is adding fuel to the fire of this worsening crisis (Heinrich, 2001). The increase in the number of higher acuity patients with the added burden of a shrinking nursing population results in a bleak picture for the future of the profession.

According to congressional testimony by the House Education and Workforce Committee, the nursing workforce is aging and there are not enough new nurses entering the profession to replace those retiring or leaving (Heinrich, 2001). According to Senator Jim Jeffords (2001), I-Vt, the average age of a nurse is presently between 42–45 and by 2010 nearly 40% of the nursing workforce will be over the age of 50 and nearing retirement. "Our nation has suffered from nursing shortages in the past. However, this shortage is particularly severe because we are losing nurses from both ends of the pipeline," Jeffords said.

---

[1] declining number

Clues to Attrition

Not only are the majority of nursing professionals aging, but many young people are choosing other careers. A recent study reported that women graduating from high school in the 1990s are 35% less likely to become nurses than women who graduated in the 1970s (Heinrich, 2001). Women today have more job options, many of which offer better pay, more job satisfaction, and perceived better working conditions ("Nursing Shortage" 2001).

6

Experienced nurses are opting out of nursing after many years, as well, looking for less stressful and more lucrative careers. A survey done by the Federation of Nurses and Health Professionals found that half of the currently employed RNs had considered leaving the patient care field for reasons other than retirement over the past two years (Heinrich, 2001).

7

Understanding the Implications

The shortage of qualified nursing personnel is an issue that affects anyone who is a provider or consumer of health care in this country. Consumers are affected directly by quality of care from nurses who feel they are overworked and overstressed due to the increasing demands on their time. Physicians are affected, as well, in their everyday practice and dealings with nurses and patients. According to one physician, "we are increasingly feeling the strain of a hospital nursing staff who are stretched too thin" (Stapleton, 2001, p. 30). The situation inevitably leads to a question of quality of care in settings such as hospitals.

8

As employers of the largest segment of healthcare professionals, administrators of hospitals and other facilities are also directly affected by the nursing shortage. A poll by the American Hospital Association (AHA) reports from a survey of 700 hospitals that there are approximately 126,000 nationwide RN positions currently vacant ("Publication," 2001). Maryland, for example, reported a statewide vacancy rate for hospitals of 14.7%, up from 3.3% in 1997. California reported a vacancy rate of 20% among its hospitals (Heinrich, 2001).

9

Proposing Solutions

There is no tried and true solution to a problem that has been seen before by this profession, but how do we stop the downward spiral as we lose current and future nurses to other, more attractive career choices? Efforts made to improve the workplace environment may both reduce the likelihood of nurses leaving the field and encourage more young people to enter the nursing profession. Governmental agencies can help

10

bring new nurses into the profession by offering money for tuition assistance as well as all related expenses. Hospitals and other healthcare agencies can offer more attractive employment packages and listen first-hand to the issues surrounding the dissatisfaction of their nursing staff. Nurse managers that work closely with top administrators and have voices that leaders listen to can take a stand for nursing as a whole. The reports show that nurses would have increased job satisfaction if they had better working relationships with supervisors who have real power and autonomy (Welch, 2001, p. 24). But the majority of the burden for improving the job satisfaction lies within each of us as nurses.

Improving the workplace environment has to start from within the profession itself. As Mueller (2001) notes in an article in *Creative Nursing*, "we know we are proceeding into a serious global nursing shortage. . . . And we are discovering that some of the solutions lie within each one of us" (p. 3). As nurses we have voices that can be heard through all the administrative and governmental offices, but we must find ways to speak collectively and constructively. Oftentimes nurses are not assertive in telling the story of what it is that causes them to be dissatisfied, and many degrade the profession by complaining and not acting to improve it. Do we not hurt ourselves as well as the profession by discouraging qualified individuals from choosing nursing as a career? To express ourselves completely and honestly, we must first look to develop personally and professionally. We, as nurses, need to implement a plan of action to further enhance our professionalism and solicit new members. My suggestions for such a plan include: 11

- First, "Do no harm"; do not degrade the profession by words, actions, or deeds.
- Become a teacher, mentor, role model to young professionals.
- Develop a strategy for community awareness and respect for the profession.
- Strive to continue to elevate our own personal standards and the standards of our profession (i.e., educational requirements should be MSN[2] for managers and teachers).
- Find ways to enhance the collective voice of nursing in your workplace, state, country.
- Finally, have pride and enjoy the wonderful and rewarding career that you have chosen.

---

[2] Master of Science in Nursing degree

These ideas can help our profession gain a sense of why it is we are important to society and why we are irreplaceable to the healthcare system. By continuing to discuss only the negative nursing experiences, we discourage many prospective nurses from entering the profession altogether. Nurses need to share stories of how wonderful and rewarding a career in nursing can be. "I have never been bored or disinterested in nursing because I've been able to have so many roles in many settings . . . nursing is intellectually stimulating as I read articles in nursing, attend conferences and meetings and use that knowledge in my practice . . . I could share that I have had the pleasure of participating in the professional growth and development and that almost everyday new opportunities present themselves to me because I am a nurse . . . and that I haven't regretted a day or a moment for having chosen nursing as a career" states Christine Mueller, RN, PhD (2001, p. 5).   12

It is stories like these that will bring those future nurses into a career that can be more rewarding than most. How many other careers allow you to be a part of the milestones of life like birth and death, recovery from illness and trauma, and make a difference in the lives of those who cross your path? Nurses are the backbone of the patient care setting, offering holistic care unlike any offered by other members of the healthcare team. And as nurses we have an obligation to save our profession from further deterioration and overall worsening of the nursing shortage.   13

Whether you are a bedside nurse or a top nursing executive, it is the responsibility of us all to make our voices heard throughout the halls of our hospitals, state legislatures, and this country. We must show why it is important to improve conditions and what a wonderful and rewarding career nursing is and can be to many individuals who have much to offer this outstanding and admirable profession. If we, ourselves, have immense pride and respect for what it is we do, we have to influence others to share this frame of mind in order to make a difference in the careers we have chosen. Be proud and speak loudly, letting everyone know what a noble and caring profession it is that we share.   14

References

Workforce: The people part of getting ready [Electronic Version]. (2001, October). AHA News, 37 (40), 6.

Boehner, J. (2001, September 25). *Nursing shortage*. FDCH Congressional testimony.

Bozell, J., Holcomb, S., & Kornman, C. (2002). Cut to the chase [Electronic version]. *Nursing Management, 33*(1), 39–40.

Heinrich, J. (2001, July 10). *Emerging nurse shortages due to multiple factors.* FDCH government account reports. Retrieved from http://ehost-vgw20.epnet.com

Jeffords, J. (2001, November 1). *Jeffords' legislation to strengthen nursing profession passes health committee.* FDCH press releases. Retrieved from http://ehostvgw20.epnet.com

Mueller, C. (2001). The breadth and depth of nursing. [Electronic version]. *Creative nursing, 7(4),* 3–5.

Nursing shortage: It's likely to get worse before it gets better [Electronic version]. (2001, August). *Occupational Health Management, 11(8),* 85.

Parker, C. (2001). Nursing shortage, working conditions interwined at congressional hearing [Electronic version]. *AHA News, 37(39),* 1.

Publication paints a bleak picture [Electronic version]. (2001, August). *Occupational Health Management, 11(8),* 89.

Romig, C. (2001). The nursing shortage demands action now—state and federal legislation passed [Electronic version]. *AORN Journal, 74(5),* 733.

Stapleton, S. (2001). Where's the nurse? [Electronic version]. *American Medical News, 44(23),* 30

Thompson, T. (2001, September 28). Tommy Thompson holds news conference on the nursing shortage. *FDCH Political Transcripts.* Retrieved from http://ehostvgw20.epnet.com

Welch, M. (2001–2002). The nursing shortage may be permanent [Electronic version]. *Connecticut Nursing News, 74(4),* 24.

QUESTIONS FOR WRITING AND DISCUSSION: LEARNING OUTCOMES

Rhetorical Knowledge: The Writer's Situation and Rhetoric

1. **Audience:** The author of this article is writing for nurses. How effectively has the author addressed this audience? What can you point to that tells you who her readers might be? To what other audience might you suggest this argument be made?

2. **Purpose:** In addition to suggesting how the nursing crisis might be solved, do you see any other purpose for Pollard's essay?

3. **Voice and tone:** How believable is Pollard? What can you point to in the essay that gives its author *ethos*?

4. **Responsibility:** What can you point to in the essay to show how Pollard is accurately using statistical information?

5. **Context and format:** How effective is the format of this essay? Why?

Critical Thinking: Your Personal Response

1. How aware were you of the impending crisis in nursing in the United States? How might this problem affect you or your family members?

2. What do you find appealing or unappealing about a career in nursing? Why?

3. To what extent do threatened or actual shortages affect your own career area? Or to what extent does your chosen field have the opposite problem: too many people attempting to enter it?

4. How important is it to you to find a career that is well respected? How important is a high salary? Why? In lean economic times, how appropriate is it for nurses to compete with other services for funds? What services do you think deserve funding under any circumstances? Why?

Critical Thinking: The Writer's Ideas

1. What do you think of Pollard's observation that experienced nurses are leaving because of stress in their work (paragraph 7)? What other possible reasons can you think of?

2. What is Pollard's solution? How concrete is it?

3. How much do you agree with Pollard's suggestions? Why?

Composing Processes and Knowledge of Conventions: The Writer's Strategies

1. Pollard lists ways the nursing profession can help itself in six bullet points. All of these steps seem easy to do from the outside. To what extent will these solutions have an impact on the problem?

2. What is the "best" solution that Pollard suggests, in your mind? Why?

3. What in the essay do you disagree with? That is, what aspects of Pollard's proposed solution do you think are unworkable?

Inquiry and Research: Ideas for Further Exploration

1. If your school has a nursing program, find out what enrollments are like. Are there more or fewer students now than there were ten years ago? What enrollment trends do you see?

2. If you are a nursing student or know any nursing students, find out what is drawing them into the nursing profession. As an alternative, do some additional research to find out more about reasons nurses are leaving the field.

3. Learn what tests or examinations nurses need to take to become certified in your state. Outline what is required to be a nurse.

4. Interview a nurse about his or her career. In no more than two pages, explain his or her "take" on a nursing career.

THOMAS L. FRIEDMAN

World War III

Thomas Friedman is a *New York Times* columnist specializing in foreign affairs. He has authored *From Beirut to Jerusalem* (1989), which won the National Book Award; *The Lexus and the Olive Tree: Understanding Globalization (1999); Longitudes and Attitudes: The World in the Age of Terrorism* (2003); and *The World Is Flat: A Brief History of the 21st Century* (2005). Friedman was born in Minneapolis in 1953, attended Brandeis University, and received a Master of Philosophy in Modern Middle East Studies from Oxford University. He began writing for the *Times* in 1981 and won Pulitzers in 1983 and 1988 for international reporting from Beirut and Jerusalem. In 1992, Friedman won his third Pulitzer for his commentary in the *New York Times*. Friedman wrote this editorial in the *New York Times* on Thursday, September 13, 2001.

As I restlessly lay awake early yesterday, with CNN on my TV and dawn breaking over the holy places of Jerusalem, my ear somehow latched onto a statement made by the U.S. transportation secretary, Norman Mineta[1], about the new precautions that would be put in place at U.S. airports in the wake of Tuesday's unspeakable terrorist attacks: There will be no more curbside check-in, he said. I suddenly imagined a group of terrorists somewhere here in the Middle East, sipping coffee,   1

---

[1] 14th U.S. Secretary of Transportation

also watching CNN and laughing hysterically: "Hey boss, did you hear that? We just blew up Wall Street and the Pentagon and their response is no more curbside check-in?"

I don't mean to criticize Mr. Mineta. He is doing what he can. And I have absolutely no doubt that the Bush team, when it identifies the perpetrators, will make them pay dearly. Yet there was something so absurdly futile and American about the curbside ban that I couldn't help but wonder: Does my country really understand that this is World War III? And if this attack was the Pearl Harbor of World War III, it means there is a long, long war ahead.

And this Third World War does not pit us against another superpower. It pits us—the world's only superpower and quintessential symbol of liberal, free-market, Western values—against all the super-empowered angry men and women out there. Many of these super-empowered angry people hail from failing states in the Muslim and third world. They do not share our values, they resent America's influence over their lives, politics and children, not to mention our support for Israel, and they often blame America for the failure of their societies to master modernity.

What makes them super-empowered, though, is their genius at using the networked world, the Internet and the very high technology they hate to attack us. Think about it: They turned our most advanced civilian planes into human-directed, precision-guided cruise missiles—a diabolical melding of their fanaticism and our technology. Jihad Online. And think of what they hit: The World Trade Center—the beacon of American-led capitalism that both tempts and repels them, and the Pentagon, the embodiment of American military superiority.

And think about what places in Israel the Palestinian suicide bombers have targeted most. "They never hit synagogues or settlements or Israeli religious zealots," said the *Haaretz*[2] columnist Ari Shavit. "They hit the Sbarro pizza parlor, the Netanya shopping mall. The Dolphinarium disco. They hit the yuppie Israel, not the yeshiva Israel."

So what is required to fight a war against such people in such a world? To start with, we as Americans will never be able to penetrate such small groups, often based on family ties, who live in places such as Afghanistan, Pakistan or Lebanon's wild Bekaa Valley. The only people who can penetrate these shadowy and ever-mutating groups, and deter them, are their own societies. And even they can't do it consistently. So give the C.I.A. a break.

Israeli officials will tell you that the only time they have had real quiet and real control over the suicide bombers and radical Palestinian groups, such as Hamas and Islamic Jihad, is when Yasir Arafat and his Palestinian Authority tracked them, jailed them or deterred them.

---

[2] An Israeli newspaper, also published in an English-language edition

So then the question becomes, What does it take for us to get the societies that host terrorist groups to truly act against them?   8

First we have to prove that we are serious, and that we understand that many of these terrorists hate our existence, not just our policies. In June I wrote a column about the fact that a few cell-phone threats from Osama bin Laden had prompted President Bush to withdraw the F.B.I. from Yemen, a U.S. Marine contingent from Jordan and the U.S. Fifth Fleet from its home base in the Persian Gulf. This U.S. retreat was noticed all over the region, but it did not merit a headline in any major U.S. paper. That must have encouraged the terrorists. Forget about our civilians, we didn't even want to risk our soldiers to face their threats.   9

The people who planned Tuesday's bombings combined world-class evil with world-class genius to devastating effect. And unless we are ready to put our best minds to work combating them—the World War III Manhattan project—in an equally daring, unconventional and unremitting fashion, we're in trouble. Because while this may have been the first major battle of World War III, it may be the last one that involves only conventional, non-nuclear weapons.   10

Second, we have been allowing a double game to go on with our Middle East allies for years, and that has to stop. A country like Syria has to decide: Does it want a Hezbollah embassy in Damascus or an American one? If it wants a U.S. embassy, then it cannot play host to a rogue's gallery of terrorist groups.   11

Does that mean the U.S. must ignore Palestinian concerns and Muslim economic grievances? No. Many in this part of the world crave the best of America, and we cannot forget that we are their ray of hope. But apropos of the Palestinians, the U.S. put on the table at Camp David a plan that would have gotten Yasir Arafat much of what he now claims to be fighting for. That U.S. plan may not be sufficient for Palestinians, but to say that the justifiable response to it is suicide terrorism is utterly sick.   12

Third, we need to have a serious and respectful dialogue with the Muslim world and its political leaders about why many of its people are falling behind. The fact is, no region in the world, including sub-Saharan Africa, has fewer freely elected governments than the Arab-Muslim world, which has none. Why? Egypt went through a whole period of self-criticism after the 1967 war, which produced a stronger country. Why is such self-criticism not tolerated today by any Arab leader?   13

Where are the Muslim leaders who will tell their sons to resist the Israelis—but not to kill themselves or innocent non-combatants?   14

No matter how bad, your life is sacred. Surely Islam, a grand religion that never perpetrated the sort of Holocaust against the Jews in its midst that Europe did, is being distorted when it is treated as a guidebook for suicide bombing. How is it that not a single Muslim leader will say that?

These are some of the issues we will have to address as we fight World War III. It will be a long war against a brilliant and motivated foe. When I remarked to an Israeli military official what an amazing technological feat it was for the terrorists to hijack the planes and then fly them directly into the most vulnerable spot in each building, he pooh-poohed me. 15

"It's not that difficult to learn how to fly a plane once it's up in the air," he said. "And remember, they never had to learn how to land." 16

No, they didn't. They only had to destroy. We, by contrast, have to fight in a way that is effective without destroying the very open society we are trying to protect. We have to fight hard and land safely. We have to fight the terrorists as if there were no rules, and preserve our open society as if there were no terrorists. It won't be easy. It will require our best strategists, our most creative diplomats and our bravest soldiers. Semper Fi.[3] 17

---

[3] Motto of the U.S. Marine Corps: always faithful

QUESTIONS FOR WRITING AND DISCUSSION

Rhetorical Knowledge: The Writer's Situation and Rhetoric

1. **Audience:** This editorial was written for readers of the *New York Times*. When you picture such readers, whom do you see?

2. **Purpose:** How serious is Friedman about his suggestions? How can you tell?

3. **Voice and tone:** What is it in how Friedman writes that makes him believable? What can you point to in the essay that gives its author *ethos*?

4. **Responsibility:** What can you point to in the essay to show how Friedman is accurately using statistical information?

5. **Context and format:** How effective is the format of this essay, written (as it is) as a newspaper editorial?

Critical Thinking: Your Personal Response

1. How do you feel about Friedman's suggestions for fighting (and winning) the war against terror?

2. How much do you agree with Friedman? Why?

3. What is your reaction to Friedman's last sentence? Why?

Critical Thinking: The Writer's Ideas

1. How viable are Friedman's suggestions? Why?

2. What is the weakest of Friedman's ideas? Why?

3. For a proposal to be effective, the problem must be understood. How does Friedman define his concept of "World War III" for his readers?

4. What in the opinion piece do you disagree with? That is, which of Friedman's ideas do you think are unworkable?

Composing Processes and Knowledge of Conventions: The Writer's Strategies

1. Friedman lists three things that this country needs to do to fight terrorism. Which is presented in the most effective manner? Why?

2. What is the "best" solution that Friedman suggests? What strategies does Friedman use that make this solution seem strongest to you?

3. How effective is Friedman's "first, second, third" approach in outlining his solution? What other approaches might he have used?

Inquiry and Research: Ideas for Further Exploration

1. Columnist Friedman wrote his opinion piece two days after the events of September 11, 2001. You have some hindsight on that date—hindsight that Friedman did not have. Looking back now at his suggestions, do you agree with them?

2. At your library or on *www.foreignaffairs.org*, read an essay in *Foreign Affairs* that deals with terrorism. Does the writer agree—or disagree—with any of Friedman's suggestions? How would you synthesize the Friedman essay along with the one from *Foreign Affairs*?

3. Look through *Longitudes and Attitudes: The World in the Age of Terrorism*, a collection of Friedman's columns since the attacks of September 11, 2001. How has his position, and how have his ideas, changed over time?

MICHAEL BÉRUBÉ

How to End Grade Inflation

Michael Bérubé teaches literature and cultural studies at Penn State University. Professor Bérubé is the author of *Public Access: Literary Theory and American Cultural Politics* (1994) and has co-edited *Higher Education Under Fire: Politics, Economics, and the Crisis of the Humanities* (1994), and *Bad Subjects: Political Education for Everyday Life* (1998). He has also published in the *New York Times, the Boston Globe, the Village Voice,* and numerous academic journals. This article originally appeared in the *New York Times* on May 4, 2004.

L ast month, Princeton University announced it would combat grade inflation by proposing that A-minuses, A's and A-pluses be awarded to no more than the top 35 percent of students in any course. For those of us in higher education, the news has come as a shock, almost as if Princeton had declared that spring in central New Jersey would begin promptly on March 21, with pleasant temperatures in the 60's and 70's through the end of the semester. For until now, grade inflation was like the weather: it got worse every year, or at least everyone said so, and yet hardly anybody did anything about it.

There is nothing inherently wrong with grade inflation. Imagine a system of scoring on a scale from 1 to 6 in which everyone gets a 5 and above, or a scale of 1 to 10 in which the lowest posted score is around 8.5. Such are the worlds of figure skating and gymnastics. If colleges employed similar scoring systems, the class valedictorian would come in with a 4.0, followed closely by hundreds of students above 3.95, trailed by the class clown at 3.4.

Critics would argue that we must be perilously close to such a system right now. Several years ago, Harvard awarded "honors" to 90 percent of its graduates. For its part, Princeton has disclosed that A's have been given 47 percent of the time in recent years, up from 31 percent in the mid-1970's. Perhaps grade inflation is most severe at the most elite colleges, where everyone is so far above average that the rules of the Caucus Race in "Alice in Wonderland" apply: everybody has won, and all must have prizes. At the school where I teach, Penn State, grade inflation over the same period has not been nearly so drastic. In the spring semester of 1975, the average G.P.A. was 2.86; in 2001 it had risen to only 3.02.

Still, we don't grade all that toughly. English departments have basically worked on the A/B binary system for some time: A's and A-minuses for the best students, B's for everyone else and C's, D's and F's for students who miss half the classes or threaten their teachers with bodily harm. At Penn State, A's accounted for 47 percent of the grades in English in 2002. The numbers are similar for sociology, comparative literature and psychology—and indeed for the College of Liberal Arts as a whole. The sciences and engineering, notoriously, are stingier.

What to do? If we so desired, we could recalibrate grades at Penn   5 State, at Princeton or at any college in the country. The principle is simple enough, and it's crucial to every diving competition: we would merely need to account for each course's degree of difficulty.

Every professor, and every department, produces an average grade—an   6 average for the professor over her career and an average for the discipline over the decades. And if colleges really wanted to clamp down on grade inflation, they could whisk it away statistically, simply by factoring those averages into each student's G.P.A. Imagine that G.P.A.'s were calculated on a scale of 10 with the average grade, be it a B-minus or an A-minus, counted as a 5. The B-plus in chemical engineering, where the average grade is, say, C-plus, would be rewarded accordingly and assigned a value of 8; the B-plus in psychology, where the average grade might be just over B-plus, would be graded like an easy dive, adequately executed, and given a 4.7.

After all, colleges keep all the necessary statistics—by year, by course   7 and by department. We know perfectly well which courses require a forward somersault with two and a half twists from the pike position for an A, and which courses will give B's for cannonballs. We could even encourage professors and entire departments to increase their prestige by lowering their average grade and thereby increasing their "degree of difficulty." Students who earn A's in difficult courses would benefit—as would students who earn B's.

Incorporating "degree of difficulty" into students' G.P.A.'s would turn   8 campuses upside down; it would eliminate faculty capriciousness precisely by factoring it in; and it would involve nothing more than using the numbers we already have at our disposal. It would be confusing as hell. But it would yield a world in which the average grade was never anything more or less than the middle of the scale.

QUESTIONS FOR WRITING AND DISCUSSION

Rhetorical Knowledge: The Writer's Situation and Rhetoric

1. **Audience:** Who is Bérubé's main audience for his discussion of grade inflation?

2. **Purpose:** What is Bérubé's purpose in writing this essay?

3. **Voice and tone:** How would you describe Bérubé's voice and tone in this essay? What can you cite from the essay to show what you mean?

4. **Responsibility:** Bérubé does not provide any citations or indications within his text of what his sources are for the facts and other details he supplies. What effect does this lack of attribution have on Bérubé's essay? Why?

5. **Context and format:** Bérubé is writing for the *New York Times* and, as such, his comments are in the form of a brief essay. How does such a format affect his argument?

Critical Thinking: Your Personal Response

1. What is your response to Bérubé's essay?

2. As a student, do you feel that grade inflation helps you or hurts you? Why?

3. What do you think about Princeton University's notion that grade inflation can be stopped by limiting the number of As? Why?

Critical Thinking: The Writer's Ideas

1. To what extent do you agree or disagree with Bérubé's comment that "there is nothing inherently wrong with grade inflation" (paragraph 2)? Why?

2. As an argument that grade inflation does not exist, Bérubé says that "in the spring semester of 1975, the average G.P.A. was 2.86; in 2001 it had risen to only 3.02" (paragraph 3). How much does this argument convince you? why?

3. How much do you agree or disagree with Bérubé's suggestion that grades be "averaged"? How do you think such averaging would affect your own Grade Point Average (GPA)?

4. Bérubé seems to be implying that any letter grading is inherently subjective and masks a real, objective numerical grade. Do you agree with this assumption? Why or why not?

Composing Processes and Knowledge of Conventions: The Writer's Strategies

1. Comment on Bérubé's tone in this essay. What does it suggest about the seriousness of the problem? What does it reveal about Bérubé's attitude toward the problem?

2. How seriously do you think Bérubé intends readers to take his ideas? What can you point to in the essay to support your answer?

3. Is Bérubé's use of statistics appropriate within the essay he has constructed?

Inquiry and Research: Ideas for Further Exploration

1. Interview several of your classmates about their views on grade inflation. Then interview several of your instructors about the same topic. In no more than two pages, write about the similarities and differences you found.

2. At your college library, look up "grade inflation" and find at least three sources that discuss the topic. In no more than two pages, how do the comments in the sources compare to Bérubé's?

Thinking about Visuals That Present a Problem and Give a Solution

Sometimes the most effective way of presenting your case is to show your audience the problem and the solution. You can illustrate problems and solutions in a number of ways. Two helpful ways are by using photographs and drawings.

The photograph in Figure 11.4 shows work being done on a parcel of land like the one in south Scottsdale, Arizona, that once was the site of the

FIGURE 11.4
A Construction Site

old Los Arcos Mall. The mall was closed, the site abandoned, and as you may imagine, the location subsequently became a problem for the community. Finally, Arizona State University presented a solution to Scottsdale's Los Arcos problem. The university proposed to enter into a partnership with the city of Scottsdale to build a mixed-use complex that would include technology research, commercial space, a hotel-conference center, and multifamily residential units. This first photograph shows heavy equipment at work— part of a proposal showing how the process of building the complex would get started.

As part of the proposal for the site, the partners also provided the architect's rendering of the project, called SkySong, which appears in Figure 11.5. The builders broke ground for the first phase of construction on January 20, 2006.

As you look at these two visual aids, consider these questions about the effective use of visuals in illustrating a proposal:

- How does each visual provide information about the proposal?

- What does the visual illustrate for a reader that would be hard to show with text alone?

- What other types of visuals might be useful in a proposal? How might they convince an audience to accept the writer's solution?

- How might a visual such as the architect's rendering shown in Figure 11.5 be used to mislead readers about the feasibility of a proposed solution?

FIGURE 11.5
An Architect's
Rendering of SkySong
Source: Courtesy SkySong,
rendering by Pei Cobb Freed
& Partners

Drawing on Research to Solve Problems

TechNote Your writing about problems and solutions can be improved if you investigate the kinds of solutions that would satisfy the larger community. To do so, you can use online resources to conduct primary research. To collect data or feedback from members of the ·community that will be affected by your solution, you can create a survey to collect their opinions, observations, and ideas, either developing a simple e-mail distribution list and sending a small number of good questions to targeted respondents or taking advantage of free spaces for collecting peoples' opinions and reactions on popular sites such as Facebook, MySpace, and SurveyMonkey.

For advice on conducting primary research, see Chapter 19.

Most of your research will probably focus on finding a viable solution to the problem that you have identified. Although your own experience may provide some evidence for the effectiveness of your proposed solution, personal experience is usually limited and needs to be supplemented by other forms of evidence: quotations from experts, examples, statistics, and estimates of time and financial resources drawn from reliable sources. As we have noted, accounts of other situations in which the problems and their solutions were similar to yours are a very powerful type of evidence for a proposal.

The problem you are writing about, the solution you are proposing, and the kind of essay you are constructing help to determine the kind of research you will need to conduct. For the scenarios in this chapter, for instance, you could conduct several kinds of research:

- If you are writing about the problems of high school dropouts (one of the problems suggested in Scenario 1 on p. 533), one effective method of conducting research would be to interview your classmates and others at your college, as well as students you knew (and know) in your own high school, asking why students sometimes stop going to school.

- If you are writing in response to Scenario 3 (p. 534) and plan to focus on a problem with a policy where you work, you could examine the history of how the policy has developed and changed over time. Researching the policy could help you understand why it was initially put into place and how it has been modified as the company's or organization's needs and personnel have changed.

 Writing Processes

For a tip on organizing your computer files, see page 97.

As you work on the assignment you have chosen, remember the qualities of an effective paper that proposes a solution to a problem (see pp. 538–40). The pages that follow will demonstrate to you how one student worked through her writing process as she used invention strategies to come up with ideas and then drafted, revised, and edited her proposal. As you will continue to notice, all of these processes are recursive—that is, writers move back and forth among all of the steps. After you engage in invention strategies and conduct some research, you may start writing, or you may decide to do some more research. In fact, the more writing experience you get, the more you will realize that no piece of writing is ever finished until your final draft.

If you are considering several problems for which you will propose solutions, or several different solutions to the same problem, you may want to keep each problem/solution in a separate computer file. That way, once you decide on the problem/solution you will write about, you'll have an easy time accessing the notes you took that relate specifically to your final proposal. Be sure to save your work frequently and back it up in two or more places—on an internal or external hard drive, on a USB flash drive, and on a rewritable CD or DVD.

Invention: Getting Started

As with any writing that you do, the more invention activities that you can draw on for your proposal writing, the more effective your paper will be. Regardless of the invention activities you decide to do (or your instructor asks you to do), try to answer these questions while you do your invention work:

- What do I already know about the problem?
- What possible solutions do I already have in mind to propose?
- Where might I learn more about this problem (in the library, on the Internet, by interviewing people, by conducting a survey)? What personal experience might I have that is relevant?
- What might my audience already know about this problem?
- What might their point of view be?
- What do I know about my audience? What don't I know that I should know?
- What questions do I have about the problem or about possible solutions?

WRITING ACTIVITY

Freewriting and Brainstorming

When you write to propose solutions, you can use freewriting and brainstorming either to come up with a problem or to find a solution once you have decided on that problem.

Keeping the questions above in mind, use freewriting to jot down everything you can think of either about possible problems you might want to solve or possible solutions for a problem you have already chosen.

Brainstorming is another way to record on paper or on screen the information you already know about your topic. Once you have several possible problems or several possible solutions written down, you may have an easier time finding the one you wish to focus on for your paper. Do not worry about putting this information into sentences or paragraphs; simply write down any words or phrases that come to mind. You might try responding to questions, as Esther Ellsworth does in the example on page 560.

For more on freewriting, brainstorming, and other strategies for discovery and learning, see Chapter 3.

Esther Ellsworth's Freewriting

Student writer Esther Ellsworth, who is planning to major in biology, decided to look at the problems of current land-use policy in Arizona—as well as solutions to these problems. She began with the following short piece of freewriting.

Arizona is such a beautiful state—lots of wide-open spaces with panoramic views of mountains. The state still has lots of undeveloped land, but what will happen to it as the population continues to explode? Arizona is one of the fast-growing states in the U.S., and there's no end in sight. What can be done to preserve as much natural beauty as possible. We owe it to future generations. Is there a way to bring government agencies, citizens' groups, and developers together so that everyone is on the same page?

Esther Ellsworth's Brainstorming

Ellsworth did some brainstorming to explore the issue of land use further, organizing her brainstorming by responding to a series of questions.

What do I already know about the problem?
I know that land is being gobbled up at an alarming rate in the fast-growing state of Arizona. I hear and read that in news stories all the time. I also know that some groups are concerned about the problem of willy-nilly land development.

What possible solutions do I already have in mind to propose?
Well, I think that there are no simple solutions. One part of this, though, is that there probably needs to be more coordination among state, county, and city governments.

What might my audience already know about this problem?
Others who live in the metro areas of the state must be aware of the tremendous population growth and the development that comes with it. It's on the television news and in the daily newspaper all the time.

What might their point of view be?
There's the rub. Some will see unplanned land-development as normal because that's what we've had for a long time. The developers will see it as good because they benefit financially. Government agencies and law makers will have a range of views.

What do I know about my audience? What don't I know that I should know?
I know that they cover a range of politics. Some want no government interference with development while others will be at the other end of the spectrum.

What questions do I have about the problem or about possible solutions?
Well, I wonder what's been tried elsewhere. What has worked elsewhere? Why? What hasn't worked? Why? If there isn't a perfect solution, what are some pretty good ones?

Exploring Your Ideas with Research

Once you have used invention techniques to decide on a problem and explore what you know about it, you need to conduct research to explore the problem further as well as possible solutions to it. One way to organize your research is to use the qualities of effective proposals to guide your research activities. Here are some possibilities:

For more on conducting research in the library and on the Internet, see Chapter 19.

- **A clearly defined problem:** As you do research on your problem, look at how others have defined it and narrowed it to make it more manageable.

- **An awareness of your audience:** Your research should give you a sense of how other writers have defined and addressed their audiences. Also, you should note how other writers have treated people's perceptions of the problem that you are trying to solve. What do they assume that people know about the problem? What do they assume that people do not know about the problem? How much do they assume that people care about the problem?

- **A well-articulated solution:** For most kinds of problems in the world, you will not be the first person to propose solutions. Look at how other writers have articulated their solutions.

- **Convincing evidence for the solution's effectiveness:** You will need to do research to find evidence that your proposed solution is viable. Look for expert testimony, the results of experimental research, and case studies.

- **A well-documented review of alternative solutions:** You cannot be certain that your proposed solution is the most effective one unless you have carefully reviewed a range of possible solutions. As you consider them, keep an open mind—you might find a solution that is more effective than the one that you first offered.

- **A call to action:** As you do your research, look at the language that other writers have used to inspire their readers to action.

WRITING ACTIVITY

Conducting Research

Using the list of qualities of effective proposals, begin by noting what you already know about your issue through experience or research you have conducted previously. Next, for each quality, note what research you still need to do and possible sources that you can consult, and then do that research.

Esther Ellsworth's Notes on Her Research

Reminder to self: Don't forget to include all the citations for the sources that I'm planning to use. Do this for everything or I'll be sorry later.

A clearly defined problem: I have a general sense of the problem from driving around the state—especially the metropolitan areas—and from the news coverage of land-use issues, but I need to look at some scholarly sources. This might be the kind of problem that the Morrison Institute for Public Policy (a respected "think tank") has considered.

An awareness of the audience: I think that I have a pretty good handle on the audience for this; it's fairly diverse. However, I should look at how others have addressed audiences. I wonder if the Sierra Club has a magazine or a local chapter? I'll bet there have been editorials and letters, too, in the local paper—I'll have to look there.

A well-articulated solution: I need to read a little more here, and I need to think about this. I have sort of a sense of what might be done, but I need to think about how to write this. One thing I want to read through is the local paper, the Arizona Republic, as it has stories all the time about land and space issues.

Convincing evidence for the solution's effectiveness: Here I need to read what the skeptics are writing. If I do that, I'll know what evidence to provide. Some of the land-use think-tanks (e.g., Lincoln Institute of Land Policy) may have information from both the advocates and skeptics. I also need to check the Government Documents section of the campus library.

A well-documented review of alternative solutions: If I don't look at a range of solutions, I might reinvent the wheel or miss a really good solution. I need to keep an open mind. Also, if I don't look at other possibilities, sceptics will think that I'm hiding something.

A call to action: I'll rely a lot on others here. I'll see how others have called for action—and how folks have responded to those calls. I know that the think-tank reports will include calls to action.

Reviewing Your Invention and Research

For more on developing a thesis, see Chapter 13.

After finding sources and reading them critically, you need to reconsider your thinking about your problem and your proposed solution in light of the qualities of an effective solution. You should also begin thinking about a tentative thesis—your statement of your proposed solution. Keep an open mind, though. As you draft and revise your proposal, you may continue to refine your thesis. In some cases, you might even change it drastically. People who develop the best solutions usually leave open the possibility that a better solution could occur to them at any time.

Esther Ellsworth Considers Her Research and Focuses Her Ideas

After reading through various sources and taking notes, Ellsworth wrote the following in her research journal:

> My reading has given me a better handle on the problem and its possible solutions. I think I'm ready to state that lawmakers need to pass laws that mandate a comprehensive—not simple—plan for land use. I think that I know what needs to be in a comprehensive plan, and I'll mention those components in my proposal.

WRITERS' WORKSHOP

Reacting to Your Classmates' Invention Work and Research

With any writing assignment, your invention materials and research can improve with peer feedback and suggestions. Working with several of your classmates, provide comments and suggestions and ask one another questions, with the overall goal of helping one another to understand your rhetorical situation more clearly so you can construct an effective proposal. Remember that a useful proposal includes the following:

- a clearly defined problem
- an understanding of what your audience needs to know and understand about that problem
- a clear explanation of your solution (and why it will work)
- a look at other possible solutions (and an explanation of why they are not as good as what you propose)
- a call to action

Comments

- I understand _____ about what you've generated so far.
- I especially like _____ in what you've generated so far.
- I agree with/disagree with _____.
- I'm confused when you write about _____.
- I'm not convinced yet about _____.
- These aspects of your solution— _____ and _____ —don't seem related, so I'm not sure why you've included them.

(cont'd)

(continued)

- The part about _____ seems promising, but the part about _____ seems underdeveloped.

- I'd suggest that you include these ideas or this information:

  _____   _____

  _____   _____

Questions

Why do you think this is an important problem?

What is a _____? (Ask this kind of question when something is unclear.)

What other solutions have people suggested for this problem?

What are the other perspectives on this problem? Why hasn't it been solved?

At this point, what do you think might be the best solution to this problem?

As your classmates respond to your invention work and research, listen carefully—and with an open mind—to what they are saying, and take notes so that you do not forget their questions, comments, and suggestions. Your classmates' responses to your writing will help you anticipate the responses of your audience. In proposal writing, your biggest challenge is to establish the viability of your solution for your readers, so you should solicit readers' responses as early and as often as feasible. You can get responses to your work in class, but you can also do so online, at the campus writing center, or even in your local coffee shop.

 ## Organizing Your Information

Once you know the problem you will be writing about and the solution you will be proposing, you need to consider how you might organize this material. The questions that you need to ask yourself when deciding on your organization are all rhetorical:

- Who is your audience?
- Why might they be concerned about the problem you are discussing, and why might they be willing to accept your solution? Is it in your audience's best interest to find a solution for your problem?
- What is your purpose for writing—that is, why do your readers need this solution?
- What is the most important aspect of the problem you are proposing to solve?

One method for organizing a solution to a problem is the **whole-problem pattern.** If you are following this pattern, you first grab the readers' attention and introduce the problem and then use the paragraphs that follow to explain and illustrate it. If you think that readers are already familiar with the problem, this part of the paper could be fairly short, consisting of only a paragraph or two. If you think that readers are not familiar with the problem, however, then you might need to devote several pages to explaining and illustrating it. Next, offer your proposed solution or set of solutions, followed by your response to objections that you think readers might have—that your proposal is too expensive, too labor-intensive, too risky. Then, if necessary, you can suggest ways to implement your proposed solution. Conclude with a call to action, encouraging your readers to do what you are proposing.

A second organizational approach is to **segment the problem.** This approach is useful if the problem is relatively complex and has several components. As with the whole-problem pattern described above, you begin by grabbing the readers' attention and introducing the problem and its background. You also explain and illustrate the problem, but in a general way. Next, you focus on a part of the problem that needs special attention, offering a solution and responding to objections that you anticipate. You continue, focusing on as many parts as necessary. Finally, you offer suggestions for implementation and conclude with a call to action.

A third organizational approach, which involves a **sequence of steps,** is appropriate if the problem can best be solved step-by-step. The introduction and conclusion are the same as in the other two approaches. After the introduction, however, you offer an overview of a series of steps that will solve the problem. You then explain each step in detail, provide evidence that it will work, and address any objections to it.

Here, then, are three organizational structures that you might consider for your proposal to solve a problem:

Options for Organization

Whole-Problem Pattern:	Segmenting the Problem:	Sequence of Steps:
• Introduce the problem and its background.	• Introduce the problem and its background.	• Introduce the problem and its background.
• Explain and illustrate the problem.	• Explain and illustrate the problem.	• Explain and illustrate the problem.
• Offer a solution or set of solutions.	• Explain and illustrate one part of the problem, offer a solution, respond to anticipated objections.	• Offer a multi-step solution with an overview of the steps.
• Respond to anticipated objections to the solution.		• Offer a detailed explanation of the first step.

(cont'd)

(continued)

Whole-Problem Pattern:	Segmenting the Problem:	Sequence of Steps:
• Offer suggestions for implementing the solution. • Conclude with a call to action.	• Explain and illustrate another part of the problem, offer a solution, respond to anticipated objections. • Deal similarly with any additional parts of the problem. • Offer suggestions for implementing the solution. • Conclude with a call to action.	• Deal with any additional steps that might be necessary. • Conclude with a call to action. • Offer a detailed explanation of the second step.

WRITING ACTIVITY

Deciding on an Organizational Approach

Before you construct a full draft of your proposal, consider which organizational approach will best serve your writing purpose, given the views that your audience is likely to have on the problem. It is sometimes useful to try several organizational approaches to see which one will be most effective for your specific purpose, audience, and rhetorical situation. Try writing a page or two using at least two organizational approaches before you settle on one. (Be sure to save each attempt with a different file name.) Note that these approaches are not inflexible; you may decide to adapt them, or combine elements of two or all three of them.

 ## Constructing a Complete Draft

Once you have chosen the organizational approach that works best given your audience and purpose, you are ready to construct the rest of your draft. After reviewing your notes and research and invention activities and carefully considering all of the information that you have generated, construct a first complete draft of your proposed solution, using the organizational approach that you have decided on. Remember that your thinking about the problem and its solution(s) will evolve as you write, so your ideas will most likely change as you compose the first draft of your proposal.

As you work on the draft, keep the following in mind:

- Draw on your invention work and your research. As you draft, you may discover that you need to do more invention work and/or more research.

- As you try out tentative solutions to the problem, ask peers about the kinds of evidence you need to demonstrate that the solution is viable.

- Ask yourself and peers whether visuals might help make your case.

- If you become so tired that it affects your thinking or productivity, take a break from drafting or turn to another activity.

For more on constructing visuals, see Chapter 18.

As you draft your proposal, stop occasionally to review your work, imagining that you are reading it for the first time. Consider the following questions:

- How am I describing the problem to someone who is unfamiliar with it?

- How am I following the organizational approach that I selected? How useful is that approach?

- As I draft, how well am I keeping track of the sources that I am using?

- How well do I explain the proposed solution?

- How am I considering and addressing objections to my solution that skeptics might raise?

- How well am I suggesting possible ways to implement the proposed solution?

- How well does my introduction grab readers' attention?

- How effectively does my conclusion call people to action?

Introduction: Regardless of the organizational approach that you choose, you need to begin with a strong **introduction** to capture your readers' attention and introduce the problem that you are proposing to solve. To accomplish these two goals in an introduction, you might do one or more of the following:

- *Provide a brief history of the problem.* In his essay "How to End Grade Inflation," Michael Bérubé uses his first three paragraphs to explain that the grade inflation problem has been present and growing since the 1970s.

- *Share an anecdote that clearly exemplifies the problem.* Thomas Friedman, in "World War III" presents the absurd situation of a terrorist responding to the U.S. ban on curbside check-in at airports after the attacks on September 11, 2001.

- *Quote an authority who knows the problem well.* In "The Nursing Crisis," Michelle Mise Pollard begins her report with an account of a nurse's testimony to Congress.

- *Cite some salient statistics that demonstrate the nature of the problem.* Pollard also demonstrates the potential consequences of the nursing problem by citing statistics that show that the average age of nurses is continually getting older, and by 2010 it will be nearing retirement age.

> • *Provide some information about the problem that will surprise—and possibly concern—readers.* In his second paragraph, Michael Bérubé makes the startling assertion that "there is nothing wrong with grade inflation."

Body: When you propose a solution to a problem, you should determine the most effective organizational approach for the purpose you are trying to achieve and the audience that you are addressing. The reading selections in this chapter, for example, use the organizational approaches outlined on pages 565–66 to good effect:

> • *Present a whole problem and then give solutions.* While she has no one solution to the whole problem of the nursing shortage, Pollard does propose that any real solution will succeed only if all of the people who have a stake in solving this problem work together to find a solution and not just try to fix small pieces of it.
>
> • *Segment the problem and offer suggestions for solutions to the individual parts.* In "World War III" Friedman breaks the complex problem faced by the United States down into three parts, using the transitional words "First," "Second," and "Third." While not presenting one solution, he explains that any real solution must address all the complexities both within the United States and around the world.
>
> • *Give a step-by-step solution to the problem.* Though satirical in nature, Michael Bérubé's "How to End Grade Inflation" does present his readers with a step-by-step process for addressing grade inflation.
>
> • *Show why other solutions won't work or have already failed.* Sometimes a problem has not been solved because previous solutions have only addressed its symptoms, not its root cause. If this is the case, you need to show how other solutions have failed because they have focused only on symptoms, whereas your solution will take care of the root problem.

Conclusion: In your conclusion you need to review your proposed solution, reach out to your audience, and, usually, call for readers to take action to implement the proposal. Your conclusion could include the following:

> • An outline of the problem you are working to solve.
>
> • A summary of your main points, with an explanation of why your solution would work.
>
> • A call to action—what you would like your reader to *do* now that he or she knows about the problem and your suggested solution.

Michelle Mise Pollard uses the "call to action" approach in "The Nursing Crisis: The Solution Lies Within" (p. 541).

Title: As you work on the process of composing your proposal, a title should emerge at some point—often very late in the process. The title should, of course, reflect the problem that you are addressing and might or might not hint at the solution. If you hint at a controversial solution in the title, however, you risk alienating readers whom you might otherwise win over with the strength of your argument.

VISUALIZING VARIATIONS

Alternative Forms for Solving Problems

Assume that rather than writing a formal report in response to Scenario 3, you decide to focus on a problem area such as the one that existed at the former site of Arizona's Los Arcos Mall (p. 556–57) and design a brochure that includes visuals to show what could replace the eyesore. Here is the first paragraph of the online sales information for SkySong, the project that replaced the Los Arcos Mall. Note that it has several potential audiences:

> Located at the intersection of Scottsdale and McDowell Road, SkySong is a mixed-use project consisting of 1.2 million square feet of office, research and retail space, and a hotel /conference center at full build-out. In addition to the commercial space, SkySong will include multi-family residential units.

What pictures or drawings might be useful to a potential customer, keeping in mind that the project is reaching out not only to businesses but also to people who might want to live in SkySong?

For the residential part of the project, this visual and the descriptive text that accompanies it is designed to catch a potential renter's eye:

Source: Courtesy SkySong, rendering by Pei Cobb Freed & Partners

- 325 one, two, and three-bedroom floor plans ranging in size from ±551 to ±1,583 SF
- Residential portion wraps around and conceals a 1,000 space parking garage for residents and tenants of SkySong

(cont'd)

(continued)

- Available to general public/market rate rents
- Private balconies
- In-unit washers and dryers
- Community pool, spa, and exercise facility
- State-of-the-art high-speed Internet and communications facilities
- Connectivity with office-research facilities at SkySong
- On-site recreational opportunities

The following visuals and details are directed at possible business clients:

Source: Courtesy SkySong, rendering by Toff & Associates

Source: Courtesy SkySong, rendering by Toff & Associates

- Two 4-story buildings, each approximately 150,000 square feet, frame the Eastern half of the east-west boulevard intersecting the center. Built with flexibility in mind, the buildings are designed to accommodate any tenant's space needs whether small start-up companies, expanding businesses, or regional operations.

- Using a palette of soft hues and natural desert materials, the buildings create a casual, relaxing backdrop for the stunning SkySong shade structure that captures the imagination of all those that experience it.

Consider these questions:

- Note that the two drawings on page 570 are the same, only the lower one shows a slightly longer view, so you can see more of the upper part of the building. Which one seems more welcoming? Why?

- Although these are all drawings—artist renderings—and not photographs, each one has the look and feel of a photograph. Why might the people who created these drawings want them to *seem real*, as if the buildings, people, and cars really exist?

- What do these three drawings contribute to the proposal for SkySong? What could similar drawings contribute to a proposal in the form of a brochure?

WRITING ACTIVITY

Constructing a Full Draft

After reviewing your notes and research and invention activities and carefully considering all of the material that you have generated, construct a first complete draft of your proposal, using the organizational approach that you have decided on. Remember that your thinking about your problem and solution will evolve as you write, so your ideas will most likely change as you compose the first draft of your essay.

An Excerpt from Esther Ellsworth's First Draft

In this excerpt from her first draft, note how Esther Ellsworth presents the problem to her audience. As she wrote, Ellsworth did not worry about grammar, punctuation, and mechanics; instead, she concentrated on getting her main ideas onto paper. (The numbers in circles refer to peer comments—see p. 575.)

Land Use Planning in Arizona

Population growth, and the urban expansion that accompanies it, is beginning to destroy Arizona's outdoor flavor. Because we have no statewide plan for land use, development goes unchecked and undirected; cities sprawl, and growth also hits both rural communities and historically unsettled areas. As people watch, the open land for which Arizona is famous begins to disappear; office buildings, housing developments, and utility plants swallow it up. Residents see this occurring, and they become worried about state land preservation and planning.❶

❷Land conservation is necessary for several reasons, first of which is the fact that open spaces can be used by virtually every member of the public, allowing all people to enjoy the outdoors. Guarding environments from exploitation by developers and businesses keeps public land available for all citizens' benefit. Protected environments offer space to everyone, space where people can go hiking or camping, where they can go boating or bird watching, where they can hunt or fish. With protected environments, people are free to enjoy the land in its most natural, undisturbed state. . . .

In order to have viable land use programs, we must have projects that are supported by all community sectors. . . . Just like education, immigration, and criminal justice concerns, land use will have to become part of Arizona's core political dialogue.❸

Arizona land preservation efforts must consider the state's present territory divisions and usage plans. . . . We can decide to save many of Arizona's wild areas from urbanization, and we can officially pledge to protect our environment's biodiversity.❹

The passage of Preserve Arizona also presents the challenge of linking small conservation areas to one another. . . . But neither boundary-specification nor Preserve Arizona is comprehensive enough to protect this state's land resources.❺

In almost any discussion of land use, developers and environmentalists put themselves at odds, polarizing the conversation and refusing any compromise. Therefore, if they are ever to recognize their roles as stewards of the land, both groups will have to take a step back from the argument. They must leave behind their extreme beliefs—advocating either no growth planning or total growth restriction—because both these approaches are harmful to the state. (If Arizona's open space is exploited, it will not be able to yield profit *for anyone* in the future, and if all development is stopped, we will endanger our present economic health.) The best approach to the question of land use, instead, is compromise. Our cities will continue to grow, but we can slow their rapid expansion by preserving areas in and around them. We can also preserve large tracts of land in the state's rural regions, thereby preventing most urbanization of these areas.❻❼❽

Revising

Once you have a draft, put it aside for a day or so. This break will give you the chance to come back to your text as a new reader might. Read through and revise your work, looking especially for ideas that are not explained completely, terms that are not defined, and other problem areas. As you work to revise your early drafts, hold off on doing a great deal of heavy editing. When you revise you will probably change the content and structure of your paper, so time spent working to fix problems with sentence style or grammar, punctuation, or mechanics at this stage is often wasted.

Revising means re-envisioning, re-seeing, and re-thinking your proposal. To revise effectively, you first need to read your text as if you were seeing it for the first time, with no preconceptions about the problem or the solutions you are proposing. Here are some questions to ask yourself:

- How effectively have I explained and outlined the problem(s), so my readers can understand those issues?
- What *else* might my audience want or need to know about my subject?
- How might I explain my solution(s) in sufficient detail and with enough examples so my readers can see how my ideas are logical solutions to the problem?
- How clearly have I explained and defined any terms my readers might not know?
- What other visual aids might help explain the problem and/or my solution?

Technology can help you revise and edit your writing more easily. Use your word processor's track-changes tool to try out revisions and editing changes. After you've had time to think about the possible changes, you can "accept" or "reject" them. Also, you can use your word processor's comment tool to write reminders to yourself when you get stuck with a revision or some editing task. If your classmates are offering feedback on your draft, they can also use track changes, the comment tool, or the peer-commenting feature of the software.

Many writers improve their ability to reconsider their own writing by having others respond to their text, which enables them to see how a real audience *reads* their proposal.

WRITER'S WORKSHOP

Responding to Full Drafts

Working with one or two other classmates, read each paper and offer comments and questions that will help each of you see your papers' strengths and weaknesses. You might share your comments and questions in a conversation, or you may have each reader write comments and questions (either with pen or pencil or electronically) on the writer's draft. Consider the following guidelines and questions as you do:

- Write a brief narrative comment that outlines your first impression of this draft. How effectively does the title draw you into the paper? Why? How might the title be improved? What part(s) of the text are especially effective at explaining the problem or the writer's proposed solution? What could use more explanation or definitions?

- What do you like about the draft? Provide positive and encouraging feedback to the writer.

- How successfully does the introduction grab readers' attention? What other attention grabbers might the writer try?

- How well has the writer explained the problem to someone who is unfamiliar with it? How might the writer explain it more effectively?

- How effective is the organizational approach that the writer has selected? What other approach might be more effective?

- How carefully did the writer document sources in this draft? What does he or she need to do with sources in the next version of the proposal?

- How well has the writer explained the proposed solution?

- How well has the writer addressed objections that skeptics might raise?

- How well has the writer explained possible ways to implement the proposed solution?

- Might visuals such as charts, tables, graphs, or photographs help the writer to present the problem or its solution more effectively?

- How effectively does the conclusion call people to action? What else might the writer do?

- In a brief paragraph, outline what you see as the main weaknesses of this paper—and suggest how the writer might improve the text.

Student Comments on Esther Ellsworth's First Draft

Using the questions above, Esther Ellsworth's classmates made some suggestions on her first draft. Below are comments she received, keyed to the excerpt from the first draft on pages 571–73.

1. You probably need to do more of an introduction that grabs our attention more than this does.
2. Here you might do something to build a link between these paragraphs—perhaps some language about the proposal.
3. Can you add something here about how to conduct these dialogues in ways that will help to solve the problem rather than make it worse?
4. What have people tried to do in the past? What will be the benefits of your proposed solution?
5. Is there anything else that needs to be done to solve the problem?
6. What about people who think that your proposal will restrict freedom and harm commerce?
7. You need some sort of conclusion.
8. Of course, in your revised version, you'll need to include all of your citations.

Responding to Readers' Comments

Once you have gotten feedback from your classmates, your instructor, and others about how to improve your text, you have to determine what to *do* with their suggestions and ideas. The first thing to do with any feedback is to really listen to it and consider carefully what your readers have to say. For example, how might Esther Ellsworth answer these reader suggestions?

- One reader was not taken by Ellsworth's introduction. When a peer reviewer indicates that an introduction does not excite him or her, that means that *some* readers might just stop reading at that point.
- Another reader asks for a better transition between two sections.
- A reader requests more historical background and information.

All of these questions or concerns are issues that Ellsworth needs to address. As with any feedback, it is important to listen to it carefully and consider what your reader has to say. Then it is up to you, as the author, to decide *how* to come to terms with these suggestions. You may decide to reject some comments, of course; other comments, though, deserve your attention. You may find that comments from more than one reader contradict each other. In that case, you need to use your own judgment to decide which reader's comments are on the right track.

In the final version of her paper on pages 578–85, you can see how Esther Ellsworth responded to her readers' comments, as well as to her own review of her first draft.

Knowledge of Conventions

By paying attention to conventions when they edit their work, effective writers help to meet their readers' expectations. Experienced readers expect proposals to follow accepted conventions, especially if they are written for the business world, where the requirements are often strictly prescribed. These include genre conventions, documentation, format, usage, grammar, and mechanics. Following these conventions allows your readers to concentrate on the content of what you are writing and not get distracted by unconventional forms.

 ## Editing

After you revise, you need to go through one more important step: editing and polishing. When you edit and polish your writing, you make changes to improve your style and to make your writing clearer and more concise. You also check your work to make sure it adheres to conventions of grammar, usage, punctuation, mechanics, and spelling. Use the spell-check function of your word processing program, but be sure to double-check your spelling personally (your computer cannot tell the difference between *compliment* and *complement*, but you can). If you have used sources in your paper, you should make sure you are following the documentation style your instructor requires.

See Chapter 20 for more on documenting sources using MLA or APA style.

Because it is sometimes difficult to identify small problems in a familiar text, it often helps to distance yourself from it so that you can approach the draft with fresh eyes. Some people like to put the text aside for a day or so; others try reading aloud, some even read from the last sentence to the first so that the content, and their familiarity with it, doesn't cause them to overlook an error. Checking conventions is a difficult task, so we strongly recommend that you ask classmates, friends, and tutors to read your work to help find editing problems. Another option is to post your paper on a course Web site and invite everyone in class to read it. You may get only one or two takers, but one or two is better than none.

To assist you with editing, we offer here a round-robin editing activity focused on inclusive language, which is an important concern when writing proposals.

WRITER'S WORKSHOP

Round-Robin Editing—With a Focus on Inclusive Language

When you propose solutions to problems, you need to be especially careful to use inclusive language—language that does not exclude people based on gender, ethnicity, marital status, or disability. Using inclusive language makes readers feel that they are included in the group that is solving the problem. For instance, consider the following two sentences:

Everyone had an opportunity to express his opinion about this solution.

Everyone had an opportunity to express an opinion about this solution.

The use of *his* in the first sentence may make the women in the audience feel that they are excluded and, consequently, may make them less receptive to the solution the writer is proposing. Instead, the writer should use *his or her* or revise to remove the pronoun altogether, as in the second example above.

Look for instances in your work where the writer may have inadvertently used language that excludes a group based on gender, ethnicity, marital status, or disability. If you are uncertain about whether a particular word or phrase is a problem, underline it and put a question mark in the margin. To resolve such questions, consult a grammar handbook or ask your instructor.

Genres, Documentation, and Format

If you are writing an academic paper in response to Scenarios 1 or 2, you will need to follow the conventions appropriate for the discipline in which you are writing. If you are writing a formal proposal in response to Scenario 3, you may decide to write a report with a cover memo. You will need to format your report so that it meets the needs and requirements of its intended audience. For Scenario 4, you will need to follow the conventions of a business letter.

For advice on writing in different genres, see Appendix C. For guidelines for formatting and documenting papers in MLA or APA style, see Chapter 20.

WRITING IN ACTION

Convention in Genre and Design

Proposals can also come in a visual form. Here are two examples from World War II. During the war, which the United States entered in 1941 and which ended in 1945,

(cont'd)

(continued)

the U.S. government realized that it had a problem. The enemy was getting information about troop locations from U.S. citizens who innocently talked about where their loved ones were stationed, and the enemy was then using that information to locate and attack allied troops. To solve the problem, the government published a series of posters that urged citizens to keep quiet about where their husbands, brothers, sons, and cousins were stationed.

As part of a community project or a proposal you write on the job, you might also construct a visual document such as a poster that illustrates the problem you are addressing as well as the solution that you are proposing.

Considering Genre and Design

1. How effective are these posters visually? Even though they were developed more than sixty years ago, how might they be adapted to fit today's needs?
2. Which poster do you find more effective? What reasons do you have for your choice?
3. These posters appeared in an era when there were no television commercials. If the government wanted to reach large numbers of people today with a similar campaign, what genre would you suggest they use?
4. With several of your classmates, brainstorm a list of the qualities of an effective poster. Think about features such as color and layout as well as the kinds of messages that work best.

 # A Writer Proposes a Solution: Esther Ellsworth's Final Draft

Below is the final draft of Esther Ellsworth's proposal. As you read her essay, consider whether you think her solutions will work.

One of Ellsworth's classmates made the following comment on her initial draft:

You probably need to do more of an introduction that grabs our attention more than this does.

Ellsworth responded with a new opening paragraph that attempts to catch the reader's attention by alluding to various American myths.

ESTHER ELLSWORTH

Comprehensive Land Use Planning in Arizona

The *American West.* What visions of grandeur that phrase brings to mind!   1
Repeating it aloud, I think of tumultuous rivers, steep mountains, deep canyons, wide expanses of desert, large stands of trees. I think of pioneers migrating to this area, of people coming in search of something more than they ever had before—money, adventure, freedom from religious persecution, rebirth—something to be found in the wide open spaces of the land.

I think of the native peoples who have inhabited this territory for centuries, not claiming ownership but instead simply living on the land for generations. I think of this place that I and so many others have called home.

Land—open land—is central to the identity of a western state. It is the very fact that our cities are two or three hours apart, that we have open areas without any significant development, that gives the West its character. Yet, more and more, we are losing this characteristic. Developers keep speculating, turning once-rural areas into huge planned communities. Cities keep sprouting up and spreading out, encroaching on the wilderness around them. And people keep moving to Arizona, attracted by the state's open land and renowned natural beauty, by the good weather and good recreation.

This population growth, and the urban expansion that accompanies it, is beginning to destroy Arizona's outdoor flavor. Because we have no statewide plan for land use, development goes unchecked and undirected; cities sprawl, and growth also hits both rural communities and historically unsettled areas. As people watch, the open land for which Arizona is famous begins to disappear; office buildings, housing developments, and utility plants swallow it up. Residents see this occurring, and they become worried about state land preservation and planning. People recognize that Arizona's lack of conservation measures is a problem, but they do not know what to do about it. They do not understand that a series of legislative actions can create the plan for comprehensive land use that Arizona needs.

Land conservation is necessary for several reasons. First of all, open spaces can be used by virtually every member of the public, allowing all people to enjoy the outdoors. Guarding environments from exploitation by developers and businesses keeps public land available for all citizens' benefit. Protected environments provide space for everyone, space where people can go hiking or camping, where they can go boating or bird watching, where they can hunt or fish. With protected environments, people are free to enjoy the land in its most natural, undisturbed state.

Open space is also important ecologically. By preserving the native species and genetic variation of an area, open space preserves biodiversity. Animals and plants thrive in unrestricted territories, because the land gives them access to migratory routes, new habitats, and new mating populations (Nabhan 37–39). Thus, land conservation allows Arizona's unique creatures and ecosystems to prosper: Our state is home to many protected species, and it is the site of several reintroduction efforts for California condor and Mexican wolf populations, both of which are endangered. Arizona is also one of the only places in the world to have Sonoran Desert flora and fauna, and regions like southern Arizona's "sky island" mountain ranges (the Tucson Mountains, Santa Ritas, and Catalinas) or northern

Ellsworth received this comment from a classmate:

Here you might do something to build a link between these paragraphs—perhaps some language about the proposal.

Her response was to add language that helps to serve as a bridge between the two paragraphs.

Arizona's Colorado Plateau provide research opportunities for numerous scientists (Ellsworth; "Colorado" 1). The importance of preserving this state's biodiversity, for both species protection and academic study, is clear.

Some people claim that preservation of biodiversity should not receive 6
as much attention as it does, that it stands in the way of states' economic health. Today, however, the opposite of that statement is true: Preserving biodiversity in Arizona is financially important and beneficial for everyone involved. Ecotourism, or "visitation to natural areas that involves no consumptive use of those areas," is an extremely profitable and reliable economic foundation for many communities (Leones 56). Ecotourism also happens to be one of Arizona's primary methods of attracting visitors to the state; each year, about five million people come to see the Grand Canyon alone, and the money they spend supports local economies ("Grand" 1). If the Canyon were only a hole in the ground without an incredibly diverse ecosystem, if it did not host an amazing variety of animals and plants, people would not be nearly so anxious to see it. But the canyon is <u>not</u> just a "hole in the ground," and like many areas in our state, its unadulterated natural beauty makes it attractive to visitors. This sort of beauty—found also in places like the Chiricauha Mountains and the West Fork of Oak Creek—brings visitors, and ultimately better financial health, to the state.

For all of these reasons, open space is worthy of conservation. We 7
realize, as Arizona citizens, that land use and planning are issues we need to address; they affect so many aspects of our lives that we cannot ignore them any longer. In Arizona, there is a growing need to develop a statewide vision for land appropriations, and the public has to decide how to set aside land for conservation.

In order to have viable land use programs, we must have projects that 8
are supported by all members of the community. The Sierra Club might advocate one approach while the governor's office and utility companies prefer another, and if no one is willing to construct a third, compromise plan, conservation efforts will fail. Many people want to approach land use planning as a problem to be solved quickly, as something they can look at once and then leave behind (Martori), but such thinking is also sure to fail. Because Arizona's land use patterns and needs will always change, it is impossible to establish policy that will not require periodic review. To be successful in conservation efforts, Arizona leaders and citizens must consider land use to be an ongoing concern, something that will be part of every future campaign and administration. "Governing growth will always require a perspective and process capable of balancing strong and independent values," ASU Public Affairs Professor John Stuart Hall says, and he is certainly correct (14). Just like education, immigration, and criminal justice concerns, land use will have to become part of Arizona's core political dialogue.

In response to a very short paragraph that briefly alluded to community involvement and political dialogue, one student made the following comment:

Can you add something here about how to conduct these dialogues in ways that will help to solve the problem rather than make it worse?

Ellsworth's response was to expand paragraph 8 in order to "show" community involvement and political dialogue rather than merely "tell" about it.

As we discuss land protection and development, we must also be care-   9
ful not to turn our conversations into tense political debates. This inclination toward divisiveness inhibits the communication and consensus that
are necessary for the successful establishment of a statewide land use plan.
If people argue continuously, they have difficulty understanding one another's
worries, and they do not work well together. Until Arizona's citizens decide
to establish common ground in conservation discussions, until they recognize
a shared desire to take care of the state's land, they will not make much
progress with planning. "We must struggle together," Phoenix writer Larry
Landry states in one opinion piece, "to replace animosity with civility in our
dialogue on the future of our community, to recognize the need to bring
balance into the growth versus no-growth debate . . ." (80). Until this happens, conservation efforts will have little success.

Advocates of land preservation in Arizona must consider the state's   10
present territory divisions and usage plans. Right now, about 80% of the
state is undeveloped. Most of these areas are managed by American
Indian tribes, local and state governments, the Bureau of Land Management, and the U.S. Forest Service ("Overview" 29). A person could rightly
ask, then, why more preservation efforts are necessary if so much land is
already held in the public's interest. The most direct response to this
query, the reason we need further conservation measures, is that many
people have tried to develop commercial and residential sites in these
so-far-undisturbed areas—areas meant for the general public's use—and
under present laws, such action is permissible. Under Arizona law, individuals and companies are allowed to purchase territory from the State
Land Department, even though the areas are designated State Trust
Lands (properties to be leased or sold only for the benefit of education
and criminal justice programs). Because of the present structure, the
Land Department manages to sell areas without much oversight from
courts or the public. Citizens therefore have no way to preserve State
Trust Lands for conservation, and they lose much of "the open landscape
[that is] so vital to [Arizona's] functioning ecosystem" (Walsh 143). If, as
some argue, we do not need to reconsider State Trust Land rules, how,
then, can we ever hope to preserve our open areas from development? If,
on the other hand, we reserve the right to decide the future of the Trust
Lands, we can create conservation codes for the state, designating certain areas for preservation and leaving others open to the possibility of
development. By taking this step, we can decide to save many of Arizona's
wild areas from urbanization, and we can officially pledge to protect our
environment's biodiversity.

People have tried to solve Arizona's land conservation dilemma sev-   11
eral times in the past, but they have not developed an all-encompassing

Here, one of Ellsworth's
classmates asks for some
historical perspective:

What have people
tried to do in the
past? What will be
the benefits of your
proposed solution?

Her response is to
describe some past
Arizona efforts at land
management.

preservation program. As recently as three weeks ago, when Arizona voters passed Proposition 303 (the Preserve Arizona Initiative), they did not effect the kind of change that can really save the state's open lands from development. Under Preserve Arizona, $20 million of state funding will be available every year to help local governments purchase land for conservation. But with this measure, citizens still have little assurance that Arizona's significant tracts of open space will be protected. The Preserve Arizona plan will help to guard small parcels from development by setting aside land in projects like the Scottsdale McDowell Mountain Preserve, but in the end, it will only create a fragmented string of conservation parks.

The passage of Preserve Arizona also presents the challenge of linking   12
small conservation areas to one another. If animals and plants living in Preserve Arizona territories are to thrive, each of the small protected parcels must be connected to other wild spaces. According to some people, such a requirement makes it necessary for cities to implement "greenbelt" or growth boundary policies. (A greenbelt is a permanent conservation area around a city; a growth boundary is a temporary development limit that is adjusted every few years.) But while these actions are helpful biologically, allowing animals to migrate, they are unlikely to solve the problem of open space preservation. Growth boundaries are simply too unpopular among politicians and developers to be viable conservation methods. Many officials maintain that boundaries make housing costs skyrocket, and politicians therefore hate the idea of implementing boundaries here in Arizona (DeGrove 88). It is wise to be skeptical of complaints against boundaries, however. In Portland, Oregon, which has had a growth boundary since 1973, residents have not noted significant cost-of-living increases (DeGrove 88), and Arizona cities could choose to adopt some version of the urban boundary idea, making it work in conjunction with Preserve Arizona. But neither boundary-specification nor Preserve Arizona is comprehensive enough to protect this state's land resources.

In addition to Preserve Arizona and urban boundary plans, the state   13
needs to develop two major policies: It must adjust State Trust Land rulings to designate some of these territories as permanent conservation spaces, and it must give individuals a way to designate their own properties as conservation lands.

Arizona lawmakers need to work with national officials to adjust the   14
federal regulations that make it impossible to designate State Trust Lands as permanent preservation zones. The easiest way to do this would be to create, with the federal government's approval, a "Conservation Area" classification within the State Land Department. The new

One classmate wants to know if there are other options:

Is there anything else that needs to be done to solve the problem?

Ellsworth responds by mentioning alternative options.

designation would give an undeveloped area permanent status as a non-development zone; its land would remain free of structures, and only the state government, with public approval, could build roads or utilities on it. The property could still generate revenue for the state by being leased to ranchers and farmers ("Overview" 29), but cities would never be allowed to encroach on the territory, companies would never be allowed to mine the land, and power plants would never pollute the area's air. The space would be free of concrete and steel; it would be open to animals, plants, and people.

Some Arizona residents would definitely object to setting aside these lands as Conservation Areas; the idea of non-development zoning is anathema for them because it seems like a restriction of freedom. But land conservation actually <u>guarantees</u> citizens' freedoms. It may prohibit certain individuals from disturbing the land, but it allows all citizens the freedom to use the area, and it is thus the most fair use for all involved. Through leasing to ranchers and farmers, Conservation Areas provide money for state education and criminal justice programs, and they ensure the preservation of places that are important and beneficial to all of Arizona. Also, not all State Trust Lands would become Conservation Areas; about 10 percent would still remain available for the Land Department to sell, lease, or preserve as it deems appropriate.

Once the Conservation Area system is in place, private individuals would have a means of designating their own properties for preservation. Currently, tax systems make it very difficult for large landowners to keep their areas free of development. If individuals who own large pieces of land do not use the territory for commercial purposes, like farming or ranching, they pay exorbitant property taxes. Upon reaching retirement age, many of these people find that they cannot afford to keep their land because the taxes are simply too high. Individuals who want to preserve their family's heritage and land have no way to do so, and consequently much of Arizona's agricultural and ranching lands have been sold to developers in the past few decades. If we were to allow landowners to make their properties Conservation Areas, however, and give them a tax break for doing so, we would make possible another way to preserve open spaces. It is true that each of the territory additions would be rather small (Arizona's remaining tracts of private land are not very extensive), but nonetheless, they would increase the amount of preserved open space in Arizona.

In almost any discussion of land use, developers and environmentalists put themselves at odds, polarizing the conversation and refusing any compromise. Therefore, if they are ever to recognize their roles as stewards of the land, both groups will have to take a step back from the

15

16

17

One of Ellsworth's classmates cautions about those who might not agree:

What about people who think that your proposal will restrict freedom and harm commerce?

She responds by trying to anticipate the position of potential critics and give arguments to show that her proposal will not restrict freedom.

argument. They must leave behind their extreme beliefs—advocating either no growth planning or total growth restriction—because both of these approaches are harmful to the state. If Arizona's open space is exploited, it will not be able to yield profit *for* anyone in the future, and if all development is stopped, we will endanger our present economic health. The best approach to the question of land use, instead, is compromise. Our cities will continue to grow, but we can slow their rapid expansion by preserving areas in and around them. We can also preserve large tracts of land in the state's rural regions, thereby preventing the urbanization of these areas.

Restricting growth and planning for conservation does not limit individual freedom; instead, these actions free us all from future problems with land use. They free us to enjoy the open spaces of Arizona. They free us to use the land for recreation and sustainable commerce (ranching and agriculture). By controlling cities' growth and general land use, we ensure every individual's ability to enjoy state lands in the years to come. We ensure the survival of our unique environment, and we ensure the beauty of this territory. Developing a comprehensive land use plan for Arizona will not be easy, but the legislation is possible, and developing it is a challenge we ought to accept.

18

Works Cited

"Colorado Plateau Information Network." 22 Nov. 1998 <http://ecosys.usgs.nau.edu/>.

DeGrove, John M. "State Responses to Urban Growth: Lessons for Arizona." Growth in Arizona: The Machine in the Garden. Tempe: Morrison Institute for Public Policy/ASU, 1998.

Ellsworth, Clare. Personal interview. 25 Oct. 1998.

"Grand Canyon National Park." 22 Nov. 1998 <http://www.nps.gov/grca/>.

Hall, John Stuart. "Arizona's Growth Continuum and Policy Choices." Growth in Arizona: The Machine in the Garden. Tempe: Morrison Institute for Public Policy/ASU, 1998.

Landry, Larry. "Restore the Focus on Planning." Growth in Arizona: The Machine in the Garden. Tempe: Morrison Institute for Public Policy/ASU, 1998.

Leones, Julie, and Bonnie Colby. "Tracking Expenditures of the Elusive Nature Tourists of Southeastern Arizona." Journal of Travel Research 36.3 (1998): 56.

Martori, Peter. "Land Use and Urban Growth in Arizona." Flinn Foundation Public Policy Seminar Series, Session 1.17, Oct. 1998.

Ellsworth didn't really have a conclusion in her initial draft, and one classmate commented on that:

You need some sort of conclusion.

She responded with a concluding paragraph.

Since the draft originally submitted to classmates didn't contain any formal documentation, one classmate reminded Ellsworth to add it:

Of course, in your revised version, you'll need to include all of your citations.

Ellsworth included a formal list works cited in her final draft.

"Overview of Growth in Arizona: Critical Statistics." <u>Growth in Arizona The Machine in the Garden</u>. Tempe: Morrison Institute for Public Policy/ASU, 1998.

Nabhan, Gary Paul, and Andrew R. Holdsworth. "State of the Desert Biome." <u>Growth in Arizona: The Machine in the Garden</u>. Tempe: Morrison Institute for Public Policy/ASU, 1998.

Walsh, James P. "Losing Ground: Land Fragmentation in Rural Arizona." <u>Growth in Arizona: The Machine in the Garden</u>. Tempe: Morrison Institute for Public Policy/ASU, 1998.

QUESTIONS FOR WRITING AND DISCUSSION: LEARNING OUTCOMES

Rhetorical Knowledge: The Writer's Situation and Rhetoric

1. **Audience:** Who is the intended audience for Esther Ellsworth's proposal? What makes you think that?

2. **Purpose:** What does Ellsworth hope will happen when people read her proposal?

3. **Voice and tone:** How has Ellsworth used language to help establish her *ethos* as someone who is knowledgeable about the problem of land use?

4. **Responsibility:** Comment on Ellsworth's use of sources to support her proposal. Has she used her sources responsibly? Why or why not?

5. **Context and format:** Ellsworth wrote this paper for a first-year writing course. How is that context evident in the paper? If she were to change this piece of writing to an editorial for her local newspaper, what revisions would she need to make? If she were to make a poster representing the land-use problem and her solution, what would be on the poster? (See the posters on p. 577)

Critical Thinking: Your Personal Response

1. What is your initial response to Esther Ellsworth's paper?

2. What personal experience have you had with land-use problems?

3. What do you find most interesting in Ellsworth's proposal?

Critical Thinking: The Writer's Ideas

1. How suitable is Ellsworth's notion that it is "necessary to compromise" for a paper like this—one that proposes a solution to a problem?

2. Which of Ellsworth's ideas is or are most important to you? Why?

3. How is Ellsworth's paper similar to other proposed solutions that you have read?

Composing Processes and Knowledge of Conventions: The Writer's Strategies

1. How effective is Ellsworth's introduction? Why?

2. How effectively does Ellsworth organize her proposal? What other organization would have worked?

3. How does Ellsworth provide evidence that her solution is viable? What other evidence might she have provided?

Inquiry and Research: Ideas for Further Exploration

1. Investigate land-use policies in your city, county, or state by considering the following questions:

   What are some problems with those policies?

   What research might you do to investigate the problems?

   What might you propose to solve those problems?

   You may prefer to consider other kinds of policies, such as those that relate to water use or mass transportation, for instance.

2. Interview family members and neighbors about their own feelings on what is happening to your own community and the surrounding areas.

 # Self-Assessment: Reflecting on Your Learning Goals

Having finished your proposal assignment, take some time now to reflect on the thinking and writing you have done. It is often useful to go back and reconsider your learning goals, which you and your classmates may have considered at the beginning of this chapter (see pp. 526–27). In order to better reflect on these learning goals, respond in writing to the following questions:

Rhetorical Knowledge

- *Purpose:* What have you learned about the purposes for writing a proposal?

- *Audience:* What have you learned about addressing an audience for a proposal?

- *Rhetorical situation:* Consider some of the aspects that you have to think about, as a writer: How did the writing context affect your writing about the problem you chose and the solution you proposed? How did your choice of problem and solution affect the research you conducted and how you made your case to your readers?

- *Voice and tone:* What have you learned about the writer's voice in writing a proposal? How did your voice and tone contribute to the effectiveness of your proposal?

Critical Thinking, Reading, and Writing

- *Learning/inquiry:* As a result of writing a proposal, how have you become a more critical thinker, reader, and writer?

- *Responsibility:* By writing your proposal, what have you learned about a writer's responsibility to propose a good and workable solution?

- *Reading and research:* What research did you conduct for your proposal? How sufficient was the research you did? Why? What additional research might you have done?

- What critical thinking, reading, and writing skills do you hope to develop further in your next writing project? How will you work on them?

Composing Processes

- *Invention:* What invention skills have you learned in writing your proposal? Describe the process you went through to identify the problem and the solution you wrote about. How helpful was this process? How would you do it next time? What research skills have you developed while writing your proposal?

- *Organizing your ideas and details:* How did you decide to organize your paper, and how successful was your organization? What drafting skills have you improved? Which of your composing skills still need the most work? How will you work to improve them?

- *Revising:* What revising skills have you improved? What one revision did you make that you are most satisfied with? What are the strongest and the weakest parts of the paper or other piece of writing you wrote for this chapter? Why? If you could go back and make an additional revision, what would it be?

- *Working with peers:* How did you make use of the feedback you received from both your instructor and your peers? List some examples of the feedback you received. Comment on how you used the comments or chose not to use them and why.

- How have you developed your skills in working with peers? How could your peer readers help you more on your next assignment? How might you help *them* more, in the future, with the comments and suggestions you make on their texts?

- Did you use photographs or other visuals to help you explain your problem and proposed solution? If so, what did you learn about incorporating these elements?

- What "writerly habits" have you developed, modified, or improved upon as you constructed the writing assignment for this chapter? How will you change your future writing activities, based on what you have learned about yourself?

Conventions

- *Editing:* What sentence problem did you find most frequently in your writing? How will you avoid that problem in future assignments?

- *Genre:* What conventions of the genre you were using, if any, gave you problems?

- *Documentation:* Did you use sources for your paper? If so, what documentation style did you use? What problems, if any, did you have with it?

If you are constructing a course portfolio, file your written reflections so that you can return to them when you next work on your portfolio.

 ## Esther Ellsworth Reflects on Her Writing

In this excerpt from her reflection, notice how Esther Ellsworth moves from thoughts and feelings about her topic to comments about her writing. Though this reflection is "free form," she still tries to tie things together.

> I first decided to write about this topic because I care about the beautiful land in Arizona. My first response was just to get my ideas out. Then, after reading what my classmates had said, I realized I needed to be more specific because not everyone would see the problem the same way I did. I knew I needed to present my solution to a larger audience.
>
> I know there's not one solution to preserving the undeveloped land in Arizona, but I want the conversation to get going and get serious. Preserving our natural heritage should be more important than some few people getting very rich.
>
> I think one of the interesting things I discovered while talking with people about this paper was that very few understood how connected everything is. They didn't understand the tourism dollars are directly connected to our state's "natural wonders" and that part of that has to do with the native animals and plants as well as the beautiful canyons and mesas.

I discovered that my classmates' comments were very helpful. I know I just like to say something and assume everyone will believe me. It's helpful for me to hear that I need to keep "proving my points" by having specific examples and using evidence. I also found it helpful to be reminded that I need to attract my readers' attention with an introduction that would capture their imagination. Finally, I needed to tie it all up with an effective concluding paragraph.

As I worked on the project, I found it helpful to work with the reference librarians, who helped me find some of the sources that I needed to develop the solution. I also learned to use our textbook to format my citations—both those in the text and those in the works-cited list.

Rhetorical Knowledge

- *Audience:* When you write about a creative work, you have to assess your audience's knowledge, interests, and biases carefully. For example, if you are writing about a story that you think few of your readers will be familiar with, then you may need to describe characters or narrative details. If you are writing about an obscure painting, you may need to describe details about the work more fully than you otherwise would. On the other hand, if you think that your audience is familiar with your subject, you can refer more casually to plot points or characters or aspects of the painting. You also need to consider whether your readers will have a negative or positive view of the work.

- *Purposes:* At the most basic level your ultimate purpose for writing about a creative work is to convince your readers that your perspective on that work is valid. Beyond that, you will usually have a secondary purpose, such as entertaining or informing your readers.

- *Rhetorical situation:* Consider the many factors that affect where you stand in relation to your subject. As you write about any work of art, it is crucial to clarify your stance for your readers.

- *Writer's voice and tone:* When you write about a creative work, you are trying to give readers a better understanding of the work. You need to be detailed and thorough, but you should avoid an "all knowing" or inflexible attitude that can be interpreted as arrogant. Instead, you should appear open to other interpretations.

- *Context, medium, and genre:* You will need to decide on the best medium and genre to use to write about the work at hand. For some works, such as plays or films, and especially for art, a visual may help you present your analysis.

 ## Critical Thinking, Reading, and Writing

- *Learning/inquiry:* Reading a creative work critically means going beyond simple comprehension. Works of literature have layers of meaning, so it is important to read them carefully, thoughtfully, and more than once. Works of visual art almost always present a myriad of possible interpretations as well. As you read, you need to analyze the work and synthesize and evaluate your ideas.

- *Responsibility:* Effective writing about any creative work often leads to critical thinking. When you write about literature, you see the nuances in the work, and it is vital to present those aspects in a responsible and accurate manner.

- *Reading and research:* Writing about a creative work can involve close reading as well as online and library research to discover what others have written about the work.

 ## Writing Processes

- *Invention:* Various invention activities—brainstorming, listing, clustering—can help you consider the parts of your subject and how they relate to one another. If you are reading a literary work, you may also find it helpful to annotate the work.

- *Organizing your ideas and details:* If your subject is large (for example, a novel or film, or several paintings, or a body of short stories), you might break it down into smaller parts, or you might begin with individual parts and examine each one in detail. You will need to make sure that each part of your analysis is presented clearly and logically.

- *Revising:* As you write, you will undoubtedly learn what you think about the work you are analyzing, and you may even qualify or change your ideas about it. You will need to read your paper with a critical eye, to make certain that it fulfills the assignment and displays the qualities of writing effectively about a creative work.

- *Working with peers:* Listen to your classmates to make certain that they understand what you are saying about the work. What do they say about how well your details justify your assertions?

 ## Conventions

- *Editing:* One of the conventions of an effective analysis of any creative work is the use and proper documentation of quotations. The round-robin activity in this chapter (p. 657) addresses the issue of using and documenting quotations correctly as well as using the appropriate tense to write about events in a literary work.

- *Genres for writing about literature:* Usually a text about a creative work is written as a formal essay.

- *Documentation:* If you have relied on sources outside of your own experience, you will need to cite them using the appropriate documentation style, which would usually be the MLA style.

Chapter 12

Writing about a Creative Work

Geometry

I prove a theorem and the house expands:
the windows jerk free to hover near the ceiling,
the ceiling floats away with a sigh.

As the walls clear themselves of everything
but transparency, the scent of carnations   5
leaves with them. I am out in the open

and above the windows have hinged into butterflies,
sunlight glinting where they've intersected.
They are going to some point true and unproven.

—Rita Dove

Is poetry what *you* think of when you think of "literature" or "creative work"? When you think of "literature," do you think of a poem like "Geometry" by poet Rita Dove, shown on the opposite page as she speaks to a college audience? How do you respond to "Geometry" or to other poems you have read or heard? Or do you associate the word "literature" with some other literary genre? You may associate writing about literature exclusively with academic courses, and certainly writing about literature is a common assignment in many high school and college English classes. In addition, if you plan to take courses in other disciplines in the humanities such as English literature, comparative literature, classics, a modern language and literature (perhaps in Spanish, French, German, Chinese, or Russian), women's studies, film studies, African American studies, Chicana/Chicano studies, or East Asian studies, you will spend a great deal of time during the next few years writing about literature.

However, people think and write about literature and other creative works in many places outside of the classroom. You may get opportunities to do this kind of writing even if you do not take college courses that ask you to analyze fiction, drama, or poetry. In presentations in civic and professional situations, speakers often allude to a scene or a character from a well-known novel, play, television series, or film to make a point. People often hold public discussions about the kinds of literature that should be taught in public schools or purchased by public libraries, and as a citizen you have the right and responsibility to join these conversations. In your personal life, you may have already joined the legions of people who post brief reviews of books on the Web sites of book vendors such as Amazon.com. And "literature" isn't necessarily restricted to books, short stories, plays, and poetry—it can be defined more broadly to include film and television shows, graphic novels, hypertext, song lyrics—basically, any story told in any kind of medium. Throughout your life, as you engage in countless spoken and written conversations about a novel you have read, a film you have seen, or the lyrics of your favorite song, you'll be continuing to think, talk, and write about literature. Literature is about life—lived and imagined—so you will have many opportunities to connect it to all four areas of your life.

Rhetorical Knowledge

You will usually write about creative works to help your readers understand that work in a new way. You need to think about why you want them to gain this understanding. You also need to decide what medium and genre will help you communicate with your audience most effectively.

Writing about a Creative Work in Your College Classes

This chapter will offer you some strategies for writing about imaginative literature or works of art, whether you are asked to write about that work for a composition or literature course or for a course in some other discipline. Here are some academic situations that might call for this kind of writing:

- In a composition course, your instructor asks the class to write an exploratory response to a short story you have all been assigned to read.
- In a women's studies course, your professor asks you to provide a feminist perspective on the main character in a novel by Virginia Woolf.
- In a history course, your professor instructs you to analyze how well a film portraying a real event, such as *Titanic* or *Pearl Harbor*, matches historical records of the event.

- In your political science course, you are asked to analyze the impact of a work of fiction on public events, such as the impact of the novel *Uncle Tom's Cabin* on the debate about slavery in the nineteenth century.

- In a psychology course, your instructor assigns you to write about a literary character who exhibits some of the psychological traits that you have been studying. For example, how does Shakespeare's Hamlet exhibit the Oedipus complex, as described by Sigmund Freud?

Writing about a Creative Work for Life

When you write about a creative work in your college classes, you will most often be asked to respond to and analyze literary works or works of art. If you are writing about a creative work in a professional, civic, or personal situation, however, you will consider literary texts or works of art in any number of ways, including explaining or evaluating ideas and concepts in the work(s) you read, comparing and contrasting ideas from them, and extracting information from them and relating it to your own situation.

Savvy **professionals** know that to make a complex idea understandable or to demonstrate that they share common ground with an audience, literary techniques and allusions to well-known fictional characters are often useful. An executive encouraging his employees to donate to charities during the holiday season might contrast their generosity to Charles Dickens's famous literary cheapskate, Ebenezer Scrooge, for example. Or another executive who wants to make the point that the company should not do something today that "will come back to haunt us in the future," could refer to another Dickens character from *A Christmas Carol*, the "Ghost of Christmas Past." Note that the effectiveness of an allusion depends on whether your audience is familiar with the work you are referring to—if they do not *know* the character or work, they will not understand the point you want to make.

Many people also use literature to help them make points in their **civic lives.** The topics may differ, but allusions to literature, films, or television shows can be powerful tools for helping audiences see the common ground that you share. The famous film *Mr. Smith Goes to Washington*, in which the main character filibusters the U.S. Senate, is often used to make the point that the country always needs strong, intelligent, and honest representatives in government. In the **personal area of life,** even people who do not think they are interested in literature often talk and write about the stories they see, read, and hear. When you see a film that your friends or family have also seen, you probably discuss it with them over dinner or in phone conversations. You may recommend it in an e-mail exchange with a friend, for example. You might also write about movies or books or music or art at blog sites devoted to these topics, or you may contribute book or film reviews or lists of recommendations to online databases or sites such as Amazon.com, which allows readers to post comments and reviews about its products and also allows feedback on those remarks.

Applying Learning Goals to Writing about a Creative Work

As with most writing you will do, writing about any creative work is a learning experience. Perhaps you will learn how you responded to the work: You liked it or disliked it, cared about and identified with its characters, empathized with situations portrayed in it, and appreciated how it relates to other things you know. The ideas or concepts in some stories, music, or works of art might even change some of your own ideas or perceptions.

With several classmates, think of a writing situation in which you would need or want to write about a creative work. Perhaps the situation is a college assignment, a piece of workplace writing, a piece of writing for a civic group or organization, or a personal circumstance. With the other members of your group, discuss your writing situation in terms of the learning goals listed on pages 590–91. Consider how you would address each of these goals within the situation you have chosen. For example, what would your purpose be? Who would your reader be, and what would your attitude be toward your subject?

Scenarios for Writing: Assignment Options

Your instructor may ask you to complete one or more of the following assignments that call for writing about a creative work. Each of these assignments is in the form of a *scenario*, which gives you a sense of who your audience is and what you need to accomplish with your writing. The list of rhetorical considerations on page 598 encourages you to think about your audience; purpose; voice, tone, and point of view; and context, medium, and genre for the scenario you have chosen.

We have provided two detailed academic scenarios (one that focuses on academic writing and the other that asks you to construct your own scenario) and one assignment that focuses on the kind of writing you might do in your personal life. Starting on page 629, you will find guidelines for responding to whatever assignment option you decide—or are asked—to complete.

Writing for College

SCENARIO 1   Writing a Literary Analysis for This Course

No matter what major you choose, especially in the humanities and social sciences, instructors in your college classes will probably require you to write about literature or other kinds of "stories," whether they are fiction or nonfiction, verbal or visual, and these stories will be open to numerous interpretations. This assignment will help you develop the skills to write about a wide range of literary works in a variety of fields such as history, economics, art, anthropology, education, business, and biology, among other disciplines.

Your instructor may ask you to write about one or more of the short stories that appear later in this chapter. Alternatively, your teacher may ask you to write about some other literary work—either one that he or she selects or one that you select.

Writing Assignment: Write an essay in which you analyze some feature (character, setting, point of view, plot, theme, style) in the work of literature chosen either by you or by your instructor.

SCENARIO 2   Writing an Analysis of a Creative Work That Matters to You

There are many options for this assignment. You might want to try your hand at writing a book review like the ones published in your local newspaper or in newspapers with a national audience such as the *New York Times*. You might want to post an analysis of the work on a Web site devoted to movies such as www.aintitcool.com. You might decide to use this opportunity to begin a blog site that you will maintain for months or even years to come. Or maybe you simply would like to practice using some of the writing-to-learn strategies described in Chapter 3. Try working through four or five strategies as you get to know the creative work you have chosen.

Writing Assignment: What do you read for enjoyment? What kinds of films do you like to see? What plays have you enjoyed? What short stories do you read? This assignment gives you the chance to focus on an area of real interest to you—and also gives you the opportunity to explain *why*.

Writing for Life

SCENARIO 3   Personal Writing: A Recommendation to a Friend or Family Member

When you read a wonderful book or short story, or when you see a movie that thrills you, or view an art collection that moves you, you probably want friends and family to share your enjoyment. Conversely, you do not want anyone you care about to have to waste their time reading a book or seeing a film that you consider pointless, dull, or even offensive. This scenario gives you the chance to influence the reading or viewing habits of people close to you.

Writing Assignment: Choose a novel, play, short story, poem, or film that you especially like. In a letter to a friend or family member, recommend that he or she read or see the work. Describe and show how the author has developed or used any of the following elements effectively: a character, the setting, the point of view, a provocative theme, a distinctive style. You can also write about how the work affects you. Be sure to point to specific evidence from the work to support your assertions.

Rhetorical Considerations

Audience: In addition to your instructor and classmates, who will read various drafts of this piece of writing, your audience might also include others who are interested in literature or art in general or in the work you select in particular. Your primary audience could include a wide range of readers—perhaps family, friends, or subscribers to a listserv that focuses on a particular author, director, or genre of literature, film, or some other medium. Assume that the audience you are addressing, including your classmates and your instructor, do not know anything about the work you are writing about. How much information will you need to supply to them?

Purpose: Your purpose for writing this analysis is to convince readers that your analysis of the creative work is valid and to add to readers' understanding of the work you are analyzing. You might want to analyze a character and explain your analysis. You might want to explain your view of the symbolism in a story and what that symbolism reveals. In addition, you might hope to persuade your readers that they ought to view or read the work you are considering. This assignment allows you to explore a work that interests you in depth, and then to explain to your readers the *why* behind that interest—what in the story, film, novel, or play is valuable to you, and why.

Voice, Tone, and Point of View: Choose a writer's role that fits your purpose: What are you trying to accomplish? What preconceptions or biases do you bring to your writing? As a writer, you will be working to balance your emotional and logical responses to the work you are writing about. It is important to monitor each kind of response throughout the process of composing the essay. Letting your reader know your biases and preconceptions will add to your credibility. If you are writing in response to Scenario 3, for example, consider your relationship with the friend or family member to whom you are writing the recommendation. How might your recommendation affect that relationship? How might that person's openness to your recommendation be affected by your relationship?

Context, Medium, and Genre: Define a context that relates to your purpose for writing. Who might be interested in what you have to say about this work? Where and how can you reach that audience? Depending on the assignment—and in consultation with your instructor—you could use any number of genres. Possibilities include a standard academic essay, a letter to the author or your friend or family member, a Web posting, a dialogue with the author or a character, or an annotated timeline.

Critical Thinking, Reading, and Writing

Before you begin to write your own analysis of a text, painting, music score, film, or other creative work, you need to consider the qualities of this type of writing. It also helps to read a sample analysis of a creative work. Finally, you might consider how visuals could enhance your consideration of a cinematic work, as well as the kinds of sources you might consult to inform and enrich your own perspective on a work.

Learning the Qualities of Effective Writing about a Creative Work

While in some instances you may be asked simply to explore a work of literature or art or music, in most cases you will be expected to make a point about the work you are writing about and provide evidence to support that point. As with most academic writing, you do not necessarily have to convince your readers to accept your point of view, but you do want readers to understand and appreciate your perspective. You may be asked to do the following:

- Evaluate the work.
- Analyze the entire work or some aspect of it (character, plot, theme, setting, sounds, colors, or another element).
- Explain the symbolism in the work.
- Detail and explain the imagery in the work.
- Compare a character or characters to characters in other works.
- Explain the significance of the work.
- Explain how the work causes a reaction in the reader/viewer and explore why that reaction occurs.
- Outline how the themes in a work relate to the themes of other works.
- Explain how the historical context in which the work was constructed affected its reception.

For more on writing an evaluation, see Chapter 9.

Effective writing about creative works includes these elements:

- **A clear thesis about the work.** Your main point or thesis statement should clearly state your main idea about the work in a single sentence or two. In the rest of your essay, you should support, explain, and expand on this main point. Most often you will be asked to interpret a creative work. Depending on the assignment or writing situation, though, you may be asked to analyze the work, explain some aspect of it, or compare it to or contrast it with another work instead.

- **Textual support for your assertions.** When writers make claims or state assertions about a work, they need to point to specific evidence in the work that provides support for their claims. Using evidence from a short story or other literary work usually involves paraphrasing or directly quoting phrases, clauses, or sentences from the text or lines or stanzas from a poem. If you claim that Kurtz, a character in Joseph

*For more information
about supporting
assertions, see
pages 331–32 in
Chapter 8: "Writing
to Convince."*

Conrad's novel *Heart of Darkness*, has been "driven to insanity" because of the situation he put himself into, for example, you would use quotations from the text—properly cited—to illustrate your point and provide evidence that your assertion is correct. To provide evidence from a film, you would need to describe specific scenes.

- **Attention to the elements of the work.** When you read or view a creative work in order to write about it, you need to pay close attention to its various elements. If you are reading a work of literature, for example, you need to read it more closely than you would read other kinds of texts. You probably read a newspaper for information: what is happening in the world, the country, and your community. When you read a college textbook, you read for information as well, but also to make connections with what you are reading for your class, what you already know, and what you are reading for your other courses.

   When you read a literary work such as a short story, which we will focus on in this chapter, you are reading not just for information— what happens in the story—but also for character development, for a theme or point the author is subtly making, for figurative language that conjures up images in your own mind, and for other elements that are commonly found in literary works. In other words, you are reading for the following **literary qualities** of the text:

   - **Character.** Who is the story about? Who does what? How? Why?

   - **Setting.** The time and location of the story.

   - **Point of view.** The perspective of the narrator—the person telling the story. The narrator may or may not be a character in the story. The story may be told from a first-person (*I*) perspective, or from a third-person (*he, she, they*) perspective, and the narrator may or may not know what other characters are thinking.

   - **Plot.** The sequence of events in a story—what happens. In a work of fiction such as a short story or film, the plot usually reaches a crisis point or climax and then a resolution.

   - **Theme.** A theme is what the story means, the general statement that the story makes about life. It is analogous to the thesis of an essay. Some common themes in fiction deal with life's big questions, such as man/woman relationships, why seemingly good people suffer, and what "love" is.

   - **Style.** Ernest Hemingway once said that the hard part of writing is "getting the words right." We see that famous quotation as a comment about writing style, which involves sentence structure and variation, word choices, the use of irony, and overall tone. Each author of the short stories included in this chapter has his or her own style, and in fact, writing style is one way literary authors define themselves and their texts. Hemingway, for example, has a reputation for spare writing—he loved to cut what he saw as unnecessary words—as well as for getting right into a story and for painting word-pictures the reader can truly see. Here is an example of Hemingway's style from the opening of his short book *The Old Man and the Sea*. Can you see the characters and situation Hemingway describes?

> He was an old man who fished alone in a skiff in the Gulf Stream and he had gone eighty-four days now without taking a fish. In the first forty days a boy had been with him. But after forty days without fish the boy's parents had told him the old man was now definitely and finally *salao*, which is the worst form of unlucky, and the boy had gone at their orders in another boat which caught three good fish the first week. It made the boy sad to see the old man come in each day with his skiff empty and he always went down to help him carry either the coiled lines or the gaff and harpoon and the sail that was furled around the mast. The sail was patched with flour sacks and, furled, it looked like the flag of permanent defeat.

- **Figures of speech/imagery.** Literary works often contain **figurative language,** which evokes images in the reader's mind, and symbols. Writers use **symbols** within a work to represent or indicate other things. For example, in the children's classic *The Wizard of Oz*, the Emerald City is a symbol of hope—a solution to all of the characters' problems. Writers also use **metaphors** to represent one thing as if it were another ("her hair is velvet"), **similes** to say that one thing is similar to another using the word *like* ("her smile is like the sun"), and **imagery** to create a group of closely related details that, taken together, evoke an idea. For example, notice how Robert Frost uses the color white to suggest death and decay in the following poem:

Design

Robert Frost

I found a dimpled spider, fat and white,
On a white heal-all, holding up a moth
Like a white piece of rigid satin cloth—
Assorted characters of death and blight
Mixed ready to begin the morning right,   5
Like the ingredients of a witches' broth—
A snow-drop spider, a flower like a froth,
And dead wings carried like a paper kite.

What had that flower to do with being white,
The wayside blue and innocent heal-all?   10
What brought the kindred spider to that height,
Then steered the white moth thither in the night?
What but design of darkness to appall?—
If design govern in a thing so small.

As you read, be open to feeling what the author or characters seem to feel; be open to viewing events through the eyes of the narrator or characters; be open to thinking about how you would solve the characters' problems.

One effective strategy is to read or view a work several times. The first time, you might simply read or view the work to comprehend or understand it. The second time, you might read or view the work with an eye for the kinds of literary features described in the list above. During this second reading, have a pen or pencil in hand to make the kinds of notes in the margins or in a journal described in Chapter 2, Reading Critically, and Chapter 3, Writing to Learn. After that second reading, review your marginal comments to see what in the work seems to have grabbed your attention the most. For instance, your comments may focus on characterization more than anything else. If so, consider that focus to be a cue to pay extra attention to characterization as you read or view the work a third time.

For more on the elements of creative works, see pages 637–40.

- **Sufficient context.** The amount of evidence, and the kinds of evidence, you provide your audience depends on who you see as that audience and your analysis of what they need to know and understand about the work if they are to accept your claim. That is, your understanding of your audience and how familiar they already are with the work helps you determine how much of the story you will need to summarize or how much detail about the work you will need to include, what characters you will need to describe, and what situations or events from the story you need to explain so that readers will understand your point.

A WRITER'S RESPONSIBILITIES

Writing about a Creative Work

When you write about creative works, you need to balance several kinds of responsibilities. First, you have a responsibility to present your own thinking about the work you are writing about instead of simply repeating the thoughts of others. Second, you have a responsibility to support your assertions about the work that you are analyzing. The best way to support your ideas is to excerpt or paraphrase relevant passages from the text carefully, making sure to present them accurately, document them correctly, and avoid claiming others' ideas or words as your own. Of course, you are also obligated to consider those passages that could be used to refute your assertions. Taking these passages into account and dealing with them by either accommodating or refuting claims that could be made about them will enhance your credibility with your readers. Third, you have a responsibility to use excerpts from the work fairly, in context. Using an excerpt out of context is a distortion, and readers who are familiar with the work will quickly recognize your dishonesty.

For more on documenting sources properly, see Chapter 20.

You have a responsibility to represent the creative work you are writing about accurately for several reasons. First, it is always unethical to misrepresent someone's work. Second, you always want to protect your reputation for truth and accuracy. Once you lose the trust of your readers, especially family members, it is difficult to regain that trust. This is especially the case if you are recommending a work that you think your reader might *not* like.

Reading, Inquiry, and Research: Learning from Literary Works

Reading short stories is not only fun and interesting, it is also useful, for literature can take you places you may never get to, show you lives very different from—or similar to—your own, and help you understand your own life and feelings and relationships. And when you *write* about literature, you open up a new world of learning, for by writing—which forces you to put your thoughts into some order and onto paper—you can learn more about what you think and believe about ideas implicit in the story, novel, poem, or play you are considering. Each of the following short stories is followed by questions based on the literary qualities discussed on page 600.

DON DELILLO

Videotape

Born to Italian immigrant parents in New York City in 1936, Don DeLillo earned his bachelor's degree from Fordham University in 1958. He is well known for his fifteen novels, including *White Noise* (1985), which won the National Book Award. He has also written plays, as well as the screenplay for the 2005 film *Game 6*, which tells the story of a playwright obsessed with the 1986 World Series between the Boston Red Sox and the New York Mets. This stroy first appeared in *Antaeus* in 1994 and was later included in his novel *Underworld* (1997).

It shows a man driving a car. It is the simplest sort of family video. You see a man at the wheel of a medium Dodge. 1

It is just a kid aiming her camera through the rear window of the family car at the windshield of the car behind her. 2

You know about families and their video cameras. You know how kids get involved, how the camera shows them that every subject is potentially charged, a million things they never see with the unaided eye. 3

They investigate the meaning of inert objects and dumb pets and they poke at family privacy. They learn to see things twice.

It is the kid's own privacy that is being protected here. She is twelve years old and her name is being withheld even though she is neither the victim nor the perpetrator of the crime but only the means of recording it. 4

It shows a man in a sport shirt at the wheel of his car. There is nothing else to see. The car approaches briefly, then falls back. 5

You know how children with cameras learn to work the exposed moments that define the family cluster. They break every trust, spy out the undefended space, catching Mom coming out of the bathroom in her cumbrous robe and turbaned towel, looking bloodless and plucked. It is not a joke. They will shoot you sitting on the pot if they can manage a suitable vantage. 6

The tape has the jostled sort of noneventness that marks the family product. Of course the man in this case is not a member of the family but a stranger in a car, a random figure, someone who has happened along in the slow lane. 7

It shows a man in his forties wearing a pale shirt open at the throat, the image washed by reflections and sunglint, with many jostled moments. 8

It is not just another video homicide. It is a homicide recorded by a child who thought she was doing something simple and maybe halfway clever, shooting some tape of a man in a car. 9

He sees the girl and waves briefly, wagging a hand without taking it off the wheel—an underplayed reaction that makes you like him. 10

It is unrelenting footage that rolls on and on. It has an aimless determination, a persistence that lives outside the subject matter. You are looking into the mind of home video. It is innocent, it is aimless, it is determined, it is real. 11

He is bald up the middle of his head, a nice guy in his forties whose whole life seems open to the hand-held camera. 12

But there is also an element of suspense. You keep on looking not because you know something is going to happen—of course you do know something is going to happen and you do look for that reason but you might also keep on looking if you came across this footage for the first time without knowing the outcome. There is a crude power operating here. You keep on looking because things combine to hold you fast—a sense of the random, the amateurish, the accidental, the impending. You don't think of the tape as boring or interesting. It is crude, it is blunt, it is relentless. It is the jostled part of your mind, the film that runs through your hotel brain under all the thoughts you know you're thinking. 13

The world is lurking in the camera, already framed, waiting for the boy or girl who will come along and take up the device, learn the 14 instrument, shooting old Granddad at breakfast, all stroked out so his nostrils gape, the cereal spoon baby-gripped in his pale fist.

It shows a man alone in a medium Dodge. It seems to go on forever.   15

There's something about the nature of the tape, the grain of the   16 image, the sputtering black-and-white tones, the starkness—you think this is more real, truer-to-life, than anything around you. The things around you have a rehearsed and layered and cosmetic look. The tape is superreal, or maybe underreal is the way you want to put it. It is what lies at the scraped bottom of all the layers you have added. And this is another reason why you keep on looking. The tape has a searing realness.

It shows him giving an abbreviated wave, stiff-palmed, like a signal   17 flag at a siding.

You know how families make up games. This is just another game in   18 which the child invents the rules as she goes along. She likes the idea of videotaping a man in his car. She has probably never done it before and she sees no reason to vary the format or terminate early or pan to another car. This is her game and she is learning it and playing it at the same time. She feels halfway clever and inventive and maybe slightly intrusive as well, a little bit of brazenness that spices any game.

And you keep on looking. You look because this is the nature of the   19 footage, to make a channeled path through time, to give things a shape and a destiny.

Of course if she had panned to another car, the right car at the pre-   20 cise time, she would have caught the gunman as he fired.

The chance quality of the encounter. The victim, the killer, and the   21 child with a camera. Random energies that approach a common point. There's something here that speaks to you directly, saying terrible things about forces beyond your control, lines of intersection that cut through history and logic and every reasonable layer of human expectation.

She wandered into it. The girl got lost and wandered clear-eyed into   22 horror. This is a children's story about straying too far from home. But it isn't the family car that serves as the instrument of the child's curiosity, her inclination to explore. It is the camera that puts her in the tale.

You know about holidays and family celebrations and how somebody   23 shows up with a camcorder and the relatives stand around and barely react because they're numbingly accustomed to the process of being taped and decked and shown on the VCR with the coffee and cake.

He is hit soon after. If you've seen the tape many times you know   24 from the handwave exactly when he will be hit. It is something, natu-rally, that you wait for. You say to your wife, if you're at home and she is there, Now here is where he gets it. You say, Janet, hurry up, this is where it happens.

Now here is where he gets it. You see him jolted, sort of wire-   25
shocked—then he seizes up and falls toward the door or maybe leans or
slides into the door is the proper way to put it. It is awful and unremarkable at the same time. The car stays in the slow lane. It approaches
briefly, then falls back.

You don't usually call your wife over to the TV set. She has her pro-   26
grams, you have yours. But there's a certain urgency here. You want her
to see how it looks. The tape has been running forever and now the thing
is finally going to happen and you want her to be here when he's shot.

Here it comes, all right. He is shot, head-shot, and the camera reacts,   27
the child reacts—there is a jolting movement but she keeps on taping,
there is a sympathetic response, a nerve response, her heart is beating
faster but she keeps the camera trained on the subject as he slides into
the door and even as you see him die you're thinking of the girl. At some
level the girl has to be present here, watching what you're watching,
unprepared—the girl is seeing this cold and you have to marvel at the
fact that she keeps the tape rolling.

It shows something awful and unaccompanied. You want your wife to   28
see it because it is real this time, not fancy movie violence—the realness
beneath the layers of cosmetic perception. Hurry up, Janet, here it comes. He
dies so fast. There is no accompaniment of any kind. It is very stripped. You
want to tell her it is realer than real but then she will ask what that means.

The way the camera reacts to the gunshot—a startled reaction that   29
brings pity and terror into the frame, the girl's own shock, the girl's identification with the victim.

You don't see the blood, which is probably trickling behind his ear   30
and down the back of his neck. The way his head is twisted away from
the door, the twist of the head gives you only a partial profile and it's the
wrong side, it's not the side where he was hit.

And maybe you're being a little aggressive here, practically forcing   31
your wife to watch. Why? What are you telling her? Are you making a
little statement? Like I'm going to ruin your day out of ordinary spite. Or
a big statement? Like this is the risk of existing. Either way you're rubbing her face in this tape and you don't know why.

It shows the car drifting toward the guardrail and then there's a jos-   32
tling sense of two other lanes and part of another car, a split-second blur,
and the tape ends here, either because the girl stopped shooting or
because some central authority, the police or the district attorney or the
TV station, decided there was nothing else you had to see.

This is either the tenth or eleventh homicide committed by the Texas   33
Highway Killer. The number is uncertain because the police believe that
one of the shootings may have been a copycat crime.

And there is something about videotape, isn't there, and this particular kind of serial crime? This is a crime designed for random taping and immediate playing. You sit there and wonder if this kind of crime became more possible when the means of taping and playing an event—playing it immediately after the taping—became part of the culture. The principal doesn't necessarily commit the sequence of crimes in order to see them taped and played. He commits the crimes as if they were a form of taped-and-played event. The crimes are inseparable from the idea of taping and playing. You sit there thinking that this is a crime that has found its medium, or vice versa—cheap mass production, the sequence of repeated images and victims, stark and glary and more or less unremarkable.

It shows very little in the end. It is a famous murder because it is on tape and because the murderer has done it many times and because the crime was recorded by a child. So the child is involved, the Video Kid as she is sometimes called because they have to call her something. The tape is famous and so is she. She is famous in the modern manner of people whose names are strategically withheld. They are famous without names or faces, spirits living apart from their bodies, the victims and witnesses, the underage criminals, out there somewhere at the edges of perception.

Seeing someone at the moment he dies, dying unexpectedly. This is reason alone to stay fixed to the screen. It is instructional, watching a man shot dead as he drives along on a sunny day. It demonstrates an elemental truth, that every breath you take has two possible endings. And that's another thing. There's a joke locked away here, a note of cruel slapstick that you are completely willing to appreciate. Maybe the victim's a chump, a dope, classically unlucky. He had it coming, in a way, like an innocent fool in a silent movie.

You don't want Janet to give you any crap about it's on all the time, they show it a thousand times a day. They show it because it exists, because they have to show it, because this is why they're out there. The horror freezes your soul but this doesn't mean that you want them to stop.

QUESTIONS FOR WRITING AND DISCUSSION

Your Personal Response

1. What is your initial emotional response to the story? Why do you think that you feel this way?

2. How do you respond to the violence in the story? Why?

3. How does your response to the story compare with your responses to depictions of violence in television news programs?

Questions about Characters

1. What is the effect of having a twelve-year-old girl videotape the murder of the man driving the car?

2. What is the effect of DeLillo's referring to the girl as "The Video Kid"?

3. Why do you think that the girl continues to videotape the driver after he has been shot?

Questions about Setting

1. The story has two settings—the setting for the events in the videotape and the setting for the viewing of the tape in the story. How do you as a reader mentally process these two settings simultaneously?

2. Which setting—the one in the video or the one that frames and comments on the video—has more of an impact on you? Why?

Questions about Point of View

1. What is the point of view of the story's narrator? Why do you think that DeLillo chose to use this point of view?

2. There are actually two points of view in the story—the point of view of the videographer (the girl) and the point of view of the story's narrator. As a reader, how do you mentally process the two points of view simultaneously?

3. Why does the narrator address the reader directly as "you"?

Questions about Plot

1. What is the structure of the story's plot?

2. What makes the story seem more like an essay about an experience than a short story at times?

Questions about Theme

1. What is the theme of DeLillo's story?

2. What is DeLillo saying about violence and death?

3. What is DeLillo saying about violence and death on television?

Questions about Style

1. Find examples of figurative language in the story.

2. Look at the language that DeLillo uses to describe the girl. How does that language affect you as a reader?

Questions for Further Exploration

1. Many people have written about DeLillo's story. Search the Web to find some of those responses. How do they compare with your reactions to the story?

2. What are some similarities between this story and the famous video of the assassination of President Kennedy in 1963 (the Zapruder film)?

3. In 2002, the Washington, D.C., area was terrorized by two serial killers. At your college library, look up details of that story. What parallels do you see between DeLillo's story and those events?

JOHN EDGAR WIDEMAN

Ascent by Balloon from the Yard of Walnut Street Jail

John Edgar Wideman is the author of *The Homewood Trilogy* (1981–83), written about life in the black middle-class section of Pittsburgh, where he was raised. After graduating from the University of Pennsylvania, Wideman won a Rhodes Scholarship to Oxford University—the second African-American to do so. He earned a master's degree in literature from Oxford in 1966. Wideman is the recipient of two PEN/Faulkner Awards; he has also received a MacArthur Foundation grant. This story was originally published in the journal *Callaloo* in 1996.

I am the first of my African race in space. For this achievement, I received accolades and commendations galore. Numerous offers for the story of my life. I'm told several unauthorized broadsides, purporting to be the true facts of my case from my very own lips, are being peddled about town already. A petition circulates entreating me to run for public office.

Clearly my tale is irresistible, the arc of my life emblematic of our fledgling nation's destiny, its promise for the poor and oppressed from all corners of the globe. Born of a despised race, wallowing in sin as a youth, then a prisoner in a cage, yet I rose, I rose. To unimaginable heights. Despite my humble origins, my unworthiness, my sordid past, I rose. A Lazarus in this Brave New World.

Even in a day of crude technology and maddeningly slow pace, I was an overnight sensation. A mob of forty thousand, including the President himself, hero of Trenton and Valley Forge, the father of our country as some have construed him in the press, attended the event that launched me into the public eye.

3

The event—no doubt you've heard of it, unless you are, as I once was, one of those unfortunates who must wear a black hood and speak not, nor be spoken to—the event that transformed me from convict to celebrity received the following notice in the Pennsylvania Gazette:

4

"On January 19, 1793, Jean-Pierre Blanchard, French aeronaut, ascended in his hydrogen balloon from the yard of Walnut Street Jail in Philadelphia to make the first aerial voyage in the United States. In the air forty-six minutes, the balloon landed near Woodbury, New Jersey and returned the same evening to the city in time for Citizen Blanchard to pay his respects to President Washington, who had witnessed the ascension in the morning."

5

Though I am not mentioned by name in the above, and its bland, affectless prose misses altogether the excitement of the moment, the notice does manage to convey something of the magnitude of the event. Imagine men flying like birds. The populace aghast, agawk, necks craned upward, every muscle tensed as if anticipating the tightening of the hangman's knot, its sudden yank, the irresistible gravity of the flesh as a trap door drops open beneath their feet. Men free as eagles. Aloft and soaring over the countryside. And crow though I was, my shabby black wings lifting me high as the Frenchman.

6

I was on board the balloon because little was understood about the effect of great height upon the human heart. Would that vital organ pump faster as the air grew thinner? Would the heart become engorged approaching the throne of its maker, or would it pale and shrink, the lusty blood fleeing, as once our naked parents, in shame from the Lord's awful gaze? Dr. Benjamin Rush, a man of science as well as a philanthropic soul, well known for championing the cause of a separate Negro church, had requested that a pulse glass be carried on the balloon, and thus, again, became a benefactor of the race, since who better than one of us, with our excitable blood and tropically lush hearts, to serve as guinea pig.

7

The honor fell on me. I was the Frenchman's crew. Aboard to keep the gondola neat and sanitary, a passenger so my body could register danger as we rose into those uncharted regions nearer my God to thee.

8

Jean-Pierre Blanchard was not my first Frenchman. Messrs. De 9 Beauchamp and De Tocqueville[1] had visited my cell in the Walnut Street Jail on a humanitarian, fact-finding mission among the New World barbarians to determine whether this Quaker invention, "the penitentiary," reformed criminals and deterred crime. The Frenchmen were quite taken with me. Surprised to discover I was literate. Enchanted when I read to them from the dim squalor of my cage the parable of the Good Shepherd, the words doubly touching, they assured me, coming from one who was born of a degraded and outcast race, one who, they assumed, had experienced only indifference and harshness.

No. Beg pardon. I'm confusing one time with another. Events lose 10 their shape, slide one into another when the time one is supposed to own becomes another's property. An excusable mistake, perhaps inevitable when one resides in a place whose function is to steal time, rob time of its possibilities, deaden time to one dull unending present, a present that is absolutely not a gift, but something taken away. Time drawn, quartered and eviscerated, a sharp pain hovering over the ghost of an amputated limb. Too much time, no time, time tormenting as memories of food and blankets when you lie awake all night, hungry shivering in an icy cell. No clocks. Only unvarying, iron bars of routine solitary confinement mark your passage, your extinction outside time.

I would meet De Tocqueville and De Beauchamp years after the flight 11 with Jean-Pierre Blanchard. By then I'd been transferred from Walnut Street Jail to the new prison at Cherry Hill. There, too, I would have the distinction of being the first of my race. Prisoner Number One; Charles Williams: *farmer; light black; black eyes; curly black hair; 5'7 1/2"; foot, 11"; flat nose, scar on bridge of nose, broad mouth, scar from dirk on thigh; can read.*

First prisoner of any race admitted to Cherry Hill. Warden Samuel 12 Wood greeted me with no acknowledgment nor ceremony for this particular historic achievement. Later that day, when I complained of dampness in my cell, he reminded me that the prison being new, on its shakedown cruise so to speak, one could expect certain unanticipated inconveniences. The good Warden Wood allowed me a berth in the infirmary until my cell dried out (it never did), but unfortunately the infirmary was also dank and chilly, due to lack of sunlight and ventilation, the cold miasma from marshy soil sweating up through the prison's foundation stones. So I began my residence with a hacking cough, the subterranean air at Cherry Hill as thick and pestilential as the air had been wholesome and bracing in the balloon.

I'm complaining too much. All lives are a combination of good times and bad, aren't they. We all suffer a death sentence. Today I wish to 13

[1] French author of *Democracy in America*, an account of his travels in the early years of the republic

celebrate the good, that special time rising above the earth. So up, up, and away then.

A cloudless morning. In minutes we drift to a height that turns Philadelphia into a map spread upon a table. The proud steeple of Christ Church a pen protruding from an ink well. After the lazy, curved snake of river, the grid of streets laid straight as plumb lines. I pick out the State House, Independence Hall, the Court House, Carpenters Hall, the market on High Street. And there, the yard of the Walnut Street Jail, there at 1, 2, 3, . . . count them . . . 4, 5, Sixth Street, the Jail and its adjacent yard from which we'd risen.   14

People are ants. Carriages inch along like slugs. Huge silence beats about my ears. A wind, clear and safe as those rare dreams that enfold me, slip me under their skirts and whisk me far from my cell.   15

But I must not lose myself in the splendor of the day until I execute the task that's earned me a ride. Once done, I can, we can, return to contemplating a world never seen by human eyes till just this unraveling, modern instant.   16

I place the glass on my flesh, count the pulse beats 1, 2, 3, . . . as I practiced counting rungs on the ladder of streets rising, no, *sliced* one after another, beginning at Water Street along the Delaware's edge.   17

Near the end of that momentous year, 1793, a plague of yellow fever will break out in the warren of hovels, shanties and caves along the river and nearly destroy Philadelphia. My Negro brethren, who inhabit that Quarter in large numbers, will perform admirably with enormous courage, skill and compassion during the emergency. Nursing the afflicted, burying the dead. One measure of the city's desperation in that calamitous year, a petition that circulates (unsuccessfully) suggesting we, the immates of the jail, be allowed to serve and, thereby risking our lives, purchase freedom. This is the year that famous prisoner, the French King, is executed and my brethren will build their separate church, the African Episcopal Church of St. Thomas at Fifth and Walnut, a location empty at the moment, though cleared and ready. See it, a mere thumb print opposite the Jail from this elevation.   18

The Quakers, with their concern for the state of my soul, their insistence I have boundless opportunity to contemplate my sins, to repent and do penance, arrange matters in the Jail so I have ample time to consider things consequential and not. I've often pondered late at night when I cannot sleep, the symmetry between two events of that busy year, 1793: the separation of black from white in God's House, the plague that took so many citizens' lives. One act, *man's*, an assertion there is not enough room in the house of worship; the second act, *God's*, making more room.   19

During the terrible months when the city teetered on the brink of   20
extinction, when President Washington together with all Federal and
City officials decamped to more salubrious locations, various treatments,
all futile, were prescribed for the deadly fever. Among the treatments,
phlebotomy, the opening of a vein to draw blood from a victim, was quite
popular until its opponents proved it killed more often than it cured.

My brethren, trained and guided by the ubiquitous Dr. Rush, applied   21
his controversial cure: an explosive purge of mercury and calomel, followed by frequent, copious bleedings. Negro nurses became experts, dis-
pensing pharmaceutical powders and slitting veins with equal dexterity.
Out with the bad air. In with the good. I couldn't resist a smile when I
pictured my brethren moving through white peoples' houses during
broad daylight as freely as I once glided through the same dwellings after
dark. Emptying purses, wallets, pockets, desk drawers, I, too, relieved my
patients of excess.

In the prison also, we must drive out bad blood. Though all of us are   22
infected by the fever of lawlessness, some prisoners are incurably
afflicted. One such wretch, Matthew Maccumsey, Number 102. His crime:
speech. Too much talk and at the wrong times and often in an obstreper-
ous, disruptive, disrespectful manner, threatening the peace and economy of the entire system of absolute silence.

Ice water ducking, bagging with black hood, flogging, the normal and   23
natural deterrents all applied and found wanting in lasting effect, the
iron gag was prescribed. Number 102 remanded for examination and
treatment to Dr. Bache, the nephew, I've heard, of the famous Dr. Franklin,
the kite-flyer.

A committee, convened a decade later to investigate continuing   24
complaints of questionable practices at the prison, described the gag in
these words: a rough iron instrument resembling the bit of a blind bridle,
having an iron palet in the center about an inch square and chains at
each end to pass around the neck and fasten behind. This instrument
was placed in the prisoner's mouth, the iron palet over the tongue, the bit
forced back as far as possible, the chains brought round the jaws to the
back of the neck; the end of one chain was passed through the ring in the
end of the other chain drawn tight to the "fourth link" and fastened with
a lock.

Rousted out of sleep before first light, groggy, frightened, I knew by   25
the hour, the hulking stillness of the figures gathered into the narrow
corridor outside my cell, I was being summoned for a punishment party.
Seeing the faces of other prisoners of color in the glaring torchlight,
I rejoiced inwardly. This night at least I was to be a punisher, not the
punished. The guards always enlisted blacks to punish whites and

whites to punish blacks, by this unsubtle stratagem, perpetuating enmity and division.

We forced No. 102's hands into leather gloves provided with rings, crossed his arms behind his back and after attaching the rings to the ends of the gag chain drew his arms upwards so their suspended weight pulled the gag chains taut, causing the chains to exert pressure on jaws and jugular, trapping blood in the averted head, producing excruciating pain, the degree of which I could gauge only by observing the prisoner's eyes, since the gag at last had effectively silenced him. 26

Niggified, ain't he, a guard exclaimed, half in jest, half in disgust as 102's lifeless, once pale face, blackened by congealed blood, was freed of the gag. 27

Again, I'm muddling time. The pacifying of 102 came later at Cherry Hill. My job on the balloon was to record the reaction of my own African pulse to heavenly ascent. Higher and higher it rose. The striped French balloon. The stiff, boat-shaped basket beneath it, garlanded with fresh flowers, red, white and blue bunting. Inside the gondola the flags of two great republican nations. We intended to plant them wherever we landed, claim for our countrymen joint interest in the rich, undiscovered lands far flung across the globe. 28

Watching the toy town shrink smaller and smaller beneath me, all its buildings and inhabitants now fittable on the end of a pin, for some unfathomable reason as I rose irresistibly to a heretofore undreamed-of height for any person of my race, as I realized the momentousness of the occasion, all the planning, sacrifice and dumb luck that had conspired to place me here, so high, at just that fantastic, unprecedented, joyous moment, as I began to perceive how far I'd risen and how much further, the sky literally the limit, still to rise, a single tear welled out from God-knows-where. 29

From my swaying perch high above everyone I watch our shadow eclipse a corner of the yard, then scuttle spider-like up the far wall of the Walnut Street Jail. 30

Observed from the height of the balloon I'd be just another ant. Not even my black hood pierced with crude eyeholes would distinguish me as I emerged from the night of my cell, blinking back the sudden onslaught of crisp January sunlight. 31

My eyes adjusted to the glare and there it was, finally, the balloon hovering motionless, waiting for someone it seemed, a giant, untethered fist thrust triumphantly at the sky. 32

From the moment it appears, I am sure no mere coincidence has caused the balloon to rise exactly during the minute and a half outdoors I'm allotted daily to cross the prison yard, grab tools, supplies 33 and return to my cell. If Citizen Blanchard's historic flight had commenced a few seconds sooner or later that morning, I would have missed it. Imagine, I could have lived a different life. Instead of being outdoors glancing up at the heavens, I could have been in my cell pounding on the intractable leather they apportion me for cobbling my ten pairs of shoes a week. In that solitary darkness tap-tap tapping, I wouldn't have seen the striped, floating sphere come to fetch me and carry me home.

How carefully I set the pulse glass above a vein. Register the measured ebb and flow, each flicker the heart's smile and amen. 34

QUESTIONS FOR WRITING AND DISCUSSION

Your Personal Response

1. Outline your initial reaction to Wideman's story. Did you at first believe that the narrator is riding in the balloon? Why?

2. What about the story stands out most to you? Why? How might you write about this aspect (these aspects)?

3. What strikes you most about the way the story comments on race?

Questions about Characters

1. How believable is the narrator?

2. How do you react to the narrator calling himself a "guinea pig" (paragraph 7)?

3. If you were asked to describe the character of the narrator, how would you characterize him?

4. The narrator says, "All lives are a combination of good times and bad, aren't they" (paragraph 13). Does his story bear that out?

Questions about Setting

1. What is the significance of Philadelphia as the setting for Wideman's story?

2. What do you make of how the narrator characterizes the size of the people and things he claims to see from the balloon?

3. What role does the yellow fever plague play in Wideman's story?

Questions about Point of View

1. What is the point of view of the story?

2. If Wideman told this story in the third person, how would that point of view have changed it? Do you think it would have been more or less effective? Why?

Questions about Plot

1. How are the events in this story related to one another? Which events in the story cause other events? Which events seem unrelated to you?

2. Choose an event in the story and explain how it affects the narrator.

3. What is significant about some of the language the narrator uses?

Questions about Theme

1. What is the theme of Wideman's story?

2. What is Wideman's narrator saying about life?

3. Do you think the narrator has been rightfully imprisoned? Why?

Questions about Style

1. Find examples of figurative language in the story. What effect does Wideman's use of figurative language have on you as a reader?

2. Which of Wideman's stylistic choices stand out the most to you? Why?

3. Were you surprised by the way the story ends? Why?

Questions for Further Exploration

1. Read other stories by Wideman and compare them with "Ascent by Balloon from the Yard of Walnut Street Jail."

2. In paragraph 28, the narrator writes that he is "muddling time." Read "A Rose for Emily" by William Faulkner. How does Faulkner's story compare to Wideman's in terms of how they "muddle" time?

AMY TAN

Alien Relative

Author Amy Tan was born in Oakland, California, in 1952 to Chinese immigrant parents. Tan went to high school in Switzerland and attended many colleges before graduating from San Jose State University. The publication of *The Joy Luck Club* (1989), about the relationships between Chinese women and their Chinese-American daughters, launched her writing career and eventually led to a film version of the novel. Tan is also the author of *The Kitchen God's Wife* (1991), *The Hundred Secret Senses* (1995), and two children's books. Her most recent works include *The Bonesetter's Daughter* (2001), *The Opposite of Fate*, a book of nonfiction, and *Saving Fish from Drowning* (2005). This story was originally published in the anthology *Charlie Chan Is Dead: An Anthology of Contemporary Asian American Fiction* (1993).

I was there at San Francisco Airport when Helen arrived in this country from Formosa. That was in 1956, maybe sooner than that. In any case, back then she was called Hulan, "Lake Mist." She said her mother named her that because she came into this world like the Queen of Clouds rising from the water at dawn. But I think Helen just made that up. I think probably her mother called her that because she was born already crying a lake of tears.

As I was saying, I was there at the airport with my husband and children, waiting for Hulan to come, this woman I call sister, although she is no such thing. I just said that for the Immigration officials, so I could sponsor her—also because I owed Hulan a debt I had to repay. She helped me leave my first marriage, that time I was married to a bad man. Actually, she did not really help, only promised not to interfere. In China, that was almost like helping. As for myself, I really did help Hulan. I helped her come to this country. In America, that meant I had to interfere.

"Hey!" I called when I saw Hulan come out of the Customs swinging door, her face bouncing up and down in the crowd. And just like her name, she had mist in her eyes, crying so hard she couldn't see us. It was seven years since the last time I saw her, but she looked as if it had been twice as long, she was so old. Her hair was unstylish, same as always, only now it was hanging down just like a washerwoman's, no curly parts to frame her round face. And she wore an ugly fur coat, the skins bent all stiff to pieces, like an old dead dog dried out on the road. So of course I didn't recognize it, my mink coat, I mean, the same one I loaned her in Shanghai last time I saw her, when I was still dreaming I could buy ten just like it in my rich new American home. Oh, I was mad when I found out later that her ruined coat was mine!

But, as I was saying, that day at the airport, at the Customs door, our   4
whole family was happy to welcome her—her husband and her children,
too. I was standing on my tiptoes, holding my young daughter's hand.
Actually, I squeezed Pearl's hand too hard. I didn't mean to, of course, but
then, with so much waiting and excitement, and then to finally see
Hulan, my old friend who knew all the troubles of my life—well, how did
I know what I had done until Pearl screamed, "Let me go, Mommy, let me
go!" In front of all those people, she said that. All my life, it seems, Pearl's
been saying the same thing. Let me go.

Anyway, we were there, only a few faces away, and still Hulan   5
couldn't see us. Of course she couldn't—she didn't have her glasses on.
So my husband, Johnny, lifted our four-year-old son high in the air to call
Hulan's attention our way. And little Samuel shouted, "Whoa, horsey!
Whoa!" and waved three cowboy hats, two white, one black, two for boys,
one for girl, because that's how many children Hulan had. Finally Hulan
saw us, and cried back, "Brother! Sister!" I think she called us that just in
case the Immigration officials were watching.

She pushed her way through the crowd. Her husband, Henry, came   6
next, just like a person still dream-walking, not believing he was really
here. He was holding the baby, Bao-bao Roger. Then came Ming-fei Mary,
so small for eight years old . . . then two suitcases . . . one box . . . no more.

Right away I noticed: Only two children, why not three? Where was   7
their middle child, the son who was six years old?

"Feng-yi Frank, where is he?" I asked, still looking.   8

"Oh, he is coming," Hulan answered slowly, "only later."   9

Johnny and I looked behind her, thinking she meant one minute   10
later. Then one minute later, when we were still waiting and looking,
Henry finally explained it this way: "The money you sent for five tickets,
later it was enough for only four."

And still we didn't understand, until Hulan began to cry in a scared   11
way. "You already did so much. How could we ask for more?" Then Henry sat
down on a suitcase and covered his face. And Ming-fei Mary started wailing.
And little Bao-bao saw all this, turned his mouth down, and cried loud, too.

So that's how we found out: They left Feng-yi behind. Too polite to   12
ask for more money! Too polite to let their middle son come to America!
Oh, isn't that the Chinese way—to make all that pain seem like just a
small inconvenience?

That day at the airport I can never forget. We were all standing   13
together at last, so many happy people rushing by us. My heart hurt,
filled with Hulan's troubles, my stomach ached, mixed with my own
anger. I wanted to shout at Hulan, "So stupid! So stupid!" Because I was
remembering how much we too had suffered. How Johnny worked

overtime, one-dollar-eighty-five for an hour, stacking boxes weekends and nights. How I always bought the fatty pork, twenty cents' saving here and there. How I scolded Pearl so hard for one sock missing, until she shouted, "Leave me alone," and I left her with a big slap mark on her face instead. All those sacrifices to bring so much unhappiness to America!

Of course, we tried to send for Feng-yi right away, as soon as we had more money. But then we found out: no applications for nephews, ten-years waiting list for sons, but first you must be a citizen, no breaking the rules. So, it was seven years more before Hulan and Henry received their citizenship papers, four years more before they were brave enough to tell the authorities, "We have another son." Eleven years altogether before they finally got Feng-yi Frank back. And telling it this way, I make it sound simple.   14

Anyway, that was long time ago, more than twenty years gone by, all those troubles now forgotten. Today Hulan's an American. Now days she calls herself Helen. Now she thinks life is so easy, doing everything the American way. Like what she said yesterday. I was complaining about my daughter, Pearl, how she never comes to visit, how she never tells me anything over the phone, just, "Oh, Mom, we're fine, don't worry."   15

And Helen said, "You want her to visit you more often, it's easy. You invite her to your house. That's the American way. These days, kids don't drop in, drop out. You have to ask. Come on this date, such-and-such a time. Like an appointment, see, easy to make."   16

And I wanted to tell Helen: Easy? You don't remember? It's not so easy to claim back your child.   17

I was with her, standing in long lines at the Department of Justice. You think Hulan could speak up for herself, a mother who left her son behind? So I came along to use the American rules to push us through first one line then another, one place to get forms, one place to ask questions.   18

Finally we found the right line, but the woman authority acted like she was too busy stamping official documents—toong! toong!—oh yes, what she was doing was more important than us. Helen pushed forward the application, the one that said, "Petition for Alien Relative." I whispered to Helen from behind, "Talk, talk, tell her your situation."   19

"I came to this country," Helen began, "but forgot my son."   20

"Forgot?" the woman said, still stamping, not even looking up. "How can you forget a son?"   21

"No, no! I can never forget my son," Hulan said, leaning back, scared. "This is not what I meant." The woman authority now looked at Hulan. Hulan looked at me. And I knew what she wanted to say, all those things she told me at her kitchen table these past eleven years. So I stepped to the counter and I told the Immigration authority how this could happen, how you can lose a child, and really, this was nobody's fault.   22

They were sitting in a courtyard in Formosa, Henry and Hulan, when   23
our telegram came. They took it inside their room, so the neighbors could
not see, these strangers who envied you if you had even one grain of rice
more. But already, people were whispering, "Overseas! They got a telegram from overseas!"

Hulan dried their hands, it was so steamy hot that day. Then care-   24
fully, so carefully, she used a small knife to cut open the envelope and
read our one-page message, the words we tried to say clearly, so there
would be no delay: "The Red Cross, the church sponsor, all of us are
saying to come now, come through. There is an opening. The money is
being wired to you."

They walked out of their room, into the courtyard. They looked at   25
their neighbors, who were by their doors watching. Hulan had waited for
the day she could do this. "Soon this room will be available," she
announced, just like a victor. "We are moving to America!"

Then came the first problem. Their daughter had a TB test, and it   26
said maybe the TB was active, maybe not. In any case, Ming-fei Mary
couldn't leave. So they gave an official some of their plane ticket money
to say it was not, and later it really turned out it was not. "But in those
days," Helen argued with me later, "who knew which way things would go
for you without paying a price?"

Now they had only enough money to buy four plane tickets. They   27
didn't think ahead that this would happen, that's how it is when you are
scared. So Henry said, "We should write to Winnie and Johnny, ask them
for more money."

But Hulan said, "They will think we were careless! Besides, too   28
much time will be wasted before they can answer us yes or no."
Because they both knew: In Formosa, wait too long and you can lose
your chance forever. Just that day, they had heard it on the radio: at
a black-market booth, hundreds of people had pushed and shoved,
shouted and fought—then fourteen people were hurt, two people
crushed—over one special visa to America, which turned out to be
illegal.

For two days and two nights, they argued and cried, deciding what to   29
do. Hulan even tried to sell the mink coat, the same one I gave her before
I left China. But then the pawnshop man told Hulan the coat was dirty,
trying to bargain her down. So Hulan washed that mink coat with soap
and water, washed it until there was nothing left to sell. After that, Henry
decided what to do.

"I will stay," he said. "You and the children, you go first." He was once   30
a military official. He knew how to be brave like that, ordering his family
to a second-place victory.

But Hulan scolded him bitterly, "What good is a family in America 31
with no father to feed them? I will stay."

Then Henry shouted, "Crazy woman! No mother to guide her children 32
to the right opportunities? You want them to become wild Americans?
We are all staying then."

That evening they felt too sick to eat. They lay wide awake on their 33
bed, grieving silently over the opportunity they could no longer use. Then
they looked at their three sleeping children, crowded on another bed in the
same room, two boys, one girl, growing bigger every day. I have done the
same with my own children, so I know. And seeing this, all their anger
turned to grief. Because at that moment, as with every moment, neighbors
were arguing: "That's my pot! Who said you can use it to cook your smelly
food!" Then more people were shouting, "Your food stinks worse!" Every
day they heard this, the cursing and shouting, accusing and pleading. They
were listening to all this hopelessness coming from rooms filled with people who had once been so rich and powerful in different parts of China,
and were now the same kind of poor in one courtyard in Formosa.

In the middle of the night, when the courtyard was finally quiet, 34
Hulan and Henry rose from the bed and went outside. They sat on the
ground, looked at the sky, but not at each other.

Hulan spoke first: "Ming-fei's health, it's always been poor." 35

Then Henry said, "And little Bao-bao—so helpless! Only one year old." 36

After that they were silent for a long time. The night was black, no 37
stars, no moon. They heard no crickets, felt no cooling wind. Finally
Hulan spoke in a trembly voice.

"Yesterday afternoon I saw Feng-yi holding a cocoon in his hand. Just 38
like this, so softly. He was blowing his breath on it, thinking this would
make the butterfly pop out and play."

"Six years old, and already so clever," said Henry. 39

"So patient, so playful," Hulan said, now starting to cry. 40

"Strong," said Henry, then more loudly, "and obedient, too." 41

"Our favorite," Hulan whispered in a hoarse voice, "and he knows 42
this, too. Old enough to never forget us."

That morning, Hulan grasped her middle child to her heart and 43
promised him, "I will never forget you, never lose you." And Feng-yi
smiled, not knowing what she meant.

In the evening, they took Feng-yi to visit his grandmother. Actually, 44
she was not the real grandmother but a bondservant who married Henry's
father after the real grandmother died. In any case, the old lady was glad
to take in the little boy. Although, after she put the boy to bed, she scolded
Hulan and Henry: "Leaving China was bad enough. Now you're going
to America, where it is even worse. What will become of us Chinese

people?" They went to the airport that night, when Feng-yi was already dreaming.

On the airplane, they practiced everything about the new country in their minds. They imagined a large Immigration official greeting them with pale eyes and a sly mouth, smiling and encouraging them, "Say anything. In our country, you are free to say anything. Do you love our government?"   45

"Yes," they practiced saying in English. "We love America, very, very much, more than China, more than Formosa."   46

And then they imagined this pale-eyed man asking them more questions, trickier ones: "Then where is your other son, the one on this document? Why did you leave him behind? Is he a Communist spy?"   47

"Oh no, not a spy, just a little boy. He loves America, too."   48

"Then why didn't you bring him?"   49

"He was sick, too sick to come."   50

"I see, and the rest of you, did you bring this same sickness here?"   51

"Actually he is not sick, nobody is. It's just that we didn't have the money to bring him. This is the truth, only that reason, no money."   52

"What! You came to our country with not enough money? You came here to beg? Police! Police!"   53

Before they landed, the visa papers with their names had one name crossed out. I always thought that was a bad-luck thing to do, crossing Feng-yi's name out, like wishing he would be banished from the world—which, of course, is what happened four months later.   54

I read the letter in Hulan's kitchen. That grandmother, who was not even the real grandmother, wrote to say she was returning to China. "Fukkien food is bad for the stomach," she wrote. "I would rather die in Shanghai than live in Formosa. No more running away. We are going home, Feng-yi and I."   55

"Henry did this!" cried Hulan. "I insisted I should be the one to stay, Feng-yi should go. Now look what's happened!"   56

"I said we all should stay," Henry shouted back. "But you! You were dreaming of American cars, a car we could drive back to Formosa to fetch Feng-yi back!"   57

Day after day, year after year, we heard them arguing like that. I used to sit in Hulan's kitchen. So many times I had to watch the steam rise from her cook pot, the mist clouding her eyes, while she whispered to me—every birthday, every festival day, every time I brought my same-age daughter to her house—how she would never forget him.   58

Let me tell you, that little boy, Feng-yi, none of us could forget him. For so many years we could not see him. We could not hear him. We could not write to him. He was just a little boy, living in Red China, cut off from the world. But I remember, it was just like he was living   59 in Hulan's kitchen all those years, shouting back, as powerful as any angry ghost.

"My sister, she only forgot to claim her son on the paper," I explained to the Immigration authority. "Now do you understand?" 60

The authority was not smiling. She said, "Then here's what you should do." 61

For her forgetfulness, Hulan and Henry had to hire an expensive immigration lawyer. The lawyer they found in the Yellow Pages was Chinese but born in this country. Hulan didn't listen when I told her, "A Chinese name doesn't mean Chinese thinking." 62

Sure enough, this lawyer said—in English—that we needed proof, "a birth certificate," to show this Alien Relative on the application paper had a true relationship with his mother. 63

"In China," I told the lawyer carefully, "you don't need a certificate to be born. See, when a baby is born, if he is crying, this is proof he is born live. If a woman sacrifices her own breast to feed him, this is proof she is his mother. Okay?" 64

"What you need," the lawyer said to Hulan, "is an affidavit witnessed by a notary public, signed by witnesses who knew you in China when your son was born." 65

Hulan shook her head quickly and said, "All those people are dead." But what she really meant was, "All those people are scared to death." Who would be willing to sign an official document when they had their own problems to hide? Maybe they were renting a room for two, when they really had eight or ten people living inside. Maybe they told the officials they were working one job, nine-to-five, but it was really three jobs—graveyard, overtime, weekends—and who knew if all that extra work was illegal to do. In any case, why should anyone lift a hand to help only to have it chopped off? 66

"Chinese people always help each other out," said the lawyer. 67

Lucky for Hulan, I remembered Old Auntie Du, her aunt married to her father's brother from long time ago. And this old aunt, over seventy years old, knew she would die soon anyway. 68

"They can kick me out of this country, okay!" laughed Auntie Du. "Send me back to China, doesn't matter. Anyway, I want to be buried there." 69

Old Auntie Du signed the affidavit, and she told the notary public several times, "I was right there. These two eyes, these two hands—right there inspecting the cord that tied mother to son, son to mother. Write that down." 70

Six months later, Feng-yi Frank, the Alien Relative on the petition, arrived at the airport. We were there, at the Customs swinging door, same 71 as in 1956, only now it was 1967. Henry brought his never-forgotten son a cowboy hat. Samuel and Pearl brought their new cousin Silly Putty and a water pistol. And Hulan, I remember, she brought her dreams. Her face had two dark spots under her eyes, two hungry hollows in her cheeks. So many nights of dreaming awake!

I saw how her eyes grew big with hope, staring at each little boy who walked through the Customs door. Her feet were ready to run toward this one—then that one—here, no, over there!   72

I was the first to know it was Feng-yi Frank standing in front of us. And Hulan was right, when she left her son, he was old enough never to forget. He stared right at his mother, nobody else. That's when Helen's eyes looked up, turned scared, searching for her memory.   73

His smooth, plump chin, the one she used to lift to her face to kiss, now it pointed down at her, rough and bony hard. His soft little hands, the ones that reached up to her, demanding to be held, now they held tight onto two boxes tied with string, and he didn't even put them down when Hulan hugged him American-style.   74

But his eyes—they had changed the most, she whispered to me later. Not curious, not eager, never looking back or farther ahead. He seemed to see only what was in front of him, and he showed no opinion in his eyes about any of it. That son, already seventeen years old when he arrived, never let his mother forget what she had done.   75

Maybe I should have felt more sorry for Hulan. But then I thought, She never told Feng-yi she was sorry. I heard what she said: how Formosa, then America, then China were the reasons for the long delay. "How could I fight three countries?" she told him at the beginning. Later, she bragged about all her hardships to bring him over: "Lawyers, money, affidavit—more complicated than you think!"   76

Now Feng-yi is an American, life is so easy. He tells everyone to call him Frank. He is almost forty, same as my daughter, Pearl. He lives with his mother and father. Lucky he still has a living father, not like my children. Every evening he has dinner at home, so polite, saying thank you, no thanks when his mother says, "Eat more, eat more!" At night he goes to his job as a security guard, signing people in, signing people out. And when he gets up late in the afternoon, he smokes too many cigarettes, or plays video games on his TV set, or lies underneath an old greasy car and sings to its stomach, "How much is that doggie in the window, the one with the waggle-ly tail."   77

An American lady from our church once asked Frank, "What was it like living in China, aren't you so glad to be here?" And Frank said, "China wasn't too bad, just boring, same old clothes, nothing to do. Oh, and they didn't let you have pets."   78

Helen then told that church lady how much Frank always wanted 79
a dog. And that's what he got, a fancy poodle dog, for his twenty-fifth birthday. Puffy head, puffy tail. I tell you this, though, that dog, all those years, lived outside on a cold little porch, because Helen didn't want it to messy up her house. And I saw that dog every time I went to visit—I saw it through the sliding glass door. It was matted and dirty, so skinny, shaking and dancing in a circle every time he saw Frank come home. But Frank didn't even look at that doggie in the window. Although sometimes he still sang that same song, the one with the waggle-ly tail.

I heard Helen complain only one time, about her son, I mean. We 80
were watching Frank, and Frank was watching cars race round and round on the TV set. He sat up, he sat back, he shook his fist and shouted, "Go, you sonabitch, go!" That's when Helen whispered to me, "Look what the Communists did to my son."

I still see Helen almost every day. But she doesn't tell me her trou- 81
bles. She doesn't cry in her kitchen. She doesn't take my advice anymore. Now she thinks she's giving me advice, helping me. Like the other day. We were sitting in her kitchen, near the sliding glass door. I was watching her dog lying outside, so sad. She was telling me how I should call Pearl.

"Make her some Chinese dumplings," Helen said. "Invite her to come 82
eat. She eats your food, she's just like your little girl again, thanking her mommy."

I pretended not to listen. What does she know? Why should I let her 83
interfere? So instead I told her, "That poodle dog looks sick, real bad."

And she said, "Oh, that dog's okay. It's just old." 84

The next day that dog died. I was in Helen's kitchen a few days after 85
it happened. I didn't say anything about the dog that was no longer there. I didn't tell Helen how I made the dumplings, how Pearl didn't come. We were just sitting and drinking tea, same as always. Then Helen started to scratch her ankles, then her legs, until she cried out, "Why are those fleas still pinching me? That dog's already dead!"

And I didn't explain to her, because I know how Helen has become. 86
She doesn't understand, not anymore, how something can still hurt you after it's gone.

QUESTIONS FOR WRITING AND DISCUSSION

Your Personal Response

1. What is your overall emotional response to Tan's story?

2. How did you respond when you read that the family had left Feng-yi, the middle son, in China?

3. How much did you enjoy reading this story? Why?

Questions about Characters

1. How would you describe the relationship between the narrator and Hulan?

2. What kind of parent is the narrator?

Questions about Setting

1. Various events in the story take place in China, Formosa (Taiwan), and the United States. How do these multiple settings affect the plot?

2. Why does Tan focus on each location as much as she does?

Questions about Point of View

1. Why do you think Tan uses a first-person narrator for this story?

2. How would the story be different if Helen were the narrator?

3. How would the story be different if Feng-yi were the narrator?

4. Why do you think Tan chose not to use a third-person narrator?

Questions about Plot

1. In a few sentences, summarize the plot.

2. Which events seem to be caused by or result from others?

3. How does the title of the story relate to the plot?

Questions about Theme

1. What is Tan saying about the immigrant experience?

2. What is Tan saying about familial relationships?

3. What is Tan saying about the choices that people make in life?

Questions about Style

1. What aspects of Tan's style—her sentence structure, word choice, and tone—seemed particularly striking to you?

2. What has Tan done to make the dialogue seem realistic?

3. How does the language of the characters affect your reading of the story? Why?

Questions for Further Exploration

1. If you have living relatives who immigrated to the United States, ask them what the experience was like. How do their experiences compare with those narrated in "Alien Relative"?

2. Interview the oldest relative you can locate, asking about his or her early life experiences, especially if this person immigrated to the United States. In no more than two pages, indicate what new information you learned about your family from this interview.

3. Conduct a family search at one of the following sites:

   http://familytreemaker.genealogy.com/

   http://www.rootsweb.com/

   http://www.familysearch.org/

   http://www.ancestry.com/

   In no more than two pages, outline what information you found about your family members.

Thinking about Visuals When Writing about Creative Works

If you are writing about a visual medium such as film, you might find it useful to include visuals as part of your discussion. For instance, artists construct *storyboards* and other drawings to illustrate what a movie will look like, what the characters in the film will wear, how specific scenes will appear for publicity purposes, and for other reasons. Figures 12.1, 12.2, and 12.3 on page 628 are illustrations from the film *Harry Potter and the Sorcerer's Stone.*

Other visuals that might be available for writing about films include publicity stills and frame enlargements. (If you post your writing on the Web, however, you will probably need permission to include these images.) As you look at these visuals, consider these questions about the effective use of visuals in writing about a creative work:

- In what ways does each illustration illuminate the film? What does it add to your understanding?

- What does the illustration show a reader that it would be hard to show with text alone?

- What other types of visuals might be useful in writing about the film?

FIGURE 12.1
Harry Potter in a
classroom at Hogwarts
School

FIGURE 12.2   Students
approach Hogwarts
School in boats

FIGURE 12.3   An owl
soars across a full moon

Drawing on Research

Your instructor may ask that you write about a creative work without consulting resources beyond those found in this textbook and in your other courses, and without citing evidence beyond what you find in the work itself. The work itself is always the best place to start your research, and often your instructor will ask you to focus only on the work, reading or viewing carefully and thoughtfully, and always taking careful notes.

For some writing situations or assignments, however, you may want or need to read what others have written about the work you are studying. If you are consulting outside sources, you need to find a way to record your own responses to the work before you read what others think about it. If you begin by absorbing others' views before thoroughly considering your own, you risk neglecting your own views and responses and simply parroting other writers' perspectives. Once you have recorded your own ideas about the work on paper or electronically, you are in a position to consider others' views more critically. For example, for the scenarios on pages 596–97, you could conduct the following kinds of research:

- For Scenario 1, which asks you to compose a literary analysis, your research should obviously include a thoughtful and thorough examination of the creative work itself: for example, critically reading a literary text or critically examining a painting. Your research may also include secondary sources—others who have commented about the work.

- For Scenario 3, which asks you to write to a family member or friend, drawing on established and recognized critics such as well-known film or book reviewers is a way to provide evidence about the creative work you are recommending.

Writing Processes

As you read, view, or listen to the creative work you are writing about, you might find it fruitful to use some of the reading strategies presented in Chapter 2 and the strategies for discovery and learning presented in Chapter 3 to help you to engage more fully and more critically in the work. As you read, view, or listen to the work, you should look for the qualities or elements discussed on pages 600–1.

As you work on the scenario you have chosen, remember the qualities of an effective paper about a creative work (see pp. 599–602). As we have noted throughout this book, this process is recursive—you will often need to return to earlier stages as you work on your assignment, and you will always need to return to the work you are writing about for fresh evidence, for more inspiration, and (possibly) for a new perspective.

If you are considering several works for your analysis, put your notes into a separate computer document for each work. Once you determine the focus

For a tip on organizing your computer files, see page 97.

of your analysis, it will be easy to access and use those notes. Also, as you work on your project, make certain that you save your computer files frequently because any work that you don't save could be lost. Many experienced writers save their files every fifteen minutes or so. Savvy writers back up their computer files in two or more places—on an internal or external hard-drive of the computer, on a USB flash drive, and on a rewritable CD or DVD, for example.

Invention: Getting Started

You should use a variety of invention activities to select and then explore your creative work. Below you will find information about the first steps in writing about a work: selecting the work, recording your responses, and finding an aspect of the work to analyze. Each step is accompanied by questions to prompt invention, and after each step is a suggested invention activity to help you begin that step. For each step, choose any invention activity that makes sense to you—and that your instructor approves. Keep in mind that doing your invention work in electronic form, rather than on paper, makes it easy to use that work later as you construct a draft.

Selecting a Creative Work to Write About

If your instructor has not assigned a particular creative work, spend some time exploring short stories or other works. Regardless of the invention activities you decide to do (or your teacher asks you to do), try to answer these questions while you do your invention work:

- Which works have you recently read or seen that pique your interest the most? Why?
- Which works have you enjoyed the most? Why?
- Which works have evoked the strongest emotional responses in you? What are those emotions?
- Which works have made you think the most?
- Which works have you read or seen multiple times?

VISUALIZING VARIATIONS

Using Visuals to Illustrate an Analysis of a Creative Work

Suppose you are writing in response to Scenario 2 (p. 597), which asks you to examine a creative work that matters to you. Perhaps you decide to select a film based on a graphic novel, which is a cross between a novel and a comic book, with the illustrations telling most of the story. As you consider possible subjects for your analysis, you might find a photo like this one from the *X-Men* films, a series you enjoyed immensely:

Browsing on the Internet, you might also find images such as these, from the graphic novels the *X-Men* films were based on:

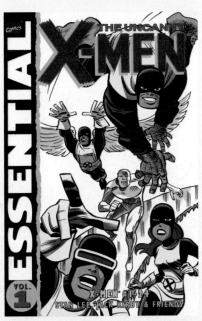

(cont'd)

(continued)

Once you decide to focus on the *X-Men* films, what other kinds of illustrations might help you to analyze an aspect of the film and/or novels for your readers? To get started, you might look for an image such as the one below from a movie site on the World Wide Web.

In addition to photographs and other kinds of images, you will also find interesting information such as mistakes in the film from Web sites such as IMDb.com, an Internet movie database:

Goofs: Continuity: When Professor Xavier and Magneto enter Jean Grey's old house and find her sitting on a chair, items in the room are levitated around her. When the items drop, the bookcase over her right shoulder hits the ground and all the books fall off, the lamp on top remains on. In a later shot the books are back in the book case and the lamp is on the floor. . . .

As you think about writing your response to Scenario 2, consider the following:

- What visual information would you include as part of your analysis?

- What textual information would you include as part of your analysis to explain the images?

- In what ways would you *use* visuals to help show what you mean?

- On what basis would you select one image instead of another?

- What links might you include? (If you were comparing one film to another, for example, you might want to include links to information on the other film.)

Considering What to Focus On

If you are responding to a college writing assignment, your instructor may suggest a focus or purpose for your project: for example, to identify and explain the theme of a creative work, to examine a character, to analyze a plot.

If you have the option of selecting the aspect of the work you will focus on, consider using the same invention techniques you have used for other assignments to help you make your choice. You can use questions such as these to help you decide:

- What strikes me about this work? How might I focus on that feature as a subject for my paper?
- What interests me the most about the work? How might I concentrate on that aspect for my paper?
- What actions, characters, plot devices, descriptions, narration, dialogue, interactions might I focus on?

Once you have some ideas, and even a tentative thesis, read back through the story (or view the film or other work again) to see what evidence you can find *in* the work that you might use to support your main idea.

TechNote

You can find many classic works of literature online in powerful literature archives. Usually these are editions and translations that are in the public domain. You can download these works from a reputable Web site such as Project Gutenberg (http://www.gutenberg.org/catalog/), then copy and paste them into a word processor. If a work is stored on your computer, you can then perform simple yet interesting types of *quantitative analysis*, which is useful for investigating and writing about the way the author uses words and phrases to develop themes and stylistic patterns in the work. For example, you can use your word processor's "Find" feature to do the following:

- Count the number of times the author uses a certain word or words, which can support the argument that the repetition of a word or

idea creates a "cumulative" effect on readers

- Focus on the consistency with which the author uses the word or words and what that might mean

- Argue that the word is used primarily by a specific character or group of characters

- Examine the actual grammar and syntax of passages in which the word appears, to show how the author explores its implications

Using technology to search for words and phrases can also turn up surprising results. Sometimes words and phrases we would expect to find are not present in the work. (Tip: Sometimes words are present in different forms. If you are looking for the word *noting*, for example, make sure you search for *note* and *notice* as well.)

WRITING ACTIVITY

Freewriting

One useful method for exploring your ideas about a creative work is freewriting. Using the questions on page 633, use freewriting to jot down everything you can think of about the work(s) you are considering.

Hanna Earley's Initial Freewriting

Student Hanna Earley was assigned to write about one of the stories she had read for an assignment for her composition class. She began the process by freewriting about "Videotape" by Don DeLillo (you can read "Videotape" on pp. 603–07). Here is a portion of Earley's freewriting:

> Wow—intense. Very different from most of the short stories I read in high school. Story: child accidentally videotapes drive-by shooting.

No. Story: man watches videotape on TV shot by child of a man shot and wants to beckon his wife to watch it with him—weird—shot/shot. But why do I say "he" for the main character when the story says "you"?

It's funny because sometimes I felt like I was in the car, riding along, but other times I felt like I was in the living room, waiting for the grainy tape to get to the end. The story felt as vivid and action-packed as a movie, even though there aren't a ton of details—the sentence "It shows a man driving a car" actually hardly says anything. And what's all this about reality, superreal, underreal? Or mentions of family, games, privacy, being exposed (the mom in the bathrobe: "bloodless" and "plucked")? This story shocks me, and I think it means to. But I know by early on that it's a videotape of a homicide—why am I still shocked? There's something going on here with the way people are exposed. But at the same time, we don't see the blood or the child's reaction (it's not like she turns the camera on herself): "It shows very little in the end"—I think there's something to this—this simultaneous showing and withholding—and it has something to do with why I feel so shocked. But how do I connect this to something I can actually write about?

Recording Your Initial Responses

Once you select the creative work, begin recording your emotional and intellectual responses to it. As noted earlier in this chapter, it is important to record your own responses to the work initially. If you do not do this step, you may be tempted to adopt someone else's views in place of your own. Regardless of the invention activities you decide to do (or your instructor asks you to do) to record your responses, write answers to the following questions:

- What kinds of emotions does this work evoke in you?
- How does this work make you think about life?
- Which character in the work do you like the most/least? Why?
- What makes this piece of literature or other type of creative work worth reading or experiencing?
- In one sentence, what is the theme of this work?
- What language in the work do you find most interesting or effective?

WRITING ACTIVITY

Freewriting and Brainstorming

Using the questions above, use more freewriting and brainstorming to jot down in a page or two everything you can think of about the work.

For more on freewriting, brainstorming, and other strategies for discovery and learning, see Chapter 3.

Hanna Earley's Additional Freewriting and Brainstorming

Student writer Hanna Earley used more freewriting as well as brainstorming to generate ideas about "Videotape," jotting down details about the story that caught her attention. Here is an excerpt:

> I want to write about that stunned feeling I have and how it connects to *how* the story is told. The author could have told this story a million ways, but it's not told just about the child and the videotape, but also about this man ("you") and something going on in the relationship with his wife. The real story is set inside the story of the man watching the tape—is that because just telling the isolated story of the shooting wouldn't make any sense? Or would be boring? Impersonal? The issues between the husband and wife are like a frame for the videotape itself. I would expect to make a story more exciting and shocking by bringing the reader closer to the event (by rubbing our faces in it?), not farther, by inserting this story about a man watching the tape in his living room. But DeLillo does—he sets us farther away by filtering the main event through this "you"/marriage situation— WHY? Does Janet see the videotape, and the repeated watching of it, as morbid? By her unwillingness to watch it, is she less willing to confront the notion that "every breath you take has two possible endings"? Does it make "you" weaker or stronger to be so drawn in to the spectacle of violence? Why does DeLillo use "you"? It almost forces me, personally, sitting here at my desk, into the story, arguably against my will (a type of violence?). The girl making the videotape "wandered into" all of this. So did I, the reader, but not the main character—he goes back to it again and again. . . . For what? Why can't we turn ourselves away from the screen (or the story)?

Possible oppositions:

The frame of the husband/wife situation	The drive-by murder and its accidental taping by a child
Inside the living room, watching the tape alone	The tape, being broadcast thousands of times
Privacy	Exposure
Anonymous, and no one cares	Anonymous, and yet famous— Video Girl, the Texas Highway Killer
Sheltered/clothed/shielded (windshield?)	Exposed, plucked
Family holiday videos	Murder
Real time	The tape seems to go on forever
Elemental truth	A joke

It exists	They show it
The girl seeing the event once, cold	Mass production, sequence of repeated images and victims
Wife (never actually enters the story, doesn't watch the tape)	Husband (can't stop watching even though he knows what happens next)
Husband (never actually named or referred to)	"You" (camera turned on reader)
You/me—reading this story as a private experience	Reality TV, technology, violence, driving on highways with thousands of strangers, millions of people watching the tape at once around the country—the world?
Controlled environment	Chaos, chance, randomness

Finding a Feature to Analyze

The following questions will help you think analytically about the various features of a story, whether you are writing about a short story, a novel, a film, or a narrative in some other genre or medium. Look for interesting possibilities about each potential feature for analysis as you do invention work for this step. Keep in mind that to consider each aspect of a creative work thoroughly, you will need to read or view it carefully and thoughtfully—never just skim—because only then will you see the details about character, language, setting, and plot that you will need to construct an effective paper. Note that whatever feature you choose (or are assigned) to focus on, you will also need to make detailed, accurate notes as you read or view the work. Your notes will help you learn what you think about the story, decide what you will finally focus on, and gather evidence from the text itself to support the claim you will make in your essay.

Character: There are many ways to analyze characters. To find an approach that works and that interests you, consider using a concept that you have learned in another course. Here are some possibilities:

- In a psychology course, you may have learned about psychological concepts you can apply to a character—for instance, the six stages people go through when accepting death or the Oedipus complex.
- In a sociology course, you may have learned about social stratification or other concepts that you can use to interpret the motivations of a character or group.

- In a philosophy course, you may have learned about concepts that will help you understand a character, such as ethical dilemmas or the collective unconscious.

As you read your text carefully, look for information about a particular character. Consider, for example, this brief passage from a short story by Ron Carlson, "Evil Eye Allen" (and consider what the title itself tells you about the main character in the story). What do you know about the character after carefully reading even this brief excerpt?

> His name, of course, was not Evil Eye. His real name was Gary, and it would be great to start with something like *He was always a strange kid,* but that isn't true. He grew up two houses down from me and we were friends from day one, that is before we went to school, and he was a regular kid, better at chess than I, better at baseball, as good with football, liked by his teachers, my parents, girls.

You can also analyze characters by thinking about them in the same way you think about people in general. To do that, you might ask the following questions:

- What motivates the actions of this character?
- What do you admire about this character? Why?
- What do you dislike about this character? Why?
- How effectively does this character communicate with other characters? What factors seem to influence those interactions the most?
- What role does this character play in the story?
- How does this character compare to some other character in another work of literature?
- Why do other characters treat this character as they do?

Setting: The physical setting is where a story takes place. Consider the picture that comes to your mind as you read this brief opening passage from "At the Jim Bridger," another short story by Ron Carlson:

> He parked his truck in the gravel in front of the Jim Bridger Lodge, and when he stepped out into the chilly dark, the dog in the back of the rig next to his was a dog who knew him. A lot of the roughnecks had dogs; you saw them standing in the bed of the four-wheel-drive Fords. It was kind of an outfit: the mud-splattered vehicle, the gear in back, a dog.

Consider how much information you can glean from the words Carlson chooses: a *truck* (not a car) parks on *gravel* (not in a driveway, or on concrete) at a *lodge* (not a house); it was *chilly* and *dark* and there are *dogs*. Is the person in the story glad the "dog knew him"? What if the dog had not known the person? What does the name "roughneck" bring to mind? What kind of "gear" might be carried in a "mud-splattered" "four-wheel-drive Ford" pickup?

Consider the following kinds of questions:

- How does the setting affect the atmosphere in which the story occurs? How does the setting affect the events that take place in the story?
- If the story is set in some specific time in history, how historically accurate are the details? What is the effect on readers of aspects of the setting such as language used by the characters, technology, dress, food—qualities that change over time?
- How does the historical setting influence what can happen and does happen in the story?

Point of view: *Point of view* is a term describing what the narrator knows (and does not know). In some stories the narrator is *omniscient;* he or she knows what all of the characters are thinking. In other stories, the narrator's knowledge is limited to what one character is thinking. If the narrator is a character in the story, his or her knowledge will be limited to what he or she sees, hears, or thinks. In "Alien Relative" by Amy Tan (pp. 617–25), the story is told from the point of view of Hulan's friend.

As you contemplate point of view, consider the following questions:

- Why do you think that the author used this particular point of view to tell the story?
- Is the narrator a character (first-person narration)? Is the narrator someone outside the story (third-person narration)? If the narration is third-person, is the narrator omniscient—that is, does the narrator know what characters are thinking? Or is the narrator limited to describing what characters do and say rather than what they think?
- How would the story be different if the author had used another point of view?
- How does the story's point of view affect readers?
- How does the story's point of view affect your perception of certain characters in the story?

Plot: A *plot* is what happens in the story—the events that take place during its course. Most plots involve a *conflict,* either between characters, within a character, or between a character and nature or circumstance. In many stories, the conflict leads to a problem or crisis, which is then resolved.

To write about the plot of a particular story, consider the following kinds of questions:

- How are the events in the story related to one another?
- Which events seem to cause or lead to others?

- Which events seem to be caused by or result from others?
- When do events begin and end?
- How do specific events in the story affect individual characters?
- Which event causes the crisis in the plot?
- How is the crisis resolved?

Theme: Most creative works have a message or an idea—a point the author is trying to get across to readers. To explore the theme of a work, you might consider the following questions:

- In one sentence, what is the author saying about life or people?
- How does the story make you think about life or people?
- What, if anything, is the moral of this story?

Style: Although many stylistic devices are used in literature and film, you are probably familiar with some of the more common ones.

- A *simile* is an indirect comparison that includes the word *like* or *as*. (*His coat was like a faded carpet.*)
- A *metaphor* is a direct comparison in which one thing is described as actually being something else. (*The hummingbird was a tiny, iridescent blue helicopter.*)
- *Personification* involves attributing human qualities to animals, objects, or even ideas. (*Sensing my frustration, the computer screen promptly went blank.*)
- *Hyperbole* is exaggeration so extreme that it is clearly not meant to be taken literally (*His car was the size of a canal barge*), while *understatement* is a statement surprising in its lack of force (*"We're experiencing some difficulties," the pilot said as we noticed the distinct smell of smoke*).
- *Irony* is a tone in which the writer's meaning contrasts sharply with, or is the opposite of, what is stated. (*"Oh I'm simply thrilled to be here," my sister said from her hospital bed.*)

Consider the following questions about style:

- What uses of language are especially interesting? Why?
- How does the creator of the work surprise the reader or viewer with his or her use of language or stylistic choices? What instances can you find?
- Can you find examples of simile, metaphor, personification, hyperbole, and understatement in the work? Identify any that you notice.
- Does the writer use irony in any way? How is it used, and why?

WRITING ACTIVITY

Analyzing a Feature of the Work

As you read or view the creative work that you plan to write about, look for the following:

- Character
- Setting
- Point of view
- Plot
- Theme

Select one of the items above and, as you reread the story or watch a film for a second time, jot down everything that comes to mind about the feature you are focusing on. Your notes will then serve as a starting point for your writing about the creative work.

Hanna Earley's Analysis

As she reread "Videotape," Earley concentrated on plot—on how DeLillo manages to build suspense in his story. Once again, she used freewriting to generate ideas on this potential focus for her analysis.

> I'm not sure if I've got a logical breakdown of things, but a story that isn't trying to surprise me is full of suspense and shock. How does DeLillo do this? By keeping the reader on the edge—the edge between stories (the frame mechanism), the edge between realities ("you"—am I involved in the story or not?), the edge between being able to access knowledge about the event and being denied the details (lack of detail, the story's resistance to letting the details "mean" anything, the anonymity of all involved), and the edge between having to watch and choosing to watch (something to do with the soul, the horror, the elemental truth—we both want to watch and want others to watch in order to understand us? But doesn't it feel almost criminal to keep watching?). I think I want to put my claim (how DeLillo keeps us on edge) early in the paper, and then make my case with examples. But I don't want to end with a conclusion that merely repeats what I've said. It might be interesting to draw readers in somehow, get them to examine their own behavior or impulses?

WRITING ACTIVITY

Recording Good Details

As you read or view the creative work that you plan to analyze in your writing, mark figurative language by underlining it or noting it and then labeling it in the margin of the text. Or you might keep a two-column notebook in which you record interesting examples of figurative language and comment on them.

When you consider *setting*, jot down details about place: what do the characters see? Where are they? How do they interact with or react to their environment? How does the setting affect the characters and the work itself? How does the weather (as shown in the painting or described in the text) affect the story and the characters?

Consider *point of view:* why do you suppose the author wrote a story from a particular point of view? Or why might an artist paint certain subjects and not others? What can you tell from the perspective that you see?

For more on two-column notebooks, see Chapter 3.

Take complete notes on each aspect of the work that you want to consider and examine (for example, character, plot, theme).

Exploring Your Ideas with Research

From your brainstorming and other invention work, select one possible focus for your analysis of the work—plot, character, narrative development, point of view, theme, or style. If you had to phrase your main idea in one sentence, what would it be? Write that sentence on the top of a sheet of paper.

Reread the work or view it again, looking for evidence that might support your claim, and write down each quotation or example that you find. If your assignment calls for it, consult other sources for their views on the work or information about the author. Use an electronic journal to record images, URLs, and other information that you find as you are conducting your research. Such an e-journal makes it easy for you to add these e-documents once you start drafting your paper.

Your instructor may ask you to share your research notes with several of your classmates, not only so that you can see what subjects they are working on, but also so you can help one another determine if you have sufficient evidence to support the claim you intend to make.

Hanna Earley's Research

Hanna Earley was interested in how "Videotape" sustains its suspense, even when the events are obvious and foretold. Here are some of the quotations she marked as she reread the story looking for information about the framing device, second-person voice, and use of detail that contribute to the suspense of the story:

"You know about families and their video cameras."	This could be me, or anyone.
"You say to your wife, if you're at home and she is there, Now here is where he gets it."	Maybe me, maybe him.
"You don't want Janet to give you any crap about it's on all the time, they show it a thousand times a day."	Exposes some minor (but seems to represent greater?) conflict between man and his wife.
"You see him jolted . . . then he seizes up and falls toward the door or <u>maybe</u> leans or slides into the door . . . " and "You don't see the blood, which is <u>probably</u> trickling behind his ear . . . the twist of the head gives you only a <u>partial</u> profile . . . "	Uncertainty woven into the details: The story seems to resist knowing or admitting too much.
"It shows very little in the end."	
"You keep on looking not because you know something is going to happen—<u>of course you do know something is going to happen</u> and you look for that reason but you . . . keep on looking because things combine to hold you fast—a sense of the random, the amateurish, the accidental, the impending."	Does DeLillo tell us outright the way he is using suspense?

Earley also wanted to make sure she was using the word "suspense" to the fullest extent, so she went to www.dictionary.com to review the definition.

"a state or condition of mental uncertainty or excitement, as in awaiting a decision or outcome, usually accompanied by a degree of apprehension or anxiety"	Excitement is positive but anxiety is negative—another opposition? The same competing feelings of compulsion and revulsion towards watching the tape?
"a state of mental indecision"	Are we somehow complicit in building this suspense?
"undecided or doubtful condition, as of affairs"	The outcome of the shooting is not in doubt, but perhaps the relationship between the husband and wife is? Does either really get resolved?
"the state or condition of being suspended"	Being on the edge between realities, stories, etc.: is the reader literally suspended, floating, between worlds in this story?

WRITER'S WORKSHOP

Evaluating Your Classmates' Invention Work and Research

With any writing assignment, your invention materials and research can improve with peer feedback and suggestions. Working with several of your classmates, provide comments and suggestions and ask one another questions, with the overall goal of helping one another to understand your rhetorical situation more clearly and to generate more useful information.

Comments

- I understand _____ about what you've generated thus far.
- I especially like _____ in what you've generated thus far.
- I agree with/disagree with _____.
- I'm confused when you write about _____.
- I'm not convinced as yet about _____.
- These aspects of your work— _____ and _____—don't seem related, so I'm not sure why you've included them.
- The part about _____ seems promising, but the part about _____ seems underdeveloped.
- I'd suggest that you include these ideas or this information:

  _____   _____

  _____   _____

Questions

- Why are you emphasizing this aspect—plot, character, setting, theme, point of view, figurative language, or something else—in your invention work? What is this focus leading you to?
- What kinds of assertions are you making about the story or other kind of work?
- What evidence from the work supports or refutes those assertions? (Invention activities—for example, brainstorming, clustering, and listing— will produce such evidence.)
- How can you explore the story or other kind of work further before writing a first draft?
- I had the following questions as I read your invention work:
- What do you feel are your keenest insights into the work?

As your classmates respond to your invention work and research, listen carefully—and with an open mind—to what they are saying, and take notes so that you do not forget their questions, comments, and suggestions. Your classmates' responses to your writing will help you anticipate the responses of your audience. You will need to evaluate your peers' feedback—questions, comments, suggestions—throughout the process of composing your analysis of the creative work. You need to decide which feedback will strengthen your writing and which will not.

Organizing Your Ideas and Details

Once you know the aspect of the work you will focus on and have a tentative or working thesis as well as evidence from the work, you need to consider how you might organize this material. The questions that you need to ask yourself when deciding on your organization are all rhetorical:

- Who is your audience?
- Will they be familiar with the work you are writing about? If they are not familiar with it, how much will you need to tell them about it?
- What is your purpose for writing—that is, why will your readers be interested in your analysis of this work?

Once you have determined your audience and purpose, you can choose the organizational approach that is best suited to it. Here are three possible organizational approaches that you might choose for your paper.

Options for Organization

A Deductive Approach:	An Inductive Approach:	A Narrative Approach:
• State, right at the beginning, the conclusion (thesis statement) that you have reached about the subject or subjects of your analysis.	• Explain, with examples, each piece of textual evidence that supports your thesis statement or claim, but without expressly stating that claim.	• Lead the reader through the story, event by event. Start by stating your thesis or claim.
• Explain why and how you reached that conclusion by providing textual evidence—quotations, examples—that support your claim.	• Each piece of evidence leads your reader to the conclusion that you are trying to assert.	• Each discussion of an event or each citation of dialogue from the story is evidence for your claim—that is, each supports the assertion you are making about the story.
• Conclude by briefly explaining all of the connections to your point—how they support your main claim.	• At the end state your claim, to which your readers have been led by the evidence you have provided.	• When you reach the end of the story, you will have presented all of your textual evidence.

Deciding on an Organizational Approach

Before you construct a full draft of your paper about a creative work, consider which organizational approach will best serve your writing purpose and help your audience understand your analysis. As with any kind of writing, it is sometimes useful to try several organizational approaches to see which one seems most effective for your specific purpose, audience, and rhetorical situation. Try writing a page or two using at least two organizational approaches before you settle on one. (Be sure to save each first attempt with a different file name.)

 ## Constructing a Full Draft

Once you have chosen the organizational approach that works best given your audience and purpose, you are ready to construct the rest of your draft. For an academic paper about a creative work, an effective strategy for constructing an early draft is to consider the claim that you are prepared to make about that work. Once you have stated that claim as clearly as you can, draw on the evidence that you have gathered to support that claim. As you work on your draft, keep returning to the major claim that you are making. Use evidence from the work itself to support your assertions.

Remember that you will learn more about your topic as you write about it. As you draft your paper, you might even discover a more interesting claim or a claim for which you have more support, so keep an open mind.

Introduction: Since in writing about a creative work you are making a point about some aspect of that work—its theme, symbolism, or use of metaphor, for example—it is often effective to start your analysis by stating your own point or thesis, especially if your readers are familiar with the work and if your thesis is bold or provocative. In order to write an introduction that captures readers' attention, however, you might want to try one of the following strategies:

- You might start with a compelling quotation or incident from the work, such as Kurtz's famous last exclamation from Joseph Conrad's novel *The Heart of Darkness:* "The Horror! The Horror!"

- If you have consulted outside sources, you might start with an incisive observation from a well-known critic.
- Consider starting with a question, something that asks the reader to respond and so to become involved with your essay.
- Make a brief comment and use an eye-catching visual to interest your reader (we use this strategy in each of the chapters in this text).
- Express a surprising opition about the work, one that goes "against the grain" of typical opinion.

Body: There are many ways to organize a paper about a creative work (see three possible organizational approaches on p. 645). In almost every case, you will state your claim, an assertion about the work, and then support that claim with evidence from the text. Usually, you will want to state your claim early in your essay, and then use the rest of your essay to provide supporting evidence for it. An alternative is the *inductive* approach, in which you present your evidence first, showing how it leads to your conclusion, which you state at the end of your analysis.

Here are two additional methods of development for analyses of creative works:

- If you are focusing on a key event in the story that either was caused by other events or caused events to happen, then another organizational approach is to identify the cause or effect, and then use your essay to provide supporting evidence that your conclusion about this event is correct.
- If you are focusing on a specific character and how he or she is developed in the story, you again could start with your main claim about this character and then present evidence from the text to support your assertion.

Conclusion: In the conclusion, you tie your essay together—that is, this is your chance to show how the examples and details you have provided support your thesis. Here are some possible ways to conclude your analysis:

- Refer back to the quotation or incident with which you began the essay.
- End with a compelling observation about a character or other element of the story.
- Construct a conclusion in which you restate all of the main ideas of your essay, noting how they connect to and support your main claim, your thesis.

Title: The title for your analysis of a creative work should give your reader some sense of your main idea or thesis, a hint about what your essay tries to show. In her analysis of Don DeLillo's "Videotape," Hanna Earley offers evidence to support her claim about DeLillo's use of suspense; the title and subtitle of her final draft, "That Doesn't Mean We Want Him to Stop: Suspense in Don DeLillo's 'Videotape,'" give readers a strong indication of what her essay will be about.

WRITING ACTIVITY

Constructing a Complete Draft

After reviewing your notes, research, and invention activities and carefully considering all of the information that you have generated, write a complete first draft of your paper about a creative work, using the organizational approach that you have decided on. Remember that your thinking about your analysis will evolve as you write, so your ideas will most likely change as you compose the first draft. As you compose this early draft, do not be concerned about the surface features of your writing—spelling, punctuation, sentence structure, precise word choice. You can attend to those matters later on.

Hanna Earley's First Draft

Here is an early draft of Hanna Earley's essay on the short story "Videotape." At this early stage, Earley did not worry about stylistic issues; instead, she concentrated on getting her main ideas about the story into her draft. (The numbers in circles refer to peer comments on pp. 654–55.)

Suspense in "Videotape" ❶

We've heard the phrases—page-turner, nail-biter, cliff-hanger—but they all communicate one idea: suspense. It doesn't matter how we experience it, but we want to know: What happened? ❷ So in a short story such as Don DeLillo's "Videotape," in which the answer to "What happened?" is revealed almost from the outset, how does he keep us reading?

The premise is simple. A videotape, filmed by a child, shows a man driving his car ❸ who is then shot and dies, and the fact that the videotape of the story's name shows a homicide is no surprise; DeLillo exposes the outcome at the beginning of the ninth of a series of brief, expository paragraphs and the outcome is delivered in the same, even, mild prose of the rest: "It is not just another video homicide. It is a homicide recorded by a child who thought she was doing something simple . . . " (page?). However, despite what we might expect—that all tension in the story is lost once the outcome is revealed—the story instead heightens its tension, paragraph by paragraph until the closing sentence: "The horror freezes your soul but this doesn't mean that you want them to stop."

DeLillo achieves this effect by keeping his reader literally on edge, using a variety of strategies that will be explored in this paper. First, by placing the central story of the homicide ❹ on film within the context of a larger story, that of a man watching the video in his living room and thinking about his wife, DeLillo creates a second opportunity for suspense, and readers hover on the border between the two "stories," one foot in each, doubling waiting for resolution, which heightens our feelings of suspense. Also, DeLillo builds tension in the story by employing second-person narration, constantly beckoning the reader into the story with "you," even though the main character is not an everyperson the reader can embody, but rather a particular man with a particular mindset and set of circumstances; the reader is both invited into and repelled from the events at hand, which could trigger the ambivalence and doubt we associate with suspense. Finally, DeLillo keeps the suspense taut through careful management of details ❺ and how they are revealed; as soon as he provides details to bring the events to life on the page, he just as quickly backs off, equivocating earlier statements or admitting there is little to know at all. So even though we know all along the man will be shot, that he will die, and his car will drift back out of the camera frame as a child watches and a murderer escapes, DeLillo compels us to read to the end—not for the answer to "What happened?" but to something else, something more elusive or ❻ accidental (not sure . . . this is getting out of control . . . help!)

In "Videotape," the reader encounters two parallel stories. The first and most obvious is that of the man being shot and his murder being caught on tape by a child, but the second is that of our main character, a married man who finds himself compelled to watch this video over and over again in his living room, even though his wife would think he's crazy for doing so.

"You say to your wife . . . Now here is where he gets it." The main character obviously has a wife and is the type of person who would egg her on to watch this tape. On the other hand, "You don't want Janet to give you any crap about it's on all the time, they show it a thousand times a day." There seems to be some conflict or tension in their marriage that was somehow amplified by the main character's viewing of this tape. "You want to tell her it is realer than real, but then she will ask you what that means." When he says this, he seems to feel more connected to the experience of watching this videotape than to his partner in life. He seems unsure what he's communicating to her by encouraging to watch: "What are you telling her? Are you making a little statement? Like I'm going to ruin your day out of ordinary spite. Or a big statement? Like this is the risk of existing?" So as the reader proceeds through the story, there are actually two storylines to follow, and as a result, we have two reasons to read, two forms of suspense. Not only do we want to learn how the tape ends—what becomes of the child? The shooter?—but we start to want to know what's happening in this relationship and why this narrator keeps talking about his wife as he watches this. In the end, both stories are somewhat unresolved: " . . . the tape ends here, either because the girl stopped shooting or because some central authority . . . decided there was nothing else you had to see." "You don't want Janet to give you any crap about it's on all the time." In some sense then, the readers' sensation of suspense, doubt and uncertainty extends beyond the end of the story.

DeLillo also achieves the unease, doubt, and anxiety we associate with suspense by using the second-person voice. At first, "You see a man at the wheel of a medium Dodge," the reader might think DeLillo is using "you" conversationally, that it isn't necessarily a strategy for suspense. "You know about families and their video cameras." Here he could be talking about any reader, or anyone at all, and seems to be establishing some common ground, as in, we've all seen this before—the family video at Thanksgiving or whatever. *This is nothing out of the ordinary.* But in fact, this situation is anything but ordinary. As soon as the reader is drawn into the story with the "you" sentence structures, DeLillo starts to show that "you" is a specific character, both similar to the reader but completely outside the reader. "You don't want Janet to give you any crap." ➐ Clearly there is a whole set of circumstances here in which the reader is not involved. So when we are both drawn into and rejected from the story, the reader is somehow both participant ⑧ and observer, but also neither, therefore unsettling our own points of view. Just where are we—in the living room with "you"? in the car with the child filming the tape" sitting outside the story as observers only? Therefore, through the second person voice in "Videotape," the reader's feelings of anxiety, doubt, and ultimately suspense are aggravated. "And you keep on looking," it says, and we do.

In addition to the use of a framing device to create two separate storylines and use of the second-person voice, the story creates suspense through its use of detail. Occasionally, the story is very detailed: "They break every trust, spy out the undefended space, catching Mom coming out of the bathroom in her cumbrous robe and turbaned towel, looking bloodless and plucked" or the girl filming the tape "feels halfway clever and inventive and maybe slightly intrusive as well." But these details actually come from imagined things, not the events of the story. The videotape and the actual murder get only vague description: "It shows a man driving a car" "He is bald up the middle of his head, a nice guy in his forties whose whole life seems open to the hand-held camera" and "You don't see the blood, which is probably trickling behind his ear and down the back of his neck . . . the twist of the head gives you only a partial profile . . . " All the details of the actual event are full of uncertainty ("seems open," "probably," "partial") so we can't ever paint a perfectly clear picture in the mind without filling in some of the details with our imaginations. The narrator likes to comment on the significance of the tape. ⑨ He says, "The crimes are inseparable from the idea of taping and playing. You sit there thinking that this is a crime that has found its medium, or vice versa—cheap mass production, the sequence of repeated images and victims, stark and glary . . . " but he seems to draw these conclusions from his own concerns rather than from the tape itself. After all, "It shows very little in the end." The story isn't going to reveal the nitty-gritty details of the story. Like the victim's car, the narrator seems to approach the details, but falls back, drifting away before we can really understand what's before us. Never being able to pin down the details of the story and being told that the videotape in fact reveals ⑩ little unsettles the reader. We want to know more, but the story withholds knowledge. We read in suspense, looking to see and understand the events, but we can never quite obtain the full scope of things.

In "Videotape," the reader is constantly on edge: on the edge between two storylines by way of the framing device, on the edge between participant and observer by way of the second person voice, and on the edge between knowledge and ignorance by the way details are made uncertain and withheld. It's no wonder, then, that even though we know the central event of the story, we are plagued by uncertainty, doubt, anxiety, and the urge to find out more, all we call suspense. So even though the story seems to show its hand early, DeLillo still manages to make a compelling, suspenseful work, one that keeps us on the edge of our seats until the end, waiting, watching, and reading. We can all think of a time when we've been stuck in a traffic jam, only to find out that we've only slowed because of other drivers gawking, trying to get a view of the mangled vehicles, a scattering of broken glass, or maybe even someone being pulled from the wreckage. The traffic from the gawking is always worse than for the accident itself. Is there something about human nature that makes us turn and watch? It must be the same force at work in "Videotape." Our desire to understand that force, like the main character's desire to watch, is what the suspense in "Videotape" is all about.

Revising

Once you have a draft, put it aside for a day or so. This break will give you the chance to come back to your text as a new reader might. Read through and revise your work, looking especially for ideas that are not explained completely, places where you need more evidence from the work, and other problem areas. As you work to revise your early drafts, hold off on doing a great deal of heavy editing. When you revise you will probably change the content and structure of your paper, so time spent working to fix problems with sentence style or grammar, punctuation, or mechanics at this stage is often wasted.

Revising means reenvisioning, reseeing, and rethinking your analysis. To revise effectively, you first need to read your text as if you were seeing it for the first time, with no preconceptions about your analysis of the work. Here are some questions to ask yourself:

- How clearly have I presented my claim about the work?

- Have I provided sufficient evidence from the work to support my claim?

- What additional evidence from the work might I provide?

- Is there a visual that I could include that would help me make my point about the work?

- Do I connect every piece of evidence (quotations from experts, examples from the work itself) to my main claim?

Technology can help you revise and edit your writing more easily. Use your word processor's track-changes tool to try out revisions and editing changes. After you have had time to think about the possible changes, you can "accept" or "reject" them. Also, you can use your word processor's comment tool to write reminders to yourself when you get stuck with a revision or some editing task. If your classmates are offering feedback on your draft, they can also use track changes, the comment tool, or the peer-commenting feature of the software.

Many writers improve their ability to reconsider their own writing by having others respond to their text, which enables them to see how a real audience *reads* their analysis.

WRITER'S WORKSHOP

Responding to Full Drafts

Working with one or two other classmates, read each others' papers, and then offer your classmates comments that will help them see their papers' strengths as well as places where they need to develop their ideas further. You might share your comments and questions in a conversation, or you may have each reader write comments and questions (either with pen or pencil or electronically) on the writer's draft. Consider the following guidelines and questions as you do:

- Read for a first impression of the text. Then, in a brief paragraph, outline your initial response.

- Write a one-sentence summary of the author's main point or thesis. If your summary does *not* match what the author thinks is the main point, that discrepancy will help the writer see what needs to be revised.

- Write a brief paragraph outlining what you liked about the essay. How effectively does the title draw you into the paper? Why? How might the title be improved? What part(s) of the text are especially effective? What could use more explanation or evidence?

- In another paragraph, indicate what you found problematic about the essay—what you needed more information about, what questions the essay did not answer, what areas of confusion exist in the text.

(cont'd)

(continued)

- Reread the introduction. How effective is it at leading a reader into the text? How might the introduction be improved?

- How well do you understand the point the author is making about the creative work? What could the author do to further clarify or explain the thesis or main point? How convinced are you that the author's thesis is sound? Why?

- Where does the text need more examples or details to show rather then tell? What claims or assertions are well-supported? Which need more textual evidence?

- How much background information about the work does the author provide? Is this context sufficient? Why or why not?

- Has the writer documented all quotations from the work correctly? If the writer used outside sources, has he or she correctly documented information and quotations taken from them?

- How logical is the organization? That is, how easy is it for a reader to follow and understand what the author is writing?

- Might a visual such as a photograph help the author to make his or her point about the work more vividly?

- Re-read the conclusion. How effective is it at connecting the writer's ideas and reinforcing the main point of the essay?

Student and Instructor Comments on Hanna Earley's Draft

Below are comments and questions from peer reviewers and her instructor that Hanna Earley received on her first draft (keyed to the draft on pp. 648–52). Note that most comments ask for further development—more information— as well as for clarification.

❶ This title is functional, but it doesn't really motivate me to read your essay.

❷ This intro feels a little flat. Maybe add some details to help the reader get into the paper?

❸ Will your reader know the short story? Do you need to say what happens if everyone already knows?

④ This seems like too much detail for an introduction. I can't tell if you are going into detail on this point or moving on to give a brief summary of where you're headed later. I wouldn't necessarily give away your whole analysis now, because what will you put in the rest of your paper? Don't be in such a rush.

⑤ This sounds out of context . . . management? Isn't it something less businesslike?

⑥ I don't really believe this yet, because I haven't seen any proof. I would save this for your conclusion, after you've made your case, so it doesn't seem like filler but actually a smart statement about the story based on the examples you've put together.

❼ Careful—sometimes your quotations seem to come out of nowhere.

❽ Are you going to use "readers" or "we"? You keep going back and forth, and it's confusing.

⑨ Not sure where you're going with this. Can you show how this commentary is connected to details and suspense?

⑩ This sentence feels backward—it takes too long to make your point.

⑪ This has been a really interesting paper so far, but I feel like this whole traffic accident thing comes off kind of weird and almost cheapens the story a bit. I would keep focusing on the story to open up the bigger issues.

Responding to Readers' Comments

After receiving feedback from classmates, teachers, and others, you have to decide how to deal with their comments and suggestions. The first thing to do with any feedback is to really listen to it and consider carefully what your readers have to say. For example, how might Hanna Earley answer these suggestions from readers?

- One reader asks her to rethink her title.
- Another reader asks her to sharpen her focus on the story to reveal larger issues.
- Yet another reader urges her to use quotations more strategically.

Earley needs to pay attention to all of these comments as she revises her essay. With any feedback, it is up to you, as the author, to decide *how* to come to terms with readers' suggestions. You may decide to reject some comments, of course, because they are not consistent with your goals for your paper. Some readers, for example, may disagree with your point of view or conclusion. Other comments, though, deserve your attention. You may find that comments from several readers contradict each other. In that case, you need to use your own judgment to decide which readers' comments will best help you achieve your goals.

In the final version of her paper on pages 658–61, you can see how Hanna Earley responded to her readers' comments, as well as to her own review of her first draft.

 # Knowledge of Conventions

When effective writers edit their work, they attend to the conventions of proper documentation, usage, grammar, punctuation, and mechanics. By following these conventions in your writing, you make reading a more pleasant experience for readers because then they don't have to work hard to understand what your main point is and how you support that point.

See Chapter 20 for more on documenting sources.

In any essay that you write about literature, you will probably need to include quotations from the work you are writing about, and you may need to quote from the work of others who have written about that work of literature. Therefore, you will need to pay close attention to the conventions of quoting and documenting primary and secondary sources. When you write about literature you will also be expected to discuss events and actions in the story in the present tense, as if they were happening now. The round-robin activity on page 657 will help you to check your essay for your adherence to these two conventions.

 ## Editing

After you revise, you need to go through one more important step: editing and polishing. When you edit and polish your writing, you make changes to improve your style and to make your writing clearer and more concise. You also check your work to make sure it adheres to conventions of grammar, usage, punctuation, mechanics, and spelling. Use the spell-check function of your word processing program, but be sure to double-check your spelling personally (your computer cannot tell the difference between *their, they're,* and *there,* but you can). If you have used sources in your paper, you should make sure you are following the documentation style your instructor requires.

See Chapter 20 for more on documenting sources using MLA style.

Because it is sometimes difficult to identify small problems in a familiar text, it often helps to distance yourself from it so that you can approach the draft with fresh eyes. Some people like to put the text aside for a day or so; others try reading aloud, some even read from the last sentence to the first so that the content, and their familiarity with it, doesn't cause them to overlook an error. Checking conventions is a difficult task, so we strongly recommend that you ask classmates, friends, and tutors to read your work to help find sentence-level problems. Another option is to post your paper on a course Web site and invite everyone in class to read it. You may get only one or two takers, but one or two is better than none.

To assist you with editing, we offer here a round-robin editing activity focused on documenting quotations and using the present tense when writing about events in a work of literature, which are two common concerns when writing about creative works, especially literature.

WRITER'S WORKSHOP

Round-Robin Editing—With a Focus on Writing about Literary Texts

For this activity, work with two of your classmates. Make sure you each have copies of the work that you are quoting from. First, concentrate on the quotations that each of you has used to support your claims about the literary text. In particular, pay attention to the following:

- The accuracy of the quotations. Check each quoted excerpt to make certain that it matches the original source exactly.

- MLA conventions for introducing quotations and citing the sources of the quoted excerpts, both in the text and on the works-cited page. (See pp. 877–904 in Chapter 20.)

Now look for places within your text where you talk about events within the work. Check to make sure that you are using the present tense, not the past tense, when describing those events.

is
There seems to be some conflict or tension in their marriage that ~~was~~
^

somehow amplified by the main character's viewing of this tape.

 ## Genres, Documentation, and Format

If you are writing an academic paper in response to Scenario 1, you will need to follow the conventions appropriate for the discipline in which you are writing and the requirements of your instructor. However, if you are responding to Scenario 2 or 3, you may decide to write a posting for a Web site, start your own blog, write a letter, or use some other format.

If you have used material from outside sources, including visuals, you will need to give credit to those sources, using the documentation style required by the discipline you are working in and by your instructor. For literary analyses, you will usually use the documentation style recommended by the Modern Language Association (MLA).

For advice on writing in different genres, see Appendix C. For guidelines for formatting and documenting papers in MLA style, see Chapter 20.

A Writer Shares Her Writing about a Creative Work: Hanna Earley's Final Draft

Here is the final draft of Hanna Earley's analysis of "Videotape" by Don DeLillo. How has she used details from the story to prove her point about the way DeLillo maintains suspense?

HANNA EARLEY

That Doesn't Mean We Want Him to Stop: Suspense in Don DeLillo's "Videotape"

We've heard the phrases—page-turner, nail-biter, cliff-hanger—but they all communicate one idea: suspense. It doesn't matter how we experience it, hairs rising on our necks, sweaty palms, or slinking down in the movie seat, but it's that distinctive mix of excitement and fear, hope and dread, that pushes us to find the answer to the primary question: What happened? So in a short story such as Don DeLillo's "Videotape," in which the answer to "What happened?" is revealed almost from the outset, how does he keep us reading, transfixed to the page as his characters are to the videotape and the event it reveals?

The premise is simple, a man's murder caught on tape by a child. DeLillo delivers the news at the beginning of the ninth in a series of brief, expository paragraphs delivered in the same sparse prose as the rest: "It is not just another video homicide. It is a homicide recorded by a child who thought she was doing something simple . . . " (1064). Despite what we might expect, however—that all excitement and suspense would be lost once the main event is revealed—DeLillo still manages to create suspense, keeping our anxiety and interest until, and perhaps beyond, the end of the story: "The horror freezes your soul but this doesn't mean that you want them to stop" (1067).

DeLillo achieves this effect, of perpetuating suspense through the story despite a revealed outcome, by keeping his reader literally on edge. The first way that DeLillo keeps us on the edge is his use of second-person narration, constantly beckoning the reader into the story with "you." "You see a man at the wheel of a medium Dodge," we learn in the first paragraph, and so we as readers feel situated inside the story itself, almost as if participating. The tone is conversational, as if to establish common ground here, in the spirit of <u>we've all seen this before</u>—the family video at

1

2

3

Thanksgiving or whatever. This is nothing out of the ordinary. But in fact, this situation is anything but ordinary. As soon as the reader is drawn into the story with the "you" sentence structures, DeLillo starts to show that "you" is a specific character, perhaps similar to the reader but completely outside the reader. For example, "you" have a wife and "[y]ou don't usually call your wife over to the TV set . . . now the thing is finally going to happen and you want her to be here when he's shot" (1065). Clearly there is a whole set of circumstances here in which the reader is not involved. So when we are both drawn into and rejected from the story, we are somehow both participant and observer, but also neither, therefore unsettling our own points of view. We are left somewhere in-between, on the edge of the story itself. DeLillo's pulling of the reader into the story, but use of "you" as a particular man with a particular point of view and circumstance, triggers the ambivalence and doubt we associate with suspense. "And you keep on looking," we read, and we have no choice but to obey.

Building upon the disconcerting and suspense-building use of second-person voice, DeLillo also generates uncertainty and anxiety by placing the central story—the murder caught on film—within the frame of a larger story, that of a man watching the videotape in his living room and thinking about his wife and the argument they'd be having about the videotape if she were there. As the moment of the murder approaches, we learn, "Now here is where he gets it. You say, Janet, hurry up, this is where it happens" (1065). Clearly, there is something about the videotape and the nature of the murder that the main character wants to express to his wife. In fact, the underlying tension in the marriage seems almost intensified by the main character's viewing of the videotape: "You want to tell her it is realer than real, but then she will ask you what that means" (1065). At this moment, he seems more connected to the videotape than to his partner in life. So as we proceed through the story, two storylines develop, and as a result, we have two reasons to read, two vehicles for suspense. Not only do we want to learn how the tape ends— what becomes of the child? The shooter?—but we want to know what is happening in this relationship and why this narrator keeps talking about his wife as he watches. Therefore, DeLillo once again puts us on edge; we hover between the two "stories," one foot in each, waiting for the resolution of both, which heightens our feelings of suspense. As the videotape rolls forward, the anxiety of the main character likewise escalates; he is unsure what he is even trying to communicate by encouraging her to watch, when he admits, "What are you telling her? Are you making a little statement? Like I'm going to ruin your day out of ordinary spite. Or a big statement? Like this is the risk of existing?" (1066). In the end, both stories are left somewhat open-ended. As for the tape, ". . . [it] ends here,

One reader had this comment:

Careful—sometimes your quotations seem to come out of nowhere.

Earley has attempted to integrate her quotations more carefully.

either because the girl stopped shooting or because some central authority . . . decided there was nothing else you had to see" (1066), and as for the relationship, we can only anticipate more conflict, as we learn "[y]ou don't want Janet to give you any crap about it's on all the time, they show it a thousand times a day" (1067). Arguably, the readers' sensations of suspense, unease, and uncertainty extend beyond the end of the text, as do the uncertainties surrounding the murder and this man's relationship.

In addition to his narrative strategies of second-person voice and a frame story surrounding the main event, DeLillo also achieves suspense through his use of detail. Occasionally, the story is very detailed; for example, "[Children] break every trust, spy out the undefended space, catching Mom coming out of the bathroom in her cumbrous robe and turbaned towel, looking bloodless and plucked" (1063) or "[The girl filming the videotape] feels halfway clever and inventive and maybe slightly intrusive as well" (1064). But these details are speculation, not truth, since they come from the main character's imagination. The key events of the story, however, get very little detail, such as "It shows a man driving a car" (1063) or "[h]e is bald up the middle of his head, a nice guy in his forties whose whole life seems open to the hand-held camera" (1064). Most noticeably, the death of the driver is clean and almost graceful: "[y]ou don't see the blood, which is probably trickling behind his ear and down the back of his neck. . . . [T]he twist of the head gives you only a partial profile. . . ." (1066). All the details of the actual event are full of uncertainty ("seems open," "probably," "partial"), so we readers are hindered from painting a clear picture in our minds—our images of the story are as grainy as the tape itself and our uncertainty adds to our feeling of suspense.

5

One reader wrote the following remark:

Not sure where you're going with this. Can you show how this commentary is connected to details and suspense?

Earley revised to clarify this important point about DeLillo's use of detail.

After all, "It shows very little in the end" (1066); like the victim's car, the narrator seems to approach the details, but falls back, drifting away before we can really understand what's before us. When we read, "If you've seen the tape many times you know from the handwave exactly when he will be hit. It is something, naturally, that you wait for" (1065), it seems the anticipation of the gunshot is more important than any detail about the murder itself. Likewise, DeLillo downplays the details in order to heighten the anticipation. We read in suspense, looking to see and understand the events, but we can never quite obtain the full picture.

6

In "Videotape," the reader is constantly on edge: on the edge between two storylines by way of the framing device, on the edge between participant and observer by way of the second-person voice,

7

and on the edge between knowledge and ignorance as details are uncertain or withheld. It is no wonder, then, that even though we know the central event of the story, we are plagued by uncertainty, doubt, anxiety, and the urge to find out more, all of which are manifested in the concept we call suspense. DeLillo, when speaking about the videotape, practically tells us outright his strategy for suspense: "You keep on looking not because you know something is going to happen—of course you do know something is going to happen and you look for that reason but you . . . keep on looking because things combine to hold you fast—a sense of the random, the amateurish, the accidental, the impending (1064)." So even though we know all along that the driver on the videotape will be shot, he will die, and his car will drift back out of the camera frame as a child watches and a murderer escapes, DeLillo compels us to read to the end. We're looking for more than an answer to "What happened?" It is something else, more elusive or accidental, something in our relationships and ourselves, something to do with that child's "clear-eyed" wander into horror, something "realer than real" (1065).

Work Cited

DeLillo, Don. "Videotape." Responding to Literature: Stories, Poems, Plays, and Essays. 5th ed. Ed. Judith A. Stanford. New York: McGraw, 2006. 1063–67.

Earley's instructor made the following final comment:

This has been a really interesting paper so far, but I feel like this whole traffic accident thing comes off kind of weird and almost cheapens the story a bit. I would keep focusing on the story to open up the bigger issues.

Earley eliminated the reference to a traffic accident in her final draft.

QUESTIONS FOR WRITING AND DISCUSSION: LEARNING OUTCOMES

Rhetorical Knowledge: The Writer's Situation and Rhetoric

1. **Audience:** What audience does Earley have in mind for this essay? How can you tell?

2. **Purpose:** What purpose(s) does Earley have for writing this essay? How well does she achieve this (these) purpose(s)? How easily can you tell what her main point is?

3. **Voice and tone:** How would you describe the tone Earley uses in this essay?

4. **Responsibility:** How accurately does Earley portray what happens in the story? How responsibly does she use quotations? If you have noticed

quotations that have been skewed to help her make her points, point them out.

5. **Context and format:** Earley is writing for her composition class. How might her essay differ if she were writing about this story for a psychology or a sociology class?

Critical Thinking: Your Personal Response

1. What is your initial response to Earley's essay?

2. To what extent do you agree with Earley's analysis? Why?

3. What did you like best about Earley's essay? Why?

4. What did you like least about Earley's essay? Why?

5. How can Earley's essay serve as a model for your own writing?

Critical Thinking: The Writer's Ideas

1. How credible is Earley's analysis? Why?

2. How effectively does Earley support her claims? Why do you think so?

Composing Processes and Knowledge of Conventions: The Writer's Strategies

1. What are the major strengths of Earley's analysis? Why do you perceive them to be strengths?

2. How effectively has Earley used quotations in her analysis? What other quotations might she have used to further support her points?

3. Examine the revisions in the final version of Earley's paper. How does each of these changes affect Earley's paper?

Inquiry and Research: Ideas for Further Exploration

1. In your library or on the Web, locate two or more critical essays on the writings of Don DeLillo (critical essays are essays written about DeLillo's stories, much as Earley's essay is). How do these essays compare to Earley's?

2. In your library or on the Internet, look up "reader response criticism" and in an essay of no more than three pages, explain how someone using the "reader response" approach would examine "Videotape."

Self-Assessment: Reflecting on Your Learning Goals

When you are finished with this assignment, reflect on all the thinking and writing that you have done while writing about a creative work. It is often useful to go back and consider your learning goals, which you and your classmates may have considered at the beginning of this chapter (see pp. 590–91). To help reflect on the learning goals that you have achieved, respond in writing to the following questions:

Rhetorical Knowledge

- *Purpose:* How successfully do you feel you fulfilled your purpose in writing about a creative work?

- *Audience:* What did you learn about your audience as you wrote about the work you chose?

- *Rhetorical situation:* Consider some of the aspects that you have to think about, as a writer: How did the writing context affect how you wrote about the work? How did your choice of topic affect the research you conducted and how you presented your argument to your readers?

- *Voice and tone:* How would you describe your own voice in this essay? Your own tone? How do they contribute to the effectiveness of your writing?

Critical Thinking, Reading, and Writing

- *Learning/inquiry:* How did you decide what to focus on in your writing about the work you chose? Describe the process you went through to focus on a main idea (or thesis). How did you judge what was most and least important in your evidence from the work?

- *Responsibility:* How did you fulfill your responsibility to your readers?

- *Reading and research:* What did you learn about writing about creative works from the reading selections you read for this chapter? What research did you conduct? How sufficient was the research you did? Why? What additional research might you have done?

- What critical thinking, reading, and writing skills do you hope to develop further in your next writing project? How will you work on them?

Processes for Writing about Literature

- *Invention:* What invention strategies were most useful to you?

- *Organizing your ideas and details:* What organization did you use? How successful was it?

- *Revising:* What one revision did you make that you are most satisfied with? What are the strongest and the weakest parts of the paper or other piece of writing you wrote for this chapter? Why? If you could go back and make an additional revision, what would it be?

- *Working with peers:* How did your instructor or peer readers help you by making comments and suggestions about your writing? List some examples of useful comments that you received. List some examples of how you revised your essay based on those comments and suggestions. How could you have made better use of the comments and suggestions you received? How could your peer readers help you more on your next assignment? How might you help *them* more, in the future, with the comments and suggestions you make on their texts?

- Did you use photographs or other visuals as part of your analysis? If so, what did you learn about incorporating these elements?

- What "writerly habits" have you developed, modified, or improved upon as you constructed the writing assignment for this chapter? How will you change your future writing activities, based on what you have learned about yourself?

Knowledge of Conventions

- *Editing:* What sentence problem did you find most frequently in your writing? How will you avoid that problem in future assignments?

- *Genre:* What conventions of the genre you were using, if any, gave you problems?

- *Documentation:* Did you use sources for your paper? If so, what documentation style did you use? What problems, if any, did you have with it?

If you are constructing a course portfolio, file your written reflections so that you can return to them when you next work on your portfolio.

 ## Hanna Earley Reflects on Her Writing

In this excerpt from her reflection on her essay, Hanna Earley addresses her knowledge and skills, as well as some connections between the academic and personal areas of her life:

> It's funny because although I really liked this story, this paper was frustrating for me. When I first read the story, I was excited and felt

flooded with ideas. The language was straightforward, I thought the story was sort of eerie and sad, and the author was able to cram a lot of complex ideas into a small space. I was curious to break it apart like an engine or a watch and leave the pieces strewn about my desk: How does this thing work?

But when I went to actually organize my ideas and put them into a coherent statement around which to organize my analysis, I felt paralyzed. I didn't know which idea to go with—especially since they all felt related. I felt like there was so much material that the paper was going to be disorganized and unwieldy. My impulse was to turn in a long freewrite and hope for the best, but I knew that wasn't really going to achieve my purpose here.

Making the chart of oppositions helped me a lot, because it became easier to examine my ideas and piece them back together, instead of getting lost again in the tangents of my freewriting. I think most importantly, just becoming aware of all these oppositions drew my attention to the whole idea of the edge, or the borderline, which seemed so crucial to the sensation of suspense. Discovering that DeLillo keeps us on the edge (builds suspense) by, well, keeping us on the edge (both in and out of the story, aware of some details but not others, etc.) felt almost inane it was so obvious and simple, but until I had that "aha" moment, I didn't really understand where this paper was going to go.

As far as the draft, I am one of those people who spend a lot of time thinking about a sentence before putting it down, but I tried to write a little more freely this time and hoped that my classmates could help focus me later. It sort of worked, but the draft still took a while, mostly because about one-third of the way through, I started to realize I had bitten off more than I could chew, and I started to worry that analyzing ALL the ways DeLillo creates suspense might just be a big mess. Once I started worrying, my draft got all the more impossible, and I just started throwing out quotes and statements, hoping it would all seem like it fit together. By the time I finished the draft, I felt sick of the whole suspense idea and didn't even feel like workshopping the paper or continuing with it for the final draft.

Luckily my peers had a few nice things to say, which at least improved my mood. A lot of them thought this was a neat idea to talk about even though it was kind of sprawling and hard to get a handle on. They agreed that the first half of my essay was too much of me talking without showing any evidence and the second half was all quotations that didn't always connect to my main idea. Instead of going right back to the paper, I went to the gym and went out to dinner with some friends—I needed a break!

Going back to the final draft, it was obvious in some places where sentences or quotations were too clumsy or unclear. I also redistributed my main points and my quotes, so the paper feels more like one whole instead of two parts. Finally, asking the reader to think about gawking at a traffic accident ended up feeling morbid and not very motivating. So I went back to my brainstorming paragraphs, when I tried to figure out what draws us back to watching things over and over again—the spellbounded quality, and all of the possibilities and feelings associated with it. I decided to move this paper more towards a questioning of "cosmic perceptions" that DeLillo himself raises within the story. Hopefully the new conclusion, though it gets a little abstract and lofty, will be grounded in enough well-supported ideas to not seem cheesy, but rather as though it's trying to feel out the truths of things, which I think is what good stories are supposed to do. I hope my audience will respond better to this kind of ending—I think it's less obvious and more interesting, which better respects my audience's intelligence and experiences.

PART FOUR

Strategies for Effective Communication

Using Strategies That Guide Readers

Chapter 13

669

The chapters in Parts 2 and 3 of this book provide guidelines for writing that have various purposes—to share experiences, inform, explore, analyze, persuade, evaluate, determine causes and effects, propose solutions, and analyze creative works. Whatever your purpose, you can use a range of **rhetorical strategies** that, by helping readers to understand your writing, will enable you to achieve that purpose.

Because sentences and paragraphs are the basic building blocks of any piece of writing, you will need strategies for writing them effectively. This is especially true for developing your thesis statement, because if readers do not understand your main point, they will not understand your text. At the level of the individual sentence, the individual paragraph, and the full piece of writing, you will need strategies to help readers make connections: to help them see how the clauses and sentences of a paragraph connect and how the paragraphs themselves connect. In longer pieces of writing, you may also need to use headings and subheadings to guide your readers. Frequently, you will want to describe, define, classify, narrate, or compare and contrast events, objects, or concepts and will need strategies to organize your paragraphs accordingly. In most pieces of writing, you will use some combination of these organizing and connecting strategies. This chapter looks in turn at each type of rhetorical strategy—writing strong thesis statements, writing paragraphs, establishing connections within and across paragraphs, using headings and subheadings, and organizing ideas.

Announcing a Thesis or Controlling Idea

A **thesis** announces the main point, major claim, or controlling idea in an essay. A clear thesis helps readers because it prepares them for what they will be reading. A well-crafted thesis also keeps you focused on what you want to tell readers.

Although a thesis statement can focus your attention as you write, it is usually a good idea to write your thesis statement after you have done invention work and research. Invention activities, such as those described and illustrated in Chapter 3 and in the chapters in Parts 2 and 3 of this textbook, can help you clarify your thinking about a topic. Research can help you learn more about it. Once you have done invention and research, a thesis statement can help you construct a well-focused draft. Of course, the exact wording of your thesis statement might continue to change as you draft your paper—and even as you revise and edit it for readers.

Thesis statements can appear in different places in an essay. If you are writing to convince readers about a controversial topic, for example, you may need to provide some background information and evidence before announcing your main claim. That is, it might be best to let the evidence prepare readers to accept your claim. On the other hand, if you are responding to an essay question on an in-class examination, you will almost always want to place your thesis statement in the first paragraph so that it can guide the rest of your response and announce to the instructor that you know the material.

The strongest and most helpful thesis statements do more than simply state facts, provide personal feelings, or offer vague generalities. If your thesis statement merely states a fact, it just informs the reader about that fact; it is not arguable. If you offer a personal feeling as a thesis ("I don't like coffee"), people could certainly argue with it, but your evidence would be purely subjective ("I don't care for the flavor") and therefore not persuasive. If your thesis statement is general and vague ("Movies are more expensive now than they were at this time last year"), there might not be much to write in support of your thesis. Providing two figures—the average price of movies last year and the average price this year—proves your assertion. Or it may be hard to get a grip on how to support your thesis. It would be difficult to decide what evidence to use to support a generalization like "Animals have a hard time living in zoos," for example. The best thesis statements are limited and focused and offer some sense of the support that is forthcoming.

WEAK	The Arizona Diamondbacks won the 2001 World Series.
REVISED	Strong pitching, especially by Randy Johnson and Curt Schilling, was a contributing factor to the Arizona Diamondbacks' victory in the 2001 World Series.
REASON	The weak version is a simple statement of fact. The revised version offers a reason for the success of the team and suggests the ideas that the paper will develop.

WEAK	I can't stand war movies.
REVISED	*Letters from Iwo Jima* is an effective war movie because it forces Americans to view, and even sympathize with, combatants traditionally seen as enemies.
REASON	There is no way to support your personal feeling—that you do not like war movies—with evidence. But you could provide evidence for the ways *Letters from Iwo Jima* helps viewers see enemy combatants in a new light.

WEAK	The National Hockey League is in trouble.
REVISED	The National Hockey League has lost fan support because of the 2004–2005 lockout.
REASON	The weaker version is too general and vague. The revised version gives a specific reason for the trouble.

It also is important to *qualify* your thesis statement by using terms like *probably* or *likely* to make it more acceptable to an audience. For example, if you write "Our local hockey team lost fan support and ticket revenue last year, so it's going broke," some readers will not agree with your conclusion. A better way to phrase your thesis would be, "Our local hockey team lost fan support and ticket revenue last year, which is probably why it's having financial problems."

WRITING ACTIVITY

Revising Weak Thesis Statements

Revise each of the following thesis statements and explain how your revision has strengthened each.

> New York City has a larger population than Chicago.
>
> Pizza is better than pasta.
>
> There are many weight-loss drugs available to consumers.
>
> I don't like it when the wind blows.
>
> Women's sports are growing in popularity.

WRITING ACTIVITY

Looking for Weak Thesis Statements

Examine a copy of your campus or local newspaper, looking at the various articles for examples of weak thesis statements. Bring some examples to share with your classmates, and be prepared to indicate how you would improve the weak statements you located.

 ## Writing Paragraphs

A **paragraph** is a collection of connected sentences that focus on a single idea. With few exceptions, your writing projects will be made up of paragraphs, each developing an idea related to the topic of your writing. To guide readers through a piece of writing, arrange paragraphs in a logical order and make the connections among them clear. They also need to support your purpose, which is often to assert a main point, or thesis. But first of all, of course, you need to structure each paragraph effectively. Consider the following simple example, which could appear in a paper about Abraham Lincoln's career.

<u>During his years as president, 1861–1865, Abraham Lincoln experienced great stress from a combination of causes.</u> **First,** the Civil War, which broke out weeks after his March 1861 inauguration, wore on him daily until its end in April 1865. **Second,** typhoid took the life of Willie, his beloved eleven-year-old son, in February 1862. **Third,** his wife, Mary Todd Lincoln, suffered from depression and other forms of mental illness, problems that became more acute during the years in the White House.

Notice that this example paragraph is fairly short. Paragraphs can vary significantly in length, depending in part on the type of writing in which they appear. Paragraphs in newspaper articles, for example, tend to be short, whereas paragraphs in articles that appear in academic journals tend to be lengthy. Notice, too, that the first line is indented. Paragraphs can be set off visually by indentation or simply by an extra blank line. In college writing, you will almost always start each new paragraph with an indented sentence. While the specifics may vary, effective paragraphs generally have the following features:

- **A Focus on a Single Main Idea.** Readers expect that a paragraph will contain a single main idea related to the topic of the piece of writing. The more tightly you focus a paragraph on a main idea, the more you will help readers navigate through the paragraph. Note that in the example paragraph about President Lincoln every sentence is focused on the causes of Lincoln's stress. If you want to alert your readers about other specific information that will come later in your paper, use a *forecasting sentence* (the sentence in the paragraph about Lincoln that mentions Mary Lincoln's depression could forecast that the paper will have more to say about that topic).

- **A Topic Sentence.** A topic sentence guides readers because it expresses a paragraph's main idea, the idea that the other sentences in the paragraph support or develop. In the example about Lincoln, the first sentence, which is underlined, serves as the topic sentence. The topic sentence often comes first because this placement helps readers see at the outset how the sentences in the paragraph fit together.

- **Different Levels of Specificity.** All paragraphs have at least two levels of specificity. In the paragraph about Lincoln, the topic sentence clearly introduces the idea of stress and its various causes, and the second, third, and fourth sentences are more specific, each discussing a particular cause.

- **Use of Connective Words and Phrases.** Used within a paragraph, connective words and phrases, discussed in more detail on pages 681–82, can show precisely how the sentences in the paragraph support the topic sentence and relate to one another. In the example paragraph, the words *First, Second,* and *Third* (in bold type) tell readers that each of the sentences they begin offers a separate cause of Lincoln's stress.

- **A Logical Connection to the Next Paragraph.** When readers finish a paragraph, they expect that the next paragraph will be connected to it in some readily apparent way. After reading the paragraph that focuses on the sources of stress that Lincoln experienced, readers expect that the next paragraph will also be related to Lincoln's stress. The final task of an effective paragraph, then, is to relate to the paragraph that follows it.

Placement of Topic Sentences

In the paragraph about Lincoln, the topic sentence is the first sentence, a placement that lets readers know right away what the paragraph will be about. Sometimes, however, you will want to place a topic sentence at the end of a paragraph in order to develop suspense or to summarize information. Consider the following paragraph, which saves the topic sentence for last for both reasons:

> Born in San Diego in 1918, she won her first swimming race at the age of eleven. In 1945, she appeared in the film *Bathing Beauty* with her former teammate Esther Williams. In 1948, she began a two-year training program to swim across the English Channel. On August 8, 1950, she swam the Channel in record time for women. In 1955, she broke the record time for both women and men. <u>These are some of the remarkable feats of Florence Chadwick.</u>

Placing a topic sentence at the end of a paragraph can be an especially effective strategy in persuasive writing because it allows the writer to present evidence before making an assertion. Here is such an example from Joseph Pace's essay "Let's Go Veggie!":

> Less than a quarter of our agricultural land is used to feed people directly. The rest is devoted to grazing and growing food for animals. Ecosystems of forest, wetland and grassland have been decimated to fuel the demand for land. Using so much land heightens topsoil loss, the use of harsh fertilizers and pesticides, and the need for irrigation water from dammed rivers. <u>If people can shift away from meat, much of this land could be converted back to wilderness.</u>

> Joseph Pace, "Let's Go Veggie!"

Although you will most often find a topic sentence as the first or last sentence of a paragraph, sometimes a topic sentence can appear as the second sentence of a paragraph, with the first sentence serving as a transition from the previous paragraph. For instance, here is a paragraph that could follow the previous one about Florence Chadwick:

Many people marvel at these athletic feats. <u>Chadwick also achieved much in other areas of life, though</u>. For instance, she was a very successful stockbroker in San Diego. Because of her business accomplishments, she became the first woman to serve on the Board of the San Diego Hall of Champions. Further, she was well known for her strong commitment to youth groups.

Sometimes a paragraph has no topic sentence. Instead, the topic sentence is implied. In cases where the point is fairly clear to readers, a writer may decide to leave it unstated. In the following paragraph, the implied (unstated) topic sentence could be something like, "Lynn had endured an abusive marriage":

When I first met Lynn, she seemed withdrawn and disoriented. She had just taken the biggest step of her 25 years; she had left an abusive husband and she was scared: Scared about whether she could survive on her own and scared of her estranged husband. He owned a small restaurant; she was a high school dropout who had been a waitress when she met him. During their three years of marriage he had beaten her repeatedly. Only after he threw her down a flight of stairs had she realized that her life was in danger and moved out. I don't think I fully grasped the terror she had lived until one summer day when he chased Lynn to the door of my house with a drawn gun.

Barbara Ehrenreich, "A Step Back to the Workhouse"

Moving to a New Paragraph

Paragraph breaks signal that a writer is moving from one idea to another—even if the shift is a small one. Consider the example paragraph on Lincoln in which every sentence is related to causes of stress. We could develop that paragraph further by adding sentences that maintain that focus. Look at what happens, though, when we add a sentence that does not fit the focus on causes of stress.

During his years as president, 1861–1865, Abraham Lincoln experienced great stress from a combination of causes. First, the Civil War, which broke out weeks after his March 1861 inauguration, wore on him daily until April 1865. Second, typhoid took the life of Willie, his beloved eleven-year-old son, in February 1862. Third, his wife, Mary Todd Lincoln, suffered from depression and other forms of mental illness, problems that became more acute during the years in the White House. <u>To alleviate the stress, Lincoln often read the plays of Shakespeare.</u>

The last sentence in this paragraph does fit the general topic of Lincoln's experience with stress, but it does not fit the tight focus on causes in this paragraph, a focus established by the topic sentence. Instead, it introduces a related but new idea—by reading plays Lincoln alleviated the stress that he felt. The solution is to make the last sentence the topic sentence of the next paragraph:

> . . . Third, his wife, Mary Todd Lincoln, suffered from depression and other forms of mental illness, problems that became more acute during the years in the White House.
>
> To alleviate the stress, Lincoln often read the plays of Shakespeare. Among those that he read most frequently were *King Lear, Richard III, Henry VIII, Hamlet*, and *Macbeth*. About his favorite play, *Macbeth*, he wrote the following in a letter to the actor James H. Hackett on August 17, 1863: "I think nothing equals *Macbeth*. It is wonderful."

Notice that this new paragraph provides details about Lincoln and stress that are even more specific than the ones in the preceding paragraph. Each sentence adds details that are even more specific than the sentence that precedes it. The second sentence elaborates on the topic sentence by naming several of the plays Lincoln often read. The third sentence discusses Lincoln's response to *Macbeth*, one of the plays mentioned in the second sentence. Depending on the complexity of what you are writing, you may need several levels of specificity to develop a paragraph's main idea sufficiently.

In any case, if the second paragraph focuses on how Lincoln alleviated stress by reading Shakespeare's plays, the third paragraph could follow logically from the first two in various ways. Consider some possible topic sentences for a third paragraph and the focus that each of these topic sentences would call for:

Possible Topic Sentence for a Third Paragraph:	Focus of the Third Paragraph:
Lincoln also alleviated stress by reading the Bible.	This topic sentence indicates that the third paragraph will continue the topic of alleviating stress. Because the second paragraph lists titles of the plays, readers might expect the third to mention Lincoln's favorite books in the Bible.
In spite of his efforts to alleviate stress, Lincoln still displayed symptoms of stress.	This topic sentence indicates that the third paragraph will include some symptoms.
Lincoln enjoyed *Macbeth* so much for several reasons.	Readers will expect an enumeration of those features of *Macbeth* that Lincoln particularly enjoyed.

In short, whatever ideas you choose to express, by organizing your ideas into paragraphs, each with a distinct focus made clear through the topic sentence, you guide your readers, making it easier for them to understand— and follow—those ideas.

Opening Paragraphs

The opening paragraphs of an essay announce the topic and the writer's approach to that topic. Because writers often develop a fuller understanding of their topic as they write, many choose to draft an opening paragraph *after* they have drafted and revised the rest of an essay. In an opening paragraph the writer needs to establish a relationship with readers and help them connect the topic to what they already know and care about. Some common strategies for opening paragraphs include the following:

- Tell an interesting anecdote.
- Raise a thought-provoking question.
- Provide salient background information.
- Offer a view that the writer and readers hold in common.
- Provide some poignant or surprising statistics.
- Forecast the rest of the essay.

In "Bipolar Iraq," for example, Michael Wolff crafts a very short introduction, one that implies the question "What's really happening in Iraq?" Wolff also promises to elaborate on the two story lines in the rest of the essay.

> Here are the two opposite story lines:
> (1) It's working.
> (2) It's a quagmire.
> Let's fill them out a little more:

(See the entire selection in Chapter 5, pp. 145–49.)

In this introductory paragraph, the writer shares an anecdote, making readers wonder what is coming next:

> On a quiet, sunny morning in the spring of 1845, six years after Abner Doubleday did not invent baseball in Elihu Phinney's Cooperstown cow pasture (or anywhere else), a black-whiskered twenty-five-year-old volunteer fireman named Alexander Joy Cartwright, Jr., walked off the pleasantly shaded Eastern Post Road, an old maple- and oak-lined New England-bound country lane on Manhattan Island, into a dewy meadow.
>
> Harold Peterson, "The Man Who Invented Baseball"

(See the entire selection in Chapter 6, pp. 200–4.)

In the following introductory paragraph to the essay "Clocking Cultures," note how author Carol Ezzell forecasts the rest of the selection, especially by stating her thesis in the last sentence:

> Show up an hour late in Brazil, and no one bats an eyelash. But keep someone in New York City waiting for five or 10 minutes, and you have some explaining to do. Time is elastic in many cultures but snaps taut in others. Indeed, the way members of a culture perceive and use time reflects their society's priorities and even their own worldview.

(See the entire selection in Chapter 6, pp. 207–9).

WRITING ACTIVITY

Introductions

For each of the following opening paragraphs, describe the strategy that the writer is using. Either on your own or with several classmates, decide how effective you think each strategy is. How much does it make you want to read more? Why? Your instructor may ask you to share your responses with the rest of the class.

> The official poverty rate in 2003 was 12.5 percent, up from 12.1 percent in 2002. In 2003, 35.9 million people were in poverty, up 1.3 million from 2002. Poverty rates remained unchanged for Hispanics, non-Hispanic Whites, and Blacks, although it rose for Whites and Asians. For children under 18 years old, both the poverty rate and the number in poverty rose between 2002 and 2003, from 16.7 percent to 17.6 percent, and from 12.1 million to 12.9 million, respectively. The poverty rate of children under 18 remained higher than that of 18-to-64 year olds and that of seniors aged 65 and over (10.8 percent and 10.2 percent, respectively, both unchanged from 2002). The poverty rate in 2003 (12.5 percent) is 9.9 percentage points lower than in 1959, the first year for which poverty estimates are available. From the most recent trough in 2000, both the number and rate have risen for three consecutive years, from 31.6 million and 11.3 percent in 2000, to 35.9 million and 12.5 percent in 2003.

> U.S. Census Bureau, "Poverty: 2003 Highlights"

> The most vulnerable victims of poverty are the world's children. Over 27,000 children die *every day*—more than 10 million per year—most from preventable diseases and malnutrition. Yet, the handful of preventable diseases that kill the majority of these children can be treated and prevented at very little cost. Measles can be prevented with a vaccine costing just 65 cents. Diarrheal disease, which results

from poor sanitation and unsafe drinking water, can be treated with pennies' worth of oral rehydration salts. Malaria kills nearly one million children each year, despite the fact that treatment for acute malaria costs less than one dollar.

"Child Survival," Results (results.org)

What does it mean to be poor? How is poverty measured? Third World countries are often described as "developing" while the First World, industrialized nations are often "developed." What does it mean to describe a nation as "developing"? A lack of material wealth does not necessarily mean that one is deprived. A strong economy in a developed nation doesn't mean much when a significant percentage (even a majority) of the population is struggling to survive.

Anup Shaw, "Poverty around the World"

Tina Taylor was a model of what welfare reform was supposed to do. Taylor, 44, a single mother, had spent six years on public assistance. After 1996, when changes were made in welfare law to push people into work, she got a job that paid $400 a week and allowed her family to live independently. For the first time in a long time, she could afford to clothe and feed her two children, and even rent a duplex on the beach in Norfolk.

Griff Witte, "Poverty Up as Welfare Enrollment Declines; Nation's Social Safety Net in Tatters as More People Lose Their Jobs"

Concluding Paragraphs

Readers remember best what they read last. Although you should not simply restate what your essay is about in your conclusion, you can use it to do the following:

- Restate your main point (your thesis) and remind readers of your key points.
- Emphasize the significance of your perspective on your topic.
- Bring your writing to closure.

Here, for example, is the concluding paragraph from Roger Ebert's review of *Harry Potter and the Sorcerer's Stone:*

During *Harry Potter and the Sorcerer's Stone*, I was pretty sure I was watching a classic, one that will be around for a long time, and make many generations of fans. It takes the time to be good. It doesn't hammer the audience with easy thrills, but cares to tell a story, and to create its characters carefully. Like *The Wizard of Oz, Willy Wonka and the Chocolate*

Factory, Star Wars and *E.T.*, it isn't just a movie but a world with its own magical rules. And some excellent Quidditch players.

Ebert's paragraph has all three qualities of a strong conclusion:

- He restates his major claim that the film will become a classic.
- He reminds readers of several features of the film, briefly noting why they are important to the claims made in his review.
- He brings his review to closure by offering a delightful observation in the final sentence.

(See the entire selection in Chapter 9, pp. 406–8.)

WRITING ACTIVITY

Conclusions

For each of the following concluding paragraphs, explain what the writer has done. Either on your own or with several classmates, decide how effective you think each conclusion is. Your instructor may ask you to share your responses with the rest of the class.

Each day of my life there are times when I reflect back to working on the farm. And every day people notice that I am different from the rest of my peers. At school, teachers and organization leaders are impressed by my time management skills and the amount of responsibility I take on. At work, my boss continues to ask me where he can find some more hard working people. I simply tell him, "Try hiring some farm girls. I hear they turn out pretty good."

Jessica Hemauer, "Farm Girl" (Chapter 4)

Blameworthiness—not whether someone did a deed or not, but the extent to which they are culpable for it—is a complicated matter, a matter of whole pictures. It would be a relief, in a way, if a diagnosis like mental retardation always settled the question of how much to blame a guilty person, but it would leave so much out of the picture. And some of those things—moral agency, the nature of the crime itself—might be the very things we care about most.

Margaret Talbot, "The Executioner's I.Q. Test"

The Supreme Court's May 17, 1954, ruling in *Brown* remains a landmark legal decision. But it is much more than that. It is the "Big Bang" of all American history in the 20th century.

Juan Williams, "The Ruling That Changed America" (Chapter 10)

Using Cohesive Devices

Within paragraphs, effective writers use a variety of cohesive devices to show readers how sentences are connected to one another. The major devices include connective words and phrases, word repetition, synonyms, pronoun reference, and collocation. To help readers understand how paragraphs are related to one another, writers use transitional sentences as well as headings and subheadings.

Using Connective Words and Phrases

You can guide readers with logically connected sentences and paragraphs, making these connections explicit through use of **connective words and phrases.** These connections fall into three main categories: temporal, spatial, and logical. Some of the more common words and phrases expressing these connections are as follows:

TEMPORAL CONNECTIONS

Time: now, then, during, meanwhile, at this moment

> I worked all weekend. *Meanwhile*, my colleagues watched football all day Saturday and Sunday.

Frequency: often, occasionally, frequently, sometimes

> Sally likes unplanned trips. *Sometimes*, she'll even show up at the airport and then decide where to fly for the weekend.

Temporal order: first, second . . . ; next; before (that); after (that); last; finally

> Let's eat dinner. *After that*, let's see a movie.

SPATIAL CONNECTIONS

Location: nearby, outside, inside

> I stood by the window. *Outside*, a moose ran down the street.

Spatial Order: first, second, . . . ; last, next

> Jane sat in the corner. *Next to her* sat Jill.

LOGICAL CONNECTIONS

Addition: further, furthermore, moreover, additionally, in addition, and, also

> Martha Flynn is a powerful council member in our city. *Further*, she may be headed for other powerful positions in the future.

Opposition/Contrast: on the other hand, however, in contrast, on the contrary, but, conversely, nevertheless, yet, instead, rather

> I don't eat meat for ethical reasons. *On the other hand*, I do wear leather shoes.

Comparison: likewise, similarly, analogously

> George H. W. Bush led the United States to war in the 1990s. *Likewise*, George W. Bush led the United States to war in 2001.

Causation: because, as a result, as a consequence, therefore, thus, accordingly, consequently, so, then, on account of

> He didn't pay his phone bill. *As a result*, the phone company discontinued his service.

Clarification: in other words, that is, that is to say

> He rarely does his homework. *In other words*, he's not a very good student.

Qualification: under the [these] circumstances, under other circumstances, under these conditions, in this context

> John McCain spent years as a prisoner of war in North Vietnam. *Under these circumstances*, it's remarkable that he is so well adjusted.

Conclusion: finally, in summary, to sum up, in conclusion

> The new Toyota Camry has been rated one of the safest cars on the road. *Therefore*, we should consider buying one.

Illustration: for example, for instance, in particular, specifically

> Luz wears colorful clothes. *For example*, yesterday she wore a bright red sweater to her math class.

Using Word Repetition

Repeating a word or phrase—either the exact word or phrase or a form of it—from one sentence to the next helps readers make a connection between those two sentences:

> In a new study on the occurrence of dating **violence** among teenagers, University of Arkansas researchers found that 50 percent of high schoolers have experienced some form of physically **violent** behavior in their relationships. More surprising, the research revealed that male and female students perpetrate **violence** at an equal rate and that, of the two, females may be inflicting more serious forms of abuse on their partners.
>
> Megan Mooney and Patricia Petretic-Jackson, "Half of High School Students Experience Dating Violence, UA Study Shows"

Using Synonyms and Near Synonyms

As an alternative to repeating words and phrases, you can also use **synonyms,** words that are close in meaning, or near synonyms to connect sentences. For instance, notice the use of synonyms in this excerpt from Elvis Mitchell's review of the film *Harry Potter and the Sorcerer's Stone* (see p. 409 in Chapter 9):

> To call this **movie** shameless is beside the point. It would probably be just as misguided to complain about the **film's** unoriginality because (a) it has assumed that the target audience doesn't want anything new and (b) Ms. Rowling's books cannibalize and synthesize pop culture mythology, proof of the nothing-will-ever-go-away ethic.

Using Pronoun Reference

Pronouns substitute for nouns. When writers use pronouns to replace nouns, those pronouns point backward or forward to the nouns that they replace:

> During **his** years as president, 1861–1865, Abraham Lincoln experienced great stress from a combination of causes. First, the Civil War, which broke out weeks after **his** March 1861 inauguration, wore on **him** daily until its end in April 1865. Second, typhoid took the life of Willie, **his** beloved eleven-year-old son, in February 1862. Third, **his** wife, Mary Todd Lincoln, suffered from depression and other forms of mental illness, problems that became more acute during the years in the White House.

Collocation

Collocation refers to words that normally occur together. The following paragraph about the luncheon meat Spam includes words, highlighted here in bold, that you would expect to find together:

> **PORK** WITH **HAM.** These are the primary ingredients. From 85 to 95 percent of Spam is **pork** from a **pig's** shoulders. The remaining 5 to 15 percent is trimmings from a **pig's** rear end, which is more commonly and appetizingly known as **ham.** (Interestingly and confusingly enough, one of the two pieces of a **pig's** shoulder is called the butt, even though it is nowhere near the animal's rear end.) The ratio of **pork** to ham varies with ham prices. By U.S. Department of Agriculture definition, luncheon **meat** may not contain **nonmeat** fillers. It also must be free of **pig** snouts, lips, and ears. Although it may contain **pig** tongues and hearts, these parts must be listed separately on the label if it does. They're blessedly absent from Spam's.

Carolyn Wyman, "Making Spam"

WRITING ACTIVITY

Focusing on Cohesive Words

Working alone or with one or two classmates, identify the cohesive devices (and lack of cohesive devices) in the following paragraph. Also, improve the paragraph by adding any cohesive devices that you think might strengthen connections between sentences. Your instructor may ask you to share your responses with the rest of the class.

> The want to consume is nothing new. It is has been around for millennia. People need to consume resources to survive. However, consumption has evolved as people have ingeniously found ways to help make their lives simpler and/or to use their resources more efficiently. Of course, with this has come the want to control such means. Hence, the consumption patterns have evolved over time based on the influence of those who can control it. As a result, there is tremendous waste within this system, to maintain such control and such disparities.

Anup Shaw, "Creating the Consumer"

Using Transitional Sentences and Paragraphs

Writers use transitional sentences and paragraphs to help readers move from one section of an essay to another. These sentences or paragraphs often summarize what has come before and forecast what will come next. Here are some examples:

- Those are the advantages of an interest-only home loan. Now let me explain their major disadvantages.
- Although after that presentation I admired her intellect even more, her next decision caused me seriously to question her judgment.
- Those are the major features of the problem. Let's now consider possible solutions.

WRITING ACTIVITY

Writing Transitional Sentences

Write a transitional sentence that might be used in each of the following essays:

- A narrative about an experience that led you, as a writer, to some new insight
- An brief narrative in which you outline how a letter you wrote really "worked"—really did what you wanted it to do

Using Headings and Subheadings

In short pieces of writing, you probably will not need to use headings or subheadings. Headings are also rarely used in certain types of writing—for instance, in writing to share experiences and in letters. For longer pieces of writing and in certain genres, though, headings and even subheadings can help readers more quickly understand the focus of the paragraphs that come after them. They give readers the following information about the paragraphs they precede:

- They are a related group.
- They are all on the same topic, specified in the heading.
- In the case of a subheading, the paragraphs are on a subtopic that is subordinate to the topic of the main heading.

To guide readers effectively with headings, keep the following guidelines in mind when you write them:

- Generally, only one level of heading is necessary for a five-page paper.
- At least two subheadings should appear under a main heading.
- All content under a heading should relate to that heading.
- Make your headings and subheadings specific.

  VAGUE   Properties of Glass
  SPECIFIC   Chemical Properties of Glass

- At each level, make headings and subheadings parallel in grammatical structure, font type, and level of specificity.

  NOT PARALLEL   The Chemistry of Glass, Physical Properties
  PARALLEL   Chemical Properties, Physical Properties

- Design headings so that they stand out from the text. If appropriate, you can use bold and italic type, capitalization and placement, and font size to highlight headings. If you are using subheadings, design them so that they look clearly different from, and less important than, the main headings.

  DOESN'T STAND OUT   Common Uses of Glass
  DOES STAND OUT   **Common Uses of Glass**

  For more on headings in MLA and APA style, see Chapter 20.

  If you are writing an academic paper, you should follow the requirements of the documentation style you are using for the style of your headings.

- Leave more space above a heading than below it. This establishes that the heading is related visually to the material that follows it.

WRITING ACTIVITY

Focusing on Headings and Subheadings

Working on your own or with several classmates, consider the headings in "The Nursing Crisis: The Solution Lies Within" (pp. 541–45 in Chapter 11). How do the headings help guide readers? Your instructor may ask you to share your responses with the rest of the class.

 ## Using Organizing Strategies

In much of the writing that you do in this course, in other courses, and in other areas of life, you will use organizing strategies to guide your readers. Among the most useful strategies are narrating, describing, defining, classifying, and comparing and contrasting.

Writing Narratives

Both in everyday speech and in many kinds of writing, **narration** is a common strategy. When you narrate, you relate an event or a series of events or, in the case of a process, you give a series of steps. Most narratives are organized by time, or **chronologically,** from the beginning to the end of an event, a series of events, or a process. Obviously, narration is relevant to much of our discourse in all areas of our lives because our lives are filled with events and processes:

- In a persuasive essay, you use narration to give the background of the issue that you are arguing, or you provide a poignant anecdote to illustrate the importance of the issue.

- At dinner, you tell your family or friends about an event at school or work that day.

- In a science course, you record what happened when you conducted a laboratory experiment.

- After watching an enjoyable movie, you tell your friends about an exciting scene in the film.

- As a witness to a traffic accident, you tell the investigating police officers what happened.

In this section we will consider two kinds of narratives: narratives that relate an event or a series of events and narratives that relate a process.

NARRATING SINGLE EVENTS OR A SERIES OF EVENTS

Often in everyday conversation, you narrate single events—you tell a friend what happened yesterday, whom you saw or spoke with, who sent you an e-mail, what movie you enjoyed. Narrating a single event is also a common way of organizing part or all of a piece of writing. You might write an essay about an event that affected your life, an article on the opening of a store in your neighborhood, or a research report on the Montgomery bus boycott in 1955, a major event in the struggle for civil rights. You can also narrate a series of events in a piece of writing. You might write an account of your life, of the growth of the McDonald's restaurant chain, or of the American civil rights movement in the 1950s and 1960s.

For more on narrating an event or a series of events, see Chapter 4.

Whether you are narrating one event or a series of events, you need to give your readers a clear picture of what happened by providing sufficient detail. You also need to clearly establish the sequence of your narration. When you narrate an event or a series of events, you will most often order your details chronologically— what happened first, what happened next, and so on. As an alternative, however, you might choose to discuss the importance of the event or events first, and then proceed to the details so that your readers will understand why they, too, ought to be interested in what happened. To make the chronological order explicit, you can use nouns referring to time such as dates or days of the week as well as temporal connectors such as those discussed earlier in this chapter (see p. 681).

CHRONOLOGICAL STRUCTURE

Because life's events occur chronologically, it is usually easiest to narrate them that way. It is also usually easier for readers to process narratives that unfold chronologically. Even a short narrative paragraph such as the following one can suggest a chronological ordering of events:

> Once my aunt found a freckle on her chin, at a spot that the almanac said predestined her for unhappiness. She dug it out with a hot needle and washed the wound with peroxide.
>
> Maxine Hong Kingston, "No Name Woman"

POINT OF VIEW

The narrator of a story can have several points of view, so when you construct a narrative, you will need to select a point of view to write from.

In the *first-person* point of view, the narrator tells the story from the perspective of a participant or character in the story:

> When I went to kindergarten and had to speak English for the first time, I became silent.
>
> Maxine Hong Kingston, "Tongue Tied"

With a first-person narrator, first-person pronouns (*I, me, my, mine, we, us, our, ours*) refer to the actions of the narrator in the story. However, if there are other characters or participants in the story, the narrator will refer to them using third-person pronouns (*she, her, hers, he, him, his, they, their, theirs*) or proper nouns (for example, *Nick, Hanna*).

In a narrative told from a *third-person* point of view, the narrator is not a participant or character in the story. The narrator consistently uses third-person pronouns or proper nouns to talk about the actions of characters:

> On December 1, 1963, shortly after President Kennedy's assassination, Malcolm X addressed a public rally in New York City. He was speaking as a replacement for Elijah Muhammad as he had done many times before. After the speech, during a question and answer period, Malcolm X made the remark that led to his suspension as a Muslim minister. In answer to a question, "What do you think about President Kennedy's assassination?" Malcolm X answered that he saw the case as "The chickens coming home to roost." Soon after the remark, Malcolm X was suspended by Elijah Muhammad and directed to stop speaking for ninety days.
>
> John Henrik Clarke, from the Introduction to *Malcolm X: The Man and His Times*

Of course, regardless of the narrator's point of view, when characters refer to themselves in dialogue, they use first-person pronouns.

DEVELOPING TENSION

Narratives that include tension are more interesting to readers. To establish tension in narratives, writers can show conflicts between characters who hold differing values or perspectives. For example, sentences such as the following can highlight tension:

- In sixth grade I wanted to wear makeup like all my friends were doing, but my parents insisted that I was too young.
- My mother's parents didn't want her to marry my father, so the young couple eloped on a blustery day in November.
- After years of working seventy hours a week, my father announced to his supervisor that he wanted to work fewer hours to that he could spend more time with family.
- Tom and I were best friends, but then one day I saw him stuff a DVD into his shirt in a department store.

RESOLVING THE TENSION OR CONFLICT

Just as readers are intrigued by narrative tension, they are interested in seeing how tensions are resolved or not resolved by the end of the story. Although readers like some suspense in a narrative, they look forward to a sense of closure by the end of the story. Of course, for tensions such as those listed above there are many possible outcomes—some more pleasant than others.

WRITING ACTIVITY

Starting a Narration

The following brief report is an Associated Press article that was posted in the business section of DenverPost.com. It relates the details of a recent lawsuit. What is your view of the acceptability of using someone else's creative product in the way that YouTube is accused of using it? With several of your classmates, construct a brief opening paragraph that introduces the narrative and outlines some of the issues as your group sees them. Your instructor may ask you to share your responses with the rest of the class.

VIACOM SUES YOUTUBE FOR $1 BILL ION

By SETH SUTEL AP Business Writer

Article Last Updated: 03/13/2007 11:08:51 AM MDT

NEW YORK—MTV owner Viacom Inc. sued the popular video-sharing site YouTube and its corporate parent, Google Inc., on Tuesday, seeking more than $1 billion in damages on claims of widespread copyright infringement.

Fans of SpongeBob SquarePants and his friends, shown here in a scene from *The SpongeBob SquarePants Movie*, will not be able to view scenes from the popular Nickelodeon cartoon show on the YouTube Web site. Viacom Inc., which owns Nickelodeon, has insisted that all of its content be removed from YouTube and is now suing the popular video sharing site for more than $1 billion, claiming copyright infringement.

Viacom claims that YouTube has displayed more than 160,000 unauthorized video clips from its cable networks, which also include Comedy Central, VH1 and Nickelodeon.

The lawsuit, filed in U.S. District Court in New York, marks a sharp escalation of long-simmering tensions between Viacom and YouTube and represents the biggest confrontation to date between a major media company and the hugely popular video-sharing site, which Google bought in November for $1.76 billion.

YouTube's soaring popularity has been a cause of fascination but also fear among the owners of traditional media outlets, who worry that YouTube's displaying of clips from their programs—without compensation—will lure away viewers and ad dollars from cable and broadcast TV.

Viacom is especially at risk because much of its programming is aimed at younger audiences who also are heavy Internet users.

Last month Viacom demanded that YouTube remove more than 100,000 unauthorized clips after several months of talks between the companies broke down.

YouTube said at the time that it would comply with the request and said it cooperates with all copyright holders to remove programming as soon as they're notified.

In a statement, Viacom lashed out at YouTube's business practices, saying it has "built a lucrative business out of exploiting the devotion of fans to others' creative works in order to enrich itself and its corporate parent Google."

Viacom said YouTube's business model, "which is based on building traffic and selling advertising off of unlicensed content, is clearly illegal and is in obvious conflict with copyright laws."

Viacom said YouTube has avoided taking the initiative to curtail copyright infringement on its site, instead shifting the burden and costs of monitoring the video-sharing site for unauthorized clips onto the "victims of its infringement."

A representative for Google didn't immediately respond to a request for comment.

Other media companies have also clashed with YouTube over copyrights, but some, including CBS Corp. and General Electric Co.'s NBC Universal, have reached deals with the video-sharing site to license their material. CBS Corp. used to be part of Viacom but has since split off into a separate company.

Universal Music Group, a unit of France's Vivendi SA, had threatened to sue YouTube, saying it was a hub for pirated music videos, but later reached a licensing deal with the company.

In addition to damages, Viacom is also seeking an injunction prohibiting Google and YouTube from using its clips.

Google shares dropped $4.82, or 1.1 percent, to $449.93 in Tuesday morning trading on the Nasdaq Stock Market, while Viacom's Class B shares rose 43 cents, or 1.1 percent, to $40 on the New York Stock Exchange.

WRITING ACTIVITY

Analyzing Narrative Strategies

After reading the preceding narrative about the lawsuit, respond in writing to the following questions. Your instructor may ask you to share your responses with your classmates.

1. What does having an image of SpongeBob SquarePants to illustrate the article add to it? Why?
2. Why does the writer end with a report on stock prices?
3. How does the writer indicate various chronologies of events in the narrative?
4. How do verb tenses function in the narrative?

For more on a type of writing that uses narration extensively, see Chapter 4, "Writing to Share Experiences."

For an example of writing that narrates, see Jessica Hemauer's "Farm Girl" in Chapter 4, "Writing to Share Experiences" (pp. 117–21). Notice how she builds tension and brings the narrative to resolution.

INCORPORATING VISUALS IN NARRATIVES

Although the distinction between narrating a single event and narrating a series of events is not always clear, when you narrate a series of events, you obviously have the opportunity to cover a significant period of time, as well as the complications involved in a more extended narration. Because the

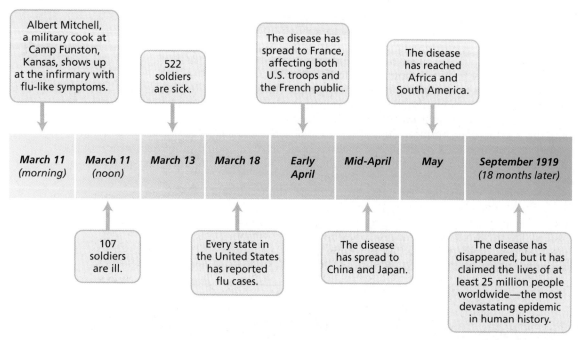

FIGURE 13.1   Timeline for the 1918 Flu Epidemic

chronology becomes complex, you might find it useful to guide readers with a summarizing visual such as a timeline. Figure 13.1, for instance, is a brief timeline for the flu epidemic of 1918.

NARRATING PROCESSES

When you narrate a process, you tell how something is done (informative/explanatory process narrative), or you tell others how to do something (instructional/directive process narrative). These types of narration, not surprisingly, are especially common in writing to inform. Like narrating events, narrating processes depends heavily on the inclusion of time connectives to clarify the sequence for readers. Writers also use illustrations, which should be labeled carefully so that readers can see precisely how the illustration is related to the process.

Informative/Explanatory Process Narratives: Informative or explanatory process narratives tell readers how something is done so that they can understand a process, not so that they can replicate the process. For example, you might write an informative process analysis about the following:

- How a legislative bill becomes a law
- How a microprocessor works

- How a seed germinates
- How a company's supply chain works

Figure 13.2 is a simple example of an informative process narrative—an account of how pencils are made.

While its purpose is chiefly informative, you might also have a persuasive purpose for narrating a process. For example, you might narrate the pencil-making process as part of a proposal that suggests more effective ways to manufacture pencils.

Instructional/Directive Process Narratives: While the purpose of informative or explanatory process narratives is to enhance the reader's understanding of a process, the purpose of an **instructional** or a **directive process**

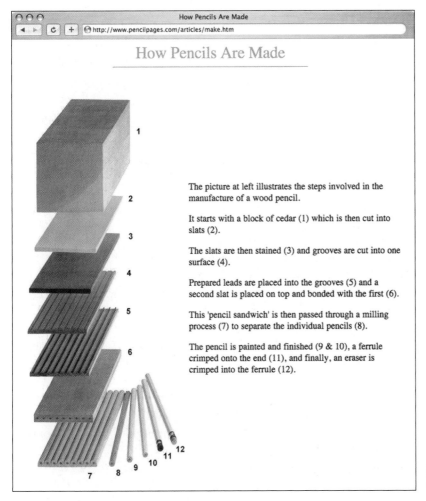

FIGURE 13.2 **The Steps in the Manufacture of a Pencil**

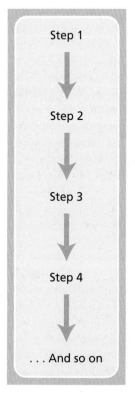

Step 1

Step 2

Step 3

Step 4

. . . And so on

narrative is to help readers learn how to do something. For instance, you might explain the following processes so that readers can replicate them:

- How to make a great pizza at home
- How to detail an automobile
- How to use the online library catalogue at your school
- How to conduct a chemistry experiment
- How to fill out a ballot petition

Figure 13.3, for example, is a narrative instructing readers how to perform cardiopulmonary resuscitation (CPR).

WRITING ACTIVITY

Analyzing Process Narratives

Respond in writing to one or more of the following questions. Your instructor may ask you to share your responses with your classmates.

1. Read the process for performing CPR that is outlined in Figure 13.3, "Learn CPR: You Can Do It!" Is the process explained effectively? What can you point to in the example to demonstrate what you mean?

2. Cover the drawings and read through the process narrative. What do the small drawings contribute to the process explanation? Why?

3. Does this process narrative make you want to learn CPR? Why or why not?

4. With two classmates and in no more than one page, explain the process you would use to make a sandwich.

5. In no more than two pages, outline your own writing process. Feel free to use a diagram if that would help to show this process to your readers.

6. In the local or campus newspaper, find several examples of a writer explaining a process. Share them with several of your classmates, and look for similarities in how each process narrative is constructed.

7. In no more than one page, outline the process a student at your school has to go through to register for classes.

8. Think of a process you recently went through or used, and outline it in writing.

LEARN CPR
You Can Do It!

CPR IN THREE SIMPLE STEPS
(Please try to attend a CPR training course)

1. CALL

Check the victim for unresponsiveness. If there is no response, Call 911 and return to the victim. In most locations the emergency dispatcher can assist you with CPR instructions.

2. BLOW

Tilt the head back and listen for breathing. If not breathing normally, pinch nose and cover the mouth with yours and blow until you see the chest rise. Give 2 breaths. Each breath should take 1 second.

3. PUMP

If the victim is still not breathing normally, coughing or moving, begin chest compressions. Push down on the chest 11/2 to 2 inches 30 times right between the nipples. Pump at the rate of 100/minute, faster than once per second.

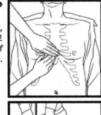

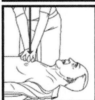

CONTINUE WITH 2 BREATHS AND 30 PUMPS UNTIL HELP ARRIVES
NOTE: This ratio is the same for one-person & two-person CPR. In two-person CPR the person pumping the chest stops while the other gives mouth-to-mouth breathing.

FIGURE 13.3   A Process Narrative for Performing Cardiopulmonary Resuscitation (CPR)

Writing Descriptions

When you describe, you sketch people, places, and things verbally, rather than visually. Usually, you will aim to establish some dominant impression—an overall feeling about what you are describing, such as the feeling evoked in the following passage:

> A dark mist lay over the Black Hills, and the land was like iron. At the top of the ridge I caught sight of Devil's Tower upthrust against the gray sky as if in the birth time the core of the earth had broken through its crust and the motion of the world was begun. There are many things in nature that engender an awful quiet in the heart of man; Devil's Tower is one of them.
>
> —N. Scott Momaday, "The Way to Rainy Mountain"

Because it is so common, **description** will be part of many of your writing projects in all four areas of life:

- In a biology course, you describe a cell that you are viewing under a microscope.
- When you meet with a realtor to search for a house, you describe the features that you are looking for in your next home.
- In an effort to have a signal light installed at a dangerous intersection, you attend a city council meeting, where you describe the aftermath of a serious automobile accident.
- At an initial meeting with a client, you describe a scene that might work well in an advertising campaign.

The approach you take to description will depend on what you are describing. Here we focus on three approaches that can be especially effective—naming, sensory, and spatial.

Naming in Description

When you describe someone or something, you need to name that person or thing, as well as its features. For example, if you were describing this book, you might name its constituent parts: chapters, table of contents, index, cover, headings, fonts, and graphic elements. If you were to describe the room where you sleep, you might name objects such as the bed, artwork, walls, ceiling, and floor. Here is an excerpt from Robert Sullivan's book *Rats: Observations on the History and Habitat of the City's Most Unwanted Inhabitants*:

> A rat is a rodent, the most common mammal in the world. *Rattus norvegicus* is one of the approximately four hundred different kinds of rodents, and it is known by many names, each of which describes a trait

or a perceived trait or sometimes a habitat: the earth rat, the roving rat, the barn rat, the field rat, the migratory rat, the house rat, the sewer rat, the water rat, the wharf rat, the alley rat, the gray rat, the brown rat, and the common rat. The average brown rat is large and stocky; it grows to be approximately sixteen inches long from its nose to its tail—the size of a large adult human male's foot—and weighs about a pound, though brown rats have been measured by scientists and exterminators at twenty inches and up to two pounds. The brown rat is sometimes confused with the black rat, or *Rattus rattus*, which is smaller and once inhabited New York City and all of the cities of America but, since *Rattus norvegicus* pushed it out, is now relegated to a minor role. (The two species still survive alongside each other in some Southern coastal cities and on the West Coast, in places like Los Angeles, for example, where the black rat lives in attics and palm trees.) The black rat is always a very dark gray, almost black, and the brown rat is gray or brown, with a belly that can be light gray, yellow, or even a pure-seeming white. One spring, beneath the Brooklyn Bridge, I saw a red-haired brown rat that had been run over by a car. Both pet rats and laboratory rats are *Rattus norvegicus*, but they are not wild and therefore, I would emphasize, not the subject of this book. Sometimes pet rats are called fancy rats. But if anyone has picked up this book to learn about fancy rats, then they should put this book down right away; none of the rats mentioned herein are at all fancy.

WRITING ACTIVITY

Analyzing Naming

After reading the excerpt from Robert Sullivan's book *Rats: Observations on the History and Habitat of the City's Most Unwanted Inhabitants*, respond to the following questions in writing. Your instructor may ask you to discuss your responses with classmates.

1. What is the effect of Sullivan's using both common names and scientific names for the various species of rats?

2. Why do you think that Sullivan offers so many common names for *Rattus norvegicus*?

3. Besides the common names that Sullivan mentions, what other names do you know for rats?

A Sensory Approach to Description

A thorough sensory description includes details from all five senses—sight, sound, taste, smell, and touch. In a vivid sensory description, the reader experiences vicariously what the writer has described. To generate such a description, you might use the questions in the following table. With minor modifications, you can use these questions to develop descriptions of a wide range of items, from roasted marshmallows to a favorite place from your childhood.

Sensory Details of _____

Sense:	Questions to Consider:	Responses:
Sight	What does it look like?	
	What do I see when I look at it?	
Hearing	What sounds does it make?	
	What sounds are associated with it?	
Taste	How does it taste?	
	What tastes are similar to it?	
	What tastes are associated with it?	
Smell	What does it smell like?	
	What smells are similar to it?	
	What smells are associated with it?	
Touch	What does it feel like to the touch?	
	What tactile associations do I have with it?	

Of course, for some subjects you will rely on details from only one or two senses and may not use others at all. The sense you will use most commonly and extensively when writing description is sight. It is important to remember that other senses can also have an impact on readers, however. The sense of smell, for example, tends to evoke memory in humans more powerfully than any other sense.

In the following description of "good bread," notice how the writer appeals to several of the senses:

Good bread. Its pleasure is deeply soul satisfying. It's not a superficial pleasure. It's down deeper than that. It may come from a perfect crust, with texture, definition, a caramelized crusty crunch with just the right give and not too thick. And it may come from a light, airy crumb, and you know it's been crafted by gentle, knowing hands that have shaped thousands of loaves just like this. And it may come from that lingering, wheaty fullness that makes you think of a soft sun-tinted breeze flowing its tide through a field of just-ripe, golden, amber-at-sunset wheat, ready for harvest. And it may make you think how the simple pleasure of a loaf of good bread, with wine, cheese, and good company, makes one of the finest of meals—inside by the fire in winter, or spread out on the grass when it's warm. And you may notice how the shape of the just-baked bread tells you an artisan did this—it bears his or her form, her mark, his signature. This is real food. It becomes a part of daily life.

Ken's Artisan Bakery and Cafáé (Portland, Oregon),
"What Is Good Bread?"

WRITING ACTIVITY

Writing Sensory Descriptions

Visit your favorite restaurant. Using the sensory-description chart on page 698, record what you see, hear, smell, taste, and touch. If you are overwhelmed by sensory data, you might focus on one sense at a time. Suggestion: When you focus on sounds, you might close your eyes because visual input can sometimes make it difficult to focus on aural input. Your instructor may ask you to share your description with the rest of the class.

A Spatial Approach to Description

When you describe something *spatially*, you describe it in terms of both its own physical dimensions and its relationship to the objects around it. Consider, for example, how you might describe a lake your family enjoys visiting. You might describe the size and shape of the lake and also how it is nestled in a valley and surrounded by small grassy hills, some covered with fir trees. You would describe the gravel paths that circle it, each just wide enough for two people to stroll hand-in-hand. Notice how an approach that is primarily spatial can include sensory details as well.

Spatial description often includes a visual, which may even be the predominant part of the description. For example, Figure 13.4 on page 700 is an x-ray of a child's hand. The paragraph below is a brief spatial description of the x-ray.

The hand is composed of many small *bones* called carpals, metacarpals and phalanges. The two bones of the lower arm—the radius and the ulna—meet at the hand to form the wrist.

The *carpal bones* are a set of eight short bones forming the wrist; they are disposed on two rows of four bones each. These bones, the size of a marble, provide the wrist's litheness and mobility.

The palm of the hand is composed of five *metacarpal bones* laid out from the wrist, as a fan. The articulation of the first metacarpal bone with the carpal bones, permits the movement of touching, with the thumb, the tips of all fingers.

FIGURE 13.4   An X-ray of a Child's Hand

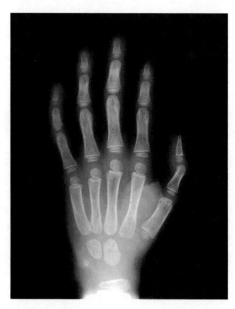

It is from this movement that the human hand can acquire the efficiency necessary to grab and manipulate objects.

Every hand is composed of 14 long bones named the *phalanges*. These bones compose the fingers and the thumb. Each finger has three phalanges and the thumb only two.

—McGill University, School of Architecture

WRITING ACTIVITY

Writing Spatial Descriptions

Find a comfortable seat at your favorite place on or off campus. Write a spatial description of the site. Your instructor may ask you to share your description with the rest of the class.

Incorporating Visuals in Descriptions

As you can see from the discussion of spatial description, there is much truth to the familiar adage "A picture is worth a thousand words." A photograph can make a description clearer or even replace several paragraphs of written description. Suppose you are describing the bird known as the great auk for a course on zoology, for example. You begin with a formal definition such as the one found in *The American Heritage Dictionary:* "a large, flightless sea bird

(*Pinguinus impennis*) formerly common on northern Atlantic coasts but extinct since the middle of the 19th century." You might continue with a basic description and include a photograph of a great auk, perhaps one of the many photos available on the World Wide Web; in a digital document, you could include a photograph or simply provide a link to a Web site that contains such a photograph. Figure 13.5, for example, is a photograph of a stuffed great auk, from a museum's Web site.

Your written description would include details that are not evident in the photograph, for instance, the fact that the adult great auk weighed five kilograms (eleven pounds) and stood seventy centimeters (twenty-eight inches) tall. Your description of the great auk would also need to answer questions that readers might ask about the creature, such as the following:

- Where did it live?
- What was its habitat?
- How was it adapted to its habitat?
- What did it eat?
- What predators and other dangers did it face?
- How long did it live?
- What were its mating practices?
- How did it care for its offspring?
- Why did it become extinct?
- To what other species was it most closely related?

FIGURE 13.5   The Great Auk

In answering these questions, you will probably use both sensory and spatial approaches to description, but you will also need to go beyond them. Many descriptions incorporate various approaches, as well as visuals, as shown in the following paragraph:

> The Great Auk or Le Grand Pingouin (*Pinguinus impennis*) was a member of the bird family *ALCIDAE*. This family of birds belongs to the large Order of birds known as the *CHARADRIIFORMES*. The family includes the Common Puffin (*Fratercula arctica*), the Dovekie (*Alle alle*), the Razorbill (*Alca torda*), the Common Murre (*Uria aalge*) and the Thick-billed Murre (*Uria lomvia*). The greatest number (16) of species from this family inhabit the North Pacific Ocean but the ones mentioned above inhabit the North Atlantic Ocean. The term Auk usually refers to the larger members of the family and the term Auklet refers to the smaller species. With the exception of the extinct Great Auk (*Pinguinus impennis*) all members of the family are small, stumpy, short-winged birds confined to the sea and coasts of the Northern Hemisphere. They are all expert divers using their wings to swim underwater, but only the Great Auk had wings too short for flight. The Great Auk was the original "Penguin." When explorers discovered the "Penguins" of the Southern Hemisphere, the name was transferred to the birds that appeared to be like the Great Auk and were found in the Southern Hemisphere. All Auks are able to withstand the rigours of wind, wave and cold weather and the cold seas in which they are found. Their wings are small and they fly direct and extremely fast. Most species however prefer to swim and be carried by currents. Food is obtained by diving from the surface of the sea and consists of crustaceans and small fish. Species of the family usually breed in large social colonies and their guano is responsible for the fertility of the isolated rocky islands that they colonise.
>
> —Royal Ontario Museum

WRITING ACTIVITY

Writing an Effective Description

For more on two types of writing that use description extensively, see Chapter 4, "Writing to Share Experiences," and Chapter 7, "Writing to Analyze."

Working on your own or with several classmates, choose a topic to describe. First, generate a list of questions that an interested reader might have about the topic you have chosen—questions similar to the ones about the great auk. Second, answer each of the questions to generate descriptive details. Third, use those details to write a short descriptive paragraph.

Your instructor may ask you to share your description with the rest of the class.

Writing Definitions

Definitions help you to make certain that your readers understand the terms that you are using. Clear definitions are especially important if you are writing about a topic that you know more about than your readers do, about an issue over which there are differences of opinion—including over the meanings of terms—or about a topic for which precision is crucial. For instance, in your professional life, your expertise may exceed that of the clients for whom you are writing a report, and so you may need to define key terms for them. You will find occasions to use definitions in all four areas of life:

- In a letter to one of your U.S. senators, you define "the working poor" as you make an argument for legislation that will assist low-income families.

- When you take a friend to a baseball game, you define "earned run average" when "ERA" appears after a pitcher's name on the big screen in left field.

- In an economics course, you define "gross domestic product" in a paper about economic growth in India and China.

- In an e-mail message to a client who wishes to purchase some income property, you define "acre"—43,560 square feet of land.

To see the importance of precise definition, consider the following famous disaster. In 1999, NASA sent the Mars Climate Orbiter to orbit Mars, but on September 23, the spacecraft burned up or broke up in the Martian atmosphere because its orbit came too close to the planet. The disaster happened because different teams of scientists had neglected to define the unit of measurement—miles or kilometers—that they were using. Some teams worked under the assumption that the unit was miles, others that it was kilometers. For all of the reasons mentioned above, then, responsible writers need to define unfamiliar, potentially controversial, or key terms for their readers and make certain that their definitions are clear, precise, and accurate.

Kinds of Definitions

You can use any of several kinds of definitions depending on how much information your readers need. Sometimes you can define a term by simply giving your readers a **synonym,** a more familiar word or phrase that could be used in place of the term you are defining. For instance, you might define the term *gaffe* by writing, "The word *gaffe* means 'social error,' which can be harmless or disastrous, depending on how it is handled." However, defining a word with a synonym has limitations. Consider some synonyms for the word *war: warfare, combat, conflict, fighting, confrontation, hostilities,* and *battle.* Each has differences in meaning, and, depending on the context, these words cannot necessarily be used interchangeably.

More useful than a synonym in many cases is an essential definition. **Essential definitions** are sentence definitions that include three parts: (1) the name of what is being defined, (2) the general category for the item being defined, and (3) the form or function that distinguishes the item being defined from other similar items in the same general category. Here are some pairs of examples:

Name	Category	Form or Function
A toaster	is a small kitchen appliance	that browns bread.
A mixer	is a small kitchen appliance	that combines ingredients.
A pencil	is a writing utensil	that contains lead.
A pen	is a writing utensil	that contains ink.

If a synonym or an essential definition is not enough, you can incorporate it in an extended definition. **An extended definition,** which can take up one or more paragraphs in a piece of writing, may include both of these briefer types of definition, as well as additional information and examples. It is especially helpful when you need to define a concept that is abstract or complex. For instance, here is an extended definition of a *mugwump:*

This archetypal American word derives from the Algonquian dialect of a group of Native Americans in Massachusetts. In their language, it meant "war leader." The Puritan missionary John Eliot used it in his translation of the Bible into their language in 1661–63 to convey the English words "*officer*" and "*captain.*"

Mugwump was brought into English in the early nineteenth century as a humorous term for a boss, bigwig, grand panjandrum, or other person in authority, often one of a minor and inconsequential sort. This example comes from a story in an 1867 issue of *Atlantic Monthly:* "I've got one of your gang in irons—the Great Mugwump himself, I reckon—strongly guarded by men armed to the teeth; so you just ride up here and surrender."

It hit the big time in 1884, during the presidential election that set Grover Cleveland against the Republican James G. Blaine. Some Republicans refused to support Blaine, changed sides, and the *New York Sun* labelled them *little mugwumps*. Almost overnight, the sense of the word changed to *turncoat*. Later, it came to mean a politician who either could not or would not make up his mind on some important issue, or who refused to take a stand when expected to do so. Hence the old joke that a mugwump is a person sitting on the fence, with his mug on one side and his wump on the other.

Michael Quinion, World Wide Words

Notice that the definition indicates what a mugwump is, explains the origin of the word and its history, and provides a concrete example.

WRITING ACTIVITY

Identifying Features of a Definition

Consider the following definition of a Luddite:

> A Luddite is a person who fears or loathes technology, especially new forms of technology that threaten existing jobs. During the Industrial Revolution, textile workers in England who claimed to be following the example of a man named Ned Ludd destroyed factory equipment to protest changes in the workplace brought about by labor-saving technology. The term Luddite is derived from Ludd's surname. Today, the term Luddite is reserved for a person who regards technology as causing more harm than good in society, and who behaves accordingly.

Tech Target Network

1. What are the features of this definition?
2. What might be added to the definition?
3. How might you clarify the definition to make it easier for readers to visualize a Luddite?

For an example of writing that defines, see Lang's "Putting in the Hours" in Chapter 7, "Writing to Analyze" (pp. 266–71). Notice how he defines each of the categories that he offers.

For more on a type of writing that uses definitions extensively, see Chapter 8, "Writing to Convince."

Incorporating Visuals in Definitions

Sometimes you may want to supplement a written definition with a visual that illustrates what you are defining. This strategy is especially useful for items that are difficult to describe. For example, here is the definition of an ellipse from Webster's dictionary: "[An ellipse is] a closed curve that is formed from two foci or points in which the sum of the distances from any point on the curve to the two foci is a constant." This definition gives readers a vague sense of what an ellipse is, but a diagram such as the one in Figure 13.6 on page 706 clarifies the geometric shape and even shows how to draw an ellipse.

FIGURE 13.6   A Diagram of an Ellipse

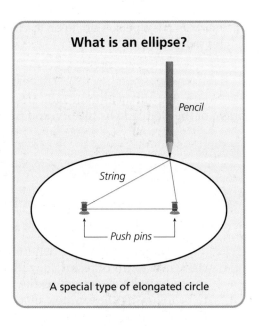

Writing Classifications

When you classify, you group—or divide—items into categories based on a principle of classification. There are three principles of division: completeness, exclusiveness, and consistency.

- **Completeness** means that all items need to be included in a classification. If you were classifying automobiles, you would need to make certain that SUVs were included in your scheme.

- **Exclusiveness** means that none of your categories should overlap with any other category. For example, the categories *movies about monsters* and *scary movies* don't work because some movies about monsters are scary (*The Thing*) and would fit in both categories.

- **Consistency** means that the same criteria need to be used to determine the contents of each category. If you are classifying animals and two of your categories are *mammals* and *birds*, your third category should not be *extinct animals* because that introduces different criteria into your system.

As the following examples show, classification systems range from simple ones with only a few parallel categories to highly complex systems, in which categories are divided into subcategories that are then divided even further, with items classified at various levels.

- In rhetoric, counterarguments can be classified into the following categories: counterarguments to acknowledge, counterarguments to concede, and counterarguments to refute.

- In biology, each species belongs to successively larger categories: genus, family, superfamily, suborder, order, intraclass, subclass, class, subphylum, phylum, and kingdom, so that each of the estimated 12,600,000 species that have lived on Earth can be classified and their degree of closeness to one another can be shown.

Many topics can be classified, which means that you will find classification a useful organizing strategy for many kinds of writing:

- In biology class you might write a paper to inform or analyze in which you discuss species according to their classification within the categories described above.
- Before purchasing a laptop computer for business travel, you might classify some possible laptops you are considering by weight—ultra-light (under three pounds), light (three to five pounds), moderate (six to eight pounds), heavy (more than eight pounds).
- In deciding which candidates to support in an election, you classify them according to their stated positions on those issues that are important to you.
- As you write a menu for your next week's meals, you use the categories in the food pyramid (see p. 708).

For more on a type of writing that uses classification extensively, see Chapter 7, "Writing to Analyze."

For an example of writing that classifies, see "Putting in the Hours" in Chapter 6, "Writing to Analyze." Notice how the writer uses description and narration as he classifies college faculty.

Incorporating Visuals in Classifications

Classification lends itself easily to illustration, especially with diagrams. The familiar food pyramid, shown in Figure 13.7 on page 708, is a convenient means of classifying foods and indicating recommended servings of each category.

Writing about Comparisons and Contrasts

The related strategies of **comparison**—looking at how subjects are similar—and **contrast**—looking at how they are different—are common not just in writing but in thinking. People find that they are crucial tools in thinking about and differentiating many aspects of the world around them. Think of something—anything—and consider how you would define and describe it: You most likely will compare it to and contrast it with other things that you perceive as being in the same category. If you have to choose between two options, you are likely to compare and contrast them as a step toward making your decision.

In all four areas of life, you will use comparison and contrast:

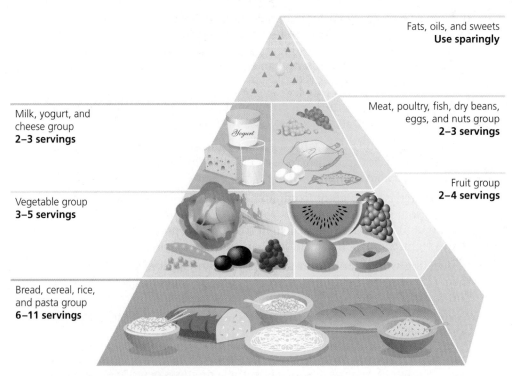

FIGURE 13.7   The Food Pyramid

- In an art history class, you might compare and contrast the features of two schools of art such as impressionism and surrealism.
- In an e-mail to a friend, you might compare and contrast two romantic comedies that you recently saw at movie theaters.
- You might write a letter to the city council to compare and contrast two plans for improving a city park.
- You might compare and contrast the features of two network servers that your company is considering for purchase.

Comparison and contrast are useful for a wide range of writing projects. For example, in Part 3 of this book, you might use comparison and contrast in Chapter 9, "Writing to Evaluate," to determine which of two items is better and in Chapter 11 "Writing to Solve Problems," to compare two possible solutions to a problem. In Chapter 12, "Writing about a Creative Work," you might compare and contrast two literary characters.

Approaches to Comparison and Contrast

The two major approaches to comparing and contrasting two items are point-by-point and block. In the **point-by-point approach,** you discuss the two items together for each point of comparison/contrast. In the **block approach,** you discuss all of your points of comparison/contrast about one item first and then all points about the other item second. Here are two abbreviated outlines for a paper comparing the sports of baseball and fast-pitch softball, each using one of the two organizational approaches.

Point-by-Point Approach

I. Pitching
   A. Method
      1. Overhand or sidearm in baseball
      2. Underhand in fast-pitch softball
   B. Speed
      1. Up to 100 miles per hour in baseball
      2. Up to 70 miles per hour in fast-pitch softball
II. Field dimensions
   A. Mound
      1. Elevated to about 12 inches in baseball
      2. Level with the field in fast-pitch softball
   B. Infield
      1. Ninety feet between bases in baseball
      2. Sixty feet between bases in fast-pitch softball
   C. Outfield
      1. Over 400 feet to the centerfield fence in baseball
      2. Usually no more than 300 feet to the centerfield fence in fast-pitch softball
III. Equipment
   A. Balls
      1. A baseball is approximately 2.75 inches in diameter
      2. A fast-pitch softball is approximately 3.5 inches in diameter
   B. Bats
      1. Baseball bats are usually over 2.5 inches in diameter
      2. Fast-pitch softball bats are usually under 2.3 inches in diameter

Block Approach

I. Baseball
   A. Pitching
      1. Overhand or sidearm
      2. Up to approximately 100 miles per hour

    B. Field Dimensions

       1. Pitcher's mound approximately twelve inches high

       2. Ninety feet between bases

       3. Over 400 feet to centerfield fence

    C. Equipment

       1. Baseball approximately 2.75 inches in diameter

       2. Bats usually over 2.5 inches in diameter

II. Fast-Pitch Softball

    A. Pitching

       1. Underhand

       2. Up to 70 miles per hour

    B. Field Dimensions

       1. Pitcher's circle level with the field

       2. Sixty feet between bases

       3. Usually no more than 300 feet to centerfield fence

    C. Equipment

       1. Softball approximately 3.5 inches in diameter

       2. Bats usually under 2.3 inches in diameter

If you are comparing two items with many features, you should usually use the point-by-point approach so that readers don't get lost. Regardless of the approach that you use, however, you can help guide your readers by doing the following:

- Focusing on the major similarities and differences.
- Including the same points of comparison/contrast for both items.
- Covering the points in the same order for both subjects.
- Using transition words to move from point to point.

WRITING ACTIVITY

Comparing/Contrasting

Read "Bipolar Iraq" on pages 145–50 in Chapter 5, "Writing to Explore." Construct an outline of the major points of comparison/contrast between the two positions about the Iraq War that Wolff describes. Does the writer use a point-by-point approach or a block approach?

Your instructor may want you to share your findings with several of your classmates.

Using Analogies to Compare

An analogy is a form of comparison in which two dissimilar objects are compared. The analogy helps to explain the unfamiliar or hard to grasp concept by relating it to something that is familiar. For example, most people are more familiar with shoes than with tires, so a writer might explain the relationship between a tire and wheel by saying, "A tire is essentially a shoe for a wheel."

For more on a type of writing that uses comparison and contrast extensively, see Chapter 9, "Writing to Evaluate."

Incorporating Visuals in Comparisons and Contrasts

Visuals can be very helpful in writing comparisons and contrasts, especially when you are comparing or contrasting items whose differences are fairly subtle. For example, people sometimes find it difficult to distinguish alligators and crocodiles. Although words can describe such subtle differences, drawings and photographs can show them. Here is a comparison and contrast of alligators and crocodiles:

> What's the difference between a crocodile and an alligator?
> Crocodiles and alligators—two creatures that share many similarities. But what are the real differences between them? This is probably the most frequently asked question when it comes to crocodilians, and while the answer may appear straightforward the real truths lie in the details.
> **1. Different families:** There are three groups (families) of crocodilians: the alligatoridae, which includes the alligator and the caimans; the crocodylidae, which includes the "true" crocodiles; and the

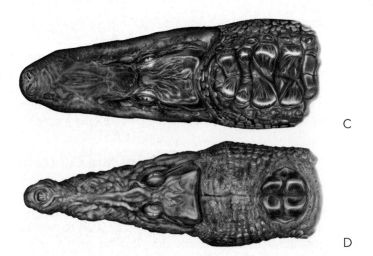

C

D

gavialidae, which contains only the gharial. So, the first difference is that alligators and crocodiles are actually in different families.

2. **Shape of the jaw:** The easiest way of telling apart crocodiles from alligators, however, is to look at their noses. Alligators (and caimans) have a wide "U"-shaped, rounded snout (like a shovel), whereas crocodiles tend to have longer and more pointed "V"-shaped noses. This is illustrated in the diagram. . . (C = alligator, D = crocodile). The broad snout of alligators is designed for strength, capable of withstanding the stress caused to bone when massive force is applied to crack open turtles and hard-shelled invertebrates which form part of their diet. Of course, alligators eat softer prey too, but hard-shelled prey are ubiquitous in their environment and it's a big advantage to be able to eat them. Conversely, the pointed snout of a crocodile isn't quite as strong as the alligatorine shape, but the crocodile is still capable of exerting massive biting power. Crocodile jaws can be thought of as being more generalized—ideal for a wide variety of prey. The full extent of the way jaw shape influences diet isn't particularly well studied in crocodilians, but it's obvious that a very thin nose like a gharial's is much better at dealing with a fish than a turtle! There are 23 species of crocodilians, though, and this simple broad vs. narrow rule doesn't always work.

3. **Placement of teeth:** In alligators, the upper jaw is wider than the lower jaw and completely overlaps it. Therefore, the teeth in the lower jaw are almost completely hidden when the mouth closes, fitting neatly into small depressions or sockets in the upper jaw. This is particularly apparent with the large fourth tooth in the lower jaw (see [A] . . .). In crocodiles, the upper jaw and lower jaw are approximately the same width, and so teeth in the lower jaw fit along the margin of the upper jaw when the mouth is closed. Therefore, the upper teeth interlock (and "interdigitate") with the lower teeth when the mouth shuts. As the large fourth tooth in the lower jaw also fits outside the

A

B

upper jaw, there is a well-defined constriction in the upper jaw behind the nostrils to accommodate it when the mouth is closed (see [B] . . .). This constriction occurs at the boundary of the premaxilla and the maxilla in the upper jaw.

Using Outlines and Maps to Organize Your Writing

Regardless of the organizing strategies that you use, outlines and visual maps can be helpful tools for getting and staying organized as you write. There are several kinds of outlines and maps, each with its own purpose. Use the one that fits best with your own situation and writing process.

SCRATCH OUTLINES

Scratch outlines work well early in the process of composing. As rough sketches of your thoughts, they can help you get ideas on paper without much concern for the final organization of the project. A scratch outline might be little more than a list of ideas in the order in which they might appear in the final project, such as this one:

Solving the Problem of Childhood Obesity

- Open with a story about obesity to grab readers' attention.
- Provide some background/history.
- Describe the problem with statistics.
- Explain the causes of the problem: poor nutrition (food pyramid), large serving sizes, lack of exercise.
- Describe the consequences of childhood obesity: diabetes, adult cardio-vascular problems.
- For each cause, offer a possible solution: teaching parents how to read nutritional labels; educating children and parents about serving sizes; persuading schools to require physical education; and persuading parents to engage their children in more exercise.
- Conclusion

FORMAL OUTLINES

Formal outlines can be useful once you have done some invention work and research and have a clearer sense of what you want to include in your draft and how you want to arrange the material. In a formal outline, you arrange your ideas in a series of levels. The first level is marked with roman numerals (I, II, III), the second level with capital letters (A, B, C), the third level with numbers (1, 2, 3), and the fourth level with lowercase letters (a, b, c). Each level must have at least two entries. The entries in a formal outline can be in sentences (a sentence outline) or in words or phrases (a topic outline).

For instance, you could convert the scratch outline on childhood obesity into the following formal outline, given as a topic outline:

Solving the Problem of Childhood Obesity

I. Opening story about obesity
II. Background/history of obesity
III. Description and explanation of the problem
    A. Statistical overview of the problem
    B. Causes of the problem
        1. Poor nutrition (food pyramid)
        2. Large serving sizes
        3. Lack of exercise
    C. Consequences of problem
        1. Diabetes
        2. Cardiovascular problems in adulthood
IV. Possible solutions:
    A. Instruction for parents on how to read nutritional labels
    B. Education for children and parents about serving sizes
    C. Recommendation that schools require physical education, and that parents engage their children in more exercise
V. Conclusion

If your wanted a more detailed plan, with sentences that you could actually use in your paper, you could prepare a sentence outline like the following:

Solving the Problem of Childhood Obesity

I. Many children, such as Heather H., begin the cycle of dieting and gaining weight as early as age 10.

II. Obesity has been increasing in the United States, especially among children and adolescents.

III. Here are some recent, and quite startling, statistics about childhood obesity.

IV. There are several reasons for this problem, including poor nutrition, ever-increasing portion sizes, and children's reluctance to exercise.

   A. The first reason is that today's children, who live in one of the wealthiest countries in the world, suffer from poor nutrition.

   B. Another reason is that we all seem to expect large serving sizes in every restaurant these days.

   C. Finally, many children don't exercise, preferring to stay indoors for video games and online chats with their friends.

V. The consequences of childhood obesity can be dire.

   A. Diabetes can be one major and severe consequence.

   B. Childhood obesity also leads to cardiovascular problems when children grow up.

VI. Fortunately, some doctors and other experts are turning their time and attention to this problem, and have come up with some unique ideas.

   A. Parents need to learn how to read food labels, so here are some instructions for doing so.

   B. Both children and parents need to understand what a reasonable "serving size" looks like.

   C. Several exercise programs are available that schools can provide to young students—exercise that will be fun and helpful to them.

VII. Childhood is too important a time to spend obsessing about weight, but children should be encouraged to eat a healthful diet and exercise regularly to avoid the dieting treadmill that Heather H. and others like her are on.

FLOWCHARTS

Flowcharts are exceptionally helpful when sequencing and specific time references are important. While Figure 13.8 shows a strictly sequential flowchart, you can also use flowcharts to help readers understand contingencies, or if/then situations. For example, a flowchart might show a situation in step 3 where if X happens, the next step is step 4. However, if Y happens, the next step is step 7.

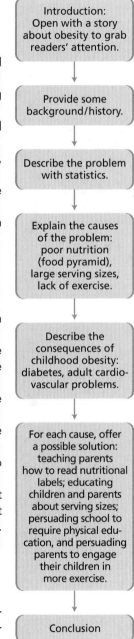

FIGURE 13.8 Flowchart for a Paper on Childhood Obesity

TREE DIAGRAMS

Like outlines, tree diagrams such as Figure 13.9 show hierarchical relationships among ideas.

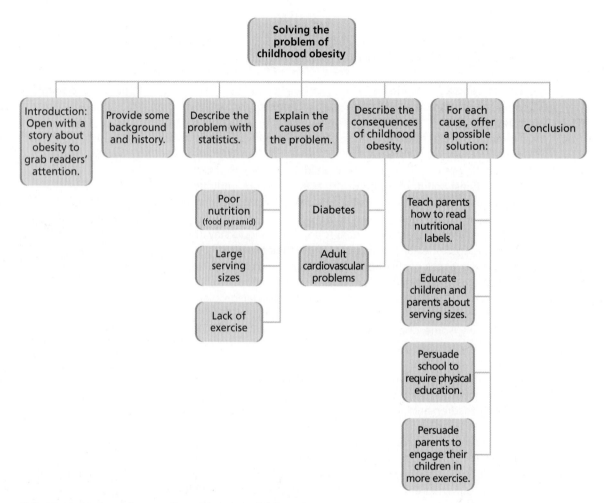

FIGURE 13.9 Tree Diagram for a Paper on Childhood

Using Strategies for Argument

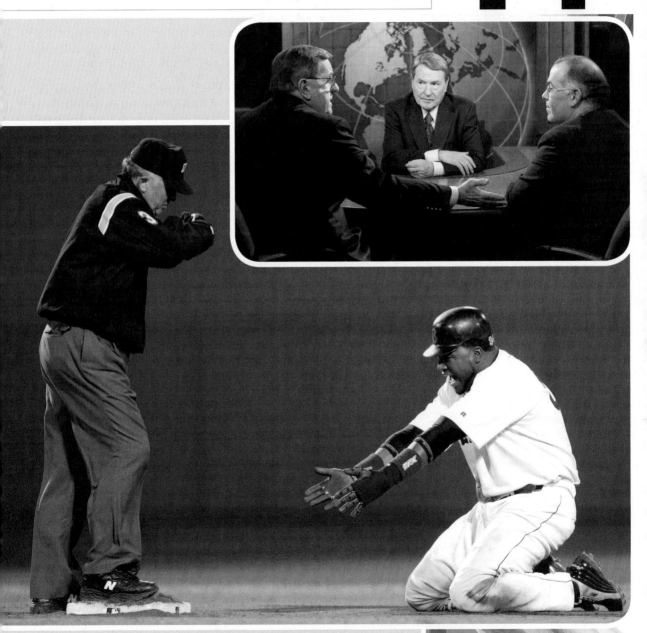

Often in our culture, the word **argument** has a negative connotation, as if to *argue* really means to *fight* about something, as children sometimes do on a playground, or as angry athletes sometimes do. But the term *argument* in many academic, professional, and civic settings and in most writing situations means to debate with someone about an issue or to attempt to convince someone to accept your point of view. That does not mean your debating partners, listeners, or readers will end up agreeing with you (or you with them), but rather that, at the end of your argument, your audience will say, "I understand what you mean and can appreciate your position. I don't necessarily agree with everything you've said, but I can see where you're coming from." This kind of *argument* must have as its thesis an assertion that is debatable, not a certainty. For instance, there is no need to construct an argument to support a factual statement such as "John Kerry lost the 2004 presidential election to George W. Bush"; it is not a statement with which people could agree or disagree. On the other hand, if a writer were to say, "John Kerry would have been an effective president of the United States," most people's responses would fall somewhere along the following continuum:

Strongly Disagree <--> **Strongly Agree**

Assertions that are capable of evoking such responses are appropriate **thesis statements** or **claims** for arguments.

The fundamental aim of an argument is to move the audience along this continuum of responses toward agreement or strong agreement if possible, but in any case farther away from strong disagreement.

Effective arguers get to know their audiences well enough to understand where on this continuum their responses to a thesis are likely to lie, and they choose argument strategies based on that knowledge of their audience. Of course, effective arguers realize that some members of the audience will be willing to move farther along the continuum than others.

WRITING ACTIVITY

Considering Your Audience

Construct two brief letters, no longer than a page or so each. For each letter, assume that you want twenty-four-hour, seven-day-a-week access to your college's library.

- For your first letter, your audience is your classmates. How would you argue for your position in a letter to them? What "shared needs" would you list, to show what needs you have in common?

- For your second letter, your audience is the president of your college or university. How would you argue for your position to him or her?

With several classmates, discuss the differences between your letters.

Sometimes instead of an actual battle, the word *argument* conjures up images of a loud and raucous debate, where the debaters do anything and everything to "win." Such images are no more relevant to argument as we define it than is the image of two people engaged in a physical fight. Of course, some people really will do *anything* to "win" an argument (for example, by presenting false data or telling fictitious anecdotes as if they were true), but if you consider our definition of argument to be a thoughtful discussion, then arguers really have no reason to stretch the truth. If "winning" an argument means that the other side sees, understands, and appreciates your position, then your goal is to present your thesis and supporting evidence in a logical manner, so that your reader can at least understand—and perhaps agree with—your position.

WRITING ACTIVITY

Considering Your Audience

Assume your audience is the president of your college. Think about what the president might already know about the topic of library hours. Your president may know, for instance, some things that might *aid* your cause:

- Not being able to conduct library research causes lower grades on papers and tests.
- Today's students often work and so cannot always get to the library during normal working hours.

But the president might also have some concerns about having a library with 24/7 access:

- More library access will increase costs for your college or university; will those costs be passed along in the form of higher tuition?
- Are there possible security issues in having students on campus in the early morning hours?
- How many students really would use the library after midnight?

How might you structure your argument to help the president accept your ideas? Revise the letter you wrote to the president of your college or university for the first activity, or draft a one- to two-page letter, if you did not complete the first activity. Be sure to address all of the issues raised above.

Argument and Persuasion

When you present an argument, you want readers at a minimum to understand what you mean and to see your perspective. The concept of *argument*, then, is somewhat different from and broader than that of **persuasion.** When you have persuaded someone, you have convinced that person to believe something (this legislative bill is better than that one) or to do something (provide the funding needed for longer library hours).

In a sense, an argument is the means of persuasion: You cannot persuade someone about anything without an effective argument. So, while you certainly hope that you will be able to persuade the president of your school to increase library hours, your overall goal is to construct and present a sound, effective argument. Put another way, after members of your audience read your argument they may or may not agree with you in part or in full, but if your argument is effective, they will at least think, "I understand this writer's position, and he or she has made a strong case." Each of the chapters in Part 3 of this book asks you to construct a certain kind of argument, with a goal of attempting to persuade your readers in the following ways:

- Chapter 8, "Writing to Convince," asks you to argue for a position on a controversial issue. When you learn about a controversial issue, your research will provide you with arguments on both sides of that issue, which will help you understand it better and more completely. And— sometimes—such research will convince you to change your initial position.

- Chapter 9, "Writing to Evaluate," asks you to argue for your judgment of the quality of a product, service, event, place, artistic work, or other subject. Your readers will probably not rush out and buy the product you have evaluated or see the film you recommend, but rather they will understand the reasons behind your evaluation.

- Chapter 10, "Writing to Explain Causes and Effects," asks you to make the argument that X is the cause of Y or that Y is the effect of X. Your readers may or may not completely agree with the cause-effect relationship you suggest, but after reading your argument they should at least understand your reasoning.

- Chapter 11, "Writing to Solve Problems," asks you to argue for a solution to some problem. While your readers may or may not agree that your solution is the best one, they should at the minimum be able to understand that the solution you have presented is plausible.

- Chapter 12, "Writing about a Creative Work," asks you to argue for your interpretation or analysis of a creative work. Readers may not agree with your interpretation or analysis, but if it is logically argued and supported by evidence from the work, they should at least be willing to consider it.

As you think about how to construct an effective argument, always consider what kind(s) of evidence will best convince your audience, along with how you might best present your evidence.

- For example, if you are writing to evaluate something (perhaps a film, a restaurant, or an art museum), quoting known and accepted authorities on the subject is often persuasive. Citing what a well-known film critic has to say about a movie is one way to provide this kind of evidence.

- If you are writing about a controversial issue or problem of some kind, statistical information is often useful, especially if you present it in a graph or table that makes the data easy to understand.

- If you are writing to solve a problem, historical information also is often useful, showing, for instance, how other communities have dealt with similar issues or problems. If you are writing to persuade your college to provide longer library hours, information about library hours from other colleges and universities would be useful to show how yours compares.

No matter what kind of evidence you use to support your argument, that evidence must come from reliable sources. For more information on evaluating sources, see Chapter 19.

Rhetorical Appeals

The philosopher Aristotle was one of the first to notice that effective speakers use three kinds of appeals to help make their arguments convincing. An **appeal** in this sense is a means of convincing your audience to agree with your argument, and perhaps of convincing them to do something. You already use these various appeals in your daily conversations when you want to convince your friends to do something with you, for example, or to talk your parents, or children, into going somewhere.

Logical Appeals

Logical appeals (or, using the Greek word, *logos*) are appeals made through your use of solid reasoning and appropriate evidence, including statistical and other types of data, expert testimony, and illustrative examples.

When teenagers attempt to convince their parents to allow them to borrow the family car by promising to fill up the car with gas before bringing it home, they present a *logical appeal*. They add to the logical appeal by showing their parents that they have cash in their wallet.

Notice how the part of a Web page about Alzheimer's disease shown in Figure 14.1 on page 722 is an example of a *logical appeal* since it offers statistical information about research on Alzheimer's disease.

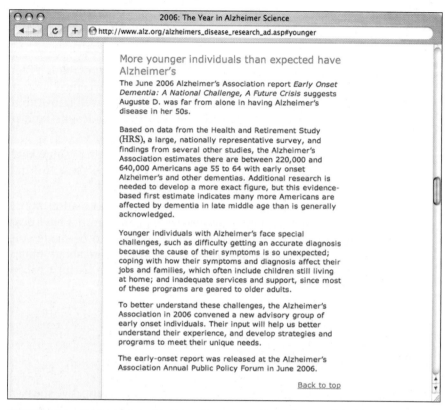

FIGURE 14.1   A Summary of Information about Early Onset Alzheimer's Disease
Source: Reprinted with permission from the Alzheimer's Association

Ethical Appeals

Ethical appeals (or *appeals to ethos*) focus on your character. When you establish your *ethos*, you communicate to readers that you are credible, intelligent, knowledgeable, fair, and perhaps even altruistic, concerned about the welfare of others. You can establish your ethos by doing the following:

- Presenting yourself as knowledgeable about your subject matter. Consider these two postings about great professional basketball players. Which blogger comes across as more thoughtful and knowledgeable?

    1. **NerdGuyDR – 2:25 AM ET September 9, 2007** (#<u>4</u> of 8075)
       I wanted to be the first one of us to use the name "Bill Russell" in this new thread. He was big and bad!
       Aaaahhhh. That felt really really good to me to say that!
       Okay, okay: I'm pathetic. Move on, children.
       ~Deywaye~
       who is sad and pathetic

2. **Hard_at_Work – 7:21 PM ET September 8, 2007** (#<u>3</u> of 8075)

. . .

I always thought that Russell was one of the first dominating big men, like Wilt Chamberlain. They had some contests, those two! But while Wilt got a lot of glory, Russell is the one who almost always came out on top, went on to a great coaching career, etc.

- Acknowledging points of view that differ from your own position, and dealing fairly with them. Sometimes dealing with an alternative position can be as simple as writing, "Other people might say that _____ is less costly than what I'm proposing, and they would be right—my plan does cost more. But the benefits far outweigh the cost, and here is why —"

- Providing appropriate information, including facts and statistics, for the audience you are addressing. Some audiences will be receptive to statistical information; others will be more receptive to quotations from experts in the field. Other audiences might look for both types of evidence.

If you present yourself in these ways, readers are more likely to be receptive to your argument. When the teenager who asks to borrow the family car mentions how conscientiously he or she has taken care of the car in the past and how responsible he or she is, that teenager is making an ethical appeal.

For example, why would you believe statistics or data that came from this source?

International Research Conference

The Alzheimer's Association hosts the International Conference on Alzheimer's Disease and Related Disorders. The next conference will be held in Madrid, Spain, July 16–20, 2006.

Conference format

This premier forum, held every two years, brings together the leading experts in dementia research to engage in a multidisciplinary, international exchange of ideas. Presentations cover the entire spectrum of dementia research, including the following topics:

- Epidemiology and risk factors
- Genetics and genetic testing
- Diagnosis, neuroimaging, and biomarkers of Alzheimer's and related disorders
- Histopathology of amyloid, tau, inflammation, and other disease mechanisms
- Cellular and animal models
- Current interventions and approaches to future therapies

- Human and animal prion diseases
- Evidence-based patient management and social-behavioral research

Conference history

The 1st International Conference on Alzheimer's Disease and Related Disorders took place in Las Vegas in 1988 with about 300 researchers in attendance. The conference was established by three prominent researchers: Khalid Iqbal and Henry M. Wisniewski of the Institute for Basic Research in Staten Island, New York, and Bengt Winblad of the Karolinska Institute of Stockholm. The conference founders and other interested researchers later formed the World Association of Alzheimer's Disease Scientists, which hosted the conference every other year. Under this group's leadership, the conference became one of the leading forums for presenting advances in dementia research.

Emotional Appeals

Appeals to readers' emotions (or *pathos*) can help readers connect with and accept your argument. However, effective arguers use emotional appeals judiciously, avoiding appeals that astute readers might consider exploitive. In the following excerpt from a Web site associated with Michael J. Fox, the film and television star who has been an active proponent of stem cell research, notice how the writer uses Fox's experience as a person living with Parkinson's disease to construct an emotional appeal for support for research into the cause and cure of this disease:

> Though he would not share the news with the public for another seven years, Fox was diagnosed with young-onset Parkinson's disease in 1991. Upon disclosing his condition in 1998, he committed himself to the campaign for increased Parkinson's research.
>
> Fox announced his retirement from *Spin City* in January 2000, effective upon the completion of his fourth season and 100th episode. Expressing pride in the show, its talented cast, writers, and creative team, he explained that new priorities made this the right time to step away from the demands of a weekly series.
>
> Though he maintains a strong commitment to his acting career and running Lottery Hill Entertainment, Fox has shifted a good deal of his focus and energies toward The Michael J. Fox Foundation for Parkinson's Research, which he launched in the year 2000, and its efforts to raise much-needed research funding for and awareness about Parkinson's disease.
>
> Fox wholeheartedly believes that if there is a concentrated effort from the Parkinson's community, elected representatives in Washington, DC, and (most importantly) the general public, researchers can pinpoint the cause of Parkinson's and uncover a cure by 2010.

There are many ways to appeal to readers' emotions. Here are some possibilities:

- Identify who is or will be affected positively or negatively by a situation or course of action that you are arguing for or against, and ask the audience to empathize or identify with them.
- Show how the situation or course of action has emotionally affected people elsewhere.
- Arouse indignation over a current situation by showing how it is inconsistent with a community's values or concerns.

You use all three appeals frequently in everyday life. To convince a reluctant friend to go to see a particular film with you, for example, you might mention that the film, while new and relatively unknown, received an award from the Sundance Film Festival, an ethical appeal in which you draw on the *ethos* of the famous film festival; you might point out that the early showings cost only half as much as the nighttime shows (a logical appeal); or you might plead that you have no one else to go with and hate going to movies alone, clearly an emotional appeal.

The Rhetorical Triangle: Considering the Appeals Together

Most effective arguments combine rhetorical appeals because audiences respond to a variety of appeals—just as you do, when you respond to someone else's argument. The three kinds of appeal complement one another, as is suggested by the rhetorical triangle shown in Figure 14.2. This model of a triangle represents visually how each aspect of an act of communication—the writer, the reader, the message—is connected to the other two aspects.

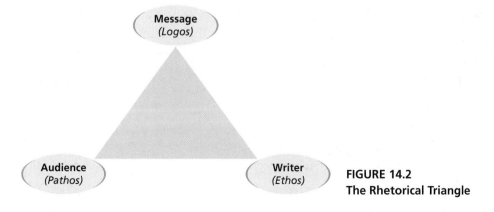

FIGURE 14.2
The Rhetorical Triangle

WRITING ACTIVITY

With two of your classmates, write a brief note to the chair of the College of Business, suggesting several possible internship projects that would count as course credit at community-service agencies. Use each of the rhetorical appeals to make your case. Possible agencies include the following:

- United Way

- Literacy Volunteers

- Kiwanis Club

- A local food pantry or homeless shelter

- The local Chamber of Commerce

Three Approaches to Argument

To aid you in responding to the assignments that call for argument in Part 3 of this text, in this chapter we cover three approaches to argument—classical, Toulmin, and Rogerian. The first approach can be traced back to the ancient Greeks; the latter two were developed in the middle of the twentieth century. All three approaches are widely used in effective arguments, so understanding how they function will help you not only to understand the arguments you read or hear, but also to construct your own written arguments.

Classical Strategies for Arguing

**FIGURE 14.3
Aristotle**

About 2400 years ago, the Greek philosopher Aristotle formalized what we now call the **classical scheme** of argument by listening to effective public speakers and then figuring out what made their arguments effective. Amazingly, Aristotle's ideas remain relevant today: You already use this approach in argument all the time. If you are using the classical scheme, this is the sequence you follow:

- Introduction

- Main claim

- Evidence supporting claim

- Discussion of other perspectives (acknowledging, conceding, and/or refuting them)

- Conclusion

This approach is called the **deductive** way to reason because you state your claim and then help the reader understand (or deduce) how the evidence supports your claim. It is a linear approach because you state your point or claim and then provide the evidence that supports that claim. Here is a simplified example of how the deductive approach might work in asking for a raise:

• Introduction and main claim	I'd like to talk with you about getting a raise. I've been with the company for two years now, and for several reasons I feel that I deserve a raise at this point in my career here.
• Evidence supporting claim	First, I am very effective now at doing work in the office as well as working with customers outside the office.
	Second, I've taken classes to learn several new software programs, and I'm now fully proficient at using them.
	Third, I've shown that I can take on lots of responsibility because I've handled several important projects in the past two years.
	Fourth, my end-of-year rankings have consistently improved every year.
	Fifth, my customer satisfaction survey numbers have improved every month.
• Discussion of other perspectives (acknowledging, conceding, and/or refuting them)	Now, I know there was that one dissatisfied customer, but if you'll recall, I managed to satisfy her (at last!) by providing extra service.
• Conclusion	Therefore, I deserve a raise.

The advantage of the deductive method is that you state your position and make your case before your reader starts thinking about other perspectives. Because readers understand what your point is *early* in your text, they find it easier to follow your argument.

If you are using another method, commonly known as the **inductive** approach, you first present and explain all of your reasons and evidence, then draw your conclusion—your main claim. In other words, you provide the evidence first and then the conclusion at the end. The advantage is that your reader may come to the same conclusion before you explicitly state your position and will therefore be more inclined to agree with your view. An inductive approach to asking for a raise would look like this:

I'd like to speak with you about my job performance here at our company now that I've been here for two years.

• Introduction

First, I am very effective now at doing work in the office as well as working with customers outside the office.

Second, I've taken classes to learn several new software programs, and I'm now fully proficient at using them.

Third, I've shown that I can take on lots of responsibility, and I've handled several important projects in the past two years.

• Evidence supporting claim

Fourth, my end-of-year rankings have consistantly improved every year.

Fifth, my customer satisfaction survey numbers have gone up every month.

Now, I know there was that one dissatis-fied customer, but if you'll recall, I managed to satisfy her (at last!) by providing extra service.

• Discussion of other perspectives (acknowl-edging, conceding, and/or refuting them)

For more on deductive and inductive reasoning, see Chapter 8.

Therefore, I deserve and would like to request a raise.

• Conclusion

Parts of a Classical Argument

Thinking about the parts or components of an argument makes the task of arguing more manageable. It allows you to focus on smaller tasks instead of trying to think of everything that you need to do all at once. When you put the parts together, the results can lead to an effective whole.

The classical argument as presented here has five parts occurring in a certain order. However, as you write your own arguments, you may find that not every part is essential in every case and you may also find it useful to rearrange or combine the parts. The five parts are as follows:

1. **Introduction** (*exordium*): In the introduction you gain the attention of the audience and begin to establish your credibility. To accomplish this, you need to have analyzed your audience so that you understand what might get their attention and what you might do to establish yourself as a credible authority on the topic. Your overall goal in the

introduction is to prepare your audience to be receptive to your case. What might you say, or what visual aids might you use, to get your audience's attention and pique their interest in reading your essay? It is usually wise to compose your introduction after you have constructed the rest of your argument, because then you will better understand your argument and how to prepare your audience to read it.

Here are some strategies that can work well in introductions for arguments:

- Show how the issue affects the audience.
- Show how the issue affects the community in general.
- Outline what a reader might do about the issue.
- Ask a question to grab the reader's attention.
- Explain what will happen if the reader does not get involved and take action.
- Begin with a compelling quotation.

TechNote

If you have ever listened closely to the words of popular songs, whether they are examples of rock, blues, jazz, musical theater, hip-hop, or rhythm and blues, you've probably noticed that many song lyrics follow the patterns of argument. Mining popular culture for examples that can help you build an argument can be quite effective.

If you are asked to write an essay that persuades, consider searching your music collection for interesting and powerful metaphors, statements, and stories you can use as quotations. Whether you collect CDs, download tunes from the Web, listen to podcasts, or even write and produce your own music, it is possible to consider your own collection of music as a collection of *arguments*. Be careful, though, to provide context and reasons for choosing the particular quotations that seem to support your view. For example, a song in which a woman claims she is going to hire a "wino" to decorate her home is actually a lament about the drinking behavior of her partner.

Often, you can insert a sound file into a *PowerPoint* presentation, which can add an interesting dimension to an in-class persuasive oral presentation. Be cautious about posting any music online, however. All music—no matter how brief the excerpt—is protected by copyright and is not considered fair use unless it is in the public domain.

---

2. **Narration** (*narratio*): Here you briefly explain the issue and provide some background or context for the argument you will make, as well as explain why it is important. If your readers understand why the issue is important to *them*, they are more likely to be interested and involved in your argument. If the audience is already familiar with the issue,

you can decide not to include a narrative in your argument. If you do include a narrative, though, you can use it to do the following:

- State the crucial facts that are generally agreed upon.
- List the main issues or aspects that you will consider in your argument.
- Introduce the main reasons that support your argument.

3. **Confirmation** (*confirmatio*): This is the main body of your argument. Here you offer evidence to support your thesis or claim. Evidence can consist of facts, statistics, expert opinion, and other information that supports your claim. For example, if you are arguing that students should get involved in the upcoming campus elections, data about tuition increases and proposed tuition hikes would be useful, so students can understand how the issues that are part of the election campaign affect them personally.

4. **Refutation** (*refutatio*): If you can argue about a statement, that means ideas or concepts or values are in dispute—that is, an issue is undecided and there is another side, or point of view, to your argument. For you to construct an effective argument, you have to deal with that objection, or **counterargument.** This is a crucial step: If you fail to deal with the opposition's counterarguments, your readers may think that you are unaware of them and consider you ignorant, or they may think that you are trying to conceal their existence and suspect that you are dishonest.

To refute counterarguments, you first need to discover what they are through research or audience analysis. As we note throughout the chapters in Part 3, classmates can be invaluable in helping you generate a list of opposing viewpoints. As you share ideas and drafts with your classmates, ask them what arguments "the other side" might make to address this issue or problem. What would they say to counteract your argument?

Another way to think about opposing arguments is to make a list of the arguments from your perspective along with those that disagree with you. Here is an example: Assume your college is considering privatizing its campus recreation facilities. What kinds of pro and con arguments might you make to such a proposal? The table on the following page offers some possibilities.

As you consider opposing viewpoints, you need to decide how to handle them. Refutation is only one of several options. Some counterarguments may not be significant enough to merit further consideration; it may be enough simply to acknowledge them. If you were trying to convince students to vote in a campus election, you might simply acknowledge the objection that one vote does not make a difference: "I understand what you mean, because I used to think that way. And it's true that one vote rarely makes 'the difference' in any election." Or you might decide to refute the objection, noting that "what one person can do is to talk to other people, and convince them that

In Favor of Privatizing Campus Recreation	Against Privatizing Campus Recreation
A wider selection and newer exercise machines of all kinds would be available to students, faculty, and staff.	Service could become worse because a private company would be looking only to make a profit. The center just wouldn't be a real part of the campus community.
The college would not have any liability in case a student got hurt using the facilities.	Hours could be restricted, once the private firm determines the times when there aren't enough customers in the facility to make it profitable to keep it open.
The college would receive rental income from the private company, for leasing campus space.	Personal, individual service is important, especially to students. That might disappear with a for-profit company in charge.
Employees could be rewarded with higher pay for more satisfactory work, like other employees.	Employees would no longer work for the local government that funds the college; some may lose their jobs.

they need to vote, and talk to them about the issues, and then all of a sudden that one person has gotten a lot of other people involved."

Other ways to deal with objections to your argument include the following:

- Agreeing that *part* of the opposing view is valid, and then demonstrating how the rest of the argument is unsound.

- Accepting that the opposing view is a valid point, but noting that what the opposition suggests costs too much / is impractical / will not work because _____, has been tried and been unsuccessful in other places, or has some other problem.

- Discrediting any authorities they cite in their favor ("Since Jones wrote that, three studies have been published showing that his conclusions were incorrect . . .").

5. **Conclusion:** (*peroration*): Here you conclude your argument and, possibly, call for action. In the conclusion, you can do one or more of the following:

- Summarize your case.

- Stir readers' emotions.

- Suggest an action or actions that the audience might take. Often a "call to action" is the most effective way to close an argument because if your reader then does what you ask, he or she has been persuaded by your argument.

- Refer back to the start of your essay, in essence tying everything together.

- List (briefly) your main points, touching on your evidence for each—basically listing why your argument makes sense.

Example: the Classical Scheme in Action

JARON LANIER

Beware the Online Collective

A pioneer in virtual reality research, Jaron Lanier invented the term *virtual reality*. In the early 1980s, he started VPL, which was the first company to offer virtual reality software. Along with his work in computer science, he is also a composer and an author. He received CMU's Watson Award in 2001 and was a finalist for the first Edge of Computation Award in 2005. In 2006, the New Jersey Institute of Technology awarded him an honorary doctorate. Among his many other awards is the first Virtual Reality Industry Award for Applications, which he shared with VPL client Matsushita in 1992. The following opinion piece first appeared in *Time* magazine in 2006.

Introduction: Here Lanier sets the stage, so to speak, as he introduces his argument.

Narration: Lanier states his point about people and groups.

Lanier tries to get readers thinking: Do people really act differently in groups than they do individually? What does he mean by "the lure of the mob"? Can you think of any examples from your own experience? Are you willing to give up some of your own personal attributes and qualities to be a member of some group? Does the Internet change people's behavior in the manner Lanier describes?

It's funny being an "old timer" in the world of the Internet. About six years ago, when I was 40 years old, a Stanford freshman said to me, "Wow Jaron Lanier—you're still ALIVE?" If there's any use to sticking around for the long haul—as computers get so much more powerful that every couple of years our assumptions about what they can do have to be replaced—it might be in noticing patterns or principles that may not be so apparent to the latest hundred million kids who have just arrived online.   1

There's one observation of mine, about a potential danger, that has caused quite a ruckus in the last half-year. I wrote about it initially in an essay called "Digital Maoism."   2

Here's the idea in a nutshell: Let's start with an observation about the whole of human history, predating computers. People have often been willing to give up personal identity and join into a collective.   3

Historically, that propensity has usually been very bad news. Collectives tend to be mean, to designate official enemies, to be violent, and to discourage creative, rigorous thought. Fascists, communists, religious cults, criminal "families"—there has been no end to the varieties of human collectives, but it seems to me that these examples have quite a lot in common. I wonder if some aspect of human nature evolved in the context of competing packs. We might be genetically wired to be vulnerable to the lure of the mob.   4

One of the most wonderful things about the rise of the Web and other Internet-based communication schemes is how anti-mob they have been. I was in heaven 10 years ago watching millions of people build web sites for the first time as a form of expression. I'm just as excited   5 today when I run across a creative web page, MySpace site, YouTube video or whatever. There are zillions of people out there who are developing themselves, reaching out to others, becoming more creative, better educated, and richer than they otherwise would have been. My personal favorite of the current batch of fast growing sites might be Second Life, where people create avatars of themselves to share in a virtual world. Bravo!

In the last few years, though, a new twist has appeared. Along with all the sites that encourage individual expression, we are seeing a flood of schemes that celebrate collective action by huge numbers of bland, anonymous people. A lot of folks love this stuff. My worry is that we're playing with fire.

There are a lot of recent examples of collectivity online. There's the Wikipedia, which has absorbed a lot of the energy that used to go into individual, expressive web sites, into one bland, master description of reality. Another example is the automatic mass-content collecting schemes like DIGG. Yet another, which deserves special attention, is the unfortunate design feature in most blog software that practically encourages spontaneous pseudonym creation. That has led to the global flood of anonymous mob-like commentary.

I remember the first time I noticed myself becoming mean when I left an anonymous comment on a blog. What is it about that situation that seems to bring out the worst in people so often? It's a shame, because the benefits of blogs (such as that citizen journalists can pool resources to do research that otherwise might not get done) get cancelled out. Blogs often lead to such divisiveness that people end up caring more about clan membership than truth after a while.

There's a pattern in recent online businesses that is sometimes called Web 2.0 that I think is distinct from the collectivity problem, but for some reason seems to be leading a lot of entrepreneurs into promoting collectives.

The Web 2.0 notion is that an entrepreneur comes up with some scheme that attracts huge numbers of people to participate in an activity online—like the video sharing on YouTube, for instance. Then you can "monetize" at an astronomical level by offering a way to bring ads or online purchasing to people in your gigantic crowd of participants. What is amazing about this idea is that the people are the value—and they also pay for the value they provide instead of being paid for it. For instance, when you buy something that is advertised, part of the price goes to the ads—but in the new online world, you yourself were the bait for the ad you saw. The whole cycle is remarkably efficient and concentrates giant fortunes faster than any other business scheme in history.

Confirmation: Lanier provides some evidence here to support his claim.
Confirmation: More evidence on how the Internet works and affects people and their work.

But now Lanier hints of a change in the way the Internet affects people—a negative change.

Example.

Another example.

Personal example.

But (Lanier provides an objection to his own argument here) the Web does some wonderful things, provides wonderful new and exciting ways for people to interact.

Refutation: Lanier answers the objection: reducing the human aspect leads to impersonal behavior. Back to his mob analogy.

Conclusion: Asks readers to think, to consider what we're becoming. Note the power of Lanier's last line.

So what's wrong with this pretty picture? All too many entrepre-   11
neurs seem to think that if you reduce the human element, the scheme
will become more efficient. Instead of asking people to create videos or
avatars, which require creativity and commitment, just watch their
clicks, have them take surveys, have them tweak collective works, add
anonymous, unconsidered remarks, etc. This trend is lousy, in my opinion, because it encourages people to lose themselves into groupthink.

What's to stop an online mass of anonymous but connected people   12
from suddenly turning into a mean mob, just like masses of people have
time and time again in the history of every human culture? It's amazing
that details in the design of online software can bring out such varied
potentials in human behavior. It's time to think about that power on a
moral basis.

WRITING ACTIVITY

With several of your classmates, find an essay in a newsmagazine (such
as *Time* or *Newsweek*) that is written in the form of a classical argument.
Identify each part of the argument:

- Introduction
- Narration
- Confirmation
- Refutation
- Conclusion

FIGURE 14.4
Stephen Toulmin

Toulmin Strategies for Arguing

Another important model of argument was developed by philosopher
Stephen Toulmin (Figure 14.4) in his 1958 book *The Uses of Argument*. As
with Aristotle's classical scheme, you already use the main aspects of
Toulmin's approach: Every day you make assertions ("All students need to be
involved in the upcoming election") and then use *"because* statements" to
provide support for those assertions ("because if they are not, they won't
have their needs and positions represented to those in power"). Toulmin

calls your assertion or thesis a **claim** and your *because* statement your **data**—the information supporting your claim, your assertion.

What Toulmin adds to this fairly intuitive way of constructing any text is the notion of a **warrant:** *why* the data support the claim. Sometimes you need to say why explicitly; other times you can assume that your reader understands this connection. For example, if you are trying to convince your classmates to become involved in campus politics, you might claim that their involvement is vital to their own interests. But unless your classmates believe that getting involved *will affect* them (in the amount of tuition they pay, for example), they will not be able to understand why they ought to take the time and make the effort to become involved. So you, as the person making the argument, must consider whether or not your audience will know why it is important for them to participate, and if you determine that they may not, it is up to you to provide those specific reasons.

In Toulmin's model of argumentation, then, three components are considered essential to any argument:

- **Claim:** the conclusion or point that you will argue and hope to convince readers to agree with. For example, your claim might be "A major objective of this country's space program should be to land a crew of astronauts on Mars."

- **Data:** the reasons you give to support your claim. Your data may take the form of *because* statements. You might support your claim about Mars by saying "because knowing about Mars will help us understand our own planet and the life it supports since Mars may have had water—and life—at one time."

- **Warrant:** the connection between the claim and the data, explaining why the data support the claim. Often this connection is obvious and can go unstated. For example, the data and claim above are connected by the idea that it is important that we understand our planet, an assumption your readers undoubtedly would share.

Three other components of an argument are considered optional: the *backing*, the *rebuttal*, and the *qualifier*.

- **Backing:** If you are not sure that your readers will see the connection between data and claim, you need to state the warrant and support it as well. The support for the warrant is the **backing.** If you felt you could not assume the warrant about understanding our planet, you might need to state it explicitly: "Understanding our own planet and the life it supports is crucial to our survival as a species, and knowing about Mars will help us do that."

- **Rebuttal:** When you **rebut** the opposition's position, you work to prove that your position is better, for example, that it is acceptable to more people. You might acknowledge the potential objection that space missions with astronauts are costly but argue that the potential benefits outweigh the costs: "While space flight with astronauts is expensive, in terms of our total economy those costs are small and the possible knowledge that we would gain by putting a human being instead of a machine in charge of data collection is priceless."

- **Qualifier:** In response to opposing positions and points, you may need to in some way limit or modify, or **qualify,** your claim. You can do this by indicating precisely the conditions under which your claim does and does not apply. Qualifiers often include words such as *sometimes*, *possibly*, *may*, and *perhaps*. For example, you could say that a major objective of the space program "may be the exploration of Mars by humans, especially if expeditions by robots continue to gather evidence that Mars may have once had life."

Example: the Toulmin Model in Action

STANLEY FISH

But I Didn't Do It!

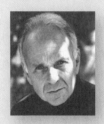

Both a professor and an attorney, Stanley Fish has held teaching as well as administrative positions in several large American universities. A world-renowned scholar on the Seventeenth Century poet John Milton, Dr. Fish is the author of more than a hundred articles and books and review articles, many of which have been translated into other languages.

Dr. Fish has also won many awards and honors, including the Hanford Book Award, the PEN/Spielvogel-Diamonstein Award, and the Milton Society Award. He also received a nomination for the National Book Award. The following opinion piece was first published in the *New York Times* in 2006.

Unstated warrant: Slavery was and is a horrible part of American history. Fish probably assumes that he does not need a *because* statement since readers will agree that slavery was terrible.

Emboldened by the State of Virginia's apology for slavery—the measure passed both houses unanimously—some Georgia lawmakers are in the process of introducing a similar resolution in their legislature. The reasoning behind the apology movement is straightforward: a great wrong was done for centuries to men and women who contributed in many ways to the prosperity of their country and were willing to die for it in battle; it's long past time to say we're sorry.

Resistance to the apology movement is also straightforward. There is the fear that because an apology is an admission of responsibility for a prior bad act, apologizing might establish a legal or quasi-legal basis for reparations. And there is also the objection that after so many years an apology would be merely ceremonial and would therefore be nothing more than a "feel good" gesture.

But the objection most often voiced is that the wrong people would be apologizing to the wrong people. That was the point made by Tommie Williams, the Georgia Senate majority leader, when he said: "I personally believe apologies need to come from feelings that I've done wrong," and "I just don't feel like I did something wrong."

Williams's counterpart in the house, Speaker Glenn Richardson, made the same claim of innocence on behalf of his colleagues. "I'm not sure what we ought to be apologizing for," given that "nobody here was in office."

Mr. Richardson's statement at least has the merit of recognizing that an apology would not be made by an individual—the idea isn't to go to some slave cemetery and speak to a gravestone—but by an institution. He just thinks that because no present member of the institution was around at the time of the injury, an apology would make no sense.

But this is very bad reasoning, and you can see why if you read just a few recent Supreme Court cases on any subject. Invariably, the justice delivering the court's opinion will cite a precedent from a case decided 50 or 100 years ago, and say something like, "In Smith v. Jones, we ruled that . . . " But of course he or she didn't actually—that is, personally—rule on anything in 1940 or 1840, so what's with the "we"?

The answer is that by using "we" to refer to an action taken before any present member of the court had reached the age of reason or was even alive, the justices acknowledge that they are part of an ongoing enterprise, and as such are responsible for its history; not as individuals, but as persons charged with the duty of carrying on a project that precedes them and will survive them.

At times "carrying on" includes revising and even repudiating earlier stages in that project. By overruling a precedent—a rare occurrence, to be sure—the justices say, collectively and on behalf of everyone who has ever donned the robe, "Oops, we got that one wrong; sorry, here's another try."

Legislatures do not overrule; they repeal, but the principle is the same. Legislators meeting on the first day of a new term don't say, "O.K., let's start all over again and figure out what laws we would like to have on the books." Instead, they regard themselves as picking up a baton passed to them by their predecessors whose actions they now "own," even in those instances when no legislator now sitting performed them.

This is the issue Fish is dealing with. He is rebutting the assertion that an apology for slavery is a bad idea because no one who is currently alive, including the individual members of the Georgia legislature, kept slaves.

Fish's claim: The Georgia lawmaker's resistance to an apology is based on faulty reasoning.

Data: The members of the Supreme Court, by relying on precedent, carry on the work of the members who preceded them and are responsible for earlier members' actions because they are all part of that institution.

Unstated warrant: The Supreme Court's authority derives from its reliance on, and respect for, precedent.

Warrant: Justices should overrule previous decisions in which the court ruled incorrectly.

Warrant: Legislatures are analogous to courts.

Data: Case where the U.S. Congress passed legislation providing reparations to Japanese-Americans unjustly treated during World War II.

Data: President George H. W. Bush formally apologized to Japanese Americans.

Qualifier: Fish admits he doesn't intend to answer the greater question of whether or not an apology should be issued, but rather he limits his argument to addressing one reason offered by members of the Georgia legislature for not apologizing.

Conclusion: The fact that the Georgia legislators did not personally keep slaves is not a valid reason to resist apologizing.

The vast majority of those actions will continue in force, but a few will be revisited, and of those, a smaller number will be modified or even reversed.   10

Sometimes a mistake now acknowledged can be remedied by changing the law. Sometimes that remedy would come too late, and another form of response is called for, as when the United States passed the Civil Liberties Act of 1988, deploring the internment of Japanese-Americans during World War II and authorizing payments of $20,000 to each surviving internee.   11

Ronald Reagan signed that act into law, and two years later President George H. W. Bush formally apologized for "the wrongs of the past."   12

Does that mean that Georgia should apologize, too? Not necessarily. The question is a political as well as a moral one, and it is not my intention here to answer it. All I am saying is that while there may be good reasons to resist apologizing, the "we didn't personally do it and those it was done to are dead" reason isn't one of them.   13

WRITING ACTIVITY

Consider some issue you think is important to you and to your classmates. Construct a brief Toulmin argument in which you identify your claim and the warrants that an audience of your classmates need to believe for them to accept your argument. It could be campus parking, the availability and quality of campus activities, or classroom amenities, or it could be an issue of national significance. Some possible issues include the following:

- The environment
- Affirmative action
- Immigration
- Health care
- The right to privacy vs. national security

**FIGURE 14.5
Carl Rogers**

Rogerian Strategies for Arguing

Rogerian argument, which is based on the work of psychologist and mediator Carl Rogers (Figure 14.5), has as its point of departure the observation that at times we will inevitably take perspectives on issues that are different from those of the people with whom we have important relationships. In the context of such relationships, the strategies of classical argument have their drawbacks. Suppose you and a close friend disagree about how to solve the problem of alcohol-related traffic fatalities, for example. Although you could use classical argumentative strategies to win this argument, in the long term your relationship might not be as well served as it would be by a conversation in which you try to see the other point of view.

Differences of opinion occur in all four areas of life—the academic, the professional, the civic, and the personal. And in all four areas, we have relationships that we value enough to want to maintain. We might therefore do better to resolve our differences without trying to "win." Although the strategies of classical argument may work well in settings where the participants are clearly opponents trying to convince a third party (two lawyers making their case to a jury, for instance), they do not work so well when the participants need to maintain a collegial, friendly, or even loving relationship. And although such strategies may work well when your topic is relatively uncontroversial or your audience is disposed to agree with your claim, they may be more likely to alienate than to persuade your audience when your topic is controversial and your audience hostile to your claim. You might think of Rogerian argument as a "kinder, gentler" way to argue—and one that might often serve you well.

The ultimate goal of Rogerian argument is to negotiate differences and cooperate to reach a resolution that benefits or is in some way acceptable to both parties. Thus, in Rogerian argument, it is useful to begin by thinking about commonalities, that is, by thinking about and understanding opposing views and asking yourself, "Even though we may have some differences, what do we have in common?" or "Even though we may not think alike, how can we work together effectively to solve this problem?"

One way to start is to consider what your intended audience already might know and believe about the issue. Once you have some sense of what your audience knows and believes, think about what beliefs you have in common.

Rogerian arguments have several component parts:

- **Introduction:** The introduction includes a description of the issue you hope to come to a consensus on. As you state a positive goal— solving a problem, reaching a consensus on some issue—keep your tone positive and invite others to participate in developing the solution to the problem, or reaching agreement if the issue does not call for a solution to a problem.

- **Summary of Opposing Views:** Be as accurate and as neutral as you can be in stating the views of those who may disagree with you. Show that you have the skills, character, and fairness to see and to appreciate the merits of opposing views.

- **Statement of Understanding:** After you have stated the opposing views accurately and neutrally, demonstrate that you understand why others might hold such views, especially in certain situations. If possible, indicate the conditions under which you too could share those views.

- **Statement of Writer's Position:** The previous three parts have prepared your readers to listen to your views, and here is the place to state them. As you state your position, acknowledge that others, especially under certain circumstance, might not share your views. Invite them to consider your views in the same way that you have considered theirs.

- **Statement of Contexts:** Building on the statement of your position, be specific about the kinds of conditions under which you hope others will find merit in your position.

- **Statement of Benefit:** Explain how your position or, if applicable, your solution to the problem, will benefit those who might oppose you. End on a positive and hopeful note, saying that you hope that your readers will accept the validity of your position.

Example: Rogerian Strategies in Action

RICK REILLY

Nothing but Nets

Rick Reilly has been voted National Sportswriter of the Year eight times. He currently writes the weekly "Life of Reilly" column for *Sports Illustrated* and also frequently contributes to *Time* magazine. Reilly's nonfiction books include *Who's Your Caddy?* and *The Life of Reilly: The Best of* Sports Illustrated's *Rick Reilly*. Reilly also has published the novel *Missing Links* and is the winner of many awards, including the New York Newspaper Guild's Page One Award for Best Magazine Story. The following article was first published in *Sports Illustrated* in 2006.

Problem: Reilly is a sportswriter who is not writing about game nets, but the need for mosquito nets.
Introduction: Reilly outlines the severity of the problem.

I've never asked for anything before, right? Well, sorry, I'm asking now.   1

We need nets. Not hoop nets, soccer nets or lacrosse nets. Not   2
New Jersey Nets or dot-nets or clarinets. *Mosquito* nets.

See, nearly 3,000 kids die every day in Africa from malaria. And   3
according to the World Health Organization, transmission of the disease would be reduced by 60% with the use of mosquito nets and prompt treatment for the infected..

Three thousand kids! That's a 9/11 every day!   4

Put it this way: Let's say your little Justin's Kickin' Kangaroos have a big youth soccer tournament on Saturday. There are 15 kids on the team, 10 teams in the tourney. And there are 20 of these tournaments going on all over town. Suddenly, every one of these kids gets chills and fever, then starts throwing up and then gets short of breath. And in seven to 10 days, they're all dead of malaria.   5

We *gotta* get these nets. They're coated with an insecticide and cost between $4 and $6. You need about $10, all told, to get them shipped and installed. Some nets can cover a family of four. And they last four years. If we can cut the spread of disease, 10 bucks means a kid might get to live. Make it $20 and more kids are saved.   6

So, here's the ask: If you have ever gotten a thrill by throwing, kicking, knocking, dunking, slamming, putting up, cutting down or jumping over a net, please go to a special site we've set up through the United Nations Foundation. The address is: *UNFoundation.org/malaria*. Then just look for the big *SI's Nothing But Net* logo (or call 202–887–9040) and donate $20. *Bang.* You might have just saved a kid's life.   7

Or would you rather have the new Beastie Boys CD?   8

You're a coach, parent, player, gym teacher or even just a fan who likes watching balls fly into nets, send $20. You saved a life. Take the rest of the day off.   9

You have *ever* had a net in the driveway, front lawn or on your head at McDonald's, send $20. You ever imagined Angelina Jolie in fishnets, $20. So you stay home and eat on the dinette. You'll live.   10

Hey, Dick's Sporting Goods. You have 255 stores. How about you kick in a dime every time you sell a net? Hey, NBA players, hockey stars and tennis pros, how about you donate $20 every time one of your shots hits the net? Maria Sharapova, you don't think this applies to you just because you're Russian? Nyet!   11

I tried to think how many times I have said or written the word "net" in 28 years of sports writing, and I came up with, conservatively, 20,000. So I've already started us off with a $20,000 donation. That's a whole lot of lives. Together, we could come up with $1 million, net. How many lives would that save? More than 50 times the population of Nett Lake, Minn.   12

I know what you're thinking: *Yeah, but bottom line, how much of our $1 million goes to nets?* All of it. Thanks to Ted Turner, who donated $1 billion to create the U.N. Foundation, which covers *all* the overhead. "Every cent will go to nets," says Andrea Gay, the U.N. Foundation's Director of Children's Health.   13

Nets work! Bill and Melinda Gates have just about finished single-handedly covering every bed in Zambia. Maybe we can't cover an entire Zambia, but I bet we could put a serious dent in Malawi.   14

Reilly works hard to put the problem into a language that everyone can understand.

Reilly points out how inexpensive the nets are.

Benefit: For $10 you can save a child's life. Note how Reilly writes about a shared, common ground with any reader who ever played a sport (which would include almost everyone).

Writer's Position: Reilly works to defuse the money objection to his proposal, and he does so in a humorous way. Sure, he says, he wants to raise a million dollars . . . but then he shows how that large amount can come from many small donations.

Benefit: no overcosts—all donations pay for nets.

Benefit: Look at how many lives could be saved.

It's not like we're betting on some scientist somewhere coming up with a cure. And it's not like warlords are going to hijack a truckload of nets. "Theoretically, if every person in Africa slept at night under a net," says Gay, "nobody need ever die of malaria again." You talk about a net profit.   15

My God, think of all the nets that are taken for granted in sports! Ping-Pong nets. Batting cage nets. Terrell Owens's bassinet. If you sit behind the plate at a baseball game, you watch the action *through* a net. You download the highlights on Netscape and forward it on the net to your friend Ben-net while eating Raisinets. Sports is nothing *but* net. So next time you think of a net, go to that website and click yourself happy. Way more fun than your fantasy bowling league, dude.   16

One last vignette: A few years back, we took the family to Tanzania, which is ravaged by malaria now. We visited a school and played soccer with the kids. Must've been 50 on each team, running and laughing. A taped-up wad of newspapers was the ball and two rocks were the goal. Most fun I ever had getting whupped. When we got home, we sent some balls and nets.   17

I kick myself now for that. How many of those kids are dead because we sent the wrong nets?   18

WRITING ACTIVITY

With several of your classmates, construct a Rogerian argument, focusing on some campus or national issue or problem (see the list on p. 738). Your instructor may want you to share your argument with the rest of the class.

◣ Some Common Flaws in Arguments

Any argument, no matter how effective, can be marred by **logical fallacies,** or flaws in reasoning. Although sometimes introduced deliberately into an argument with the aim of misleading readers, such flaws are often inadvertent, and avoiding them requires the kinds of critical thinking discussed in Chapter 2 of this book. The following list of flaws in arguments is by no means exhaustive, but it does include the most common and easily avoided ones.

- **Appealing to irrational fears:** All humans have fears, and it is often easy to exploit those fears. Someone making the argument that even though there have been only a few isolated cases of Mad Cow Disease in the United States, cattle ranchers should test each cow every month would be exploiting an irrational fear.

  As we are writing this chapter, several cases of infection from the dangerous E. coli bacteria have been traced back to tainted spinach and lettuce. Even though such cases are rare, it would be easy for a writer to exploit fears about food-borne illness and thus harm a restaurant chain.

- **Appealing to pity:** Although appeals to pity and other emotions can be justified at times, this kind of appeal can mask an otherwise weak case. If a student who is earning a failing grade in a course because she has missed many class sessions, neglected to hand in assignments, and performed poorly on examinations appeals to her instructor by pleading tearfully, "If I fail this course, I won't graduate on time," she is obviously masking a weak case.

- **Appealing to prejudice:** Also known as "*ad populum*," this fallacy occurs when the writer appeals to a preexisting positive or negative prejudice. A common example is the practice of putting an image of the American flag on a bumper sticker that advocates a particular product or stance, with an appeal to patriotism thus substituting for an argument for the product or stance. For example, the book shown in Figure 14.6 was written by the executive vice president of the National Rifle Association (NRA). Figure 14.7, an advertisement for the American Civil Liberties Union (ACLU), is another example of using the image of the American flag to

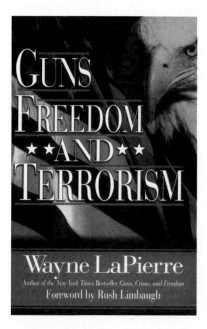

FIGURE 14.6 The Cover of a Book Written by the Executive Vice President of the NRA, with the Flag in the Background

FIGURE 14.7 An Advertisement for the ACLU, Using the Familiar Stars and Stripes as Part of Its Appeal

TAKE A STAND FOR YOUR FREEDOM

At the heart of Freedom lie our basic civil rights. And we hold these rights to be sacred. It takes more than a display of pride to protect those rights. It takes action.

advocate a cause. How do the images in Figures 14.6 and 14.7 work to create your own initial reaction to the book and advertisement.

- **Appealing to tradition:** The most common form of this appeal is the statement "We've always done it this way in the past." If a corporate executive responds to an innovative way of packaging a product by saying, "The old packaging has always worked for us," this reply would be an appeal to tradition.

- **Arguing from a lack of knowledge or evidence:** We can illustrate both forms of this flaw with the following example: You have looked for a sewing needle in a twenty-foot-tall stack of grass clippings, and your search has been unsuccessful. From this lack of evidence, one person might argue that there must be a needle in that stack of grass clippings, if you would only search more carefully. From the same lack of evidence, a second person might argue that there is no needle in the stack of grass clippings. In reality, of course, neither conclusion can be supported.

- **Attacking the opponent's character:** Often called an *ad hominem* attack, this fallacy is sometimes used in an attempt to direct attention away from the logic of a case—usually a strong case—by evoking a negative emotional response to the person making the case. In an effort to make an opponent seem like a hypocrite, a person might say, "My opponent argues that vegetarianism is a moral choice, but I notice that he wears leather shoes—so it is acceptable to *wear* part of an animal, but not to eat part of one? That is hypocritical!" The opposite fallacy (*pro hominem*), which is also common, involves directing attention away from a case—usually a weak case—by evoking a positive emotional response to the person making it. A legislator might appeal to the public to support an unworthy bill by praising the record of the colleague who introduced it: "Since Representative Smithers has produced good ideas in the past, we should vote for her plan to drill for oil in Central Park."

- **Attributing false causes:** Usually called *post hoc, ergo propter hoc* ("after this, therefore because of this"), this fallacy occurs when someone assumes that Event A caused Event B because Event A occurred before Event B. A common example is superstitious thinking: "I've been having so much bad luck recently because I broke a mirror/walked under a ladder/crossed the path of a black cat." This fallacy is common in civic life. In political campaigns, for example, an incumbent will often claim that his or her policies have caused the economy to improve, whereas a challenger will charge that the incumbent's policies have caused crime rates to increase. All sorts of events occur before other events in the world, but that does not mean that they cause those other events.

- **Bandwagon appeal:** Here the arguer is essentially saying "Many people are doing it, especially people whom you admire, so it must be a good thing to do. You should do it too." Television beer commercials frequently use this appeal when they show a group of young, attractive people having a great time at a party: If those people are having such a good time drinking that brand of beer, anyone who drinks it will also have a good time.

- **Begging the question (circular reasoning):** This fallacy treats a questionable assertion as if it has already been answered or fully explained. For instance, suppose someone says, "My friend would never cheat because he's an honest person." To assert that someone is honest is not to provide evidence that he did not or would not cheat; this assertion just restates the idea that the person would not cheat but has nothing to do with whether he actually did cheat.

- **Complex question:** In this ploy, an arguer asks a question that actually has two parts and demands a one-part response. For instance, the question "When did you stop beating your dog?" has embedded in it the assumption that you used to beat your dog. The person to whom it is addressed would be right to reply, "Hold on. Let's first establish whether I have ever beaten my dog in the first place."

- **Either-or reasoning:** Also known as "false dichotomy," this fallacy occurs when writers give readers two opposing choices (either A or B) when other possibilities also exist. For instance, a person might state, "You can major in business administration, or you can plan on getting a crummy job." Many attractive jobs do not require a degree in business administration, of course.

- **Faulty analogy:** In this fallacy, the writer makes a comparison that is in some way misleading or incomplete—or that does not even relate to the topic being discussed. A reporter who writes "The President hit a home run with his labor bill" is using a faulty baseball analogy. The President is not a baseball player and is supposed to be working with Congress, not "playing" against them.

- **Guilt by association:** This fallacy occurs when a writer seeks to discredit an opponent by associating the opponent with some unpopular person, group, or idea, as when politicians attempt to brand their opponents with labels such as "free-spending liberal" or "hard-right conservative." Such labels imply that *all* liberals are "free spending" or that all conservatives are "hard-right"—and both terms (*free-spending* and *hard-right*) have negative connotations.

- **Overgeneralization:** This fallacy occurs when someone reaches a conclusion based on insufficient evidence, especially atypical examples. For instance, your best friend engages in overgeneralization when, after an automobile accident in which she was not wearing a seatbelt but sustained only minor injuries, she says, "See. Seatbelts aren't necessary." Of course, anyone who has read studies on seatbelt use knows that they save many lives each year.

- **Oversimplification:** People sometimes search for simple answers to complex problems. For instance, some might say that the solution to gang violence in high schools would be simply to require students to wear uniforms in school. Of course, the problem of gang violence is complex, and its solution will not be that easy.

- **Red herring (or non sequiter):** This fallacy occurs when the writer introduces irrelevant material to divert attention from the issue being considered. The fallacy gets its name from the practice of dragging a red herring—a fish—along the ground to distract hunting dogs from the scent that they are following. A student who says to the teacher, "I know that I was late for class today, but I've been on time every other day" is using a red herring to throw the teacher off the scent of the real issue: the student is late.

- **Slippery slope:** This fallacy claims that once something starts, it must continue, just like a person sliding down a slippery slope. The person will not be able to stop sliding. An example is the student who says, "We've got to fight that proposed fee for using the computer center. If that fee is enacted, pretty soon they'll be charging fees for using the restrooms on campus."

- **Stacking the deck:** Here the writer presents evidence for only one side of the case. A student who says, "I should get an 'A' in this class because I handed in all my homework," while neglecting to mention that she got a "C" on the midterm and final exams, is stacking the deck in a rather blatant way.

- **Straw person:** This fallacy occurs when an arguer distorts the opponent's argument and then attacks that distorted argument. For instance, a few decades ago when equal rights for women was a hotly contested issue, some people made statements such as "Equal rights for women means that women will have the right to use men's restrooms. What is this country coming to?" Unisex restrooms were not part of what women's rights advocates were arguing for—so they served as a straw person.

- **Universal statements:** Such statements often include words such as *always, never, all, everyone, everybody, none,* or *no one.* Of course, some statements that include those words are true—for instance, "All humans are mammals." However, when writers use those words to describe human behavior or beliefs, those statements are usually problematic. For example, the statement "Men never share their feelings, but women always do" could be easily contradicted with just one or two cases.

WRITING ACTIVITY

To help you learn to identify logical fallacies, in your local or campus newspaper, find several instances of logical fallacies (hint: often, letters to the editor provide rich material!). Bring copies to class, share them, and explain the logical fallacies to your classmates.

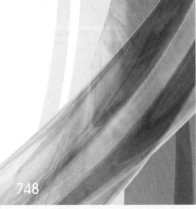

Although writing can be a solitary activity, it is often a collaborative endeavor. For instance, researchers in the physical and life sciences, social sciences, education, and engineering often co-author research proposals and reports. In business, teams often write project proposals and reports. In local, state, or national legislatures, many people collaborate to write bills to present to their colleagues. When groups of neighbors or parents are concerned about some local problem or issue, they will often collaborate on a letter to the editor of their local newspaper or to the school board. In your writing classroom, you will probably have the opportunity to get feedback on your writing from your classmates, and you may also work with your classmates on a project. In other courses throughout your college career, you are likely to encounter assignments that require you to work as part of a team.

Working with Peers on Your Single-Authored Projects

As you work on your own writing projects, working with peers—whether they are your classmates this semester or your colleagues in the workplace now or in the future—can yield many benefits. Early in the process of crafting a project, peers can help you generate ideas by challenging you to consider perspectives that you may not consider on your own. Later in the process, peers can point out ways to revise your writing so that readers will find it more understandable, informative, or persuasive. Peers can also help edit your prose by seeing problems that your tired eyes might miss.

In the chapters in Parts 2 and 3 of this book, you will find various Writer's Workshop activities that will help you solicit feedback from peers. As you gather comments from peers, it is your responsibility to encourage reviewers to offer candid assessments of your work. Peers should not be nasty, of course, but they *should* give you a clear sense of how well your writing is fulfilling its purpose. One sequence of responses that can work for almost any piece of writing at almost any point in the composing process appears in the following chart:

Feedback from Peers	Your Response to This Feedback
"I identify with you when you write . . . ."	Make a note of what peers identify with.
	Ask, "Why do you identify with me when I write . . . ?"
"I like the way that you have . . . ."	Make a note of what peers like.
	Ask, "Why do you like that?"

(continued)

Feedback from Peers	Your Response to This Feedback
"What do you mean when you write . . .?"	Make a note of peers' questions.
	Respond to their questions.
"I have these suggestions that you might consider: . . . ."	Make a note of peers' suggestions.
	Later, evaluate each of the suggestions; don't automatically accept or reject any of them.

Strategies for Working with Peers on Your Projects

As noted in the assignment chapters in Parts 2 and 3, peers can offer perspectives that can help you at any point in a project—invention, research, revising, editing. Although it is important to seek and use the perspectives that peers can offer, it is equally important to remember that you—not your peers—are ultimately responsible for the project. Given this principle of responsibility, the following guidelines can be useful:

1. Peers can indicate what is working well—and not so well—in a draft. When peers ask questions that are requests for more information, you should consider adding that information to your next draft.

2. Peers' questions are usually more helpful than their suggestions. Questions keep the responsibility for the project on your shoulders.

Using Digital Tools for Peer Review

Because students often have to balance class loads with part- or full-time jobs, commitments to community organizations, and even parenting responsibilities, it can be a challenge finding time to meet face-to-face outside of class. Digital tools for peer review can help you meet these challenges. Even if it is easy to meet face-to-face, though, writers still work with digital texts, and therefore need to use digital tools. Here are some common tools that you can use:

1. The track-changes feature of your word-processing software makes it easy to see the changes that different reviewers are suggesting in a document. You can then accept or reject any or all suggested changes.

2. The "comment" feature of most word-processing software makes it easy to offer a suggestion or pose a question to the writer.

3. Many instructors use *WebCT, Blackboard,* or some other course-management system to offer courses either completely or partially online. Such course-management systems make it possible for the

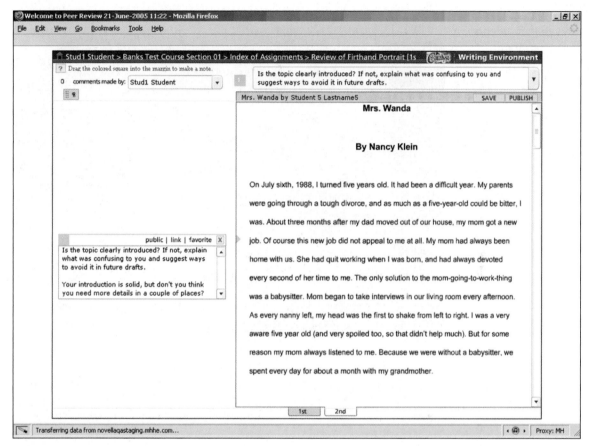

FIGURE 15.1   A Peer Editing Screen in *Catalyst*

Source: Copyright © The McGraw-Hill Companies, Inc. Reprinted by permission of The McGraw-Hill Companies, Inc.

instructor to set up online work areas in which students can hold online conversations and share their work online.

Using *Catalyst* for Peer Review

McGraw-Hill, the publisher of this book, offers a useful set of online learning, writing, research, and editing tools, collectively called *Catalyst*. The site includes specialized software that allows you and your classmates to comment on one another's work, as shown in Figure 15.1.

 ## Working with Peers on Multiple-Authored Projects

Working with your classmates on multiple-authored projects can have many benefits. One long-term benefit is that it will prepare you for co-authoring

**FIGURE 15.2
University Students
Using Library
Computers**

documents with your colleagues in the workplace. Another benefit is that working with a group can infuse a project with a rich array of perspectives. Co-authoring can enhance the quality of a project because more than one mind is developing and organizing ideas, revising content, and editing surface features.

Group work also presents challenges, however. Some members of the writing team may be inclined to contribute too much to the project while others sometimes seem to contribute too little. Another challenge is that some co-authors may insist on doing things their way without listening to potentially effective ideas from others.

Strategies for Working with Peers Effectively

Working with peers can be challenging because they can question your thinking in new and sometimes uncomfortable ways. In college, this kind of interaction is especially likely because your classmates may have personalities and/or cultural backgrounds that differ substantially from yours. Although encountering a variety of backgrounds and perspectives can move you out of your comfort zone, it can also be a powerful catalyst for accelerated learning. For example, in some cultures blunt statements are valued, but in other cultures blunt statements are considered rude and inconsiderate.

Also, while some people are more introverted, others are more extroverted. People who tend to be introverted often prefer to listen and think

> **TechNote**
>
> When working in groups with other students, remember that not everyone in the class will have the same level of access to the Internet or to computer technologies. Among any given group of college students, the level of experience with and knowledge about computers will vary.
>
> Never assume that everyone uses the same programs on his or her personal computer. Some students do not even own computers, although most college campuses and dormitories have computer labs available for student use. It is a good idea to ask your friends and classmates what kinds of programs they use regularly, rather than simply assuming everyone is familiar with the services you use most often.

before they speak. However, people who tend to be extroverted often prefer to use talking to think about a topic.

To make the most of your work with peers, try some of the following strategies:

1. **Listen empathically to your group members' comments and questions.** Empathic listeners strive to understand why someone is making a particular comment or raising a particular question.

2. **Assign roles to members of the group.** One member of the group can be the *recorder*, whose duty is to keep track of who says what. Another member of the group can be the *question-asker*, posing questions to encourage everyone to think more critically or deeply. Yet another group member can be the *facilitator*, whose role is to keep the discussion focused and moving forward, to keep everyone on task. It is important that every group member have some *specific responsibility* to perform for the whole group to succeed.

3. **Provide positive and constructive feedback.** Every piece of feedback can be stated more-or-less negatively or more-or-less positively. Further, every negative or less positive statement can be recast into a more positive form:

Less Positive	More Positive
There's an error in his sentence.	You could edit the sentence this way:
This paragraph is underdeveloped.	You could develop this paragraph by adding this:
You don't have a conclusion.	What are you planning to say in the conclusion?

4. **Pay attention to interpersonal dynamics.** Before the group begins discussing the assigned topic, ask each member of the group to respond to the following kinds of questions:

    a. What can the group do to function most effectively?

    b. What seems to impede our group from functioning effectively?

    c. What encourages you to contribute effectively to the group?

5. **Do round-robin sharing.** Sometimes some group members contribute more than their fair share to the discussion while others contribute less than they could. To ensure that every member of the group contributes equally, go around the table clockwise, with each person contributing one after the other. Keep going around the table as many times as necessary to solicit everyone's contributions.

6. **If possible, keep the group relatively small—three or four members.** Just as your instructor will probably form groups of three or four students in class, you should try to keep your informal out-of-class group that size. Larger groups become hard to manage, and it becomes difficult to coordinate calendars or to come to consensus.

7. **Consider your class and your peer group to be intertwined communities.** Make a commitment to improve the work of each community and each member of the community. If every member of the class and the group makes such a commitment, everyone will benefit.

8. **Celebrate your accomplishment.** When the project is completed, treat yourselves in some way, perhaps by enjoying coffee or lunch together.

One way to ensure the success of any group endeavor is to plan. The charts that follow will help you to plan various aspects of your work with your group. Before the group decides on items to include on a chart, it is helpful to give each member an opportunity to have his or her items included:

1. Have each member of the group jot down some items individually.

2. Show each member's items to the group.

3. If everyone has jotted down the same item, add it to the group's list.

4. When there are discrepancies between or among individuals' lists, negotiate those differences to come to agreement.

5. Use planning sheets such as the charts on pages 756–57.

DEFINE SUCCESS FOR THE GROUP

What will count as success, and how can the group achieve it? You might use the following chart, for example, to define success and to identify the means for achieving that success. We have provided several example items here to illustrate the kinds of signs and methods that you might include.

Defining Group Success

Sign of Success	Method(s) for Achieving
Everyone shows up for our out-of-class meetings at the agreed-upon time.	Add meetings to daily planners and/or PDAs.
Everyone participates equally.	Use a round-robin approach for sharing ideas during discussions.

IDENTIFY POTENTIAL ROADBLOCKS TO SUCCESS

Once you have identified such hurdles, brainstorm ideas for getting over them. We have provided several example items here to illustrate the kinds of roadblocks and methods that you might include.

Overcoming Roadblocks to Success

Potential Roadblocks	Method(s) for Overcoming Roadblocks
There is too little time available in class for the group to meet.	Find a time and place to meet outside of class, or agree to work online.
We're engaged in group-think.	To get everyone's diverse perspectives on the table, each member of the group will write down his or her ideas and then read them to the group.
Some members of the group are engaged in ego-think. (They only see things their own way.)	To encourage these members to listen empathically, ask them to paraphrase what a peer has just said.

DEVELOP A PLAN FOR DEALING WITH GROUP PROBLEMS

Potential problems include a group member who dominates a discussion, doesn't carry a fair share of the load, or misses a deadline. If a problem does surface, deal with it immediately. Dealing with small problems immediately can keep them from becoming bigger problems. If a problem arises, do *not* focus on who is to blame; instead, focus on finding a solution. We have provided several example items here to illustrate the kinds of problems and methods that you might include.

Dealing with Group Problems

Potential Problem	Method(s) for Dealing with the Problem
A dominating group member	Use a round-robin approach so that each person contributes no more or no less than everyone else. Develop a gentle, perhaps humorous, method for telling a group member that he or she is dominating.
A group member who is not carrying a fair share of the load	Note in a group meeting that for your group project to work, everyone must do his or her fair share.
A group member who misses a deadline	Discuss and agree on all deadlines, noting that agreement commits each member to meet the deadlines.

SET SHORT-TERM AND LONG-TERM GOALS

Before the group begins a particular work session, decide what you want to accomplish in the session, your short-term goal. As you work, stay focused on that goal until you achieve it. If the group will work together over multiple sessions, decide on a long-term goal to achieve by the last session. Then establish short-term goals for each session along the way. Keep focused on both your long-term goal and the short-term goals that will enable you to achieve it. We have provided several example items here to illustrate the kinds of long-term and short-term goals that you might include.

Project Goals

Long-Term Goals	Short-Term Goals
Complete the project by November 16.	Complete library research by October 3.
	Complete interviews by October 10.

DEVELOP A PLAN FOR COMPLETING THE PROJECT

Identify the subtasks that need to be completed along the way, as well as a timeline for completing each subtask. Write down who is responsible for each task, and make certain that each member of the group has a list of everyone's responsibilities. As each deadline for a subtask approaches, ask the responsible member or members to report on progress. Keep track of every team member's progress throughout the project. We have provided several example items here to illustrate the kinds of subtasks, deadlines, and individual responsibilities that you might include.

Project Plan

Subtask	Deadline for Subtask	Individual Responsibilities
Complete interviews of rental-property owners.	October 10	Hanna
Complete interviews of renters.	October 10	Molly
Complete interview of city attorney.	October 10	Meghan

MAKE A CALENDAR OF GROUP MEETINGS

Group meetings can be held face-to-face, by telephone, or in online chat rooms. For each meeting, establish an agenda and identify what each person needs to do before the meeting. Also, decide who will serve as the discussion leader for each meeting. Assign a different discussion leader for each meeting so that no one group member dominates. We have provided an example item here to illustrate the kind of calendar item that you might include.

Calendar for Meetings

Meeting Date	Agenda Item(s)	Individuals' Preparation	Discussion Leader
October 11	Examine interviews	**Hanna:** Bring three copies of transcripts of interviews with rental-property owners.	Hanna
		Molly: Bring three copies of transcripts of interviews with renters.	Molly
		Meghan: Bring three copies of transcript of interview with city attorney.	Meghan

Using Digital Tools for Facilitating Multiple-Authored Projects

Here are some tried-and-true suggestions for using digital tools so that your co-authoring experience is a happy, productive one:

1. Agree on a sequence for working on each digital file to avoid duplication of effort. That is, indicate in writing who will draft each section of the project. Once all the sections have been drafted, decide—and write down—who will do the first round of revisions, who will be second, and who will be third.

2. For revising, use the track-changes and the comment features of your word-processing software. That way other members of the group can

see the changes that you are making. For editing, it is less important to use track changes and comments, but you might use them for that work too.

3. When you send a digital file to another member of the group because it is his or her turn to do the next round of revising or editing, copy the other members of the group so that they can be certain who is working on the document. This practice also gives them an opportunity to see the progress on the project.

4. When you name digital files, make certain to include the current date in the file name. For example, using a file name such as "rental_paper_10–18–08" will help everyone know what version of the paper it is. Don't delete older versions of files because you may need them to recover a deleted paragraph or to recover a file that has become corrupted.

Making Effective Oral Presentations

Along with invention, arrangement, memory, and style, *delivery*—the way you present a message—is one of the five "canons" of rhetoric. In most of this book, we have dealt with written or visual forms of delivery. In this chapter, however, we will consider oral presentations, a form of delivery that is becoming increasingly important in all areas of your life.

- In your **academic life**, you will be asked to make presentations in some of your classes—to discuss a class reading, for example, or to make a presentation as part of one of your class assignments.
- In your **professional life**, you will often be asked to present your ideas to your colleagues and to clients.
- In your **civic life**, you may speak before the local school board, or to the city council, or in front of any number of civic or political organizations.
- In your **personal life**, you may be called upon to give a speech at an occasion such as a wedding, a funeral, or a school reunion, or you may speak at a less formal gathering of your family or friends.

As with written communication, oral presentations are *rhetorical acts*. To prepare an effective oral presentation, you need to ask yourself the same questions that you would ask for any writing situation:

- **What** do I want to accomplish? In other words, what is the purpose of this presentation? To inform? To persuade? To explain? To analyze?
- **Who** is my audience? What do they already know about my topic? What information do I need to supply in order to achieve my purpose? What is the best way to present this information—charts, graphs, photos, handouts, a *PowerPoint* presentation, overhead slides?
- What is the **context** surrounding this presentation? Will I make a classroom presentation, or will I present in a more formal setting? Why have I been asked to speak to this group at this particular time and place?
- How much do I already know about my **topic,** and what else do I need to learn about it? Am I expected to be an expert (for example, in a business setting)? Am I speaking as someone concerned about an issue (for example, in a civic setting)? Am I speaking as someone learning about a subject and sharing what I've discovered (for example, as a student)?

Once you decide what you want to accomplish with a particular audience on a specific occasion, you will have a better understanding of how you need to prepare: what kind of research you need to conduct, the types of information you need to collect, whether you should prepare handouts, or *PowerPoint* or overhead slides.

Developing Your Presentation

To develop an oral presentation, you can use several approaches. For more formal presentations on complex topics, you might decide to write the full text of your presentation, using the composing strategies detailed in Parts 2 and 3 of this textbook. In some situations you might decide to read that full text, especially if you have to use specific words at specific moments during your presentation. In other situations you might write the full text and then prepare an outline of it. You might then speak from that outline on a sheet of paper and/or on a set of *PowerPoint* slides.

Establishing a Clear Structure

As with any piece of discourse that you construct, an oral presentation needs to have a clear organization that helps you to achieve your purpose. For most oral presentations, you will need to do the following:

- Construct an effective, thought-provoking, and attention-grabbing **introduction.** Remember that during your presentation, your listeners may be tempted to let their attention wander. Therefore, part of your job is to draw them in, to tell them something that will interest them, and to indicate quickly how your topic affects them. If your audience—even part of your audience—does not understand why they should care about your presentation, that group simply will not pay attention to you.

- Let your audience know the **main point(s)** that you plan to make. Often called **forecasting,** this technique is especially important in oral presentations because your audience will not usually have something they can refer back to, as they can with a written text. If you have five main points that you want to cover, name them. Each time you move to the next point, make note of that, too ("The third point I want to make is . . ."). It often helps to provide the audience with a written outline of your points.

- Include sufficient evidence to **support** each one of your claims. You will be much more credible as a speaker if you support your claims with facts, examples, statistics, and testimony from experts. As one of us tells our students, while you are a nice person and I want to believe you, unless you can provide some evidence, I may not buy what you are selling.

  For more on supporting claims with evidence, see Chapters 8 and 14.

- Always be sure to **point back** to your main point so that it will be easy for your listeners to understand exactly how each point that you make or piece of information that you provide relates to your thesis. Because your audience won't have a full text that they can refer back to, you have to remind them of your main point in your presentation itself. Of course, if you provide your audience with a handout or slide

For more on using transitions, see Chapter 13.

with an outline of your main points, it will be easier for them to recall your main points.

- Use **visual aids** to outline the structure of your talk, if the situation calls for them. Your *PowerPoint* or overhead slides should outline the points you want to make, which you will then elaborate on (for more on using visuals, see the box that follows). You can use visuals to announce each of your points, but the message of each visual needs to be readily apparent.

- Use your **conclusion** to summarize and emphasize your main point, and to outline briefly how everything in your presentation supports it.

VISUALIZING VARIATIONS

Effective Visual Aids

Consider the most **ineffective** ways to use overhead slides or a *PowerPoint* presentation:

- The speaker uses very small type, so any text would be hard for the audience to read.
- The speaker spends part of the designated speaking time setting up or becoming familiar with the projection equipment.
- The speaker simply reads the visuals to the audience, without adding any new information or ideas.
- The speaker uses every *PowerPoint* special effect on every slide.
- The speaker faces *away from* the audience as she reads the text on the screen.
- The speaker walks to the screen and uses a finger to point to words on the screen.

Ouch! That presentation would be excruciatingly boring, wouldn't you say? Now contrast that to a presentation like the following:

- Each visual aid uses appropriate type sizes, colors, and graphics to illustrate the speaker's main points.
- Before the presentation the speaker learns how to use the equipment and sets it up. He or she has already made sure needed equipment is available and functional.
- The speaker talks directly to the audience, using the text on each visual only as starting points, which he or she then elaborates and explains.
- The speaker uses *PowerPoint* special effects sparingly—perhaps to help emphasize major points.
- The speaker talks directly to the audience, making eye contact, looking for signs of affirmation (smiles, nodding heads) that the audience is "getting" what the presentation is about.
- If necessary, the speaker uses an inexpensive laser pointer to point to specific words on the screen.

Now that's better, isn't it?

If you were assigned to write the academic paper in Chapter 6, focusing on whether or not college students are "slobs," for example (see p. 192), and you needed to prepare an oral presentation as part of that assignment, the slide in Figure 16.1 is one possible way for you to start a *PowerPoint* presentation on that topic.

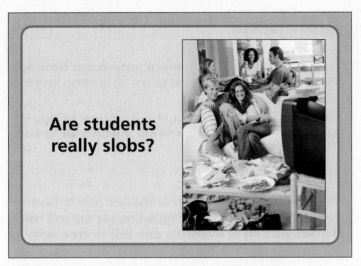

FIGURE 16.1   An Opening Slide for a Presentation

The photograph can help you get your audience's attention and focus them on your topic. Each subsequent *PowerPoint* slide can contain the same heading, but provide the points you want to discuss in your presentation. Your second slide (Figure 16.2) might offer examples that suggest that students really are *not* slobs.

> ## Are students really slobs?
>
> Not necessarily. At our college, students
> - help with the campus recycling program.
> - are responsible for cleaning their dorm rooms.
> - are subject to weekly inspections.
> - are fined if their bathrooms are not clean.
> - serve on a task force to keep our
>   campus beautiful.

FIGURE 16.2   A Second Slide

(Cont'd)

(continued)

You will elaborate on these **talking points** as you make your presentation, discussing each one in detail and providing more information to support each point as you make it. For example, for the first point you make—that students help with the campus recycling program—you could add the following information:

- Student organizations collect all recycled products in classrooms and office buildings.
- Student groups make money through this recycling effort.
- Students work together in the dorms to collect recycled products.
- Several student leaders serve on the Campus Recycling Board (CRB), which is responsible for making all decisions regarding the recycling program.

As you speak, then, you will flesh out each point with specific examples that are not on the slide, but that provide information and details for your audience. The following list gives the typical order you would follow when using slides with a presentation:

Typical Order of Slides for an Oral Presentation

1. Speaker's Name and Title (one slide)
2. Forecast the Gist of the Presentation (one slide)
3. Outline of Presentation (one slide)
4. Major Points (one to three slides per point)
5. Summary/Conclusion (one slide)
6. Request for Questions from Audience (one slide)

For more on visuals for presentations, see Chapter 18.

Figure 16.3, for example, is a *PowerPoint* slide listing the "plan" for today's presentation (slide 2 in the example sequence above).

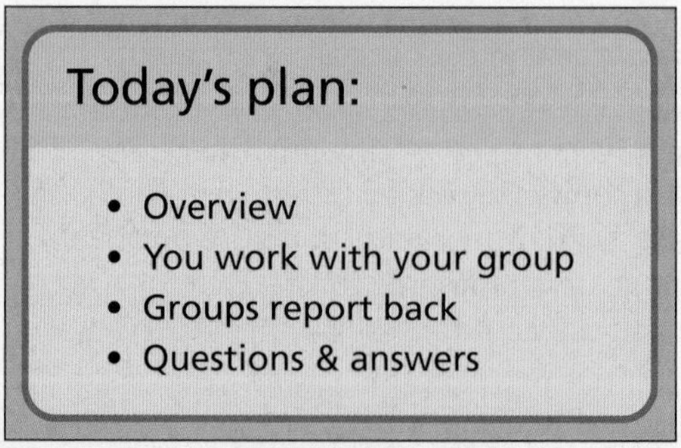

Today's plan:

- Overview
- You work with your group
- Groups report back
- Questions & answers

FIGURE 16.3   A Second Slide in a Presentation

Considering Your Audience

Your *audience* is your primary concern as you plan, develop, and give your presentation. Every decision you make depends on your awareness of that audience, from considering what they already know about your subject to what they need to know to believe what you tell them to how you should present yourself to that audience. Or, as author Dale Dauten has put it, "It

---

TechNote

Using graphic, audio, and video files to enhance your oral presentations is not just a good idea—in this day and age, it's often expected. Audiences are not usually critical of video that is less than perfect as long as it illustrates an important point. Before incorporating media into your oral presentation, however, use the following checklist to make sure your presentation goes smoothly:

- Examine the room, lecture hall, or space where you will be presenting—note the size and shape of the room, the seating arrangements, and the available equipment.

- If you are using video or sound media, make sure you have allowed enough time within your allotted presentation time for the video or audio clip to play.

- Keep it brief. Do not give the audience time to get uncomfortable or restless while the video or sound is playing. Follow the rule used by pop radio: Most people will endure almost anything for two and a half minutes.

- *Always* plan a fallback handout, visual chart, or anecdote in the event that the technologies available in the room suddenly fail.

- Choose music, video clips, and images that are relevant to your presentation, and that strengthen your claims and positions. (Importing the *Saturday Night Live* "More Cowbell" skit may make the audience laugh, but it will not improve your presentation unless it is directly relevant to it.)

- Practice your presentation, including the time it takes to start and stop each video or sound element. If you are still fumbling with computer files, start and stop buttons, and projection issues by the third rehearsal, it's time to consider using simpler fallback materials, such as handouts or overhead slides, until you can work out the glitches.

- Ask a friend, coworker, or classmate to be your test audience and be open to this person's feedback. Video and sound elements should illustrate, add meaning to, and clarify main points, not distract or confuse your audience. If your test audience tells you that it's not clear why you have incorporated media, ask for comments and suggestions. These may lead you to add more effective setups for and lead-outs from the media you've chosen.

- Give the audience time to react. If they *do* enjoy the media you've incorporated, give them a moment or two to laugh, applaud, or just babble exuberantly before you continue with your presentation.

took my giving a hundred speeches over the period of three or four years to come to this critical realization about giving a speech: IT'S NOT ABOUT YOU." So consider: How do you want to come across to your audience? As informed and logical? As thoughtful? Probably. Or as someone shouting at them? Or droning at them? Probably not.

One way to move your audience in the direction you would like them to go is through what magician and author Steve Cohen calls "command [of] the room." You are the one presenting; you are the one in charge; you are the one who determines the pace, what is said (and not said), what visuals are used, and so on—put another way, you are in control of the situation. Cohen recommends that you do the following:

- Look listeners in the eye. This might seem hard to do, especially if you are speaking before a large crowd, but you can always find someone to look at and speak to directly. Find these folks in several parts of your audience, and soon it will look like you are speaking personally to *everyone* in that audience.
- Hold that eye contact longer than you might expect to.
- Search out "key people" in the audience who are really listening, and speak directly to them.
- Speak in a conversational tone and manner.
- Remember the 45-degree rule: If you are concerned that you might "wobble" as you speak, make sure to put one foot in front of the other, at about a 45-degree angle. It's impossible to wobble when you stand that way.

Finally, always make certain that your listeners can hear you, projecting your voice to the farthest member of your audience. Actors have a technique in which they speak to an imaginary person in the back row who is hard of hearing. If you use that technique, everyone else in the room will be able to hear you, too. You do not need to shout but, rather, to project your voice. Remember that if your audience cannot hear you, they will not pay attention to what you say—how can they? To make certain that the audience can hear you, begin your presentation by asking, "Can folks in the back of the room hear me if I speak at this volume?" It's also a good idea to ask people to raise their hands and cup their ears if your volume becomes so low that they can't hear you.

WRITING ACTIVITY

Analyzing and Evaluating a Speech

Dale Dauten suggests listening to the "top 100 speeches" and other speeches available at http://www.americanrhetoric.com/. Visit that Web site and listen to a famous speech. In no more than two pages, write a brief analysis by responding to the following questions:

- What do you think made this speech famous?
- How effective do you think it was? Why?
- How effective do you think its original audience found it? Why?
- How was it organized?
- What were the main points of the speech?

Discuss your responses with several of your classmates.

Eliminating the Fear of Speaking in Public

In every list of the common fears that people have, the fear of speaking in public is always at or close to the top of the list. Even the famous illusionist Howard Thurston used to throw up before every show—and he performed thousands of times.

In fact, a bit of nervousness before a presentation can be a positive thing. If you are not nervous, you can be overconfident and not do a very effective job. Here are some techniques that can help you overcome stage fright:

- Always be overprepared. Know what you want to say. Know your subject. If you plan to use visual aids, be prepared for the unexpected—for example, a broken projector (see Figure 16.4). When one of the authors of this text has to make a presentation, he does the following:
  - Prepares *PowerPoint* slides.
  - Also prepares overhead slides, in case the computer or projector isn't working.
  - Also has handouts on hand, so listeners can follow along if the technology breaks down completely. For instance, you can print *PowerPoint* slides in "Notes Pages" mode, which allows you to include 1–6 slides per page, with lines for the audience to record their notes.
- Remember the five Ps: *Proper Planning Prevents Poor Performance.*
- Practice *out loud* several times before your presentation. The more you practice, the better your presentation will be, period. *Thinking* what you want to say and actually *saying it aloud* are really two different things. When you just think about a presentation, your mind tends to fill in the gaps and blanks and words you leave out. But when you force yourself to practice presenting out loud, you will end up with a much more thoughtful, articulate, and polished presentation. If you have the technology available, videotape your presentation and then watch—and critique—yourself.

FIGURE 16.4
If a projector is not available, it's good to have substitutes.

- Time your presentation, so you will know that it fits whatever time parameters you have been given. There's nothing worse than having your host hold up a sign that says "TWO MINUTES LEFT" when you still have eight minutes of material left in your presentation.

- Another way to eliminate the fear of speaking, or at least to avoid showing that fear, is always to use a clipboard to hold your notes. A piece of paper held in your hand might shake, but a clipboard will not.

- *Visualize* making a successful presentation before you make it. *See yourself* in front of your audience. *Listen* to them applaud. *See* them nod in agreement. *See yourself speaking with them* afterwards, as they congratulate you for your effective speech. Picture what you want to happen, and it will.

- As you speak, do not let minor distractions bother you. If you hear noise from an adjoining room or from the street outside, ignore it. Do not assume that the person in the back row who appears to be laughing is laughing at you. If you hear a cell phone ring, do not stop speaking and glare at the offending party. Any number of things will distract you. You need to ignore them and concentrate on what you want to say.

Other Tips for Making Effective Oral Presentations

- Show enthusiasm.
- Use hand gestures purposefully.
- Finally, always say "thank you" at the end of your presentation. You will be surprised at how many speakers do *not* use this ending, and you will find it to be surprisingly effective (and thoughtful).

ACTIVITY

Making an Oral Presentation

Using one of the papers that you wrote for Part 2 or 3 of this textbook, prepare and deliver an oral presentation. To do so, use these steps:

1. Reread the paper.
2. Construct an outline of the main points in your paper.
3. If you did not use visuals in the paper, find or develop some visuals to illustrate your main points.
4. Prepare a series of *PowerPoint* slides for the presentation. On each slide, include a main point from the outline and/or a visual element. Print a "Notes Pages" version of your slides to serve as a handout for your audience and for you to refer to as you speak.
5. Rehearse your oral presentation in front of a mirror or a video camera. Practice using your *PowerPoint* slides as you speak.
6. Make sure whatever hand gestures you use do in fact add to your presentation.

If you have a video camera and can record your presentation so you can play it back and critique yourself, so much the better. But in any case when you practice, think of your work as *rehearsal*: Go through your presentation from start to finish, without stopping. If you get tongue-tied or drop your notes or the projector does not work, just continue as if you were actually giving your speech.

This is the kind of work actors or professional magicians do to get good—try it!

 ## Impromptu Presentations

In many situations you will find yourself called upon to make impromptu presentations of your ideas, whether in the classroom or on the job. One key to making effective impromptu presentations is preparation. For example, if a professor asks you to speak on the spot on a topic that you have been studying in class, you will speak more effectively if you have been doing your homework diligently throughout the semester. That is, if you have been using the kinds of activities described in Chapters 2 and 3 of this book in your classes, you will know the material that you have been studying.

Besides being prepared, you can also use some time-tested strategies for making impromptu presentations:

- Give yourself a few moments to prepare by standing slowly and taking several steps away from your chair. Better yet—walk to the front of the room. As you walk, think about your major point(s) and perhaps your first sentence.
- Speak slowly and use pauses—not *um* or *like*—to think of what you want to say next.
- Announce your point before making it.

PART FIVE

Technologies for Effective Communication

Choosing a Medium, Genre, and Technology for Your Communication

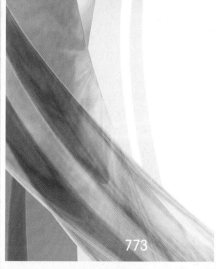

As long as humans have recorded their experiences, they have used technologies that act as tools to record their ideas. Historically, "written on paper in pen or pencil" and "print or electronic" have been fairly recent options for communicating messages. We can see evidence of an older technology by looking at the image that opens this chapter.

A portion of a prehistoric cave painting from caves in Lascaux, France, this image is approximately 17,000 years old. Although this cave painting undoubtedly had a purpose when it was created, that particular purpose has not survived. Some people suspect that part of the purpose may have been supernatural or magical. The specific meaning of the individual images in this ancient work has been lost in time. While we know little about the person or people who made this image, we can surmise that painting was a useful technology for communicating with the intended audience. We do know that this medium (painting on a cave wall) allowed ancient humans to record images that might be decorative, might be symbolic, might tell a story, or might have performed a combination of these functions. Although the form of communication—or *genre*—this cave painting was created in has been lost, its medium is certainly durable, having survived for thousands of years.

Communication technologies are as varied as paint on a cave wall or a canvas, a piece of chalk, a ballpoint pen, or a word-processing program. Whatever a writer's purpose, the availability of a particular tool often helps to determine what **medium**—method of delivery—that writer uses to communicate. Depending on the tools at a writer's disposal, he or she might write a message on a chalkboard, print it on paper, or publish it in an electronic format such as a newsgroup posting or a Web page.

When writers use a specific communication technology, they need to understand the impact that the technology will have on that communication. Some technologies can be very effective for some kinds of communication and much less effective for others. You do not always have a choice of which technology or medium you can use, but when you do, you need to understand the potential and limitations of each and you need to make your choice in a rhetorically sound way. You also need to decide whether the message you are trying to communicate to a particular audience will be most effective in color or black and white; with or without headings, boxes, and other design elements; and as plain text or illustrated with photographs or tables or charts. This chapter will provide guidelines for choosing the most effective genre and medium for your written work, a brief discussion of your options for publishing and designing documents (more detailed guidelines for designing documents are provided in Chapter 18), and an overview of the technologies for computer-mediated communication.

Communication Technologies

As we have seen, a **communication technology** is not necessarily an electronic device. Because writing is itself a technology, every tool that we use to write is a kind of communication technology. Indeed, any tool that facilitates communication between humans is a communication technology—whether it is as simple as a pencil and its eraser or the latest version of a complex presentation software program such as *PowerPoint*. Sometimes technology hinders—rather than helps—communication, however. For example, our friend and colleague C. J. Jeney demonstrates how technology can impede communication with the following anecdote:

> To my humiliation and dismay, my first-grade teacher one day "demoted" me to the use of eraser-less pencils because I made "too many corrections" and changes as I wrote, and as a result, often accidentally tore the writing paper. From *my* perspective, I had a great enthusiasm to edit, to correct, to reshape my sentences. From *her* perspective I was a destructive paper-shredder. She said I would not be allowed to erase until I learned how to "write better." When I asked why I couldn't just have a *better* eraser, or some *stronger* paper, she became furious with me. During parent-teacher conferences, she explained to my mother that I was "inept" at using erasers and had to write without them because I had torn too many holes in the school writing paper. My mother offered to buy more paper, but the teacher rejected this solution out of hand—the *point* was not that I was correcting mistakes, the *point* was that I had not learned properly how to care for the school's cheap, triple-lined paper. I was not careful enough when I wrote. The poor quality of the writing technologies—erasers, pencils, paper—was not the problem, my poor usage of it was the problem.

In commenting on the story from her childhood, Jeney recognizes that her difficulty was not in the communication itself, but in the inadequate technology that she had at her disposal. Jeney's story suggests an important lesson for all of us as we are faced with an ever-expanding selection of writing technologies. Writing is inextricably linked to the technology that produces it. Some communication technologies, such as word-processing software, encourage revision while others, such as the cheap paper and hard erasers in Jeney's first-grade class, act to discourage it. On the other hand, a handwritten letter, while difficult to revise, may make a more personal connection with your reader than a word-processed document. And pens, pencils, and note paper are easier to carry than laptop computers and do not require an electrical outlet, a battery, or an Internet connection to function.

Because communication technologies clearly have an impact on your writing process, understanding your own process and what communication technologies will work most effectively and efficiently for you in a given writing situation is important to your success as a writer.

For an overview of technologies for computer-mediated communication, see pages 780–90.

Publishing Your Work

When you write letters or even when you write for an academic purpose, you are usually writing to one person or to a small number of people. As a result, your communication is generally private—between you and that small audience. When you *publish* your written work, however, you make it public. You can publish your writing in a variety of ways, from printing a newsletter and distributing copies to a limited group of people to constructing a page on the World Wide Web that is accessible to anyone in the world who has a computer connected to the Internet. Although publishing your work can be exciting, it also involves both responsibilities and risks.

As recently as the 1970s, the only way to publish a piece of writing was in some kind of print medium. Publishing meant typesetting a manuscript and reproducing it on a printing press, a process that was both time-consuming and expensive. Fortunately, the technological breakthroughs of the past thirty-five years have enabled average people to gain access to technologies that allow them to publish their own work or the work of others easily and inexpensively.

With the advent of the huge network of computers known as the Internet, and specifically the hypertext environment of the World Wide Web, today's students have technology and publishing options and opportunities that were unheard of in the past. Now anyone who constructs a Web page on a server connected to the Internet publishes a document that is available to the entire world. The ability to publish work in this way gives student writers a power they never had before, but it also gives them a tremendous responsibility. And if you are like our students, you probably spend some time with MySpace and FaceBook. These areas of the Internet give people a way to communicate and to share information that has never been available before.

If you publish to a broad audience, and especially if you publish on the Web, you need to remember that those who view your work will be forming an opinion of you and your ideas that is based solely on what they see and read. Comments made in haste, without thought and reflection, can sometimes come back to "haunt" their authors. Members of your audience will also respond in some way to the design of your document or Web page—to the colors, the typeface, the size of type, how items are arranged on the page or screen. If you make assertions, they will expect you to provide proof. As with any other form of written communication, they will also expect you to follow the conventions of spelling, grammar, punctuation, and mechanics. If you do not, you will weaken the credibility of your document or Web page.

Whether you publish in print or in an electronic medium, you will enhance your credibility with your audience if you choose an appropriate genre for your message.

Selecting a Genre and a Medium

At the beginning of any writing task that has an audience beyond their immediate circle, then, writers need to decide which established form of writing, or **genre,** to write in and the best medium in which to publish their work. Often, the best way to reach your audience will be to publish your work in print. It is now possible, however, to choose an electronic medium instead of print.

For more on genre, *see Chapter 1, page 11.*

So how should you make these decisions? When choosing a genre and medium, you need to consider carefully the audience, the context, and the purpose for your writing. For example, if you are writing a set of instructions for the operation of a propane camp stove, you can expect that the people who will read those instructions will usually be outdoors and often in isolated locations. The instructions will be more useful and effective, then, if they are published in print and in a size that is easy to pack and carry. On the other hand, if you are providing information about the academic support resources available on your college campus and most of the students on the campus have high-speed Internet access, the best way to reach this audience may be to publish the information on a Web site. You may even decide to use sound, video, or animation.

Deciding on a Genre for Your Work

Because the genre you choose is usually determined by your purpose, it is a rhetorical decision. If your purpose is to obtain funding for a project or permission to implement a change, you will usually write a proposal (a type of writing covered in Chapter 10), a relatively easy decision. However, if your purpose is to provide information about a project you are working on, you have many choices. You might write a formal, authoritative report, called a white paper, a brochure, or a set of frequently asked questions (FAQs) among other genres for informative writing (for more on informative writing, see Chapter 6). Determining what genre you use in this situation will depend on not only your purpose but also your audience. Ultimately, you will have to decide which genre will be most effective for the people you are trying to reach. (For more on some common genres, see Appendix C.)

Once you have decided on the appropriate genre (say you decide on a brochure), you will have to decide which medium will be most effective in presenting that brochure to your audience (you might provide it in print form and as a PDF file on the Web, for example).

Deciding Whether to Use Print, Electronic, or Oral Media

Although in-class essay examinations are usually written by hand, few academic papers are handwritten these days. Usually, you need to turn in an assignment printed in type on paper or in some kind of electronic medium.

Often you have no choice; your instructor will specify a medium and format. However, in other situations, your instructor might not specify the medium and format and, instead, expect you to make the proper rhetorical choice. If you decide to prepare an electronic document (or any kind of document, for that matter), you have another decision to make: What format should it take?

Because the same information can usually be provided in both print and electronic forms, the medium you choose often depends on how that information is going to be used. Both paper and electronic documents have physical limitations. However, each one also helps you accomplish different tasks better than the other.

Features of Paper and Electronic Documents

Criteria	Medium: Print on paper	Medium: Electronic
Portability	Easily portable	Needs devices for portability such as a laptop, PDA, or Smartphone.
Control of design	Relatively easy to control	Less easy to control—issues can be screen size and resolution
Ability to search	More difficult to search—needs a good index	Easy to search—can use hot-linked keywords
Transportability	Needs to be carried or mailed over distance	Can be sent almost instantly over the Internet
Revision	Once printed, paper is difficult to revise. You must go back to the electronic version	Most electronic documents are easy to revise

Paper documents work best when you are providing information in a narrative or sequential organization. Much academic writing, which is often argumentative, works well in print form because argument, which involves presenting and supporting a thesis, is best presented as a linear sequence of points. On the other hand, if you are providing information that does not need to be read sequentially or chronologically, then hypertextual electronic formats, in which readers can use links to move easily from one section to another, offer a distinct advantage over paper documents.

In some situations, you may need to deliver your assignment in the form of an oral presentation to your class or to another group in addition to or instead of in writing. Oral presentations are ubiquitous in the work world, and they may be required in some civic and personal situations as well. Chapter 16 provides some guidelines for oral presentations.

WRITING ACTIVITY

Selecting a Medium

With several of your classmates, consider the following writing tasks. For each one, decide what medium might be appropriate to get your message across to the audience indicated.

- Your group wants to notify your school's president about the deplorable conditions of the dormitory or other college housing or another college building. The housing or other building is in disrepair, and your group wants the college to take action.

- A group consisting of you and your neighbors wants to collect comments and information on a problem with an illegal dump near a school and present them to the town council.

- To increase public awareness of the different organizations on campus, your group has been asked to send information to various civic clubs such as the Rotary, Kiwanis, and Elks. With the material will be a request for donations for your school organizations.

 ## Considering Design

In addition to choosing a genre and medium for your work, you will need to decide on a design for it. We know that many people are visual learners: They seem to absorb information more readily when it is presented in a diagram or a chart. And we know that how a document (an advertisement, for instance) looks will affect our response to it. Chapter 18 covers the principles of good design and provides guidelines for incorporating visual material effectively in your writing. Because even the word-processing software you use regularly can be a powerful design tool, understanding the principles of good design can give you real advantages in conveying your message to a given audience. While many word-processed documents have simple, straightforward designs, and for many college papers such simplicity is all that is required, the current generation of word processors offers options for design and formatting that give users tremendous power and flexibility. With the click of a mouse, writers using word processors can easily do the following:

- Construct a bulleted list such as this one
- Change the size of the text
- Change the color of the text
- **Boldface**, <u>underline</u>, *or italicize the text*
- Highlight the text

In addition, you can insert a table with any given number of cells:

Writing task	Audience	Due date	Length
Directions to my place	Friends	Before this weekend's party	Less than one page
Essay	Instructor	Friday	750 words

Or you may simply want to emphasize some text by placing it in a box.

No matter what design functions you use, your goal in using them should be to make your message more effective.

Technologies for Computer-Mediated Communication

Your choice of a medium for your work may depend not only on the writing situation and the genre you have chosen, but also on the availability of computers and the Internet to you and your audience and your—and their—comfort level with using them. It is likely that you and your classmates may have had very different experiences in using computers and have various perspectives on them and on the technologies that surround them. If you are an older student, computers may still be a relatively new technology to you. On the other hand, if you graduated from high school in the past few years, you have no doubt had plenty of experience with computers at home and/or at school. Therefore, each of you may have different answers to the question "What do we use computers for?"

Although you probably use computers to do your schoolwork, you may also use computers to play games, send e-mail, and surf the Web. You may even use them to play and record music, edit images and video, and for many other tasks. The way you use computers for recreation—in the personal area of your life—can help you get more benefit from them in your academic work. For example, if you play a computer game on the Internet with an opponent who is in another state, the idea of working with people in other places and communicating over the Internet probably already feels comfortable to you. Likewise, if you find a particular game appealing because of its interesting graphics, you will understand more clearly how the right graphics might help you construct a more powerful oral presentation or a more effective Web site.

When you think about the way you use computers during your writing process, you probably think about using word-processing software to compose, revise, and edit your various drafts. While these uses are important, they are not the only way that computers can help you during your writing process. Thinking about the ways in which you use computers in other areas of your life can give you ideas about how computers can help you as you do research, write, revise, and edit your work. You might use a computer to find information on the Internet or to access a variety of library databases. In addition, you can use word-processing software at other stages of the process besides composing, such as when you are taking notes or using brainstorming, listing, and other invention strategies. You can even use other technologies, such as e-mail and instant messaging, for exploring topics and sharing ideas and drafts with peer reviewers.

The following technologies give you additional tools and options for writing and publishing your work in different media.

E-mail

Many of us use **e-mail** frequently. We e-mail our family and friends. We may e-mail business associates, and most of you probably e-mail your classmates and teachers. E-mail can be very useful for trying out possible writing topics, exchanging ideas and drafts, and asking a quick question. In civic and work contexts, it is also a means of delivering information to your audience. Familiar though it may be, e-mail is a powerful technology. To make the best use of it, you need to be aware of some basic rhetorical issues.

- **Tone:** E-mail messages range from very informal to formal, depending on your audience. If you are writing to a close friend, a family member, or even a classmate, you may feel comfortable using nonstandard words such as "gonna" or "dunno" or acronyms such as BTW (by the way), ASAP (as soon as possible), or LOL (laughing out loud). Sometimes writers get so accustomed to using nonstandard language in their e-mails that they use these abbreviations inappropriately in e-mail correspondence with their supervisors, their instructors, or people they don't know well, thus harming their credibility with their audience.

- **Audience:** Once you send an e-mail message, you lose control of who will see and read it, so be aware of and cautious about what you say. While you may send an e-mail to a specific person, *that* person might forward your e-mail or include it in another e-mail to someone you don't even know.

- **Ethos:** Your e-mail address will be seen by everyone you send e-mail to. If you send e-mail from work or school, your address is often assigned to you—and usually consists of a form of your name. However, when you set up a personal e-mail account, you can choose your own address, which will therefore say something about you. Like a vanity license plate on a car, addresses that are overly cute (FroggyBoy), slightly edgy (Earthling), or too personal (ILuvBill), might be fine for your closest

*For more on e-mail as a
genre, see Appendix C,
pages. A-32–A-33.*

friends but are likely to be highly inappropriate in a professional environment. If you feel that you don't want to be limited by a bland e-mail address, consider using different addresses for different purposes.

Threaded Discussions

A **threaded discussion** is simply e-mail that, instead of being sent to individual addresses, is posted on the virtual equivalent of a bulletin board, usually as part of a Web site. Participants simply add their comments on a particular topic in the appropriate place—either as an extension of a previous message or as a new topic or "thread." The advantage is that everyone who is participating in the discussion can see what the other participants are saying.

Threaded discussions can help instructors and students perform a variety of writing tasks. If the class is being offered entirely online, threaded discussions are a substitute for in-class discussions. If the class meets face-to-face, then threaded discussions are one way to work collaboratively on a class assignment or participate in a discussion outside of class. When students want to continue a fruitful classroom discussion after the class time has ended, for example, they can start a threaded discussion on the topic. A threaded discussion such as the one shown in Figure 17.1 is also an ideal place to post a great idea about a classroom topic that did not surface until several hours after class ended.

One of the responses to the question posed in Figure 17.1 looks like this:

> I'd contact all the employees in multiple ways. First of all I'd send an e-mail to all employees that some practices needed to be changed. I'd then find a way to visit one-on-one with as many employees as possible. I'd do this by visiting their cubes.
>
> Still I think it would take a long time.

Synchronous Chat

At its most basic level, **synchronous chat** is simply a way to communicate with someone else in real time using text. Two types of synchronous chat that may be familiar to you are the virtual text-based worlds in MUDs (Multi User Domains) and MOOs (MUDs Object Oriented). These days most people who use synchronous chat are likely to be using some kind of instant messaging (IM).

Although you may think that instant messaging and other forms of synchronous chat are a great way to communicate with distant friends or relatives while avoiding long-distance phone charges, you can also use the same technology for a variety of group or team activities. Aside from enabling

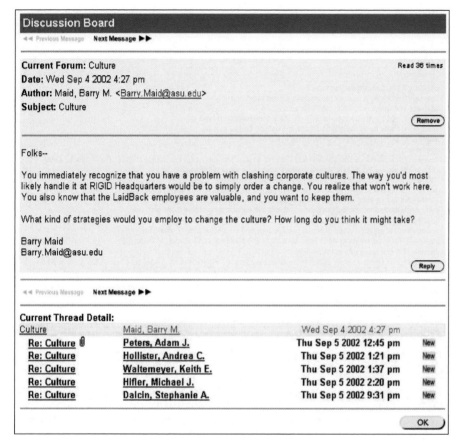

FIGURE 17.1
A Threaded Discussion

you simply to keep in touch with friends or to ask a question immediately to clarify a comment that you do not understand, synchronous chat provides an incredibly powerful environment for brainstorming. Because most chat software has a logging function, you can keep a written record of your conversation or brainstorming session and use it later in your writing. Chat seems to be especially helpful in the invention and planning stages of projects (see Figure 17.2 on p. 784).

For a definition of brainstorming, see Chapter 3, page 44.

Blogs

Blogs or **Web logs** are a type of online journal. Like pen and paper journals, blogs often feature personal, reflective writing. Most paper journals are private documents written for the writers themselves or a select, small audience. In contrast, blogs are posted on the Web and are therefore public documents. Since blogs are consciously written as public documents, they are often about subjects that might interest large numbers of people such as politics or sports or entertainers. However, they tend to retain their personal

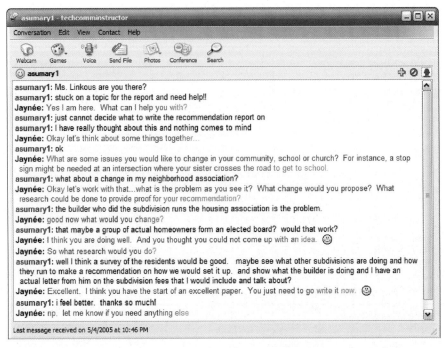

FIGURE 17.2   Synchronous Chat Used at the Invention Stage of a Project

flavor because there is seldom, if ever, any accountability for what gets written in a blog. Although you might find a blog maintained by someone who expresses exactly how you feel about a certain politician or political position, you need to evaluate carefully the accuracy of what is written on that blog. While some blogs are the work of a single author, others are interactive. They allow, and even encourage, multiple writers to take part in the conversation. In this way they are like threaded discussions; however, blog entries tend to be longer and more reflective than the typical posting on a threaded discussion board. An Internet site like Globe of Blogs (www.globeofblogs.com) lists thousands of blogs on a wide variety of topics and interests.

Word-Processing Software

Word processors such as Microsoft *Word, OpenOffice,* and *WordPerfect* have always performed four basic functions: inserting text, deleting text, copying and moving text, and formatting text. Today's high-end word processors retain those four basic functions, but they can do much more. One important advantage that word processors offer is that they are a very forgiving technology. Changes are incredibly easy to make—whether you spot a misspelled word or need to rephrase a sentence or rewrite a paragraph. This ability to revise texts easily opens up all kinds of possibilities for writers. Major revisions become easier because moving chunks of text from one place to another takes only a few simple manipulations of the mouse. Editing your text becomes easier because you can make minor changes with just a few keystrokes instead of retyping the entire paper. In addition, other functions allow a writer or writers to edit a text and peer reviewers to make comments on it. Here is an example of how easy it is for different people to edit and add comments to the same text:

> In addition, many ~~newer~~ word-processing programs <u>incorporate</u> special features, such as the "track-changes" and "comment" functions, <u>that</u> give writers the opportunity to consider reviewers' suggested revisions and comments as they work on a piece of writing.

> Page: 21
> [E2] The highlight in the text indicates where a reader has added a comment or question.

In this sentence, the word "newer" has been deleted; the deletion is indicated with a line through the word. The words "incorporate" and "that" were added to the original text, so they are shown underlined and in color. The comment feature in Microsoft *Word* and *OpenOffice* lets readers highlight (in this case, the part of the text [in brackets] or highlighted), and then insert a comment (shown in red, below the paragraph). "E2" in brackets refers to the second editor or reader who has made comments on this text. (For more on peer-review applications, see the next section.)

Finally, the options for designing a word-processed document are increasing all the time. While all documents need to be well written, their content can no longer be divorced from their format, and readers now expect word-processed documents to look professional. Formatting options include, but are not limited to, type fonts in different sizes, tables, boxes, and visual effects such as numbered and bulleted lists. If a writer needs to include graphics, they can be inserted directly into the word-processed document.

WRITING ACTIVITY

Using Editing Features

Using whatever word-processing software you have available, investigate some of its editing features. Is there a "track-changes" feature? If so, try it. Use the help function to learn how to turn this feature on and off. Is there a "comment" feature?

Working in teams of two, each student should write a paragraph or two on what you think is the most interesting or challenging feature of your word-processing program. Save your writing as an electronic file and then share it with your teammate. Edit your teammate's file, using the track-changes and comment features.

TechNote Use the barter system to discover how you and your classmates can help one another become more proficient with various software applications:

1. Make a list of all of the computer programs (software applications) you have used.

2. Beside each one, rate your familiarity with the application on a scale of 1 to 5. Give a rating of "1" to programs you have opened and used only once or twice. Give a "5" to programs you use frequently, and whose features and flaws you know well.

3. Now list all of the programs you rate either 4 or 5, ranking them in order from the most difficult or complicated to the least complicated.

4. Make another list of the programs you rated 5, ranking them from most to least popular among your classmates (this will be a guess, but it can help you think through what kind of knowledge you have to share vs. what kind of knowledge will be in demand).

5. Compare your list with those of your classmates, and agree to help one another with programs that you would like to learn, or learn to use more effectively.

For more on effective document design and the use of visuals, see Chapter 18, pages 791–824.

TechNote Computers are like toothbrushes: people really don't like to share. Letting someone use your computer can result in downloads and icons you don't want or need and resource issues that can mean an expensive visit to a tech support service. It's better to limit the number of people who use your college computer and to resist the urge to use someone else's computer. Most colleges provide computer labs on campus, and the staff at the computer lab can usually help you with any problems that arise.

Peer-Review Applications

As increasing numbers of writers use computer software to collaborate in both educational and workplace environments, the software that facilitates collaborative writing keeps improving. The programs that writers use for this purpose fall into two distinct categories: collaborative tools built into standard word-processing programs, as discussed on pages 784–85 in the preceding section, and web-based editing programs.

One type of Web-based editing program is a Wiki: software that allows for open editing of Web documents. When a document is placed in a Wiki, it can be edited by anyone who views it through any Web browser, using any computer operating system. Some Wikis, however, require that users be logged in before they are allowed to edit a document. A Wiki is useful when writing teams work over distance and do not necessarily share the same computer operating systems or Web browsing software. The flexibility that a Wiki allows also makes it useful for student projects. However, since a Wiki is a Web page, unless it is password protected or sits on an intranet (a private computer network), any document in a Wiki becomes accessible to anyone in the world with Internet access. As a result, Wikis are used most often in workplace situations where there is a local intranet.

For more on the peer-review software that is available with this text, see Chapter 15, page 751.

One Web-based program that allows peers to comment on your work is available to you as part of the Online Learning Center for this text. This software permits you and the other members of your assigned peer group to make comments about one another's writing and to view and respond to those comments.

Graphics Software

Today, it is possible to enhance your documents using a variety of visual information: tables, charts, and graphs as well as photos, drawings, and other visual images. While you can create some tables in your word-processing program and graphs and charts using a spreadsheet, other images need to be digitized (that is, put into a form that can be read by a computer) in order to include them as part of your computer document. The easiest way to render many visuals in a digital format is to use a graphics program such as *PaintShopPro, Illustrator,* or *FreeHand*. If you are taking photographs yourself, you can use a digital camera. If you have a printed image, however, you can easily digitize it by using a scanner.

Once the image is digitized, you can manipulate it in a variety of ways by using graphic editing software such as *PhotoShop*. Image-editing software allows you to change the size or resolution of the digital image, crop out unneeded elements, or change the contrast so that the image becomes clearer. However, image editing software also makes it possible to change images inappropriately. Just because it is easy to change a photo does not mean that you *should* change it. The ease with which we can now alter images raises serious ethical questions.

We have all seen examples of famous photographs that have been altered to include a person who was not in the original image, a relatively easy change to make with the right software. Although some doctored photos might be considered funny, others are created with the intention of misleading readers. For example, a fake photo of a young John Kerry attending an anti-war rally with Jane Fonda surfaced during the 2004 presidential campaign season. Figure 17.3 shows the fake photo, along with the two photos that were combined to construct the fake.

Fonda Speaks To Vietnam Veterans At Anti-War Rally

Actress And Anti-War Activist Jane Fonda Speaks to a crowd of Vietnam Veterans as Activist and former Vietnam Vet John Kerry (LEFT) listens and prepares to speak next concerning the war in Vietnam (AP Photo)

FIGURE 17.3 This photograph of John Kerry and Jane Fonda, supposedly appearing together at an anti-war rally, is fake. It was fabricated by combining the two photographs shown below it.

The fake photo enraged many people because John Kerry, who was using his status as a Vietnam War veteran as part of his presidential campaign, is standing next to Jane Fonda, well known for her controversial visit to North Vietnam during that war. Perhaps not surprisingly, this fake photo was cited as evidence that Kerry was unpatriotic. Clearly, some people were fooled by the fake.

A WRITER'S RESPONSIBILITIES

Using Image-Editing Software Ethically

If you are thinking of altering a photo, the first question you need to ask yourself has both ethical and legal implications: Do I have the right to change someone else's image without that person's permission? Unless you already own the image or have the owner's permission to use it and alter it, making changes may very well violate the creator's copyright. Because you will need the owner's permission to use the image, make sure you also get permission to change the image if you would like to do so. You may think that cropping out what you consider to be unnecessary parts of a photo might not be an issue, but the copyright owner might see the issue differently. Second, even if you are within your rights to change the image, you need to be sure that by making changes you are not misrepresenting your subject or misleading your readers, as the people who altered the photos of John Kerry and Jane Fonda did.

Desktop Publishing Software

Desktop publishing software such as *Quark*, *Pagemaker*, or *InDesign* allows writers to produce documents on their personal computers that are ready to be professionally printed. While people who are comfortable with computers and have some training in layout and design can readily do some simple tasks in desktop publishing software, most people need either training or practice to get comfortable in its use. Most desktop publishing software programs are designed to construct short documents, and people often use them to prepare flyers, brochures, newsletters, and similar publications. While many of the functions that used to be available only in desktop publishing software can now be done by word processors, there are still good reasons to use software that is designed solely for desktop publishing. The primary reason is that it gives you more control over your document, such as the following:

- More precision in placing and manipulating images.
- More control over *leading*, the spacing between the lines, and *kerning*, the spacing between letters.
- The ability to incorporate sophisticated design features such as sidebars into your document (sidebars are messages that provide extra

information to readers and are set off to the side of a text. You can see them in the margins of this text).

Once you import your text into desktop publishing software, however, you will be unable to make any but the most basic editorial changes to it.

Presentation Software

At some point in their careers, almost all professionals make oral presentations, and you will most likely be asked to make presentations to some of your classmates while you are still a student. Sometimes professionals need to make a presentation to an audience of peers or higher-level employees. At other times they may need to do a sales presentation, or present a new idea or report on a project in a more informal setting. Most professional presenters include some kind of visual component in their presentations in order to help keep their audience's attention focused on the presentation. This visual component often includes images that are important to the topic as well as information that is best presented in charts or graphs. In the past, presenters often used large charts or posters, slides, or overhead transparencies. Now, most professionals use presentation software such as *PowerPoint* to complement their oral presentations. Presentation software allows you to format slides for a presentation easily and professionally. The standard format is a heading followed by a bulleted list, but other formats are available, as well as graphics and sound. Figure 17.4 is an example of a standard *PowerPoint* slide. If you do not have access to *PowerPoint*, you can use *Impress*, a compatible, open source (free) program that is part of the *OpenOffice* desktop software suite. *Google Docs*, another free Web-based presentation program, allows you to import *PowerPoint* files and easily share and collaborate on presentations online.

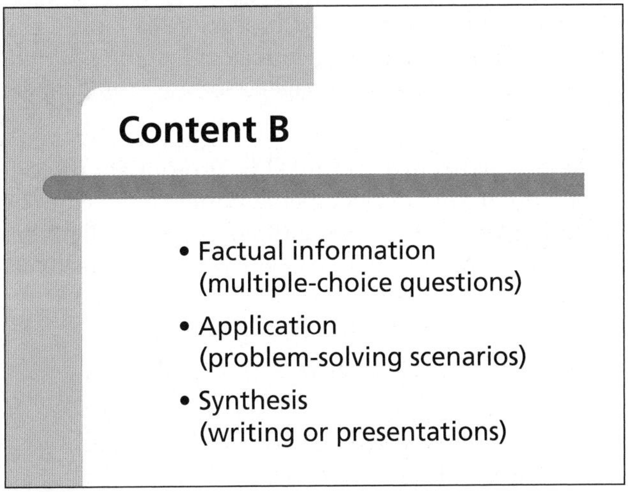

Content B

- Factual information
  (multiple-choice questions)
- Application
  (problem-solving scenarios)
- Synthesis
  (writing or presentations)

FIGURE 17.4   A Standard *PowerPoint* Slide

When using presentation software, you need to remember that your slides should complement your presentation, not be its focus. When you give a presentation, you want your listeners to pay the most attention to what you say, not to the slides being shown behind you. If you use a graphic, the graphic should add to, not detract from, the content of the slide. Think of your bullet points as "talking points." They are simply reminders to you of all the things you need to say. You might also think of them as hyperlinks. What you actually say is the equivalent of clicking on a link in a Web page for more information. In fact, presenters often distribute handouts of their slides as ready-made notes for the members of the audience so they can spend more time listening to the talk.

For more on oral presentations and presentation software, see Chapter 16.

Technologies for Constructing Web Pages

Web pages are computer files that can be viewed using software called a **browser.** Examples of browsers are *Internet Explorer*, *Netscape*, and *Firefox*. Web pages are coded using hypertext markup language (html). The html coding places information in the document that allows the browser to display the page properly. Currently, there are four ways to construct a Web page:

- Use the "save as a Web page" option in your word-processing software. This option has the advantage of being easy and is appropriate for very simple, straightforward Web pages. For more complex pages, you may need to choose one of the other two options.

- "Hand code" the html (this means writing the actual mark-up tags in a text editor like *Notepad* or *TextEdit*). This option gives you more control over the design of your site, but it is time-consuming.

- Use an html editor like *Dreamweaver*. Because html has become increasingly complex, most professionals now use html editors.

- Use a Web-based page construction tool like *Google Page Creator*. Web-based tools usually have both visual (word processor-like) and html editor modes. They also have the added advantage of instantly providing you with an opportunity to view your page exactly as it will appear online before you publish it.

For more on writing Web pages, see Appendix C.

Constructing effective Web pages involves making appropriate rhetorical choices, just as with any other kind of document. While you need to be sensitive to the look and feel of your Web pages, ultimately what will matter most is their content. The most important question will be, "How effectively am I getting my message across to the audience that I am targeting?"

Communicating with Design and Visuals

Chapter 18

First United Nations Decade for the Eradication of Poverty, 1997-2006

"Eradicationg poverty is an ethical, social, political and eonomical imperative of humankind."

Millennium development goal:
"...To halve, by the year 2015, the proportion of the world's people whose income is less than one dollar a day

Q. If I'm a high school student struggling in one of my classes, how can I get extra help?

A. FREE tutoring at ABCD Parker Hill/Fenway!

Neighborhood ABCD Parker Hill/ Fenway Service Center
Providing opportunities... because we care

For more information contact:
Tejwattie Balgobin
Special Projects Coordinator

ABCD Parker Hill/Fenway N.S.C.
714 Parker St.
Roxbury, MA 02120

Phone: 617-445-6000 ext. 232
Fax: 617-445-6005
Email: balgobin@bostonabcd.org

Subjects Available:
- Algebra • Trigonometry
- Calculus • Grammar
- Essays • Biology
- Physics • American History/Literature
Plus More!

Think you need tutoring?
Do you want:
- To improve your grade in algebra?
- To get a better understanding about the periodic tables in chemistry?
- To get help writing an essay?
- To get assitance with tonight's homework?
If you answered yes to any of the above questions you may qualify for our FREE tutoring program! Call us to-day for more information!

The two documents that open this chapter combine both written and visual elements. To craft a poster like the one for the International Day for the Eradication of Poverty, a writer needs specialized graphics software, which is commonly available in university or college computing labs. To design a flyer similar to the one for the tutoring program for high school students offered by the Fenway Neighborhood Service Center, however, a writer can use any of several widely available word-processing software programs, which provide graphics such as the image of the beakers and the shading in the text box. Whether you are designing an elaborate document like the poster or a simpler document like the flyer, you can use the same standard design principles that are the focus of this chapter.

Any time you apply the principles of design, and any time you decide to use images in your own texts, you need to consider your writing situation and make rhetorical choices. Here are some questions to consider:

- What are you trying to accomplish with your text, and how might your design and images (photographs, charts, diagrams, tables) help you achieve your goals?

- Who is your audience? What kind(s) of design elements and images (or data presented in graphic form) might interest and appeal to your audience? What might make it easier for your readers to understand the information you are providing?

- What is the context in which you are writing? How does that context limit the kinds of design choices you might make and the images you might use? Many academic writing situations, for example, require the use of specific styles such as the one recommended by the Modern Language Association (MLA).

- How might the available technology affect the design and image choices you make? If you do not have access to a color printer, for example, that obviously restricts your use of color in your document.

For a discussion of reading visuals critically, see Chapter 2.

In addition to discussing the principles of document design that you can apply to any document that you prepare, this chapter offers guidelines for choosing suitable visuals for your paper.

 ## Principles of Document Design

Whatever their rhetorical choices might be, writers can use the design principles of proximity, contrast, alignment, and repetition to craft more effective texts.

Proximity

Whenever you vary the amount of space between and around text elements so that related items are close to one another and unrelated items are separated from one another, you are employing the principle of **proximity.** For instance, consider the following three versions of a shopping list:

Version A	Version B	Version C
wireless network router	wireless network router	wireless network router
t-shirt	wireless mouse	wireless mouse
water colors	blank CDs	blank CDs
English dictionary	English dictionary	
blank CDs	thesaurus	English dictionary
pastels	book of quotations	thesaurus
thesaurus	oil paints	book of quotations
skirt	water colors	
wireless mouse	pastels	oil paints
socks	socks	water colors
oil paints	t-shirt	pastels
book of quotations	skirt	
		socks
		t-shirt
		skirt

Which list would make it easier for you to find these twelve items in the shortest amount of time? Most people would probably find the third list easiest to use because the information is organized into categories, with space above each one.

For some documents, such as brochures and newsletters, writers can also use borders and color to group common items and separate them from dissimilar items. (Color type may not be appropriate for many academic papers.) Most word processors allow you to add these elements to your document.

As illustrated by the flyer advertising tutoring services at the beginning of this chapter, borders can also make sections of your written text stand out. The two versions of the same text that follow also illustrate this principle.

TEXT WITHOUT A BORDER

Elizabeth Moore lost a gold bracelet as she walked home from the park last night. If you find it, please contact her at 555-7846.

TEXT WITH A BORDER

The use of color is covered on pages 795–97.

> Elizabeth Moore lost a gold bracelet as she walked home from the park last night. If you find it, please contact her at 555-7846.

Contrast

You can use **contrast** by employing design features such as bold or italic type, underlining, indentation, and color to indicate the hierarchy of importance among text elements and to create certain effects. For instance, you can use contrast to make headings at different levels of importance visually

Version A	Version B
Shopping List	**Shopping List**
Computer Store	*Computer Store*
wireless network router	wireless network router
wireless mouse	wireless mouse
blank CDs	blank CDs
Bookstore	
English dictionary	*Bookstore*
thesaurus	English dictionary
book of quotations	thesaurus
Art Supply Store	book of quotations
oil paints	
water colors	*Art Supply Store*
pastels	oil paints
Clothing Store	water colors
socks	pastels
t-shirt	
skirt	*Clothing Store*
	socks
	t-shirt
	skirt

distinct. Notice how we can use the principle of contrast by adding two levels of headings to identify the groups in our shopping list. Version A uses contrast alone: The higher level heading is in bold type and the lower level one is in bold italics. Version B adds the principle of proximity to contrast: Spaces separate each of the four groups.

Color can also add visual interest and contrast to your texts. If you use more than one color in a document, however, consult the color wheel shown in Figure 18.1 to determine which colors work best together.

As the color wheel indicates, the **primary colors** are red, yellow, and blue. The **secondary colors,** located at points halfway between the three primary colors on the wheel, are formed by combining primary colors: Red and yellow combine to make orange; blue and yellow combine to make green; and red and blue combine to make violet. Other colors are formed by combining primary colors with secondary colors.

Complementary colors are directly across from each other on the wheel—for instance, yellow and violet, red and green, and blue and orange. Placing complementary colors next to each other has the effect of **jarring** the reader. Placing adjacent colors together, on the other hand, has a **pleasing** effect. Pairing colors separated by two or three positions on the color wheel can have a **vivid** or **bold** effect, as illustrated in Figure 18.2 on page 796. Note, for example, that yellow and yellow-orange work well next to each other, but that red and green, when next to each other, are not as visually pleasing.

Colors are sometimes considered to be "warm" and "cool." Warm colors—red, orange, and yellow—are energetic and bold. Cool colors—green, blue, and violet—sometimes have a soothing, calming effect. Consider the poster shown in Figure 18.3 on page 796. Two warm colors, yellow and red,

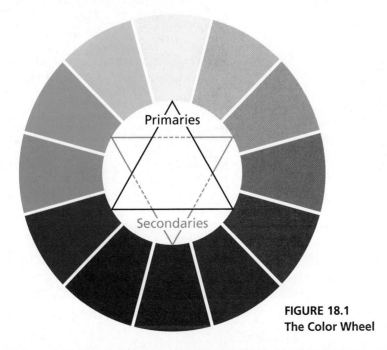

FIGURE 18.1
The Color Wheel

FIGURE 18.2
Color Combinations and Their Effects

Putting complementary colors together		Putting adjacent colors together		Putting primary and secondary colors together	
Jarring effect		*Pleasing effect*		*Vivid or bold effect*	
Red	Green	Yellow	Yellow-orange	Violet	Red

appear together in this poster. Because red and yellow are also both primary colors, the red text on the yellow background is especially eye-catching. After the poster grabs our attention with the "blazing" red letters, we encounter the more subdued message in black.

Now consider another poster, shown in Figure 18.4, this one announcing a conference on ecology and environment. The background for this poster includes large patches of green and blue, both cool colors that have a

FIGURE 18.3   A Poster Using Warm Colors

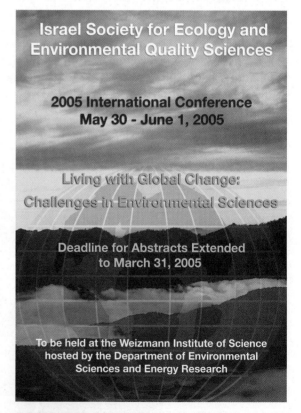

FIGURE 18.4   A Poster Using Cool Colors

calming effect. The conference theme and dates stand out to readers because they appear in two warm colors, orange and yellow. Other information in the poster appears in colors that are not as eye-catching: blue and white.

Alignment

Writers also use **alignment** to indicate relationships among text elements and make their documents easier for readers to process. As readers of English, we are accustomed to text that is aligned on the left side of the page. Other alignments are possible, however, and you can vary alignments to achieve different effects. Consider the following paragraph from "Beware the Online Collective" by Jaron Lanier (the complete essay appears on pp. 732–34 in Chapter 14), aligned in four different ways. Which is easiest to read?

LEFT ALIGNMENT

One of the most wonderful things about the rise of the Web and other Internet-based communication schemes is how anti-mob they have been. I was in heaven 10 years ago watching millions of people build web sites for the first time as a form of expression. I'm just as excited today when I run across a creative web page, MySpace site, YouTube video or whatever. There are zillions of people out there who are developing themselves, reaching out to others, becoming more creative, better educated, and richer than they otherwise would have been. My personal favorite of the current batch of fast growing sites might be Second Life, where people create avatars of themselves to share in a virtual world. Bravo!

RIGHT ALIGNMENT

One of the most wonderful things about the rise of the Web and other Internet-based communication schemes is how anti-mob they have been. I was in heaven 10 years ago watching millions of people build web sites for the first time as a form of expression. I'm just as excited today when I run across a creative web page, MySpace site, YouTube video or whatever. There are zillions of people out there who are developing themselves, reaching out to others, becoming more creative, better educated, and richer than they otherwise would have been. My personal favorite of the current batch of fast growing sites might be Second Life, where people create avatars of themselves to share in a virtual world. Bravo!

CENTER ALIGNMENT

One of the most wonderful things about the rise of the Web and other Internet-based communication schemes is how anti-mob they have been. I was in heaven 10 years ago watching millions of people build web sites for the first time as a form of expression. I'm just as excited today when I run across a creative web page, MySpace site, YouTube video or whatever. There are zillions of people out there who are developing themselves, reaching out to others, becoming more creative, better educated, and richer than they otherwise would have been. My personal favorite of the current batch of fast growing sites might be Second Life, where people create avatars of themselves to share in a virtual world. Bravo!

LEFT AND RIGHT JUSTIFIED

One of the most wonderful things about the rise of the Web and other Internet-based communication schemes is how anti-mob they have been. I was in heaven 10 years ago watching millions of people build web sites for the first time as a form of expression. I'm just as excited today when I run across a creative web page, MySpace site, YouTube video or whatever. There are zillions of people out there who are developing themselves, reaching out to others, becoming more creative, better educated, and richer than they otherwise would have been. My personal favorite of the current batch of fast growing sites might be Second Life, where people create avatars of themselves to share in a virtual world. Bravo!

Unless your text is very brief, your best choice for most academic writing is usually to align your text at the left margin to make it easier for your readers to process. For other contexts—for example, for a professional report—you might choose to align your text at both margins, or *justify* it, for a professional look; most books and many periodicals make extensive use of this type of alignment. If your text is short and you want to achieve an eye-catching effect on a poster or a brochure, you might consider using right or center alignment.

Repetition (or Consistency)

When you use **repetition** or **consistency,** you apply the same design features to text elements with similar rhetorical functions. The general principle is that a writer should use design features consistently throughout the text. For example, note how the consistent use of bullets in front of the items in our grocery list sets them off even more for readers.

SHOPPING LIST

Computer Store

• Wireless network router

- Wireless mouse
- Blank CDs

Bookstore

- English dictionary
- Thesaurus
- Book of quotations

Art Supply Store

- Oil paints
- Water colors
- Pastels

Clothing Store

- Socks
- T-shirt
- Skirt

There are many ways to follow the principle of repetition or consistency in a document: following a documentation style accurately; using typefaces and fonts consistently; using a carefully developed heading structure; and using bullets, numbers, and graphics consistently.

USING A SINGLE DOCUMENTATION FORMAT

Chapter 20 provides guidelines for the systems for citing sources and formatting academic papers recommended by the Modern Language Association (MLA) and the American Psychological Association (APA). Following a single, consistent format throughout your paper makes it easier for readers to determine the type of source you are citing (a book or a periodical article, for instance), find it in your works-cited or references list, and consult it themselves if they choose to do so.

USING TYPEFACES AND TYPE SIZES CONSISTENTLY

A typeface is a design for the letters of the alphabet, numbers, and other symbols. A type font consists of all of the different styles and sizes that one typeface is available in. For most academic documents, you probably need to use only one or possibly two typefaces. Typefaces belong to one of two general categories: **serif** and **sans serif.** A serif typeface has small strokes or extenders at the top and the bottom of the letter, and letters may vary in thickness. Sans serif ("without serif") type has no small strokes or extenders, and the letters have a uniform thickness. Usually, serif type is considered easier to read, especially in longer texts. For that reason, most newspapers, magazines, and books, including this one, use serif type for body text and sans serif type in headings and other kinds of displayed type, for contrast. Here are some examples of serif and sans serif type:

Serif Typefaces	Sample Sentence
Times New Roman	Carefully select the typeface that you use in your texts because the type can affect how easily readers can process your text.
Courier New	Carefully select the typeface that you use in your texts because the type can affect how easily readers can process your text.

Sans Serif Type	Sample Sentence
Arial	Carefully select the typeface that you use in your texts because the type can affect how easily readers can process your text.
Century Gothic	Carefully select the typeface that you use in your texts because the type can affect how easily readers can process your text.

All of the samples above are in 12-point type, which is a standard size for academic papers (a point is equivalent to 1/72 of an inch). Notice that different typefaces take up different amounts of space. In some writing situations, space costs money; if so, you should consider a smaller face such as Times New Roman or Arial over a larger one such as Courier or Century Gothic. In other situations, such as a slide presentation, you may need a larger face because it will be easier to read from a distance.

Most computers offer a wide range of typefaces to choose from, including unusual and ornate varieties. You should use these typefaces sparingly, however, because they can be difficult to read, especially for longer texts. Consider the following examples:

| Monotype Corsiva | *Carefully select the typeface that you use in your texts because the type can affect how easily readers can process your text.* |
| Haettenschweiler | **Carefully select the typeface that you use in your texts because the type can affect how easily readers can process your text.** |

Whatever typeface or typefaces you decide to use, be sure to use typefaces, sizes, and styles such as italic or bold consistently throughout your documents, especially when styling your headings.

USING HEADINGS CONSISTENTLY

Headings signal the content of your paper and help readers understand its organization. When headings are worded and styled consistently, readers know which sections are at a higher or lower level of generality than others. You can use different sizes of type; different typefaces; and underlining, bold, and italics to signal different levels of generality. When you use headings to signal different levels of generality, it is important that you treat headings at the same level the same way—the same font size and style (for example, 12 point Times New Roman), the same location on the page (for example, at the left margin, centered, or indented), and the same capitalization.

TechNote

Projects written for digital media should integrate visual and graphical elements in ways that make logical and intuitive sense to your audience. Here are some suggestions:

- Break up long blocks of text into paragraphs or boxes.

- Choose color schemes that are easy on the readers' eyes.

- Create labels and captions that clarify visual information.

- Create elements that explain and contextualize images, video, and sound—don't assume that the image, video, or audio by itself will indicate to online visitors the point you are trying to get across.

- Be prepared to prove ownership and/or rights to the media and images you have incorporated.

You should also use parallel structure for all headings at a given level, as in the following examples:

Parts of the City
    Business District
    Residential Areas
    Waterfront
    Parks

Parts of the City
    Shopping in the Business District
    Discovering the Residential Areas
    Enjoying the Waterfront
    Relaxing in the Parks

USING BULLETS, NUMBERS, ROMAN NUMERALS, OR LETTERS CONSISTENTLY

You can use bullets, numbers, Roman numerals, or letters—or some combination of these elements—for several purposes. Most frequently, they are used to indicate items in a list or an outline. Any of these markers can be effective for a short list of items, as shown below.

If you are presenting steps in a process or items in a certain order, numbers are usually a better choice, and a combination of Roman numerals, let-

Bullets	Numbers (with Bullets)	Roman Numerals (with Letters)	Letters (with Numbers)
Car Models	Car Models	Car Models	Car Models
• Ford	1. Ford	I. Ford	A. Ford
• Taurus	• Taurus	A. Taurus	1. Taurus
• Focus	• Focus	B. Focus	2. Focus
• Mustang	• Mustang	C. Mustang	3. Mustang
• Chevrolet	2. Chevrolet	II. Chevrolet	B. Chevrolet
• Impala	• Impala	A. Impala	1. Impala
• Malibu	• Malibu	B. Malibu	2. Malibu
• Corvette	• Corvette	C. Corvette	3. Corvette
• Chrysler	3. Chrysler	III. Chrysler	C. Chrysler
• Sebring	• Sebring	A. Sebring	1. Sebring
• Crossfire	• Crossfire	B. Crossfire	2. Crossfire
• PT Cruiser	• PT Cruiser	C. PT Cruiser	3. PT Cruiser

ters, and numbers is standard in outlines. Bullets can be used to set off the items in a displayed list effectively, although they can be problematic in longer lists because readers may have to count down the list of items manually if they need to discuss a particular point in the list ("Joe, look at the fourteenth bullet item in the list" or "Joe, look at the item that begins with . . .") Of course, you should use bullets, numbers, Roman numerals, and/or letters consistently throughout a text to make it easier for readers to process your writing. For example, you might choose to set up all lists of recommendations in a proposal as bulleted lists.

For more on how to construct an outline, see Chapter 13, pages 713–15.

USING WHITE SPACE CONSISTENTLY

White space is any part of a document that is not covered by type or graphics. The margins at the edges of a document are white space, as are the spaces between lines and above and below titles, headings, and other elements. Use white space consistently throughout a document. You should always leave the same amount of space above headings at the same level. (If you are using MLA or APA style, you will need to follow the guidelines provided by the style you are following for margins and spacing—see Chapter 20.)

Consistent Spacing	Inconsistent Spacing
As you will notice, this short text uses consistent spacing between lines. To be precise, it has double spacing. This makes it easier for readers to mentally process a text.	This short text, on the other hand, uses inconsistent spacing between lines. To be precise, it has two kinds of spacing. This makes it more difficult for readers.

USING GRAPHICS EFFECTIVELY

Graphics—photographs, charts, drawings, diagrams, cartoons, graphs, and tables—can appear in academic papers as well as a number of other types of documents that you might prepare. The different kinds of graphics that a writer might choose are discussed on pages 805–20. Generally, you should use the same kind of graphic to illustrate similar points or concepts. To achieve consistency, you need to consider the following:

- What you want to accomplish with the graphic
- The overall look of the image

- How the graphics are marked in the text in terms of their labels and captions
- How you should introduce the graphics within your text

Select the kind of graphic that best accomplishes your purpose—what you are trying to show to your readers. To best indicate the composition of a pizza, for example, you might choose a pie chart like that shown in Figure 18.5, which shows the ingredients used to make a sausage and mushroom pizza weighing 1.6 kg. The sum of the numbers shown equals 1.6 kg, the weight of the pizza. The size of each slice shows us the fraction of the pizza made up from that ingredient.

Figure 18.6 shows the same data but given as a bar graph—as you can tell, the bar graph does not explain or present the information as effectively as the pie chart does.

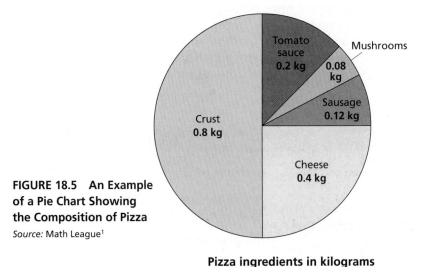

FIGURE 18.5 An Example of a Pie Chart Showing the Composition of Pizza

Source: Math League[1]

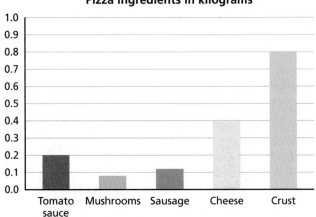

FIGURE 18.6 A Bar Graph Presenting the Same Data as the Pie Chart

[1] Complete source information for the figures in this section can be found in the Credits on page C-4.

To present graphics effectively, follow these guidelines:

- Give the graphics in your document a consistent look. For example, use one-color or multi-color drawings rather than mixing one-color and multi-color drawings. If you use multiple colors, use the same ones in each graphic (for more on the use of color, see pp. 795–97).

- Be sure you introduce and explain each graphic, just as you need to do with each quotation you insert into your text. If you do not do so, then it is possible that your readers will not "see" the image in the same way that you do. They may not understand why it is there or what it is intended to convey. For the bar graph in Figure 18.6, for example, you would want both to introduce it before putting it into your text ("This next graph shows how mushrooms make up the least amount, in weight, of the ingredients in a typical pizza") and to follow the image with an explanation of how the bar graph connects to your topic ("In pizzas, as in many other dishes, mushrooms make up in quality what they lack in quantity").

- Place graphics in a document strategically. To help your readers connect your words with your graphics, place each visual as close to the text discussion that refers to it as possible. Try to avoid placements that force readers to flip back and forth from the page that discusses the visual to the page on which the visual appears. If you are following APA style, however, you have the option of placing visuals at the end of your paper.

Common Kinds of Visual Texts

When you consider adding a visual image or images to a document, you should do so to help accomplish your overall purpose: to persuade or inform your readers, to help demonstrate something to your readers, or to entertain your readers. Do not add a visual just to have a picture or chart or table in your text; rather, use it as a way to support your thesis and achieve your goal for that piece of writing. The following visuals can help you in various ways:

- Tables
- Bar and line graphs
- Charts
- Photographs
- Drawings
- Diagrams
- Maps
- Cartoons

Tables

Tables organize information in columns and rows for readers, helping them make comparisons between or among pieces of information or sets of numerical data. Consider, for instance, the following table, which compares cereal use across many countries. This table shows what percentage of the total domestic cereal supply was used for direct human consumption, was used for feeding animals, or was wasted.

The same data given in a paragraph would be difficult to compare. By reviewing the table, however, readers can easily make comparisons up and down rows, across columns, and across rows and columns. Notice how the table focuses on cereal as food for humans rather than feed for cattle or waste

Domestic Cereal Supply: Food, Feed, Waste

	Food	Feed	Waste
Sri Lanka	**92.2**	**0.5**	**4.7**
Pakistan	88.9	3.5	2.8
India	88.0	0.9	4.4
Viet Nam	84.6	2.6	7.8
Nepal	83.9	2.2	11.0
Indonesia	82.6	8.3	6.6
China	**72.3**	**18.5**	**5.2**
Egypt	70.3	18.0	9.0
Philippines	68.2	23.9	1.1
Korea DPR	68.0	6.1	6.8
Thailand	59.5	28.0	8.7
World	**57.1**	**32.5**	**4.7**
Malaysia	54.7	40.4	2.8
Korea Rep.	50.3	31.5	2.7
Japan	44.3	44.2	0.8
Germany	23.9	59.1	2.8
Austria	17.4	67.8	3.1
U.S.A.	12.6	68.5	0.2
Denmark	**8.8**	**80.3**	**3.7**

Source: FAOSTAT, 1997

by listing countries in descending order in terms of the percentage of cereal that is used for human food.

USING TABLES EFFECTIVELY IN YOUR TEXTS

Word-processing programs will usually allow you to format information into tables automatically—consult the Help screen for the program you are using. Spreadsheet programs also allow you to construct tables.

To decide if a table will be appropriate for your purpose and audience, answer the following questions:

- Do I have data or information that could appear in tabular form?
- How would a table help me organize this data or information for readers?
- How do I want my readers to use the table?
- How do I want or need to organize the data or information in the table so that readers can find the information they need, or that I want them to see?

Bar and Line Graphs

Bar and line graphs provide another way to present numerical information to your readers. Both types of graphs plot data along a horizontal line (the *x* axis) and a vertical line (the *y* axis). Like a table, a **bar graph** allows readers to make comparisons. For example, the graph in Figure 18.7 allows readers to compare actual or projected energy use in three different parts of the world over a period of fifty years.

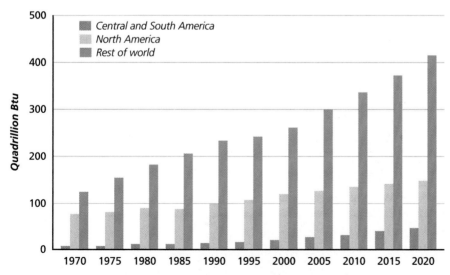

FIGURE 18.7   A Bar Graph Showing Energy Consumption in the World from 1970 to 2020 *Source:* U.S. Government Energy Information Administration

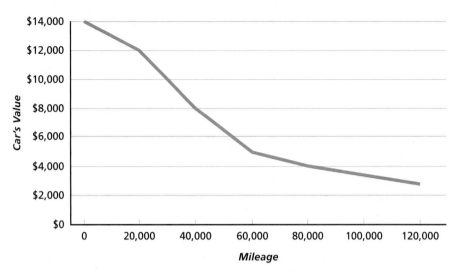

**FIGURE 18.8   A Line Graph Illustrating the Relationship between Mileage
and Value**   *Source:* Math League

A **line graph** shows readers a change or changes over a period of time.
Figure 18.8 is a line graph illustrating the relationship between a car's mileage and its value.

WRITING ACTIVITY

Analyzing Bar and Line Graphs

Analyze the preceding bar and line graphs by responding to the following questions:

- What are the components of the graphs?
- How has the writer used color in the bar graph?
- How has the writer organized the data in the graphs?
- How effective is the organization in the graphs?
- What would happen if the writer reversed the x axis and the y axis in either of the graphs?
- What stories do these graphs tell?

USING GRAPHS EFFECTIVELY IN YOUR TEXTS

You can use bar or line graphs that have been constructed by others in your
paper as long as you give proper credit to the source of the graph. You can

also use a spreadsheet program or *PowerPoint* to construct your own bar and line graphs from data you have discovered or generated on your own, or you can use an online graphing site, such as "Create a Graph" (http://nces.ed.gov/nceskids/Graphing/), hosted by the U.S. government's National Center for Educational Statistics (http://nces.ed.gov). If you do not have access to a computer, however, you can always construct the graph yourself, using graph paper. If you use data from a source to construct your graph, you need to give credit to that source.

See Chapter 20 for help with citing sources for your data.

To use bar and line graphs effectively in your texts, consider the following questions:

- Do I have sets of numerical data that I would like readers to compare?
- Do I have data that indicate a change over a period of time?
- What could a bar or line graph add to my text?
- If I am using a bar graph, how should I organize it?
- How should I explain the graph in my text?
- Do I have access to the technology (a color printer, for example) that will enable me to construct the graph and/or present it effectively?

Charts

A **chart** is a visual text that allows you to show the relationships among different items or among the parts of a whole. Consider Figure 18.9 on page 810, which shows what various stain colors look like on oak. Notice how the chart holds one variable constant—the kind of wood—so that readers can make consistent comparisons among stain colors.

Two kinds of charts that are very common in academic writing, as well as in writing for other areas, are pie charts and flowcharts.

A **pie chart** shows readers the components that make up the whole of something. Pie charts are ideal for showing the percentages of each part of an item. The pie chart in Figure 18.5 on page 804 shows the ingredients used to make a sausage and mushroom pizza. In the pie chart shown in Figure 18.10 on page 810, the weight of each ingredient is given as a *percentage* of the whole. We see that half of the pizza's weight, 50%, comes from the crust. Note that the sum of the percentages is 100%.

FLOWCHARTS

A flowchart shows how a process works. Although you can usually describe processes with words alone, a flowchart can do so in a visual way. Many readers find it easier to understand processes when they see flowcharts. Figure 18.11 on page 811 illustrates the complex process of launching a water rocket. Notice that the chart is also a kind of *decision tree,* with yes or no responses that direct readers' progress through the chart.

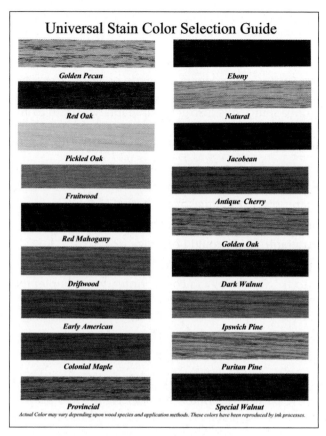

FIGURE 18.9   A Chart Showing Wood Stains

Source: ComeToBuy.com

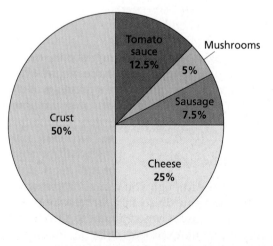

FIGURE 18.10   A Pie Chart Showing Pizza Ingredients by Percentage

Source: Math League

Bigfoot Rocket Launcher Flowchart

FIGURE 18.11
A Flowchart That Is Also a Decision Tree
Source: Gary Ensmenger

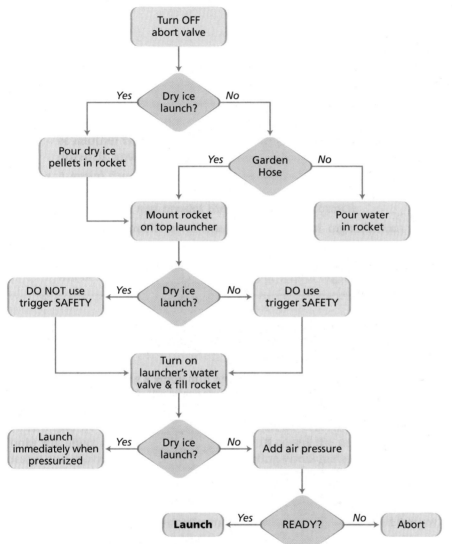

USING CHARTS EFFECTIVELY IN YOUR TEXTS

As with graphs, you can use charts that have been produced by others in your paper as long as you give proper credit to the source of the chart. You can also construct your own chart the old-fashioned way—drawing it by hand—or by using a drawing program. Spreadsheet programs and *PowerPoint* also enable you to produce pie charts and flowcharts and import them into your paper.

To use charts effectively in your texts, consider the following questions:

- Is there a process, a key relationship, or the components of something within my text that I could illustrate with a chart?
- How will the chart help my audience better understand a particular point in my paper?
- How will a chart support my purpose?
- How can I organize the chart so that readers can see patterns in the information?
- Do I have access to the technology (a color printer, for example) that will enable me to construct the chart and/or present it effectively?

Photographs

Photographs are common in our lives. We collect photographs of friends and family, and we see them daily in magazines and newspapers, as well as on Web sites, billboards, and posters. Because photographs are filled with details, a single photograph can replace hundreds or even thousands of words. Imagine how difficult it would be to describe your best friend's physical appearance to a stranger using words alone, without a photograph. On the other hand, a photograph could not give your reader a detailed view of your friend's personality; for those characteristics, words are needed.

Consider two well-known photographs of Abraham Lincoln. The first photo (Figure 18.12) portrays Lincoln with his son Tad. The second photograph (Figure 18.13) portrays Lincoln with Allan Pinkerton, who developed the federal Secret Service and who headed the Union spying operations, and Major General John A. McClernand. A writer could use either photograph to illustrate what Lincoln's life was like during the Civil War years, which corresponded with his years in the White House. The photograph that shows Lincoln reading

FIGURE 18.12 Abraham Lincoln with His Son Tad *Source:* Library of Congress

FIGURE 18.13 Lincoln with Allan Pinkerton (left) and Major General John A. McClernand *Source:* Library of Congress

to his son gives readers a sense of his personal life, specifically his closeness to his sons. It does not tell the whole story, however, including his love for Tad and his other two children—Willie and Robert—and his heartbreak when his favorite child, Willie, died from typhoid fever in 1862, at the age of eleven. These are details that a writer would include in the text. Similarly, the photograph of Lincoln with Pinkerton and McClernand does not give a complete picture of his working relationship with them; for that, words are needed.

WRITING ACTIVITY

Considering Photos

With your classmates, prepare a list of six well-known places, people, or objects—for example, the Alamo, Martin Luther King, Jr., a castle. Bring one photograph of each place, person, or object to class. Compare and contrast your photos with those that other students have brought by responding to the following questions:

- What does each photograph reveal about its subject? What does each photograph leave out?
- What does each photograph reveal about the classmate who selected it?
- What does each photograph reveal about the person who took it?
- How could you use each photograph in a piece of writing?
- What purposes could each photograph have in a given type of writing? For example, if you were writing a paper about Lincoln for a history course, why might you include the photo of him reading to his son as opposed to the photo on the battlefield with Pinkerton and McClernand?

USING PHOTOGRAPHS EFFECTIVELY IN YOUR WRITING

With the advent of inexpensive digital photography, it is easy to store, retrieve, manipulate, and send photographs. Although it is easy to integrate digital photographs into your documents, note that low-resolution photos are grainy when printed on paper. *Resolution* refers to the number of pixels (or dots) in the image. High-resolution photos have more pixels per inch than low-resolution photos. The following table gives the recommended resolutions (300 dots per inch) for several photograph sizes:

Size of Photo	Recommended Resolution for Printed Photograph
2" × 2"	600 × 600 pixels
2" × 3"	600 × 900 pixels
4" × 6"	1200 × 1800 pixels
5" × 7"	1500 × 2100 pixels

In your written texts, you may use photographs that have been produced by others if you give proper credit to the source of the photograph. If you are publishing the photograph on a Web site or in some other print or electronic medium, you will need to obtain permission to use it from the copyright holder unless it is in the public domain. (If a photograph is in the **public domain,** no one owns the copyright for the image, and you may use it without obtaining permission.)

To decide when and how to use photographs in your writing, consider the following questions:

- What kind of photograph will best support my purpose?
- What impact will a photograph have on my text?
- How will my audience respond to each of the photographs that I am considering?
- Where might I place the photograph in my text? Why?
- Do I need permission to use a particular photograph?
- How might I ethically manipulate the photograph to use in my text? For example, can I cut out, or "crop," part of the photograph that includes extraneous material?
- If the photograph is an electronic document, is the resolution high enough for use in a print document?
- Will the technology that is available to me accurately reproduce the photograph?

Drawings

Like photographs, **drawings** enable readers to visualize a subject. Drawings are common in technical and scientific writing because writers in those fields frequently need to give readers detailed descriptions of objects, many of which are so small (atoms or strands of DNA) or so far away (stars in other galaxies) that it is difficult to see and photograph them. You may also need to illustrate something that you witnessed in a split second or something that you have seen only in your imagination. Some phenomena, such as black holes, are impossible to view altogether. Drawings, however, can show readers scientific and technical objects and other phenomena that cannot be photographed. Consider the drawing of a cell nucleus in Figure 18.14 on page 816. Notice how this drawing of a cell nucleus includes **labels,** words that name its parts. What is missing from this drawing, however, is an explanation of the functions of the nucleus and its many parts. Only words can provide that information, and only writers can provide those words. In other words, the visual and verbal elements in a text need to complement and supplement each other.

WRITING ACTIVITY

Considering Drawings

Find an example of a drawing in one of your textbooks, in a newspaper, in a magazine, or on a Web site. Discuss how successfully the text and drawing you have found work together to achieve the writer's purpose.

FIGURE 18.14
A Drawing of a Cell Nucleus

Source: Spector Lab

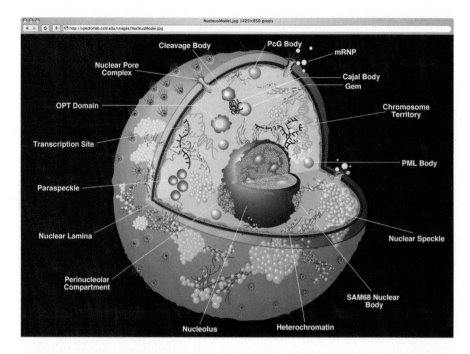

USING DRAWINGS EFFECTIVELY IN YOUR TEXTS

You can produce a drawing by hand. If you have access to a scanner, you can then scan your finished drawing, generating a computer file. Alternately, a drawing program allows you to generate a digital file directly on your computer. If you pick up a drawing from a source for use in your paper, you will need to give proper credit to that source. If you are publishing the drawing, you will need to obtain permission to use it.

To use drawings effectively in your texts, consider the following questions:

- What in my text could I illustrate with a drawing?
- How could a drawing meet the needs of my audience?
- How would a drawing support the purpose of my text?
- Can I use an existing drawing, or do I need to construct one?
- Do I need permission to use an existing drawing?
- Do I have access to software that I can use to construct the drawing? Or should I make the drawing by hand and scan it?

Diagrams

Diagrams are drawings that illustrate and explain the arrangement of and relationships among parts of a system. Venn diagrams, for example, consist of circles representing relationships among sets. Consider the Venn diagram

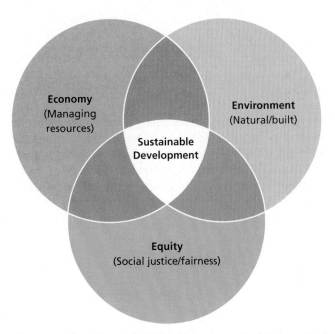

FIGURE 18.15   A Venn Diagram Illustrating Sustainable Development

Source: Manchester Development Education Project

shown in Figure 18.15, which illustrates how sustainable development depends on relationships among the environment, the economy, and equity. Of course, this diagram by itself does not explain the exact nature of these relationships. To do that, a writer needs to define each of the terms in the diagram—*environment, economy, equity*—and then explain how they interact to form sustainable development.

USING DIAGRAMS EFFECTIVELY IN YOUR WRITING

As with drawings, you can either construct a diagram by hand and scan it or use a drawing program. If you use a diagram from a source in your paper, you will need to give proper credit to that source. If you are publishing the diagram, you will need to obtain permission to use it.

To use diagrams effectively in your writing, consider the following questions:

- What in my text could I illustrate with a diagram?
- What effect will the diagram have on my readers?
- How would a diagram support my purpose?
- Can I use an existing diagram, or do I need to construct one?
- Do I need permission to use an existing diagram?
- Do I have access to software that I can use to construct the diagram? Or should I construct the diagram by hand and scan it?

Maps

Cartographers use **maps** to record and show where countries, cities, streets, buildings, colleges, lakes, rivers, and mountains are located in the world or in a particular part of it. Of course, consumers of maps use them to find these places. We use printed or downloaded maps to drive from one location to another. On the evening news we see maps showing where events take place and what kind of weather is occurring in neighboring states and countries. We even use maps to help us visualize fictional places such as the territories described in the *Lord of the Rings* trilogy (Figure 18.16).

Many different academic disciplines use maps. Anthropologists use maps to illustrate where species have lived, as in the map in Figure 18.17, which shows the range of the Neanderthals—an extinct species of human—in Europe.

WRITING ACTIVITY

Analyzing Maps

Choose one of the two maps in Figures 18.16 and 18.17 and respond to the following questions:

- What is the purpose of this map?
- What additional information would make the map more useful?
- What would a writer need to explain to readers within the text so that they could use the map effectively?
- How does the map adhere to the principles of proximity and contrast (see pp. 793–97)?
- How might the captions for the maps be revised to be more informative?

USING MAPS EFFECTIVELY IN YOUR TEXTS

In most cases, you will need to use maps from other sources, giving credit and obtaining permission to use them if necessary. If you produce your own map, you can either draw the map by hand and scan it or use a drawing program.

To use maps effectively in your texts, consider the following questions:

- What information could a map offer to my audience?
- If there is an existing map that will serve my purpose, do I need permission to use it?
- If I need to draw my own map, what tools do I need?
- What data do I need to create the map?
- What information do I need to include in the caption for the map?
- Do I have the technology available to present the map effectively?

FIGURE 18.16   A Map from the *Lord of the Rings* Trilogy
Source: New Line/Saul Zaentz/Wing Nut/The Kobal Collection

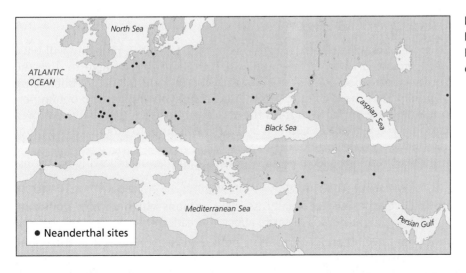

FIGURE 18.17 Neanderthal Range Map   *Source:* National Geographic Society

FIGURE 18.18
Cartoon
Reprinted by
permission of
Randy Glasbergen

GLASBERGEN

"My presentation lacks power and it has no point.
I assumed the software would take care of that!"

Cartoons

To find evidence of how much people enjoy cartoons, you need only walk the halls of any office building on your campus. You will notice that people display cartoons on their office doors, cubicle walls, and bulletin boards. Cartoons make humorous—and sometimes poignant—observations about people and events. Consider the cartoon in Figure 18.18, for example.

This cartoon offers a humorous perspective on a fairly serious topic: Because we have come to rely so much on technology in our daily lives, we sometimes expect that the technology can do more than it is capable of doing. One feature of most cartoons is that their visual and verbal elements complement each other. The visual part of the cartoon gives the topic a human or human-like face, and the verbal part offers a specific comment.

USING CARTOONS EFFECTIVELY IN YOUR TEXTS

In most cases, when you use cartoons in your text, they probably will have been produced by other people. Make sure that you are able to give the source information for any cartoon that you include. If you are publishing your paper on the Web or in another medium, you will need to obtain permission to use the cartoon from the copyright holder. If you draw your own cartoon, you will need to draw it by hand and scan it to produce a computer file that you can incorporate into your text.

To use cartoons effectively in your texts, consider the following questions:

- How will a cartoon support my purpose?
- Given that readers usually associate cartoons with humor and/or satire, how might humor or satire affect my readers?
- Do I need permission to use a published cartoon, or is it in the public domain?

Using Visuals Rhetorically

As you consider using the visuals we have covered in this chapter, you need to think about using them rhetorically to achieve some specific purpose with a specific audience.

Considering Your Audience

Readers are more likely to expect visuals in some genres than in others. Lab reports, for example, commonly include tables and graphs. This principle applies to any visuals that you plan to use in your writing as much as to the words that you write. As you consider using a particular visual, ask yourself the following questions:

- Does my audience need this visual, or is it showing something that my readers already know very well? What information might a visual add?
- How will this audience respond to this visual? How do I know what their response will be?
- What other visual might they respond to more favorably?
- Will this audience understand the subtleties of this visual?
- How do I need to explain this visual for this particular audience?

Considering Your Purpose

As we have seen throughout Parts 2 and 3 of this book, you will have a general purpose for any writing project—to record and share experiences, to explore, to inform, to analyze, to convince or persuade, to evaluate, to explain causes and effects, to solve problems, or to analyze creative works. To the extent possible, every section, paragraph, and sentence of your paper should contribute to that purpose. Any phrase, clause, sentence, paragraph, or section of your paper that does not support your purpose needs to be revised or deleted. The same principle applies to any visual that you are considering. Diagrams, for example, most often have an informative purpose. A cartoon, by contrast, is almost always humorous but often makes a statement. The cartoon on page 820, for example, plays with the name of the Microsoft product *PowerPoint*, but also makes the statement that software cannot determine the message (point) a writer wants to make. Photographs are often used to make the rhetorical appeal of *pathos*, as they can create an emotional response in the reader. Figure 18.19 on page 822, for example, is a photograph from the Web page for Feed the Children, a well-known charitable organization.

Before using any visual, you should ask yourself these questions:

- How will this visual support my purpose?
- How might this visual detract from my purpose?
- Why is this visual necessary?
- What other visual or visuals might support my purpose more effectively?

FIGURE 18.19   A Photograph from the Web Page for Feed the Children, a Charitable Organization *Source:* Feed the Children

 ## Using Visuals Responsibly

Just as you need to consider the purpose of using any visual, you also need to consider how using visuals responsibly will enhance your credibility as a writer.

Permissions

Whenever you plan to use a visual, you need to make certain that you have permission to use that visual. If you have constructed a table, graph, or chart from data that you have gathered, then permission is not needed. If you use a visual prepared by someone else, or use data from a source to produce a visual, you should always give credit to your source, even if the visual or data are from a government source and/or are in the public domain (that is, outside of copyright and available to anyone who wants to use it). For most academic papers, it is usually not necessary to request permission to use a visual. If your writing will be made available to an audience beyond your classroom, however, you will need to ask for permission to use any visual from a source that you include. Some visuals that you find on the Web are in public domain, but if you are in doubt about a particular visual, contact the Web manager of the site where you found it to ask what permissions are required.

The subjects of photographs have certain rights as well. If you take a photograph of a friend, you need to ask your friend for permission to use it if your project will have an audience beyond the two of you. If your friend does not want the photo used in a course paper or on a Web site, you are ethically and legally obligated to honor those wishes. To be certain that there is no misunderstanding, ask your friend to sign an agreement granting you permission to use the photo for clearly specified purposes. If you later want to use the photo for other purposes, ask your friend to sign another agreement. You should never put undue pressure on someone to sign such an agreement.

Distortions

Just as you should not distort quoted or paraphrased material (see Chapter 20), you should also be careful not to distort the content and the physical properties of any visuals you include in your paper. In Chapter 17, for instance, we show a fabricated photo of Jane Fonda and John Kerry on stage together—a fake photo that circulated and caused controversy when Kerry was running for the presidency in 2004 (pp. 787–88). A related example also appeared in the same presidential campaign, with charges that someone altered military records to misrepresent part of George W. Bush's service in the Air National Guard. Sometimes the data in charts and graphs is misrepresented—consider, for example, Figure 18.20, which shows the pass rates for students in English 101. Clearly, the pass rate improved by year 3 and has remained fairly stable since then. *If* this chart maker wanted to show a dramatic improvement in the pass rate, then it makes sense to use a "scale" that runs from 75% to 100%. On the other hand, a full scale (from 0 to 100%) makes the improvement in pass rates much less obvious and dramatic, as shown in Figure 18.21.

Edward R. Tufte has written several books on the subject of displaying visual information, including *The Visual Display of Quantitative Information,* which is considered to be the classic in this field. Tufte's books include not

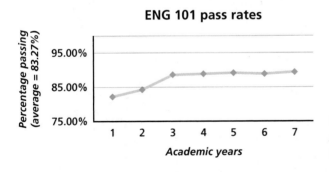

FIGURE 18.20
A Chart That Distorts
Information

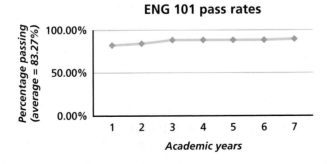

FIGURE 18.21
A Chart That Presents
the Same Information
Honestly

only warnings on how visuals can impart *inaccurate* information, but also guidelines for designing and presenting effective—and honest—visuals.

There may be times, however, when some forms of distortion can be helpful and ethical. For instance, consider the two maps shown in Figure 18.22. The first one shows the forty-eight contiguous states as they typically appear on a map. Such maps show the relative sizes—measured in square miles—of the states. The second map, on the other hand, is designed to show the distribution of wire-service news stories about certain cities and states. Notice that New York and Washington, DC, get lots of attention in wire-service news stories. This deliberately distorted image helps to make a serious point about the news.

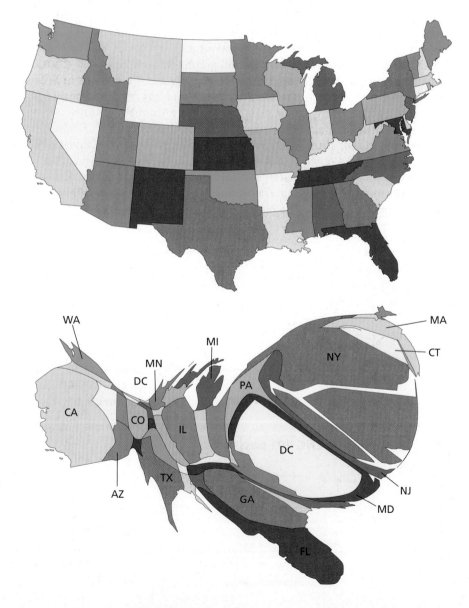

FIGURE 18.22
A Regular Map of the United States and a Distorted Map That Illustrates a Point about News

Source: Maps by M.E.J. Newman and M.T. Gastner

PART **SIX**

6

Using Research for Informed Communication

Finding and Evaluating Information from Sources and the Field

To older generations, **research** meant searching through actual library stacks. Because of the almost instant access to a wealth of sources that technology makes possible, however, finding information today may appear to be much easier than it was in the past, but the reality is that it is simply different. While you can still find books and print journals on library shelves, and they are still useful resources, print indexes such as the *Reader's Guide to Periodical Literature* are increasingly a thing of the past. Today researchers often start a project with a search of the library's online catalog and a database such as *Academic Search Premiere* or a similar subscription service, or they may start with a search of the World Wide Web using www.google.com or some other search engine before moving on to other types of sources. The speed with which such electronic resources provide us with mountains of information gives the appearance of ease. But this appearance is deceptive.

Before the advent of electronic sources, researchers usually assumed that they could generally rely on the accuracy of the printed texts found in college or university libraries. While those sources still exist, of course, anyone can now publish anything on the World Wide Web or more easily self-publish content as a book. So much information is available on the Internet that it is vital to focus your search as carefully as possible so that you turn up only the most relevant sources. It is also more critical than ever for researchers to learn effective ways not just to locate useful information, but also to evaluate the quality of what they do find.

Finally, researchers still go "out into the field" to conduct other kinds of research. In this kind of hands-on investigation, researchers gather information through observation and experimentation as well as, when working with humans, interviews, and surveys.

Conducting Effective Research: An Example

You already have plenty of experience in conducting research. Have you ever determined a classmate's opinion of an author or a band and tried to use it to influence a friend to read that author's book or buy a ticket to see that band? If so, you were using the results of a type of *field research* called *interviewing* as evidence. Your interview was undoubtedly informal—you probably conducted it over the telephone or via e-mail—but the result was the same as it would have been had you conducted a formal interview: You relied on an opinion given to you by another person to try to influence someone else.

For more on field research, see pages 861–69.

The research that you do for any writing task—whether for a college class, in a letter to a friend, or for a report to your supervisor—is a rhetorical act. That is, you conduct research for a specific purpose, with a particular audience in mind, in a specific writing situation. Consider how you might approach the following assignment for a psychology class:

Respond to this question: Why do adolescent males (and sometimes females) change their behavior when they join a gang? Based on your own research, write a 3- to 4-page paper that provides compelling reasons for this behavior, providing specific evidence to support your position.

This assignment is fairly straightforward: Your purpose is to fulfill this assignment, and your audience is your psychology professor. The assignment even provides you with a **research question:** Why do adolescent males (and sometimes females) change their behavior when they join gangs? Your answer to this question will form the thesis of your research paper. But where will you find the evidence that will help you decide on your answer to this question—your thesis—and support that thesis? How will you locate it? How will you be able to tell if the evidence is credible and reliable?

Sometimes your instructor will provide you with a **research question,** as in the example cited above. However, often it will be your responsibility to formulate your own research question. When you find yourself in that situation, keep these principles in mind:

- Keep the question focused. For example, "What caused the Civil War?" is a huge question. However, "Why did Confederate forces fire on Fort Sumter on April 12, 1861?" is much more manageable.

- Make sure you will be able to get good information on your question. You may be interested in the role Venezuelan oil plays in the U.S. economy, especially from the Venezuelan perspective. However, if you discover that most of the information for this topic is in Spanish and you can't read that language, you will probably not be able to go forward with this question.

- Consider whether you can find an adequate number of resources to answer your question. For example, are the people you hope to interview available and willing to speak with you? Can you really arrange to do field research at that far-off location?

Library Research

Often the first place to look when conducting research to answer a question is the reference section of your college library. There you will find sources such as general and specialized encyclopedias and dictionaries that can give you background on a given topic. For example, you might start your research for the psychology paper about gangs and adolescents by defining the word "adolescent," perhaps by looking it up in a medical dictionary:

A young person who has undergone puberty but who has not reached full maturity; a teenager.

—The American Heritage® *Stedman's Medical Dictionary*

Based on this definition, you determine that your research will focus on males and females between the ages of thirteen and nineteen. You decide to conduct a search in your online college library catalog. While you may decide to begin your search before you actually go to the library, asking the Research Librarian at your college library's Reference Desk for help is also a good idea. (Librarians are also available online in many libraries, in some cases twenty-four hours a day, seven days a week.) He or she will probably be able to point you to some reference sources that might be useful in your research project.

All college libraries have a book **catalog** of some kind—usually that catalog is online. In addition to the book catalog, your library probably subscribes to various electronic **databases** such as *Academic Search Premiere*. Databases are indexes of articles that are available in periodicals; many also provide complete texts of the articles themselves. To look for articles in popular or trade magazines, for instance, you would search one database, while you would use another database to find articles in academic journals, and still another library database for articles in newspapers. The TechNote below lists some popular databases.

TechNote

Here are some popular academic databases that can help you with research in different disciplines. Keep in mind that the names of academic databases do change; your reference librarian can help you find a database that will be useful for your particular project.

Academic Search Premier: A valuable resource that provides the full-text articles for more than 8,000 scholarly publications.

ERIC: A popular education database with articles going back to 1966. It also provides access to over 100,000 full-text documents.

General Science Index: A helpful index for science students, especially for introductory courses.

Humanities Index: An index that lists articles from publications in the humanities

disciplines, including modern languages and literature, history, and philosophy.

JSTOR: An electronic archive of scholarly journals in different disciplines.

LexisNexis Academic: An online service that offers full-text articles from over 6,000 newspapers and other publications.

ProQuest: A resource that offers access to journals and other publications, including the full texts of many articles, going back to 1996. It also offers information on sources going back to 1986 and historical sources that date to the nineteenth century, including a Historical Newspapers database.

Social Science Index: An index that lists articles from publications in the social sciences, including economics, psychology, political science, and sociology.

SEARCHING A LIBRARY CATALOG

For any electronic search, you need to come up with an appropriate word or phrase, or **keyword,** that will be found in the kind of source you are seeking. To find useful keywords for a search of your library's catalog, it is often a good idea to start by consulting the *Library of Congress Subject Headings* (LCSH), a book that lists subject headings in use in most library systems. It will tell you how subject areas are categorized in the library and will therefore help you come up with search terms that will turn up books on your subject.

However, a search using the main terms in your paper assignment, "adolescent gang behavior," produces only one book, as shown in Figure 19.1. You decide to broaden the phrase to "gang behavior," which leads you to four books in your college library, as shown in Figure 19.2 on page 832.

Note that the search term "gang behavior" is just one of a range of possibilities. It is often useful to use a number of search terms because that will provide you with a range of sources to choose from. Many of the titles your search turns up seem to have possibilities in terms of your research. You decide to look at them a little more closely. You pull up more information on the first entry and note that it includes a number of references that might be useful to your research (Figure 19.3 on p. 833).

Here is a research hint: Whenever you find a book on your research subject in your college library, spend a few minutes examining the *other* texts that surround the one you just located. Books about the same topic are

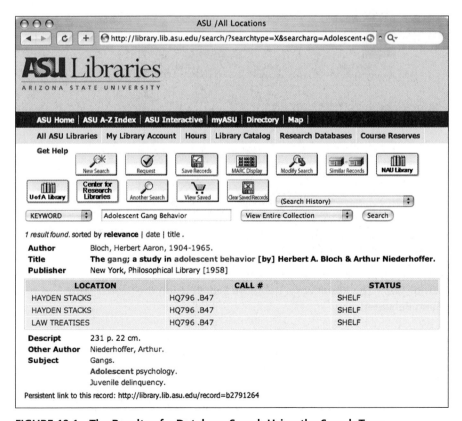

FIGURE 19.1   The Results of a Database Search Using the Search Term "Adolescent Gang Behavior"   Reprinted by permission of the Arizona State University Libraries

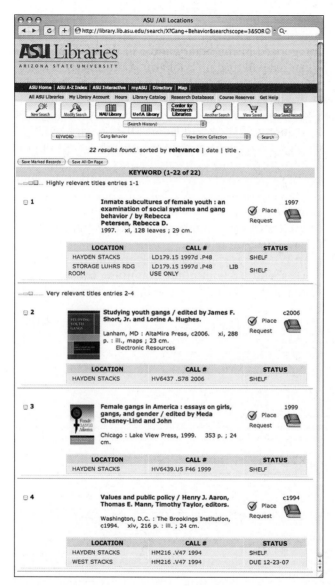

**FIGURE 19.2 The Results of a Database Search Using the Search Term
"Gang Behavior"**

shelved together, so once you find one book on the topic you are researching, many others will be nearby. Because you are standing right there, it is
easy for you to conduct further library research.

SEARCHING AN ONLINE DATABASE

Now that you have several books that you might want to examine for
information on gang behavior, you should also search one or more of the

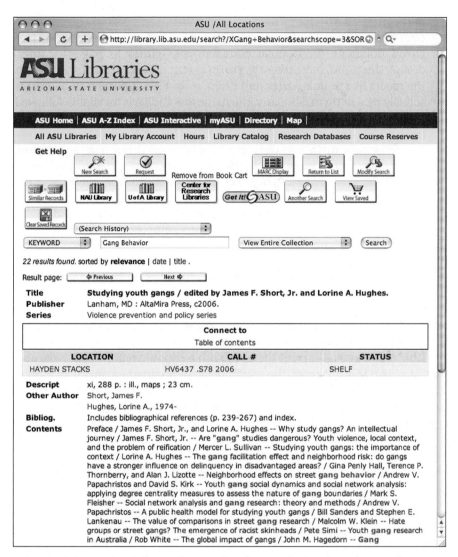

FIGURE 19.3   Further Information on the First Book Listed on the Results Page, Using the Search Term "Gang Behavior"

databases your college's library subscribes to. A search of a typical database—in this case, *Academic Search Premier*—using the keywords "male" and "gang" might turn up abstracts (summaries) of articles like this one:

> ***GANG*** WORLD. By: Papachristos, Andrew V.. Foreign Policy, Mar/Apr2005 Issue 147, p48–55, 8p, 3c, 1bw; Abstract: The article discusses the rise of street ***gangs*** around the world. The image of a young, minority, "inner-city," ***male gang*** member is transmitted, exploited, and glamorized across the world. The increasing mobility of information via cyberspace, films, and

music makes it easy for *gangs, gang* members, and others to get information, adapt personalities, and distort *gang* behaviors. Two images of street *gangs* dominate the popular consciousness—*gangs* as posses of drug-dealing thugs and, more recently, *gangs* as terrorist organizations. Although the media like to link *gangs* and drugs, only a small portion of all *gangs* actually deal in them. Similarly, the name Jose Padilla is inevitably followed by two epithets—al Qaeda terror suspect and street *gang* member. The link between the two is extremely misleading. One of the most urgent challenges for policymakers is distinguishing between the average street *gang* and groups that operate as criminal networks. Globalization and street *gangs* exist in a paradox: *Gangs* are a global phenomenon not because the groups themselves have become transnational organizations, but because of the recent hypermobility of *gang* members and their culture. Individual *gangs* flaunt their Internet savvy by posting complex Web sites, including some with password protection. As the global economy creates a growing number of disenfranchised groups, some will inevitably meet their needs in a *gang*. INSETS: Want to Know More?; When *Gangs* Go Bad.; (*AN 16195307*) 📄 **HTML Full Text**   📄 **PDF Full Text** (1.7MB)

Note that the abstract indicates that this article deals with "gang culture," so this one seems especially promising (and because the full text of the article is available online, you can print the essay with a click of your mouse). Note also that *Academic Search Premier*, the search database we used for this search, may not be available in all libraries. We use it here to illustrate a possible search database; your college or university will provide a similar search database.

Another online database that many colleges offer their students is *Lexis-Nexis*, which indexes a range of newspapers, other periodicals, and a wide range of other kinds of documents. Figure 19.4 shows the first part of a search using the keyword "adolescent gangs," a search term that focuses on both the subject of gangs and the youth involved in those activities.

Several of the articles listed by *LexisNexis* appear to be potentially useful. Since they are available as full-text articles, you can click on the title and immediately check them for relevance.

Research on the World Wide Web

You continue your search on the **World Wide Web,** which is the largest part of the global network of computers known as the **Internet.** The Web is hyperlinked, which means that one useful site will often provide you with links to many more.

If you have conducted Web searches, you probably quickly learned that different **search engines,** software programs that find sites on the Web, locate different information—that the search engine Google (www.google .com), for example, will give you different results from what does Yahoo! (www.yahoo.com), and both return somewhat different lists of sites for a given keyword than would be provided by a search conducted using AltaVista

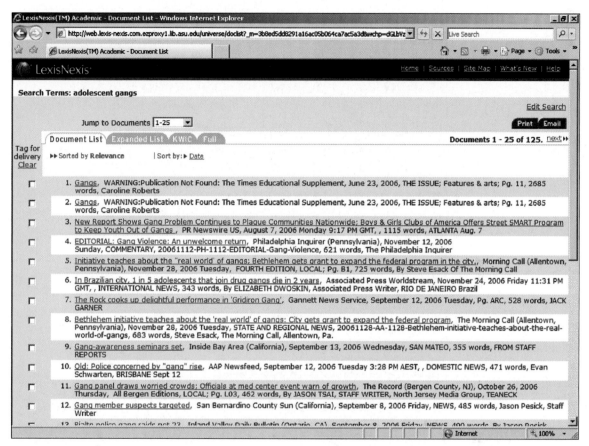

FIGURE 19.4   A Search of the LexisNexis Database Using the Search Term "Adolescent Gangs"

LexisNexis and *Knowledge Burst* logo are registered trademarks of Reed Elsevier Properties Inc. Used with permission of *LexisNexis*

(www.AltaVista.com). You may also have used a "meta-search" engine such as Dogpile (www.dogpile.com), which searches *other* search engines, so the results you retrieve are from a range of searches. Usually, it is a good idea to use several different search engines.

A search of the Web using Google, one of the most commonly used search engines, and the keywords "gang behavior," for example, turns up over 1,470,000 hits, as shown in Figure 19.5 on page 836.

Clearly, this result provides an unmanageable number of choices. The best way to limit the number of hits that a search engine returns is to narrow what the search engine is looking for. You can do this easily on Google by enclosing multiple keywords within quotation marks so that the search engine looks for them when they appear together as a phrase. (To see how to narrow search terms on another search engine, consult the Help screens for that engine.) Simply by enclosing the search term "Gang Behavior" in quotation marks, you can limit the result to 46,700 hits, for example. This helps, but 46,700 options

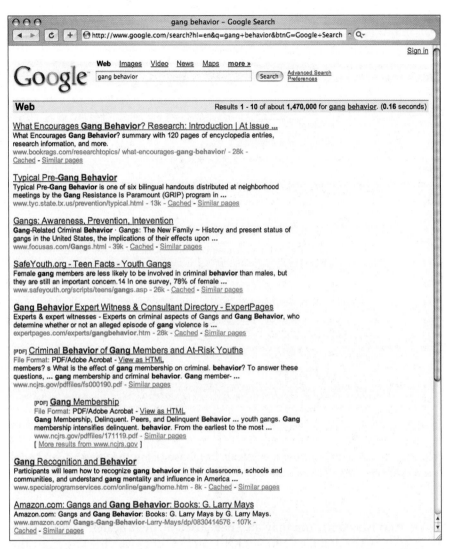

FIGURE 19.5   The Result of a Search Using the Google Search Engine and the Keywords "Gang Behavior"   Reprinted by permission of Google Brand Features

are still far too many. As a next step, you might qualify the search even more. If you are looking for information about female gangs, for example, you might try searching with the keywords "gang behavior" + "female." Doing so gives you a list of 13,000 hits. While that's still better, it's not really good enough. You can then modify the search even further by trying this combination of keywords: "gang behavior" + "adolescent female." This time the response, shown in Figure 19.6, is only twenty-four hits, a manageable number. By closely defining your search terms and using them in combination, you can narrow your search and come up with the best possible online sources. Most

FIGURE 19.6 The Result of a Search Using the Google Search Engine and the Keywords "Gang Behavior" + "Adolescent Female"

search engines such as Google also have an advanced search screen that can help you narrow your search.

One other option you might consider using if you are working on an academic paper is Google Scholar, which searches only scholarly Web sites. Searching Google Scholar using the keywords "gang behavior" + "adolescent female" gives you the result shown in Figure 19.7 on page 838.

You can also search for images on the World Wide Web. Using an image search on Google, for example, you may find a photo of gang activity such as the one shown in Figure 19.8 on page 839, which you can use to illustrate your paper.

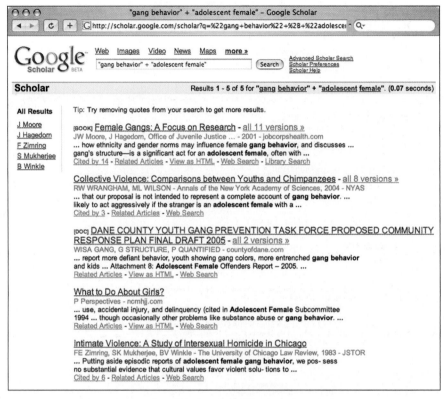

FIGURE 19.7   The Result of a Search Using the Google Scholar Search Engine and the Keywords "Gang Behavior" + "Adolescent Female"

WRITING ACTIVITY

Develop a List of Questions and a Research Plan

For one of your current writing projects, develop a list of intriguing research questions. These are questions that require complex answers, not just facts. After each question, indicate where you would go to find answers (for example, the library) and what you would do there (for example, search a database for newspaper articles on your topic).

Your instructor may ask you to share your lists and research plans with several of your classmates.

FIGURE 19.8   A Photograph of Gang Graffiti Located Using the Google Search Engine

Selecting Sources

Whenever you do research you will encounter a wide range of sources. You have to determine what sources will be useful to you for your particular writing situation. We will outline a number of sources here, and then discuss how you might *evaluate* the various kinds of information you locate.

The kind(s) of sources that you select depend on what you are trying to learn. You would not, for example, expect to find information in books on events that took place less than a year ago. For that kind of information, you would need to look for publications that publish more current information.

Each type of source has advantages and disadvantages, so it is usually best to use a variety of sources.

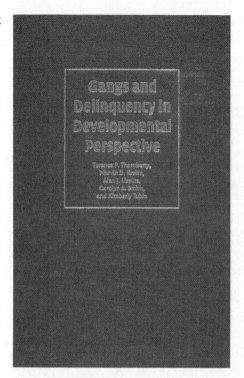

FIGURE 19.9   A Book from Cambridge University Press

Books

Books such as the one shown in Figure 19.9 have historically been a researcher's first choice for much academic research because what you learn from them has almost always been well-researched and the statistical information validated. However, even books have to be subjected to more intensive questioning these days, as it is now relatively easy for just about anyone to publish a book. Books in an academic library, however, have been carefully evaluated by librarians and are usually reputable. One disadvantage of the research you will find in a printed book is that it often takes several years to write, review, and publish a book—so the information often is not as current as that in newspapers, academic journals, the Internet, and other media.

Academic Journals

Academic essays appear in **journals** such as the *American Journal of Psychiatry*, shown in Figure 19.10. Journals are most often sponsored by universities. Because journals are nonprofit, many do not carry advertisements. Essays in most academic journals are written by scholars in the field and are "peer reviewed," which means that other scholars have read, commented on, and made a judgment about the article's validity and usefulness. Journal articles are usually well-researched. Also, academic essays most often come with a

FIGURE 19.10 A Scholarly Journal

"works cited" or "references" page, which lists all of the sources the writer used in his or her essay. Often, these lists are gold mines of information for you, as they point to useful sources about the topic you are working on.

For example, your library search focusing on adolescent males and females and gangs might turn up this essay, published in the *American Journal of Psychiatry:* "What Happens to 'Bad' Girls? A Review of the Adult Outcomes of Antisocial Adolescent Girls" by Kathleen A. Pajer, M.D., M.P.H. In addition to the essay, which might contain useful information, you find a "works cited" section with eighty-three entries, references to other journal articles and books that Dr. Pajer used in her text. These will lead you to more information about teenage gangs.

Newspapers

Newspapers, especially those with a national focus such as the *New York Times,* the *Washington Post,* the *Los Angeles Times,* and the *Wall Street Journal,* are considered reliable sources. Often, local papers will get their information from national sources. They always acknowledge when they do—so you can tell where their information comes from. Local newspapers are a useful source for just what you might expect: local news and information.

A *LexisNexis* search for newspaper articles on a topic will provide you with recent information. You do need to remember, however, that while newspapers are very current sources, because they are following stories in progress, sometimes the information they provide may change as more complete information on a story becomes available.

Popular Magazines

Magazines, especially newsmagazines such as *Time* and *Newsweek*, have a broad perspective on national issues and often provide useful background and historical information. Most magazines now have online versions. Many make the contents of the print magazine available online, either to anyone who visits the site or to registered users. Often the magazine will offer additional content online, as well as forums for readers to respond to articles and to one another.

A search at Time.com, for example, turns up possible sources for your paper on gangs, as shown in Figure 19.12.

FIGURE 19.11
A Popular Magazine

FIGURE 19.12   A Search of the Time.com Web Site Using the Keyword "Gangs"
Copyright © 2007 Time Inc. Reprinted by permission

Trade or Commercial Magazines

Trade or commercial/professional magazines have a specific audience, which consists of the members of a group with a common interest or profession. Figure 19.13 on page 844, for example, is a magazine for business travelers. If the magazine is published for a professional organization, a portion of the members' dues usually pays for the magazine. Other magazines are for-profit publications that serve the industry as a whole. These publications often have a point of view and are written specifically for their target audience. They also can provide lots of information from an insider's perspective, so you may need to be very familiar with the field to really understand the context.

FIGURE 19.13　A Commercial Magazine

Public Affairs Magazines

Magazines that focus on public affairs, such as *Harpers*, *Public Affairs*, or *Foreign Affairs*, shown in Figure 19.14, generally publish articles on large national issues, so they are useful sources for papers about these issues. Their essays are usually thoughtfully researched and documented.

Specialty Magazines

Magazines about travel, different regions of the country, cooking, and other specialized topics are often useful if you are searching for the kinds of information they provide. Examples include *Alaska*, *Southern Living*, and *Arizona Highways*, shown in figure 19.15. Others, like *Business Week*, cater to a specific field and often have useful statistics and other types of information related to that field.

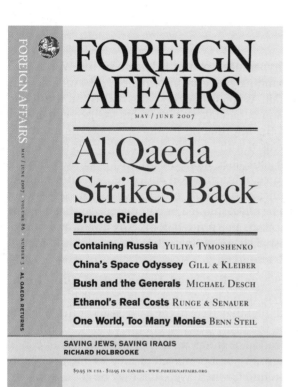

FIGURE 19.14 A Public Affairs Magazine

FIGURE 19.15 A Specialty Magazine

The Internet

The Internet, especially the hyperlinked part of it known as the World Wide Web, offers a huge and expanding range of information, all available very quickly and often in great detail. As you will see on pages 850–61, in the discussion of evaluating sources, it sometimes takes a bit of work to figure out exactly who controls a Web site and the information it presents, so information you obtain from the Web must be used with caution, depending on its source.

It is extremely difficult to generalize about the Internet because it remains a dynamic, ever-evolving source of information and, often, misinformation. What may seem like a significant new type of resource as this sentence is being written may appear to be old-fashioned or completely outdated by the time this sentence actually appears in a printed book. Any attempt to categorize Internet sources is, at best, a rough estimate, but we can point to at least five different kinds of online resources.

1. **Web sites that serve as what used to be called the "home page" of an organization.** Most of these are now much more complex and sophisticated than they were in the early years of the Web, but they may very well be the first place you choose to look for information about any organization or group, no matter whether it is an educational institution, a business, or a nonprofit agency. While the quality of the information you find on these Web sites may be good, you need to remember that because they are maintained by the organization itself, they tend to give a very positive view of the organization.

2. **Web sites that provide information to the general public.** Many of these Web sites are maintained by governmental agencies. Their subject matter and complexity vary depending on whether they are constructed and maintained by local municipalities, state agencies, or the federal government. In most instances the information found on these sites is very reliable. Figure 19.16, for example, is the home page for the site maintained by the Internal Revenue Service, a highly reliable source for information on the federal income tax.

3. **Online periodicals and newspapers.** As noted in the discussion of popular magazines on pages 842–43, almost every print publication now has its own online version. Some local newspapers, such as the *Daily Hampshire Gazette* (www.gazettenet.com) of Northampton, Massachusetts, which serves the Northampton/Amherst area (Figure 19.17 on p. 848), have a free news section and a section only for paid subscribers. Much of the content from each day's edition of the *New York Times* (www.nytimes.com), considered by many to be a national newspaper, is available for free online, but only to those who have registered for free. Many magazines allow online viewers to read most of their articles, while others publish snippets online and allow full access only to subscribers.

   Some academic journals such as *Kairos* (http://english.ttu.edu/Kairos/) are published only online (Figure 19.18). Like most academic

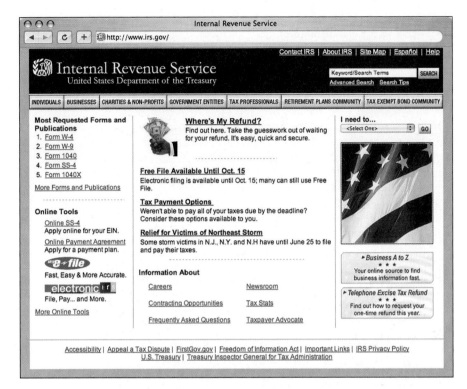

FIGURE 19.16
The Home Page for the Internal Revenue Service

journals, they are peer-reviewed and the information in them is as reliable as that found in print academic journals.

4. **Blogs.** A Weblog, or **blog,** is a kind of Web journal, usually maintained by one person who shares his or her thoughts on a given topic or set of topics and may post links to other sites on the Web as well as comments from other writers. It's sometimes difficult to determine the soundness of the information that you find in a blog. While some blogs are maintained by experts in a particular field, others are written by people who want to spread their own point of view on anything from politics to what kind of software is better and most everything in between. Use them with caution. Figure 19.19 on page 850 is an example of a blog on dieting.

5. ***Wikipedia.*** A collaborative online encyclopedia, *Wikipedia* is a fairly new phenomenon. All the articles on *Wikipedia* are written by volunteers, and it is possible for anyone to edit already existing articles. Though there are some safeguards to protect certain pages, it is possible that some information found on *Wikipedia* may be suspect. You may think of it as a good starting place, in much the same way that a traditional encyclopedia, whether in print or online, is a place to start for background on your research topic—but you should not rely on it for all of your information on a topic. It is always wise to look for additional sources of information beyond *Wikipedia.* You should also be cautious about citing it as a source in your academic papers. Figure 19.20 on page 851 shows the *Wikipedia* entry for "textbook."

See the information on evaluating sources on pages 850–61.

For more about Wikipedia, see "Growing Wikipedia Revises Its 'Anyone Can Edit' Policy" by Katie Hafner, in Chapter 6.

FIGURE 19.17   The Home Page for the *Daily Hampshire Gazette*

Copyright GazetteNET.com. Reprinted by permission of *Daily Hampshire Gazette*

WRITING ACTIVITY

Planning Your Research

For a college class in which you have been asked to conduct research on a particular topic, select a potential topic and then list the sources you might look at and what you might expect to find in them. Also plan when and where you will conduct your research. Your plan might look like this:

Where I plan to look	What I hope to find	When and where I'll do the work
Electronic book catalog	Background information and statistics	College library; Saturday afternoon
National newspapers	Current information	Newspaper index, college library; also Saturday afternoon

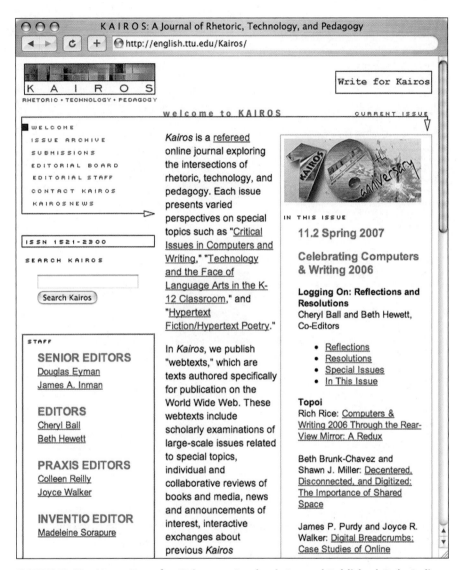

FIGURE 19.18 Home Page for *Kairos,* an Academic Journal Published Only Online

Reprinted by permission of *Kairos*

**FIGURE 19.19
A Page from
*Diet Blog***

Reprinted by permission
of Jim Foster, Editor, www.
diet-blog.com

Evaluating Your Sources: Asking the Reporter's Questions

Finding sources is only the beginning of your task in conducting research;
you also need to evaluate the information you locate. How do you determine
that a source is credible and accurate? Usually, asking the questions a reporter
asks when he or she is working on a story will help you.

Who Is the Author?

Who is the author of the research? What can you learn about that author? If
the work is an essay or an entire book, you may be able to find biographical
information about the author or authors. For example, let's say you were

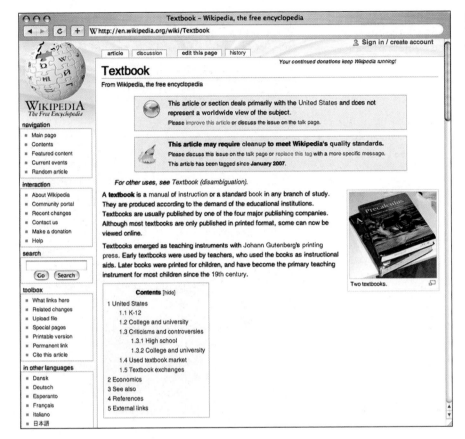

FIGURE 19.20
The *Wikipedia* Entry for "Textbook"

conducting research on gangs and found this book in your college library: *Teen Gangs: A Global View*, edited by Maureen P. Duffy and Scott Edward Gillig (Figure 19.21 on p. 852). This book was published by Greenwood Press. Here is what the publisher says about the two editors in its online catalog:

MAUREEN P. DUFFY is Associate Professor and Chair of the Counseling Department at Barry University, Miami Shores, Florida.

SCOTT EDWARD GILLIG is Professor and Coordinator of the mental health counseling specialization at Barry University.

Both editors are university professors, which means the book most likely contains thoroughly researched and well-documented articles by respected authors. In fact, each of the editors has written one chapter of the book, and Duffy has also written the introduction. If you examine Greenwood's catalog or Web site, you will see that it specializes in nonfiction books primarily for schools—middle school through college level—and that it also publishes library reference titles. So you know the editors are both professors and the book is not self-published, and although you cannot tell much about the

FIGURE 19.21
A Scholarly Book on the Subject of Gangs

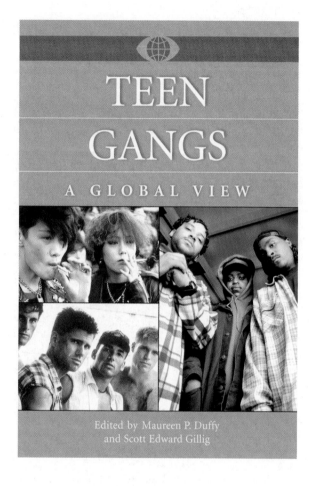

TEEN

GANGS

A GLOBAL VIEW

Edited by Maureen P. Duffy
and Scott Edward Gillig

reputation of Greenwood Press from its Web site alone, all of the information you have found indicates that the articles in this text were probably written by people who are credible authorities in their field.

What Is the Text About? What Is the Quality of the Information?

To determine the answer to this question, you will need to ask the following additional questions:

- What is the focus of the printed or online text you are considering?
- How thoughtful and research-based is it?
- Does the text seem designed to sensationalize its topic, or does it take a more balanced, thoughtful approach?

You'll also want to make sure the text is relevant to your topic. It is possible to find interesting and well-researched information that may not have much to do with your topic.

For instance, in your research on why adolescent males or females change their behavior when they join gangs, suppose you visit the Web site at www.streetgangs.com. If you searched the site on March 27, 2007, you would have seen the opening page shown in Figure 19.22.

The mission statement shown in Figure 19.23 on page 854 indicates that the site appears to be controlled by an individual and has been since 1995. This does not mean the information on the site is not credible, only that you will need to consider this information about the source if you decide to use anything from this Web site. The final paragraph of the section about the history of the Web site adds this information:

> We receive dozens of email every day so forgive us if we cannot personally respond to your message, but we will do our best to answer ALL serious questions. We receive over 6 million page visits monthly so please do not email us to help you with your high school paper or to ask silly questions. Please see the *bibliography* for tips on good books to read and for articles to download, or visit the *topics* to read recent news articles. If you have a serious question about gangs visit the *billboard* where your question may have

FIGURE 19.22 Links to Information on Gangs from the Web Site Streetgangs.com

Reprinted by permission of Alex Alonso, Editor, www.Streetgangs.com

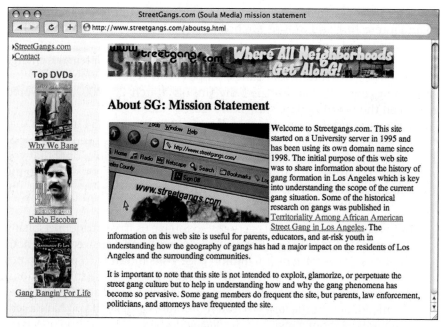

FIGURE 19.23   The Mission Statement for the Web Site Streetgangs.com

already been asked. If you would like to write an article for *Street Gangs Magazine* please follow the *submission guidelines* and forward your essay. Media requests should be made from the *contact page*.

With so much interest in street gangs, it is certainly possible that this Web site gets "over 6 million page visits monthly." How does the tone of these comments (to not ask silly questions, for example) affect how you think about this site?

At the same time, even at sites or blogs maintained by individuals (and blogs are a good example of this), you can sometimes learn valuable information and find useful links. For example, Streetgangs.com offers a "100 page bibliography" for sale, but the site includes a few sample pages to give you a sense of the information the site makes available.

When Was the Text Published or the Web Site Last Updated?

Generally, the more current the information a source provides, the more useful it is to you. In academic research, new data is generally a response to *older* data. In fact, one of the benefits of reading books and articles by university scholars is that they almost always refer to earlier research as they outline how their new research relates to it, giving you the best of both worlds—the older information as well as the latest data.

At www.streetgangs.com, there is no notice that tells you when the Web page was last updated, but in the copyright section you will find the following notice:

Copyright © Notice, Terms & Conditions
Copyright © 1995–2006, Street Gangs, Gangs in Los Angeles
P.O. Box 18238, Los Angeles CA, 90018, USA
800.249.1324
All Rights Reserved

This notice tells you that someone has worked on this Web site sometime in 2006. The page also includes a link to the biography and contact information for A. Alonso, who is evidently responsible for the site, another bit of evidence that the site is controlled by a person rather than by a group or company.

Why Was This Information Published?

What can you determine about why the information was published? What is the text's purpose? Who appears to be the target audience for this text? If you can determine to whom the text appeals, you might gain a sense of its purpose.

Of course, you cannot know for sure why an essay was published, or a book printed, or a Web site constructed, but you can make some good educated guesses:

- **Essays in academic journals** are often published to share new knowledge. This is especially true of articles in scientific journals, which publish the results of scientific research, but even in journals that focus on the humanities or on professional fields, professors publish what they have learned and concluded from their reading and thinking.

  Because articles in academic journals are peer-reviewed, other scholars in the field will get the chance to comment on and make suggestions (and criticisms) about any essay before it is published. So generally you can expect the information in journal articles to be reliable. Journals are also one of the major ways that scholars and practitioners communicate and share information within professional and scientific fields: Attorneys read law journals, physicians read medical journals, and writing teachers read journals about composition and rhetoric.

- **Academic books** provide professors with a way to distribute large amounts of information and insight to their peers, and while some make money for their author and publisher, many do not, so the profit motive is not a strong factor in publishing an academic text. Academic texts are also peer-reviewed, just as academic essays are, so other scholars in the field will have examined the information, data, and conclusions in a text prior to publication. During the publishing process, those peer reviewers will have the opportunity to contribute their ideas, criticisms, and suggestions—always with the goal of making the text the best possible. Academic texts are generally published by university presses (Harvard University Press, for instance).

- **Articles in newsmagazines and newspapers** present items in the local, national, or worldwide news. Most often, editors work hard to present the news in an unbiased manner, but most newspapers and even some magazines have editorial pages or sections.

  As with anyone else, newspaper and magazine editors and writers have their own particular viewpoints and ways of looking at what they report on—in other words, there always is *some* bias in anything that is said or written. At any particular time and place, you might be able to label newspapers and magazines according to their general tendencies. As we write this in the fall of 2007, for example, we can say with some confidence that the *New York Times* would be considered a somewhat left-leaning/liberal newspaper, but not as far left as, say, the magazine *Mother Jones*. But these ways of seeing and writing about the news vary over time, as editors and writers come and go.

  How can you, as a reader, get some sense of the biases of the newsmagazines and newspapers you read for your research? One way is to compare how the same information is presented in the different magazines or newspapers you are looking at. Reading two or more editorials on the same topic will give you some sense of how the editors of each newspaper see the world. Look for facts related to a story that appear in one publication but that do not appear in the other: What might that tell you about each publication? Consider how the same story is presented in two different publications. What photographs are included? How big is the headline? How much space is devoted to the article? Is it on the front page or on an interior page?

- **Web sites** give all kinds of information. However, not all Web sites give completely accurate and reliable information. You have to evaluate the value of a Web site just as you would any other source. You'll need to ask yourself questions like the following:

  - Who constructed the Web site?

  - What makes that person or organization credible?

  - What clues can you find within the Web site that indicate it is more or less credible? For example, what kind of sites do the links lead to?

    Knowing who hosts the Web site might help you answer these questions. A site hosted by a governmental agency is most likely very credible. A private site might not be as credible, though it might provide some very good information.

WRITING ACTIVITY

Newspaper Analysis

Most newspapers do have a particular political slant, which is often clear in their editorials but is also evident in the way various news stories are presented. If you examine the newspapers from several large cities, such differences will be readily apparent. Your college library will have copies of major newspapers such as the *New York Times* and the *Washington Post*, and all major newspapers now have online versions. Select a major story that is currently in the news and compare how three newspapers cover it. What kind of photographs have they printed about the story? What do their editorials say about it? How much "newsprint" space is devoted to the story? Where do the stories appear?

Compare what you have learned with the information that several of your classmates have gathered about coverage of the same story or another similar story.

WRITING ACTIVITY

Examine a Web Site to Determine Its Audience

Select one of the following Web sites and, in no more than two pages, outline who you think is the intended audience for the site, what you think its purpose is, and why you make that assertion. Indicate who maintains the site (if you can tell) and when it was last updated. Use examples from the site to help prove your claim about the intended audience and purpose.

> http://www.gangwar.com/dynamics.htm
> http://www.csun.edu/~hcchs006/gang.html
> http://ojjdp.ncjrs.org/pubs/reform/ch2_e.html
> http://www.gangstyle.com/

Your instructor may ask you to share your findings with several of your classmates.

Where Was the Item Published?

It is becoming more and more difficult to differentiate between library research and online research because so many traditional library resources are now located online. In addition, many libraries provide portals to online databases and other online sites. As a result, whether information resides in a physical building or is stored on a server, you will need your critical thinking skills more than ever to determine its value.

As with any research activity, your decision about where to search for information depends on what you are trying to learn. If the answer to your research question requires demographic data, you might find that all the best and most current census information you need is on different Web sites maintained by a variety of agencies of the U.S. government. Web-based research is rarely sufficient for a project of any depth, however. For example, you probably can learn more about local census trends and data from your local newspaper.

One question to ask about any publication, whether it is in print or online, is whether it is local, regional, or national. National magazines or newspapers will generally be more up to date on national and international news than local papers tend to be; however, local papers or regional magazines will generally have more and better coverage of local news.

Articles and other source materials published on the World Wide Web can appear professional and unbiased, but it is often difficult to find information that allows you to evaluate fully the credibility of a Web page. To do so, you need to determine what person, company, or organization constructed the site and stands behind it. If you learn that you are examining a personal Web site instead of one sponsored by a government agency or a university, you need to take that fact into account when judging its reliability. While organizations will often have their own agenda, of course, usually an organization can devote more resources to the construction and maintenance of a Web site than an individual can. Web suffixes generally indicate the source of a Web site:

- **.edu** indicates an educational institution (www.asu.edu, for instance, is the Web address for Arizona State University). Information you find at such a location has generally been approved by the college or university. However, many colleges and universities also provide Web space for students and faculty members, and those individuals may post information that has *not* necessarily been approved by the school. You can usually recognize such sites by the content of their Uniform Resource Locators, or URLs. For example, the URL http://www.public.asu.edu/~dhroen/ will take you to the Web site constructed and maintained by one of the authors of this text. Note the word "public" in the URL as well as the tilde (~)—these elements often appear in college or university Web addresses that are not maintained by the school.

- **.com** indicates a for-profit company (www.cnn.com is the Web address for the Cable News Network). The suffix *.com* is a shortened form of the word *commercial* and usually designates a business-oriented site.

- **.org** indicates an organization (www.pbs.org is the Web address for the Corporation for Public Broadcasting). The *.org* Web suffix is generally used for nonprofit organizations.

- **.gov** indicates some level of government (state, national, or local). The URL http://www.loc.gov/ is the Web address for the site maintained by the Library of Congress.

- **.net** These Web sites are generally used by Internet service providers (ISPs) and companies that provide Web hosting like www.concentric .net. Some commercial businesses also use the *.net* extension, but usually not as their main Web site. Some Internet service providers allow their customers to use their "net" extension, for sharing things like photographs, such as www.photo.net.

- **.biz** is most often used for small business Web sites such as www .minimus.biz, a Web site that sells travel-size products.

- **.info** is, like *.com*, an unrestricted domain. Anyone can use it. According to Network Associates, the company that assigns and allocates Web addresses, *info* is the most popular extension beyond *.com, .net*, and *.org*. An example is www.microbes.info, a portal for information on microbiology.

For more information on Web suffixes and addresses, see http://www .networksolutions.com/. Network Solutions offers a "WhoIs" search function for nearly all sites on the Web except personal ones. Conducting a "WhoIs" search will give you information about the creator of any particular Web page. This search not only tells you who "owns" the domain name, but also provides e-mail contact information. If the Web page you're looking for is not listed, then it is probably a personal page.[1]

How Accurate Is the Information in This Source?

Do you believe everything you read? Anyone who checks out in a supermarket and sees newspaper headlines about aliens and Elvis sightings understands that not all news stories that appear in print are necessarily accurate. How do you know what information to believe and what information to view with skepticism?

- One of the best ways of determining accuracy in any publication is finding out who published it. As we have noted, books published by university presses and articles published in academic journals are peer-reviewed. That means experts in the field have reviewed the manuscript before it was published. You can usually expect that large newspapers such as the *New York Times* will print the most accurate information available at the time. Over time, some information published in reliable periodicals or newspapers may change or be corrected. The publication is then likely to publish the updated information. Publications of this caliber also tend to be credible because

---

[1] Thanks to William Sherman, University of Northern Colorado, for this information.

they have a history of firing writers who knowingly publish false information.

- Another way of determining accuracy is to investigate the author's track record. You might check the author's academic credentials, for example, as we have done for authors Duffy and Gillig on page 851. Of course, it's important to make sure that the author's area of expertise is in the subject you are researching. A famous actor who writes a diet book may or may not be a credible source of information on proper nutrition.

To determine the accuracy of information on a Web site, you might consider the Web sites the site provides links to. Often, following some of the links will give you a good deal of information about the site's credibility. For example, the Web site Streetgangs.com showed these links in December of 2006:

> ➤ Gang Member receives 50 years, Dec 8, 2006
> ➤ Stopping gang activity is a noble goal, but the end doesn't always justify the means, Nov 30, 2006
> ➤ Delgadillo names U.S. prosecutor as 'gang czar', Nov 28, 2006
> ➤ Police, FBI target San Fernando Valley gang crimes, Nov 22, 2006

Links that connect to reputable newspapers or television stations would indicate that whoever is maintaining the Web site is providing readers with connections to legitimate news articles, thus adding to the credibility of the Web site. However, the links listed above lead to stories that have bylines but give little indication of what organization the writer works for. Some simply say "Times Staff." What impact do links such as these have on the way you view the information available on this site?

A WRITER'S RESPONSIBILITIES

Evaluating Web Sites

Ask yourself the following questions when evaluating the credibility of a Web site.

- Who is the author or sponsor of the site? What can you find out about the author or sponsor?
- What does the site's address tell you about it? What does the suffix that appears at the end of the address tell you about it: *edu* for educational, for example, or *com* for commercial? Is there a tilde (~) in the address, which indicates a personal site?
- What is the purpose of the site? Is the purpose to provide information? Is the site trying to sell a product or service? To persuade readers to accept a particular point of view?
- How professional is the tone, and how well designed is the site? How carefully has it been edited and proofread? How many grammatical and spelling errors are there?

- Consider the quality of the author's arguments. Does the content contain logical fallacies? How fairly does the author deal with opposing views?
- Can you find a date when the site was published or most recently updated?
- What kinds of links does the site provide? How legitimate or credible are the sites the links lead to ? Are there links to questionable sites or to sites that no longer exist?

Field Research

As we have seen, much of the time you will gather information for your research projects from books, periodicals, the World Wide Web, and other preexisting sources. At other times, you may need to gather first-hand information. Sometimes you can get the information you need by simply observing people, wildlife, or natural phenomena. At other times, the best method of gathering information from human subjects may be to ask questions of individual people or groups of people, either directly or in writing. However you do it, the act of gathering information on your own, instead of relying solely on information obtained in the library, on the Internet, or in a laboratory setting is called **field research** because, in order to obtain this information, you need to go out "into the field." The most common kinds of field research you might find yourself doing are observation, personal interviews, and surveys.

Working with Human Subjects

Much of what you may study as you conduct field research has to do with human behavior. Any time you are doing research that involves human subjects, you are expected to behave ethically and to do or say nothing that might in any way hurt your subjects. In order to ensure that researchers follow ethical practices, all academic institutions (and many private organizations) have Institutional Review Boards (IRBs). All research projects that use human subjects must be approved by your organization's IRB or its designated representative. In most colleges and universities, the IRB designates that the instructor will serve as the IRB's representative for most undergraduate classroom research projects. Special, large undergraduate projects such as senior thesis projects may need specific IRB approval. All IRBs have their own rules. Check with your instructor about your school's human subject policy.

Informed Consent

Whether you are required to submit a formal proposal to your school's IRB or simply need to work closely with your instructor, if you are going to be working with human subjects, you need to get their permission by having all of the participants in your field research—whether it is an interview, an observation, or a survey—sign an Informed Consent Form. Most institutions have templates for these forms readily available.

Observations

Sometimes, seeing really is believing: Watching and recording what you see might be the best way to get good information that will help you answer your research question. If viewing people, animals, or other phenomena over a short period of time will provide you with good information, you may choose observation as your research method. On the other hand, though a phenomenon like soil erosion may be observable, it usually takes place over too long a period of time for personal observation to be useful.

OBSERVING HUMANS

If you are writing an informative or analytical paper, you may need to observe human behavior as part of your research. To make your observations, you might station yourself at a particular place in a shopping mall, at an athletic event, or at a busy intersection and record, in detail, certain behaviors. At the shopping mall you might note how many people passing by are carrying a certain food item or a beverage that has clearly been purchased at one of the restaurants in the mall's food court. At the athletic event, you might note how many people entering the stadium or arena are wearing items that clearly mark them as supporters of one team or the other. Or you might record how many vehicles passing through an intersection near your college actually come to a complete stop at the stop sign. In each of these examples, you would need to keep track of the total number of people or vehicles passing by as well as the specific number of people or vehicles that demonstrate the particular behavior you are watching for. It is, of course, possible to make even more detailed observations. Are more men wearing items identifying their allegiance to an athletic team than women? What car models are drivers who run the stop sign driving? To make detailed observations such as these, it helps to make preparations before you start your observation by setting up categories. Once you are in the field observing and recording, you probably won't have time to develop new ones.

OBSERVING OTHER PHENOMENA

For writing projects that lend themselves to observation, see Chapters 5, 6, and 7.

You can also observe other natural and human-influenced phenomena, of course. Some researchers observe animal behavior; others watch volcanoes, tornadoes and other weather patterns, or cosmic activity. The specific nature of what you are observing will determine the tools you will need as well as the appropriate methods you will use. People who observe weather phenomena such as tornadoes or hurricanes, for example, use different instruments and methods than those who observe volcanic action.

WRITING ACTIVITY

Conduct an Observation

People often comment on how tied to technology students are. Do you think this is true? One way to test this assumption might be to sit for an hour in your student union or some other place where students from your campus gather. Watch the behavior of the students. Are students talking with one another in person, or are they using technology to, for example, communicate with one another, listen to music, or watch videos? Take notes of what you see. You might want to create some categories. Are students talking on cell phones? Are they using laptops? Are they listening to iPods? After you've watched and taken notes, write a short report on your findings.

Interviews

Because most of us are comfortable talking with other people, we often think that interviewing someone will be easy. Interviews are rarely an easy way to do meaningful research, however. Good interviews that yield useful information happen only when the interviewer prepares ahead of time. As you prepare, it's important to remember that some of the interviews you may see on television or listen to on the radio are not necessarily good examples of interviewing. The aggressive, "in your face" nature of many media interviewers is rarely suitable for the purpose of gathering information.

You can employ several strategies to prepare and conduct a successful interview:

- Be sure to call ahead to make an appointment instead of just showing up in your subject's office. A little bit of courtesy will often make your subject more comfortable and, as a result, you might obtain more information than you might otherwise have been able to get.

- Do your homework ahead of time so that you have good questions ready to ask, have anticipated the nature of the responses, and have good follow-up questions at hand. While it is impossible to predict exactly what your subject will say, being able to anticipate the nature of the interview will enable you to steer the interview in the direction in which you need it to go.

- Be prepared to take notes using either a laptop computer or paper and pencil. The best way to learn how to take notes during an interview is to practice ahead of time. Before you interview someone for an assignment, practice (using your interview questions) with a classmate or a friend.

- Consider bringing along some kind of recording device. Recording the interview not only gives you a record of what was said, it also eliminates the problem of trying to get answers to your questions down on paper while your subject continues to talk. However, if you plan to record the interview, make sure you have your subject's permission before the interview begins. Some people are willing to talk but do not wish to be recorded. They have the right to say "no" to you.

- Be polite and friendly during the interview. It is usually a good idea to follow up an interview with a thank-you note.

While your specific interview questions will depend on your topic and the person you are interviewing, you will usually want to prepare two kinds of questions: open-ended and directed. **Open-ended questions** let the person being interviewed develop his or her answers at length. You ask **directed questions** to get more specific kinds of information. As part of her research for a paper on violence in the movies, for example, Magda is interested in learning about how people actually react when they are watching violent movies. To find out, she has decided to interview the local manager of a theater chain that sometimes shows violent, R-rated movies. To prepare for the interview, Magda has come up with the following list of questions:

1. What would you consider a violent movie?
2. What specific content in a movie makes it violent?
3. Are all movies that contain scenes with (the content from the previous questions) necessarily violent? If not, why not? What's the determining factor?
4. Do you show many movies like that? If so, how many per month?
5. Why do you think people like violent movies?
6. What age groups seem to like violent movies?
7. Do audiences at violent movies behave differently from audiences at other types of movies, such as comedies?
8. Are audiences at violent movies likely to buy more at the concession stand?
9. Do audiences at violent movies leave behind more trash in the theater?
10. Are audiences at violent movies more likely to leave through an unauthorized exit?
11. Are audiences at violent movies generally noisier, rowdier?

Some of the questions in Magda's list, such as the first three, are open-ended. Others, such as questions 7–11, are more directed and may indicate the direction of her thinking as she develops her thesis.

You should always avoid what can be called "forced-choice questions," questions that presuppose only a few specific choices and force your subject to answer one of them. Asking "Do you think the football team is bad or just plain awful this year?" assumes the team really is bad and that your subject will agree. A better question would be, "What's your opinion of the football team this year?"

You should also stay away from leading questions that have built-in *assumptions* the person you are interviewing might not agree with. A question like "Don't you think that conducting surveys provides a richness that other research methods can't match?" assumes (1) that the interviewee will interpret "richness" in the same way you do, and (2) that both of your definitions of "can't match" will also agree. It would be better to ask the question in a more neutral way: "Are there any advantages, in your view, to surveys over other kinds of field research? If so, what might they be?"

WRITING ACTIVITY

Conduct an Interview

Assume that you are a reporter for your school's newspaper. Your editor has assigned you to interview the president of your campus on a topic of your choice. Develop a list of ten questions, some open-ended, some directed, that you want to ask the president.

Surveys and Questionnaires

While interviews are helpful sources of information and have the advantage of enabling a direct exchange between the subject and the interviewer, the number of people that one person can interview is of course limited. Some research projects require you to collect information from a larger number of people than you could possibly interview. To get information from a large number of people quickly and efficiently, you can use a **survey** or **questionnaire.** Though on the surface a survey may look like just a set of questions, a good survey is carefully designed, and its questions are very specifically framed. A good survey will either target a particular group of people or solicit information about the participants in order to provide you with a context for their answers.

Several strategies will enable you to put together an effective survey:

- Keep the survey a reasonable length. Ask only those questions that are really necessary. Many people think that all surveys need to start with questions that ask for certain basic demographic information, but you need gather only information that is important for your research. If you are not going to sort your data by age groupings, for example, there is no need to ask your respondents their age.

- Make sure the questions you ask call for an appropriate response. If a reasonable answer to the question is "yes," or "no," make sure there are only two possible responses. If a wider range of responses is appropriate, a scale such as "strongly agree, agree, no opinion, disagree, strongly disagree" may be more useful.

- Consider whether you want to ask only *closed-ended* or *directed* questions that call for specific answers, such as "List your age," or if you also want to ask *open-ended* questions, such as "Describe your experience at the Math Testing Center." Closed-ended questions are easier to tabulate, but open-ended questions will provide you with more examples and narrative detail.

- If you ask open-ended questions that call for written responses, make sure that you give your respondents enough room on the form to answer fully.

- Make sure that the question itself doesn't influence the response. Asking a question like "Do you think there are not enough parking spaces on campus?" leads the respondent to say "yes." A better way to get the same information would be to ask, "What is your opinion of the campus parking situation?"

- Make sure you have a way of tabulating the open-ended responses. Are you going to try to categorize them? Are you planning to use them as anecdotal examples?

One of the authors of this text conducts a student survey, administered anonymously, at mid-semester of every term in order to get feedback on how well the class is going and determine if changes need to be made and, if so, what those changes might be. The survey author asks for anonymity in the hopes of eliciting honest feedback. He wants students to say what they wish to say, in as much detail as they would like. In this survey, he uses open-ended questions such as the following:

- What is the best thing about this class?
- What is the worst thing about this class?
- Do you feel your writing is improving? Why or why not?
- What can I do to make the class more effective for you?
- Do the grades you're getting seem too high _____ too low _____ about right _____?
  Comments:
- Are the comments I make on your papers useful?
- What can I do to make my comments more effective?

CONSTRUCTING A SURVEY: AN EXAMPLE

As part of her dissertation research, PhD student Katherine Mason constructed a survey designed for students just completing their first-year composition

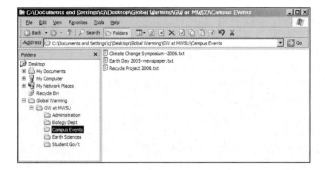

FIGURE 19.24 Organizing Files for a Research Project on Climate Change

TechNote Tired of scrolling endlessly up and down a huge document, looking for chunks of information to paste into your draft? Instead of lumping all of the information in the form of quotations, paraphrases, and summaries that you have gathered from sources and field research into one long text file, divide your research into a number of documents, giving each piece of information from a source an easy-to-identify file name. These files will function more or less like electronic "note cards" that you can easily find by their names. The example in Figure 19.24 shows three files for a research report on the topic of campus responses to climate change. Be sure to include bibliographic information for each source as part of each file.

For help with quotations, paraphrases, and summaries, see Chapter 20.

classes. Look at Mason's final survey, shown in Figure 19.25, and consider how you would answer some of her questions.

One consideration Mason had to deal with when constructing her survey was whether or not she should describe some of the activities she asked about. For example, look at her first question on invention. What if she had asked this initial question as shown in Figure 19.26 on page 869? Leaving out the description of what "invention activities" consist of could adversely affect the responses to this question in Mason's survey because students whose instructors perhaps did not use the term "invention activities" in their classroom discussions might answer "never," even if they did in fact use free-writing, brainstorming, and the other activities Mason listed. It is vital, then, to word your questions carefully and to explain any terms that might be unfamiliar or potentially confusing to respondents.

ADMINISTERING YOUR SURVEY

It is a good idea to test your survey before you administer it. That way, if a question or two prove to be faulty, you have a chance to make changes. Have

Part I: Personal Information

Please circle or write the answer that best describes you.

1. Gender:	Female	Male			
2. Current FYC Course:	ENG 102	ENG 105	ENG 108		
3. Age:	18–20	21–23	24–26	27–29	30 or older
4. Country where you attended high school:	United States	Other (please write in): _____			
5. Where you took ENG 101/107 or equivalent:	Arizona State University	Other (please write in): _____			
(not applicable for ENG 105 students)					

FIGURE 19.25 A Survey of Student Experiences in First-Year Composition (continued on page 868)

Part II: Academic Writing within First-Year Composition

For the following question, please refer to your writing within your First-Year Composition courses, and circle the one answer in each row that most closely describes your experience. **On average, how often do you participate in the following activities for writing assigned within First-Year Composition?**

	3 or more times for every assignment	2 times for every assignment	1 time for every assignment	Never or hardly ever	I don't know	Comments: Please feel free to write comments about your responses in this area. Thank you.
Invention activities (i.e., freewriting brainstorming, listing, webs)	3	2	1	0	?	
Talking about or showing your ideas and writing to **your peers or family** before handing in your final draft (for example, peer review)	3	2	1	0	?	
Talking about or showing your ideas and writing to **your instructor** before handing in your final draft	3	2	1	0	?	
Producing a draft of your paper	3	2	1	0	?	
Revising (making changes to your writing's overall content and/or organization)	3	2	1	0	?	
Editing (making changes to spelling, punctuation, grammar, and word choice)	3	2	1	0	?	
Showing or reading your final draft to someone other than your instructor	3	2	1	0	?	
Reflecting on (writing, talking, or thinking about) your writing process at any time	3	2	1	0	?	

FIGURE 19.25 Continued

	3 or more times for every assignment	2 times for every assignment	1 time for every assignment	Never or hardly ever	I don't know	Comments: Please feel free to write comments about your responses in this area. Thank you.
Invention activities	3	2	1	0	?	

FIGURE 19.26 Alternative Wording for a Question in the First-Year Composition Survey

several people respond to your survey, asking them to indicate any confusing questions. For example, one of the authors of this book was involved in a survey in which a question that asked

- What state do you live in? _____

was followed by this question:

- What area of the country do you live in? _____

The second question was meant to help categorize respondents by sections of the country (North, Southwest). Unfortunately, because it immediately followed the "state" question, many respondents thought the second question was asking what area of the *state* they lived in. In the end, the researchers had to disregard the answers to both questions.

Also consider whom you would like to respond to your survey, targeting your audience as specifically as possible. A general rule of thumb is that the more people you can ask to take your survey—the larger the data set—the more useful the results will be. It is also important to make sure that you are surveying the right population. If you are looking for information on what kind of coffee drinks are most popular on your campus (mochas, lattes, cappuccinos, and the like), for example, you will need to make sure you survey only coffee drinkers.

WRITING ACTIVITY

Develop a Survey

Often people who are thinking of opening a small business conduct a survey of their potential clientele to test their business plan's chances for success. Think of a possible product or service that seems to be lacking in your community. Then identify the customers your business will serve. Develop a set of survey questions that will give you a good sense of whether others share your perceived need for this business.

Chapter 2

Synthesizing and Documenting Sources

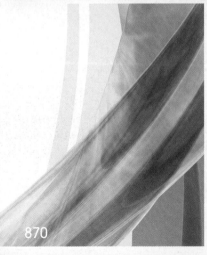

Effective academic writing does not just emerge out of a writer's mind. Academic writers are expected to know what others have said on their topic, using the work of other writers to help establish a foundation for an argument, substantiate an argument, or set up a point that they will then challenge or support. This process of building your own arguments using support and arguments from other writers is called **synthesis.** As they synthesize ideas, all academic writers need to use sources, acknowledging the thinking that already exists on an issue and giving credit to those who developed it. When developing an argument in an academic essay, for instance, you will be expected to review the relevant work of previous researchers and summarize their results. You will then be able to build your own arguments, working from theirs. And you will need to give these researchers credit.

For more on synthesis, see Chapter 2, pages 37–38.

When you document sources appropriately, you accomplish several important purposes.

- Documentation indicates what you as the writer did not produce—in effect, it indicates where you have used summary and paraphrase: "This isn't my idea and here is where it came from." Or it indicates a quotation: "These aren't my words, and here is the name of the person who wrote them."

- Documentation that follows a system such as the one recommended by the Modern Language Association (MLA) or the American Psychological Association (APA) provides readers with a list of sources—called the list of Works Cited in MLA style or References in APA style—so if a reader wants to learn more about the topic, he or she can consult the works listed.

- Proper documentation, within the text and in the list of sources, makes it easy for the reader to locate and read a particular source the writer has cited or even a specific quotation in that source. In this way sources function like hyperlinks do in Web-based documents.

- Proper documentation of appropriate sources lends ethos and credibility to you as a writer and enhances your argument.

Different academic disciplines have different style guides that offer a range of conventions for writers to follow, including conventions for documentation; to some extent, the differences among these style guides reflect the different needs of the disciplines that use them. Here we will present the conventions for documentation given in the style guides of the MLA and the APA. MLA style is used for papers in humanities disciplines, including English; APA style is used for papers in social science disciplines. The current editions of both manuals are as follows:

> Gibaldi, Joseph. *MLA Handbook for Writers of Research Papers*. 6th ed. New York: MLA, 2003.

American Psychological Association. (2001). *Publication manual of the American Psychological Association* (5th ed.). Washington, DC: Author.[1]

Although we are concentrating here on the documentation styles recommended by the MLA and APA, other disciplines recommend a variety of styles. Here are some of those other options:

- *Scientific Style and Format: The CSE Manual for Authors, Editors and Publishers* (7th ed.). If your academic work is in the sciences, you may be required to use the style suggested by the Council of Scientific Editors (CSE), formerly the Council of Biology Editors (CBE).

- *Information for Authors,* published by the Institute of Electrical and Electronics Engineers (IEEE), is used by engineers, both academics and practicing professionals.

- *The Chicago Manual of Style* (15th ed.) (CMS) is another widely used style. In fact, if you are expected to do on-the-job writing that requires documentation, more likely than not you will use CMS.

For help with avoiding plagiarism, see pages 874–76.

When you use information from sources to support your thesis, you must be careful to give appropriate credit to the author of each source. Failing to do so is plagiarism. You can choose from among several options for presenting information that you have taken from other writers' work: quotations, paraphrases, or summaries.

Quotations

When the most effective way to make a point is to use another author's exact words, you are using a **quotation.** Use a direct quotation in the following situations:

- When the exact wording is particularly striking, such as in a literary quotation
- When the author is considered to be especially authoritative
- When you take issue with the author's statement

If you are using MLA style and your quotation is shorter than five lines, you should enclose it in quotation marks and incorporate it into your text. Because the quotation is incorporated into the sentence, a comma is used after the introductory phrase. At first it might feel a bit awkward or clumsy when you integrate quoted material into your writing; however, you will get better with practice. Using verbs such as *notes, comments, observes, explains,* or similar words will help you introduce quotations smoothly and meaningfully.

---

[1] APA has also published the *APA Style Guide to Electronic References* (2007), which covers electronic sources.

Writing about the power of computers, Sherry Turkle says, "When I want to write and don't have a computer, I tend to wait until I do" (29).

For information on how to cite quotations, paraphrases, and summaries within text, see pages 878–80 for MLA style and pages 905–7 for APA style.

When the quotation is longer than four lines and you are using MLA style, start the quotation on a new line and indent all lines of the quotation ten spaces. The quotation should be double spaced and does not need to be enclosed in quotation marks. Because the quotation is introduced with an independent clause, that clause is followed by a colon.

An early researcher in virtual environments writes of their compelling nature:

> Why is it so hard for me to turn away from the screen? The windows on my computer desktop offer me layers of material to which I have simultaneous access: field notes; previous drafts of this book; a list of ideas not yet elaborated but which I want to include; transcripts of interviews with computer users; and verbatim logs of sessions on computer networks, on bulletin boards, and in virtual communities. (Turkle 29)

If you are using APA style, quotations of fewer than forty words should be enclosed in quotation marks and incorporated into the text, as follows:

Writing about the power of computers, Sherry Turkle (1995) says, "When I want to write and don't have a computer, I tend to wait until I do" (p. 29).

Block quotations are used in APA style when the quotation is at least forty words long. They are indented only five spaces and double spaced, and are not enclosed in quotation marks.

An early researcher in virtual environments writes eloquently of their compelling nature:

> Why is it so hard for me to turn away from the screen? The windows on my computer desktop offer me layers of material to which I have simultaneous access: field notes; previous drafts of this book; a list of ideas not yet elaborated but which I want to include; transcripts of interviews with computer users; and verbatim logs of sessions on computer networks, on bulletin boards, and in virtual communities. (Turkle, 1995, p. 29)

Paraphrases

Use **paraphrases** when you put someone else's ideas into your own words. It is important to understand that because you are using someone else's ideas in a paraphrase, you need to make appropriate citations. However, in a paraphrase you will use your own words and sentence structure. If you choose to borrow unique phrases from the original, those phrases should be placed in quotation marks. Here, for example, is a block quotation in APA style:

> In his book, *The World Is Flat, New York Times* columnist Thomas L. Friedman (2005) notes that when Netscape went public in 1995, it had significant ramifications for the emerging global economy:
>
>> Looking back, what enabled Netscape to take off was the existence, from the earlier phase, of millions of PC's, many already equipped with modems. Those are the shoulders Netscape stood on. What Netscape did was bring a new killer app—the browser—to this installed base of PC's making the computer and its connectivity inherently more useful for millions of people. (p. 57)

If you don't want to use a direct quotation, you can paraphrase Friedman's information by changing it into your own words. However, you need to be careful in paraphrasing that you do not commit **plagiarism** by using language and/or sentence structures that are too close to the original. The following paraphrase is guilty of using language that too closely mimics the original. (The language that is too close to the original is highlighted.)

Faulty Paraphrase

> In *The World Is Flat* (2005), Thomas L. Friedman looks back to 1995 and notes that what enabled Netscape to take off when it went public was that it could stand on the shoulders of the millions of already existing PC's, many already equipped with modems. Its new killer app—the browser—helped millions of people make connecting more useful. (57)

By contrast, the following paraphrase is entirely in the writer's own words and sentence structures, yet it contains essentially the same ideas as the original quotation from Friedman.

Acceptable Paraphrase

> In *The World Is Flat* (2005), Thomas L. Friedman looks back to 1995 and notes that Netscape could make a significant impact on the emerging global economy when it went public because of its browser. When Netscape brought this new software application—the browser—to the users of modem-enhanced PC's, it made those connected computers much more useful. (57)

Suppose you were writing about the film *Harry Potter and the Sorcerer's Stone* and wanted to cite ideas from Roger Ebert's review of it. Here is a paragraph from Ebert's review (the entire review appears in Chapter 9):

> *Harry Potter and the Sorcerer's Stone* is a red-blooded adventure movie, dripping with atmosphere, filled with the gruesome and the sublime, and surprisingly faithful to the novel. A lot of things could have gone wrong, and none of them have: Chris Columbus' movie is an enchanting classic that does full justice to a story that was a daunting challenge. The novel by J. K. Rowling was muscular and vivid, and the danger was that the movie would make things too cute and cuddly. It doesn't. Like an Indiana Jones for younger viewers, it tells a rip-roaring tale of supernatural adventure, where colorful and eccentric characters alternate with scary stuff like a three-headed dog, a pit of tendrils known as the Devil's Snare and a two-faced immortal who drinks unicorn blood. Scary, yes, but not too scary—just scary enough.

A faulty paraphrase would mimic Ebert's sentence structure in the original text. Here is an excerpt from Ebert's paragraph:

> The novel by J. K. Rowling was muscular and vivid, and the danger was that the movie would make things too cute and cuddly. It doesn't.

A poor paraphrase would look similar:

Faulty Paraphrase

> According to Ebert, the novel by J. K. Rowling was brawny and brilliant, and the danger was that the movie would make things too delightful and cuddly. It does not.

The following acceptable version conveys Ebert's idea but with a different sentence structure:

Acceptable Paraphrase

> According to Ebert, the film avoids the trap of making Harry's story too cutesy while remaining true to the novel's power.

Summaries

When you include a **summary** of your source's ideas, you condense the material presented by another author into a briefer form. While similar to paraphrasing, summaries condense information into a substantially smaller number of words. Paraphrases might be similar in length to the original. Summaries vary in length depending on what is being summarized. You might summarize a paragraph or even a page of material in only a sentence or two. To summarize a chapter, you might need several paragraphs. A summary of a larger work might be several pages in length. Once again, however, a summary must be entirely in your own words and sentence structure to avoid plagiarizing the original. Here are acceptable and unacceptable summaries of the Ebert passage on page 875 (in the unacceptable passage, wording from the original and sentence structure that is too close to the original are highlighted):

Unacceptable Summary

> Roger Ebert notes that the film is an adventure movie with lots of atmosphere and that it does full justice to Rowling's challenging novel. Colorful and eccentric characters alternate with scenes that are scary but not too scary.

Acceptable Summary

> In Roger Ebert's opinion, the film is a faithful rendition of the first Harry Potter novel, a rousing adventure story in the tradition of the *Indiana Jones* films. It offers a not overly frightening experience along with Rowling's "colorful and eccentric characters."

For more on writing a summary, see Chapter 2, pages 35–37.

Note that if you use phrases from the original in your summary, you should enclose them in quotation marks.

Ellipses

If you decide that a quotation is too long and you want to condense it, you can do so by placing an ellipsis (three periods with a space between each) in place of the omitted words. If the ellipsis occurs at the end of the sentence, you will need to place the sentence's period preceding the first ellipsis with a space between the first ellipsis period and the period of the sentence. Make sure when you use an ellipsis that you are careful not to change the meaning of the original quotation. For example, compare the original quotation from Marshall McLuhan and the condensed version.

> As the alphabet neutralized the divergencies of primitive cultures by translation of their complexities into simple visual terms, so representative money reduced the moral values in the nineteenth century.

> In <u>Understanding Media</u>, Marshall McLuhan compares the visual technology inherent in the alphabet with money, saying, "As the alphabet neutralized the divergencies of primitive cultures . . . so representative money reduced moral values in the nineteenth century" (141).

Brackets

If you find that something within a quotation is not clear and you need to add information so that your readers will understand it better, you can do so by using square brackets [ ]:

> In their book <u>Freakonomics</u>, Steven D. Leavitt and Stephen J. Dubner confirm that often commonly held stereotypes seem to apply to reality:
>> For instance, men [on online dating sites] who say they want a long-term relationship do much better than men looking for an occasional lover. But women [on the same sites] looking for an occasional lover do great. (82)

MLA Documentation Style

There are two components to MLA style: parenthetical in-text citations and a works-cited list that appears at the end of the paper. Every source cited within the body of the paper appears in the works-cited list.

MLA Style: In-Text Citation

In MLA style, parenthetical in-text citations are used in conjunction with the list of works cited to give readers the information they would need to locate the sources that you have quoted, paraphrased, or summarized. The intent in MLA style is to give only as much information in the text as the reader needs to find the detailed bibliographical information in the list of works cited—generally, the author and the page number of the material cited. The following are examples of how to cite different types of sources within your text using MLA style, starting with the most basic citation: a work with one author.

A WORK WITH ONE AUTHOR

Suppose that you quote from page 282 of Deborah Tannen's *You Just Don't Understand: Women and Men in Conversation*, published in 1990. In MLA style, your in-text citation would be *(Tannen 282)*. MLA in-text citations do not include punctuation, and the page number is given simply as a number.

The parenthetical citation is placed directly after the cited material. Here is an example using a block quotation in MLA style:

> In talking about gender differences, this phenomenon is noted:
>
> > Complementary schismogenisis commonly sets in when women and men have divergent sensitivities and hypersensitivities. For example, a man who fears losing freedom pulls away at the first sign he interprets as an attempt to "control" him, but pulling away is just the signal that sets off alarms for the woman who fears losing intimacy. (Tannen 282)

In this example, the author's name is not mentioned in the text that precedes the quotation. When the author's name is mentioned in the preceding sentence, however, the parenthetical citation includes only the page number, as in the following example:

> Deborah Tannen, a researcher who has written extensively about the language differences of men and women, notes, "Understanding each other's styles, and the motives behind them, is a first move in breaking this destructive cycle" (282).

Note that when a quotation is given within a sentence of your text, the period ends *your sentence*.

A WORK WITH MORE THAN ONE AUTHOR

Use all the authors' last names. If there are more than three authors, you can use the first author's last name with *et al.* following it.

Glassick, Huber, and Maeroff state that "teaching, too, must in the end be judged not merely by process but by results, however eloquent a teacher's performance" (29).

Ultimately, it is the results of teaching, not the method or the quality of the teacher's performance, that we must evaluate (Glassick, Huber, and Maeroff 29).

TWO OR MORE WORKS BY THE SAME AUTHOR

If you are citing ideas from two or more works by the same author, use the title of the work (in a shortened version if appropriate) to distinguish which source you are citing.

It is important to establish good relations with the people you work with by engaging in non-work related conversation. Both men and women do so, but the subjects of their conversations differ (Tannen, <u>Talking from 9 to 5</u> 64).

AN UNKNOWN AUTHOR

Use a shortened version of the title.

Employees of Google believe their corporate culture to be antithetical to that of Microsoft ("Google" 15).

A GOVERNMENT AGENCY OR A CORPORATE AUTHOR

Use the name of the organization. You can shorten lengthy names in the parenthetical citation.

Policy makers and citizens are warned that "Arizona is not positioned well to attract and keep the knowledge workers it needs" (Morrison Institute 6).

AN ANTHOLOGIZED WORK

Cite the author of the anthologized piece, not the editor of the collection. However, give the page numbers used in the collection.

John Perry Barlow asks the important question: "The enigma is this: If our property can be infinitely reproduced and instantaneously distributed all over the planet without cost, without our knowledge, without its even leaving our possession, how can we protect it?" (319).

A SECONDARY SOURCE

Whenever possible, cite the original source. However, if you do need to use a quotation from a secondary source, use *qtd. in* to let your readers know that you are doing so.

Jonathan Shaw muses, "I don't think mankind is ready, spiritually or mentally, for the transformations it's undergoing in the technological era: tattooing is a mute plea for a return to human values" (qtd. in Dery 284).

AN ONLINE SOURCE

Unless your source has some kind of numbering system or is a pdf file, you will not usually be able to provide page numbers for your quotation or paraphrase. Give the author or, if the author's name is not available, the title of the online work you are citing.

According to Christopher Beam, there are a number of methods that Internet service providers can use to block Web sites if a government orders them to do so.

MLA Style: Constructing a List of Works Cited

Because the list of works cited at the end of your paper is intended to work together with your in-text citations, it includes only the sources you cite within your text, not the works that you read but did not cite. The list should be double-spaced, and its entries are listed alphabetically by the last name of the first author. The first line of each entry is even with the left margin; any subsequent lines are indented by one-half inch or five spaces so that it is easy for a reader to skim down the left side of the page and find the author he or she is looking for.

All entries in the list are formatted following the same rules—this standardized format makes it easy for readers to understand the information in each entry. In the following pages you will find, for each common type of entry, a sample entry for a work in MLA style and, on pages 908–20, for many of the same works in APA style. First, though, to see some important differences between the two styles, consider these pairs of entries:

MLA   Paivio, Allan. <u>Mental Representations</u>. New York: Oxford UP, 1986.

APA   Paivio, A. (1986). *Mental representations*. New York: Oxford University Press.

MLA   Miller, George A. "The Magical Number Seven, Plus or Minus Two: Some Limits on Our Capacity for Processing Information." <u>Psychological Review</u> 63 (1956): 81–97.

APA   Miller, G. A. (1956). The magical number seven, plus or minus two: Some limits on our capacity for processing information. *Psychological Review, 63,* 81–97.

Notice in particular the following:

- In both styles, entries consist of three essential pieces of information, separated by periods: author, source (a book in the first pair, an article from an academic journal in the second), and publication information for the source (place of publication and publisher for the book; journal title and volume number for the article). Note the difference in the placement of information: Because of the importance of the year of publication to social scientists, in APA style it immediately follows the author's name rather than coming later in the entry as it does in MLA style.
- In MLA style, authors' first and middle names are given in full if that is how they are given in the source; in APA style, only initials are given.
- In MLA style, all major words in titles are capitalized; in APA style, only the first word, words following a colon, and names are capitalized in the titles of books and articles. All major words are capitalized in the titles of periodicals, however.
- In MLA style, titles of books and periodicals are underscored, and titles of articles are enclosed in quotation marks; in APA style, titles of books and periodicals are given in italics, and titles of articles are not enclosed in quotation marks.

The section that follows includes model entries for different types of print and nonprint sources in MLA style. Figure 20.1 provides you with a flowchart that will help you find the model entry that is closest to the source that you need to cite.

FIGURE 20.1
MLA Style: A Flowchart for Determining the Model Works-Cited Entry You Need

Is My Source a Complete Print Book or Part of a Print Book?

No	Yes, go to the next question below.	Go to this entry.
	Is it a book with only one author?	1
	Are you citing more than one book by this author?	2
	Is it a book with multiple authors?	3
	Is the book by an organization of some kind?	4
	Is the author unknown or unnamed?	5
	Does the book also have a translator?	11
	Is it a later publication or edition of the book?	6, 7
	Is it a multivolume work or part of a multivolume work?	13
	Is it part of a series?	14
	Does the book have an editor or a translator?	8, 11
	Is the book an edited collection or anthology?	8
	Is it a work in a collection or anthology?	9
	Is it an introduction, a preface, a foreword, or an afterword?	12
	Is it an entry in a dictionary or reference work?	22
	Is it a published interview?	10

Is My Source from a Print Periodical Such as a Journal, a Magazine, or a Newspaper?

No	Yes, go to the next question below.	Go to this entry.
	Is it from a scholarly journal?	
	Do the journal's page numbers continue from one issue to the next?	15
	Does each issue start with page 1?	16
	Is it from a magazine?	17
	Is it a review?	20
	Is it from a newspaper?	18
	Is it an editorial?	19
	Is it a letter to the editor?	21

Is My Source a Print Source but Not from a Journal, a Magazine, or a Newspaper?

No	Yes, go to the next question below.	Go to this entry.
	Is it an entry in a dictionary or reference work?	22
	Is it a government document?	23
	Is it a pamphlet?	24
	Is it the proceedings from a conference?	25
	Is it an unpublished doctoral dissertation?	26
	Is it a published or an unpublished letter?	27
	Is it a map or chart?	28
	Is it a cartoon?	29
	Is it an advertisement?	30

Is My Source a Nonprint Source from an Online Subscription Database or the World Wide Web?

No	Yes, go to the next question below.	Go to this entry.
	Is it a professional or personal Web site?	31
	Is it an article?	
	Is it a scholarly article retrieved from a database?	32
	Is it an article from an online journal?	34
	Is it an article from an online magazine?	35
	Is it an article from an online newspaper?	36
	Is it an online book?	33
	Is it a blog entry?	37
	Is it an entry on a wiki?	38
	Is it a posting to an electronic forum?	39
	Is it an e-mail message?	40

Is My Source a Nonprint Source That Is Not Published Online?

No	Yes, go to the next question below.	Go to this entry.
	Is it a television or radio program?	41
	Is it an audio recording?	42
	Is it a film, video recording, or DVD?	43
	Is it a nonperiodical publication on CD-ROM?	44
	Is it a personal, e-mail, or telephone interview?	45
	Is it an oral presentation?	46
	Is it a performance?	47
	Is it a work of art?	48

Consult with Your Instructor about How to Cite Your Source.

FIGURE 20.1   Continued

PRINT DOCUMENTS

Books

The basic items in an entry for a book are the author's name or authors' names, the title, and the publication information, consisting of the place of publication, publisher, and date of publication. See Figure 20.2 on pages 884–85 for guidelines on where to find the elements of a works-cited entry for a book in MLA style.

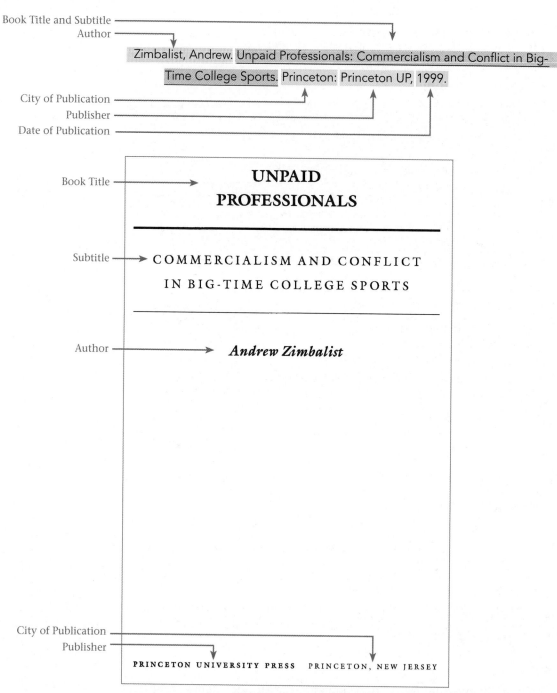

Book Title and Subtitle ——————————————————————

Author ——————

Zimbalist, Andrew. Unpaid Professionals: Commercialism and Conflict in Big-Time College Sports. Princeton: Princeton UP, 1999.

City of Publication ——————

Publisher ——————

Date of Publication ——————

Book Title ——————→

UNPAID PROFESSIONALS

Subtitle ——→ COMMERCIALISM AND CONFLICT IN BIG-TIME COLLEGE SPORTS

Author ——————————→ *Andrew Zimbalist*

City of Publication ——————

Publisher ——————

PRINCETON UNIVERSITY PRESS   PRINCETON, NEW JERSEY

FIGURE 20.2   The Parts of a Works-Cited Entry for a Book in MLA Style

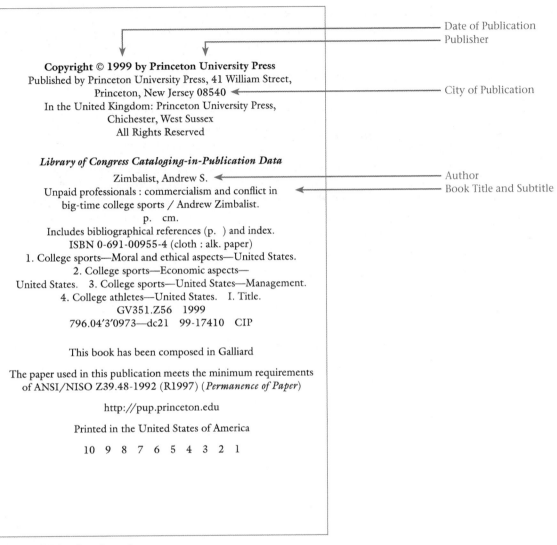

FIGURE 20.2 Continued

1. Book with one author: The most basic form includes the author's name, the title of the book, underlined, and the publication information.

publication information

author   title   city   publisher

Gould, Stephen Jay. <u>The Mismeasure of Man</u>. New York: Norton,

date

1981.

2. Two books by the same author: MLA style gives the author's name only in the first entry. For all subsequent entries, three hyphens are used instead of the name. The entries are listed in alphabetical order according to title.

Tannen, Deborah. <u>Talking from 9 to 5</u>. New York: Morrow, 1994.

- - -. <u>You Just Don't Understand: Women and Men in Conversation</u>. New York: Ballantine, 1990.

3. Book with multiple authors: In MLA style, only the first author's name is inverted; the other authors' names are given first name first. MLA style uses *and* before the last author's name. In MLA style, if a book has more than three authors, you may give all the names or give the name of the first author followed by *et al*. (For an example of the use of *et al.*, see #8.)

Covey, Stephen R., A. Roger Merrill, and Rebecca R. Merrill. <u>First Things First</u>. New York: Simon, 1994.

4. Book by a corporate entity or organization:

Adobe Systems Inc. <u>Adobe Acrobat 5.0: Getting Started</u>. San Jose, CA: Adobe, 2001.

5. Book by an unknown author:

<u>The Chicago Manual of Style: The Essential Guide for Writers, Editors, and Publishers</u>. 15th ed. Chicago: Chicago UP, 2003.

6. Republished book: Including the original date of publication is optional in MLA style. If you do include this date, place it immediately following the title.

Dickens, Charles. <u>Hard Times</u>. 1854. Ed. David Craig. Baltimore: Penguin, 1969.

7. Book in a later edition:

Corbett, Edward P. J. <u>Classical Rhetoric for the Modern Student</u>. 3rd ed. New York: Oxford UP, 1990.

8. Edited collection:

Inman, James A., and Donna N. Sewell, eds. <u>Taking Flight with Owls: Examining Electronic Writing Center Work</u>. Mahwah: Erlbaum, 2000.

Harrington, Susanmarie, et al., eds. <u>The Outcomes Book: Debate and Consensus after the WPA Outcomes Statement</u>. Logan: Utah State UP, 2005.

9. Work in a collection or an anthology: In MLA style the page ranges come at the end of the citation.

Anson, Chris M., and Richard Jewell. "Shadows of the Mountain." <u>Moving a Mountain: Transforming the Role of Contingent Faculty in Composition Studies and Higher Education</u>. Ed. Eileen E. Schell and Patricia Lambert Stock. Urbana: NCTE, 2001. 47–75.

10. Published interview:

Hawisher, Gail. "Making the Map: An Interview with Gail Hawisher." <u>Feminist Cyberscapes: Mapping Gendered Academic Spaces</u>. Interview with Kristine Blair and Pamela Takayoshi. Ed. Kristine Blair and Pamela Takayoshi. Stamford: Ablex, 1999. 177–91.

11. Translation:

Eliade, Mircea. <u>The Sacred and the Profane: The Nature of Religion</u>. Trans. Willard R. Trask. New York: Harcourt, 1959.

12. Introduction, preface, foreword, or afterword:

Burns, Hugh. Foreword. <u>Technology and Literacy in the Twenty-First Century: The Importance of Paying Attention</u>. By Cynthia L. Selfe. Carbondale: Southern Illinois UP, 1999. ix-xvii.

13. A multivolume work: If you have used more than one volume of a multivolume work, place that information after the title.

Campbell, Joseph. <u>The Masks of God</u>. 4 vols. New York: Viking, 1972.

If you have used only one volume of a multivolume work, however, cite only the volume you have used.

Elias, Norbert. <u>The History of Manners</u>. Vol. 1. New York: Pantheon, 1982.

14. A book in a series: If you are using a book that is part of a series, include the title of the series with no underlining or quotation marks before the publication information. Include the number of the series as well if it is present.

> Marshall, Margaret J. <u>Response to Reform: Composition and the Professionalization of Teaching</u>. Studies in Writing & Rhetoric. Carbondale: Southern Illinois UP, 2004.

PERIODICAL ARTICLES

The basic items in an entry for a periodical article are the author's name or authors' names, the title of the article, and information about the publication in which the article appeared, including its title, volume number (if applicable), date, and the page range for the article. See Figure 20.3 for guidelines on where to find the elements of a works-cited entry for a periodical article in MLA style.

15. Article in a scholarly journal with continuous pagination: The volume number follows the title.

> *authors' names*   *title of article*
> Thayer, Alexander and Beth E. Kolko. "Localization of Digital Games: The Process of Blending for the Global Games Market."
> *title of periodical*   *volume no. and date*   *page range*
> <u>Technical Communication</u> 51 (2004): 477–88.

16. Article in a scholarly journal that is paginated by issue: When an article is from a journal that restarts its page numbers with each issue, the issue number follows the volume number and a period.

> Howard, Rebecca Moore. "Power Revisited: Or, How We Became a Department." <u>Journal of the Council of Writing Program Administrators</u> 16.3 (1993): 37–49.

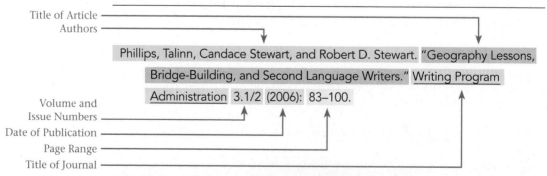

Title of Article
Authors

Phillips, Talinn, Candace Stewart, and Robert D. Stewart. "Geography Lessons, Bridge-Building, and Second Language Writers." <u>Writing Program Administration</u> 3.1/2 (2006): 83–100.

Volume and Issue Numbers
Date of Publication
Page Range
Title of Journal

FIGURE 20.3   The Parts of a Works-Cited Entry for a Journal Article in MLA Style

W P A

Writing Program Administration

Journal of the
Council of Writing Program Administrators
Volume 30.1/2 (Fall 2006)

————————— Title of Journal

————————— Date of Publication

Volume and
Issue Numbers

Contents

————————— Title of Article

————————— First Page of Article
————————— Authors

Reviews

FIGURE 20.3
Continued

17. Magazine article: Magazines may or may not include volume and issue numbers. *Business Week*, for example, does not use volume numbers. In any case, in MLA style volume numbers are not given. Instead, dates are provided. If magazines are published weekly or biweekly, the day is included along with the month, which is abbreviated. If the entire article does not appear on consecutive pages, give only the first page number and a plus sign (+).

> Foust, Dean, Michael Eidem, and Brian Bremner. "AFLAC: Its Ducks Are
>> Not in a Row." Business Week 2 Feb. 2004: 52–53.

> Wilson, Chauncey E. "Usability and User Experience Design: The Next
>> Decade." Intercom Jan 2005: 6–9.

18. Newspaper article: Entries for newspaper articles include the edition, when it is given (since different editions print different items), along with the date of publication and the section and page numbers. You should include the city of origin of a local newspaper within square brackets if it is not part of the title of the newspaper (for example, *Capital Times [Madison, WI]*). You should also eliminate *The* at the beginning of the names of newspapers. When articles appear on discontinuous pages, as they often do, MLA style calls for using a + sign.

> Fatsis, Stefan. "A More Modern Masters." Wall Street Journal 9 Apr. 2002:
>> B1+.

19. Editorial:

> "Moral Scoreboard." Editorial. Arizona Republic [Phoenix, AZ] 18 Feb.
>> 2004: B10.

20. Review: If there is no author for the review, alphabetize it by the title of the review. If the review also has no title, alphabetize by the title of what is being reviewed. When citing a review, use the format appropriate for its place of publication. If it appears in a magazine, use the format for magazines. If it appears in a newspaper, use the format for newspapers.

> Jablonski, Jeffrey. Rev. of The New Careers: Individual Action and Economic
>> Change, by Michael B. Arthur, Kerr Inkson, and Judith K. Pringle.
>> Technical Communication Quarterly 12 (2003): 230–34.

21. Letter to the editor:

> Rosati, Colette. Letter. Arizona Republic [Phoenix, AZ] 18 Feb. 2004: B10.

Other Print Sources

22. Entry in a dictionary or reference work: In MLA style, entries in reference works are treated like entries in collections. If the author is known, begin with the author. Otherwise, start with the title of the entry. If the reference work is commonly known and regularly updated, you can simply give the edition and the date of publication. Otherwise, full publication information is necessary.

"Express Mail." Merriam-Webster's Collegiate Dictionary. 10th ed. 1993.

Pfeiffer, Robert H. "Sumerian Poetry." Princeton Encyclopedia of Poetry and Poetics. Ed. Alex Preminger. Enlarged Ed. Princeton: Princeton UP, 1974.

23. Government document: When the author of the document is not known, the agency is given as the author. Most publications from the U.S. federal government are published by the Government Printing Office (GPO). Give GPO as the publisher unless the title page indicates otherwise, as in the citation below.

United States. Dept. of Health and Human Services. National Institutes of Health. Toxicology and Carcinogenesis Studies of Resorcinal (CAS No. 108-46-3) in F344/N Rats and B6C3F$_1$ Mice (Gavage Studies). Research Triangle Park: National Institutes of Health, 1992.

24. Pamphlet: Pamphlets are short documents and are usually held together by staples rather than a more formal binding. They are treated as books.

A Guide to Visiting the Lands of Many Nations & to the Lewis & Clark Bicentennial. St. Louis: National Council of the Lewis & Clark Bicentennial, 2004.

25. Published conference proceedings: The entire collection is treated as a book. Individual articles are treated as though they were in a collection by different authors.

Buchanan, Elizabeth, and Nancy Morris. "Designing a Web-Based Program in Clinical Bioethics: Strategies and Procedures." Proceedings of the 15th Annual Conference on Distance Teaching & Learning. Madison: U of Wisconsin, 1999. 65–70.

26. Unpublished doctoral dissertation:

> Edminster, Judith R. "The Diffusion of New Media Scholarship: Power,
>
>   Innovation, and Resistance in Academe." Diss. U. of South Florida,
>
>   2002.

27. Letter: If the letter you are citing has been published, treat it as you would a work in an anthology, but also include the date.

> Hemingway, Ernest. "To Maxwell Perkins." 7 February 1936. Ernest
>
>   Hemingway: Selected Letters, 1917–1961. Ed. Carlos Baker. New
>
>   York: Scribner's, 1981. 437–38.

If the letter you are citing is a personal letter, start with the writer's name followed by *Letter to the author* and the date.

> Morris, Patricia M. Letter to the author. 28 Dec. 2005.

28. Map or chart:

> San Francisco Bay. Map. San Francisco: California State Automobile
>
>   Association, 2004.

29. Cartoon:

> Benson, Steve. Cartoon. Arizona Republic [Phoenix, AZ] 28 Dec.
>
>   2006: 17.

30. Advertisement: Identify the product or company being advertised. If the ad appears in print or in the media, give the appropriate publication information.

> Bristol-Myers Squibb. Advertisement. Time. 25 Dec. 2006: 81.

ONLINE SOURCES

Because online sources change constantly, citing them is more complicated than citing print sources, although the principles, and many of the specifics, are the same. In addition to the author's name (if known) and the title and date of the document, MLA asks for the date the document was accessed and for its electronic address or Uniform Resource Locator (URL). Since some URLs are very long and complicated, MLA suggests giving URLs for pages containing links that will lead to the document, such as search pages for large sites. When the document you are citing has a print as well as an electronic version, MLA requires you to provide publication information for both versions. See Figure 20.4 for guidelines on where to find the elements of a works-cited entry for an article accessed from an online database.

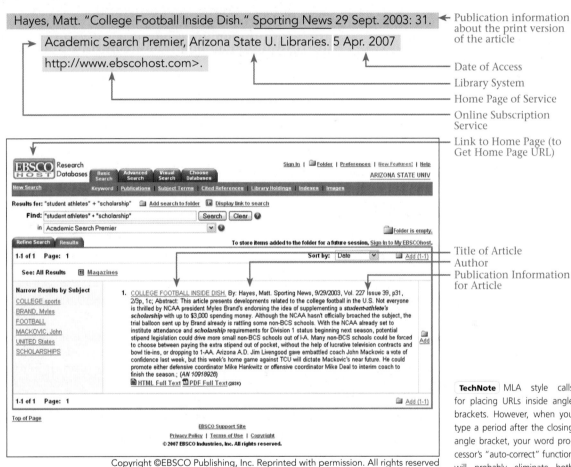

Hayes, Matt. "College Football Inside Dish." *Sporting News* 29 Sept. 2003: 31. ← Publication information about the print version of the article

Academic Search Premier, Arizona State U. Libraries. 5 Apr. 2007 http://www.ebscohost.com>.

Date of Access
Library System
Home Page of Service
Online Subscription Service
Link to Home Page (to Get Home Page URL)

Title of Article
Author
Publication Information for Article

FIGURE 20.4   The Parts of a Works-Cited Entry for a Periodical Article Accessed from an Online Subscription Database

31. Basic professional or personal Web site:

American Medical Association. Home page. 17 Feb. 2004

<http://www.ama-assn.org/>.

TechNote MLA style calls for placing URLs inside angle brackets. However, when you type a period after the closing angle bracket, your word processor's "auto-correct" function will probably eliminate both angle brackets, so you will have to go back and retype them. To avoid having to do this step each time, modify your word processor's auto-correct settings so that they do not include angle brackets. Try to avoid breaking URLs across lines; if you must break them, break them only after a slash (/).

32. Scholarly article retrieved from a database:

author   title of article

Selber, Stuart A. "Beyond Skill Building: Challenges Facing Technical

     Communication Teachers in the Computer Age." Technical

      title of journal   volume no., date, page range   database

     Communication Quarterly 3 (1994): 365–91. EBSCOHost.

    subscribing system   date of access

     Arizona State University. 18 Feb. 2004

           URL of database

     <http://www.ebsco.com/home/>.

Bennet-Kastor, Tina. "Spelling Abilities of University Students in

     Developmental Writing Classes." Journal of College Reading and

     Learning, 35.1 (2004): 67–82. ERIC. Arizona State University.

     30 March 2007 <http://www.eric.ed.gov/ERICDocs/data/

     ericdocs2/content_storage_01/0000000b/80/2c/a4/f2.pdf>.

33. Online book:

Howells, William Dean. Familiar Spanish Travels. Project Gutenberg.

     18 Feb. 2004 <http://www.gutenberg.net/etext05/sptrv10.txt>.

34. Article from an online journal: When the online article is a digitized version of a print document, include the page numbers that you would find in print. However, if the document appears only in electronic form, as in the example below, page numbers will not exist.

Salvo, Michael J. "Deafened to Their Demands: An Ethnographic

     Study of Accommodation." Kairos 7.1 (2002). 17 Feb. 2004

     <http://english.ttu.edu/kairos/7.1/binder2.html?coverweb/salvo/

     ctx.html>.

35. Article from an online magazine: If the online source is a digitized version of an original print source, give the page numbers.

Cooper, Matthew, and Karen Tumulty. "Bring on the Cash!" Time. 16

     Feb. 2004. 17 Feb. 2004: 18–21 <http://www.time.com/time/

     election2004/article/0,18471,591298,00.html>.

36. Article from an online newspaper:

> Novovitch, Barbara. "It's Home Stupid Home, but the 'Clods' Can
>
>   Read." New York Times. 17 Feb. 2004. 23 Feb. 2005 <http://
>
>   www.nytimes.com/2004/02/17/education/17PROF.html>.

37. Blog entry: Use the MLA format for general Web sites. Include the name of the author (bloggers often use pseudonyms), the name of the entry, enclosed in quotation marks, the name of the blog, the date of the entry (if available), the date of access, and the URL.

> Rice, J. "Network Academics." Yellow Dog. 30 Mar. 2007 <http://
>
>   ydog.net/?page_id=345>.

38. Wiki entry: Include the title of the entry, in quotation marks, the title of the wiki, underscored, the date you accessed the entry, and the URL for the entry.

> "Rhetoric." Wikipedia, 30 Mar. 2007 <http://en.wikipedia.org/wiki/
>
>   Rhetoric>.

39. Posting to an electronic forum such as a mailing list (listserv): This basic format is used for all online forums including Web-based postings.

> Peckham, Irvin. "Re: Update on AP and Dual Enrollment." Online posting.
>
>   21 Sept. 2003. WPA-L. 17 Feb. 2004 <http://lists.asu.edu/cgi-bin/
>
>   wa?A2=ind0309&L=wpal&D=1&O=D&F=&S=&P=52156>.

40. E-mail message:

> Bernhardt, Stephen B. "RE: Congrats!" E-mail to the author. 17 Feb. 2004.

OTHER NONPRINT SOURCES

41. Television and radio programs: The basic elements for entries that cite radio and television programs include the following: the title of the episode, the title of the program, the title of the series, the name of the network, the call letters and the city of the local station, and the broadcast date.

> "Dogs and More Dogs." Nova. Narr. John Lithgow. PBS. KAET, Phoenix.
>
>   3 Feb. 2004.

"Scientists Succeed in Cloning Human Embryo." <u>All Things Considered</u>.

      Narr. Joe Palca. NPR. WGBH, Boston. 12 Feb. 2004.

42. Audio recording:

Jackson, Alan. "Drive." Perf. Jackson. <u>Drive</u>. Arista, 2002.

43. Film, video recording, or DVD: In MLA style the citation starts with the title and the director. The distributor and year of release are necessary. Other items, such as performers, are optional.

<u>The Lord of the Rings: The Two Towers</u>. Dir. Peter Jackson. Perf. Elijah Wood

      and Ian McKellan. 2002. DVD. New Line Home Entertainment, 2003.

44. A nonperiodical publication on a CD-ROM:

<u>The OWL Construction and Maintenance Guide</u>. Ed. James A. Inman and

      Clinton Gardner. CD-ROM. Emmitsburg: IWCA, 2002.

45. Personal, e-mail, or telephone interview: Indicate whether the interview was conducted in person (*Personal interview*), by e-mail (*E-mail interview*), or by telephone (*Telephone interview*) following the name of the person you interviewed.

Schwalm, D. Personal interview. 21 Feb. 2004.

46. Oral presentation:

Russell, David R. "Teacher's Perception of Genre across the Curriculum: Making

      Classroom/Culture Connections Visible." Conf. on College Composition

      and Communication Convention. Atlanta Hilton, Atlanta, 26 Mar. 1999.

47. Performance: If you are citing a play, an opera, a concert, or a ballet performance, start with the title, followed by the authors (*By*), and any other pertinent information (such as the director, identified as *Dir*), the site where performed, the city, and performance date.

<u>The Norse Family</u>. By Jerry Jones. Dir. Walter Onger. Mesa Performing Arts

      Center, Mesa. 28 Dec. 2007.

48. Work of Art:

di Chirico, Giorgio. <u>The Philosopher's Conquest, 1914</u>. Joseph

      Winterbotham Collection. Art Institute of Chicago, Chicago.

MLA Style: Sample Student Paper

Follow these guidelines if you are required to use MLA style:

- A separate title page is not required in MLA style. Instead, on the first page, put your name, your professor's name, the course number, and the date in the upper-left-hand corner, one inch from the top of the page, and follow with the title of your paper. The title should be centered, with every word capitalized except articles and prepositions, and should not be underlined or in a special typeface.

- Double-space the entire paper, including the information mentioned above as well as block quotations and the entries in your list of works cited.

- Leave one-inch margins on all sides.

- Put page numbers in the upper-right-hand corner, one-half inch from the top. Just before each page number, put your last name.

- Indent paragraphs one-half inch, or five spaces, from the left-hand margin.

- Begin your list of works cited on a new, consecutively numbered page. Include the title *Works Cited* one inch from the top. Center the title; do not use a special typeface for it.

- In quoting and citing sources, use the guidelines for MLA style given in this chapter.

The student paper that follows, "Money for Nothing" by Jessie Katz, is an example of a paper that uses MLA style.

Student's name   Jessie Katz

Professor's name   Professor Wilson

Course title   English 105

Date   February 15, 2006

Title centered;   Money for Nothing
important words
capitalized   For followers of college sports, February is a particularly exciting time of

                             year. With the recent culmination of the football season in the bowl games and

                             the anticipation of upcoming March Madness, all eyes seem glued to ESPN

                             and the sports section of the newspaper as the drama of the season's games,

                             rivalries, and players unfolds. In this charged atmosphere, the public turns its

                             attention toward student-athletes and has ample occasion to contemplate the

                             extraordinary lives that these young people lead. Indeed, some student-ath-

                             letes apparently have it all: Aside from their national recognition and virtual

                             stardom on and off of their campuses, these athletes also often receive special

                             on-campus housing, state-of-the-art training facilities, and, perhaps most nota-

                             bly, substantial scholarships from their schools.

                                      According to the National Collegiate Athletic Association (NCAA), col-

                             leges and universities award $1 billion in athletic scholarships annually to over

Shortened version of   126,000 student-athletes (Online). NCAA defines athletic aid as "a grant,
the title of an online
source is enclosed in   scholarship, tuition waiver, or other assistance from a college or university
parentheses.
                             that is awarded on the basis of a student's athletic ability"; and a student-

                             athlete is a member of the student body who receives athletic aid from

                             his or her school sometime during his or her freshman year. Regardless

                             of financial need or academic promise, athletic scholarships may cover

                             tuition, fees, room and board, and books. Although nearly all Division I

                             and Division II schools grant athletic scholarships, awarding this type of

                             aid does little to benefit the academic prestige, community, or economic

Thesis statement   condition of colleges or universities. Giving scholarships based solely

                             on athletic merit may in fact undermine the purpose of institutions of

                             higher education, so colleges and universities need to reexamine the

                             extraordinary amounts of money they currently spend on athletic aid to

                             their students.

Like any social institution, colleges and universities exist to promote a certain set of goals. Even though mission statements differ from school to school, these organizations usually share three major objectives: academic scholarship through instruction and research, service to the university's community, and economic development of the university and its surroundings. For instance, Arizona State University, one of the nation's premier research institutions and member of the PAC-10, has a mission statement typical of a state university. Its 2005–2006 General Catalog reads as follows:

> Arizona State University's goal is to become a world-class university in a multicampus setting. Its mission is to provide outstanding programs in instruction, research, and creative activity, to promote and support economic development, and to provide service appropriate for the nation, the state of Arizona, and the state's major metropolitan area. To fulfill its mission, ASU places special emphasis on the core disciplines and offers a full range of degree programs—baccalaureate through doctorate, recognizing that it must offer quality programs at all degree levels in a broad range of fundamental fields of inquiry. ASU will continue to dedicate itself to superior instruction; to excellent student performance; to original research, creative endeavor, and scholarly achievement; and to outstanding public service and economic development activities. (23)

Quotation longer than four lines is indented 1 inch or 10 spaces and double-spaced. The sentence that introduces it ends with a colon. Page number is given at the end.

Universities, including ASU, promote their goals through their facilities, through their academic and community programs, and especially through their people, the large majority of whom are students. Students represent both a college's main source of income and its main product; and when a school awards a scholarship, it makes an investment in an individual who it feels will make a special contribution to its goals. However, granting athletes aid does not directly contribute to the three primary goals that most colleges and universities share.

Although they are part of institutions that society entrusts with the passage and creation of knowledge through scholarship and research, people often suspect that athletics departments disregard the academic success of student-athletes.

Katz 3

Certainly not all student-athletes fit the "dumb jock" stereotype, but an alarming amount of data shows that these individuals fall behind their peers in the
classroom. Academic underachievement in student-athletes starts at the
recruitment level. To become a member of the NCAA and gain the privilege of
practicing and playing sports and obtaining a sports scholarship at a Division
I or Division II college, incoming freshmen must graduate from high school,
complete at least fourteen core courses (including English, math, and physical
and social sciences), have a minimum grade point average of 2.0, and achieve
a minimum score of 820 on the SAT (Online). While these requirements appear reasonable, NCAA receives too many applicants and has a staff that is too
small to carefully examine each potential student's high school record. Thus,
academic advisors "cheat the system," as is evidenced in a 1997 scandal in
which exceptional high school athletes attended and paid certain high schools

*Source is cited in
parentheses, with
page number.*

that adjusted their deficient standardized test scores (Zimbalist 35). In the most
extreme cases of academic under-preparedness, student-athletes enter institutes of "higher" education without basic literacy and math skills. Since NCAA
evaluates high school courses rather than college courses, after student-athletes
are accepted into college, the regulation of student-athlete academic education
becomes less centralized, falling to the universities' athletic departments, which
may be motivated to keep student-athletes in the game and not on the academic chopping block. Instances abound in which advisors recommend lenient
professors and classes with titles like "Leisure and the Quality of Life," "Sports

Organization as author.

Officiating," and "Popular Music" (Arizona State University). Surely, if and when
academic education becomes subordinate to athletics, colleges and universities
are counterproductive in funding their student-athletes' "scholarship."

One of the most disturbing facts concerning athletics in colleges and
universities is that a substantial number of athletes are leaving these schools
without a degree. In an effort to remedy the academic deficiencies prevalent
in college sports, NCAA instituted the Academic Progress Rate (APR) program
in 2004 (Bartter 1). Using a complex formula to assign each team an APR,
NCAA supports teams with an APR of 925, the minimum value that predicts
that the team will graduate at least half of its athletes, and higher. According to

Katz 4

a recent study by the University of Central Florida, of the fifty-six Division I football teams selected to play in the 2006 Bowl games, twenty-three teams (including the previous national champion, University of Southern California) received an APR below 925, and twenty-seven teams had a graduation rate under 50%. For all Division I student-athletes, the U.S. Department of Education reports a 62% graduation rate, although the graduation rates for "the elite sports" (men's basketball and football) are considerably lower, with a basketball graduation rate of 44% and a football graduation rate of 54% (Wolverton). Admittedly, the total student-athlete graduation rate exceeds the graduation rate (60%) of non-athletes, but the success of many of these student-athletes may be bolstered by the financial support they receive. Consequently, a vast sum of the money that colleges give to their athletic students does not support the achievement of a degree, the most important tangible reward that a college or university can give a student. Indeed, unlike academic or music scholarships, which directly contribute to a college degree, athletic scholarships fund a pursuit unrelated, and at times even counterproductive, to what ASU's mission statement calls "fundamental fields of inquiry." Considering the tough odds of playing professional sports (1 in 1,233), student-athletes who do not graduate miss out on the invaluable and marketable skills and knowledge that a degree signifies (Zimbalist 31). Thus, granting athletic scholarships does not necessarily lead to academic returns for the university or the student-athlete.

Katz cites studies to support her thesis about athletic aid.

Despite the academic arguments against granting athletic scholarships, some institutions defend their awarding of financial aid based solely upon athletic performance with the argument that athletics contribute to the community service facet of a college's or university's stated mission. Certainly, a strong athletic program may benefit the community in a variety of healthy ways; a winning team engenders school spirit in its students and faculty, entices the citizens who live near the college to take an active interest in at least one aspect of the school, and earns state and national recognition and exposure, which may attract students and lead to increased enrollment. However, college athletics can be seen as having as many detrimental as positive effects on its community. In some instances, the same school spirit that fills the students with a sense of pride and place leads to very disreputable, unsportsmanlike conduct in the student body. In 2001, about 2,000 University of Arizona basketball fans flooded streets, destroyed cars, and set fires after the NCAA tournament in Minneapolis (Rotstein); and in 2003, University of West Virginia students set over 100 fires and rioted in the streets after their football team defeated Virginia Tech (French 89). The athletes themselves also sometimes engage in activities that harm the communities; underage drinking and drug use occur in the athlete population as they do the general college population, and more serious events (such as allegations of rape against members of the University of Colorado football team in 2001 and the 2005 Baylor University incident in which one basketball player murdered his team-mate) become highly publicized scandals. These events weaken considerably the positive impacts college athletics may have on schools' communities and undermine other community services, such as volunteer work, that students

Katz responds to a counterargument about the possible benefits of student athletics.

without any sort of scholarship perform. While athletics may benefit the community in many ways, they also have too many harmful effects on the community for colleges to justify the current levels of spending that many of them devote to athletic scholarships.

Perhaps the most common justification for granting student-athletes athletic scholarships is that college athletics is a major source of revenue for institutes of higher learning: through scholarships, athletes are allowed a portion of the money that they bring to their schools. This justification operates on the assumption that athletics do indeed attract capital to colleges and universities; yet an increasing amount of evidence shows that athletics departments actually cause a substantial deficit to the institutions that house them. The financial information from college athletics departments can be very misleading: in 1994, NCAA reported that Division I-A athletics programs earned an average of about $13,632,000 and spent about $12,972,000, yielding an apparent profit of $660,000 (French 80). These numbers, though, did not account for the fact that some universities subsidized their athletic departments. If the direct transfers to athletics programs from their universities that year were subtracted from the average earnings, the result would reveal that these programs actually had a $174,000 deficit. In fact, some athletics departments had so little money that they could not even afford to fund their athletes' scholarships; instead, there is evidence of some universities dipping into the scholarship funds reserved for students with demonstrated financial need or academic merit (French 82).

Another misconception about athletic funding is that winning teams attract more monetary gifts from donors and alumni. A study by Cornell University management and economics professor Robert Frank, discussed in a 2004 Sports Illustrated article, demonstrates that "the presumed indirect benefits of sports, such as the spike in alumni giving and an enlarged applicant pool, are by all indications minimal." In fact, Frank discovered that "the revenues needed to compete have escalated to the point where the average big-time athletic program runs in the red. And when success brings a spike in donations, the money is routinely earmarked for the athletic program—not the general university fund" (Fish). Therefore, even if a profit from student athletics is earned, universities usually cannot and do not use the money to advance their missions. Southern Methodist University President Gerald Turner confirms these conclusions: "I've been a university president now for about 20 years and I have never found any relationship between alumni giving to academic programs and the success of the athletic program" (qtd. in Fish). When colleges and universities award athletic scholarships, it may be less of a sound financial investment than boosters hope.

Without a doubt, athletics have an important entertainment role in a university setting. Yet, behind the Rose Bowl and March Madness, athletics programs are not as beneficial to their scholarly institutions as they may seem. It's time for colleges and universities to concentrate on their central missions—to promote academic scholarship, service to the university's community, and economic development of the university and its surroundings—instead of justifying the exorbitant expenditures of funds on programs that are more popular than they are useful to the school, the student, and the community at large.

Information from an authoritative source introduced by a signal phrase within the text.

Katz responds to two additional counterarguments. She responds to the second counterargument by citing a study and quoting an expert.

Secondary source introduced in text, with *qtd. in* used in parenthetical citation.

New page, title centered; double space between title and first line of works-cited list.

Entries double spaced, in alphabetical order

First line of each entry at left margin; all other lines indented 5 spaces or 1/2 inch.

Works Cited

Arizona State University. Office of the Executive Vice President and Provost of the University. <u>Arizona State University: 2005–2006 General Catalog</u>. Tempe: Academic and Administrative Documents, 2005.

Bartter, Jessica. "Institute Study by Lapchick Looks at APR Rates and Graduation Rates for 2005–06 Bowl-Bound Teams." 5 Dec. 2005. Devos Sport Business Management Program, College of Business Administration, University of Central Florida. 8 Feb. 2006 <http://www.bus.ucf.edu/sport/public/downloads/2005_Football_APR_Grad_Rate.pdf>.

Fish, Mike. "Separate Worlds: Studies Show Big-Time Athletics Don't Impact Academic Donations." <u>Sports Illustrated</u>. 14 Sept. 2004. 9 Feb. 2006. http://sportsillustrated.cnn.com/2004/writers/mike_fish/09/14/straight.shooting/index.html.

French, Peter A. <u>Ethics and College Sports: Ethics, Sports, and the University</u>. Lanham: Rowman, 2004.

<u>The Online Resource for the National Collegiate Athletic Association</u>. 2005. NCAA. 7 Feb. 2006 <http://www.ncaa.org/wps/portal>.

Rotstein, Arthur H. "Arizona Fans Turn Rowdy." <u>Associated Press</u>. 3 Apr. 2001. 12 Feb. 2006 <http://www.usatoday.com/sports/other/2002-04-09-fan-violence.htm>.

Wolverton, Brad. "Under New Formula, Graduation Rates Rise." <u>Chronicle of Higher Education</u>. 52.21 (2006): A41. 10 Feb. 2006 <http://chronicle.com/weekly/v52/i21/21a04101.htm>.

Zimbalist, Andrew. <u>Unpaid Professionals: Commercialism and Conflict in Big-Time College Sports</u>. Princeton: Princeton UP, 1999.

APA Documentation Style

APA Style: In-Text Citation

In APA style, parenthetical in-text citations are used in conjunction with the list of references at the end of a paper to give readers the information they would need to locate the sources that you have quoted, paraphrased, or summarized. In research in the fields in which APA style is used (the social sciences, business, and so on), often currency is crucial and dates of publication are extremely relevant, so in-text citations include year of publication along with the author and page number. Suppose, for example, that you are quoting from page 282 of Deborah Tannen's *You Just Don't Understand: Woman and Men in Conversation*, published in 1990. In APA style, a parenthetical in-text citation would be *(Tannen, 1990, p. 282)*. If you give the author's name within your sentence, however, the date appears in parentheses following the name. APA parenthetical citations have commas between the elements and "p." before the page number. Page numbers are needed only when you are citing a quotation or specific information.

The following are examples of how to cite different types of sources within your text using APA style.

A WORK WITH ONE AUTHOR

Deborah Tannen (1990), in talking about gender differences, observes, "Complementary schismogenisis commonly sets in when women and men have divergent sensitivities and hypersensitivities" (p. 282).

A WORK WITH MORE THAN ONE AUTHOR

For a source with up to five authors, use all the authors' last names in the first citation. If you give their names in parentheses, put an ampersand (&) between the last two names. After the first citation, use the first author's name followed by *et al.* for a work by three or more authors.

Glassick, Huber, and Maeroff (1999) state that "Teaching, too, must in the end be judged not merely by process but by results, however eloquent a teacher's performance" (p. 29).

Ultimately, it is the results of teaching, not the method or the quality of the teacher's performance, that we must evaluate (Glassick, Huber, & Maeroff, 1999, p. 29).

For a source with six or more authors, use *et al.* with every citation, including the first.

AN UNKNOWN AUTHOR

Use a shortened version of the title.

> Employees of Google believe their corporate culture to be antithetical to that of Microsoft ("Google," 2006).

A GOVERNMENT AGENCY OR A CORPORATE AUTHOR

Give the complete name of most organizations every time you use them. After the first use, however, you can use an abbreviation for organizations with unwieldy names and well-known or easily understood abbreviations.

> The Federal Emergency Management Agency (FEMA) (2007) offers officials many suggestions in a new brochure. You can obtain a copy of FEMA's brochure at our main office.

A SECONDARY SOURCE

If you need to use a quotation from a secondary source, use *as cited in* to let your readers know that you are doing so.

> Jonathan Shaw muses, "I don't think mankind is ready, spiritually or mentally, for the transformations it's undergoing in the technological era: tattooing is a mute plea for a return to human values" (as cited in Dery, 1996, p. 284).

AN ONLINE SOURCE

Cite in the same way that you would cite a print source. For a source with paragraph numbers, use *para.* or ¶ for *p.* If you cannot find a date for the source, use the abbreviation *n.d.* (for "no date").

> According to Christopher Beam (2006), there are a number of methods that Internet service providers can use to block Web sites if a government orders them to.

A BLOCK QUOTATION

In APA style, block quotations are used for quotations of more than forty words and are indented one-half inch or five spaces, as in the following example:

> Tannen (1990), in talking about gender differences, notes this phenomenon:
>> Complementary schismogenesis commonly sets in when women and
>> men have divergent sensitivities and hypersensitivities. For example, a

man who fears losing freedom pulls away at the first sign he interprets
as an attempt to "control" him, but pulling away is just the signal that
sets off alarms for the woman who fears losing intimacy. (p. 282)

Note that the year of publication is given in parentheses immediately following the author's name and not with the page number.

APA Style: Constructing a References List

For a comparison of the MLA and APA styles for citing books and periodical articles, see page 881.

The section that follows includes model entries for different types of print and
nonprint sources in APA style. Figure 20.5 provides you with a flowchart that will
help you find the model entry that is closest to the source that you need to cite.

Is My Source a Complete Print Book or Part of a Print Book?

No	Yes, go to the next question below.	Go to this entry.
	Is it a book with only one author?	1
	Are you citing more than one book by this author?	2
	Is it a book with multiple authors?	3
	Is the author unknown or unnamed?	5
	Is the book by an organization of some kind?	4
	Does the book also have a translator?	10
	Is it a later publication or edition of the book?	6, 7
	Is it a multivolume work?	12
	Does the book have an editor or a translator?	8, 10
	Is the book an edited collection or anthology?	8, 9
	Is it a work in a collection or an anthology?	9
	Is it an introduction, a preface, a foreword, or an afterword?	11
	Is it a published interview?	13
	Is it an entry in a dictionary or reference work?	22

Is My Source from a Print Periodical Such as a Journal, a Magazine, or a Newspaper?

No	Yes, go to the next question below.	Go to this entry.
	Is it from a scholarly journal?	
	Do the journal's page numbers continue from one issue to the next?	14
	Does each issue start with page 1?	15
	Is it from a magazine?	16
	Is it a review?	19
	Is it from a newspaper?	17
	Is it an editorial?	18
	Is it a letter to the editor?	20
	Is it an article in a newsletter?	21

(continued on page 908)

FIGURE 20.5   APA Style: A Flowchart for Determining the Model References Entry You Need

FIGURE 20.5
Continued

Is My Source a Print Source but Not from a Journal, a Magazine, or a Newspaper?

No	Yes, go to the next question below.	Go to this entry.
	Is it an entry in a dictionary or reference work?	22
	Is it a government document?	23
	Is it an unpublished doctoral dissertation?	24
	Is it an academic report	25

Is My Source a Nonprint Source from an Online Subscription Database or the World Wide Web?

No	Yes, go to the next question below.	Go to this entry.
	Is it a professional or personal Web site?	26
	Is it an article?	
	Is it a scholarly article retrieved from a database?	27
	Is it from an online journal?	29
	Is it from an online magazine?	30
	Is it from an online newspaper?	31
	Is it an online book?	28
	Is it a posting to an electronic forum?	32
	Is it an e-mail message?	33
	Is it a blog entry?	34
	Is it an entry in a wiki?	35
	Is it computer software?	36

Is My Source a Nonprint Source That Is Not Published Online?

No	Yes, go to the next question below.	Go to this entry.
	Is it a television or radio program?	37
	Is it an audio recording?	38
	Is it a film, video recording, or DVD?	39
	Is it an oral presentation?	40

Consult with Your Instructor about How to Cite Your Source.

PRINT DOCUMENTS

Books

The basic elements in an entry for a book are the author's name or authors' names, the date of publication, the title, and the publication information, consisting of the place of publication and the publisher. See Figure 20.6 for guidelines on where to find the elements of an entry in a list of references for an edited collection in APA style.

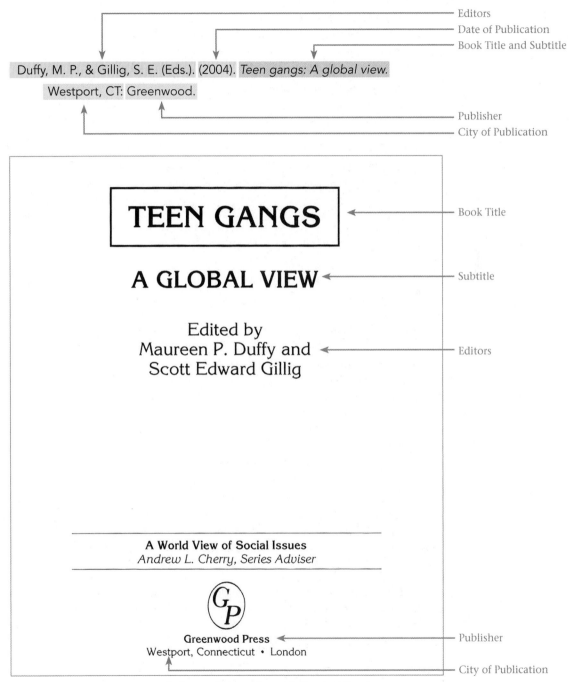

Editors
Date of Publication
Book Title and Subtitle

Duffy, M. P., & Gillig, S. E. (Eds.). (2004). *Teen gangs: A global view.*
Westport, CT: Greenwood.

Publisher
City of Publication

TEEN GANGS ← Book Title

A GLOBAL VIEW ← Subtitle

Edited by
Maureen P. Duffy and
Scott Edward Gillig ← Editors

A World View of Social Issues
Andrew L. Cherry, Series Adviser

Greenwood Press ← Publisher
Westport, Connecticut • London
City of Publication

FIGURE 20.6 The Parts of a Reference Entry for an Edited Collection

(cont'd)

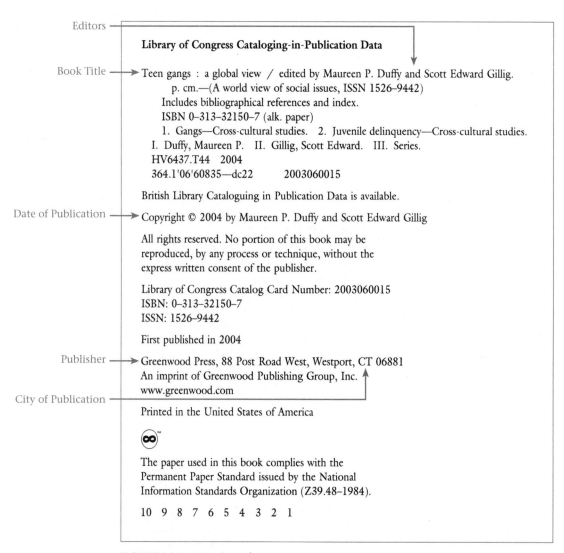

Editors

Book Title

Date of Publication

Publisher

City of Publication

Library of Congress Cataloging-in-Publication Data

Teen gangs : a global view / edited by Maureen P. Duffy and Scott Edward Gillig.
    p. cm.—(A world view of social issues, ISSN 1526–9442)
    Includes bibliographical references and index.
    ISBN 0–313–32150–7 (alk. paper)
    1. Gangs—Cross-cultural studies. 2. Juvenile delinquency—Cross-cultural studies.
  I. Duffy, Maureen P. II. Gillig, Scott Edward. III. Series.
  HV6437.T44   2004
  364.1'06'60835—dc22   2003060015

British Library Cataloguing in Publication Data is available.

Copyright © 2004 by Maureen P. Duffy and Scott Edward Gillig

All rights reserved. No portion of this book may be
reproduced, by any process or technique, without the
express written consent of the publisher.

Library of Congress Catalog Card Number: 2003060015
ISBN: 0–313–32150–7
ISSN: 1526–9442

First published in 2004

Greenwood Press, 88 Post Road West, Westport, CT 06881
An imprint of Greenwood Publishing Group, Inc.
www.greenwood.com

Printed in the United States of America

The paper used in this book complies with the
Permanent Paper Standard issued by the National
Information Standards Organization (Z39.48–1984).

10 9 8 7 6 5 4 3 2 1

FIGURE 20.6 Continued

1. Book with one author: In APA style, the date of publication follows the author's name. The author's first and middle name are given as initials, and the title of the book is italicized, not underlined. Only the first word of the title is capitalized, as well as any proper nouns and the first word following a colon.

   author   date of publication title   city   publisher
Gould, S. J. (1981). *The mismeasure of man*. New York: Norton.

2. Two entries by the same author: The entries are listed in chronological order, with the earliest publication first. If more than one work was published in the same year, the works are ordered alphabetically based on the first letter of the title. Each work is given a lowercase letter after the date: for example, (2004a) for the first entry published in 2004 and (2004b) for the second entry. These letters would appear with the dates in the in-text citations.

> Tannen, D. (1990). *You just don't understand: Women and men in conversation.* New York: Ballantine Books.

> Tannen. D. (1994). *Talking from 9 to 5.* New York: Morrow.

3. Book with multiple authors: All authors' names are inverted. Use an ampersand to separate the last two entries. Give the names of all authors for up to six authors; if there are more authors, follow the sixth name with *et al.*

> Covey, S. R., Merrill, A. R., & Merrill, R. R. (1994). *First things first.* New York: Simon & Schuster.

4. Book by a corporate entity or organization: When the publisher is the same as the author, use the word *Author* where the publisher's name is usually given.

> Adobe Systems Inc. (2001). *Adobe acrobat 5.0: Getting started.* San Jose, CA: Author.

5. Book by an unknown author:

> *The Chicago manual of style: The essential guide for writers, editors, and publishers* (15th ed.). (2003). Chicago: Chicago University Press.

6. Republished book: Including the original date of publication is obligatory in APA style.

> Dickens, C. (1969). *Hard times.* (D. Craig, Ed.). Baltimore: Penguin Books. (Original work published 1854)

7. Book in a later edition:

> Corbett, E. P. J. (1990). *Classical rhetoric for the modern student* (3rd ed.). New York: Oxford University Press.

8. Edited collection:

> Inman, J. A., & Sewell, D. N. (Eds.). (2000). *Taking flight with owls: Examining electronic writing center work.* Mahwah, NJ: Erlbaum.

See also Figure 20.6.

9. Work in a collection or an anthology: In APA style the page numbers come after the title and before the publication information.

> Anson, C. M., & Jewell, R. (2001). Shadows of the mountain. In E. E. Schell & P. L. Stock (Eds.), *Moving a mountain: Transforming the role of contingent faculty in composition studies and higher education* (pp. 47–75). Urbana, IL: NCTE.

10. Translation:

> Eliade, M. (1959). *The sacred and the profane: The nature of religion* (W. R. Trask, Trans.). New York: Harcourt. (Original work published 1957)

11. Introduction, preface, foreword, or afterword:

> Burns, H. (1999). Foreword. In C. L. Selfe, *Technology and literacy in the twenty-first century: The importance of paying attention* (pp. ix–xvii). Carbondale: Southern Illinois University Press.

12. A multivolume work published over more than one year:

> Campbell, J. (1959–1968) *The masks of god* (Vols. 1–4). New York: Viking.

13. Published interview:

> Blair, K., & Takayoshi, P. (1999). Making the map: An interview with Gail Hawisher. [Interview with G. Hawisher] In K. Blair & P. Takayoshi (Eds.), *Feminist cyberspaces: Mapping gendered academic spaces* (pp. 177–191). Stamford, CT: Ablex.

You should cite an interview published in a periodical as you would a periodical article (see #s 14, 15, and 16). APA categorizes personal interviews as personal communications: Because such an interview cannot be recovered, there is no need to include an entry for it in a reference list, but the interview should be cited in the body of the text (see #s 33 and 40).

Periodical Articles

The basic items in an entry for a periodical article are the author's name or authors' names, the date of publication in parentheses, the title of the article, and information about the publication in which the article appeared, including its title, volume and issue number (if applicable), and the page range for the article. See Figure 20.7 below and on page 914 for guidelines on where to find the elements of a reference entry for a periodical article in APA style.

14. Article in a scholarly journal with continuous pagination: In APA style the volume number is italicized. APA style also uses full page numbers.

> authors   date of publication   title
> Thayer, A. & Kolko, B. E. (2004). Localization of digital games: The
>
>   title of periodical
>   process of blending for the global games market. *Technical*
>
>   volume no. and page range
> *Communication, 51,* 477–488.

15. Article in a scholarly journal that is paginated by issue: When an article is from a journal that restarts the page numbers with each issue, the issue number follows the volume number in parentheses in APA style.

> Howard, R. M. (1993). Power revisited: Or, how we became a department. *Writing Program Administration: Journal of the Council of Writing Program Administrators, 16*(3), 37–49.

16. Magazine article: Magazines may or may not include volume and issue numbers. In an entry in APA style, the volume number should be included, placed within commas between the name of the magazine and

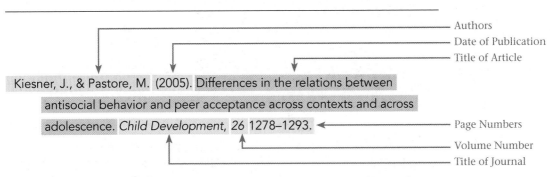

FIGURE 20.7 The Parts of a Reference Entry for a Journal Article

(cont'd)

Volume Number

Title of Journal
Date of Publication

Child Development, November/December 2005, Volume 76, Number 6, Pages 1129–1317

Contents

Title of Article ⟶

Authors ⟶
First Page of Article

FIGURE 20.7   Continued

the page numbers of the article (*Scientific American, 290,* 54–61). In the first example below, *Business Week* is a magazine that does not use volume numbers.

Foust, D., Eidem, M., & Bremner, B. (2004, February 2). AFLAC: Its ducks are not in a row. *Business Week,* 52–53.

Wilson, C. E. (2005, January). Usability and user experience design: The next decade. *Intercom, 52,* 6–9.

17. Newspaper article: When articles appear on discontinuous pages, as they often do, APA style requires you to list all the page numbers.

Fatsis, S. (2002, April 9). A more modern masters. *The Wall Street Journal,* pp. B1, B4.

18. Editorial: If there is a title, it should precede [*Editorial*].

Moral scoreboard. (2004, February 18). [Editorial]. *The Arizona Republic,* p. B10.

19. Review: If the review is titled, give the title in the usual position, preceding the bracketed information.

Jablonski, J. (2003). [Review of the book *The new careers: Individual action and economic change*]. *Technical Communication Quarterly, 12,* 230–234.

20. Letter to the editor:

Rosati, C. (2004, February 18). Let's throw the book at Valley street racers [Letter to the editor]. *The Arizona Republic,* p. B10.

21. Newsletter article, no author: Unsigned articles should be alphabetized in the list of references by the first word of the title. If there is a volume number, place it between the name of the publication and the page numbers, separated by commas. The following example from the newsletter of the Heard Museum of Native Cultures and Art has no volume number.

Shared images: The jewelry of Yazzie Johnson and Gail Bird. (2007), (January/February), *Earthsong,* 8.

Other Print Sources

22. Entry in dictionary or reference work: APA style uses page numbers even when the entries are alphabetical.

> Express Mail. (1993). In *Merriam-Webster's new collegiate dictionary*
>
>   (p. 411). Springfield, MA: Merriam-Webster.

> Pfeiffer, R. H. (1974). Sumerian Poetry. In *Princeton Encyclopedia of*
>
>   *Poetry and Poetics* (pp. 820–821). Princeton: Princeton University
>
>   Press.

23. Government document: Like MLA style, APA style lists the agency as the author of the report when the author is not known. If you list a sub-department or agency, make certain that you also list the higher department if the sub-department is not well-known. If the publisher is not the Government Printing Office (GPO), list the highest known agency or department as the author. If the document has a specific publication number, list it after the title.

> National Institutes of Health. (1992). *Toxicology and carcinogenesis studies*
>
>   *of Resorcinol (CAS No. 108-46-3) in F344/N rats and B6C3F$_1$ mice*
>
>   *(Gavage Studies)* (NIH Publication No. 92-2858). Research Triangle
>
>   Park, NC: Author.

24. Unpublished doctoral dissertation:

> Edminster, J. R. (2002). *The diffusion of new media scholarship: Power,*
>
>   *innovation, and resistance in academe.* Unpublished doctoral
>
>   dissertation, University of South Florida.

25. Academic report:

> Melnick, R., Welch, N., & Hart, B. (2005). *How Arizona compares: Real*
>
>   *numbers and hot topics.* Tempe: Arizona State University, Morrison
>
>   Institute for Public Policy.

ONLINE SOURCES

Unlike MLA, APA prefers that the exact URL be given in the reference entry. When the document being cited has a print as well as an electronic version, APA requires you to provide publication information for both versions. If the content is likely to change, give a retrieval date. For content that is

Publication Information about the Print version of the Article

Sullivan, M. L. (2005). Maybe we shouldn't study "gangs": Does reification obscure youth violence? *Journal of Contemporary Criminal Justice 21*(2), 176. Retrieved from CSA Illumina database.

Online Subscription Service

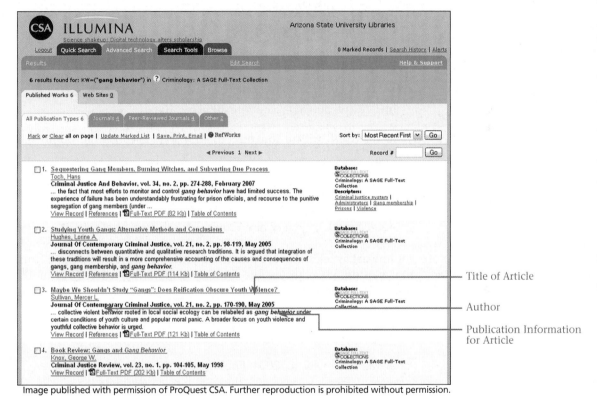

Title of Article

Author

Publication Information for Article

Image published with permission of ProQuest CSA. Further reproduction is prohibited without permission.

FIGURE 20.8 The Parts of a Reference Entry for a Journal Article Accessed from an Online Subscription Database

fixed, such as a journal article, no date is necessary. See Figure 20.8 for guidelines on where to find the elements of a reference entry for an article accessed from an online database in APA style.

26. Basic professional or personal Web site:

American Medical Association. (2004). Home page. Retrieved February 17, 2004, from http://www.ama-assn.org/

27. Scholarly article retrieved from a database: Include the issue number as well as the volume number.

author   date of publication   title of article
Selber, S. A. (1994). Beyond skill building: Challenges facing technical

communication teachers in the computer age.

          title of journal   volume no. and page range
Technical Communication Quarterly, 3(4), 365–391. Retrieved

      name of database
from EBSCOHost database.

28. Online book:

Howells, W. D. (1913). *Familiar Spanish travels*. Retrieved from

http://www.gutenberg.net/etext05/sptrv10.txt

29. Article from an online journal: In APA style the volume number is italicized.

Salvo, M. J. (2002). Deafened to their demands: An ethnographic study

of accommodation. *Kairos 7*(1). Retrieved from http://english.ttu.

edu/kairos/7.1/binder2.html?coverweb/salvo/ctx.html

Note: For journal articles that are published online and are unchanged from their print version, you can use the format for a journal article (#14 or 15) but add [*Electronic version*] following the title of the article. A retrieval statement is not necessary.

30. Article from an online magazine:

Cooper, M., & Tumulty, K. (2004, February 16). Bring on the cash! *Time*.

Retrieved from http://www.time.com/time/election2004/

article/0,18471,591298,00.html

31. Article from an online newspaper:

Novovitch, B. (2004, February 17). It's home stupid home, but the "clods"

can read. *New York Times*. Retrieved from http://www.nytimes.com/

2004/02/17/education/17PROF.html

32. Posting to an electronic forum such as a mailing list (listserv): In APA style, list only electronic references that have been archived and are retrievable.

Peckham, I. (2004, February 17). Update on AP and dual enrollment.

Message posted to WPA-L. electronic mailing list, archived at

http://lists.asu.edu/cgi-bin/wa?A2=ind0309&L=wpal&D=1&O=
D&F=&S=&P=52156.

33. E-mail message: In APA style, e-mail is considered personal communication and is cited only in the text as "personal communication," followed by the date of the communication. Since personal communications are not recoverable data, they are not listed in the references.

34. Blog entry: Provide the name of the author (bloggers often use pseudonyms), date, title of entry, the words *Message posted to,* name of blog, and the URL.

Rice, J. (2007, March 30). Re: Network academics. Message posted to

http://ydog.net/?page_id=345

35. Wiki entry:

Rhetoric. (n.d.). Retrieved March 30, 2007, from *Wikipedia*: http://

en.wikipedia.org/wiki/Rhetoric

36. Computer software: If you download software, inlcude *Available from* and the URL.

AllWrite! 2.0 with Online Handbook. (2003). [Computer software]. New

York: McGraw-Hill.

OTHER NONPRINT SOURCES

37. Television and radio programs: In APA style the names of the writers, directors, and producers are given as appropriate. In addition, after the name of the series, the reference indicates whether the source is a television or radio broadcast in square brackets.

Buckner, N., & Whittlesey, R. (Writers, Directors, Producers). (2004,

February 3). Dogs and more dogs. *Nova* [Television broadcast].

Boston and Washington, DC: Public Broadcasting Service.

Turpin, C. (Executive Producer). (2004, February 12). Scientists succeed

in cloning human embryo. *All things considered* [Radio broadcast].

Washington, DC: National Public Radio.

38. Audio recording:

Jackson, A. (2002). Drive. On *Drive* [CD]. New York: Arista.

39. Film, video recording, or DVD:

> Jackson, P. (Director). (2002). *The lord of the rings: The two towers* [DVD]. United States: New Line Home Entertainment.

40. Oral presentation: Because live lectures are not recoverable data, in APA style they are cited parenthetically in the text but are not included in the list of references. However, when professional presentations are made from texts that can be recovered, they are cited.

> Russell, D. R. (1999, March). Teacher's perception of genre across the curriculum: Making classroom/culture connections visible. Paper presented at the Conference on College Composition and Communication Convention. Atlanta, GA.

APA Style: Sample Student Paper

The student paper that follows, "How Do Gangs Affect Adolescent Behavior" by Aaron Zook, is an example of a paper that uses APA style.

If you write a paper using APA style, follow these guidelines:

- Include a separate title page. Center the title one-third of the way down the page, using capital and lowercase letters, and do not use a special typeface for it. Give your name, the course number, and the date, all also centered and double spaced, on separate lines below the title. In the upper-right-hand corner give the page number, preceded by a short version of the title, which you will include on each page of your paper.
- On the second page of your paper, provide an abstract of the paper if your instructor requires one. The abstract should be a short (about 100–120 words) summary of your paper's contents. If you include an abstract, the paper itself begins on the third page. Repeat the title on the first page of your paper, centering it one inch from the top. Double-space to the first line of your text.
- Double-space the entire paper, including any block quotations and the items in your list of references.
- Leave one-inch margins on all sides.
- Place page numbers in the upper-right-hand corner after the running head, five spaces after the shortened version of the title.
- Indent paragraphs one-half inch from the left margin.
- Some papers use headings to label sections of the text. If you use headings, center them and double-space above and below them.
- Put your list of references on a new page, with the title "References" centered at the top.

How Do Gangs Affect Adolescent Behavior?

Aaron Zook

Psychology 101

Professor Jones

March 23, 2007

Title is centered, one-third of the way down the page.

Name, title of course, name of professor, and date all centered and double-spaced on separate lines below the title.

How Do Gangs Affect Adolescent Behavior?

Since the early 1920s, researchers have closely studied the relationship between street gangs and violent crime from a variety of perspectives: criminological, sociological, and psychological (Thabit, 2005). Whatever the underlying causes for gang membership, the results seem clear; members of street gangs admit to a far greater rate of serious crime, and to far more severe acts of violence (Penly Hall, Thornberry, & Lizotte, 2006) than non-gang members of the same age, race, and socioeconomic background (Battin-Pearson, Thornberry, Hawkins, & Krohn, 1998). According to the Web site Safeyouth.org (n.d.), gang violence is certainly cause for concern:

> Gang members are responsible for much of the serious violence in the United States. . . . Teens that are gang members are much more likely than other teens to commit serious and violent crimes. For example, a survey in Denver found that while only 14% of teens were gang members, they were responsible for committing 89% of the serious violent crimes.

Many researchers have therefore come to the conclusion that gangs necessarily cause violence and deviant behavior. As a matter of policy, then, it seems clear that the solution to a number of social ills is to break up, disrupt, or prevent the formation of gangs. Other programs seek to prevent young people from joining gangs through interventions of various types and levels of effectiveness. Most of these efforts take it as a given that gangs seriously distort behavior, even among individuals who already belong to "high-risk" demographic groups. Adolescents living in poverty or other disadvantaged circumstances; those attending violent and/or failing schools; members of criminalized peer groups; and children from violent and/or extremely dysfunctional households or demonstrating a predisposition toward antisocial behavior all seem to be at greater risk for future gang membership (Battin-Pearson et al., 1998), but a number of studies have shown that their own behaviors are considerably more violent while they belong to a gang than they were before or after membership (Gordon et al., 2004). After years of study, researchers still do not clearly understand how and why gangs exert such a powerful influence on behavior.

Side annotations:

Title repeated on first page of paper, centered.

Double-space from title to first line of paper.

Information from sources cited with parenthetical references.

Quotation longer than forty words is indented 1/2 inch or 5 spaces and double-spaced. The sentence that introduces it ends with a colon. Because no date is given in the source, the abbreviation *n.d.* is included.

Et al. used after the first citation for Multiple authors. *Et al.* used for first citation of a work with six authors

How Do Gangs   3

A crucial answer might be found in the typical composition of a gang. Overwhelmingly, gangs are made up of adolescents and young adults. The median age of violent gang members has been estimated to be eighteen; members tend to join in their late teens, and contrary to popular fallacies and urban legends, youths generally leave a gang with few or no consequences within a year of joining (Thomas, 2005). Clearly, then, the gang problem can and should be understood in large part as a youth problem; researchers might come to a deeper understanding of the nature and impact of gangs by shifting some emphasis in their research from violence to adolescent adjustment behaviors.

Opening paragraph sets up the issue.

The research community has by no means reached a consensus as to the precise definition of street gangs, however. The telltale sign that a group is a gang—one that most researchers, police organizations, the popular media, and gang members themselves agree on—is a tendency to commit violent acts (Katz & Jackson-Jacobs, 2004), but violence is not an adequate condition in itself. Why, for example, are Crips and Bloods considered gangs, but not Skinheads? Likewise, organized crime is now rarely considered "gang behavior," though early studies included these types of organizations. Yet all of these form distinct social groups and are involved in criminal behaviors (Thomas, 2005). One common distinction researchers draw is based on the motivation behind the group's violent activities. Does the group sell drugs or stolen merchandise? Do they operate according to an ideology or shared set of racial or cultural prejudices? Or are they primarily concerned with "turf," status, or violence for its own sake (U.S. Department of Education, n.d.)? Contemporary studies tend to maintain that only the latter group of motives typify "gangs" and have been particularly concerned with the seemingly random nature of the various criminal behaviors that many such gangs exhibit. The criminal acts seem to have largely symbolic value, consistent with the way many street gangs are associated with the use of emblems, dress, and a shared name easily identified by all of their members (Katz & Jackson-Jacobs, 2004).

Government agency given as author.

First point: Difficulty of defining gangs.

Experts in gang behavior have advanced numerous explanations for the most troubling examples of violent gang behavior: random drive-by shootings, seemingly unmotivated killings and aggravated assaults, car-jackings, and so on. Ritual initiations, turf wars, cycles of retribution between competing gangs, and intra-gang status have all been identified as motivators (Fagan & Wilkinson, 1998). Other hypotheses focus on the greater availability of guns and drugs, and still others on the model of shared or diffuse moral culpability (Thornberry, Krohn, Lizotte, & Chard-Wierschem, 1993), a phenomenon that has also been observed in riots and cases where soldiers have committed wartime atrocities. Yet another explanation has involved the culpability of the media and the police in promoting gang imagery: The very definition of gangs as violent entities increases members' levels of violence. In other words, certain youths seek the rewards they think gang membership will afford them—status; protection; group identity; and entertainment, drugs, and sex (U.S. Department of Education, n.d.)—and are willing to engage in violent acts because "that's what a gang is." The image is reinforced by the news and popular media and by the folklore of the gang itself. It has also been argued that both gang members' own accounts of their activities and police statistics may be misleading. Because of the status violence confers on a perpetrator, a subject could conceivably exaggerate his or her criminal behavior in surveys and interviews as a means of bragging. Further, crime statistics reflect arrest and incarceration rates which, considering the general conspicuousness of gang members and police efforts to target these groups, could conceivably skew higher for gang offenders than for criminals who do not belong to gangs. A number of studies, less sensational in their findings and therefore less visible in the mainstream media, have found that most gang members spend the majority of their time simply "hanging out," albeit often within the context of drug or alcohol use (Katz & Jackson-Jacobs, 2004). In a sense, then, lacking any overarching objective such as profit or ideology, some gangs may see continued violence as a means of justifying their own existence and retaining members who would otherwise grow restless and leave.

> Second point: Various explanations of gang behavior, leading to the most satisfactory one.

If retention is indeed the motivation for violent gang behavior, then it seems unlikely that some special feature of gangs in their day-to-day operation enables violent extremes of behavior; rather, it is the symbolic value of the gang "family" that makes them sufficiently attractive to justify violence, the risk of death or imprisonment, and the common perception (however false) that one can never leave the gang. It seems likely that certain characteristics typical of adolescents—the desire to create a self-identity, establish a sense of belonging, and both derive status from and earn status within groups (Ausubel, 2002)—make them vulnerable to the allure of such symbolism. It also seems likely that, in addition to environmental and psychological factors such as peer pressure and/or facilitation (Gifford-Smith, Dodge, Dishion, & McCord, 2005) or poor self-esteem ("At last," 1995), cultural factors also aggravate the problem of gang violence. That is to say, while many studies have rightly focused on how crumbling inner cities, poverty, and lack or loss of opportunity and hope affect a teen's predisposition toward gang affiliation, it might be worthwhile to examine how society itself provides gangs with false or mythical status that might add to their attraction.

Citation of a source with no author indicated.

Concludes with assertion that his arguments have led to: cultural factors contribute to gang violence.

References

At last—a rejection detector! (1995, November). *Psychology Today*. Retrieved from http://www.psychologytoday.com/articles/pto-19951101-000034.html

Ausubel, D. P. (2002). *Theory and problems of adolescent development* (2nd ed.). Lincoln, NE: iUniverse.

Battin-Pearson, S. R., Thornberry, T. P., Hawkins, J. D., & Krohn, M. D. (1998, October). Gang membership, delinquent peers, and delinquent behavior. *Juvenile Justice Bulletin*. Retrieved from http://www.ncjrs.gov/pdffiles/171119.pdf

Fagan, J., & Wilkinson, D. L. (1998). Social contexts and functions of adolescent violence. In D. S. Elliott, B. Hamburg, & K. R. Williams (Eds.), *Violence in American schools: A new perspective* (pp. 55–93). New York: Cambridge University Press. Retrieved from http://www.colorado.edu/cspv/publications/factsheets/schoolviolence/FS-SV03.html

Gifford-Smith, M., Dodge, K. A., Dishion, T. J., & McCord, J. (2005). Peer influence in children and adolescents: Crossing the bridge from developmental to intervention science. *Journal of Abnormal Child Psychology, 33*(3), 255–265. Retrieved from SpringerLink.

Gordon, R. A., Lahey, B. B., Kawai, E., Loeber, R., Stouthamer-Loeber, M., & Farrington, D. P. (2004). Antisocial behavior and youth gang membership: Selection and socialization. *Criminology, 42*(1), 55–88. Abstract retrieved from Blackwell Synergy.

Katz, J., & Jackson-Jacobs, C. (2004). The criminologists' gang. [Electronic version]. In C. Sumner (Ed.), *The Blackwell companion to criminology*. Malden, MA: Blackwell Publishers.

National Youth Violence Prevention Center. (n.d). *Youth gangs*. Retrieved February 13, 2007, from http://www.safeyouth.org/scripts/teens/gangs.asp

Penly Hall, G., Thornberry, T. P., & Lizotte, A. J. (2006). The gang facilitation effect and neighborhood risk: Do gangs have a stronger influence on delinquency in disadvantaged areas? In J. F. Short, Jr., & L. Hughes (Eds.), *Studying youth gangs*. Lanham, MD: Altamira Press.

New page, title centered; double-space between title and first line of reference list.

Entries double spaced, in alphabetical order.

First line of each entry at left margin; all other lines indented 1/2 inch or 5 spaces.

Thabit, W. (2005). How did East New York become a ghetto? Retrieved February 13, 2007, from http://faculty.ncwc.edu/toconnor/301/301lect08.htm

Thomas, C. (2005). Serious delinquency and gang membership. *Psychiatric Times 22*(4). Retrieved from http://www.psychiatrictimes.com/showArticle.jhtml?articleID=162100156

Thornberry, T. P., Krohn, M. D., Lizotte, A. J., & Chard-Wierschem, D. (1993). The role of juvenile gangs in facilitating delinquent behavior. *Journal of Research in Crime and Delinquency, 30* (1), *55–87*. Abstract retrieved from Sage Journals Online.

U.S. Department of Education. (n.d.). *Youth gangs: Going beyond the myths to address a critical problem.* Retrieved from http://www.ed.gov/admins/lead/safety/training/gangs/problem_pg3.html

Walker-Barnes, C. J., & Mason, C. A. (2001). Ethnic differences in the effect of parenting on gang involvement and gang delinquency: A longitudinal, hierarchical linear modeling perspective. *Child Development, 72*(6), 1814–1831. Abstract retrieved from IngentaConnect.

Appendix A
Constructing a Writing Portfolio

Constructing a writing portfolio gives you the opportunity to select, display, and reflect on the work you have done in this course. Although there are many ways to construct a portfolio, this chapter offers you some common suggestions and guidelines that others have found useful. An important purpose for constructing the portfolio is to provide you with support for the claims that you will make about your writing in the course: In short, a portfolio helps you support this statement: "Here is what I have learned this semester, and here is the evidence that I have learned these writing strategies and conventions."

Your instructor will guide you on how much evidence to include in the portfolio to support your claims about what you have learned. In some cases, a single example of your work will be sufficient evidence. In other cases, you may need to provide multiple pieces of evidence. For instance, to demonstrate that you know how to adapt a message for a particular audience, you might need to show how you have done so for two or three different audiences.

What Is a Portfolio and Why Should I Construct One?

In the past, graphic artists or photographers were the only professionals who tended to keep portfolios of their work. These artists used portfolios to show potential clients their previous work and to give them a sense of what to expect in the future. More recently, many other professionals, such as technical or professional writers, have found that keeping a portfolio is helpful when they look for work.

While no one will deny that the quality of the final product is important, from an educational perspective how you arrived at that final product may be just as important as, or even more important than, the result you achieved. By looking at your process (the path you took to get to your endpoint) in a portfolio, your instructor can better assess your strengths and weaknesses as a writer.

When instructors or other readers look at a single piece of your writing, they may come away with a narrow view of your writing capabilities. They may see only a particular kind of writing, with its strengths and weaknesses. However, when readers look at a portfolio of your work, they gain a fuller picture of the writing you have accomplished.

Because the portfolio represents what you have learned throughout the course, the ideal time to read this appendix and to begin constructing your portfolio is during the first week of the course. That will give you many opportunities to select and reflect on your work while that work is still fresh in your mind. Students who construct the most effective portfolios usually work on them a little each week.

 ## Selecting Materials for Your Portfolio

As you decide what to include as part of your portfolio, consider the following questions:

1. What have I learned about writing in each of the four areas of life—academic, professional, civic, personal?
2. What have I learned about writing for various purposes?
3. What rhetorical skills and knowledge have I developed?
4. What critical reading skills have I developed?
5. What critical thinking skills have I developed?
6. What have I learned about composing processes—invention, drafting, revising, editing?
7. What have I learned about working effectively with peers?
8. What knowledge of conventions have I developed?
9. What have I learned about writing responsibly?
10. What have I learned about using technology?

As you respond to each of the questions listed above, consider a follow-up question: *What evidence will demonstrate that I have developed this set of skills or knowledge?* Think about all the work that you have done in the course. Among the print or electronic evidence—tangible evidence—available to you are the following:

- Invention work (lists that you constructed; brainstorming; clustering; freewriting)
- Research notes (from your library and online research; field research; interviews)
- Reading notes (comments you made on the reading you did for the class)
- Drafts of papers
- Peers' written comments on your work
- Online discussions about your work
- Polished versions of your papers
- Reflections on your papers (that you write when you submit your papers)

Among the evidence that may not appear on paper or disk are the following:

- Discussions with peers about your writing
- Discussions with your instructor about your writing

You will, of course, need to transcribe evidence that exists only in your memory so that you can make it available to those who read your portfolio.

Reflecting on What You Have Written

As noted earlier, it is a good idea to reflect on your work regularly throughout the semester while that work is fresh in your mind. A week or a month later, you may not remember why you followed up on a peer's comments or how you would approach the topic differently if you were to write about it again. Remember that *reflective writing* asks you to do just what its name suggests: to think back on, to consider, to reflect on the work you did for the course. Consider answering the questions at the end of each chapter in Parts 2 and 3 as a way to start that reflective process.

There are several ways to keep track of your reflective writing. You may choose to keep a handwritten or electronic journal, or you may want to keep your own course blog where you regularly reflect on your course writing.

As you reflect on the work that you use as evidence in your portfolio, you might consider another question: *Why does this piece of evidence effectively demonstrate that I have developed a certain set of skills or knowledge?* Your response to that question should also appear in your portfolio because it illustrates that you are confident about what you have learned during the course.

As you reflect on your polished essays, you might wish to include a paragraph for each that begins, "If I had the opportunity to revise this paper further, I would . . . ." This kind of statement acknowledges the situation that exists in most courses: There is rarely enough time to revise as thoughtfully as you could if the course were two semesters long.

Organizing Your Portfolio

There are many ways to organize your portfolio, and your instructor will let you know how he or she would like your portfolio arranged and organized. Some colleges and universities have specific portfolio requirements; if yours does, you will receive guidance on what you need to do.

Sometimes, your teacher will ask you to organize your portfolio in a *chronological* manner: You would start with the first piece of writing you did for the class and end with the final piece of writing. Other organizational schemes you may find especially useful include the following:

- **By Learning Goals:** This is an efficient and effective way to organize your portfolio. For example, the Writing Program Administrators Outcomes Statement, which is prominent in this book, includes four categories of learning goals: (1) Rhetorical Knowledge; (2) Critical

Thinking, Reading, and Writing; (3) Processes; and (4) Knowledge of Conventions. If you use this scheme, you may wish to follow the order given here, or you may wish to reorganize the categories to reflect what you consider to be most important. Once you have decided on the order of the learning goals, those goals can become headings in your portfolio. Under each heading, then, you could respond to the three questions noted earlier:

- What have I learned? How have I grown as a writer?
- What evidence demonstrates that I have learned this—that I have grown?
- Why is this evidence the best possible evidence that I can choose?

For an example from a writing portfolio organized by learning goals, see pages A-6–A-12.

- **By Purpose:** If you use this organizational scheme, you could list the chapter titles from Parts 2 and 3 of this book as your headings—for example, "Writing to Explore," "Writing to Convince," "Writing to Propose Solutions." This pattern may allow you to focus on each purpose more fully, but it also may cause you to repeat statements about learning goals. That is, for each purpose, you might have to say, "Here's how I learned to adapt my message to an audience." If you do use this organizational pattern, you still can use the same questions:
    - What have I learned? How have I grown as a writer?
    - What evidence demonstrates that I have learned this—that I have grown?
    - Why is this evidence the best possible evidence that I can choose?

Portfolio Formats

You may decide to submit—or your instructor may request that you submit—your portfolio in one of the following formats:

- **As a print document** in a three-ring binder.
- **As an electronic file,** either on a floppy disk, flash drive, or CD. If you use this format, consider constructing a hypertext document so that readers can click on links to see other parts of your portfolio.
- **As a Web site.** This format enables you to provide links to other parts of your own portfolio as well as links to other Web sites or pages that you have found useful during the semester.

In the example shown in Figure A.1, note how student Eileen Holland has organized her electronic portfolio. As background for her work in her first-year writing course, she provides examples of her writing from elementary and secondary school. Because she is an avid reader who believes that reading

Electronic Portfolio
Introduction and Table of Contents
by Eileen Holland

Welcome to my writing portfolio for first-year composition. As my contents indicate, I've been interested in writing since elementary school because my teachers gave me fun writing projects and lots of encouragement. In high school, I was fortunate enough to work with teachers who offered me lots of constructive feedback; some of my friends did the same. I've also been inspired by writers such as Garrison Keillor, Jared Diamond, and Sarah Vowell.

In this portfolio I demonstrate how I have developed skills and knowledge in this course. In particular, I demonstrate how I have learned in four areas: (1) Rhetorical Knowledge; (2) Critical Thinking, Reading, and Writing; (3) Processes; and (4) Knowledge of Conventions. In addition to describing what I have learned, I also offer evidence from my work this semester to prove that I have learned the kinds of knowledge and skills that we have studied.

When I finished high school, I thought that I knew all that I needed to know about writing. In this course, though, I have come to appreciate that learning to write is a never-ending journey. My teacher, who has been writing for more than five decades and teaching writing for almost three decades, told us that she's still learning to write. In class we talked about all sorts of people who keep learning to perform well in their fields until they retire— teachers, professional athletes, entertainers, engineers, painters, architects. Humans keep on learning.

helps her as a writer, she provides information about several of her favorite writers. Then she includes materials to demonstrate that she has learned skills and knowledge from the four areas of the Writing Program Administrators Outcomes Statement. Finally, she looks to the future by projecting what she hopes to learn in upcoming semesters.

A Portion of a Sample Portfolio

The following portfolio excerpt comes from Chelsea Rundle, who constructed it in a second-semester writing course. Note how she has used the Writing Program Administrators Outcomes Statement to organize her portfolio. Also note how she uses evidence from her work to demonstrate what she has learned.

Portfolio

Chelsea Rundle

I cannot believe the semester is coming to a close already. Even though it has seemed quite short, I have learned a lot over the course of this semester. In English 102, I learned that a good paper topic is one that I am passionate about and is feasible. Picking topics that were particular to my major—applied biology—helped me explore different issues/trends in the field of biology and medical science through writing my English papers.

In my first paper, I explored the concept of personalized medicine by researching what others thought about it and then stepping back and forming my opinion on the topic. For the second paper, writing to convince, I addressed a topic I am very passionate about—CT scans causing radiation cancer. I was able to look at how these two topics affect one another because CT scans are an integral process in personalized medicine.

The topic for my evaluation was the biology program at ASU Tempe versus the biology program at another ASU campus. I picked this topic because I am planning on attending one campus for one more year, but I do not know what campus to attend after that. Even though in my evaluation I came to the conclusion that the other campus's biology program would be better for me—I am still not sure. You made the comment on one of my drafts that I should try taking a biology course at ASU Tempe. I may take your advice and try taking a course over there before making a final decision regarding which university to attend. Also, I am not certain what future career I want to enter into. It may be best for me to figure that out before picking which campus I want to attend.

For my proposing a solution paper, I chose a topic that I am passionate about but is not particular to my major. Instead, I chose a topic personal to me and those living in my neighborhood—a new parking regulation passed by the Home Owner's Association (HOA) that does not allow any vehicles to be parked on the street. I chose this topic because my sister will be getting her driver's license soon and I just bought a new truck, so my family will have too many vehicles to fit in our garage and driveway. You suggested that I go to the city council with my final paper, and I just might. The parking regulation has been a problem for a number of families in my neighborhood. If I get enough people to side with me and show the HOA why the regulation is a problem and what some possible solutions to the problem are, I have faith we can get the HOA to change their minds. We'll see.

While writing these four papers and revising them, I have expanded my writing knowledge and have learned how to strengthen my writing skills. I will demonstrate what I have learned in this portfolio. In the portfolio for writing goals and objectives, I used only examples from English 102 because it is the only class I took this semester in which I learned about writing.

RHETORICAL KNOWLEDGE

- Focus on a Purpose

In writing the first argument, I stayed focused on a purpose: persuading the audience to see the dangers of CT scans. To do this, I used a claim, support for my claim, and the refutation of counterarguments. In refuting counterarguments I addressed multiple viewpoints on the issue while showing the reader why my claim is correct. The following is a refutation of a counterargument I used to strengthen the paper:

> Some argue that radiation cancer is not caused by CT scans, but can be caused by other factors. This is absolutely true, for radiation, or the release of energy, can be given off by a number of

sources including household electrical appliances, heaters, the sun, and x-ray machines. For example, I recall my parents telling me that they were always warned as children not to stand too close to the microwave, or they would get cancer. This is hardly the case, for the type of radiation given off by electrical appliances and heaters isn't harmful enough to cause cancer. However, radiation cancer is caused by high exposure to the sun and x-ray machines. Therefore, as exposure to CT scans—a form of x-ray technology—increases, so does the risk of radiation cancer.

- Respond to the Needs of Different Audiences

When writing a paper particular to my major, I had to think about the needs of my audience. It is important to explain a topic and give background information at the beginning of the paper to avoid confusion. It is hard for the reader to form an opinion from reading your paper if they don't understand the topic you are writing about. It is also important to not offend your audience, so the writer must determine how to use the three appeals—logos (logic), ethos (ethics), and pathos (emotions)—appropriately. Balancing logos, ethos, and pathos is a major challenge in writing an effective paper. Peer reviews helped me determine where more background information was needed.

To provide background information to the reader in a draft of my argument on the topic of CT scans, I wrote:

> The word <u>tomography</u> originates from the Greek word <u>tomos,</u> meaning "slice," and <u>graphia,</u> or "describing." CT scans, a form of tomography, have been used for years as the predominate method for medical imaging. The scans produce a three-dimensional image of an object's internal structure based on several x-ray images. Original uses of CT scans are to diagnose different cancers, guide biopsies and similar procedures, and to plan surgery or radiation treatment ("Computed").

Also regarding how to respond to the needs of audiences—I learned that it is crucial to maintain a negotiable stance while writing an argument. Arguments are rarely two-sided, so it is important to be open to all sides. If you form an opinion without getting all the facts and hearing other viewpoints, you can't honestly say your claim is correct. It is difficult to persuade your audience to see things from your perspective if you don't know all the perspectives yourself.

- Respond Appropriately to Different Kinds of Rhetorical Situations

The different types of writing situations we encountered over the course of this class all required different approaches. Homework and the learning logs were informal and focused more on content than spelling and grammar. On the other hand, the assignments and this writing portfolio are formal and require the use of correct spelling, grammar, usage, punctuation, and, if possible, the use of visuals to enhance appearance.

Writing in English 102 also had to be approached differently to address specific audiences. For example, in my proposing a solution project I wanted to address one specific person: Kathy Olsen, the Association Manager of my neighborhood's Home Owner's Association (HOA). In my letter I wanted to make sure that I reminded Ms. Olsen of our previous conversation, that I maintained a reasonable tone, and that I respected Ms. Olsen's point of view.

Kathy Olsen

Community Association Manager

Dear Ms. Olsen:

My name is Chelsea Rundle. I came in last Tuesday to discuss with you why the Home Owner's Association passed the new parking regulation prohibiting vehicles from parking on the street in my neighborhood—Finley Farms South. You told me that the HOA passed the regulation for three reasons: they thought emergency vehicles could not pass through on a street with vehicles parked on it, a few neighbors had complained that vehicles parked on the street looked bad, and the HOA was worried that drivers would not see children darting into the street from behind parked vehicles.

Further, you informed me that the HOA only fines the owners of vehicles parked on the street after midnight because there are too many vehicles parked on the street during the day to fine the owners. Also, you noted that the fines started out at $100 per vehicle parked on the street per night, but were reduced to $25 because of homeowners' complaints. . . .

On the other hand, in the introduction to my classical argument, I addressed a general audience—explaining the concept of *personalized medicine* for those who do not already know what it is:

> In recent years, computed tomography scans, or CT scans, have been used in personalized medicine—a medical revolution based on the theory of predicting what will happen to one's body any number of years from now and how to fix it. Paranoid people are now flocking to CT scans, desperate to know what is "wrong" with them. Little do they know that the scans themselves cause what they are trying to avoid. I think CT scans cause radiation cancer because of the high amount of radiation a person undergoing a scan is exposed to.

- Adopt Appropriate Voice, Tone, and Level of Formality

Different tones and levels of formality should be used for different genres of writing and in different writing situations. For example, in my argument paper it was important to present the technical background information in a way that could be easily understood by the reader, so I maintained a semiformal tone:

> CT scans are a form of medical imaging process. The CT scan machine creates a series of x-ray image slices of the scanned body area. The series of x-rays can be manipulated to produce a 3-D image (see Fig. 1) of the body's internal structure. Original uses of CT scans are to diagnose different cancers, guide biopsies and similar procedures, and to plan surgery or radiation treatment ("Computed").

A semiformal tone was appropriate because it informed the reader without seeming too wordy or technical. However, some genres of writing are less technical and more informal, allowing the writer to incorporate more of his or her own voice. For example, a short narrative (for lack of a better word) from my learning log is much more informal. The following excerpt is not only less formal, but has a lot of my own voice as well:

> Earlier this evening, I was reading Leonard Pitts Jr.'s argument entitled "Spare the Rod, Spoil the Parenting." At the same time, my sister and dad were having an argument about I don't know what, but my sister wouldn't stop talking back. She was saying, "It's a free country, I can say whatever I want." To which my dad replied, "Yah, but the family is more of a dictatorship." Still reading Pitts' argument, I came to the sentence "As a culture, we seem to have forgotten that the family is not a democracy, but a benign dictatorship." What a coincidence . . . it made me laugh!

- Write in Several Genres

In English 102, I learned the structural aspects of various genres of writing. In the analysis essay, for example, I began with an introduction that included a question I wanted to answer: *How can treatment for disease be adapted to an individual's genetic makeup?* I then gave brief summaries of two texts that answered the question. Next, I analyzed the texts. Finally, I synthesized the texts with my thoughts and opinions to answer the beginning question. Overall, I have realized what an amazing impact on medical technology personalized medicine can potentially have. It will not only add to our knowledge of the causes of disease, but it will also help scientists and doctors alter medicine to treat specific variations of diseases:

> In this early stage, however, I do not think scientists should focus on curing a specific disease. Instead, they should research the causes of many diseases and how they are related on the DNA level. This will help them gain enough knowledge to develop the most effective treatments.

In the argument paper, I began with a claim: *CT scans cause radiation cancer due to the high amount of radiation a person is exposed to.* Next, I provided any background information on the topic my audience might need. Then, I provided evidence to support my claim. Next, I addressed and refuted counterarguments to my claim and concluded.

For the evaluation, I first stated, within the introduction, the topic I would be evaluating: *My original plan was to begin attending ASU's Tempe campus after next year. However, I am not sure this is the best path for me . . . so instead, I am strongly considering transferring to another ASU campus. I evaluated programs at both campuses because they are the two campuses I will be choosing between.*

Next, I evaluated the topic based on criteria. These criteria were my personal criteria a university biology program should meet, or what is ideal: *how many credit hours are required for a degree, the cost of the program, faculty credentials and resources, availability of specialized degrees, and overall location/atmosphere.* Then, I concluded with a restatement of my thesis and showed the reader why the other campus is good/better/ best:

> Overall, I think the biology program at the other campus will be better for me. It will require me to take more credit hours of biology and biology-related courses than at the Tempe campus— allowing me to decide if I want to specialize my major and if so, what I want to specialize in. Also, if I decide to change my major to specialize in a particular field, the credits I take for the general biology major will count for the specialized biology major as well. Attending the other campus will be a little more expensive than attending ASU's Tempe campus, but I think it will be well worth it. I feel the other campus's overall atmosphere will be a good change for me, and their biology program will help me discover what aspects of biology really interest me. Ultimately, attending the other campus will help me choose what biology-related career field I want to become a part of.

After taking English 102, I am confident I know how to effectively structure a paper from all of these genres. Also, I have learned a lot about writing in different genres in general—and I can apply what I have learned to papers in other classes.

Writing Effective Essay Examinations

In many of your college classes, you will be asked to take essay examinations: to sit and write (sometimes on a computer, most often by hand), for a specified period of time, about the material you have learned. Writing essay exams differs in several ways from writing academic papers that you might work on for several weeks. When you write an essay exam, you will find that the following is true:

- You usually have to rely on your memory.
- You don't have much time to figure out what you would like to say.
- You can't get feedback from your instructor and classmates.
- You usually do not have much time for revision.

It is no wonder, then, that some students worry about in-class essay examinations. Our purpose here is to help you overcome any possible fears about essay examinations by giving you some specific strategies to use before and during such tests.

Keep in mind that essay examination situations may come along throughout your life. In your career or in a civic organization, for example, you may be asked to write quickly and without the luxury of invention work or peer feedback:

- As a small business owner, you might have to draft and complete a cost estimate and quotation in a customer's home.
- As a member of a city council or town board, you may need to comment on a political issue at a town meeting or in response to a question from the media.
- If you write advertising copy or are a journalist, you will frequently have tight deadlines to contend with.

Think of college essay examinations as a way of preparing for life after college, when you often will have to write from memory in a short period of time.

To write an effective response to a question on an essay examination, you will need to do the following:

- Know and understand the information that the examination will cover.
- Be able to relate that information to other topics and ideas you have read about and discussed in class.
- Analyze and understand the question(s) that you are asked to address.

- Construct a thoughtful answer to the question(s) and get your ideas down onto paper, in the available time.

- Deal with any pre-exam stress issues that you might have (much of what causes stress for any kind of examination occurs when students are not prepared for the exam, so just being ready can make a big difference in your anxiety level).

- Deal with the examination *scene*—whether you are writing by hand or with computer, what distractions there might be (other students, noise), and so on.

 ## Getting Ready: Information Gathering, Storage, and Retrieval

When you read and take notes for your college classes, remember that one day you probably will be tested on this information.

Chapter 2 provides useful strategies for reading effectively, and Chapter 3 offers strategies for writing about course material, so we suggest you revisit those chapters with an eye to using them to help prepare you for essay examinations. Teachers don't expect students to remember everything covered in classes, but you will be expected to recall and understand the main concepts and to relate them to other ideas. As you read and listen in class, make note of the major concepts, and be sure you can explain them.

One reading strategy, for instance, requires you to annotate what you read, not only listing the main points but also jotting down any comments and questions you have about the text. This "talking back" to the text helps you remember what you've read and develop your own ideas and positions on the issues you read about—positions you may be asked to argue in an in-class essay examination.

For more on annotating, see Chapter 2, pages 25–27.

 ## Considering Questions

As you read and listen to class lectures and participate in class discussions, consider the kinds of questions an instructor might ask you to write about. What are the big issues or ideas that have been covered in class or that you have encountered in your reading? As you think of possible questions, record them in your journal. Then set aside some time to write responses to those questions.

For example, in a humanities class where you are considering various periods in the world of art, it is quite possible that, for an in-class essay examination, your teacher will ask you to situate a group of specific artists in the historical context in which they lived and worked. In a political science class, you may be asked to write about how the specific political issues of the day influenced a particular political party or movement. In your history class, you may be asked to explain how the historical events that took place over a period of time led to the start of a war. The important thing for you is to realize that you probably can make a good guess at what questions a teacher will ask on an essay examination, so it is worthwhile for you to consider what those questions might be—before the exam—and how you might answer them.

 ## Analyzing Questions

In addition to thinking about and predicting what questions you might be asked, it is equally important to understand what the questions are asking you to do.

Because instructors know that students have only a limited time to respond to an essay examination, they generally will ask questions that have a narrow focus. For example, in a history class, a question for a major writing assignment might be worded like this:

- Discuss the events that led up to the second Iraq war.

For an in-class examination, where students have only a brief time to respond, however, a question might be worded like this:

- In no more than two pages, explain what was Iraq's "no fly zone."

The following question is a writing prompt designed to elicit a brief response, and is similar to prompts used on placement examinations—those tests that determine which writing class is appropriate for a student. How might you answer it?

> Ernest Hemingway once commented, "As you get older, it is harder to have heroes, but it is sort of necessary." To what extent do you agree or disagree with his observation? Why? Support your opinion with specific examples.

What is this essay question asking you to *do*? If you have not studied Hemingway, this question might worry you, but consider this: The question is not about Hemingway but rather asks for your response to what he said about having heroes. Do you think that in order to construct an effective essay, you might want to define what a hero is to you? That you might want to provide some examples of your own heroes? That when you answer the real question—whether or not you agree with Hemingway's comment—you will need to provide some specific examples to show what you mean?

When you see the test question(s) for your essay examination, ask yourself what the question(s) asks you to *do:*

- Does it ask you to *analyze* something—to explain how the parts make up the whole? Consider how you might answer this question:

For more on analysis, see Chapter 7.

Analyze the use of the magic of flying in relation to the other illusions in the *Harry Potter* films.

- Does the question ask you to *evaluate* an idea or text or work of art? Consider how you might answer this question:

For more on evaluation, see Chapter 9.

  Of the short stories we read in our English class this semester, explain which makes the most effective use of *imagery*.

- Does the exam question ask you to *show connections* between historical trends, or causal chains—to demonstrate that one event led to or caused other events? Here, of course, your answer will need to show clearly the connections that you see. How might you answer this question?

For more on cause and effect, see Chapter 10.

  How did the Gulf of Tonkin incident influence the start of the Vietnam war?

- Does the test ask you to *compare* one or more ideas or texts with others? Or does it ask you to *contrast* concepts or ideas or texts? If you are asked to compare things, then you will look for similarities between them; if you are asked to contrast, then you will look for (and provide examples of) differences. How might you answer the following question, from a political science class?

For more on comparison and contrast, see Chapter 13 on rhetorical strategies, pages 707–10.

  Briefly compare Canada's and Australia's reactions to the second Iraq war.

- Does the question ask you to *define* something? When you define something, you most often explain what you think it *is*, and then also set it against what it is *not*. Usually questions that deal with definitions ask for more than just a dictionary definition.

For more on definition, see Chapter 13 on rhetorical strategies, pages 703–06.

- Does the question ask that you *discuss* an idea or concept or text? In examination terms, "discuss" means to present the most important features of an idea or concept and then analyze them. You will need to provide examples or other kinds of evidence to support your analysis. "Discuss" in an examination question also leaves your options fairly open—that is, you can discuss briefly or discuss in detail. In an essay *exam*, you can only discuss *briefly*, so consider only the main points you want to make, and how you can support those specific points.

- Does the question ask you to *illustrate* something—that is, to provide specific examples to explain the characteristics of the idea or concept?

- Does the examination ask you to *explain* an idea or concept? Think about how you might answer this question:

  Explain the significance of *rills* on the lunar surface.

- Does the exam ask you to *critique* something (a work of art, a short story, a poem, an idea), outlining and explaining the object's strengths and weaknesses? Consider how you might answer this question:

For more on evaluation, see Chapter 9.

  Critique William Faulkner's use of *time* in "A Rose for Emily."

- Does the exam question ask that you *review* or summarize a particular philosophy or train of thought?

If you are faced with a multiple-part question that perhaps seems impossible to answer, draw some lines between each section—in effect, break down the question into its component parts. For example, here is a multi-part question:

Noting the recent changes in campus safety problems, argue that your campus needs more or less police protection, but without creating a siege- or locked-in mentality for the student body.

Go through and mark each part of a multi-part question (here set off with lll):

lll Noting the recent changes in campus safety problems lll

lll argue that your campus needs more or less police protection lll

lll but without creating a siege- lll

lll or locked-in mentality for the student body lll

The first part of the question (*Noting the recent changes in campus safety problems*) asks that you outline what campus safety issues have recently taken place.

The second part of the question (*argue that your campus needs more or less police protection*) asks that you take a position on the amount of police protection your campus needs (if you argue for more protection, what does that mean: more police on campus? More police on foot patrol? Bicycle police? Should they be more heavily armed? Should there be police dogs?).

The third part of the question (*but without creating a siege-[mentality]*) asks that you define what a "siege-mentality" would be for the teachers as well as the students. The last part of the question asks much the same: for a definition and explanation of what a "locked-in mentality" means.

Breaking down a complex question in this manner allows you to see and thus consider each part of the question, an analysis that helps ensure that you will answer all of its parts.

WRITING ACTIVITY

Construct a Test Question

Select one of your current college classes and construct a "test question" for an essay examination based on information you have learned in the class.

Share your question with several of your classmates. What similarities do you see in the questions each of you generated? Your instructor may ask your group to report its findings to the rest of the class.

Constructing Thoughtful Answers

Once you understand exactly what the question is asking you, it is a good idea to jot down your main ideas quickly. Then think about what organizational method you might use.

Also think about whether your professor considers the exam to be a *short-* or *long-answer* essay examination. If you have an hour for the essay exam, for example, and there are ten questions, that gives you an average of six minutes to answer each question, a fairly good tip-off that you are working with a *short-answer* examination. For your answers to be effective, you will need to get right to the point and then state any supporting evidence as concisely as possible.

On the other hand, if you have 90 minutes to respond to one question on an exam, then you have time, perhaps, for some brainstorming about the ideas you think you might like to present, to construct a brief cluster diagram of how the parts of your answer relate to each other, and other invention work. And as you are writing the examination, you will have time to explain each aspect of your answer in greater detail than you could with only a few minutes to answer the question.

Often, the test question itself will give you a strong clue as to what kind of organization might be effective. For example, consider this sample question from a history class:

> **An understanding of the past is necessary for understanding the current situation.**
>
> *Explain what you think the above statement means. Discuss the similarities between the "Republican Revolution" of 1994 and the fact that the Democrats regained control of both houses of Congress in 2006. How does an understanding of past events help us to understand events that happen in the present?*

This is a three-part question, which means a three-part answer might be the most efficient and effective way to answer it. If you break down the question into its parts, you have the following:

- *Explain what you think the above statement means.* The first part of your answer should do just what the question asks, in your own words and from your own perspective: What do you think the statement means?

- *Discuss the similarities*, as the question asks you to do. What historical trends and events brought about the 1994 Republican Revolution? What has happened since 1994 to reverse that situation and put the Democrats in control?

- *Discuss* how past events (in this case, the Republican Revolution and what took place in the years afterward) help us understand a similar event that took place twelve years later. Do these two events mean that another similar event might happen again, in 2018?

One type of organization that works well for essay examinations is what is commonly called the "Classical Scheme." This method of organizing ideas dates back at least to Aristotle, who noticed that effective speakers most often

A. State their position and what is important (what is "at stake" in the argument).

   a. State their first piece of evidence, always connecting it back to the main point

   b. State their second piece of evidence, connecting it back to the main point

   c. State the third piece of evidence . . .

   d. And so on

B. Briefly outline any objections to the main point; explain why those objections are incorrect, or at least show how their position can accommodate the objection.

C. Summarize their position, restating their main points.

If you follow the Classical Scheme, you will do the following:

For more on the Classical Scheme, see Chapter 14, pages 726–31.

- Construct a solid thesis statement, clearly indicating the main point that you want to make in your answer.

- Provide an effective and logical organizational pattern to follow.

- State your main point right at the start, forcing you to use supporting details that always relate back to that main idea (if an idea or piece of supporting evidence does *not* help you accomplish what the test question asks you to do, then why is it there?).

- Acknowledge the other side of an issue or situation or idea, which tells your instructor that you are aware that there are other perspectives or approaches.

- Tie everything together at the end (which is what a conclusion should do).

Dealing with the Examination Scene

You probably have your favorite place to write, where it is quiet (or there is music playing), where everything you need is at hand (pencil, pen, computer, paper, erasers, coffee), and so on. But, you *rarely* will have such an ideal setting for an in-class examination—unless you construct it.

Since you usually know when an exam will take place, it's a good idea to prepare your test-taking environment as best you can, so the writing situation the examination presents is as normal and comfortable as possible. If you usually use a pencil to write, then make sure you have several sharpened pencils with you—or better yet, a good quality mechanical pencil. If you are allowed to use notes as you write the exam, make sure your notes are clearly written and legible. Here are some other ways to prepare to construct an effective essay examination:

See Chapter 3, "Writing to Learn for College and for Life," for more on study strategies.

- Know the material that you will be tested on, by using effective studying techniques (tape recording and then listening to your notes, rewriting your in-class notes on your computer, to help impress them in your memory and also to make them available in readable form; working with others in study groups, and so on).

- Consider what questions you might be asked by constructing your own test questions. This activity forces you to look at the material from a different viewpoint (teacher rather than student), by asking, What would I like my students to know and understand about this material? What way might be the best way for them to demonstrate that knowledge?

- Think about how you will spend the time you are allotted for the examination, *before* taking the examination. Surprisingly, few students really think about how they will spend the hour or 90 minutes or whatever time they will be given for the exam. If you have a plan of attack, so to speak, going into the exam, then you will use your time more wisely. So think about how to use the time you will be allowed effectively and then consider how much time you might plan to spend on each of these tasks:
    - Understanding the question
    - Getting some ideas onto paper
    - Organizing those ideas
    - Actually writing the exam
    - Revising your response, once you have it on paper
    - Editing your work
    - Proofreading your work

Note whether some questions are worth more points than others; if so, then it makes sense to spend *more time* on the questions that are worth more. If you encounter a question that you cannot immediately answer, skip it and go on to other questions. That gives you some time to think about it as you work on other answers.

Terry Dolan Writes an Essay Examination

College student Terry Dolan received this prompt for a 60-minute essay examination:

PROMPT

In his 2005 book *The World Is Flat*, Thomas Friedman talks of "ten forces that flattened the world." Name three of Friedman's ten forces and explain how they helped to flatten the world.

TERRY DOLAN'S RESPONSE

In his book *The World Is Flat*, Thomas Friedman talks of ten forces that flattened the world. I will discuss how three of these forces—the fall of the Berlin Wall, Netscape going public, and open-sourcing—helped to flatten the twenty-first-century world.

On November 9, 1989, the Berlin Wall fell. While this was a major victory for the forces of democracy in East Berlin and East Germany, it also stood as a symbol for the eventual fall of communism in all of Europe. By opening up Eastern Europe, and eventually the old Soviet Union, to free market capitalism, the end of the Berlin Wall was Friedman's first "flattener." Friedman also talks about the IBM PC computer and how its introduction helped to facilitate the flattening process begun by the fall of the Berlin Wall. The computer with a modem helped to connect people in the old communist bloc with new computer and economic networks.

Friedman's second flattening force happened when the browser Netscape went public. Netscape was a major force because it really opened up the World Wide Web and the Internet for the general population. Before Netscape, the only way people had access to the Internet was in text-only environments. While that type of access may have been interesting, it mainly attracted scientists and educators. Netscape let people use graphics, and eventually sound and video, online as well. One of the important advantages Netscape offered is that it could be used on any type of computer—PCs, Macs, or Unix boxes.

One important off-shoot of Netscape that helped flatten the world was the fact that when people began to send pictures, audio, and video files over the Internet, they needed more bandwidth. To accommodate this need, companies started laying more fiber optic cable. As a result, phone prices started dropping as well, enabling people to communicate more and faster.

Another flattener, according to Friedman, is the open-source movement. Unlike most software, you can download open-source software for free. Friedman explains that it works on the same model as scientific peer review. People participate in developing the software for the good of the group and the notoriety it gives them. The main open-source software that Friedman discusses is the Apache Web server. Friedman talks about how many of the main Internet Web sites run on Apache servers. Because there is no cost involved in buying the software, just about anyone who knows how can run a Web server.

An even more important example of open-source software is probably the Linux operating system. Linux is a kind of Unix, a powerful computer operating system. The advantage to Linux is that it's cheap (you can download it for free) and flexible (lots of computer people are constantly working to make it even better). The disadvantage to Linux is that most software is written to run on PCs. But more and more open-source software is being written to run on Linux boxes. You can now get Open Office and similar open-source programs that will let you do just about anything you could do with Microsoft software. All the open-source programs are free. You can also get Firefox, a web browser that runs on Linux. In other parts of the world, lots of computers run on Linux and use open-source software.

Finally, what I think is the most interesting point about all of Friedman's flatteners is that they're all about technology, mainly computer technology, and how that helps all of us connect to one another faster and better. Technology is what's making the world flat.

Standard Document Forms

Selecting and using a particular "form" for your text involves making rhetorical choices. Before selecting any kind of format for your text, then, you first need to ask (and answer) the following questions:

- What do you want your writing to accomplish? Do you want to inform your reader, or persuade your reader to do something, or evaluate some product, service, or creative work for your reader?
- What form will best serve your purpose?
- Who is your audience?

You already make these kinds of decisions about form all the time when you communicate with your friends, family members, and professors. For some communications (a letter to your great-aunt), a handwritten, personal letter will suffice; for others (asking a professor for a letter of recommendation to get into law school), a more formal business letter is a better choice.

In addition, you also select the size and kind of font to use as well as photographs and drawings, charts and graphs, and other visual aids; you decide whether to use headings in your document, whether bulleted or numbered lists are appropriate and useful, where a colored background or type is useful, and so on. These are all rhetorical choices that you as a writer make, whatever document you are constructing.

For more on designing documents, see Chapter 18, "Communicating with Design and Visuals."

This appendix presents guidelines for designing ten different types of print or online documents, along with examples of each type.

Business Letters

Features of an Effective Business Letter

The audience for any piece of business writing will have specific expectations. The most obvious expectation is that you should address your colleagues more formally than you address your college classmates. As with any text, business letters (and memos—see p. A-26) have real audiences and purposes, and the form that you use needs to fit your readers' concept of business correspondence:

- Use margins of at least one inch on all four sides of the letter.
- Use a standard 12-point font such as Times New Roman.

- Single-space addresses and paragraphs.
- If you use a block or modified block format (see below), double-space between sections of the letter—return address of sender, date, name and address of person to whom the letter is being sent, salutation, paragraphs, and closing. If you use an indented format, you do not need to double-space between paragraphs.
- Use a colon after the salutation.
- Use formal, but not stilted, language.
- After the closing (usually "Sincerely"), use a comma.
- After the closing, include four blank lines for your signature; then type your name, and give your professional title, if applicable. If you are using your company's letterhead, then of course you do not need to duplicate the address, telephone numbers, and so on that are already printed on the letterhead.
- After your name and professional title, include a "cc:" (copy) line and/ or an "Enc:" (enclosure) line if necessary.
- Because error-free letters give readers a positive impression, proofread your letter carefully and ask a friend or colleague to proofread it if possible. A second set of eyes is an effective insurance policy.
- Be sure to keep the electronic version of the letter. Back it up—just as you would for any important document.

Figure C.1 is an example of a business letter.

Letters of Application

Your purpose in writing a letter of application is just what you would expect it to be: You want your letter to *get* something for you—most often a job interview (and sometimes even the job itself).

Features of an Effective Letter of Application

- Use the features of the business-letter format described on pages A-23–A-24.
- Use the exact job title from the job announcement to indicate the position for which you are applying. Businesses sometimes advertise for more than one position at a time, so it is crucial to get the job title right.
- Briefly summarize your qualifications for the job. Don't simply repeat what is on your résumé, which will be attached to your letter.
- If the job announcement includes "required qualifications" and "desired qualifications," you must discuss all of the required ones, and you should discuss as many of the desired ones as possible.

Hanna Olsen
1111 Lutefisk Lane
Olso, WI 55555

Return address of sender

Double-space between sections

October 1, 2005

Date

Kirsti Andersen, Director
Office of the Registrar
413 Lefse Hall
Oslo College
Oslo, WI 55555

Name and address of person to whom letter is being sent

Dear Ms. Andersen:

Salutation

I am writing to request that you adjust my tuition payment for this semester. Because of health problems, I have been forced to withdraw from two of my courses. I am requesting a partial tuition refund for those six credit hours.

Double-space between paragraphs

Three weeks after the semester began, I was diagnosed with mononucleosis, which has limited the number of hours that I can attend class and study. Fortunately, I am doing well in my other two courses, and I am confident that I will be able to carry a full course load next semester.

To document my illness, I have attached a note from the Campus Medical Center. If you need further evidence, I will be happy to provide it.

I look forward to hearing from you soon.

Sincerely,

Closing

4 blank lines

Hanna Olsen

Signature

Hanna Olsen

Name

Enc: Note from Campus Medical Center

Enclosure line

FIGURE C.1 Business Letter (Block Format)

- Indicate how you can meet the needs of the hiring organization. Show that you are eager but not desperate.
- Subtly show that you have done your homework in learning as much as possible about the organization, the unit within the organization that you would be working for, and the job itself.
- Never misrepresent your skills, knowledge, or background. Honesty is the best approach.

Figure C.2 is an example of a letter of application.

Memos

As with business letters, business memos have their own specific requirements as to format—and memos, too, always have a rhetorical purpose. Ask yourself the following questions when writing a memo:

- What do I want this memo to accomplish?
- Who is my audience? What will my readers already know about my topic? What additional information do I need to provide to accomplish my goals?
- What is the situation or context in which I'm writing this memo? How does that affect what I write and how I write it?

Features of an Effective Memo

- If your office or organization has a memo template, use that format. If it does not, follow the generic format: Include a separate line for a "To" entry, a "From" entry, the date, and a "Regarding" or "RE" designation.
- For printed memos, use margins of at least one inch on all four sides.
- In the "RE" line, use a clear, concise subject heading.
- For printed memos that have legal significance, include your initials or legal signature, in ink.
- For memos that need to be shared with other people besides the primary recipient(s), add a "cc" (copy) line after the body of the memo.
- Use bold type sparingly for emphasis and to highlight any information that requires immediate attention.

Figure C.3 on page A-28 is an example of a memo.

Kirsti Brones   Return address of sender
1234 Raaen Way
Modum, MN 55555

                                 Double-space between sections

July 5, 2007   Date

Anna Drolsum   Name and address of person to
Personnel Director   whom letter is being sent
Super Computer Company, Inc.
2222 E. Cyberspace Dr.
Minneapolis, MN 55444

Dear Ms. Drolsum: Salutation

I am writing to apply for the sales representative position recently
advertised in the *Minneapolis Star-Tribune.* The skills that I have developed in my degree program support my strong interest in the position.

                    Double-space between paragraphs

In my recent internship with Excellent Computer Company, I had sales
responsibilities similar to those described in your advertisement and on
your Web site. Thus, I gained experience in maintaining sales accounts
and in making cold-calls to prospective corporate customers. Prior
to my internship, I learned how to handle customer concerns by
working for several years at the Customer Service desk of a Bull's-Eye
Department Store.

I am especially interested in working for Super Computer Company
because you have such a strong reputation for offering quality products and being responsive to customers' needs.

I am eager to speak with you about the sales representative position.
If you have any questions about my enclosed résumé, please call me at
400-555-4371. Thank you for considering my application.

Sincerely,   Closing

Kirsti Brones   Signature

Kirsti Brones   Name

Enclosure   Enclosure line

FIGURE C.2   Letter of Application

FIGURE C.3 Memo

> **Date:** March 29, 2006
> **To:** Information Technology Staff
> **From:** Norman Jones, Assistant Director, Division of Information Technology
> **RE:** Installing New Computers
>
> At the end of this fiscal year, we will be purchasing 124 new desktop computers for employees in the Division of Research and Development. The machines are scheduled to arrive on June 30, but the delivery date could vary by a day or two.
>
> Because we need to have all the new computers installed and fully operational by July 10, **all Information Technology staff need to be on the job between June 28 and July 10.** For that reason, I cannot approve any requests for vacation time during that period.
>
> I hope that this early notice affords you ample time to plan your summer vacations accordingly. I regret any inconvenience that this computer installation might cause.
>
> Thank you for your good work.
>
> cc: Linda Searcy, Director, Division of Information Technology

Résumés

At first glance, writing a résumé might seem easy: just list your work history and when you did it. But constructing an effective résumé involves a great deal of time and effort. To begin with, you need to consider carefully the audience to which you are addressing your résumé: Who will see your résumé? What information will they need, and what format should it be in? Should it be a paper résumé, or should it be in an electronic form? If you are adapting your résumé for a specific position, what does the *job advertisement* call for? You want to ensure that everything the advertisement asks for is included.

Features of an Effective Résumé

- You may—or may not—choose to include a concise career objective at the beginning of your résumé. Although such job objectives were common until recently, some experts now advise résumé writers not to include an objective because the objective is to acquire the job for which you are applying.

- Include current contact information—name, mailing address, e-mail address, phone numbers.

- Use descriptive headings to label the sections of your résumé, such as "Education," "Work Experience," "Skills," "Activities," "Awards," and "References." Include activities if they demonstrate additional skills, such as leadership. Include awards that reveal qualities or achievements that are an asset to the job you are seeking.

- Do not include personal information such as age, race, ethnicity, marital status, sexual orientation, or health status because employers are not allowed to consider such information.

- If requested to do so, list your references. Before you list someone as a reference, make certain that he or she knows your work and feels comfortable recommending you for a job. As an alternative, you can add the line "References available upon request." If you post your résumé on a Web site, do not list your references.

- If you limit your résumé to a single page, hiring personnel can read it quickly. However, it is more important to include the information that will help you get a job—even if it takes several pages—so consider your audience and what they expect from you. In business, for example, one-page résumés are common; in colleges and universities, résumés are usually much longer and more detailed.

- Use good quality paper.

- A résumé must not have any errors, so be sure to proofread carefully. Ask friends to help with this task if possible. Do not rely solely on the spell-check function of your word-processing program.

- If you post your résumé on a Web site, keep in mind that readers will see it one screen at a time rather than one page at a time.

- Although it is easy to embellish an online résumé with ornate graphics, a simple online résumé is actually more effective.

- Because employers sometimes conduct Web searches for résumés, adding some key terms such as the word *résumé* itself to your online résumé will make it more likely that a search engine will detect your résumé.

Different Kinds of Résumés

The two most common kinds of résumés are the chronological résumé and the functional résumé. In a **chronological résumé,** you list all of the jobs you have held in the past in reverse chronological order with the most recent listed first. Your work history should appear just below your personal information. Figure C.4 on page A-30 is an example of a chronological résumé. In a **functional résumé,** you make sure to highlight skills you possess or tasks you have accomplished in previous jobs. Another option is to combine the

FIGURE C.4
A Chronological
Résumé

>
>
> **Kirsti Brones**   Name, centered
>   and bold font
>
> 1234 Raaen Way   Contact information,
> Modum, MN 55555   centered
> 400-555-6981
> kbrones@email.com
>
>
> **Work Experience**   Heading, flush left and in bold
>   Double-space before and after headings
>
> Marketing Intern, Excellent Computer Company, Anoka, MN, Spring 2006
> Customer Service Representative, Bull's-Eye Department Store,
>   Edina, MN, 2002–2005
>
> **Education**
>
> Bachelor of Science, Marketing, College of Business, University of
>   Minnesota, 2006
>
> **Activities**
>
> President, Undergraduate Student Marketing Club, University of
>   Minnesota, 2005–2006
> Volunteer, Habitat for Humanity, 2004
> Volunteer, Boys and Girls Club of America, Edina, MN, 2002–2004
>
> **References**
>
> Available upon request.

two formats by listing jobs chronologically and highlighting the tasks that you performed while employed in each job.

Electronic Résumés

As you enter today's employment market, you are likely to encounter employers who ask you to submit electronic résumés. Sometimes the electronic résumé can be nothing more than a digital copy (a *Word* document or a pdf) of your paper résumé. However, you might be asked to fill out a web-form that will serve as a résumé. When you are submitting an electronic résumé of any kind, in all likelihood the first reader of your résumé will not be a human but a machine. When they read résumés, machines are programmed to search for predetermined keywords or phrases. That means that every résumé that contains the right keyword or phrase will go on to the next phase of screening—maybe by a human. Reading job ads closely will give you a good idea of what keywords or phrases might be important for the specific job you're applying for. While you already know the importance of proofreading a paper résumé, proofreading becomes even more important with electronic résumés. A human reader might forgive one small typo in a paper résumé. A machine can't forgive a typo because unless the words are all spelled correctly, they won't match the words the program is looking for. Figure C.5 is an example of a mixed chronological and functional résumé. Potential keywords or phrases that would be helpful in an electronic résumé are highlighted.

Kirsti Brones   Name, centered
                            and bold font

1234 Raaen Way   Contact information,
Modum, MN 55555   centered
400-555-6981
kbrones@email.com

Work Experience   Heading, flush left and in bold
                           Double-space before and after headings

Marketing Intern, Excellent Computer Company, Anoka, MN, Spring 2006
  ➢ Facilitated focus groups
  ➢ Wrote questions for focus groups
  ➢ Wrote brochure copy
  ➢ Assisted with marketing research
Customer Service Representative, Bull's-Eye Department Store,
  Edina, MN 2002–2005
  ➢ Helped with solving problems for customers
  ➢ Responsible for inventory of returns

Education

Bachelor of Science, Marketing, College of Business, University of
  Minnesota, 2006

Activities

President, Undergraduate Student Marketing Club, University of
  Minnesota, 2005–2006
Volunteer, Habitat for Humanity, 2004
  ➢ Coordinated volunteers
  ➢ Trained new volunteers in reading blueprints
Volunteer, Boys and Girls Club of America, Edina, MN, 2002–2004

References

Available upon request.

FIGURE C.5 A Mixed Chronological and Functional Résumé, with Keywords Highlighted

E-mail Messages

Especially in business environments, e-mail is everywhere, and often everyone seems to be checking e-mail all the time, every day. Constructing an e-mail, like any other kind of text, requires that you consider the rhetorical situation, who your audience is, and what you want the e-mail to accomplish.

In addition, because it is so easy to forward an e-mail (readers do not even need to cut and paste any of the text), it is important to understand that what you say to one person in an e-mail *might* be shared widely with people whom you did not intend to receive it.

Features of an Effective E-mail Message

- Use relatively short block paragraphs to make it easier for your readers to read the message. Single space, and include a blank line between paragraphs.
- Be very careful when using "reply to all" when you respond to an e-mail message, especially on listservs.
- Before sending a "BCC" (blind copy) to other people, think carefully about the implications of secretly sharing the message with people besides the primary recipient(s).
- Use a font that is easy to read on a screen, such as 10-point or 12-point Times New Roman or Arial.
- If you use an electronic signature for your e-mail, make certain that it includes relevant contact information. For business messages, use a signature that is suitable for business. Don't use a font that is too flashy, and if you do include a photograph or drawing, make sure it is not so large that downloading your message takes a long time (many people send and receive their e-mail over a telephone line, which is slow).
- In business e-mail, it is best to not use emoticons such as smiley faces.
- If you intend to attach a file to the message, develop a system that helps you remember to attach the file. Also make certain that the file is free of viruses.

Figure C.6 is an example of an e-mail.

 ## Threaded Discussion Groups and Listserv Postings

A number of publicly available Web sites such as Yahoo, MSN, and Google offer online discussion groups (sometimes called **threaded discussions**). Organized by topic or interest area, these groups allow members to view and participate in written discussions over the Web. After a member posts a mes-

FIGURE C.6
E-mail Message

> **Date:** Thu, 24 May 2007 16:58:31 -0400
>
> **From:** O_DOOL@XYandZ.com
>
> **To:** needshybrid@cox.net
>
> **Subject:** Your new vehicle
>
> I am happy to tell you that your new Toyota Prius has arrived. We will have it prepared for you to pick up after 5:00 pm tomorrow evening.
>
> I think you'll find the colors you chose to your liking.
>
> Please respond to this e-mail to tell us when you'll pick up your new Prius. Could you also please make sure to bring a copy of your proof of insurance card? Our finance officer forgot to make a copy when she was doing your paperwork. We do need a copy for the files.
>
> Thanks for your business,
>
> Oscar Doolittle
> Sales Manager
> X,Y, & Z Toyota/Scion
> Yuma, AZ 85365
> (928) 555-4567

sage about a particular topic, others may then post their responses. As the discussion proceeds, a Web page is automatically built around the discussion. Threaded discussions allow members to see all the postings in context on one Web page. This makes participating in and viewing the discussion easy.

A **Listserv** is another kind of online forum. Although the word *Listserv* technically should be capitalized because it is a registered trademark of a company called L-Soft International, Inc., the word is increasingly used as a common noun—the way that *kleenex* is often used to mean "facial tissue," rather than as a brand name, Kleenex. A listserv distributes e-mail to the addresses of all people who have subscribed to that listserv. That is, when a subscriber sends a message to a listserv, the listserv automatically distributes it to all other subscribers. Listservs allow participants to transmit information to large numbers of people who share an interest or are involved in an organization and are effective for discussing important issues, sharing ideas, and making announcements.

Features of an Effective Threaded Discussion or Listserv Posting

- If you are posting a message as part of an ongoing discussion in a threaded discussion group or on a listserv, become familiar with

FIGURE C.7
Listserv Posting

> **Date:**   Tue, 19 Oct 2005 23:00:10 −0500
> **Reply-To:**   Writing Program Administration <[log in to unmask]>
> **Sender:**   Writing Program Administration <[log in to unmask]>
> **From:**   CJ <[log in to unmask]>
> **Subject:**   Re: names for FYC 2
> **In-Reply-To:**   <[log in to unmask]>
> **Content-type:** text/plain; charset=ISO-8859-1; format=flowed
>
> Our FYC sequence is titled
>
> Semester 1: College Writing and Rhetoric
> Semester 2: College Writing and Research
>
> Could be better . . . . could be a lot worse . . . .
>
> Best,
>
> CeeJ

previous postings on the topic so that you don't repeat what has already been written. Repetition may annoy other subscribers.

- Stay on the topic at hand unless it is appropriate to move to a new topic.
- If you disagree with someone's opinion on a topic, express your views clearly and politely. Do not engage in personal attacks (called **flaming**).
- Because server space costs money and online readers do not enjoy scrolling through prior messages, do not include in your posting the message to which you are responding. If you want to respond to a specific section of a previous posting, copy and paste the specific text instead, making sure to distinguish the text so that it is not confused with your own.
- Do not post personal messages ("thanks for that information, Joe") to the group or listserv, when that message is intended for just one person.
- And above all, *be sure* that you want to reply to the group or listserv as a whole rather than to an individual. Sometimes, people post a reply to a group or list that was *intended* for an individual. As you might imagine, such messages can be embarrassing.

Figure C.7 is an example of a listserv posting.

 ## Brochures

As with your résumé, you want a brochure to accomplish something: to sell a product or service (or to get a reader more interested in a product or service), perhaps, or to provide information (a voter's guide, for example).

Features of an Effective Brochure

- Include a headline that is informative and attention-getting.
- Include a visual element such as a photo or drawing if it adds to the content of the brochure and if it grabs readers' attention.
- If the brochure advertises an event, make certain that you include all relevant information—date, time, place, cost (if any), phone number interested parties can call or Web site address they can visit for further information.
- Your layout will depend on the number of folds that your brochure has. If you are using standard 8-1/2″ × 11″ paper, you may decide to have no fold, a bi-fold, or a tri-fold. A no-fold sheet fits well into a notebook. A tri-fold can fit into a shirt pocket.
- Consider the principles of proximity, contrast, alignment, and repetition described in Chapter 18.
- If you use photos or graphics that are not your own, make certain that you have permission to display them publicly.

Figure C.8 on page A-36 is an example of a brochure.

Posters

While posters often seem to be only large sheets of paper with a small amount of text and lots of illustrations and a colored background, they also have a rhetorical purpose: What do you want a poster to *do*? Provide information? Show people how to get somewhere? Explain something?

Features of an Effective Poster

- Include a headline that is informative and will grab viewers' attention.
- Include a visual element such as a photograph or drawing if it adds to the content of the poster and if it grabs viewers' attention.
- The quality and color of the paper will affect the cost of the poster. At a certain point, you need to consider how much you are willing to spend in terms of your overall budget.
- Because using colored ink can also affect cost, determine what colored ink will add to the poster.
- Determine what size poster and what size font will be necessary for readers. Both will depend on the location of the poster and how close to the poster readers will be. Will they be whizzing by on their bikes, or will they be walking within a few feet of it?

Join us at the
15th Annual Patuxent
Wildlife Art Show and Sale

Artists' Reception
Friday, March 26th, 2004 6 p.m. -10 p.m.

Art Show and Sale
Saturday & Sunday, March 27th – 28th, 2004,
10 a.m. - 4:30 p.m.

Over 50 nationally recognized artists will display and sell wildlife art. Painters, sculptors, master carvers, renowned photographers, and superb artisans will be present.

Spend a weekend surrounded by nature, exquisite wildlife art, and interesting activities-all taking place at the marvelous National Wildlife Visitor Center which offers hiking trails, wildlife and conservation exhibits, outdoor education, and guided tram tours.

An Artists' Reception with the artists and the Silent Auction will be held Friday evening from 6 p.m. - 9 p.m. Tickets to the Artists' Reception will be $25.00 per person. *Admission to the Art Show and Sale is free.*

Special Events and Activities

•Maryland Migratory Game Bird Design Contest (Maryland Duck Stamp Contest) Saturday, March 27th 12:00 noon

•Wildlife tram tour

• Adopt a Whooping Crane display

All proceeds from the show support the outreach and educational programs of the Patuxent Research Refuge and research activities at the Patuxent Wildlife Research Center, America's premier wildlife research institution.

FIGURE C.8   A Brochure for an Art Show   Reprinted by permission of Friends of Patuxent Wildlife Research Center and Patuxent Research Refuge, Inc.

- Consider the principles of proximity, contrast, alignment, and repetition described in Chapter 18.
- If you use photos or stock graphics, make certain that you have permission to display them publicly.
- If the poster advertises an event, make certain that you include all relevant information—date, time, place, cost (if any), phone number or Web site address where further information is available (if applicable).

Figure C.9 is an example of an effective poster.

FIGURE C.9 A Poster Advertising an Event

Newsletters

Newsletters most often have a specific audience (usually employees or members of a club or organization of some kind). Those who produce newsletters for a group also have specific purposes. At our university, for example, we get newsletters from a number of places, including the following:

- The university itself, including a "wellness newsletter," which tells of various workshops employees can attend to lose weight, stop smoking, and so on, as well as information on how to become better managers, learn new computer software, and other useful advice.

- The faculty senate, which lets us know about political issues on campus.

- Our department, letting us know about upcoming speakers, recent publications by our colleagues, and other news of interest.

Features of an Effective Newsletter

- It is very important to determine who your readers will be because you need to include information that will be interesting and useful to those readers.
- Determine a purpose for the newsletter, and keep that purpose in mind as you decide what to include and what to exclude.
- Use headlines that clearly indicate the content of the stories that follow them.
- Consider the principles of proximity, contrast, alignment, and repetition described in Chapter 18.
- If you use photos or graphics that are not your own, make certain that you have permission to include them in your publication.

Figure C.10 is an example of a newsletter.

Web Sites

Do you have your own Web site (a collection of Web pages)? Would you like to? These days, more and more of us do have Web sites. For example, as a student you might develop a portfolio as a Web site, one in which you display your work. (See Appendix A.) As a member of an organization, you might develop a Web site that describes the activities of the organization. Or, like many people do these days, you might develop a Web site in which you tell your family's history.

As with any text, one primary consideration is *audience*—and for a Web site, that can mean just about anyone. Consider the following questions as you create your Web site:

- What do you want your Web site to do? To tell about you and who you are? About the work you do?
- What do you want to include on your Web site? Photos? Drawings?

Features of an Effective Web Site

When designing a Web site, there are several points you should keep in mind. First of all, your Web site should be rhetorical. You should keep both the purpose of the site and its intended audience in mind. That means that you will definitely design a personal Web site, intended to be viewed by your friends and family, very differently from a Web site that is intended to portray you as a professional. On your personal Web site you might have pictures of your family, your friends, your pets, or some of your favorite places. You might have links to your favorite restaurants or your favorite sports teams. On the

FIGURE C.10
A Newsletter for
a Community
Organization

Volume 5, Issue 3

Fall 2003

Perspectiva Latina

The Hispanic Federation — Strengthening Latino Agencies and the Communities they Serve

Federation Leads Coalition's Push for Smaller Classes, Improved Learning

Inside this issue:

National Latino AIDS Awareness Day 2

Ayúdenos A Ayudar, cont. 3

Federation Agencies Ease Transition 3
for Immigrants

Community Calendar 4

HF's 2002-2003 Supporters Insert

The Hispanic Federation is playing a lead role in a coalition of parents, community organizations, labor unions, and public school educators advocating for smaller classes for New York City public school students.

The coalition, known as New Yorkers for Smaller Classes, is working to have a ballot question that would create a commission to study smaller class size for New York City schools. The commission's recommendations to amend the charter would be voted on by the public in the November 2004 election.

"Parents know what the research has shown over and over again: smaller

> "Parents know what the research has shown over and over again: smaller classes are key to improving learning."

classes are key to improving learning," said Lillian Rodriguez Lopez, the Federation's vice president and co-chair of the Coalition.

In fact, the Federation's 2003 survey found that Latinos in New York City consider smaller classes to be the most important priority for improving public schools. And New York City, where 40% of all public school students are Latino, suffers from the most overcrowded classes in the state.

Last August, the Coalition delivered more than 115,000 petition signatures endorsing the ballot question to New York's City Clerk, the most petitions ever gathered in New York City history. ☼

Ayúdenos a Ayudar: Helping The Federation Help Our Community

Latino Children's Day at the Met is just one of the programs made possible thanks to Hispanic Federation supporters.

Message from HF's President
Lorraine Cortés-Vázquez

I'm certain that many of you are beginning to prepare for the holiday season—a time when we renew our ties to families and friends, give thanks for the blessings we have received, and look forward to the New Year.

But while this season is a time of warmth and comfort for some of us, many in our communities continue to face serious hardships—challenges that are felt more deeply during the holidays. In response, the Hispanic Federation began its "Ayúdenos a Ayudar" (Help us

to Help Others) Campaign in 1997 to encourage all Latinos to give what they can to help Latino families in need. Over the years many of you have answered our call and made the Hispanic Federation's work possible through your contributions.

We are pleased to dedicate this issue of *Perspectiva Latina* to the individuals, corporations, and foundations who supported the Federation and the Latino community in 2003. The successes we highlight in *Perspectiva Latina*, like more funding for English language learners, services for recent immigrants, better access to

health care, and HIV/AIDS awareness programs, are made possible by the generous supporters listed in this issue.

But more remains to be done. The weak economy, increasing unemployment, and the rising cost of living has hurt countless Latino children and families. And Hispanic agencies are once again being asked to care for more people in need with less funding from public and private sources.

Fortunately, there is hope. Like the supporters highlighted in this edition of

continued on page 3

---

other hand, on a professional Web site you might have links to a professional organization and include your résumé. What both sites should share, however, is some clear sense of how to navigate the site. You might have a navigation bar along the top or on the side, with buttons that link to different pages on the site, including the home page. In any event, you should provide a clear way for the people who visit your site to move around the site and return to the home page.

One other factor to keep in mind is that although we call the parts of a Web site *Web pages*, we are really talking about screens. While paper pages are a uniform size, Web pages can vary in size depending on the size and resolution of the monitor on which they appear.

- Break text into smaller chunks, and write as concisely as possible. Give readers "breathers." Bulleted lists work especially well on the Web.

- Graphics can enhance the informational value and aesthetic appeal of Web pages, but they can also make pages download more slowly. Use graphics if they highlight, elaborate on, or replace words on the screen. Not everyone who visits your page will have a high-speed connection.

- Try to design each page of your site so that readers can view the entire page with only a minimal amount of scrolling.

- To make pages usable to a wide audience, make them accessible to people with visual impairments. To determine if your site is accessible, you can use *Bobby*, a free, Web-based tool that will analyze your site and tell you if you need to make changes so that people with disabilities will be able to view it (http://bobby.watchfire.com/bobby/html/en/index.jsp). There are also pages on the site that will give you information on how to design your site so that it is more accessible.

- Each page on your Web site should have a design that is consistent with the other pages on your site. Although you have more flexibility on a personal Web site than with a professional site, you still want to give each page the same overall look and feel. A lack of consistency may make your viewers suspect that they have left your site for another.

- Organization and navigation work hand-in-hand on the Web. Organize material on the site so that the organizational principle is apparent to readers. Web designers frequently organize sites either sequentially or hierarchically. You might choose to organize the site sequentially, which would be similar to a numbered list. Or you might choose to organize hierarchically, where you begin with the most important or most general topic and then have your viewers "drill down" further into the site for the specific details.

- If you include links to external sites, periodically check to see if any links are "dead"—links to sites that are no longer active.

- Regularly examine the page to make certain that the information is current. Including a "last date updated" line helps to assure your viewers that you are keeping the site current.

Figure C.11 is a Web page from a student oral history project. Notice the navigation bar on the left side of the page and the title identifying the project at the top. Every page on this site has the same general design as this one.

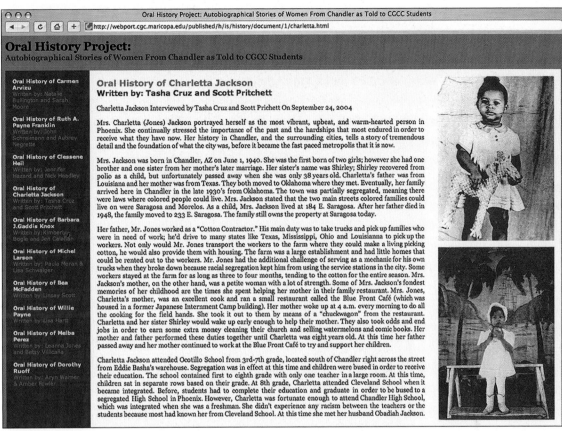

http://webport.cgc.maricopa.edu/published/h/is/history/document/1/charletta.html

Oral History Project:
Autobiographical Stories of Women From Chandler as Told to CGCC Students

Oral History of Carmen Arvizu
Written by: Natalie Bullington and Sarah Moore

Oral History of Ruth A. Payne Franklin
Written by: John Schreimann and Aubrey Negrette

Oral History of Clessene Heil
Written by: Jennifer Hazard and Nick Headley

Oral History of Charletta Jackson
Written by: Tasha Cruz and Scott Pritchett

Oral History of Barbara J.Gaddis Knox
Written by: Kimberly Bogle and Jen Calahan

Oral History of Michel Larson
Written by: Paula Moran & Lisa Schwalger

Oral History of Bea McFadden
Written by: Linsay Scott

Oral History of Willie Payne
Written by: Lisa Hartt

Oral History of Melba Perez
Written by: Leanna Jones and Betsy Villicaña

Oral History of Dorothy Ruoff
Written by: Aryn Warner & Amber Fowler

Oral History of Charletta Jackson
Written by: Tasha Cruz and Scott Pritchett

Charletta Jackson Interviewed by Tasha Cruz and Scott Prichett On September 24, 2004

Mrs. Charletta (Jones) Jackson portrayed herself as the most vibrant, upbeat, and warm-hearted person in Phoenix. She continually stressed the importance of the past and the hardships that most endured in order to receive what they have now. Her history in Chandler, and the surrounding cities, tells a story of tremendous detail and the foundation of what the city was, before it became the fast paced metropolis that it is now.

Mrs. Jackson was born in Chandler, AZ on June 1, 1940. She was the first born of two girls; however she had one brother and one sister from her mother's later marriage. Her sister's name was Shirley; Shirley recovered from polio as a child, but unfortunately passed away when she was only 38 years old. Charletta's father was from Louisiana and her mother was from Texas. They both moved to Oklahoma where they met. Eventually, her family arrived here in Chandler in the late 1930's from Oklahoma. The town was partially segregated, meaning there were laws where colored people could live. Mrs. Jackson stated that the two main streets colored families could live on were Saragosa and Morelos. As a child, Mrs. Jackson lived at 184 E. Saragosa. After her father died in 1948, the family moved to 233 E. Saragosa. The family still owns the property at Saragosa today.

Her father, Mr. Jones worked as a "Cotton Contractor." His main duty was to take trucks and pick up families who were in need of work; he'd drive to many states like Texas, Mississippi, Ohio and Louisiana to pick up the workers. Not only would Mr. Jones transport the workers to the farm where they could make a living picking cotton, he would also provide them with housing. The farm was a large establishment and had little homes that could be rented out to the workers. Mr. Jones had the additional challenge of serving as a mechanic for his own trucks when they broke down because racial segregation kept him from using the service stations in the city. Some workers stayed at the farm for as long as three to four months, tending to the cotton for the entire season. Mrs. Jackson's mother, on the other hand, was a petite woman with a lot of strength. Some of Mrs. Jackson's fondest memories of her childhood are the times she spent helping her mother in their family restaurant. Mrs. Jones, Charletta's mother, was an excellent cook and ran a small restaurant called the Blue Front Café (which was housed in a former Japanese Internment Camp building). Her mother woke up at 4 a.m. every morning to do all the cooking for the field hands. She took it out to them by means of a "chuckwagon" from the restaurant. Charletta and her sister Shirley would wake up early enough to help their mother. They also took odds and end jobs in order to earn some extra money cleaning their church and selling watermelons and comic books. Her mother and father performed these duties together until Charletta was eight years old. At this time her father passed away and her mother continued to work at the Blue Front Café to try and support her children.

Charletta Jackson attended Ocotillo School from 3rd-7th grade, located south of Chandler right across the street from Eddie Basha's warehouse. Segregation was in effect at this time and children were bused in order to receive their education. The school contained first to eighth grade with only one teacher in a large room. At this time, children sat in separate rows based on their grade. At 8th grade, Charletta attended Cleveland School when it became integrated. Before, students had to complete their education and graduate in order to be bused to a segregated High School in Phoenix. However, Charletta was fortunate enough to attend Chandler High School, which was integrated when she was a freshman. She didn't experience any racism between the teachers or the students because most had known her from Cleveland School. At this time she met her husband Obadiah Jackson.

FIGURE C.11   Web Page from a Student Oral History Project Chandler's Pioneer Women: Oral History Project conducted by Chandler-Gilbert Community College students in partnership with the City of Chandler Public History Department. Tapes and transcripts are property of the Chandler Historical Society.

Credits

TEXT CREDITS

Front matter
WPA Outcomes Statement for First-Year Composition is reprinted by permission of the Council of Writing Program Administrators.

Chapter 1
P. 4: Aristotle, *Rhetoric*. Trans. W. Rhys Roberts. 19 Nov. 2007 <http://classics.mit.edu/ Aristotle/rhetoric.html>: I, ii.; Bain, Alexander. *English Composition and Rhetoric*. 1866. New York: Appleton, 1890; Burke, Kenneth. *A Rhetoric of Motives*. 1950. Berkeley: U of California P, 1969: 43; Getty, John. *Elements of Rhetoric*. 1831. Philadelphia: Littell, 1881; Lunsford, Andrea. "Some Definitions of Rhetoric." 2 Feb. 2007 <http://www. stanford.edu/dept/english/courses/sites/lunsford/pages/defs.htm>; **p. 5:** Quintilian. *Institutes of Oratory*. London: George Bell & Sons, 1892: Section 38. Chapter XV, Book II. **p. 5:** Richards, I. A. *The Philosophy of Rhetoric*. New York: Oxford UP, 1936: 3; **p. 6:** Moffett, James. *Teaching the Universe of Discourse*. Boston: Houghton Mifflin, 1968: 115; **p. 12:** Lindeman, Erika. "Some Definitions of Rhetoric." 2 Feb. 2007 <http://www.stanford.edu/dept/english/courses/ sites/lunsford/pages/defs.htm>; **p. 13:** Bulwer-Lytton, Edward. *Richelieu. Choice Readings for Public and Private Entertainments and for the Use of Schools and Colleges and Public Readers with Elocutionary Advice*. Ed. Robert McLean Cumnock. Chicago: McLurg, 1898; **p. 15:** Brooks, Cleanth, and Robert Penn Warren. *Modern Rhetoric*. 3rd ed. New York: Harcourt, Brace & World, 1970: 6.

Chapter 2
p. 27: "A Purpose Greater Than Oneself," Miss Hall's School. Reprinted by permission of Miss Hall's School, www. misshalls.org; **p. 32:** Elbow, Peter. "Writing without Teachers," *Everyone Can Write: Essays Toward a Hopeful Theory of Writing and Teaching Writing*. New York: Oxford, 2000; **p. 34:** "Choosing the Sex of Your Baby," *The New York Times*, September 30, 2001. Copyright © 2001 by The New York Times Co. Reprinted with permission.

Chapter 4
p. 69: Excerpt from "Katrina & The Waves," Richard Connelly, Ray Hafner & Todd Spivak, *Houston Press*, September 8, 2005. Reprinted by permission of the Houston Press; **p. 81:** Excerpt from *Growing Up* by Russell Baker. Copyright © 1982 by Russell Baker. New York: Congdon & Weed, Inc.; **p. 85:** "Se Habla Espanol," Tanya Barrientos from *Border-Line Personalities* by Michelle Herrera Mulligan and Robyn Moreno. Compilation copyright © 2004 by Michelle Herrera-Mulligan and Robyn Moreno. Reprinted by permission of HarperCollins Publishers; **p. 91:** Excerpt from *All Deliberate Speed: Reflections on the First Half-Century of Brown vs. Board of Education* by Charles J. Ogletree, Jr. Copyright © 2004 by Charles J. Ogletree, Jr. Used by permission of W.W. Norton & Company, Inc.; **p. 116:** "26 Days and I'm Out!" excerpt from *Ed's Girl on the Hunt* is reprinted by permission of the author, Rachel Sturtz.

Chapter 5
p. 139: "Scientist at Work: Terence Tao; Journeys to the Distant Fields of Prime," Kenneth Chang, *The New York Times*, March 13, 2007. Copyright © 2007 by The New York Times Co. Reprinted with permission; **p. 145:** "Bipolar Iraq," Michael Wolff, *New York Magazine*, November 17, 2003. Reprinted by permission of *New York Magazine*; **p. 151:** "Memoir Essay," P. J. O'Rourke, *The New York Times Magazine*, March 1, 1998. Copyright © 1998 by The New York Times Co. Reprinted with permission; **pp. 178, 179:** Images from Denver's CowParade Web site are copyright © 2007 CowParade Holdings Corporation. Reprinted with permission.

Chapter 6
p. 188: *The New York Times* online front page from February 23, 2007 is reprinted by permission of The New York Times Co.; **p. 199:** Excerpts from *The Man Who Invented Baseball* by Harold Peterson. Copyright © 1969. New York: Charles Scribner's Sons; **p. 206:** "Clocking Cultures," Carol Ezzell, *Scientific American*, September 2002. Reprinted

It!" Stanley Fish, *The New York Times,* March 21, 2007. Copyright © 2007 The New York Times Co. Reprinted by permission; **p. 740:** "Nothing But Nets," Rick Reilly, *Sports Illustrated,* May 1, 2006. Reprinted with permission.

Chapter 16
pp. 765–66: Dauten, Dale, "Giving Speeches: It's Not about You." *The Arizona Republic* 9/1/2005: D2; **p. 766:** Cohen, Steve, See Chapter 6, *Win the Crowd,* by Steve Cohen. New York: HarperCollins, 2005.

Chapter 17
p. 775: Jeney, C. J. Personal communication, July 12, 2002.

Chapter 18
p. 791: ESOL Flyer from Fenway Neighborhood Service Center is reprinted by permission of Action for Boston Community Development, Inc.; **Fig. 18.1:** Colorwheel is reprinted by permission of Stanford Brands, Newell Rubbermaid, Inc.; **Fig. 18.4:** Poster for Israel Society for Ecology and Environmental Quality Sciences is reprinted by permission of Weizmann Institute of Science; **Figs. 18.5, 18.6, 18.10:** Pie charts showing composition of a slice of pizza are reprinted by permission of Mathematics Leagues, Inc.; **p. 806:** "Domestic Cereal Supply: Food, Feed, Waste" is compiled by the Land Use Change Program of the International Institute for Applied Systems Analysis (IIASA) using data from the Food and Agriculture Organization of the United Nations. Reprinted with permission; **Fig. 18.8:** Relationship between a Car's Mileage and Its Value is reprinted by permission of Mathematics Leagues, Inc.; **Fig. 18.9:** Universal Stain Color Selection Guide is reprinted by permission of Come To Buy, Inc., www.ComeToBuy.com; **Fig. 18.11:** Bigfoot Water Rocket Launcher Flowchart is reprinted by permission of Gary Ensmenger, President, Bigfoot Stilt Company; **Fig. 18.14:** Drawing of a cell nucleus is reprinted by permission of David L. Spector, Cold Spring Harbor Laboratory, New York; **Fig. 18.15:** Venn diagram on sustainable development is reprinted by permission of Manchester Development Education Project; **Fig. 18.17:** Neanderthal Range Map is reprinted by permission of Richard G. Klein; **Fig. 18.22:** Two maps of the U.S., one plain and one distorted, from "Diffusion-based methods for producing density-equalizing maps," Michael Gastner and Mark Newman, *PNAS,* May 18, 2004. Copyright © 2004 National Academy of Sciences, USA. Reprinted with permission.

Chapter 19
p. 829: Definition of "adolescent" copyright © 2007 by Houghton Mifflin Company. Adapted and reproduced by permission from *The American Heritage Medical Dictionary;* **pp. 833, 834:** Search result for keywords "male" and "gang" are reprinted by permission of EBSCO Publishing; **p. 851:** Blurb about authors Duffy and Gillig from the Greenwood Press online catalog is reproduced with permission of Greenwood Publishing Group, Inc., Westport, CT.

Chapter 20
Fig. 20.2: Title and copyright pages from *Unpaid Professionals* by Andrew Zimbalist are reprinted by permission of Princeton University Press; **Fig. 20.3:** Journal table of contents is reprinted by permission of Council of Writing Program Administrators; **Fig. 20.6:** Title and copyright pages from *Teen Gangs* are copyright © 2004 by Maureen P. Duffy and Scott Edward Gillig. Reproduced with permission of Greenwood Publishing Group, Inc., Westport, CT; **Fig. 20.7:** Journal table of contents are reprinted by permission of Blackwell Publishing.

Appendices
Fig. C.10: Front page of *Perspectiva Latina* newsletter is reprinted by permission of the Hispanic Federation.

PHOTO CREDITS

Chapter 1
P.3: Getty Images/Digital Vision, (inset) DigitalVues/Alamy.

Chapter 2
p. 19: Getty Images/Digital Vision; **p. 24:** © AP/Wide World Photos; **p. 25:** © Mark Richards/PhotoEdit.

Chapter 3
p. 40: Stockbyte/PunchStock; **p. 45:** © SuperStock, Inc./SuperStock; **p. 51:** United States Environmental Protection Agency; **p. 52:** © Digital Vision.

Chapter 4
p. 68: © AP/Wide World Photos, (inset) Courtesy of Todd Spivak/Houston Press; **p. 73:** © A. Ramey/PhotoEdit; **p. 75:** (top) Ryan McVay/Getty Images, (bottom) © Andrew Paterson/Alamy; **p. 81:** Jeffrey MacMillan for WGBH/Masterpiece Theatre; **p. 85:** David Cruz/Newscom; **p. 91:** Photo courtesy of Charles Ogletree; **pp. 96, 101, 102:** Courtesy of the authors.

Chapter 5
p. 128: Courtesy of NASA, (top inset) NASA Jet Propulsion Laboratory, (bottom inset) Courtesy of NASA and STScI; **p. 134:** Jack Hollingsworth/Getty Images; **p.135:** © Bill Aron/PhotoEdit; **p. 139:** Courtesy of *The New York Times*; **p. 145:** © Najlah Feanny/Corbis SABA; **p. 151:** Michael Buckner/Getty Images; **p. 169:** Quarter-dollar coin image from the United States Mint.

Chapter 6
p. 193: © BananaStock/PunchStock; **p. 195:** Courtesy Mike Bayouth; **p. 199:** National Baseball Hall of Fame Library, Cooperstown, NY; **p. 206:** Photo courtesy of Carol Ezzell Webb; **p. 211:** © *The New York Times*/Redux Pictures; **p. 224:** © RF/Corbis.

Chapter 7
p. 252: © AP/Wide World Photos; **p. 254:** Graphic Design by Leslie Ernst. Reprinted with the permission of the University of Texas at Austin. All Rights Reserved; **p. 255:** Jonathan Wood/Getty Images; **p. 259:** © RF/Corbis; **p. 261:** Copyright © 2007. Courtesy of Alaska Wildland Adventures, www.alaskawildland.com; **p. 266:** Photo courtesy of James Lang; **p. 271:** Matthew T. Stallbaumer/*Mother Earth News*; **p. 279:** Courtesy Demos: A Network for Ideas & Action www.demos.org.

Chapter 8
p. 320: Courtesy of Mexico Tourism Board; **p. 325:** The McGraw-Hill Companies, Inc./Christopher Kerrigan, photographer; **p. 326:** The McGraw-Hill Companies, Inc./John Flournoy, photographer; **p. 328:** The McGraw-Hill Companies, Inc./Lars A. Niki, photographer; **p. 334:** Photo courtesy of Anne Applebaum; **p. 337:** Fred R. Conrad/*The New York Times*/Redux; **p. 339:** Courtesy of Dr. Brian Pereira; **p. 342:** (top) Courtesy of Arthur Levine, (bottom) Courtesy of Jeanette Cureton; **p. 355:** © RF/Corbis; **p. 356:** © The McGraw-Hill Companies, Inc./John Flournoy, photographer; **p. 369:** © Brand X Pictures/PunchStock.

Chapter 9
p. 390: © RF/Corbis, (inset) RKO Radio Pictures Inc./Photofest; **p. 397:** © RF/Corbis; **p. 398:** The McGraw-Hill Companies, Inc./John Flournoy, photographer; **p. 399:** © The McGraw-Hill Companies, Inc./Lars A. Niki, photographer; **p. 404:** © 2004 by Consumers Union of U.S., Inc. Yonkers, NY 10703-1057, a nonprofit organization. Reprinted with permission from the February 2004 issue of Consumer Reports ™ for educational purposes only. No commercial use or reproduction permitted. www.ConsumerReports.org; **p. 406:** © Frank Trapper/Corbis; **p. 409:** Michael Germana/SSI Photo/Landov; **p. 414:** Courtesy of Matthew Power; **p. 423:** © 2004 by Consumers Union of U.S., Inc. Yonkers, NY 10703-1057, a nonprofit organization. Reprinted with permission from the February 2004 issue of Consumer Reports ™ for educational purposes only. No commercial use or reproduction permitted. www.ConsumerReports.org; **p. 438:** Jules Frazier/Getty Images; **p. 439:** Photodisc/Getty Images; **p. 447:** WARNER BROS./THE KOBAL COLLECTION.

Chapter 10
p. 458: © Lauri Kangas; **p. 463:** © Index Stock Photography Inc./Photodisc/Getty Images; **p. 465:** © Digital Vision/PunchStock; **p. 466:** © RF/Corbis; **p. 473:** PRNewsFoto/SeniorNet/Newscom; **p. 479:** Courtesy *Business Week*; **p. 483:** © AP/Wide World Photos; **p. 489:** © moodboard/Corbis; **p. 490:** Nick Koudis/Getty Images; **p. 491:** D. Falconer/PhotoLink/Getty Images.

Chapter 11
p. 533: Kent Knudson/PhotoLink/Getty Images; **p. 535:** © RF/Corbis; **p. 536:** The McGraw-Hill Companies, Inc./John Flournoy, photographer; **p. 541:** Courtesy of Michelle Mise Pollard; **p. 548:** Fred R. Conrad/*The New York Times*/Redux; **p. 553:** © Steve Tressler; **p. 556:** © *Arizona Republic*; **p. 557:** Courtesy SkySong, The ASU Scottsdale Innovation Center, rendering by Pei Cobb Freed Architects; **p. 569:** Courtesy SkySong, The ASU Scottsdale Innovation Center, rendering

by Todd & Associates Architects; **p. 570:** Courtesy SkySong, The ASU Scottsdale Innovation Center, rendering by Pei Cobb Freed Architects; **p. 577:** (both) Office of War Information Posters ca.1941-9145, National Archives.

Chapter 12
p. 592: JP Beato III Photography; **p. 603:** © Jurgen Frank/Corbis; **p. 609:** Lawrence Lucier/Getty Images; **p. 617:** © Marc Brasz/Corbis; **p. 628:** (top and middle) Warner Bros./Photofest, (bottom) © Jeffrey Jackson/Alamy; **p. 631:** (top) Twentieth Century Fox/Photofest, (bottom) © Marvel Entertainment, Inc.; **p. 632:** (top) © Marvel Entertainment, Inc., (bottom) 20TH CENTURY FOX/THE KOBAL COLLECTION.

Chapter 13
p. 669: BananaStock/JupiterImages; **p. 690:** © Paramount Pictures/Bureau L.A. Collection/Corbis; **p. 700:** Jim Wehtje/Getty Images; **p. 701:** With permission of the Royal Ontario Museum © ROM; **p. 711:** (left) © age fotostock/SuperStock, (right) Photodisc/Getty Images; **p. 712:** © Encyclopedia Britannica, Inc.; **p. 713:** (top) © Fred Whitehead/SuperStock, (bottom) © ANUP SHAH/Animals Animals - Earth Scenes. All rights reserved.

Chapter 14
p. 717: © Mike Segar/Reuters/Corbis, (inset): Courtesy of MacNeil/Lehrer Productions; **p. 726:** © SuperStock, Inc./SuperStock; **p. 732:** PRNewsFoto/Newscom; **p. 734:** © sijmen hendriks; **p. 736:** Courtesy of Stanley Fish; **p. 739:** © Roger Ressmeyer/Corbis; **p. 740:** Courtesy of *Sports Illustrated;* **p. 743:** Cover image courtesy of WND Books; **p. 744:** © Copyright 2007 American Civil Liberties Union. Reprinted with permission of the American Civil Liberties Union http://www.aclu.org.

Chapter 15
pp. 748, 752: BananaStock/JupiterImages.

Chapter 16
p. 759: Keith Brofsky/Getty Images; **p. 763:** BananaStock/JupiterImages; **p. 767:** Photodisc Collection/Getty Images.

Chapter 17
p. 773: © images-of-france/Alamy; **p. 787:** (top) Ken Light, (bottom left) © Ken Light/Corbis, (bottom right) © Owen Franken/Corbis.

Chapter 18
p. 791: United Nations Graphic Design Unit/Outreach Division/DPI, (inset) Courtesy of ABCD Parker Hill/Fenway Neighborhood Service Center; **p. 796:** (left) USDA Forest Service; **p. 810:** Courtesy of FUHR Industrial, www.furhindustrial.com; **p. 812:** Library of Congress, Prints and Photographs Division, LC-USZ62-11897; **p. 813:** Library of Congress, Prints and Photographs Division, LC-DIG-cwpb-04326; **p. 819:** NEW LINE/SAUL ZAENTZ/WING NUT/THE KOBAL COLLECTION; **p. 822:** Courtesy of Feed the Children, Inc.

Chapter 19
p. 827: BananaStock/JupiterImages, (top inset) © Stockbyte/PunchStock, (bottom inset) USDA; **p. 839:** © PictureNet/Corbis; **p. 840:** Reprinted with permission of Cambridge University Press; **p. 841:** Courtesy of American Psychiatric Publishing, Inc.; **p. 842:** PRNewsFoto/NEWSWEEK/AP/Wide World Photos; **p. 844:** PRNewsFoto/*Business Traveler* magazine, Nathan Jalani/AP/Wide World Photos; **p. 845:** (left) Courtesy of *Foreign Affairs*, (right) Courtesy *Arizona Highways*; **p. 852:** Maureen Duffy, *Teen Gangs: A Global View*, Copyright © 2004 by *Greenwood Press.* Reproduced with permission of Greenwood Publishing Group, Inc. Westport, CT.

Chapter 20
p. 870: The McGraw-Hill Companies, Inc. / Christopher Kerrigan, photographer.

Appendix C
p.A-36: Courtesy Friends of Patuxent; **p.A-37:** Courtesy Mayor's Office of Special Events, Chicago, IL.

Index

Useful Boxes in *The Brief McGraw-Hill Guide*

Guide to MLA Documentation Models in Chapter 20